Approaches to Psychology

Approaches to Psychology

FIFTH EDITION

William E. Glassman and
Marilyn Hadad

The McGraw·Hill Companies

London Boston Burr Ridge, IL Dubuque, IA Madison, WI New York San Francisco St. Louis
Bangkok Bogotá Caracas Kuala Lumpur Lisbon Madrid Mexico City Milan Montreal
New Delhi Santiago Seoul Singapore Sydney Taipei Toronto

Approaches to Psychology, Fifth Edition
William E. Glassman and Marilyn Hadad
ISBN-13 978-0-33-522885-0
ISBN-10 0-33-522885-2

Published by Open University Press/McGraw-Hill Education
Shoppenhangers Road
Maidenhead
Berkshire
SL6 2QL
Telephone: 44 (0) 1628 502 500
Fax: 44 (0) 1628 770 224
Website: www.openup.co.uk

British Library Cataloguing in Publication Data
A catalogue record for this book is available from the British Library

Library of Congress Cataloging in Publication Data
The Library of Congress data for this book has been applied for from the Library of Congress

Head of Development: Caroline Prodger
Editorial Assistant: Katy Hamilton
Marketing Manager: Lin Gillan, Mark Barratt
Senior Production Editor: James Bishop

Cover design by Hybert Design • www.hybertdesign.com
Printed and bound in Italy by Rotolito Lombarda S.p.A.

ISBN-13 978-0-33-522885-0
ISBN-10 0-33-522885-2

The McGraw·Hill Companies

To Lies, Dave and Danny
with love and gratitude.

and

In memory of my father, for teaching me
that vision is more than simply eyesight,
and wisdom is more than simply knowledge.

WEG

To my niece, Michelle Tomlinson, whose determination
and courage are inspirational, and whose unflagging
love keeps us all warm.

MH

Brief Table of Contents

Detailed Table of Contents

List of Illustrations

Figures

Boxes

Preface to the Fifth Edition

At most universities, introductory psychology is one of the most popular courses. This reflects the interest which most people have in understanding human behaviour – both their own, and that of others. While an introductory course should acknowledge this interest, it must also be an introduction to psychology as a discipline, providing a coherent understanding of the nature of psychology. In meeting these goals, the choice of a textbook is often crucial.

There are many possibilities in selecting course materials for introductory psychology. While using a textbook might seem to present a simple solution, there are literally dozens of introductory texts in print, and most seem to follow a formula which is less than satisfactory. With over 50 years of teaching experience between us, we have encountered many texts, and used more than a dozen in our classes. From our experiences as teachers, and the feedback from several thousand students, we have come to recognize certain factors which seem important in a textbook.

Most textbooks today tend to be rather large volumes which provide an impressive amount of factual knowledge. Unfortunately, as teaching tools, these texts tend to have several limitations. First, they are both too large and too expensive. No student can really hope to assimilate all the detail which is provided, and often they find the mass of information overwhelming. So, they end up paying for content that isn't needed. Second, most students come to psychology with an interest in human behaviour, yet often find a large proportion of their text is devoted to research on other species. While such research clearly is part of psychology, it is often not handled in ways that help students to understand its relevance to understanding human behaviour. Third, by presenting a survey of various sub-areas such as 'perception', 'development' and 'motivation', texts fail to provide a coherent framework for the discipline as a whole. In the end, it becomes disjointed for students.

Out of these concerns emerged this book, which is designed to offer a relatively brief, coherent introduction to psychology which emphasizes the understanding of human behaviour. The emphasis on human behaviour was the easiest goal to meet, since much of psychological research is focused on people; animal research is included only where it clearly relates to our understanding of human behaviour. The goal of brevity was met by making a conscious decision to be selective rather than encyclopaedic. In order to define criteria for such selection, it was necessary to choose some organizing principles – which in fact related to the third goal, coherence.

The organizing structure of this book is based on the historical reality that psychology has been based on several different conceptual frameworks, each with its own assumptions, methods and theories. Thus, the examination of five such frameworks (or approaches, as they are called in this text) forms the central focus of the book. Underlying this structure is a concern with the process of how we arrive at knowledge of behaviour – not just that different approaches exist, but how and why they arose. A central theme of the book is that the processes of perception are important for understanding both human behaviour and the nature of psychology as a discipline. This organizing structure has proven popular with both students and instructors in previous editions, and this edition remains faithful to those basic concepts and goals.

The changes in this edition involve three goals: first, to clarify and update the material of the previous edition where necessary; second, to provide coverage of new topics where appropriate;

and third, to provide more structural aids to readers. With regard to the first goal, this book includes almost 250 recent references (both research and theory), selected for both currency and significance. In terms of the second goal, this edition includes a new feature: The World Today boxes. These boxes discuss some aspect of information in the chapter in terms of issues that are interesting and relevant to students today. Specifically:

■ Chapter 1 (Behaviour and Psychology): discusses how magicians exploit some psychological phenomena to work their tricks.

■ Chapter 2 (The Biological Approach): examines how Ecstasy affects the brain.

■ Chapter 3 (The Behaviourist Approach): describes the reinforcement values in video games.

■ Chapter 4 (The Cognitive Approach): contains two boxes, one which explains how attribution theory is used in sports psychology and one which discusses terrorism as examined by cognitive dissonance theory.

■ Chapter 5 (The Psychodynamic Approach): gives an analysis of the character of Harry Potter as a Jungian archetype.

■ Chapter 6 (The Humanistic Approach): describes how coaching psychology may be applied to project management.

■ Chapter 7 (Perspectives on Development): contains two boxes, one which discusses how hormones affect women's preferences in men, and one which describes how parents react to their children's gender nonconformity.

■ Chapter 8 (Perspectives on Social Behaviour): briefly discusses how each of the five approaches might explain the behaviour of serial killers.

■ Chapter 9 (Perspectives on Abnormal Behaviour): contains a discussion of the relationship between creativity and psychopathology.

In terms of providing guidance to readers, it was felt important to retain, and build on, existing features intended to make the book more helpful. One feature, 'Putting it all Together', is a linked set of discussions at the end of Chapters 1–6. Chapter 1 provides a detailed case study which has been expanded in this edition. This case study is then discussed in Chapters 2–6, illustrating how each approach can assist in understanding some aspect of the case. The purpose of these discussions is to show how the approaches can be complementary, and thereby provide both a sense of integration, and also counterweight the student's desire to view the approaches in terms of 'right' vs. 'wrong'. By expanding the scope of the case study to include a more detailed social network for the character, we increase the degree to which students can understand and identify with 'Sam'.

In addition, discussion questions are dispersed throughout the book with the label 'Try it Yourself'. Some are completely new and others have been expanded from the discussion questions ('For Further Consideration') in the fourth edition to be more engaging to students. These questions are meant to encourage readers to apply the ideas within the text as a means of enhancing understanding. In general, they go beyond simple rote review, but are not intended to be completely open-ended. Some ask students to reflect on their own experiences, others may prove amenable to group discussions. While 'critical thinking' has become a much-abused buzzword in recent years, these questions are intended to provoke involvement and reflection.

In addition to an extensive end glossary, important terms are also highlighted and defined in context where they first occur, with formal definitions being provided in the margin. The fifth edition now begins each chapter with a list of Learning Objectives, and continues, as in the fourth edition, to include an overall Chapter Contents to help readers grasp the structure of what lies ahead. Each chapter concludes with a point-form Summary and list of Key Terms and Concepts. It is hoped that these features will aid students in the process of studying and reviewing, without distracting from the flow of the text itself.

A note on style: the handling of the third person singular in non-sexist ways is continuing to evolve, but this book adopts the (increasingly accepted) usage of 'their' rather than the awkward 'his/her'.

This edition marks the thirtieth anniversary of this book. The first edition arose as a collaborative effort of six people, including William E. Glassman (WEG). The second and third editions saw WEG as the sole author. Marilyn Hadad (MH) was brought on board for the fourth edition, and has played a major part in this edition. The intervening years and editions have seen the book evolve, but the writers of the first edition were part of its origin: Gordon R. Emslie, Paul H. Hirschorn, Judith Kelly Waalen, John Medcof and John Roth. To all of them, we give our thanks.

A further debt must be accorded to those readers and reviewers who provided comments on the previous edition, and thereby contributed to making this book better. Making psychology accessible and enjoyable for readers has always been a key goal, and the feedback and comments from students have been useful as well as gracious – it is yet one more reason why teaching is such a worthwhile endeavour. Many reviewers, who must go unnamed, have also contributed to this book, and their comments have been both supportive and extremely useful. In addition, we want to acknowledge our colleagues at Ryerson University, who have provided thoughtful comments and valuable criticism. Their support has been much appreciated.

WEG:

I also wish to thank my family, who have sacrificed in many ways over many editions. My sons, Dave and Danny, aged 19 and 14 respectively, have been understanding of the many days, nights and weekends that this project consumed; in some ways, their lives are intertwined with the life of this text. Their interruptions have been a frequent relief when the task has grown heavy, and their curiosity and enthusiasm are constant reminders of just how remarkable our existence is. My wife, Lies Weijs, has been invaluable emotionally, intellectually and logistically. She has provided encouragement when I needed it, and bore the burdens of family demands when I could not fulfil them. Further, as a reader who is a non-expert in psychology, she provided insightful and intelligent feedback on clarity and readability. Family life and career often seem at odds in our society; in this case, my family has my gratitude and love for all that they have given to this project, and to my life.

I also wish to thank Marilyn Hadad, who has been all that one could wish for in a collaborative partner, as well as a friend and colleague for much of my career. Her energy and creativity have moved this edition forward in new ways, and it is my fond hope that she will do so in editions yet to come. I know that if she does, the book will be in good hands.

MH:

I wish to express my gratitude to my friends who supportively allowed me to 'disappear down the rabbit hole' for weeks at a time as I worked on this book, and brought me food and wine to sustain both the body and the spirit.

Most particularly, though, I wish to thank Bill Glassman for providing not only the superb basis for subsequent editions to this book, but also for allowing me to become part of this enterprise. Without his mentorship and constant faith and encouragement, it is unlikely that I would have the opportunities and the soul-satisfying career that I have today.

WEG and MH:

Finally, we wish to thank the staff of McGraw-Hill/Open University Press. Open University Press has supported the development of this book through several editions, and their direction and encouragement have been crucial. Caroline Prodger, the head of development, has been the guiding light on the fifth edition; her enthusiasm, insight and wit have kept us on track and encouraged. To Caroline and all the staff at McGraw-Hill/Open University Press who have made this book possible, thank you.

William E. Glassman
Marilyn Hadad
Toronto, May 2008

Guided Tour

Chapter Introduction and Learning Objectives

Each chapter begins with an overall outline to help you grasp the structure of what lies ahead, including learning objectives which outline the main ideas you'll encounter in the chapter, and what you should understand once you have read it.

Try it Yourself

Psychology is a living subject that is about how we think, feel and behave. Therefore, each chapter contains 'Try it Yourself' activities and exercises that encourage you to explore the ideas in the chapter yourself – either through a class exercise or on your own. Additional boxes, figures and examples throughout also help you to see how psychological concepts apply in practice.

Key Thinkers

Psychology has been influenced by many thinkers and theorists and it is important to appreciate how the discipline has developed through time under the influence of different schools of thought. The 'Key Thinker' boxes give a brief recap of a notable psychologist and a brief overview of their key contributions to the field.

Key Terms

Psychology has its own vocabulary which can be daunting if you are new to the subject. To help you make sense of concepts, each new term that is introduced appears in the margin with an accompanying definition for easy revision.

Putting It All Together

In psychology there may not be right or wrong answer, but there may be different perspectives on the same problem. The purpose of the 'Putting it all Together' discussions at the end of chapters is to illustrate how different approaches can be complementary, and thereby provide a sense of integration.

Chapter Summary

Each chapter concludes with a summary of the issues discussed that captures the key points in that chapter, and helps you to revise the main ideas you have read about.

Test Yourself Questions

These questions provide you with a chance to test what you have learnt. They also give you an opportunity to apply the ideas within the text as a means of enhancing understanding. You may also find them useful as revision or as test questions for exams and assessments.

Suggestions for Further Reading

Each chapter concludes with a number of references to sources of additional information outside the book. These include books, journal articles and pieces of research which can form a starting point for study, or for an essay or assignment. A full reference section at the end of the book also provides an excellent source of contemporary international resources in psychology.

Technology to Enhance Learning and Teaching

Visit www.openup.co.uk/glassman today

Online Learning Centre (OLC)

After completing each chapter, log on to the supporting Online Learning Centre website. Take advantage of the study tools offered to reinforce the material you have read in the text, and to develop your knowledge of psychology in a fun and effective way.

Resources for students include:

- *Additional 'Try it Yourself' Exercises*
- *Self-test questions*
- *Glossary*
- *Weblinks*
- *Background to each chapter*
- *Suggested answers to 'Try it Yourself' exercises and end of chapter questions*

Also available for lecturers:

- *Workshop activities*
- *Additional teaching resources*
- *Artwork from the book*
- *Testbank of questions for tests and exams*

A note for instructors:

If you are a lecturer adopting this textbook, or evaluating this book for adoption on your psychology module, please visit the OLC website. On the website you will be able to review all of the student support materials. To access the lecturer materials, click on the link on the homepage to request the password and submit your request. Alternatively, if you are in touch with your McGraw-Hill sales representative, they will be happy to supply the password to you.

Custom Publishing Solutions: Let us help make our content your solution

At McGraw-Hill Education our aim is to help lecturers to find the most suitable content for their needs delivered to their students in the most appropriate way. Our **Custom Publishing Solutions** offer the ideal combination of content delivered in the way which best suits lecturer and students.

Our custom publishing programme offers lecturers the opportunity to select just the chapters or sections of material they wish to deliver to their students from a database called Primis at www.primisonline. com.

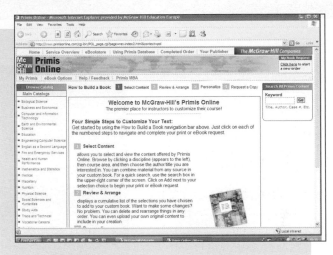

Primis contains over 2 million pages of content from:

- textbooks
- professional books
- case books – Harvard articles, Insead, Ivey, Darden, Thunderbird and BusinessWeek
- Taking Sides – debate materials

Across the following imprints:

- McGraw-Hill Education
- Open University Press
- Harvard Business School Press
- US and European material

There is also the option to include additional material authored by lecturers in the custom product – this does not necessarily have to be in English.

We will take care of everything from start to finish in the process of developing and delivering a custom product to ensure that lecturers and students receive exactly the material needed in the most suitable way.

With a Custom Publishing Solution, students enjoy the best selection of material deemed to be the most suitable for learning everything they need for their courses – something of real value to support their learning. Teachers are able to use exactly the material they want, in the way they want, to support their teaching on the course.

Please contact your local McGraw-Hill representative with any questions or alternatively contact Warren Eels e: warren_eels@mcgraw-hill.com.

  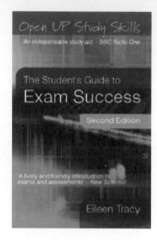

Acknowledgements

Our thanks go to the following reviewers for their comments at various stages in the text's development:

Beverly Plester – Coventry University
Matt Jarvis – Totton College of FE and HE
Juan Gomez – University of St Andrews
David Alcock – University of the West of England
Mohamed Ally – University of Lethbridge, Canada
David Holmes – Manchester Metropolitan University
Eric Shiraev – George Mason University (Virginia/DC)
Cornelia Kranczioch – University of Portsmouth
Ana da Cunha Lewin – Birkbeck College
John Devaney – Queen's University Belfast

The authors and publishers would like to extend their grateful thanks to the following for permission to reproduce images and photographs:

Margot Adler for photograph of Alfred Adler
Albert Bandura for photograph of Albert Bandura
Daniel and Amy Starch, Harvard University, for photograph of Jerome Kagan
Archives of the History of American Psychology, University of Akron, Ohio, for photographs of Abraham Maslow and John B. Watson
Nobel Institute for photograph of Ivan Pavlov
Nobel Institute for photograph of Konrad Lorenz
Nobel Institute for photograph of Herbert Simon
Nobel Institute for photograph of Roger Sperry
Archives Jean Piaget for photograph of Jean Piaget
Martin Seligman for photograph of Martin Seligman
Istvan Berczi, University of Manitoba, for photograph of Hans Selye
Natalie Rogers for photograph of Carl Rogers
B. F. Skinner Foundation for the photograph of B. F. Skinner
Wikipedia: the free encyclopedia for the photograph of Wilhelm Wundt

And to the McGraw-Hill Companies for permission to use photographs and images from Santrock: *Psychology*, 7th edn, copyright year 2000, McGraw-Hill, for Figures 1.8, 1.12, 2.6, 2.10, 3.5, 3.7, 4.6, 4.7, 7.2, 9.2 and Box 9.5.

Every effort has been made to to trace and acknowledge ownership of copyright and to clear permission for material reproduced in this book. The publishers will be pleased to make suitable arrangements to clear permission with any copyright holders whom it has not been possible to contact.

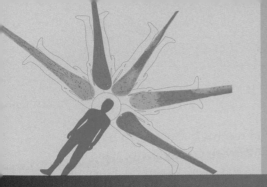

Chapter 1

Behaviour and Psychology

Never did any science originate,
but by a poetic perception.

Ralph Waldo Emerson

Chapter contents

LEARNING OBJECTIVES

In this chapter, the objectives are to learn:

- ☑ what psychology is
- ☑ why the study of psychology provides special challenges
- ☑ why different approaches to the study of psychology are necessary
- ☑ how perception affects the study of psychology
- ☑ the origins of psychology
- ☑ why the scientific method is used in psychology
- ☑ the methodologies used in the study of psychology
- ☑ the ethics of psychological research

THE MAGIC OF BEHAVIOUR

When I (WEG) was a child, my father sometimes took me to see magic shows. To a boy of 10, this was a wondrous and exciting event. The tricks performed were usually pretty standard – producing objects from hats or boxes, making things disappear, and so on. I knew even then that these feats were not supernatural, but based on some sort of deception or gimmickry – in a word, 'tricks'. Nonetheless, they held me spellbound, wondering how it was all accomplished.

As children and as adults, we are curious about the world, and when faced with the unexpected or unexplained, we are driven to increase our understanding. Magic shows represent a special kind of mystery, because what we *think* we see is somehow different from the underlying reality. Indeed, one of the most basic tools in a magician's repertoire is *misdirection* – getting the audience to focus on an irrelevant detail, while ignoring a crucial manoeuvre by the magician. By manipulating our attention and expectations, magicians draw us into a world which entertains us precisely because it is hard to understand.

For us (WEG and MH), magic and psychology are linked, because the mechanics of magic are based on exploiting perceptual processes that are a basic concern in psychology. Even more fundamentally, both evoke a sense of wonder and the desire to understand. Consider the case of a horse called 'Clever Hans'. Hans had been 'educated' by his owner for four years, and subsequently seemed capable of answering questions in history, geography, mathematics and more. People came from near and far to see Clever Hans, and most went away convinced that he really was educated. Ultimately, it was a psychologist named Oskar Pfungst who figured out the true explanation. (Of course, Hans really didn't understand history and so on; later in this chapter, we will discuss what was really happening.) Although an 'educated' horse is unusual, it is not really surprising that a psychologist was involved in understanding it. Understanding behaviour in all its forms is, after all, the primary goal of psychology.

INTRODUCTION

Throughout human history, people have sought ways to make sense of the world, and there have been many attempts to formalize the understanding of behaviour. Astrology, for example, arose out of the belief that human actions were influenced by the stars. Often, theories of behaviour have been stimulated by developments in other fields. For instance, in the eighteenth century, anatomists studying the brain proposed that there was a relationship between brain size and mental abilities. This led to the development of **phrenology**, which asserted that one could assess people's various abilities by examining the shape of the skull. While phrenology and astrology have been largely discredited, their goal of understanding and explaining the way people act seems similar to that of psychology. So what makes psychology different?

phrenology a now-discredited eighteenth-century theory which asserted that one could assess ability by examining the shape of the skull.

psychology the scientific study of behaviour and experience.

The simple answer is that psychology differs in the method it uses in the search for understanding. Unlike astrology, phrenology, or even 'common sense', **psychology** utilizes a form of systematic observation and analysis that is often called 'the scientific method'. In fact, psychology is often defined as 'the scientific study of behaviour'. Definitions, of course, have limitations, and this one does, too. For example, some psychologists would interpret 'behaviour' to mean both overt responses and conscious experience, that is, actions and thoughts or feelings; while others would be more restrictive, omitting thoughts and feelings because they cannot be

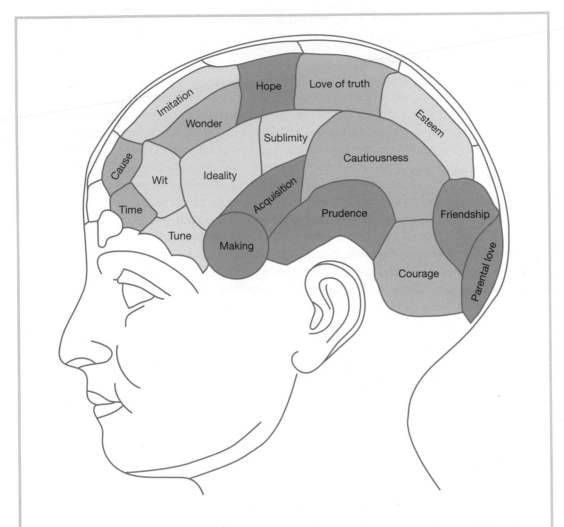

Figure 1.1 Phrenology This reproduction of a nineteenth-century phrenology diagram divides the head according to abilities. The idea that the shape of the head could indicate relative abilities was derived from the concept of localization of function (see Chapter 2) – but in fact the shape of the head has little relation to brain size and shape.

directly observed. Similarly, some psychologists include the behaviour of other species, while some are concerned only with human behaviour. Despite such variations in the focus of interests, the *methods* used in psychology are *scientific*. These methods, which involve both how observations are made and how theories are assessed, are primarily based on a tradition which originated with the natural sciences of physics, chemistry and biology.

The Challenge of Psychology

All scientists emphasize certain common principles, like the importance of careful observation, minimizing sources of error and testing alternative explanations. At the same time, the methods of psychologists differ from those of physicists or chemists, because what psychologists study is different: rather than dealing with inanimate particles, psychologists explore the actions (and interactions) of living creatures. This means that psychological researchers face four particular challenges which are unique to their discipline.

- *Complexity.* One challenge in psychology relates to the **complexity** of behaviour. Physicists studying atomic particles typically deal with only a limited number of particles at once – a hundred particles interacting would be a very complex system. By contrast, a physiological psychologist studying the human brain is dealing with a structure composed of several *billion* interconnected cells – the most complex structure in the known universe! Even for non-physiological researchers, there is tremendous diversity to consider – for example, studying language is complicated because there are several thousand languages and dialects known, each with its own vocabulary and grammar. Given the richness of human behaviour, psychologists must contend with a vast range of possibilities, and a correspondingly large variety of data (observations). By comparison, the possible interactions between two chemical elements, or the dynamics of a moving object, are relatively simple.

complexity a characteristic of systems composed of large numbers of interacting units (such as neurons in the brain), resulting in new patterns or phenomena not found in individual units.

- *Self-awareness.* Psychologists also face challenges related to the human capacity for **self-awareness** (Hofstadter 1979). While physicists studying atoms are themselves composed of atoms, most researchers would say that this has no impact on the problems they study. By contrast, psychologists studying human behaviour are simultaneously *producing* human behaviour. At first glance, this may not seem like a problem – it might even be seen as a convenience. In fact, historically, a number of noted psychologists studied their own behaviour as part of their broader studies: Sigmund Freud, the founder of psychoanalysis, studied his own dreams as well as those of his patients (Freud 1900). William James, a pioneering American psychologist, favoured introspection – studying the contents of one's conscious awareness – over laboratory research. In doing so, he popularized the phrases 'stream of consciousness' and 'armchair psychology' (James 1890). Eventually, however, it was recognized that self-observation is prone to many sources of error, not the least of which is bias – researchers, like other people, may misinterpret their own behaviour to fit their theoretical ideas. (For example, consider the possible distortions in trying to recall one of your dreams.)

self-awareness the capacity for individuals or other living organisms to consciously observe their own behaviour.

- *Reactivity.* A concern related to self-awareness also arises when observing the behaviour of others. While measurement can be demanding even in simple physical systems, psychological observation is complicated by the fact that one is dealing with independent, living organisms, not inanimate particles. In particular, observing human behaviour can lead to reactivity, the tendency for people to alter their behaviour when they know that they are being observed. (As a simple case, consider how if you are singing to yourself, you may stop if you realize someone is listening.) In order to deal with **reactivity**, psychologists often resort to complicated research designs, sometimes including deliberate deception to increase the chances of people behaving naturally. (The methods used will be discussed in more detail later in this chapter.) In the end, observing human behaviour proves more difficult than observing simple physical systems.

reactivity the tendency for people to alter their behaviour when they are being observed.

- *Causality.* Another challenge arises in terms of identifying the causes of behaviour. Traditionally, science has viewed **causality**, the study of what actions or events produce an outcome, as an important part of 'understanding', and psychology has tended to accept this goal. However, the reality is that many different factors can influence behaviour in a given situation. Consider the following example. The child welfare authori-

causality the study of how actions or events produce (cause) a particular outcome

ties are called in when someone is reported to have hit their child. It turns out that the father was drinking, had just lost his job, and was himself abused as a child. Is the cause of his abusive behaviour the alcohol, the job loss, his early upbringing, a combination of these, or some factor not identified? In any situation, there are many factors which influence behaviour: some are internal, some are part of the immediate situation, and some are related to past experience. Each of these represents a type of cause, but developing a complete description of such causes in a given situation is a difficult (if not impossible) task.

WHY DIFFERENT APPROACHES?

It is not surprising, given the richness and complexity of behaviour, that psychologists have evolved different approaches to understanding behaviour. Ideally, we would have one simple set of principles which would explain every aspect of human experience. At present, no such theory has been developed which has met with broad acceptance. Instead, there are a number of different approaches which differ from each other in terms of their basic assumptions, their methods and their theoretical structures. In effect, each approach represents a distinct framework for the study of behaviour. While most introductory psychology books emphasize the research findings in psychology, organized according to traditional topic areas like learning and perception, this book focuses instead on the frameworks which have been developed in psychology, as defined by the major approaches. Examining how these frameworks arose, and how they differ, provides a way to understand the significance of each approach, and to make sense of the field as a whole.

The traditional model of science says that scientists formulate theories based on the information they have gathered from research. Hence, one might imagine that each approach arose as an attempt to improve on existing theories. This viewpoint, while a bit simplistic, is partially valid. In some cases, theorists *do* react against what they see as limitations or errors in the work of others. For example, Carl Jung split from his mentor, Sigmund Freud, partly because of disagreements about the meaning of sexuality. At the same time, other factors also come into play. Thomas Kuhn (1970), a specialist in the philosophy of science, has argued that the acceptance or rejection of particular frameworks or approaches (which he calls 'paradigms') depends on human preferences as well as the available evidence. That is, the development and evaluation of a theory depend not simply on the available data, but also on social and personal factors, including the experiences of the researcher and the influence of the prevailing culture. (See Chapter 10 for more on Kuhn's ideas.)

To summarize briefly, the complexity of behaviour means that currently no single theory can effectively explain all aspects. In addition, the nature of theory formation in science means that different approaches developed in response to that complexity, but also as a result of personal and cultural factors. To understand how this happens, let us start by examining how we actually perceive the world.

Perception and Experience

perception the process of selection, organization and interpretation of information about the world conveyed by the senses.

Most individuals tend to assume that what we experience depends on what is 'out there' – that is, that our senses simply convey information about the physical stimuli that we encounter. This implies a direct record of the external world, similar to the way a video camera records a scene. The idea that we see things simply as they are is sometimes called 'naive realism'; however, the process of perceiving is actually much more complex. **Perception** is an *active* process involving selection, organization and interpretation, not a passive mirroring of the external world.

Let us consider first the process of *selection*. At every moment, we encounter a tremendous variety of stimuli – sights, sounds, smells, etc. Unfortunately, the human brain has a limited capacity to deal with incoming information. Imagine going to a television store, and trying to watch several channels on different televisions simultaneously – parts of one or more programmes are inevitably missed. In order to cope with the sensory barrage, our perceptual system focuses on some aspects of the situation, while ignoring others. This process of choosing stimuli is called **selective attention**. One example is the way we focus on one conversation, while filtering out other voices and sounds, at a party or other crowded location. (The nature of attention, and its limits, will be discussed further in Chapter 4. See *The World Today: Magic*, below, as well.)

selective attention the perceptual process of selectively focusing on particular stimulus elements.

Perception, then, is partly determined by the external stimuli that we encounter, as filtered by selective attention. This stimulus-based process is sometimes called 'bottom-up' processing. At the same time, perceptual experience is also influenced by various internal factors, such as our prior experience and expectations. These factors (referred to as 'top-down' processing) influence both the way that we interpret selected stimuli, and also what we select. Consider two examples: in Figure 1.2, what do you see? (Look *now*!) While the figure *could* be interpreted as either a duck or a rabbit, most native English speakers see the rabbit first, because they have learned to scan

The world today: **Magic**

Psychology may or may not be 'magical', but it's undeniable that magicians make use of psychological phenomena in their acts. Massimo Polidoro (2007) has reviewed some of the ways that magicians have (usually unwittingly) done this. First, magicians make use of misdirection. What this means is that magicians influence where we will direct our attention. For example, in making a coin 'disappear' from their hand, magicians will verbally direct us to look at the coin in their hand and will reinforce this by directing their own attention to their hand. Then, the magician makes the coin 'disappear' (actually by passing it to the other hand). At this point in the trick, they look at the audience and tell a joke to distract them away from the hand and focus attention on the magician's face instead. Attention is diverted away from the hand at this critical point and not directed back at the hand until the magician instructs the audience to notice that the coin has 'disappeared' from that hand (i.e., directs attention back to the hand). Note that we, the audience, are further disadvantaged because magicians usually do not tell us what they are going to do at the beginning of the trick: the situation is ambiguous, so we have little idea beforehand of where to direct our attention.

Magicians also take advantage of our expectations in performing their tricks: very often, we see what we expect to see, whether it is visually there or not. When magicians do a card trick, for example, they often open a new sealed deck of cards. We expect that the new sealed deck will contain all the cards, so even if the audience is allowed to examine the deck, they typically fail to notice that it is not complete. This removal of one or more of the cards and the resealing of the deck allow the magician to take advantage of our expectations and perform a number of card tricks. In addition, magicians often make use of our memory systems which reconstruct events rather than recording them as they happen. For example, the magician may say, 'You will notice that I never touched the deck of cards,' when a videotape of the event shows clearly that he or she did, in full view of the audience. Yet, most of the audience who witness this report afterwards that the magician never touched the deck of cards!

As we will see in Chapter 4, attentional processes, seeing what we expect to see, and memory reconstruction not only play a large part in the fun of magical tricks, they also play a problematical part in eyewitness testimony.

images in a left-to-right sequence. In this case, past experience influences the processing order. (Individuals brought up to read in a different sequence, like the right-to-left sequence of Hebrew, would often perceive it differently. To explore this issue further, try making a copy of the image reversed, and show it to a friend to see what happens.)

A different source of influence is illustrated in the next two figures: in Figure 1.3, what are the letters? Now, compare this with Figure 1.4. What are the elements in the centre – numbers, or the letter B? In this situation, the presence of other letters or numbers – what we might call the *context* of the stimuli – leads us to interpret the same elements differently.

So-called **ambiguous figures**, which can be interpreted in different ways, have long been of interest to psychologists studying perception. Such figures illustrate that what we perceive is not based simply on what is 'out there', but is also influenced by internal processes. On first encounter, it may seem that ambiguous figures have little to do with everyday experience – but they actually underscore the processes which are part of *all* perception. In trying to make sense of the world, we look for familiar patterns, and we interpret what we encounter based on our prior experiences. When faced with a situation where there is incomplete information, we fill in the gaps according to what seems probable. For example, in a noisy environment, we fill in small gaps in what someone says based on the words we *do* hear. 'Do you want to get [gap] [gap] here?' says your friend, looking somewhat uncomfortable. Most of us readily recognize that the words in the gaps are 'out of', and we may not even be aware that we filled in the gaps, thinking that we 'heard' the words. This view of perception as an active, creative process was pioneered in the early part of the twentieth

ambiguous figure a picture or other visual stimulus which can be perceived in more than one way.

Figure 1.2 Ambiguous Figures Is the figure at left a rabbit, or a duck? Is the one at right a cat or a dog? (Look upside down!) What we see can change, even when the stimulus stays the same.

A B C

Figure 1.3 Ambiguous Figures What do you see between the A and the C? Compare this to Figure 1.4.

12 13 14

Figure 1.4 Ambiguous Figures What do you see between the 12 and the 14? Compare this to Figure 1.3; note how context alters our expectations, and thereby what we perceive.

Gestalt theory a theory of behaviour pioneered in the early part of the twentieth century by Kohler, Wertheimer and others, which emphasized the active, creative nature of perception and learning (Gestalt is German, and means roughly 'organized whole).

similarity a Gestalt principle of perceptual organization, based on grouping together similar elements (for example, shape or size).

proximity a Gestalt principle which states that elements which are close together tend to be perceived as a group.

closure in perception, the tendency to fill in incomplete patterns to produce a coherent whole.

century by the developers of **Gestalt theory** (the word *Gestalt* is German, and means roughly 'organized whole').

Gestalt psychologists argued that perceptual experience is the result of active synthesis, and one of their goals was to identify the basic factors that affect how we organize and interpret sensory data. Over time, they identified a number of organizational principles which are sometimes called 'laws of grouping'. Among these are the principles of **similarity** (grouping similar items together) and **proximity** (elements which are close together tend to form a group) (see Figures 1.5 and 1.6). In general, the Gestalt view was that we are naturally inclined to seek ways to organize sensory data; perception is not random.

Gestalt theory also argued for the importance of *interpretation* in perception. This is clearly seen in the concept of **closure**, which is the tendency to fill in incomplete patterns to produce a coherent whole (see Figure 1.7). Rather than perceiving a complex set of unconnected elements, we interpret sensory data to create a meaningful pattern – even if this means modifying in some way the original stimulus information. Closure helps to explain why tasks like proofreading can be difficult: we tend to see what we expect to see (a correct word), instead of what actually appears on the page (an error).

The interpretations we make when perceiving are seldom random; instead, they reflect the way we have structured our previous knowledge and experience. From early infancy, we organize and interpret our experiences, seeking patterns to help us make sense of the world. Some of these patterns are fairly simple concepts, like 'food' or 'chair'. As our experience and knowledge grow,

schema (pl., 'schemata') a mental framework which organizes knowledge, beliefs and expectations, and is used to guide behaviour.

we form more complex structures called **schemata**. Some schemata are scripts to guide our actions in particular situations. For example, a 'restaurant' script tells us that when we dine out we order from a menu, are served by someone, and are expected to pay for what we order, among other things. Schemata can also be used to organize our knowledge of objects and people. For example, a schema for 'bedroom' would include knowledge of the various objects found in a bedroom, as well as their functions.

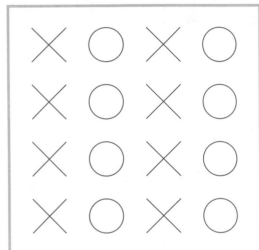

Figure 1.5 The Gestalt Concept of Similarity Note how we tend to see the figure as columns rather than rows, because of grouping the similar shapes.

Figure 1.6 The Gestalt Concept of Proximity Note how we tend to see the figure as rows rather than columns, because of grouping those which are closer together.

Figure 1.7 The Gestalt Concept of Closure What do you see in these two figures? Note that both are easily recognizable, even though both are based on incomplete outlines.

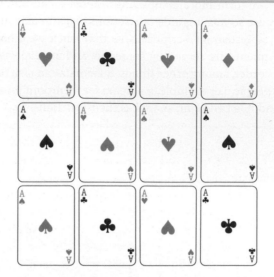

Figure 1.8 Expectations and Perceptions Quickly count how many spades you see in this picture. If you found only two or three, this can be understood in terms of the fact that past experience led you to expect that spades should be black (a cognitive schema about cards); non-black spades violate your expectations, which in turn influence what you perceive.

Whether simple or complex, schemata influence the way we perceive the world around us. Depending on the schema one has, the same situation may be interpreted differently: an old chair at a flea market may be perceived as junk by one person; another person, more knowledgeable about furniture, may recognize it as a Georgian antique. A Brazilian settler may see a rainforest as something to be cleared in order to create a farm; an environmental activist may see the same forest as a priceless ecosystem.

In many cases, it is impossible to label a particular interpretation as correct or incorrect. Thus, in each of the above examples, both points of view have meaning. At the same time, it should be obvious that the use of schemata also creates the risk of distortions in the way we see the world. Sometimes the distortions may be relatively benign, but in other cases the errors may be more serious – especially when our schemata involve faulty or inaccurate assumptions. Consider our attitudes towards people: such **stereotypes** can also be considered schemata (Baldwin 1992). Social stereotypes are often formed initially from some specific experience, or from observations of one or more individuals. These specific impressions become a stereotype when this information is then generalized to apply to *all* members of a group, regardless of circumstances. This creates difficulties when circumstances change, but the stereotype does not, or when a stereotype is used as a substitute for gathering accurate information about a person. For example, a friend once reported an experience that his 6-year-old son had at school. The teacher had asked the children to 'draw a picture of your father relaxing'. When the teacher saw the boy drawing a picture of a man chopping wood, she said, 'No, I said draw him *relaxing*.' Bursting into tears, the 6-year-old exclaimed (correctly), 'But my Daddy *does* chop wood to relax!' (By contrast, his father's 'work' involved sitting at a desk all day.) The teacher's stereotype, not the boy's drawing, was the problem. Stereotypes, as mental schemata, can lead us to prejudge others – and *all* schemata carry this risk of distorting reality.

Even when we are not consciously aware of using schemata, they are part of our perceptual process. Our perceptions of friends and family members are based on many, many experiences. Over time, the schemata we create from these experiences can have more influence on our perceptions than the present reality. Consider the following examples: as parents, we tend to overlook the changes in our maturing children, and fail to recognize that they are no longer as dependent as they were as toddlers. As adults, we can be shocked to realize that our elderly parents now need to be cared for as if *we* were the parents. Friends may change both physically and emotionally, but we still perceive them as they *used* to be. In each case, the mental schema is inconsistent with the person before us. Typically, we are unaware of these distortions; somewhat ironically, we tend to believe that family and friends are the people we know best, because we have such elaborate schemata to deal with them.

confirmation bias a form of cognitive error based on the tendency to seek out information which supports one's beliefs, and to ignore contradictory information.

The likelihood that we will recognize such distortions is reduced by a phenomenon called **confirmation bias**. Generally, we tend to focus on information that confirms our beliefs, and ignore potentially contradictory information. Ironically, the more confident we are in our beliefs, the more likely is the danger of distortion, because we are less likely to look for information that might reveal our error. Thus, a doctor with 30 years of experience is less likely to recognize when he has made a diagnostic error than a newly-graduated intern – precisely because greater experience instils greater confidence (Halpern 1989). As another example, when we fall in love, we become supremely confident that we know the object of our affections well, and we point out all his or her wonderful qualities to our friends. Sometimes we are amazed that our friends are sceptical of our appraisals, seeing other qualities which are significantly less than wonderful in our loved one. But we, in our infatuated state, ignore or find justifications for all the information that does not fit our conviction that our beloved is magnificent. Sometimes, later, we wonder how we could have been so blind – now that we have a new, less positive schema of the former beloved, we can see only his or her negative qualities, and this now confirms our new opinion!

This is not to say that schemata are undesirable – most of the time, they aid us in efficiently and accurately processing the vast amount of sensory information that we encounter. Rather, it is to emphasize that perception is an imperfect process, even as it is a crucial one in our dealings with the world. Schemata help us to make sense of the wealth of sensory information around us. On balance, the risk of errors is largely offset by the benefits gained from organizing our experiences. In addition, by *understanding* the perceptual process, we are more likely to avoid the kinds of errors we have discussed.

Perception and Theorizing

We began this discussion of perceptual processes in response to the question, 'Why different approaches?' By now it should be obvious that researchers depend on the same perceptual processes as other people, with the same limitations. Still, it may not be apparent how these perceptual limitations have led to divergent approaches within psychology. To understand this, recall what was said earlier about the challenges involved in studying behaviour. In particular, we noted that human behaviour is almost infinitely complex and variable. Faced with this complexity and variability, how is a researcher to proceed?

Since 'studying everything' is impossible, some degree of selection is inevitable in research. Researchers make choices, focusing on one aspect or type of behaviour (for example, physiological processes, or a problem like aggression), or sometimes one species (humans, primates or bees, etc.). The choices made may reflect the researcher's interests, theoretical assumptions, or other aspects of the individual's schemata. In other words, the process of deciding what to study, and how to study it, is influenced by the processes of perception which we have been discussing.

Thus, the process of doing research involves selection in the same sense that perception in general does. Faced with a range of choices, many individuals interested in behaviour decide to follow a research path already defined by others. In some cases, however, circumstances and schemata combine in a way that leads certain individuals to break new ground. In effect, they make choices of what to study, and how, that come to define a new framework or approach to the study of behaviour. In the long run, the development of any approach involves the contributions of many people, but in the beginning there is usually a key figure, whose personal choices play a key role in defining the nature of the approach.

Psychology as a discipline is characterized by not one, but several, different approaches. Most of this book will be devoted to exploring five major ones: the biological, behaviourist, cognitive, psychodynamic and humanistic approaches. In each case, we will explore the origins of the approach, the individuals involved in its development, and the assumptions and methods which characterize it. Inevitably, you will find points of disagreement between the approaches, as well as apparent limitations in each. Faced with this situation, you may well wonder which approach is the 'real' psychology. While such a query is natural, it may not be the most productive way to view the situation.

It is frequently noted in introductory texts that psychology is a relatively young field, tracing its origins back only about 100 years or so. This is just as frequently followed by statements about how one cannot expect much coherence from a young field, as if apologizing for a toddler who is a messy eater – that is, one shouldn't expect much more. This sentiment not only downplays the accomplishments of psychology, but is also likely erroneous, because it assumes that coherence is *necessary* to a mature field. (Modern physics, by comparison, still grapples with differing models of basic forces, without having a unified theory.)

This general issue deserves more detailed exploration, but the purpose here is to suggest that disagreement is not always a weakness. (See Chapter 10 for a further discussion.) Physics, a much older discipline than psychology, has long recognized the concept of

complementarity a concept developed by physicists to deal with the existence of two models which are both useful, but not directly reconcilable.

complementarity – different frameworks may be separately valid, without being reducible one into the other (Blackburn 1971). For example, light can be described as a wave or a particle, depending on the circumstances. Each representation has value, without implying that one is right and the other is wrong in an absolute sense. In the same way, the differing approaches to behaviour that we will consider may also reflect complementarity. Seen in this way, the basic concern becomes how *useful* each approach is, not which is completely correct. Indeed, despite the historical disagreements, it is not unusual today to see researchers combining concepts and methods of different approaches (such as the biological and cognitive) in order to advance the understanding of behaviour. (See also *Putting It All Together* at the end of this chapter.)

If the preceding discussion of complementarity seems abstract, consider the following story: a group of blind men were making a pilgrimage together in India, when they met a man leading an elephant. None of the blind men had ever encountered an elephant before, and they proceeded to touch it. One man, grasping the trunk, exclaimed, 'Oh! An elephant is like a snake!' Another, wrapping his arms around one of the elephant's legs, said, 'No! An elephant is like a tree, with rough bark!' A third, grasping the end of the elephant's tail, countered, 'You're both wrong! An elephant is hairy, like a camel!' They proceeded to argue vehemently, never realizing that they were each partly right, but that none was completely right. Their disagreements stemmed from making different observations, and making different interpretations based on those observations. In a similar way, each approach to psychology may be only a partial view of the whole subject. And, like the interpretations of the blind men, each approach may have something valuable to offer in our attempt to understand behaviour, even if no one approach can answer all questions.

In considering the five approaches, the process of perception can help us understand how the origin of each approach is related to the experiences and schemata of the individuals who pioneered it. In addition, we will need to consider the intellectual and social context in which the approaches were developed, because people do not live (or work) in a vacuum; each of us is influenced by the ideas and attitudes of the society we live in. (Consider, for example, differences in social customs and attitudes in London today compared to a hundred years ago, or the prairies of Canada compared to the jungles of the Amazon.) In this sense, the lives of the pioneers of psychology, and the cultural contexts in which they lived, are not simply historical details, but important clues to understanding each approach.

The impact of culture is a broad issue, and no complete analysis can be given here. As should be evident, people in all cultures have striven to understand human behaviour, and have developed different types of frameworks and explanations. In that sense, the five approaches on which we will focus represent frameworks that have been particularly significant, not the only possible ways of seeking to understand behaviour. Throughout the book, we will look at examples of how culture influences both individual behaviour and the way people think about behaviour (see Box 1.1).

In the end, it is important to remember that psychology is a science, but all science is a human endeavour. Understanding the richness of that endeavour requires acknowledging the people who contribute to its development, and the social contexts in which they live. For the moment, let us consider the general context in which psychology as a discipline emerged (for further discussion of the issues of theory formation, see Chapter 10).

THE ORIGINS OF PSYCHOLOGY

Psychology did not exist as a specific discipline until the end of the nineteenth century. Formally, its inception is usually traced to the creation of Wilhelm Wundt's laboratory of experimental psychology, established in Leipzig in 1875. While it is convenient to point to a specific date, psychology is not a baby with a specific birth date; its genesis really involved a number of elements, from the creation of laboratories, to the formation of university psychology departments, to the growth of public recognition of the discipline. In this sense, its 'birth' really extends over roughly the last three decades of the nineteenth century.

In a broader sense, it can be argued that the origins of psychology go back even further. What has been called the first 'psychology experiment' was performed in ancient Egypt, in about 700 BCE (Hunt 1993). In order to explore the origins of language, the king of Egypt arranged for a child to be reared by a shepherd, who was ordered never to speak to the boy. When the grown child was later presented to the king, supposedly the first sounds he made sounded like the Egyptian word for bread. The king concluded that the Egyptian language must be innate, thus demonstrating the inherent superiority of Egyptian culture!

Box 1.1 *The Problem of Interpretation in Research*

Interpretation is a basic part of research in psychology as well as everyday perception. While psychologists may observe specific behaviours, they then often make inferences about the intent or meaning of these behaviours. Like all human beings, researchers tend to interpret behaviour in terms that are meaningful to them. But are these interpretations necessarily objective and unambiguous? Often, the answer is no. Consider the following example (inspired by a television comedy): if Malcolm calls Dewey a nerd, what does this mean? Psychologist A says, 'Malcolm feels contempt for Dewey. If I called someone a nerd, it would be because I was angry and had contempt for that person.' Psychologist B says, 'No, Malcolm loves Dewey. If I called someone a nerd, it would be because I was comfortable enough with that person and respected that person enough that I could affectionately tease him or her.' Which psychologist is right? Only by standing in the shoes of the actors can we know; otherwise, we are making assumptions that can't be directly tested, and that may in fact be wrong.

The problem with interpretation becomes more acute when we look at the behaviour of people from cultures other than our own. For example, is Yäel being an unthinking conformist when she agrees to go along with a class plan that she has private reservations about? Or is she reflecting the spirit of collectivism, emphasizing group interest, that is part of her upbringing on a kibbutz in Israel? Is Mr Takehashi being unfriendly when he fails to join his new American workmates for lunch? Or is he reacting according to the Japanese norm that says it would be rude to join his co-workers without an explicit invitation? How one answers these questions may depend on the culture in which one lives.

Psychologists can also be influenced in various ways by the culture in which they live and do research. Ideally, researchers are seeking to develop theories that apply to human beings in general, but there is always the possibility that interpretations are limited by culture and/or historical context. While this does not mean that theories can never apply to all people, the question of cultural influence is relevant to understanding how theories are developed and evaluated. Of course, culture is not the only factor that influences how people (including psychologists) interpret the world, but it is easily overlooked because it is always present, surrounding us, like the air we breathe. As we consider the different approaches discussed in this book, we will look at a number of specific examples of the challenges involved in interpreting behaviour, including the role of culture.

Try it Yourself

Schemata influence how we perceive more complex social situations. To understand the variability we show in our schemata and how our own perceptions of the world may be influenced by our previous experiences, indicate how you would interpret the following situations. Then ask one or two friends how they would interpret the same situations. Are there differences?

1 Someone you barely know suddenly becomes very friendly and helpful, even offering to run errands for you and lend you money.

2 Your closest friend is uncharacteristically withdrawn and quiet.

3 You have a choice as to which of the following people you will have dinner with: an artist, an accountant, a car mechanic, a nuclear physicist. What would you expect the dinner conversation to be like with each? Which would you choose? Is your choice based on a stereotype, or some personal schema?

In general terms, psychology emerged out of two traditions: philosophy and natural science. Philosophers have always been concerned with understanding the meaning of human experience, and many basic concepts in psychology trace their origin back to philosophy. For example, John Locke was deliberating the role of learning in behaviour in his *Essay Concerning Human Understanding*, published in 1690. In addition, philosophy, like the humanities more generally, has posed questions about awareness, motivation and values that have also been of concern to psychologists. Along with philosophy's interest in human experience, psychology has been influenced by the study of the natural world. Physics and the other natural sciences have been important to psychology both conceptually and in terms of methods of study. In particular, the success of the physical sciences in using experiments to develop explanations based on causation led to psychology seeking to do the same. Later, as the biological sciences began to develop, they too became sources of influence in the development of psychology. An often-cited example is the impact of Darwin's work on evolution, with its emphasis on understanding the innate origins of behaviour.

Hence, both philosophy and science have been influential in shaping the nature of psychology. The continuity of these influences is indicated in a review of research on memory by Tulving and Madigan (1970). Looking at the then-current findings, they began by suggesting, only partly in jest, that there was very little that would have surprised Aristotle (perhaps the greatest of the early Greek philosopher-scientists)! To see more clearly how psychology developed from these sources, we will consider two of the great pioneers: Wilhelm Wundt and William James. Taken together, their contributions laid the foundation for most of modern psychology, while reflecting the impact of philosophy and natural science.

The son of a Lutheran pastor, Wilhelm Wundt was born in Baden, Germany, in 1832, and received a medical degree at the University of Heidelberg, graduating at the top of his class in 1855. Shortly after, he went to Berlin to study under Johannes Müller, who had earlier established the first laboratory of experimental physiology. While Wundt's association with Müller was fairly brief, it had a significant influence on him, inspiring him to give up medicine to pursue research in physiological processes. Wundt's training led him to study behaviour by examining elementary sensory processes. His background in medicine made it natural to emphasize physiological aspects of behaviour, though he also hoped that eventually psychology could analyse higher mental processes. He was a prolific writer, publishing almost 500 articles and books and writing papers on all aspects of psychology, from physiological processes to social behaviour. By today's standards, his equipment and techniques were primitive, but the impact of his work was far-reaching.

At this time, psychology did not exist as a distinct discipline; as a result, Wundt's appointment at the University of Leipzig was as a professor of 'scientific philosophy' (as opposed to classical philosophy). Thus, a man whose training was in medicine and physiology became a founder of psychology, while teaching as a philosopher! Out of these unusual circumstances emerged the new discipline, and Wundt played a significant role, both through his own work and his impact on his students: although Wundt himself was designated a 'philosopher', he advocated the creation of a new field of experimental psychology. By the end of the century, psychology departments had been created at several universities, and some of the founders of these programmes (for example, E. B. Titchner and J. M. Cattell) studied under Wundt. As a result, Wundt's conception of an experimental psychology – physiologically-oriented, emphasizing basic sensory processes – was an important influence in the early development of psychology, and many regard him as the founder of modern psychology.

Key Thinker: **William Wundt**

Wilhelm Wundt (1832 – 1920) was born in Baden, Germany, the son of a Lutheran pastor. He received a degree in medicine from the University of Heidelberg in 1855, graduating at the top of his class. Over time, his interests turned toward research in physiology, particularly sensory processes. This led him to an interest in psychology, and in 1875 he founded what is regarded as the first laboratory of experimental psychology at the University of Leipzig. Wundt hoped that eventually the study of sensory processes would lead to an understanding of higher mental processes, and he wrote papers on all aspects of psychology, from physiological processes to social behaviour. A prolific writer as well as researcher, he published almost 500 articles and books, totalling almost 60,000 printed pages. As a teacher and researcher, he influenced many early psychologists, but the approach he took to the study of behaviour, called structuralism, has been supplanted by other approaches within psychology. Despite this, Wundt is often regarded as the founder of modern psychology.

Interestingly, one of the other early giants of psychology, William James, also began as a medical student. James, the elder brother of the novelist Henry James (*The Turn of the Screw* is often considered the first of the psychological novels), was born to a wealthy family in Boston, Massachusetts, in 1842. Unlike Wundt, James was an indifferent student, and tried several fields before finally receiving a medical degree from Harvard when he was almost 30. At this point (1872), he was asked to teach half of a course in physiology at Harvard; within three years the course had evolved into a study of 'The Relations Between Physiology and Psychology'. Three years after that, he dropped the physiological component, and began teaching a course which was explicitly psychological.

It was at this time that James was asked by publisher Henry Holt to prepare a textbook on psychology. He accepted, thinking it would be a straightforward task. After all, he was fluent in German and French as well as English, and knew most of the existing literature (including Wundt's work). Writing the book turned into a mammoth enterprise, consuming almost 12 years, and resulting in two massive volumes totalling approximately 1000 pages. James himself was ultimately dissatisfied with his efforts, telling Holt, '*1st*, that there is no such thing as a *science* of psychology, and *2nd*, that W. J. is an incapable' (quoted by Fancher 1979, p. 160). In fact, by the time of the publication of *Principles of Psychology* (1890), James's interests had turned towards philosophy, and with the exception of *Varieties of Religious Experience* (1902), his significant later work was all philosophical, not psychological. In his later years, his appointment at Harvard was in philosophy.

From this brief biography, and James's own comment, one might conclude that his efforts in psychology had little impact on the developing field. In fact, nothing could be further from the truth. Like his brother Henry, William James was a gifted writer, and his *Principles of Psychology* was both influential and widely read – it is probably the best-selling textbook in the history of psychology (and is still in print). More importantly, he was an incisive thinker, and his analysis of basic problems set the framework for later research in many areas, from emotion to consciousness. Doing experiments did not particularly appeal to James (although he *did* set up a laboratory for teaching purposes in 1875, the same year as Wundt); he preferred analysing how the mind functioned rather than trying to observe its basic parts. Consequently, he expressed little interest in Wundt's approach, which he

Key Thinker: **William James**

William James (1842 – 1910) was one of the most influential and articulate of the early American psychologists. Indeed, his writing is so clear and engaging that it has been said that he wrote like a novelist. (Interestingly, his younger brother Henry is often regarded as the creator of the psychological novel.) He came from a wealthy family, and travelled extensively during his career, from the salons of Europe to the jungles of Brazil. His academic career was spent at Harvard University, first as a student, then as a professor. His student career was undistinguished: he started in chemistry, switched to medicine, took a foray into biology and eventually, after several interruptions, finished his medical degree when he was almost 30. He began his teaching career as an instructor in physiology at Harvard, but gradually incorporated more psychological content, so that by 1878 the course was purely psychological in focus. At this time, he was approached to write a psychology textbook; the task took more than a decade to complete, but his *Principles of Psychology* became one of the most influential texts in the history of the discipline, and is still in print. Over time, however, his interests shifted towards philosophy, and he ended his career in the philosophy department at Harvard. Within psychology, he is perhaps best known for coining the phrase 'the stream of consciousness'; the approach he founded, called functionalism, has remained influential, particularly among cognitive psychologists.

once compared to trying to understand a house by studying each of its bricks (James 1884). In turn, Wundt was less than impressed with James, saying of *Principles of Psychology*, 'It is literature, it is beautiful, but it is not psychology' (quoted by Fancher 1979, p. 128).

Wundt and James each played a major role in shaping the direction of psychology as a discipline. As contemporaries, they each began as a medical student and ended as a professor of philosophy (at least in title, if not content). In this sense, they highlight the double heritage of psychology – the natural sciences and philosophy. At the same time, they differed significantly in their approach to the study of behaviour and the mind. James's approach, with its emphasis on how the mind works, came to be known as **functionalism**, while Wundt's study of basic mental processes became known as **structuralism**. Wundt was a precise and prolific experimenter, while James cared little for the laboratory. Yet, taken together, they point toward two crucial aspects of modern psychology: the importance of making careful observations, and the importance of asking the proper questions. While neither man's views are accepted completely today, their efforts and insights provided much of the foundation for the new discipline. If psychologists today seem to see further than they did, it is partly because (as Isaac Newton once said of his own accomplishments) they are standing on the shoulders of giants.

Psychology, then, traces its origins to rather divergent roots. This diversity is still evident in the current form of the discipline, which extends in many directions. Today, there are individuals involved in psychology who look at everything from intracellular chemistry, to the causes of forgetting, to the nature of romantic love. In some cases, they may feel more comfortable talking with colleagues in other disciplines than with other types of psychologists. Some would see this as a failing, and it is *possible* that time will support that view. At present, though, one can view

functionalism an approach to the study of behaviour pioneered by William James, which emphasizes the analysis of the processes by which the mind works.

structuralism an approach to psychology pioneered by Wundt which attempted to analyse the contents of the mind, using the introspectionist method.

this diversity as simply a reflection of the complexity of both psychology's origins and its subject matter. One might draw an analogy to the medieval world view, which saw man as the measure of all things, and therefore pla◉d humanity at the centre of the universe: psychology is clearly not the measure of all things, but it is perhaps fitting that the study of human behaviour should have links extending into all the domains of human knowledge, from the natural sciences to the humanities.

Try it Yourself

William James emphasized asking good questions over gathering data; Wilhelm Wundt was concerned with gathering data. Which aspect appeals to you? Examine your own behaviour: do you prefer thinking about why a situation is occurring or why people are behaving in certain ways, or do you prefer to bide your time while closely observing people and situations to gather information? Are these two orientations necessarily antagonistic? Could you find a way to reconcile the orientations of Wundt and James? How could you convince each man that the orientation of the other was necessary?

METHODS OF STUDYING BEHAVIOUR
The Role of the Scientific Method in Psychology

Given the complexity and diversity of human behaviour, how does one go about studying it? While the five approaches differ in the methods they emphasize, all psychologists share a belief in the observational methods of science as the foundation of psychological research. We noted earlier that psychology is distinguished from pursuits like astrology or phrenology, or even common-sense wisdom like proverbs, by being a science. But what exactly does that mean?

empirical based on making observations, as in an empirical theory.

First and foremost, psychology is **empirical** – that is, it is based on making observations. Precisely what observations researchers are interested in varies according to the approach, but there is a common emphasis on *objective* observation; normally, this means that observations can be verified by different observers. In this sense, psychology is a public endeavour, which cannot depend on secret knowledge or mystic inspiration. (More will be said about this in conjunction with introspectionism.)

The emphasis on empiricism is important, but does not directly tell us what to observe, and how. Suppose someone likes to 'people watch' by sitting in a sidewalk café; if a friend joins in, does that make their observations scientific? To decide, one has to remember that the goal of psychology is to understand behaviour – and understanding requires more than a random cataloguing of observations. By itself, counting how many people go past a sidewalk café has no scientific value. At the very least, one must *classify* those observations in some way, which may lead to relating them to something else (perhaps the weather, or time of day, or some other factor). That is, science depends on *organized observation*, based on the belief that classification of observations will ultimately lead to an explanation of those observations (Robinson 1985). Understanding and explanation require the formulation of general principles; at the highest level,

theory a structured set of principles intended to explain a set of phenomena.

a structured set of principles is called a **theory**. A theory provides a coherent structure for relating various observations, and often permits prediction of future observations. Traditionally, theories in science have explained observed events by identifying their causes; at the very least, a theory provides a way of generalizing across specific observations. Hence, observations and theories are complementary to each other: observations suggest a theory, a theory is tested by observations, observations suggest modifications of the theory, and so on.

Essentially, observations and theory are connected by two basic cognitive processes – inductive and deductive reasoning. **Induction** involves forming general principles from specific observations. The story of Isaac Newton discovering gravity by being hit by a falling apple is doubtless folklore. What is *not* folklore is that Newton saw a connection between falling apples and orbiting planets – that is, gravity was a general principle that was derived from the specific observations of falling apples and orbiting planets, and could be used to link these observations. **Deduction**, by contrast, involves drawing specific conclusions from a set of general principles. For example, Freud believed that aggression is an innate drive which can be expressed in destructive behaviour (a general principle). From this, it follows that if someone commits murder, it is because of this innate drive (a specific conclusion). Most commonly in science, deduction is used to derive a **hypothesis** – a specific outcome or prediction derived from a theory, which can then be evaluated by making further observations.

induction a process of reasoning based on forming general principles from specific observations.

deduction the process of drawing specific conclusions from a set of general principles.

hypothesis a statement describing a proposed relationship between variables; a specific outcome or prediction derived from a theory which can be evaluated by making further observations.

Which comes first, you may ask – inductively forming principles from observations, or deductively deriving hypotheses to be tested by observing? In reality, this is much like the old chestnut about whether the chicken or the egg comes first: there is no clear answer. In practice, researchers use both processes, in a more or less continuous interaction (see Figure 1.9). Sometimes, past experience will lead to an interest in particular phenomena, and then observations will lead to a theoretical insight. Alternatively, thinking about a theory may lead to the discovery of a new implication, which then must be tested for accuracy by making appropriate observations. As we will see in the following chapters, both processes have played important roles in the development of the five approaches. As supporters of the scientific method, all approaches share common concerns: to make careful, consistent observations, to avoid errors, and to develop clear theories. Despite the general agreement on these principles, there is still room for a range of particular techniques when gathering information.

Introspectionism and Public Observation

At first glance, it might seem that the best way to learn about behaviour would be to carefully analyse your own behaviour. After all, whom do you know more intimately than yourself? This approach, called **introspectionism**, was, in fact, used in various forms by a number of early psychologists, including Wundt and James. Despite its early popularity, introspectionism (literally, 'looking within') proved to be a questionable technique. Even when it involved carefully structured forms of self-analysis, as in Wundt's case, the method ultimately failed to provide clear answers. In part, this was due to the limitations inherent in the process of perception, as we have discussed. But a second weakness stems from trying to use private experiences as data. Suppose two people, trained in Wundtian introspection, view two colour samples. One person says one sample is red, and the other is pink – that is, they differ in one sensory characteristic, colour. The other person says that both samples are the same colour, but that they differ in

introspectionism a method of gathering data in which the individual attempts to analyse the content of their conscious mind; associated with the structuralist approach.

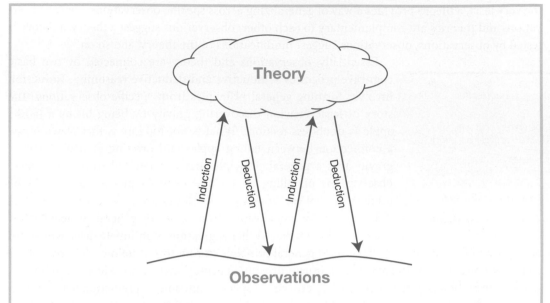

Figure 1.9 The Interaction of Induction and Deduction in Research Research involves an interaction between generalizations derived from observations (induction) and the formulation of predictions about reality derived from theory (deduction). Most researchers use both, and trying to say which comes first is rather like the question about the chicken and the egg.

saturation (purity of the colour), with the 'pink' one being a mixture of red and white. In essence, the two observers disagree as to whether their experience of the stimuli reflects one quality, or two. How can we resolve this dispute? One may be wrong, or each may be correct about their own experience, but since we have no way to determine, we are no closer to a general understanding of what is involved in perceiving a colour sample.

To indicate the importance of this interpretation issue, consider what happened in the history of taste research. One of Wundt's students, named Federico Kiesow, did pioneering research on taste, and borrowed an analogy from colour in order to describe taste phenomena – that is, he argued that we experience *mixtures* of salty, sour, bitter and sweet, just as we experience mixtures of colours. It turned out that this interpretation is wrong, and although another researcher, Hjalmar Ohrwall, argued that the four taste qualities were *discrete*, his view was overlooked for almost a hundred years, creating a major setback in taste research! (Bartoshuk 2003).

To avoid the problems of introspection, psychology, like other forms of science, has come to emphasize *public* techniques of observation, which make it possible for observers to agree on what has occurred. Even so, this principle takes many forms, since researchers sometimes disagree as to what is 'public'. In general, any aspect of behaviour which can be observed consistently (that is, produces agreement among observers) is considered open for possible study. For example, an arm movement is public. Many physiological responses can also be considered public, in that the technologies used for measuring them produce results which observers can agree on. When one refers to mental states, it becomes more ambiguous: some psychologists believe that reports of mental states are inherently unreliable, and cannot be considered public. Others argue that as long as the *results* of such reports are consistent, then it is possible to devise public measures of mental events. For example, studies of memory depend on what people are able to report remembering, and those reports are typically considered a public measure of memory.

Some researchers also extend the requirement for public obser-

operational definition a term whose meaning is defined by the processes or observable events used to measure it.

vation to the way terms are defined. So-called **operational definitions** must be based on observable events. For example, to define *love* as 'a feeling in the heart' is not acceptable as an operational definition, because it is not based on an observable event. However, defining it as 'giving a dozen roses to someone' is operational. The difficulty with such definitions, as this example suggests, is that sometimes an operational definition seems unrelated to the concept which it supposedly defines. Defining love as giving roses may be operational, but does it really reflect what people mean when they talk about love? If not, how is the definition useful? Similarly, cultural differences can make it difficult to define the meaning of gestures in operational terms. For example, an 'O' formed by the thumb and index finger may mean 'OK' in North America, but 'zero' or 'no' in France (Hall 1981). In the end, while all researchers accept the importance of using public processes to confirm observations, not all psychologists see value in operational definitions.

Try it Yourself

Basing a definition on something observable is not itself enough to make a definition operational, because different observers may still define what is to be observed differently. Try this simple example: light a candle and sit quietly around it with two or three other people. For five minutes, let each person silently count the number of times the candle flame flickers. After five minutes, compare your counts. Do not be surprised to see numbers varying from 2 to 2000. Yet each of you was watching the same candle flame! The problem was that each of you was defining 'flicker' in a different way. Now, work as a group to develop a common definition of 'flicker', and then watch the flame again for five minutes. Using this agreed-upon definition of 'flicker', do the individual number counts of the group come closer to agreement?

How could you measure the following so that the observations would meet the requirements of an operational definition?

hunger   joy   fatigue   grief   aggression

Measures of Behaviour, Research Settings and Research Methods

In doing research on behaviour, there are a number of ways to gather information. As a result, a researcher must make choices in terms of how to measure behaviour, what sort of setting to use, and what type of research method to employ. In the remainder of this chapter, we will be looking at the various possibilities in some detail. However, before doing so, it is useful to describe briefly the kinds of options that exist.

Since research requires making observations, the most basic question

self-report a method of gathering data which involves asking an individual to describe their behaviour or mental state in some way, such as an interview, survey or psychological inventory.

is what sort of *measure of behaviour* to use. Generally speaking, observation can be based on two different ways of measuring behaviour: self-report and direct observation. **Self-report** involves asking the person to indicate their behaviour or mental state in some way; that is,

think-aloud protocol a transcript of the comments made when an individual is asked to describe their thoughts and behaviour while working on a task such as problem solving.

what they have done or are doing and what they are thinking or feeling. Such procedures are used in many situations, but most commonly in interviews, surveys and psychological testing. For example, a survey might ask individuals how often they consume alcohol. Self-report has the attraction of seeming very direct, and in some cases it allows researchers to access information which is otherwise unobtainable, such as mental processes. For example, in cognitive research, experimenters may ask people to think aloud while trying to solve a problem. The comments are transcribed as **think-aloud protocols**, which may reveal information about the participants' thought processes.

direct observation any observational technique which depends on direct measurement of behaviour by the researcher, rather than asking an individual to report their behaviour.

The alternative to self-report procedures is for researchers to use **direct observation** of the behaviour of interest; in this case, the researcher observes behaviour in some way that does not depend on what the individual says. Direct observation by an independent person tends to be more neutral or objective than self-report, and is more easily verified by having multiple observers. Overall, direct observation is used most frequently in experiments, although observational methods take many forms, as we will see. The choice between self-report and direct observation as a method of measuring behaviour represents one of the basic decisions a researcher must make when beginning the study of a particular issue. In addition, there are decisions about what type of setting to use, and the type of research method.

research setting the context in which research is conducted, either a laboratory setting (which involves having participants come to a special location), or a field setting (which requires going to where the people are whom the researcher wishes to study).

The choice of **research setting** concerns whether to observe behaviour in a *laboratory setting*, which involves having participants come to a special location (the laboratory), or in a *field setting*, which requires the researcher going to where the people are that he or she wishes to observe. In a laboratory setting, it is possible to create particular conditions, in order to see how people behave in that situation. However, bringing individuals to a laboratory is also somewhat artificial, since participants will be very aware of being observed. (Recall the earlier comments about self-awareness and reactivity.) A field setting may seem more natural, but is necessarily more difficult to control. For example, a researcher may be interested in how children interact while playing. Bringing them into a laboratory would make it possible to control what toys are available and other factors, but may also lead to non-spontaneous behaviour. By contrast, going to a playground to observe such interactions would be more natural, but would allow no control over what was played, by whom, or for how long, thus making comparisons more difficult. Hence, each type of setting has advantages and disadvantages.

research method a procedure for examining a problem and gathering observations; in broad terms, research methods are either experimental or non-experimental

non-experimental methods research methods which do not involve direct control of any factor, in contrast to experiments; sometimes called descriptive/correlational designs.

The choice of setting is often closely linked to the **research method** chosen. An *experiment* is a procedure whereby a researcher systematically varies one or more factors in order to see what effect the changes have on behaviour. For example, in order to examine the effects of alcohol on coordination, a researcher might systematically vary the amount of alcohol which different subjects consume in the experiment. Experiments are normally conducted in a laboratory setting, since this makes it easier to control the factors one wishes to systematically vary. **Non-experimental methods**, sometimes called descriptive/correlational designs, do not involve direct control of any factor, in contrast to experiments. For example, testing individuals' coordination before and after they visit a bar would not provide any direct control over how much alcohol people drank. Consequently, such comparisons would not directly tell us anything about how alcohol affects coordination. Non-experimental methods include naturalistic observation, case studies and surveys, among others. *Quasi-experiments*, as the name suggests, are similar to experiments, but do not provide the same degree of control. Typically, quasi-experiments are used when studying characteristics which cannot be manipulated by the researcher (such as gender, age or medical condition), or in circumstances where manipulation would be unethical (for example, requiring people to smoke in order to see if smoking causes health problems). All three types of research method will be discussed in more detail later in this chapter.

The three characteristics of research – method, setting and measurement type – can be used to describe virtually all of the techniques used in psychological research. As we consider some specific techniques, you should ask yourself where they fit in terms of these characteristics.

At this point, the description of research techniques may seem very abstract. Why, for example, would a researcher choose to use self-report in a particular situation? To understand how psychologists make such decisions, let us consider a real-world problem: why do people help or not help in an emergency? In recent years, there have been all-too-frequent reports in the media of situations where someone is in trouble, and onlookers don't get involved. In one well-known case, a young woman named Kitty Genovese was on her way home from her job as a waitress in a New York restaurant. It was late, and the street was virtually deserted as she neared the building where she lived. Unfortunately, before she reached it, a man attacked her, stabbing her. She screamed, and her assailant ran off. Before she could reach home or other shelter, he returned. This time, a man leaned from his apartment window to yell at the attacker, who then retreated again. Kitty then tried to seek refuge in the lobby of an apartment building, only to be attacked again. Sadly, she died as a result of the attack (Latané and Darley 1969).

As shocking as this story is, most people were more shocked to learn that despite her screams, *no one telephoned the police*, even though the whole sequence took nearly 40 minutes. At first glance, it appears to be a case of utter callousness: someone must have heard; why wouldn't they call? The police and reporters combed the area to seek witnesses, and found 38 people living close to the scene who acknowledged having been home at the time. (One man said the sound of his window air conditioner blocked outside noise – on a night when it was nearly freezing!) Obviously, none of these people phoned the police. How can we understand this? Is it really the result of callousness and apathy? The tragic death of Kitty Genovese, and other similar incidents, led to the coining of a new term: **bystander apathy**, used to describe situations where people do not intervene in an emergency. For researchers, as for society in general, the challenge is to understand why such incidents happen; ideally, such understanding might lead to ways of increasing helping behaviour in the future. Faced with a problem like this, it is possible to proceed in many ways. Let us explore this situation further, seeing how psychologists might try to learn more about the underlying behaviour.

bystander apathy the failure of onlookers to intervene in an emergency; despite the label, the cause is often unrelated to apathy.

Non-experimental Methods: Interviews and Surveys

interview a method of gathering data in which a researcher asks an individual questions; the format may be pre-planned and highly structured, or relatively free-flowing and unstructured.

The police and reporters in the Kitty Genovese case used **interviews** as a research method. In an interview, a researcher asks questions, which may be pre-planned and highly structured, or relatively free-flowing and unstructured. The responses from the person interviewed

Try it Yourself

To understand how self-reports and direct observations can yield different results, consider the example of eating. How much do you eat during a typical day? How many calories do you consume? Give a rough estimate. Now spend a day actually recording what you eat and calculate the number of calories you consumed. Do the results match your estimate? Did measuring your consumption make you feel self-conscious about your eating behaviour? Is it possible your food choices changed because of this? When people are asked how much they normally eat, they are usually quite inaccurate. This is why a standard technique used to help people diet is to ask them to keep a record of their food consumption: many people are appalled at how many calories they ingested without being aware of it! Not surprisingly, being aware can itself cause changes in (eating) behaviour (*reactivity*). As a result, the choice between self-report and direct observation can be a complicated decision for a researcher.

represent *self-report* data, since the person is describing his or her own behaviour. In the Genovese case, for example, a number of the people interviewed reported hearing the screams, or even watching the attack from their windows, and wondering why the police hadn't arrived. Rather than being apathetic, these people seemed very upset. When questioned as to why they hadn't phoned the police, these people typically stated that they *assumed someone else* had done so already. (The reality was that no one had.) If we accept the self-reports as accurate (as opposed to being a rationalization for not having helped), the interviews showed that these people had failed to phone because of a faulty assumption, *not* because they were apathetic. By suggesting an alternative to apathy as an explanation of the incident, the self-reports were very useful.

survey a technique for determining attitudes of many individuals by providing a pre-planned series of questions to which individuals respond.

Another approach to the issue of bystander apathy would be to do a survey. A **survey** is a technique for determining the attitudes of a large number of people. Some surveys use predetermined response options; this is commonly called a *fixed-alternative* survey. For example, a researcher might ask, 'Would you be willing to aid a stranger in distress?' and allow the answers, 'Yes', 'No' or 'I'm not sure'. To provide a bit more choice, the researcher might give a rating scale, with several options, from very positive to very negative, or from very likely to not at all likely. The fixed-alternative technique has several advantages, including being easy to administer and analyse. Its major limitation is that it allows little flexibility in answers, and thereby limits how much information can be obtained from respondents; in the worst case, the questions and response alternatives may be seen as inappropriate by the person responding. For example, asking a traditional Muslim woman if she would be willing to help a male stranger may lead to a 'no' – not because she wouldn't care, but because her religious beliefs and/or culture prohibit contact with male strangers. Rephrasing the question to ask, 'Would you be willing to ask your father or brother to help a male stranger?' might well lead to a 'yes' response. Thus, culture is one of many factors that affect people's responses, and how one asks the question is often crucial to getting meaningful results.

By contrast, *open-ended* surveys use skilled interviewers; they ask prearranged questions, but allow the respondent to give a spontaneous response. At first glance, this may seem more useful than a survey with fixed alternatives, but it has several drawbacks. First, it requires a skilled interviewer to get clear responses without coaching or leading the interviewee. (Coaching could of course lead to **bias**, a systematic distortion of results.) Second, it takes considerable effort to analyse the sometimes lengthy responses, and it becomes difficult to summarize responses from a large group of people. Even if one is willing to face these obstacles, responses may not always be very meaningful. In one survey which asked people 'What do you think is the most pressing problem facing the world today?', the majority of responses simply restated the day's newspaper headlines! Without adequate time to reflect on the questions, there is a danger of such superficial responses; the more complex the issue, the greater this problem is likely to be. In such cases, a series of carefully developed fixed-alternative questions may actually give more meaningful information about people's views than will open-ended questions.

Surveys, even when open-ended, are more structured than interviews, and are employed to gather information from a relatively large number of individuals. Today, surveys are used extensively by government, political groups, corporations, the news media and other groups. Sometimes it seems as if we are bombarded by reports of survey results, many of which are less than insightful. (Does it surprise you, for example, that people who have lost their job are less optimistic about the economy than those who are employed full-time, as one survey reported?)

Surveys and Sampling Procedures

Whether the issues are earth-shaking or trivial, all surveys face a common problem: who to survey? At first glance, this may seem very straightforward – simply select a large number of people. Unfortunately, large numbers do not guarantee that a survey will provide meaningful results. To understand why, we need to consider two concepts: population and sample. A **population** is the group whose views one wishes to determine; a **sample** is the sub-group of the population which one actually studies. For example, if a political party wished to determine the attitudes of Canadian voters towards the prime minister, the population would be all Canadians eligible to vote. Since contacting some 20 million people would obviously be impossible, the researchers must use a smaller sample group. (In a case like this, they would probably contact between 200 and 1000 people, depending on the number of sub-groups and desired variance.) In selecting a sample, the goal is to obtain a **representative sample** – that is, one which fairly represents the population of interest – and thereby reduce the likelihood of bias in the results. In the case of the election poll, suppose the researcher went to a large shopping centre in Toronto at lunch time, and stopped every third person that went by. This procedure would not result in a representative sample, since not all Canadian voters are equally likely to be found at that site. (For example, it is unlikely that anyone working a night shift would be in a mall at lunchtime!) While various techniques exist for selecting a sample, they all share the goal of seeking a balanced representation of the population of interest.

As you might expect, sampling procedures in surveys (and in other forms of research) always have some potential for error. In order to deal with this, proper surveys always calculate the probable margin of error, and report this with the results. If you don't see such figures indicated, be cautious – especially in comparing numbers which are close in size. For example, an election survey reported the percentage of people who favoured each political party in an upcoming election (Toulin 1993). In this survey, the margin of error was ± 2 per cent, meaning if a reported value was 12 per cent, the actual figure in the population was likely to be between 10 and 14 per

population in statistics, the group whose characteristics one wishes to determine, and from which a sample is chosen.

sample in statistics, a sub-group drawn from a population; in research, the group which one actually studies.

representative sample in statistics, a sample whose composition matches the population from which it is drawn.

cent. In this case, the margin of error meant that the apparent difference between the third place party (12 per cent) and the fifth place party (8 per cent) was more apparent than real.

Obviously, the process of obtaining a sample for a survey is not a simple matter, and one must be cautious in looking at survey results – especially when the numbers are taken out of context. Nonetheless, when properly conducted, surveys provide an excellent tool for determining the views of a large group of people. (For further information on sampling, see the Appendix.)

Limitations of Self-reports

Self-report procedures, like interviews and surveys, are an important method of measuring behaviour; but their use also poses some problems (Schwarz and Oyserman 2001). One basic concern is *accuracy*: is self-report an accurate reflection of behaviour? After all, individuals may not always be clear about their own behaviour, owing to lapses of attention, memory distortions or other factors. This problem was highlighted by a classic study of racial discrimination, which examined attitudes of restaurant and hotel owners toward racial minorities (LaPiere 1934). Because the study was done in the USA in the 1930s, there was little human rights legislation to influence behaviour and attitudes. Travelling across the country with a young Chinese couple, LaPiere kept records of their experiences. Out of 251 establishments visited, only *one* refused to serve the couple (who typically went in first). Six months after their trip, a letter asking about policies was sent to the same establishments. The letter asked, 'Will you accept members of the Chinese race in your establishment?' Overall, 51 per cent replied to the letter, and of these, 92 per cent said they would *not* serve Chinese people. In this case, the owners *claimed* to be more discriminatory than they actually *behaved*!

More commonly, a person may lie to a researcher in order to create a more favourable impression. For example, the man who said his air conditioner prevented him from hearing anything when Kitty Genovese was attacked was presumably lying, given the cold weather; in this case, the lie served to justify his failure to intervene. Because of such uncertainties, researchers using self-report procedures must always consider the possibility that what people say is not what they really do (Wicker 1971). Furthermore, in many cases, such as surveys of sexual behaviour, there is no way to determine the accuracy of what people say (Rutter 2002). Consequently, researchers do not rely solely on surveys and similar self-report procedures as a means of understanding behaviour.

Naturalistic Observation and Unobtrusive Measures

Since self-reports may be distorted in various ways, one might prefer to study behaviour through direct observation. One form of direct observation is **naturalistic observation**, which, as the name suggests, involves observing behaviour in a natural setting. Depending on the type of behaviour a researcher is interested in, this technique may be relatively simple, or quite difficult. In the case of bystander apathy, a major hurdle is the unpredictability of emergencies, which makes it almost impossible for a researcher to be present as events unfold. When the behaviour of interest is more frequent and/or more predictable, naturalistic observation has the advantage of presenting behaviour in a real-world context. Observing in a natural setting avoids the potential artificiality of the laboratory, and for many behaviours, such as social interactions, this can be a great benefit. For example, naturalistic observation has frequently been used in studying children's play.

naturalistic observation a research method which is based on observing behaviour in a natural setting, without interfering or attempting to control conditions.

At the same time, naturalistic observation has some limitations. One obvious concern, referred to earlier, is *reactivity*: when people know they are being watched, they may act differently. In practice, this is often not a serious concern, since there are a number of ways to conceal the observation process. One technique, made famous by the American television show *Candid Camera*, is to use a hidden camera. In other cases, researchers will be able to use a one-way mirror, or other form of blind, to make their presence less noticeable. (The day-care centre at our university has a one-way mirror, allowing students in the early learning programme to observe the children at play.) Sometimes, simply staying in a situation long enough to make one's presence familiar is sufficient to reduce reactivity. Alan King, a Canadian documentary filmmaker, is noted for spending weeks or months with the people he wishes to film. He has commented, 'I carry the camera from day one, but there's no film in it for the first week or so. After that, they're so used to it, they forget about my presence.' In one memorable film, *A Married Couple*, King ended up recording the break-up of a marriage (King 1971).

participant observation a non-experimental research method in which the researcher becomes part of a group he or she wishes to observe.

Very close to King's approach is a variation of naturalistic observation called **participant observation**, in which the researcher becomes part of a group he or she wishes to observe. One example is described in *Among the Thugs*, where author Bill Buford joined a group of English rowdies to learn more about fan violence (Buford 1991). His involvement became so intense that he was injured during a post-game riot! Apart from personal risk, participant observation also poses a risk of biasing the results, since the researcher's interaction with the group may alter what would otherwise occur. In addition, as involvement with the group increases, the researcher's objectivity is likely to be reduced.

unobtrusive measure an indirect measure of behaviour intended to avoid the reactivity which can occur with direct observation; such measures typically require making complex assumptions about the relationship of the measure to actual behaviour.

In order to avoid the problem of reactivity, researchers will sometimes use **unobtrusive measures** as a means of recording behaviour. As the name implies, unobtrusive measures involve recording behaviour indirectly, rather than possibly disrupting it by direct observation. Examples would include checking the frequency of borrowing of various library books as a means of determining which is most popular, or checking sales of travel insurance after an airline crash to measure changing levels of anxiety among travellers (Webb *et al.* 1972). Inventing unobtrusive ways to measure various behaviours can be a creative exercise, but such measures can also be very difficult to interpret. In one instance, an archaeologist attempted to determine whether men or women lived longer in ancient Rome by counting the number of tombstones for each sex. The assumption was that among married couples, the first to die would be more likely to receive a tombstone; thus, finding more tombstones for men meant women lived longer! Of course, this ignores a wide number of possible factors, from cultural norms about death to the impact of war on male mortality rates. Consequently, when using unobtrusive measures, there is always a need to make sure that the characteristic observed is in fact measuring what one intends.

Case Studies

case study a detailed description of a single individual, typically used to provide information on the person's history and to aid in interpreting the person's behaviour.

One of the most fascinating aspects of psychology for many readers is the use of case studies. A **case study** is a detailed description of a single individual. Like a well-written biography, a good case study seems to capture the essence of a particular person's behaviour. While this sense of drama is certainly one of the attractions of case studies for general readers, the value of this method as a research tool stems from the contextual detail it provides on the behaviour of an individual. Case studies basically arose out of medical practice, where developing a clear picture of a patient's background and current symptoms served as an important diagnostic tool. Many basic advances in psychological understanding have come from case studies, particularly in the area of brain function.

Try it Yourself

Imagine you want to measure soft drink preferences unobtrusively. How would you do this? Think about this before you go on reading.

You probably thought about sitting in a restaurant or school cafeteria and counting the number of people who bought certain soft drinks. But did you consider that not all soft drinks may be available in this particular location? Did you consider the time of day (since some people may prefer caffeinated soft drinks but will avoid them in the evening, or some people who don't normally choose caffeinated drinks might choose them in the late afternoon when their energy level is low)? What about other factors that could affect your measurements? Thinking about this now, do you trust your original method to give accurate results?

For example, the discovery of the speech area in the brain came about through the study of a patient who lost the ability to speak after a head injury (see Chapter 2 for more detail). Case studies are found in other areas as well. For example, Sigmund Freud (whose training was in medicine) emphasized case studies as a basic tool of psychoanalysis.

An effective case study can aid treatment, and can also deepen our insight into behaviour in general. However, like other methods, case studies have their limitations. One important concern is *representativeness*: a case study is essentially a sample of one, and consequently a researcher must be careful in generalizing to a larger population. For example, if a researcher studying Kitty Genovese's death focused on a single observer to the crime, the person might or might not reflect how other observers reacted. Fortunately, in many situations, the important aspects of a case may well be applicable to a broader group – for example, when studying basic neurological functions. (One of my (WEG) early psychology mentors, whose specialization was the visual system, used to comment, 'In physiology, a sample of one is sufficient.') Unfortunately, one cannot always be certain whether a case is representative or not. In one well-known instance, Russian neurologist A. R. Luria reported on a man who had a remarkable memory – so remarkable that he essentially never forgot *anything* (Luria 1968). In fact, the man (referred to as S.) would write down things which he *wanted* to forget, in the hope that his mind would no longer be obliged to retain them! As Luria studied S., he discovered that he was also unusual in that his senses appeared 'cross-wired': sounds could create visual images, and had textures and colours as well. This sensory linkage, called *synaesthesia*, apparently was a factor in his unusual memory. Luria's account makes remarkable reading, but it is not clear how relevant the case is to our general understanding of either memory or sensory functioning. Such cases are extremely rare: Richard Cytowic, an American neurologist who has studied another individual with synaesthesia, estimates that fewer than ten people in a million show any real indications of the phenomenon (Cytowic 1993). Consequently, such cases seem rather unrepresentative. As disappointing as this is, it does point out one of the ways that researchers evaluate representativeness – by looking for similar cases. If similar cases are found, this bolsters the representativeness of the behaviour.

A second limitation of most case studies is not so easily remedied. By their nature, clinical cases arise when someone seeks treatment; as a result, the doctor/researcher is presented with a situation whose causes are not directly known (one of the purposes of developing a clinical history, of course, is to try to learn what preceded the current situation). This frequently limits the ability to draw conclusions about causation, particularly for behaviour. For example, a doctor examines a teenage boy who has been in trouble with both school officials and the police. The case history reveals that the boy's delivery at birth was difficult, which may have resulted in minor brain damage. His mother died when he was 7, and his father, who has remarried, is emotionally remote and physically abusive. Which of these factors, if any, account for the boy's current problems? In this type of situation, it is difficult to draw clear conclusions, and there is a risk of confusing factors which may be significant and those which may be coincidental. Even in situations where some type of pre- and post-treatment comparisons might be possible, ethical standards require that concerns for the patient's well-being transcend any research goals. Consequently, case studies can be helpful in suggesting further directions for research, but are generally a poor tool for understanding the *causes* of behaviour.

Try it Yourself

Case studies can be fascinating reading and are often very compelling. The presentation of a real person instead of vague numbers (e.g., 'Sam' instead of '200 people') induces us to relate more to the person in the study, and we often put more faith in the case study because of this. (This is the reason why advertisers rely more on testimonials from satisfied customers than on statistics.) Unfortunately, the vividness of a case study does not demonstrate that it is representative. For example, an advertisement may relate the story of 'Joan's' success with an exercise programme, even though 'Joan' may be the only person to have been satisfied!

Think of an example of a testimonial ad you've seen: on what basis do you decide whether the case is representative or not? What else might you want to know in making your assessment?

Correlations and Non-experimental Research

Like surveys and naturalistic observation, most case studies represent non-experimental forms of research. Typically, the purpose of a case study is simply *descriptive*, to provide an accurate portrait of behaviour in a particular situation. While accurate descriptions of behaviour are an important starting point in research, description cannot conclusively tell us why behaviour occurs. Instead, a researcher may look for patterns which link different aspects of behaviour, such as age and willingness to help in an emergency. Any characteristic which can vary (like age) is called a **variable**; a pattern observed between two variables is called a **correlation**. Thus, if people's willingness to help others increases with age, then this would represent a correlation. This correlational approach is commonly used in non-experimental studies, since finding patterns is one of the important ways of increasing our understanding of behaviour. Correlational methods are used to identify possible relationships between factors being studied (in the example above, age and willingness to help).

Correlations can enable researchers to make sense out of what might otherwise seem a jumble of data. For example, Figure 1.10 shows performance on a term examination compared to term

variable any measured characteristic which shows variation across cases or conditions.

correlation a pattern or relationship observed between two variables.

correlation coefficient a descriptive statistic measuring the degree of relationship between two variables. For positive correlations, it is a number which varies between 0.0 and +1.0, and for negative correlations between 0.0 and −1.0; in both cases, the closer the value is to 1, the stronger the relationship between the two variables.

paper grades for students in a course I (WEG) recently taught. In this situation, I wanted to see how performance on the exam compared to that on the papers, since the scores reflect different types of assessment. By using a measurement called a **correlation coefficient,** it is possible to show that there is a moderately strong relationship between the two variables – that is, students tended to get similar grades on the two evaluations. Without the aid of correlational techniques, it would be difficult to know if there is a pattern or not. Thus, a researcher looking for links between measured variables can find correlations very helpful. (For a more detailed discussion of correlations and how they are measured, see the Appendix.)

The desire to find patterns in observational data is part of a larger goal, which is to understand how and why behaviour occurs. In fact, the desire to find correlations as a way of making sense of what we observe is not restricted to researchers. Studies have shown that the search for patterns is a natural human trait. Most of the time, finding patterns in our environment is adaptive – for instance, a young child quickly learns that brightly glowing objects, like stove burners and lights, are usually hot. Unfortunately, sometimes we see patterns where none actually exist; when this happens, it is called an **illusory correlation** (Halpern 1989). B. F. Skinner, the behaviourist, suggested that many forms of superstitious behaviour arise when people falsely perceive connections between their behaviour and a desired or feared outcome (Skinner 1948a). In essence, such superstitions arise out of illusory correlations. Our favourite example from everyday life is what people do while waiting for elevator doors to close: often they tap the edge of the door, push the 'Close' button repeatedly,

illusory correlation a cognitive error in which an individual perceives a relationship between variables where none actually exists.

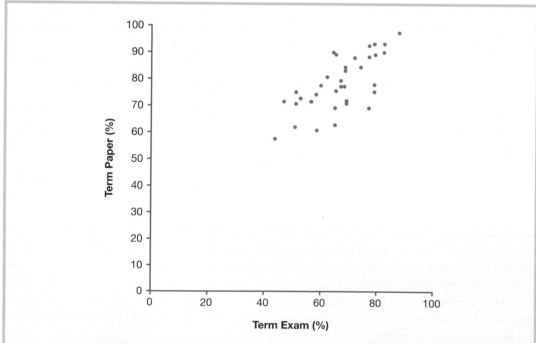

Figure 1.10 Correlation of Academic Grades These data, obtained from an actual class, show that there is a positive correlation (+.75) between performance on term exams and on term papers.

or engage in other actions which may actually do nothing to alter the programmed cycle of the elevator. In fact, this behaviour has been observed in an elevator in which the 'Close' button was disengaged and the door closed after a set period of time. Yet, because the action sometimes coincided with the doors closing, people become convinced it worked! Hence, while seeking patterns can be useful, in everyday life we should be wary of our tendency to see patterns even where none exist.

While finding patterns can help us to make sense of the world, correlations (including those found in non-experimental research) are limited in what they can tell us. The most important limitation concerns explaining *why* an observed pattern occurs. Ideally, we would like to be able to say something like 'A causes B' when we observe a correlation between variables A and B. Unfortunately, a correlation does *not* prove causation. In the example given above, rather than exam performance directly causing term paper performance (or vice versa), it is likely that there are underlying factors (such as ability and hard work) that affect both types of grades.

It can be very tempting to draw conclusions about cause and effect when we see a pattern in events, but this is also a very error-prone process. For example, most people know that different species of birds have distinctly different songs – robins vs. sparrows vs. finches, for instance. That is, there is a relationship between song type and species. From this, one might conclude that each species sings its particular song *because* of its species (that is, that the song is genetically programmed). While this is consistent with everyday observations and plausible in terms of genetic theory, in fact it is wrong – birdsong requires *learning*, somewhat like human language does (Marler 1970). Or consider this example: a study done in Hamburg, Germany, found that over a period of years, there was a correlation between the number of storks nesting in the city and the number of human babies born. That is, more storks were found nesting in those years in which more human babies were born. Obviously, folk tales about storks bringing babies are not true, despite this observed pattern! (The reason for this pattern *may* be a series of underlying links in terms of storks choosing chimneys as nesting sites, and the number of chimneys increasing as human population grows – *or*, it may be coincidence!)

In the end, finding a correlational pattern doesn't tell us *why* the pattern occurred; further research is required to find out its origin. Generally, one of three possible explanations applies:

1 one variable actually causes changes in the other;
2 there is a third factor linking the observed variables (for example, ability in the case of student grades); or
3 the observed pattern is really coincidental, and would not reoccur in a new set of similar observations.

Try it Yourself

Have you ever thought about someone when suddenly they telephoned you or appeared? This is the 'speak of the devil' effect. Given the three possible explanations of correlations, how would you interpret this phenomenon? Test the correlation yourself: concentrate on a friend you haven't seen for quite a while, and wait five minutes. Did he or she call or appear? Try concentrating on a few more friends in this way. How often do they call or appear as you concentrate? Does your testing affect your view of the 'speak of the devil' effect?

While one might gather further information by doing additional descriptive or correlational research, the best way to address questions of causation is by doing experiments.

Experiments

All of the methods we have discussed thus far, from interviews to naturalistic observation, share the same limitation: they cannot answer questions about the causes of behaviour. This difficulty stems partly from the complexity of behaviour, but also relates to the fact that non-experimental research methods cannot assess the many possible influences on it. To understand this, let us consider again the case of Clever Hans, the 'educated' horse. As was described in the introduction to this chapter, Hans's owner spent several years trying to teach him maths, geography and other information, and seemed to have succeeded: Hans was able to answer questions correctly by tapping his foot to spell words, or shaking his head to answer yes or no. Finally, after Hans had become rather famous, a psychologist named Oskar Pfungst came to observe (Pfungst 1911).

Mr von Osten, the horse's owner, had already invited a number of psychologists and animal trainers to observe Hans, and all had come away convinced that the horse's ability was real. However, their assessments were limited to observing Hans perform – a type of *naturalistic observation*; by comparison, Pfungst asked Hans to perform some simple experiments. One experiment showed that Hans could still perform if his owner was absent (thus ruling out fraud by the owner). A second test involved comparing how Hans performed with or without a blindfold. The results led to the conclusion that Hans used some sort of visual cues to determine his responses, since his performance was poor when wearing blinkers. Eventually, by varying the conditions, Pfungst was able to identify the mechanism by which Hans figured out answers: members of the audience who knew the answer would unconsciously make minor head and facial movements in anticipation of Hans's response (for example, slightly tilting the head down when expecting him to tap). While the cues varied from person to person, the general conclusion was supported by a further experiment, in which no one in the horse's view knew the answer; under these conditions, Hans could not answer correctly. Thus, rather than learning mathematics, history and geography, Hans had learned to read non-verbal cues in the onlookers, as a way of getting rewards of praise and carrots!

experiment a research design in which the experimenter uses a controlled situation and manipulates one or more factors (called independent variables) in order to determine their effect on one or more measures of behaviour (called dependent variables).

field experiment an experiment done in a natural setting, usually without the explicit awareness of participants; as contrasted to experiments done in a laboratory setting.

What is most striking in this story is how successful Hans was, and how long it took to discover the truth. Note that his owner was *not* engaged in deliberate fraud – he genuinely believed Hans was clever, and encouraged scientists and others to find an explanation. Only Pfungst was able to do so – by conducting a series of experiments. **Experiments**, unlike the most careful of descriptive and correlational methods, allow us to manipulate and control conditions in ways that make determining causation possible. In essence, these two factors – manipulation of a variable of interest, and control of factors that might confuse the situation – are what distinguish experimental methods from other forms of research. The experiments that Pfungst did all involved testing the same subject (Hans) under various conditions (for example, with or without blinkers). As we will see, most experiments involve comparing different groups of individuals under different conditions (a procedure commonly called a 'between-groups design'). Since Pfungst did his tests in Hans's ordinary environment, it represents an example of a **field experiment** (as compared to experiments done in a *laboratory setting*).

independent variable a variable in an experiment which is systematically varied by the researcher, in order to see what effect it has on behaviour

dependent variable in an experiment, the behaviour measured in order to evaluate the effects of the independent variable.

In any experiment, the researcher begins with a *hypothesis*, a statement describing a proposed relationship between two types of variables; the experiment is then designed as a way of testing the accuracy of this hypothesis. One type of variable, called an **independent variable**, is controlled by the researcher, in order to see what effect it has on behaviour. For example, Pfungst looked at the effect of Hans wearing blinkers vs. no blinkers. The other type of variable, called a **dependent variable**, is a measure of the behaviour under study. In Pfungst's experiments, the dependent variable was always whether Hans answered correctly or not. In the simplest form of experiment, there is a single independent and a single dependent variable, although as we will see, more complex designs are frequently used.

In order to see how researchers use experiments to test hypotheses, let us return to the problem of bystander apathy. As you may recall, the results of interviews with nearby residents indicated that although no one intervened, those who observed the attack on Kitty Genovese were hardly apathetic about the experience. Faced with the phenomenon that people seemed concerned, but did not react, two social psychologists named Bibb Latané and John Darley decided to explore the issue further (Latané and Darley 1969). As noted previously, the interviews suggested that most people assumed *someone else* had already telephoned the police. Given that several apartment buildings overlooked the location, it seemed reasonable for someone to imagine that other people were also aware of the attack, and therefore that others would have telephoned already. This meant that people had acted according to what they thought others were doing. Latané and Darley recognized that emergencies represent an unfamiliar and sometimes ambiguous situation, and that in such circumstances people often guide their behaviour by what others do. Consequently, the researchers decided to explore the effects of the presence of others on behaviour in an emergency. They did a series of experiments, of which we will discuss two.

participant (alt., 'subject') in research, an individual who is the object of study or the participant in an experiment.

The first experiment was done in a laboratory, and was dubbed 'A Lady in Distress'. **Participants** were recruited through ads asking for volunteers to take part in a consumer research study. (Latané and Darley recognized that telling people the true purpose of the study might distort their responses.) Participants came either alone or with a friend; if alone, they found either another volunteer, a confederate of the researchers who was pretending to be a volunteer, or no one. These variations represented the levels of the independent variable – being alone, with a friend, with a stranger or with a stooge (confederate of the researchers). Latané and Darley wanted to see what effect these variations had on the likelihood of someone intervening in a (staged) emergency, so the measure of intervention became the dependent variable. In this experiment, the emergency involved an apparent injury to the woman conducting the consumer survey: when the subjects arrived, they were greeted by a woman wearing a white lab coat, who gave them a questionnaire, and then went into the next room. Through the partially opened door, subjects could hear the sounds of someone climbing on a chair, and then a crash, followed by a scream and sounds of evident distress. If you were sitting in the waiting room, would you go to help? Would it matter to you if a friend or stranger was present? What do you think Latané and Darley found?

The primary measure of helping behaviour was whether subjects did anything to intervene, ranging from going next door to simply calling out. (Latané and Darley also measured a second dependent variable – how long subjects waited before responding. While we will not discuss the results for this variable here, it is worth noting that experiments can have more than one dependent variable.) The main result was that individuals who were alone were the most likely to help – 70 per cent intervened. Groups consisting of two friends also showed a 70 per cent response rate, but since there were two people present, this is actually lower than would be expected if they acted independently. (Probability theory says the likelihood that at least one would respond, given the 70 per cent figure for a single person, is 91 per cent.) When two strangers witnessed the emergency, only 40 per cent of the time did one or both react (again, this is significantly less than the 91 per cent expected if they acted independently). When a stooge was present who deliberately ignored the emergency, the rate of intervention by subjects dropped to 7 per cent! Clearly, in this situation, the presence of another person reduced the rate of intervention.

Despite the relatively high level of response by individuals who were alone, Latané and Darley were concerned that the situation may have been too artificial. After all, the participants had come to a laboratory for a form of psychological research, and may have been suspicious. While it would be difficult to conduct research on bystander apathy without some form of deception, Latané and Darley felt that the use of a laboratory design may have limited the usefulness of the research in terms of what is called **external validity** (which concerns the degree to which one can generalize the results beyond the specific situation). Obviously, if participants saw this situation as different from other types of emergencies, the experiment would have low external validity.

external validity an assessment of the degree to which one can generalize research results beyond the specific situation studied.

Faced with this concern, Latané and Darley decided to try a further experiment, which would be a *field experiment*. Like naturalistic observation, field experiments are done in a natural setting, without telling participants that their behaviour is being observed. Unlike naturalistic observation, field experiments involve the same elements of manipulation and control which are found in laboratory experiments. In this case, Latané and Darley decided to examine how people respond to a perceived theft in a store. Dubbed 'The Case of the Stolen Beer', the experiment involved repeatedly staging a 'theft' at a store selling beer in suburban New Jersey. (The store operator, of course, was a knowing participant, and the 'thieves' were actually confederates of the researchers.) As in the previous experiment, Latané and Darley were interested in the influence of another person's presence on response rates, but in this case they also added a second *independent variable*: the number of robbers (one or two). As before, their hypothesis was that an individual would be more likely to intervene when alone than when others were present. The robbery scenario was rehearsed to be consistent: while one or two customers (remember, the number of people present is an independent variable) were in the store, the robber (or robbers) would enter, ask the lone clerk for an item not on display, and while the clerk went to check the storeroom, would glance around, pick up a case of beer from a floor display, and walk out. When the clerk returned, he would ask the other customers if they'd seen what happened to the now-disappeared person(s). The customers, of course, did not know this was a staged event; from their point of view, the robbery was genuine. To measure rates of helping (the dependent variable), Latané and Darley defined helping as telling the clerk about the theft. (They felt it was unreasonable to insist on actively attempting to prevent the theft!)

One of the challenges of doing field experiments is the need to preserve consistency of conditions, while at the same time not revealing to participants that an experiment is in progress. (Note that, as in the previous study, this involved an element of deception.) In order to fulfil the conditions of the Latané and Darley experiment, it was necessary that the number of customers required (one or two) did not change during the staging of the robbery; thus, if a customer entered or left the store *during* the scenario, the staging was aborted. While a number of aborted trials occurred, eventually the researchers obtained results from 92 trials, half involving one

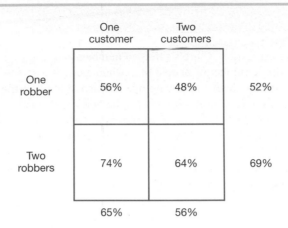

Figure 1.11 Latané and Darley's Field Experiment This experiment actually used two independent variables: the number of customers present, and the number of robbers involved. As the figure shows, both variables had an influence, with people being most likely to report the theft when it was a single customer faced with two robbers. (Data from Latané and Darley 1969)

customer, and half involving two. Since the customers did not know that the robbery was staged, a secondary concern was to prevent harm to the confederates who were acting as robbers. Fortunately, no one attempted any heroic intervention that posed risk to those involved.

What would *you* do if you witnessed a theft like this? Would you attempt to stop the thieves, tell the clerk, or pretend you didn't notice the theft? The results from The Stolen Beer experiment are shown in Figure 1.11. Note that the data are presented in a two-dimensional matrix, because there are two independent variables: the number of customers (subjects) and the number of robbers (confederates). Look carefully at the results: note that overall, people were more likely to respond when there were two robbers rather than one! Why do you think this was the case? (One possibility overlooked by Latané and Darley is that failure to actively intervene was *easier to justify* when there were two robbers because of the increased risks, so that customers were more willing to admit having seen the robbery in this circumstance.) The pattern found in the previous study was also supported: people are more likely to intervene when alone than when others are present.

diffusion of responsibility a lessening of an individual's feeling of responsibility in a situation which involves other people.

social influence a general term for the various ways in which an individual's behaviour is affected by others, such as conformity pressures and social expectations and norms.

Therefore, the experiments by Latané and Darley support the hypothesis that the presence of others reduces helping behaviour in emergencies. This takes us a step further than interview data or naturalistic observation, in suggesting that it is not apathy, but a social process of some sort, that inhibits helping behaviour. What exactly is the nature of that social process? Latané and Darley offered two possibilities: diffusion of responsibility and social influence. **Diffusion of responsibility**, which can occur in any group situation, including committees, is the tendency to feel less personal responsibility when others are also perceived as responsible. (This is consistent with the reports in the Kitty Genovese case, when people assumed someone else must have called the police. While no real group existed, people apparently *perceived* themselves as part of a social unit defined by the locale.) **Social influence**, which is more subtle, reflects how others affect our behaviour – such

Try it Yourself

Have you ever heard the expression 'There's safety in numbers'? This saying reflects the belief that people are safer when with a number of people than when alone. Given the research on bystander apathy, what do you conclude about this saying now? Which study had the greatest influence on your outlook? Did you find the laboratory experiment, the field experiment or the case study of Kitty Genovese the most compelling? Why? Do you think that bystander apathy can be plausibly studied by doing experiments which simulate emergencies? Or should it be studied using naturalistic observation in real emergencies?

It may happen that in the future you will be with other people when you see someone have a minor accident (tripping, a sports injury, etc.). Knowing what you know now, what will you do?

as the tendency to look to others for guidance when facing an unfamiliar situation. For example, if you were at a formal banquet, and were uncertain which fork to use for the salad, you might try to see what fork other people were using. Unfortunately, the experiments described above cannot determine which of these two explanations is more important. However, in the Genovese murder, social influence seems less likely than diffusion of responsibility as an explanation, since the people who saw the crime were isolated from each other. (Subsequent work has indicated that in fact *both* factors play a role in most emergency situations, as will be discussed in Chapter 8.) What the research *does* tell us is that 'bystander apathy' is a misnomer, since when people don't intervene it doesn't necessarily mean they don't feel concern.

Quasi-experiments

Although experiments provide a powerful tool for exploring the causes of behaviour, it is not always possible to do experiments, for practical or ethical reasons. For example, it is unethical to perform experiments which might violate individuals' basic human rights. (Note that the customers in the second Latané and Darley experiment were not asked if they wished to participate; by some standards, this creates a violation of their rights.) Apart from ethical concerns (which will be discussed below), it is not always possible to establish the control of a variable which is required for a true experiment. For example, experiments which compare different groups of subjects (called 'between-subjects designs') require that subjects be randomly assigned to the various groups (Jones 1995). Yet if a variable like age, sex or height is being studied, the researcher clearly cannot alter the characteristics of an individual in order to create random groups. To deal with these situations, researchers use a method called a **quasi-experiment** (Campbell and Stanley 1966). In a quasi-experiment, the subjects are assigned to groups according to the particular characteristic under study (for example, smokers vs. non-smokers, or 8-year-olds vs. 10-year-olds). In this type of situation, any observed differences in behaviour may be due to *either* the identified characteristic, *or* some other systematic difference between the groups (for example, smokers may tend to exercise less than non-smokers). Clearly, quasi-experiments do not provide as clear an outcome as do true experiments, but they offer a middle ground between experiments and correlational methods.

quasi-experiment a research design in which participants are assigned to groups based on variables which cannot be manipulated by the researcher (e.g., age, height, sex)

To better understand how quasi-experiments work, let us consider an example related to sexual roles. People have long debated whether homosexuality is innate or learned. A study by LeVay attempted to address this by looking for structural differences in a part of the brain called the hypothalamus, which is believed to play a role in sexual behaviour (LeVay 1993). Because of the measurement techniques used, the study required using brains of individuals who had died. To determine sexual orientation (and thus determine which group each brain belonged to), LeVay used *case-study* data indicating whether the individuals were known to have been homosexual, or presumed to have been heterosexual. As a control group, LeVay also examined the brains of women who were presumed to be heterosexual. Thus, the quasi-independent variable was sexual orientation, and the dependent variable was the size of the hypothalamus. The results indicated that the brains of the homosexual men were more like those of the women than those of the heterosexual men, implying that there is a biological link between brain structure and sexual orientation. Unfortunately, like all quasi-experiments, there are other possible interpretations of the results – for example, all of the homosexual group had died of AIDS, which might have resulted in changes in the brain. Alternatively, since brain structure can be influenced by experience, the structural differences might have been the *result* of sexual orientation rather than the *cause*. (While LeVay was very careful not to over-interpret his results, the popular press tended to be hastier in their coverage of the study – an example of why one should be cautious when reading media coverage of research results!)

In the end, quasi-experiments have their place in the repertoire of research methods, just as the other methods we have discussed do (see Box 1.2). Doing research requires making many choices, and good researchers always seek to balance a range of competing factors – not the least of which is a concern for ethical conduct.

Box 1.2 Basic Types of Research Methods in Psychology

Each method has its advantages and disadvantages, and researchers must consider the specifics of the research issue in order to determine which method is most appropriate for a particular situation.

Method	Description	Uses and limitations

CORRELATIONAL
  Survey
  Naturalistic observation
  Non-obtrusive measures
	Observing without controlling variables
	  Verbal self-reports of behaviour
	Observing in real-world setting
	
	Indirect measures of behaviour
		Useful where practical and/or unethical limitations prevent doing experiment, or for preliminary exploration of an issue
		Not possible to interpret cause of observed behaviour

EXPERIMENT
 	
  Laboratory
  Field
	Controlling situation and manipulating independent variable(s)
	Subjects come to experimental setting
	Done in real-world setting
		Only method to permit making interpretation of causation
		Can be difficult to execute; sometimes not practical/ethical

QUASI-EXPERIMENT
 	
  Laboratory
  Field
	Controlling situation and selecting subjects according to characteristic of interest (e.g., age, gender)
	Subjects come to experimental setting
	Done in real-world setting
		Necessary for studying variables which cannot be controlled
		Provides only limited information about possible causes

Try it Yourself

It's often assumed that older people like different music than younger people. Try to design a quasi-experiment to test this. Try this before you read on.

Presumably you decided to ask older and younger people their music preferences. Did you specify what constitutes 'older' and 'younger' people? That is, did you consider that 20-year-olds and 15-year-olds (all of whom might be considered 'younger') may have different tastes? Similarly, what age groups did you designate as 'older people'? It is likely that your parents and your grandparents might differ from each other in their tastes in music as well. Clearly, the terms 'younger' and 'older' need to be specified. But there's more: are there other factors that may play a part? For example, older people raised in different countries may well have different preferences in music. Or younger people raised in a rural area as opposed to a city may differ. What other factors do you think might contribute to any differences observed?

Ethics in Psychological Research

As we have seen, the desire to understand behaviour has led to the development of a variety of methods based on scientific principles. Over time, the application of these methods has significantly increased our understanding of human behaviour. While it would be comforting to portray psychology as simply the neutral and impartial pursuit of understanding, it is also true that research can be intrusive, and possibly even harmful. To say this is not meant to portray psychologists as evil, like some lab-coated villain in a low-budget movie, but to acknowledge that no human activity is value-free. The concern for values applies to all scientific endeavours, but the focus on living beings (animals as well as people) in psychology makes concerns about ethics more immediate than in the natural sciences. In part to foster high standards, the psychological associations in every major country publish codes of ethics for their members (for example, American Psychological Association 2002a; British Psychological Society 2006; Canadian Psychological Association 2000). Despite this attempt at uniformity, ethical standards in research, like all social standards, are shifting thresholds, which seldom produce universal agreement. Nonetheless, concern for ethics in the conduct of all research is an increasingly significant issue for both researchers and society, as Joseph Rotblat, a winner of the Nobel Peace Prize, has affirmed (Rotblat 1999).

The most basic ethical concern is the desire to avoid causing harm. While this seems very straightforward, in practice it can be more ambiguous (see Box 1.3). Consider this example from medical research: in the late 1980s, it was discovered that the drug AZT had some possible benefit in the treatment of AIDS. Since the drug was unapproved, doctors began a double-blind study to test its safety and effectiveness. However, because no other treatment existed for AIDS (a fatal disorder), trials were halted before the study was completed, in order to provide AZT to all participants. In this case, the concern was that it was unethical to withhold a promising drug from those in need (the placebo group). Unfortunately, cancelling the study had the negative effect of slowing the process of evaluating AZT; consequently, it was not discovered until 1993 that AZT was not as beneficial for those who were HIV-positive but not yet showing symptoms of AIDS. Should the researchers have continued the original study, even if it meant denying some individuals with AIDS full access to AZT? Or did the immediate need outweigh the concern for future knowledge, and therefore the welfare of other individuals in the future? In circumstances like this, one sometimes finds conflicts between different ethical principles.

obedience to authority the tendency to act in accordance with instructions from someone who is perceived as having social authority, even when it is counter to one's own inclinations.

A case which directly involves psychological research relates to a famous study of **obedience to authority** (Milgram 1963). This study was concerned with how people respond to authority figures when instructed to do something they feel unwilling to do. (While often referred to as an 'experiment', Milgram's original study actually had no control group.) Participants were recruited through a newspaper ad to participate in 'a study of learning and teaching methods'. When they arrived at the laboratory, a researcher in a white coat showed them an impressive-looking device which, it was explained, was used to punish wrong answers with a series of electric shocks (see Figure 1.12). The volunteer was to be the 'teacher', while a 'learner' in the next room would receive the shocks. The teacher met the learner (actually a confederate of the experimenter) and watched while the electrodes were strapped to his wrists; the learner expressed some apprehension as to how the shocks might affect his heart condition. The researcher stated that, 'Although the shocks can be extremely painful, they cause no permanent tissue damage.' During the actual 'learning' session, the teacher and learner communicated from adjacent rooms, via an intercom. As the experiment progressed, the researcher instructed the subject to increase the shock each time a wrong answer was given.

debriefing discussing the nature of a research study with participants at its conclusion, in order to explain the true nature and goals of the research and to answer any questions or concerns.

(The shock apparatus had a series of switches in 15-volt increments, going from 15 to 450 volts – the latter was also labelled 'Danger XXX'.) Despite possible personal misgivings, protests from the learner, and finally, no sound at all from the learner, the subject acting as teacher was instructed by the researcher to go to the highest voltage level. It is hard, while sitting comfortably reading this account, to imagine how upsetting the participants found this situation. It may be even harder to understand why they continued – for in Milgram's original study, 65 per cent continued to the maximum shock level!

Milgram's study has subsequently become well known, both for its results and the controversy over its methods. After taking part in the study as described above, participants discussed the experience with the researcher. During this **debriefing**, participants were told that the apparatus,

Box 1.3 *Research Ethics in a Multicultural World*

A basic principle of ethics in doing research is respect for persons (Smith 2003). Among other things, this means that one should try not to offend or insult people. But how can one be certain about what is acceptable or appropriate? This can be very tricky when we try to do research in a multicultural setting, or in cultures other than our own. What seems like a perfectly reasonable question or task may be perceived by people of other cultures as being inappropriate or even offensive. For example, it may be considered acceptable to ask couples about their sexual activity in downtown New York City, but it may be highly unacceptable in Islamic Pakistan. How one interprets research data can also vary with culture. Thus, a clinician attempting to diagnose a mental disorder is more likely to err when clinician and patient are from different cultural backgrounds (see Chapter 9). How does one define research ethics in a multicultural world?

In general, ethical codes expect psychologists to show cultural sensitivity (including awareness of, and respect for, cultural differences) – but applying this in practice is not always simple (Rice and O'Donohue 2002). It is a particular challenge when one considers individuals who are vulnerable, such as those seeking help for mental disorders (Baeaernhielm and Ekblad 2002; Bolling 2003). In such cases, researchers must seek to balance the interests and rights of the individual, along with the scientific concerns for representativeness and completeness. As with many such issues, there is no simple answer, but recognizing the problem is an important first step.

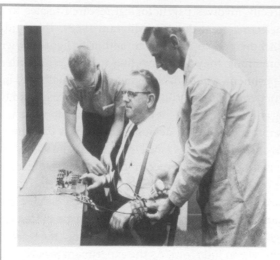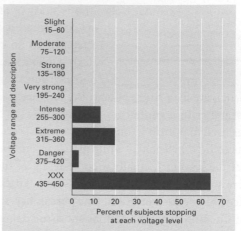

Figure 1.12 Milgram's Obedience Experiment The man being strapped in the chair and having electrodes attached is the 'learner' whom participants were instructed to punish for wrong answers by delivering electric shocks. As the graph shows, most participants continued to the maximum voltage level.

as well as the entire situation, was simply a ruse; the learner was never actually shocked, and his protests were carefully scripted acting. The *real* purpose of the study was to see how far people would go to obey an authority figure. The fact that most people went to the top of the scale, Milgram has argued, shows how important it is to understand the roots of obedience.

At the same time, many of Milgram's volunteers found that complying was very upsetting, since they believed that the learner was actually suffering real shocks. For those who fully complied, this upset was perhaps compounded by the realization that, had the shocks been real, they might have killed someone. The debate then comes down to this: does the knowledge gained about obedience offset the emotional upset to the subjects? Milgram himself has gone to great lengths to justify the study, and has used follow-up studies of the original subjects to indicate that no enduring trauma ensued: after one year, 84 per cent were either glad or very glad to have taken part (Milgram 1964). However, this might be explained by the theory of *cognitive dissonance*, which says we tend to alter beliefs to fit with past actions (Festinger 1957); from this viewpoint, the subjects might have been trying to justify their original behaviour.

Critics have suggested that Milgram was insensitive to the suffering of his subjects. For example, Baumrind criticized Milgram for statements like 'a mature and initially poised businessman … within 20 minutes … was reduced to a twitching, stuttering wreck' (Baumrind 1964). Brandt has offered a meta-analysis of the situation, suggesting that participants' willingness to inflict suffering in the name of research was paralleled by Milgram's own willingness in the same cause. From this viewpoint, Brandt argues, the experiment was unnecessary, since Milgram's own attitude would tell him how others would respond (Brandt 1982). It seems clear that Milgram was not deliberately malevolent, and did in fact take considerable care to debrief his volunteers after their participation. At the same time, it seems probable that a less harmful technique could have been found to test the concept of obedience. (It is also possible that the results of a less dramatic situation might be perceived as less applicable to the real world.) Ultimately, ethical standards *do* evolve, and it is probable Milgram's research would *not* be approved if it were to be proposed today. (At our university, the rules of the ethical standards code state that the perceived benefits of research cannot be used to justify causing harm to research subjects.) In the end, Milgram's study highlights the difficulties of achieving consensus on ethical matters.

Milgram's study also points out the ethical conflicts raised by another issue: the use of deception in research. Technically, *deception* occurs whenever participants are not fully informed about their participation in research – although this is a rather stringent, and possibly unrealistic, standard. As has been noted already, the phenomenon of reactivity makes it impossible to provide full disclosure in all research situations. In naturalistic observation, for example, the researcher cannot typically seek the consent of those being observed before doing research, since that could lead to altered behaviour. In social psychology in general, whether observing in the field or doing experiments in the laboratory, research requirements often make it necessary to withhold information or even to actively deceive participants. Obviously, deception (and with it, the lack of opportunity for informed consent) is open to abuse, and must be used with caution. Most ethical codes allow deception to be used, with certain restrictions (American Psychological Association 2002a; British Psychological Society 2006; Canadian Psychological Association 2000). The guidelines typically require that the research cannot be done otherwise, that participants are not coerced to take part, that they will be fully debriefed after participating – and that there be a justifiable value to the outcome of the research (normally, an increase in understanding of behaviour). Most researchers agree with this approach, and argue that under these conditions no real harm occurs to participants (Christensen 1988). Nonetheless, the issue is still contentious. Kelman has argued that the use of deception can undermine the relationship between researcher and participants, and suggests that deception should be used only when there is no alternative way to do the research (Kelman 1967). Warwick goes even further, suggesting that the willingness to use deception contributes to undermining public perceptions of the trustworthiness of public institutions (Warwick 1975). Brandt has argued that essentially the APA code amounts to saying the end justifies the means – it's all right to deceive subjects if society gets something out of it (Brandt 1982).

The concern about long-term effects of deception is illustrated by a follow-up to Milgram's study, which sought to demonstrate that the same effects could occur in the real world (Hofling *et al.* 1966). In this case, researchers set up a field experiment, in which nurses at a hospital received a telephone call from an unfamiliar staff doctor, instructing them to administer what appeared to be a toxic dose of medication to a patient. The doctor explained that he was on his way to the hospital and would sign the authorization when he arrived (of course, the situation was designed to ensure no actual harm came to patients). True to expectation, 21 of 22 nurses tried to administer the 'toxic' dosage. This study demonstrated the external validity of Milgram's results, and is cited approvingly by Zimbardo (1992) for this reason. What is *ignored* by both the original researchers and Zimbardo is the question of how this experience affected the nurses subsequently: did it make them more distrustful, and if so, is that ultimately good or bad? The consequences of such deception seems to extend well beyond the confines of the experiment itself.

In the end, it is impossible to find universal agreement on this issue. Having served on ethical review boards, we know that good researchers recognize that they bear a moral responsibility for their work, although cases do arise where researchers are not sufficiently sensitive to possible ethical conflicts. Ethical boards exist, in fact, to ensure that the proponent of a study is not the only one to evaluate its suitability. In some research, such as research on cognitive processes, deception is not an issue, and the greatest risk to subjects is the possibility of boredom. However, some types of researchers have no such luxury, and must often balance the desire for knowledge against other kinds of values. At the very least, it is to the credit of the discipline that the debates about ethical issues are publicly argued. Psychology exists to enhance our understanding of ourselves, and as long as researchers remain sensitive to the ethical responsibility this entails, then psychology will represent *humane* behaviour as well as *human* behaviour.

Try it Yourself

Imagine that you are a researcher asking an ethical review board to approve an experiment similar to Milgram's obedience study. What arguments would you make to the board? Now imagine that you are a member of the board. Are you convinced by the arguments? What alternatives might you suggest to address the underlying research goals?

CONCLUSION

In this chapter, we have looked at the history and nature of psychology as a discipline. In the process, two basic themes have emerged. The first is that psychology, like all science, is a human endeavour, and the process of understanding behaviour is influenced by the perceptual processes which we use in interpreting everything which we experience. One aspect of this is the selective nature of perception. Given the complexity of behaviour, researchers cannot avoid being selective in what they study, and this is reflected in the nature of the different approaches to psychology which this book considers. Perception is also important in that we actively interpret the world as a way of trying to make sense of it. The interpretations we make are based on the schemata which we use to organize our thinking, and reflect both our experiences and the culture in which we live. Psychological theories are a result of attempts to organize our understanding of the world. Hence, the existence of different approaches within psychology can be partly understood in terms of the processes of perception.

The second basic theme is that psychology faces specific challenges in the process of studying behaviour. Like the natural sciences, psychology is empirical, and emphasizes the importance of observations in developing an understanding of behaviour. However, physics or chemistry deal with inanimate matter, and the concepts can seem remote from personal experience. By contrast, psychology is concerned with the understanding of our own actions and experiences. Because people are self-aware, researchers must be careful that the process of observing does not alter the behaviour of interest. This concern underlies many of the research methods employed, from naturalistic observation to field experiments. In addition, because psychology deals with living creatures, ethical concerns exist which do not arise in the natural sciences. These two factors make psychology very different from the natural sciences.

At this stage, you may feel that the challenges are overwhelming, not only for psychologists as researchers, but also for you as a reader. If so, don't despair. This chapter has tried to outline some basic themes, but it cannot tell the whole story. Indeed, while much of the meaning lies in the themes, the excitement lies in the details – the specifics of how we act, and why. In the chapters ahead, you will encounter more of the specifics, and also develop a better understanding of the broader themes and issues. As you proceed, you will find that each chapter adds to your understanding of both behaviour and the way psychologists study it.

Each of us has wondered what we are, and why; psychologists have dedicated their lives to answering these questions. While no final answers can be offered, in the chapters ahead, we will see that even partial answers can offer both excitement and insight.

Putting It All Together

As you read about the various approaches in the next several chapters, you will find that there are many issues on which different approaches disagree. This is not surprising, given that competing theories are a natural part of the scientific process, and currently no one approach can fully explain human behaviour. However, while competition exists, it is also true that in many ways the approaches can provide complementary insights. Consequently, when taken together, they can often provide a more complete view of human behaviour than does any one approach alone. To help you understand this, consider the example presented below. As you read about each approach you will find another section like this one, discussing a different aspect of the person and behaviour. By putting the discussions together as you go, you can gain a more complete understanding of the underlying behaviour, and of how the approaches relate to each other.

Scenario

Sam is a first-year university student. He is bright, friendly and easy-going, the type of person that people say is a 'really good guy'. He comes from a stable, middle-class family, and his parents have always been loving and supportive. They instilled in him a desire to work hard in order to achieve success in life. Both parents work; one is an accountant, and the other is an interior designer. They always told him, 'You have the ability to be the best, and that's what we know you will be.'

Sam worked hard to get into university, and he thought that he was well prepared for the challenges. He was admitted to a well-regarded university (his first choice) in a city some distance from the small town where he grew up. At first he found being away from home difficult, but now he has begun forming new friendships. He is now midway through the school year, and to his dismay, things have not gone as well academically as he had anticipated. In his first semester, he found the workload to be much greater than he expected, and he found himself worrying about whether he would be successful. He started getting very anxious about tests, and as the semester went on, he began feeling overwhelmed with the amount of work he had to do. But instead of tackling the work, Sam found himself procrastinating. He would put off getting started on his studying and his assignments until the last minute, choosing instead to socialize with his friends, Nigel and Rajiv, play video games, and watch TV. At the same time, these activities were not that enjoyable, because thinking that he should have been working left him feeling guilty. He has met Vanessa too, and he found himself spending a great deal of time fantasizing about whether she might become his girlfriend in the near future. But he's afraid to ask her to go out with him – what if she says no? She's an independent young woman with a strong desire for a career, and Sam fears that he might be too traditional a man for her. By cramming for exams and staying up all night writing essays, Sam managed to pass his first semester, but found he was exhausted, and ended up in bed with flu for a week during the semester break. Now, facing his second semester of university, Sam is even more anxious: the workload is not going to decrease, and just thinking about it leaves him feeling knots in his stomach. Yet Sam is already finding himself procrastinating, and feeling badly about himself; he wonders if he really is capable of succeeding academically. And will he get the courage to ask Vanessa for a date before she finds someone else?

Given Sam's background and prior behaviour, how can we understand his current situation?

CHAPTER SUMMARY

- Psychology is defined as 'the scientific study of behaviour'. By *behaviour*, researchers variously mean observable responses, inner experience (thoughts, feelings, etc.) or both – the variations are one of the factors that distinguish the different approaches within psychology. It is *scientific*, in that it is based on the methods of systematic observation and analysis which are part of all science.

- The task of understanding behaviour can be related to *perception*. Rather than being a passive representation of sensory input, perception is an active process of *selecting* and *interpreting* the information provided by our senses. Faced with the complexity and diversity of behaviour, psychologists make choices in terms of what aspects to study, the research methods to be used, and other issues.

- These choices are reflected in the various *approaches* to the study of psychology, which differ in their basic assumptions about behaviour, as well as their methods and theories. In effect, each approach represents a distinct framework for the understanding of behaviour.

- Psychology developed from two different traditions, associated with philosophy and natural science. The influence of the natural sciences is seen in the work of Wilhelm Wundt, who founded the first major laboratory for psychology at Leipzig in 1879. The influence of philosophy is reflected in the ideas of William James, an American contemporary of Wundt's who wrote a highly influential text on psychology.

- Five major approaches have been influential within psychology: the *biological, behaviourist, cognitive, psychodynamic* and *humanistic.*

- In psychology there are many possible ways of collecting observations, which vary in terms of *measurement techniques* (*self-report* or *direct observation*), *setting* (in a *laboratory* or in the *field*) and *research method* (*experimental, non-experimental* and *quasi-experimental*).

- Non-experimental techniques include *interviews, surveys, case studies, naturalistic observation* and the use of *unobtrusive measures.* Non-experimental methods are *correlational* – that is, they assist us in finding patterns in behaviour, but do not directly identify the causes.

- Experimental methods always involve systematically varying one or more *independent variables* in order to see how the changes affect behaviour. This systematic manipulation, together with control of other factors in the situation, is intended to aid in understanding the *causes* of behaviour.

- Quasi-experimental methods are used to study variables that cannot be directly controlled, like age or gender, or in situations where manipulating a variable would be unethical. Quasi-experiments offer more insight into causation than do non-experimental methods, but can be more susceptible to interpretation problems than true experiments.

- One issue which is common to all psychological research is the importance of *ethics.* Among particular concerns are the possibility of causing harm, and the role of deception vs. informed consent.

🔑 Key terms and concepts

psychology
causality
perception
Gestalt theory
schema
empirical
theory
hypothesis
self-report
interview
survey
sample

population
complexity
representative sample
naturalistic observation
unobtrusive measure
case study
correlation
experiment
independent variable
dependent variable
quasi-experiment
debriefing

Test yourself questions

1 Why are different approaches to psychology necessary?
2 How does perception affect the study of psychology?
3 Why does psychology use the scientific method?
4 What are the differences between correlational methods and experiments?

Online
Learning Centre

When you have read this chapter, log onto the Online Learning Centre website at
www.openup.co.uk/glassman where you will find answers to these Test Yourself questions and
suggested answers to the Try it Yourself activities, plus many more learning resources to help
you study psychology.

Suggestions for Further Reading

- **Fancher's** *Pioneers of Psychology* (1996) provides a highly readable historical overview of psychology, focusing on the major figures who helped shape the discipline.
- **Luria's** *The Mind of a Mnemonist* (1968) is a short book which shows the value of case studies, while also providing a vivid account of an individual with a truly remarkable memory.
- **William James** was both an influential psychologist and a wonderful writer. *The Varieties of Religious Experience* (1902), his last book on psychology, offers both an excellent introduction to James's thinking, and a still-relevant exploration of one of the most profound aspects of human experience.
- If you are interested in learning more about research methods, you should read **the Appendix** of this book (which also includes suggestions for further reading).
- *Unobtrusive Measures: Non-reactive Research in the Social Sciences* (1972), by **Webb** *et al.*, is an interesting account of how to do research without intruding.
- *On Being a Scientist: Responsible Conduct in Research*, published by the **National Academy of Science,** provides a thought-provoking discussion of ethical issues, including many specific examples. (It is available on the web at www.nap.edu/readingroom/books/obas/contents/values.html.)

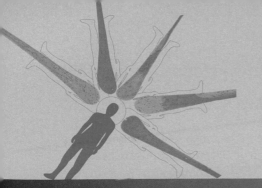

Chapter 2

The Biological Approach

LEARNING OBJECTIVES

In this chapter, the objectives are to learn:

- ☑ the basic structure of the nervous system

- ☑ techniques for studying the brain, including electrical recording and stimulation, and computerized imaging

- ☑ the role of neurotransmitters and hormones in behaviour

- ☑ the way drugs affect the nervous system, and their effects on behaviour

- ☑ the effects of separating the two cerebral hemispheres

- ☑ the nature of stress and options for coping with it

- ☑ the basic mechanisms of heredity, and how heredity and environment interact in influencing behaviour

- ☑ how evolutionary psychology seeks to understand the origins of behaviour

LOOKING FOR THE MIND

Most people think of medicine as a profession that takes care of our bodies. Yet sometimes doctors are confronted with cases where the problem seems to go beyond the body. Instead, the focus becomes the individual's awareness of themselves and their surroundings – in short, the mind. Such cases can be extremely puzzling, but may also be useful in helping us understand the mind. Let us briefly consider two such examples.

Oliver Sacks, a neurologist who is also a gifted writer, has described a remarkable case that he encountered (Sacks 1985). 'Dr P.' was a music professor who was referred to Sacks because of a visual problem – he often confused common objects. On one occasion, he thought his wife's head was his hat. Given a live rose to identify, he described it as 'a convoluted red form with a linear green attachment'. Shown photographs, he could identify only those with a distinguishing feature, such as Einstein's unruly hair. On the street, he sometimes patted a fire hydrant, thinking it was the head of a child. Indeed, he could only recognize people by voice, not by sight. Yet his eyes were fine – he could even spot a pin on the floor. In other respects, Dr P. seemed normal; in fact, his musical gifts (with the exception of no longer being able to read music) were considerable. The only evident symptom, apart from his problems with visually recognizing faces and complex shapes, was a slight abnormality of reflexes on the left side. Here was a bizarre puzzle: how could someone find a pin, yet think that his wife's head was a hat? How is our awareness related to what our senses tell us?

phantom limb a mysterious phenomenon in which individuals who have lost a limb will often continue to experience sensations which seem to come from the missing limb.

If that seems puzzling, consider the phenomenon known as **phantom limb**. When individuals lose an arm or other limb, they will often continue to experience sensations which seem to come from the missing limb. Sacks has reported one case of a man who experienced his missing finger as extending straight out – accompanied by the fear that if his hand came near his face, the phantom finger would poke him in the eye! He knew the finger didn't exist, but could not escape the sensation, or the accompanying fear. Despite great efforts to understand and treat the problem, the full explanation of phantom limb remains a mystery.

mind the inner subjective experience of conscious awareness; the term has no direct reference to physical form.

Both of these phenomena call into question the relationship between mind and body. Traditionally, **mind** is used to refer to our experience of awareness, or consciousness; it has no direct reference to physical form. The *body*, of course, refers to our physical being, and includes what many feel is the basis of mind – the brain. Are mind and body separate, and does their separateness account for cases like those above? Or are mind and body simply different aspects of an underlying unity? If they are a unity, then what accounts for the sometimes bizarre discrepancies between the two? William James, in his *Principles of Psychology*, stated that, 'The explanation of consciousness [i.e., mind] is the ultimate question for psychology.' Although James made the statement over a hundred years ago, and much has been learned since, the answer to the question is still beyond our grasp. However, if we *do* find the answer, many believe it will come from research based on the biological approach.

INTRODUCTION

The biological approach to psychology, as its name implies, views man as a biological organism. What we do, and even what we think, is seen as having its basis in our physical structure. The approach arose out of attempts to understand two major issues: the relationship between mind and body, and the influence of heredity on behaviour. Each is a reflection of our biological nature, and the study of them sometimes overlaps, but the two aspects have separate histories.

As one might guess, biological researchers tend to view behaviour as being purely physical. As a doctor commented while discussing possible physical causes of schizophrenia, 'Of course it has to be physical. There isn't anything else up there.' By 'up there', he was referring to the brain. Thus, his reasoning was based on the assumption that the brain determines behaviour. Although you may not find that very surprising, in earlier times it would have been seen as very radical. Even in the seventeenth century, most people believed the body was controlled by an intangible soul. Among those who believed in the soul was the French philosopher René Descartes (noted for his assertion, 'I think, therefore I am'). A keen observer, but also deeply religious, Descartes tried to reconcile the apparent physical nature of the body with the intangible nature of the soul. The human body, he felt, was constructed like that of an animal – both were basically machines. However, he also believed that people (unlike animals) had a soul, which interacted with the physical body through a small gland in the brain called the pineal gland. Since in French the same word (*l'âme*) can be used for both 'mind' and 'soul', Descartes' idea came to be interpreted as referring to the relation between the mind and body; his view that mind and body are distinct, but can interact, became known as **dualism**. While Descartes saw the body's functioning in machine-like terms, his interactionist view (physical body interacting with intangible soul) was also a compromise. By separating the mind from the body, dualism created a split which has been the subject of much subsequent controversy (Damasio 1994). Rightly or wrongly, the concept became so well known that for the better part of two centuries, dualism was the dominant view in western culture.

dualism the view, first attributed to Descartes, that mind and body are distinct; Descartes believed the two could interact via the pineal gland in the brain.

Despite its long history, dualism poses many contradictions (for example, how can a non-physical mind control a physical body?). Today, researchers in the biological approach reject dualism in favour of *monism*, the belief that mind and body are a single entity (in most respects this is equivalent to **materialism**, which assumes all behaviour has a physical basis). As a starting point, materialism avoids many of the problems of dualism – but that does not prove it is true. Like dualism, materialism is an *assumption*, and not every person (or every culture) holds the same assumptions about the world. As recently as 1994, researcher Francis Crick (better known as the co-discoverer of the structure of DNA) felt justified in claiming that materialism was 'so alien to the ideas of most people alive today that it can truly be called astonishing' (Crick 1994, p. 3). Still, the materialist view which lies at the heart of the biological approach is increasingly influential in psychology today, and it is worth considering how this came about. Like many changes in our understanding, the shift from dualism to materialism occurred slowly, and was influenced by a series of discoveries.

materialism the assumption that all behaviour has a physiological basis.

Interestingly, one crucial insight came about almost by accident. In 1745 (about a hundred years after Descartes), a French priest-turned-physician named Julien de La Mettrie contracted a fever, and noticed that this physical condition affected his mental state as well as his physical state. Reflecting on this after his recovery, he wrote a book called *L'histoire naturelle de l'âme (The Natural History of the Soul)*. In the book, he argued that the body is but a machine, and that the soul is no different from the mind. Further, he said the mind was part of the body. This assertion, which clearly went beyond the position proposed by Descartes, caused a tremendous outcry, but La Mettrie held fast to his views. Ultimately, the opposition from religious and political authorities forced him to leave France for his own personal safety.

By the time of the French Revolution (less than 50 years after La Mettrie), a physician named Cabanis was able to argue that guillotine victims were not conscious after beheading, because consciousness was the function of the brain, just as digestion was the function of the stomach. Still, no one had shown a specific connection between physiological structures and behaviour. Then, in 1861, a French doctor at the insane asylum at Bicêtre, Paul Broca, encountered a case in which a man lost the ability to speak coherently after a head injury. When the man died several years later, Broca was able to demonstrate by an autopsy that the cause of the man's deficit lay in damage to a specific point in the brain. Demonstrating this **localization of function** (connecting a specific behaviour to a specific brain area) was the final step in the progression of ideas. The acceptance of Broca's finding completed the gradual change in attitude, from seeing behaviour as governed by an intangible soul, to the modern view of behaviour as having a physiological basis. Of course, many others also contributed to our current knowledge and ideas. The brief history given here is simply meant to indicate how the basic assumptions about mind and body arose.

localization of function the assumption that specific functions are associated with specific areas of the brain.

heredity the biological transmission of characteristics from one generation to another.

The other main aspect of the biological approach, the role of **heredity** in behaviour, also had a gradual development. In the eighteenth century, people believed that each species of plant and animal had been independently created: as the Bible says, 'every living creature after his kind'. Still, there were indications that this might not be literally true. The great biologist Linnaeus had published a catalogue of over 4000 plant and animal species in 1735, and his orderly categories suggested connections among species. Then, in 1809, a French naturalist named Lamarck presented the first widely known theory of species development, or evolution. Lamarck believed that variations developed through inheritance of acquired characteristics. For instance, giraffes acquired long necks because each generation strained a little further to get food, slightly stretching their necks, and passed this difference on to their offspring. Today, Lamarckian theory is generally discredited, but it was a significant step forward in suggesting that characteristics have a hereditary basis.

natural selection the evolutionary process by which those random variations within a species which enhance reproductive success lead to perpetuation of new characteristics; in essence, individuals possessing traits which enhance survival and reproduction are likely to have more offspring.

The real revolution in thought came with the work of Charles Darwin. Darwin's theory, published in *On the Origin of Species* (1859), was that variations among individuals of a species would occur by chance, but could in turn be passed on. His doctrine of 'survival of the fittest' meant that only those variations which helped the individuals survive long enough to breed would be passed on. Through this process, which he called **natural selection**, Darwin was not only advocating the inheritance of characteristics, but also an evolutionary link between humans and all other species. In 1872 he made this even clearer by writing *The Expression of the Emotions in Man and Animals*. (Actually, Darwin proposed the *concept* of inheritance, but specified no biological *mechanism* for its operation; it remained for the rediscovery of the work of an Austrian monk, Gregor Mendel, for a specific mechanism for heredity to be suggested.)

Like La Mettrie, Darwin came into conflict with religious doctrine, this time with the view that man was created 'in God's image'. In part, the controversy concerned how literally one should interpret the biblical concept. The controversy raged for many years, and is still not completely ended, but in time the evolutionary viewpoint expressed by Darwin became dominant. Despite not specifying precisely how heredity operated, Darwin's theory laid the basis for the study of hereditary influences on behaviour.

Today, these two concepts – *materialism* and *heredity* – are the foundation of the biological approach to psychology. The assumptions involved (that mind has a physiological basis, and that behaviour can be inherited) influence both the questions asked and the type of data collected. Compared to other approaches, the biological approach emphasizes 'getting inside the black box' – that is, looking at the internal structure of the organism. Broca showed that a specific defect in the brain could destroy speech in an otherwise normal person. Darwin showed that what we are is at least partly due to what our parents are. In this chapter, we will look at how these ideas have been applied to enhance our understanding of behaviour.

THE NATURE OF THE PHYSIOLOGICAL SYSTEM

As previously noted, the biological approach emphasizes the physiological basis of behaviour. While the approach can be applied to any aspect of behaviour, the most challenging questions seem to be those relating to the interactions between mind and body. In everyday life, we encounter situations where the body affects the mind (as when coffee makes you tense), and also situations where the mind affects the body (as when executives get high blood pressure). What is the mechanism of such interactions? In this section, we will try to deal with this question in terms of what is currently known about the physiological basis of behaviour, and also consider some of the problems psychologists face in trying to develop answers.

Mind, Brain and the CNS

In trying to understand the interaction of mind and body, the first difficulty encountered is dealing with the terms involved. For instance, where is 'the mind'? Where is the 'self' that we experience? Terms like these, while seemingly clear in everyday usage, are not so clear when one tries to relate them to physiological structures.

Most people would equate 'mind' with 'brain', and this is partially correct. But in more precise terms, the word 'mind' refers to a psychological concept, not a physiological one; and is usually regarded as the seat of consciousness or awareness, not as a physiological structure. Current knowledge indicates that the brain is, indeed, involved in our experience of consciousness, but no one is currently certain just how, or whether consciousness involves only the brain, or the entire physiological system. So, in discussing interactions of the physical (brain) and mental (mind), one is restricted to saying that somehow the two are connected, or even fundamentally the same, but the specific relationship is not clear. (As noted earlier, in part, this is an *assumption* that researchers make. However, the alternative – that the mind is non-physical, perhaps a 'soul' – would not only take us back before Descartes, but would also make scientific study irrelevant.) While no final answers can be given here, we will examine what is known about the structure of the physiological system and its influence on behaviour.

Neurons and the Nervous System

The human body is a remarkably complex system, comprised of trillions of individual living cells of many specialized types. Certain cells in the stomach lining, for example, do nothing but produce digestive secretions. Other cells fight disease, transport oxygen or store energy. Coordinating the activity of the body's many systems requires communication, which is one of the key functions of the specialized cells which make up the *nervous system*. These cells, called nerve cells or **neurons**, are like

neuron (alt., 'nerve cell') a cell of the nervous system.

synapse the junction between two neurons, represented by a small physical gap which is bridged by the flow of neurotransmitter chemicals from the terminals of the 'sending' neuron.

central nervous system (CNS) the brain, together with the nerve pathways of the spinal cord.

wires in that they carry an electro-chemical message from one point to another. Each time a neuron connects to another neuron, at a junction called a **synapse**, it is possible for a message to be switched to other areas. The *brain*, together with the nerve pathways of the *spinal cord*, forms the **central nervous system** (or **CNS**). Although the brain is responsible for integrating incoming information and directing muscle activity, the spinal cord is a vital relay station. For instance, the first connection (or synapse) between your big toe and the brain is where the pathway enters your spinal cord. For protection, the spinal cord passes within the bones (vertebrae) of the spinal column, like wires in a flexible casing. Despite this protection, a back injury can result in disruption of the spinal cord, which can cause loss of all feeling (sensory input) and movement (motor control) below the point of injury (see Figure 2.1).

Try it Yourself

We all experience conscious awareness, but the connections between this awareness and behaviour are complex. Consider the following examples:

- Do you breathe in or out when you hit a ball (for instance, in tennis, golf or baseball?
- Have you ever walked or driven a familiar route and found that upon arrival at your destination you really didn't remember the trip? How would you explain your being able to get there without being aware en route?
- Have you ever accidentally cut yourself, but not felt pain until after you noticed the cut?
- When you get up from a chair and start to walk, do you start with your left foot or your right foot?

In all these cases, you seem to be performing behaviours which you are not consciously aware of. If we are not aware of such things, do you think that means that the mind is separate from the body? Why or why not? What is governing these behaviours? Which do you see as being your 'self', the part of you that is performing what seem to be automatic behaviours, or the part of you that is concentrating on other things while you perform these behaviours?

peripheral nervous system (PNS) those nerve pathways which lie outside the central nervous system, involving sensation, motor control and regulation of internal organs.

sensory neurons neurons in the PNS which carry information from the sense receptors to the CNS.

motor neurons those neurons in the PNS which are responsible for initiating muscle activity.

interneurons neurons which are part of the central nervous system.

nerve impulse the electrical signal generated when a neuron is active, which normally passes from the dendrites, along the axon, to the terminals.

The nerve pathways outside the central nervous system form the **peripheral nervous system** (or **PNS**). **Sensory neurons** in the PNS carry messages from the outside world to the CNS via the sense receptors, such as those located in the eyes and ears, while **motor neurons** are responsible for initiating muscle activity, under the direction of the CNS. (The neurons which comprise the CNS are often called **interneurons**, because they are intermediate between sensory and motor neurons.)

The basic unit of the nervous system is the neuron. As noted above, a neuron is like a wire through which an electrical signal passes. This signal, called a **nerve impulse**, stays essentially the same (i.e., in amplitude) as it passes along the 'wire' or *axon*, and is also the same in every neuron (see Figure 2.2 for details of neuron structure). While all neurons show the same basic structure and serve the same basic purpose, they show many differences in their details. One of the most striking variations is in size – the central wire or axon may range from less than 1 millimetre (for neurons in the brain) to about 1 metre (for peripheral neurons between the spinal chord and the toes)! Another difference among neurons is whether they are insulated or not: as with ordinary electrical wires, insulation improves efficiency by reducing signal losses. In neurons, the insulation consists of a fatty substance called *myelin* (the myelin is actually composed of another specialized type of cell called a Schwann cell, which wraps itself around the axon to provide an insulating sheath). Not all neurons in either the CNS or PNS are insulated ('myelinated'), although most of those in the brain of a healthy adult are. The process of forming myelin begins in the foetus, and a major part of the process is completed by about age 3, though formation (and repair) continue throughout life. Across species, the degree of completion at birth is roughly paralleled by the degree of behavioural capacities; a new-born calf, for example, is both better myelinated and more capable at birth than a human infant. At the same time, destruction of the myelin sheath (in disorders like multiple sclerosis) can have disastrous effects on the nervous system and behaviour by disrupting the efficiency of communication. When the electrical impulse reaches the terminals of the neuron, there is a small physical gap called a *synapse*. Communication across the synapse occurs when the nerve impulse triggers the release of chemicals called **neurotransmitters**. As we will see in the next section, neurons can differ in terms of what neurotransmitter chemicals they use.

neurotransmitter a chemical released by the terminals of a neuron which plays a role in communication between neurons, across the synapse.

While the pathways of the peripheral nervous system are crucial in providing our links to the outer world for both sensation and movement, the central nervous system, with responsibility for integrating and controlling the whole system, is much more complex. As noted above, damage to the spinal cord can result in loss of feeling and also movement (paralysis); the brain itself is also vulnerable. In the peripheral nervous system, severed nerves will often repair themselves; cases of a severed arm or leg being successfully reattached after an accident attest to this. Unfortunately, nerves in the central nervous system do not normally regenerate – hence damage to the spinal cord can result in permanent paraplegia.

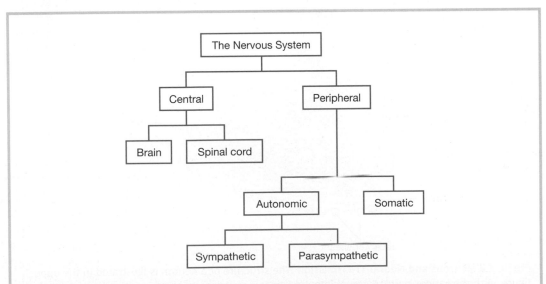

Figure 2.1 The Central and Peripheral Nervous Systems As the figure shows, the nervous system is sub-divided into various sub-systems, with the major distinction being between the CNS (brain and spinal cord) and the PNS (all those nerves not part of the CNS). The somatic system includes both sensory pathways (to the CNS) and motor pathways (from the CNS).

The Brain

Considered visually, the **brain** is not very impressive – a greyish lump weighing approximately 1.4 kilograms, with an irregular surface of ridges and valleys. However, that superficial impression belies both its complexity and its capabilities. The brain consists of about 100 billion neurons (no one knows the exact number, since estimates are based on examining

brain the portion of the central nervous system which lies within the skull.

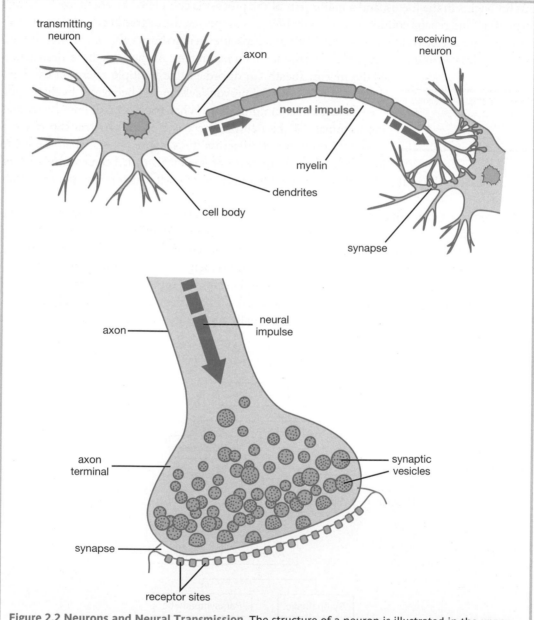

Figure 2.2 Neurons and Neural Transmission The structure of a neuron is illustrated in the upper figure, with the various parts. A neural impulse ('signal') travels from the dendrites, along the axon, to the terminals, where it must cross a physical gap, the synapse. Transmission across the synapse is by means of neurotransmitters, chemicals released by the synaptic vesicles, which then flow across the gap, to lock into receptor sites on the receiving neuron (see lower figure).

a small region, and extrapolating the number found there to the whole structure). In turn, each neuron makes and receives connections with hundreds or possibly thousands of other neurons, resulting in a network of some one million billion connections in the cortex (the outer layer of the brain) alone (Damasio 1994; Edelman 1992).

Like the nervous system as a whole, the brain can be subdivided into many areas. Early anatomists looked for physical divisions (like the fissures on the cortex, or the characteristic almond shape of the amygdala in the limbic system), and then tried to deduce the functions. They *assumed* that specific functions are associated with specific areas, and this assumption, called *localization of function*, has led to many insights, as we will see. At the same time, the brain is a highly interconnected system, and it is worth keeping that in mind as we discuss what is known about the functions of different parts of the brain.

cortex the pink, somewhat wrinkled outer layer of the brain which controls many of our higher functions like speech and perception; from the Greek for 'bark' (as on a tree).

If you were to remove the top portion of a person's skull, you would see the pink, somewhat wrinkled outer layer of the brain, called the **cortex** (see Figure 2.3). Its wrinkled ('convoluted') appearance results from the cortex being folded on itself. Since maximum surface area seems important (simpler organisms have both smaller and less convoluted brains), this crumpling effect allows a large sheet to be compressed into the relatively small confines of the skull. (Imagine crumpling a large sheet of paper into a small wad.)

The cortex is made up of two distinct hemispheres, left and right, each of which essentially controls the opposite side of the body (for example, muscle movements in your right hand are initiated by your left hemisphere). In turn, the hemispheres can be broken down into smaller

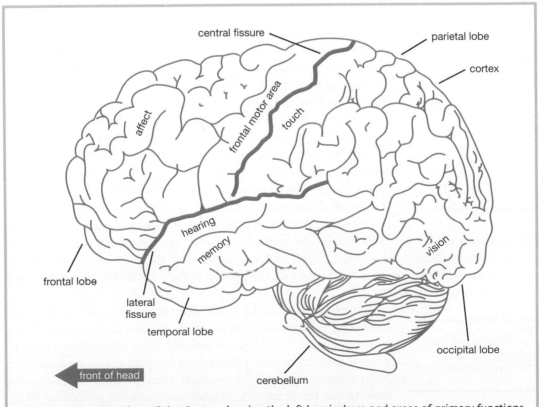

Figure 2.3 Exterior View of the Cortex showing the left hemisphere and areas of primary functions.

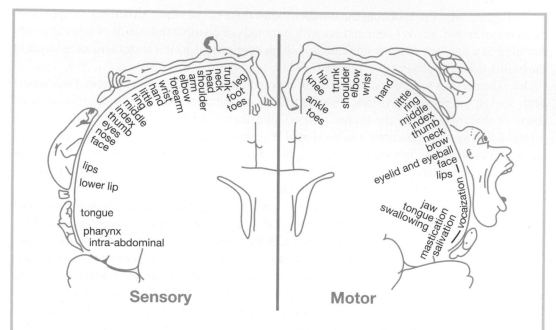

Sensory   **Motor**

Figure 2.4 Tactile and Motor Representation in the Cortex Penfield's research using electrical stimulation of the cortex has helped clarify the localization of touch and motor control along the central fissure. (In the figure, the brain has been cut vertically along the fissure which divides the frontal motor area from the sensory region of the parietal lobe – compare Figure 2.3.) The relative size of the body parts shows the relative degree of cortical representation. (After Penfield and Rasmussen 1957)

frontal lobe the area of the cortex in front of the central fissure, and above the lateral fissure; it is involved in the interpretation of emotion and experience.

frontal motor area the area of the frontal lobes just before the central fissure which controls all voluntary movements of the muscles.

parietal lobe the portion of the cortex just behind the central fissure and above the lateral fissure, whose primary function is the sense of touch.

regions called lobes, which are identified by the valleys or 'fissures' on the surface. Surprisingly, there is considerable variation across individuals in the exact shape and location of the convolutions; despite this, the ridges and valleys make reliable landmarks for distinguishing major regions of the cortex. The two major landmarks are the *central fissure*, which divides each hemisphere roughly in half front-to-back, and the *lateral fissure*, which runs along the side of each hemisphere. In each hemisphere, the **frontal lobe** is the area in front of the central fissure, and above the lateral fissure; the portion of the frontal lobes just before the central fissure is called the **frontal motor area**, because it controls all voluntary movements of the muscles. Interestingly, the body areas capable of very subtle motor control (such as the hands or lips) show a greater representation in the frontal motor area than other body regions. In fact, researchers have created maps of the frontal motor area, detailing the body areas controlled. A similar mapping for the sense of touch exists for the portion of the **parietal lobe** just behind the central fissure (see Figure 2.4).

association areas areas of the cortex which have no primary function (such as receiving direct sensory data), but rather play a role in integrating activity from other brain areas.

In contrast to the frontal motor area, much of the frontal lobes seem to have no primary function (such as receiving direct sensory data); such regions of the cortex are referred to as **association areas**. In general, association areas play a role in integrating activity from other brain areas; in the frontal lobe, these areas are involved in decision making and the processing of emotional response (Goldberg 2001).

frontal lobotomy an operation, popular in the 1940s and 1950s, which involved sectioning or removing portions of the frontal lobes, in an attempt to treat cases of bipolar mood disorder or chronic pain; later shown to be largely ineffective as a therapeutic procedure.

Because of the frontal lobe's role in emotions, an operation called a **frontal lobotomy**, which involved isolating or removing portions of the frontal lobes, was once used in an attempt to treat cases of bipolar mood disorder or chronic pain. The rationale behind this was that if the frontal lobes were removed or deprived of input from other brain areas, the person would not be able to form an emotional response, and thus would have no extreme moods (such as depression in the case of bipolar disorder), or distress (in the case of chronic pain). The procedure, popular in the 1940s and 1950s, was ultimately shown to be a poor treatment, and frontal lobotomies have been largely abandoned today (Goldstein 1950; Shorter 1997).

temporal lobe the region of the cortex below the lateral fissure; its primary functions are hearing and memory.

occipital lobe the rear-most portion of the cortex, which is devoted solely to vision.

We also have some understanding of other portions of the cortex. The **temporal lobe**, located in the region below the lateral fissure, plays a role in hearing, language and memory for objects. In terms of language, a region of the left temporal lobe called Wernicke's area is crucial to make language meaningful. Patients with damage to this area typically have difficulty understanding words and sentences, and produce 'word salads' (sequences of speech which are fluently spoken, but make little sense, such as 'Lizards spell nothing bluely'). The **occipital lobe**, at the rear of the cortex, is devoted solely to vision. Given the large area devoted to it, one might speculate that vision is either very complex, or very important, or both; the evidence suggests that it is indeed both. The experience of seeing, like other senses, is dependent on brain activity as well as sensory activity. In the extreme case, a person with damage to the occipital lobe would be functionally blind, despite having perfectly functioning eyes. Recognition of this connection between brain function and sensory experience is another reason why many researchers feel comfortable identifying the mind with the brain.

visual agnosia a general term for disorders which result in disruption of visual recognition.

At the beginning of this chapter, we discussed the peculiar case of Dr P., who could see, but often failed to recognize what he saw, including faces. His problem is an example of **visual agnosia**, which refers to problems with visual recognition. Clearly, the primary visual areas of the brain were intact, since he could recognize simple forms like a pin, and had no difficulty avoiding obstacles in his path. Instead, his problem involved integrating the sensory information into a coherent whole, and relating it to other information, such as his memories of people. Disorders like this can be very perplexing, and indeed, in describing this case, Sacks (1985) does not specify the precise regions of the brain affected, or the cause of the damage. However, based on the symptoms, it is likely that it involves the role of the association areas for vision, which link visual sense data to functions in other parts of the brain. In particular, the pattern of problems (trouble in integrating complex patterns, along with abnormal motor reflexes on the left side of the body) suggests damage to the association areas of the right occipital lobe.

While there are clearly differences in the functions of the various parts of the cortex, these functions are often interlinked. For example, when we recognize an object as familiar, we often make use of both sight and touch: children asked to identify an object like a rubber ball often take the ball in their hand before giving an answer. The process underlying this can involve complex interactions between the occipital and parietal lobes (James *et al.* 2002), Thus, despite the apparent localization of many cortical functions, we must always remember that the brain functions as a whole.

limbic system a series of subcortical structures which connect the cortex with other parts of the brain and which are important in many basic functions; among the main parts of the limbic system are the thalamus, hypothalamus, amygdala and hippocampus

hypothalamus one of the most important elements in the limbic system, the hypothalamus both regulates behaviours associated with hunger, thirst, sex and other basic drives, and also plays a role in regulating hormonal functions.

hippocampus a structure within the limbic system which is important to memory function.

amygdala an almond-shaped structure in the limbic system which plays a role in basic emotions, and possibly memory and stimulus evaluation..

The cortex received its name (Greek for 'bark') both because of its wrinkled appearance, and because it covers other sections of the brain, much as the bark of a tree covers the interior. Below the cortex are sub-cortical networks which connect the cortex with other parts of the brain, notably the *limbic system* and the *brain stem*. These regions are sometimes referred to as the 'primitive brain'. As the name implies, these structures control fundamental aspects of behaviour that we share with many lower organisms. The main parts of the **limbic system** are identified in Figure 2.5; among these, the most important is the **hypothalamus**, which both regulates behaviours associated with hunger, thirst, sex and other basic drives, and also plays a role in regulating hormonal functions. The **hippocampus** is important to memory function; in a well-known case, a man who suffered damage to the hippocampus lost the ability to retain experiences which occurred subsequent to the surgery, but left prior memories intact (Milner 1965). (The damage disrupted transfer to *long-term memory*, as will be discussed in Chapter 4.) Next to the hippocampus is the **amygdala** (from Latin for 'almond', because of its shape), which plays a role in basic emotions like fear and rage. Emotions are a fundamental, yet complex, part of our behaviour. Research indicates that the amygdala may be involved in aspects of emotion ranging from forming emotional memories (via its links to the hippocampus) to identifying emotionally significant stimuli, such as facial expressions indicating anger or fear (LeDoux 1995; Ohman 2002).

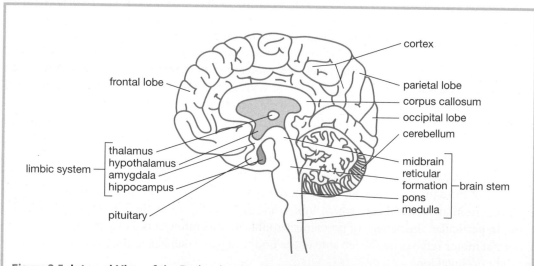

Figure 2.5 Internal View of the Brain, showing the relatively 'old' parts of the brain, such as the limbic system, which are normally hidden by the surrounding cortex.

cerebellum ('little brain' in Latin) two small hemispheres located beneath the cortical hemispheres, at the back of the head; the cerebellum plays an important role in directing movements and balance.

Nestled beneath the large cortical hemispheres, at the back of the head, are two smaller hemispheres. These two hemispheres form the **cerebellum** (literally 'little brain' in Latin). The cerebellum plays an important role in directing movements and balance, particularly fine motor control activities like sewing or playing the piano, and also complex movements like gymnastics. It does this by receiving information from both the sensory nervous system and the cortex, with much of this information passing through an adjacent centre, the brain stem. In addition to guiding movements, the cerebellum also seems to play a role in sensory processing (Nixon and Passingham 2001).

brain stem the region at the top of the spinal cord, composed of three primary structures: the medulla, the pons and the midbrain

medulla a small swelling at the top of the spinal cord composed of the cell bodies of neurons whose axons extend to the heart and other internal organs; its role is to regulate basic bodily processes.

pons (Latin for 'bridge') a region in the brain stem above the medulla which provides connections between the cortex and cerebellum.

reticular formation a diffuse network of nerve fibres which runs through the brain stem and limbic system, with connections both up to the cortex and down to the spinal cord; the reticular formation acts as a relay network controlling sensory inputs, and thereby plays a key role in regulating arousal level, alertness and sleep.

The **brain stem** is the region at the top of the spinal cord, and is composed of three primary structures: the medulla, the pons and part of the reticular formation. The **medulla**, a small swelling at the top of the spinal cord, has neurons whose axons extend to the heart and other internal organs; its role is thus to regulate basic bodily processes. Above it, the **pons** (Latin for 'bridge') provides connections between the cortex and cerebellum. A significant structure of the brain stem is the **reticular formation** (reticular means 'finely interwoven'), a diffuse network of nerve fibres which runs through the brain stem and limbic system, with connections both up to the cortex and down to the spinal cord. The reticular formation acts as a relay network, controlling sensory inputs; as such, it plays a key role in regulating our arousal level, controlling alertness and sleep.

Thus, the brain and nervous system are made up of a number of specific structures, which must function as an integrated system to regulate our behaviour. For example, when we expect to be shown an unpleasant or disgusting picture, there is increased activity in a variety of areas in the brain, including the prefrontal cortex, thalamus and hypothalamus, among others (Herwig *et al.* 2007). The description given here should not be taken as complete, but simply as an introduction to this incredible system. At the same time, this discussion has said little about *how* we know these things – for example, how do we know that motor functions are located in the frontal lobe?

Try it Yourself

Based on what we have discussed about the workings of the brain, consider the following science fiction scenario: a mad scientist kidnaps you, and renders you unconscious. Then he takes your brain, and places it in a bowl that provides nutrients, and is connected to a computer to provide 'sensations'. When you awake, would you be able to tell your brain was no longer in your body? Why or why not? If the computer were providing all your 'sensations', would it matter to you that your physical body had been discarded? What would be the disadvantages of being a 'disconnected' brain? Can you think of any advantages?

Studying the Brain

In order to develop an understanding of the brain, researchers have long been dependent on observation. At one time, clinical cases were the primary method available to study the workings of the brain. The use of clinical observation (*case studies*) has its drawbacks, however, particularly in terms of lack of control. For example, a person may receive a severe blow to the back of the head, and subsequently complain of numbness in one arm. Unfortunately, one cannot easily interpret the connection between the blow and the symptom, because the impact would have been transmitted throughout the skull. Thus, in this case, it does *not* mean that the occipital lobe (the area closest to the site of the blow) is involved in the sense of touch (the symptom). Occasionally, though, the clinical method can lead to important breakthroughs: Broca's discovery of the speech centre is one example. In this case, it was possible to study the patient in detail, since the problem existed for many years. In addition, after the patient's eventual death, an autopsy clearly showed a lesion (tissue injury) in the left frontal lobe, providing the basis for Broca's conclusion. Today, researchers have available a variety of techniques for identifying the function of various brain structures, beyond the use of clinical cases.

Electrical Recording and Stimulation

It has long been known that the brain is somehow involved in electrical activity. In ancient Rome, Pliny the Elder recommended the shock of an electric fish, applied to the forehead, to ease the pain of childbirth. Without knowing the mechanism, Pliny recognized that the shock stunned the patient, reducing conscious awareness (including pain). The electrical nature of nerve activity was first recognized by Luigi Galvani, an Italian anatomist, in 1791 when he observed that a frog's leg could be made to twitch at the touch of dissimilar metals. Apparently he first noticed the effect when a butcher used metal tongs to reach for some frogs' legs hanging on a hook! (Galvani thought, wrongly, that the frog's leg generated the impulse, rather than being activated by the metal tool, which actually created a battery.) While it was not long before the true nature of the process was recognized, the possible implications were ignored for nearly a century. It was only about 80 years ago that researchers began to study electrical activity in the brain in a systematic manner.

electroencephalograph (**EEG** – 'writing the electricity of the brain'). A device for recording the electrical activity of the brain by means of electrodes placed on the scalp.

In the 1920s, the first recordings of brain-wave activity (as the electrical signals are called) were made using the **electroencephalograph** (**EEG** – 'writing the electricity of the brain'). The EEG allowed researchers to record activity, and is still an important tool today. Recently, EEGs were used to identify synchronized patterns of activity associated with perceptual recognition; researchers found that there was a burst of activity at the moment when an ambiguous visual stimulus was recognized as a face, most particularly, a human face (Rodriguez *et al.* 1999; Zion-Golumbic *et al.* 2008). Similarly, based on EEG evidence, it is surmised that frontal brain regions are involved in the

Key Thinker: **Wilder Penfield**

Wilder Penfield (1891–1976) was born in Spokane, Washington. He was educated at Princeton University, and subsequently attended Oxford University as a Rhodes scholar. It was at Oxford that the direction of his career took shape, as he met the distinguished neurologist Sir Charles Sherrington. After returning to the USA to obtain a medical degree at Johns Hopkins University, he returned to Oxford to study with Sherrington for two more years. Eventually, he established a practice in neurosurgery, first in the USA, and then in Montreal, Canada. At Montreal, he became a professor at McGill University, and founded the Montreal Neurological Institute. This institute became one of the world's leading centres for neurology, and it was here that Penfield did his pioneering work on the mapping of cortical functions. In the course of doing surgery for epilepsy and other disorders, Penfield would identify the functions of various cortical regions by using electrical stimulation as the patient lay conscious on the operating table. This work has been widely hailed, and among other honours, Penfield became a member of the Royal Society. He died in Montreal at the age of 85.

craving for nicotine experienced by smokers (Knott *et al.* 2008). More dramatically, researchers were able to demonstrate by using EEG recordings that a man paralysed in an accident, and assumed to have lost all cognitive functions, was actually aware. This led to his receiving intensive rehabilitation which enhanced his recovery (Connolly 2000). Despite such successes, a limitation of the EEG is that it is essentially passive, allowing researchers to observe the brain, but not directly alter brain activity.

electrical stimulation of the brain (ESB) artificial stimulation of neurons by means of a current applied through an implanted electrode.

In the 1950s, techniques developed that permitted more direct intervention, by means of **electrical stimulation** of nerve cells (sometimes called **ESB**, for 'electrical stimulation of the brain'). In this technique, small clusters of cells are activated by inserting a fine wire into the desired area, and then applying a small electric current. (Note that since the brain itself has no sense receptors, the simple presence of an electrode does not cause pain or other sensations.) In 1954, researchers at Yale University discovered that electrical stimulation of certain regions of the limbic system and midbrain in animals seemed to trigger aversive reactions (Delgado *et al.* 1954). That is, Delgado's results seemed to identify a pain centre that was distinct from a simple sensory response. Then, in the same year, James Olds discovered that stimulation of certain areas of the limbic system could also produce pleasure (Olds and Milner 1954). Delgado and Olds were studying areas of the 'primitive brain' (below the cortex) in animals, and the effects they discovered seemed to reflect primitive emotions and drives. These techniques, while striking in their findings, also raised questions: Could the results be applied to people? And what of the cortex? As it happens, initial answers came quickly, due to the work of Wilder Penfield, a neurosurgeon at the Montreal Neurological Institute.

Penfield's discovery occurred while working with individuals suffering from epilepsy; as part of the surgical procedure used to treat the disorder, he identified the effects of stimulation of the cortex in conscious individuals. In many cases, epileptic seizures are triggered by random bursts of activity in a focal region, which then spread to other parts of the cortex. To treat individuals suffering from severe seizures of this type, Penfield would sometimes operate, destroying cells in the area where the seizure originated. In order to avoid damage to essential functions, Penfield needed to know what functions would be affected by the tissue he planned to remove. To find out, he would first stimulate various areas of the cortex, and observe the effects reported by the patient (who was conscious throughout the operation). From this, he would produce a 'map' of the cortex and its functions, making the surgery itself more accurate. In this way, Penfield was able to help his patients more effectively, and also advance our understanding of the brain.

Electrical stimulation poses some basic questions about the brain and mind. One issue concerns the localization of functions. The materialist view argues that all functions of the mind are based on activity in the body. The simplest form of this view says that each aspect of behaviour is produced by a specific location in the brain – that is, that functions are localized. Broca offered support for this position when he pinpointed speech functions in the left cortical hemisphere. Similarly, Penfield's work indicated that specific regions of the cortex control particular movements, sensations and even memories (refer back to Figure 2.4 for his findings). Thus, it would seem that electrical stimulation may allow us to identify – and ultimately control – all aspects of behaviour. How far one can take such control is unclear, though researchers continue to extend the boundaries of application: one recent study demonstrated that rats implanted with electrodes and equipped with a tiny video camera could be remotely controlled to explore where the researcher directed (Talwar *et al.* 2002).

This line of thought can give rise to all sorts of scenarios, ranging from people using ESB instead of drugs to control mood, to governments enforcing laws by means of computer-controlled systems implanted in each citizen's brain. These possibilities can seem frightening and Orwellian, and critics have been quick to raise questions. Typically, the questions focus on the moral aspect: who is to control the computers that control the ESB, and what sort of behaviours should be rewarded or punished? But before accepting this as a purely moral crisis, one should look more carefully at the scientific basis of the issue.

Problems *do* exist with ESB, and in some sense they are all connected with the issue of localization of function. If one accepts it in its simplest form, then there exists a specific centre responsible for any type of behaviour. At present, there is inadequate evidence to support this view. Lower animals show a great degree of physiological predetermination of their behaviour (often called 'instincts'). In humans, however, there appear to be relatively few such patterns, even for comparable behaviour. For example, while male stickleback fish show stereotyped courtship rituals, human males do so only to the extent that their culture dictates – so it is unlikely to be based on a specific neural structure in humans. If true localization of function does not exist, one must question whether complete control of every action would ever be possible. A second problem concerns variability across individuals. Gerald Edelman, a Nobel laureate in physiology, has noted that while the general patterns of brain structure are similar across individuals, the details of neural connections differ significantly. This implies that the mapping of functions must still be done on a case-by-case basis, even if localization exists (Edelman 1992).

While electrical stimulation has greatly aided our understanding of the brain, it does have limitations as a research tool. First of all, ESB is an artificial process. Inserting an electrode destroys a few hundred cells in the immediate vicinity, and the effects of the stimulation itself are not the same as normal neural activity. Typically, the current applied is either some form of alternating current, or a series of brief direct-current pulses. The effect in either case is to artificially stimulate all the neurons in the immediate area, perhaps a few thousand cells. These cells then fire *in synchrony*, which is hardly typical of normal neural function over such a region. Thus, current techniques of ESB initiate brain activity, but do not duplicate the normal workings of the brain. Since there are approximately ten *billion* neurons in the cortex alone, it is unlikely that ESB will ever mimic the brain's patterns over any significant area. Given these difficulties, it is worth noting that researchers have had more success using electrical stimulation in peripheral nerves (called 'functional electrical stimulation', or FES) than in the CNS. For example, doctors are developing a system to enable paralysed individuals to walk by using FES to stimulate the leg muscles (von Wild *et al.* 2002). FES has also been used to enable quadriplegics to grasp with their paralysed hand (Popovic *et al.* 2006) and holds promise for enabling people with spinal cord injuries to control a sitting posture (Wilkenfeld *et al.* 2006).

Try it Yourself

The notion of implanting electrodes has fascinated many people, including writers. For example, Michael Crichton – himself trained as a doctor – wrote a science fiction novel entitled *The Terminal Man* in which a man with uncontrollable epilepsy was treated by the implantation of electrodes in the pleasure centre of his brain, with unexpected side-effects. The idea could also appeal in cases where there is no existing disorder: if technical and ethical constraints did not prevent it, would you be interested in having electrodes planted in a pleasure centre of your brain? What would you see as the advantages and disadvantages?

Electrical stimulation has been useful in increasing our understanding of the brain. In addition, clinical work like Penfield's has led to better, simpler methods of treating disorders like epilepsy. At the same time, it is inherently limited, in that it cannot tell us how the brain functions as a whole. This means that larger-scale functions, like consciousness, are unlikely to be revealed by ESB. For that, we must look to other approaches.

Computerized Imaging Techniques

More recently, a variety of techniques have been developed to study activity across large regions of the brain. These **computerized imaging** techniques, which use computers to assist in the analysis of information, are enabling researchers to gain new insights about brain function (Barinag 1997; Kevles 1996). While the details of each technique differ, they are similar in that the computer is used to convert a series of two-dimensional images into a three-dimensional model of the brain which can be viewed on a television monitor. The first technique, the *CAT scan*, was developed by British engineer Godfrey Hounsfield in 1971. It uses a series of X-ray images which are combined by a computer to create a 3-D picture of the brain. The limitation of the CAT scan, however, is that, like any X-ray, it shows physical structures, but reveals nothing about the activity within the brain.

computerized imaging techniques for studying brain function which use computers to convert information into a three-dimensional model of the brain which can be viewed on a television monitor.

Since the development of the CAT scan, newer techniques have provided doctors and researchers with more detailed information about the brain. In **positron emission tomography** (PET) scans, a short-lived radioactive substance is injected into the bloodstream along with glucose, which is used by cells (including brain cells) for energy. Consequently, when the injection is given, the active areas of the brain absorb more of the glucose, and with it the radioactive tracer (see Figure 2.6). Sensitive detectors then pinpoint the location of the tracer – and thereby tell researchers which parts of the brain are most active. PET scans have been used to study links between brain function and a variety of cognitive processes – for example, the role of the frontal lobes in language (Ravnkilde *et al.* 2002). While PET scans are very useful in helping to study activity in the brain, they have two significant limitations: the use of a radioactive tracer is rather invasive, and activity patterns must be averaged over intervals of about 30 seconds, because the absorption of glucose occurs gradually.

positron emission tomography (PET) a technique for studying brain activity by monitoring the absorption of a radioactive tracer injected via the bloodstream.

By contrast, **magnetic resonance** scans (variously identified as either 'nuclear magnetic resonance' or '**magnetic resonance imaging**' – MRI – scans) do not require injection of a radioactive tracer; instead, they utilize the response of electric charges within cells to a rapidly changing magnetic field – a process called *resonance*. Depending on how it is used, magnetic resonance can be used to study structures or activity patterns; the latter is often referred to as *fMRI*, for 'functional magnetic resonance imaging'. Because it does not depend on the use of a radioactive tracer, magnetic resonance is non-invasive, and fMRI is able to identify activity changes over intervals of only a few seconds – both of which make it somewhat more attractive than PET scans. The use of fMRI has enhanced our understanding of important aspects of brain function; for example, the study of cerebellar activity during sensory and motor tasks has led to recognition that the cerebellum does more than coordinate movement (Gao *et al.* 1996). In another study, MRIs have indicated that Penfield's classic mapping of the cortex (see Figure 2.4) may contain errors in the

magnetic resonance imaging (MRI) a technique for studying the brain by observing the effects on electrical charges in cells in a rapidly changing magnetic field; variants can be used to study either body structures or activity.

regions associated with the face; in particular, the parts associated with the forehead and chin should be reversed (Servos *et al.* 1999).

The new generation of scanning techniques provide a powerful tool for research into brain functions, enabling researchers to examine aspects of brain function never before possible. At the same time, scanning methods also assist in the treatment of a range of disorders. For example, PET scans have identified markedly reduced activity in the cortex of depressed patients compared to normal individuals, and reduced frontal-lobe activity in individuals with schizo-phrenia (Kasper *et al.* 2002); MRI studies have detected abnormalities in the temporal lobe, the hippocampus and the amygdala of people with major depressive disorder (Caetano *et al.* 2007). Further, brain imaging techniques can help assess the effectiveness of drugs used in treating depression (Drevets *et al.* 2002). By using fMRI to study language in bilingual individuals, researchers were able to identify different areas of the frontal lobes involved in native language, compared to a second language learned as an adult. This helps to explain why bilingual stroke victims sometimes only lose one language, and has implications for therapy (Kim *et al.* 1997). An intriguing alternative to the standard polygraph test for detecting deception may also one day arise from work with fMRI: researchers in one recent study reported that they can tell whether someone is telling the truth or lying 78 per cent of the time by examining brain activity patterns in the prefrontal cortex (Langleben *et al.* 2005).

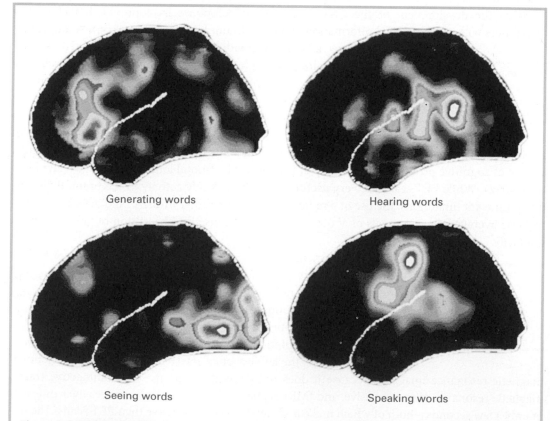

Generating words

Hearing words

Seeing words

Speaking words

Figure 2.6 PET Scans of Brain Activity These images of the left hemisphere show how PET scans can show changes in the pattern of brain activity associated with different behaviours. In these images, the lightest areas indicate regions with highest activity.

While very useful, computerized scanning techniques also have two major limitations. First, they are very expensive, and their use is unlikely to become routine for some time to come. Second, at present they are limited in their ability to pinpoint the location of activity precisely – less than electrical stimulation, for example. However, since PET scans and magnetic resonance are fairly recent, further improvements are likely to be seen in the future.

Each of the above methods has contributed to our understanding of the brain, but there are cautions to be added. These methods provide new ways to *observe* brain activity, but the results of the research must still be *interpreted*, and that can involve various assumptions and potential limitations.

- *Interconnectedness and complexity.* In many cases, the evidence seems to support the concept of localization of function. However, one must remember that the brain is highly interconnected, and its activity is highly integrated. (It is worth noting that more of the brain is devoted to integration, via association areas, than to primary functions.) Despite the existence of specialized functions, no one part can really be considered alone (an analogy might be a car: examining one part, such as the transmission, will not reveal the way the system as a whole functions). As the example of Dr P. (the music professor described by Oliver Sacks) shows, we see the psychological processes most clearly when considering the whole brain.

- *Correlational data.* A major limitation of brain imaging studies is that they typically produce data that are correlational in nature. That means that no *causal* inferences can properly be drawn from this data. For example, when it is found that there is reduced frontal lobe activity in people with schizophrenia, it cannot be determined whether the reduced frontal lobe activity has caused the schizophrenia, whether the schizophrenia has caused reduced frontal lobe activity, or whether another factor (such as neurotransmitter levels) has caused both.

Try it Yourself

A few years ago, researchers noted that when some people with temporal lobe epilepsy had a seizure, they also had what seemed to be a mystical or religious experience. The media quickly dubbed areas in the temporal lobe of the brain the 'God spot' and speculated that belief in a deity is a natural function of this area in the brain. More recently it has been demonstrated that mystical or religious experience is not correlated with any one localized spot, but is correlated with activity in several brain areas (Beauregard and Paquette 2006).

Researchers have sometimes tended to regard religious belief as 'simple' faith, but the reality is probably much more complex. Any belief system (whether belief in a deity, a political ideal or a philosophical concept) involves many elements: knowledge and memory of concepts involved in the belief, understanding of the meaning of the concepts, the decision to accept certain concepts as truths, and application of the concepts to facets of the individual's life and of the world; it is reasonable to assume that there are also emotions that are associated with a faith or belief. Given this partial list of elements involved in religious belief, is it realistic to suppose that all aspects would reside in one small area of the brain?

Suppose for a moment that there is a 'God spot'. How would one account for atheism? What if a surgeon had to excise this area of the brain because an individual had a tumour there? Would the post-operative person now be an atheist? What about agnostics? Would their 'God spots' be considered to be malfunctioning?

■ *Variability.* As noted earlier, there is significant variability in detailed brain structure across individuals. Studies of the activity levels of the brain using brain imaging techniques may detect a location of 'high' activity in one person that is, in fact, only normal activity in another person. In addition, given the expense of doing such studies, most fMRI studies use very few participants. Under these conditions, it is very difficult to determine what the true norms are and what differences in activity are both meaningful and reliable.

In fact, 'If a scan shows that a brain area "lights up" when someone is doodling, that doesn't mean the area is a doodling center!' (Wade 2006, p. 24).

Chemical Processes in Behaviour

As discussed in the preceding section, the CNS plays an essential role in coordinating behaviour. Neurons transmit sensory messages and allow motor responses to occur almost instantaneously; the process of touching a hot stove and quickly removing one's hand is a good example. (This represents an example of a so-called *spinal reflex arc*, the simplest form of neural circuit; it involves only a sensory neuron and a motor neuron, which connect via a synapse in the spinal cord.) Despite the impression we may have from such experiences, nerve conduction is not truly instantaneous: the fastest speed for nerve impulses is about 150 metres per second in large myelinated sensory nerves, slowing to a mere tenth of a metre per second (point-to-point) in the brain stem.

reaction time the time required to make a response to a stimulus, as measured by the interval between the stimulus and the response.

Our **reaction time** to respond to a stimulus is a reflection of the limits of this communication system. For example, when driving a car, it takes about three-quarters of a second to begin lifting your foot off the accelerator pedal, from the moment of seeing something you should stop for. At 80 kph, you cover almost 17 metres in that time – and that doesn't count the time for the brakes to physically stop the car!

Neurotransmitters

Despite being less than instantaneous, the nervous system is very effective in fulfilling its role as the body's communication network. Messages continually criss-cross, enabling us to perceive and respond to both our internal and external environments. In this system, the primary signals are the nerve impulses, racing along the axons. While the axon of a neuron may be compared to a wire which relays an electrical signal, a nerve impulse only travels within the neuron which generated it. At the junction between two neurons is a physical gap, the *synapse*. In order to bridge this gap, communication between neurons depends on an exchange of chemicals. These chemicals, called *neurotransmitters*, are released by the terminals of one neuron, and flow across the synaptic gap to the receptors of the next neuron.

The first neurotransmitter to be identified was *acetylcholine*, which is released by motor neurons to activate muscle fibres; in the CNS, it has been implicated in learning and memory (Butt *et al.* 1997). Since acetylcholine was first identified in the 1930s, approximately 100 chemicals have been found which are involved in neural transmission (Cooper *et al.* 1991). *Dopamine*, for example, plays a role in both motor control and sensory processing; low levels in motor pathways result in Parkinson's disease, while high levels in sensory pathways have been partially linked to schizophrenia. A study found that playing battle-simulation video games raises dopamine levels, which may account for their 'addictive' attraction to players (Koepp *et al.* 1998). Dopamine's relationship to addictive behaviour may also be seen in a phenomenon known as 'punding'. **Punding** consists of stereotyped, purposeless behaviour

punding stereotyped, purposeless behaviour that is maintained for long periods of time.

Box 2.1 *Major Neurotransmitters and their Functions*

A range of neurotransmitters exist in the nervous system, often serving different functions in different parts of the brain.

Neurotransmitter	Where found in nervous system	Examples of functions
Acetylcholine	Throughout the brain Neuromuscular synapses	Learning and memory Control of muscles
Dopamine	Many locations, including cerebellum, basal ganglia, limbic system	Motor activity, coordination Emotion and memory
Epinephrine	Many locations, including sympathetic nervous system	Emotion, stress
GABA	Major inhibitory neurotransmitter found throughout brain	Anxiety, arousal, learning
Glutamate	Major excitatory neurotransmitter found throughout the nervous system	Anxiety, mood
Serotonin	Many locations, including thalamus, brain stem	Sensory processing Sleep, arousal

that is maintained for long periods of time. Examples of this include piling stones, dressing and undressing, various types of game playing, manipulating and sorting small objects, and doodling. In these cases, the people performing the actions get little or no pleasure from the activities, and consider them to have no purpose, yet the activities are repeated endlessly. Punding has been found in patients with Parkinson's disease who have been treated with medications which increase the action of dopamine; the behaviours decrease with the removal of these medications (Kumar 2005; McKeon *et al.* 2007; Miwa and Kondo 2005). While it is not possible to review all the types of transmitters, it is worth noting some basic concepts of neurotransmitter function (see Box 2.1 for an overview of some of the major neurotransmitters and their functions).

Neurotransmitter substances can function in various ways. Some neurotransmitters trigger activation of the neuron, called *excitation*; this is a bit like stepping on the accelerator while driving a car. Others act to prevent the neuron from firing, called *inhibition*; by reducing neural activity, this is somewhat like stepping on the brakes while driving. Still other substances act to block the excitatory or inhibitory chemicals, or to clear them away after they have done their job. As we will see when we discuss drug effects, this system provides the basis for a wide range of outcomes.

While well adapted to providing quick responses, neuronal control has its limitations. Neurons only communicate while they are active, and while changes in activity can take place over fractions of a second, a neuron cannot remain active indefinitely. Faced with constant stimulation, neurons begin to reduce their response, a phenomenon called **habituation**. This means that the nervous system is not well suited to the regulation of slower-changing processes like metabolism, growth and reproduction. To understand how such processes are regulated, we must look at another type of chemical process.

habituation a reduction in neural response due to continual stimulation.

Hormones

In contrast to the transient processes of nerve conduction, some bodily processes are based on another class of chemicals produced by glandular cells. These cells 'communicate' by means of

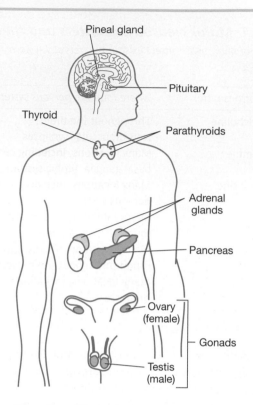

Endocrine Glands and their Functions

Pineal – melatonin (circadian rhythm)

Pituitary – growth hormone

ACTH – stress hormones for labour and milk production

Thyroid – metabolism

Parathyroids – calcium levels

Pancreas – insulin

Adrenals – stress response metabolism

Gonads – sex hormones

Figure 2.7 The Endocrine System and Hormonal Functions The major hormone-secreting glands are illustrated, along with the functions of some of the major hormones produced.

endocrine glands (ductless glands) glands which secrete chemicals called hormones directly into the bloodstream.

hormone a chemical secreted by an endocrine gland; hormones are involved in many aspects of metabolism and long-term functioning of the body.

chemical secretions. The most significant glands, from this standpoint, are the **endocrine glands**. These are a number of glands which secrete chemicals called **hormones** directly into the bloodstream, where they are carried to all parts of the body (see Figure 2.7). Given the time it takes for circulation through the body, the effects of these chemical messengers are not as swift as neural transmission – often it can be minutes, hours, weeks or longer before the response occurs. Not surprisingly, though, the effects are typically much longer-lasting than those processes which are under direct neural control. In this sense, neural and hormonal processes are not competitive, but complementary.

At one time, the distinctions between neural and hormonal processes seemed both clear-cut and neat: the nervous system handled short-term functions with fast responses, and the endocrine system handled slower, long-term functions. But research in the past decade has shown that the boundaries are not quite so distinct. One reason for this view is the realization that the two systems directly interact. The *pituitary gland*, for example, which is sometimes called 'the master gland' because of its role in regulating other endocrine glands, also has direct linkages to the *hypothalamus*, whereby it can influence the nervous system. The hypothalamus, in turn, releases small amounts of hormones, which affect the endocrine system. While such interactions actually make sense – links between the systems presumably let the body function more effectively overall – the interactions make separating their roles much harder. A couple of examples will indicate the concept. *Norepinephrine* (also called noradrenaline) is one of the primary secretions of the adrenal glands, and also a neurotransmitter found in many parts of the nervous system. (The neurons which use it as a neurotransmitter are called 'noradrenergic neurons'.) *Vasopressin*, first identified as a hormone which influences blood pressure, is also used as a neurotransmitter by the hypothalamus, and has been shown to enhance memory and learning. While the method of delivery for neurotransmitters vs. hormones differs (i.e., release into the synapse, or into the bloodstream), both processes involve receptors on the target (a neuron or a bodily organ), which are activated when the appropriate chemical binds to the receptor.

neuropeptide a chemical, comprised of a short chain of amino acids, which can function both as a neurotransmitter and as a hormone; also called a neurohormone.

In addition, it has been discovered that some chemicals influence neural transmission, while retaining their roles as hormones. One example is the family of chemicals called *endorphins*, which can enhance our mood and reduce pain (Hoffman 1997). (The function of endorphins will be discussed further in relation to drug effects.) Variously called **neuropeptides** (a peptide is a short chain of amino acids) or neurohormones, they have further influenced our ideas about how the body functions, even as we try to puzzle out their role (Cooper *et al.* 1991). As time goes on, our understanding of the chemical processes which underlie behaviour will doubtless increase. At present, the new-found complexity is exciting, even as it reminds us never to assume that we have the complete picture.

Try it Yourself

Clearly, chemical processes are vital to the regulation of the nervous system, yet we rarely think about our 'dopamine level' or how our neuropeptides are doing. But consider this everyday example: caffeine is a chemical that many of us use regularly in tea, coffee, cola drinks and chocolate; we may even joke about not being able to get started in the morning without our caffeine jolt. And we're right in thinking that caffeine does increase our arousal: in moderation, it makes us more energetic, alert and attentive, as well as improving our mood. The basis for these effects is that caffeine increases the receptivity of dopamine receptors, which has been found to increase our arousal level (Lorist and Tops 2003). How would you explain the tension we feel when we ingest too much caffeine? And how would you expect your behaviour to change if you suddenly stopped using caffeine?

INTERACTIONS OF MIND AND BODY IN BEHAVIOUR

Both neural and chemical processes are important to our understanding of the relationship between the brain and behaviour. In this chapter, we cannot cover all that is known about these processes. Rather, the intention is to give a basic description of how these physiological processes fit into the biological approach as a means of understanding behaviour. At the beginning of this chapter, we noted that the biological approach assumes that the mind is ultimately a product of the brain, with a physical basis. This assumption is often referred to as *materialism*. At the same time, no one can presently explain precisely *how* mind and brain are connected, despite the progress made in understanding more basic functions. A person may be a type of 'machine' in the materialist sense, but it is an exceedingly complex machine. To help us understand this more clearly, we will examine some of the interactions between mind and body.

As already noted, it is impossible to identify the mind with one particular brain structure, or portion of the body. Consciousness may depend on a normally functioning cortex, but other aspects of behaviour depend on other elements of the system. If we cannot localize the mind to a specific structure in the body, then how is it possible to study interactions of the two? It is precisely because mind and body are separate conceptually, and require different types of description, that one can seek parallels. It is almost like trying to translate between two languages – words may not always be easy to match up, but in the end the ideas can be communicated. In this case, we are trying to translate between physiologically-based 'body' and psychologically-based 'mind'.

The Effects of Body on Mind

When we speak of effects of the body on the mind, we are referring to the effects of physically identifiable events (for example, changes within the body) on psychological functioning and behaviour. Nearly all of the identifiable events can be described in terms of neural and/or chemical processes. Obviously, this can include a wide range of effects, both transitory (such as a cup of coffee as a drug) and enduring (such as spinal injury or alcohol-induced memory deficits). In this section, we will focus on two issues: drugs and their effects, and separating the cortical hemispheres ('the split brain').

The Study of Drug Effects

Technically, a drug is any substance that has an effect on living cells. Since this could include virtually any substance, including water, we will use a more restrictive meaning of the term. *Drugs* are chemical substances which are foreign to the body, either totally or in the form introduced (for example, adrenaline is a hormone, but it may also be injected as a drug). It is worth noting that not all drugs are medically prescribed: a morning cup of coffee is an example of drug use (or abuse), as is the illegal use of cocaine. Also, not all drugs are of interest to psychologists, because they do not have discernible effects on behaviour. For example, penicillin reduces infections, but does not directly affect how we act. The study of **psychoactive** (mind-affecting) **drugs** is a concern in both psychology and medicine, and has given rise to a hybrid field called *psychopharmacology*.

psychoactive drug a chemical agent which has a discernible effect on mental state or behaviour.

The use of psychoactive drugs is probably as old as recorded history. Nearly every culture has used some type of fermented grain or vegetable to produce an alcoholic drink. Some South American tribes have long traditions of eating plants in order to alter perceptions as part of religious rites. But it is only relatively recently that doctors have considered the use of drugs as a therapeutic tool, or that researchers have had effective methods to study drug effects.

Psychopharmacology today has become a complex field, but in the early days of drug research, techniques were very pragmatic. Many psychoactive substances were first identified by studying plants which had already been used for folk remedies. For example, reserpine, one of the first tranquillizers, was originally isolated from Indian snakeroot; aspirin was isolated from willow bark. In other cases, researchers even explored drugs by experimenting on themselves. Heinrich Kluver, a man noted for his contributions in other areas of physiological research, wrote a paper on his experience with mescaline, a hallucinogenic drug derived from a type of cactus (Kluver 1966). Today, research techniques have become more formal and sophisticated.

The methods typically used today for research on psychoactive drugs are much like those for other types of drugs. Typically, experimental animals are used to assess toxicity, strength and basis of effects. These assessments may involve intricate techniques and precision chemical analyses, such as injecting tiny amounts of the drug directly into specific regions of the brain, and then examining changes in neurotransmitter concentrations at nearby synapses. These methods often yield important information about the mechanism of drug actions, which is important to the preliminary screening of new drugs. Unfortunately, they do not provide sufficient information for a full understanding of drug effects.

Ultimately, psychoactive drugs must still be assessed by use on human subjects. There are several reasons for this: first, even the use of closely-related species like chimpanzees does not always produce the same results as with people. Second, even if the effects are the same, assessing them in animals can be difficult. By definition, the key aspect of psychoactive drugs is their effect on behaviour, which can include changes in alertness, responsiveness, mood, memory and even perceptions. Obviously, it is difficult to assess these effects in animals. This leads to the most basic problems in studying drugs: how to describe and categorize the effects.

By their nature, drugs operate on the physical system, yet the behavioural changes are primarily mental (perception, memory, etc.). This leads back to the problem of linking mind and body. Consider some of the possible difficulties:

1 Some drugs will affect only certain clinical groups, and not other types of patients or healthy individuals.

2 Some drugs affect sensory capacities in ways that are not directly expressed in behaviour. Consequently, even with verbal reports from subjects, it can be difficult to determine what is happening.

3 It is convenient to categorize drugs, but the categories may not always fit well with the subtleties of drug effects.

For example, the label 'antidepressant' focuses on one aspect of mood; however, drugs operate by affecting all neurons which have appropriate receptors, and this may involve much more than mood functions. The result can be a tendency to focus on an intended effect while overlooking various side effects. For instance, many drugs used to treat schizophrenia do so by affecting a neurotransmitter called *dopamine*. While such drugs can often reduce delusional thoughts and hallucinations, they also can affect motor responses, which also depend on dopamine. In the end, it can be very difficult to match behavioural descriptions, which are partly based on culture, to the physiological effects of a drug, which depend on complex sets of neural pathways (Snyder 1980). These problems are not insurmountable, as the increasing sophistication of psychopharmacology shows, but they do present continual challenges to researchers.

In addition to understanding in what ways a drug alters behaviour, we need to understand how it operates in the body. In this regard, there has been tremendous progress in recent years. Essentially, all psychoactive drugs operate by affecting communication between neurons. As was described earlier, communication across the synapse is dependent on neurotransmitters. These chemical messengers are released by the terminals at the end of the axon, and flow across the synaptic gap to the receptors on the next neuron (see Figure 2.2). The relationship between the receptor and the neurotransmitter may be compared to a lock and a key only a particular shape of neurotransmitter molecule will fit in a given receptor. (There are also variations on this basic theme. Sometimes, a molecule will seem to fit, but not influence the neuron; this is something like a key which fits a lock, but won't turn. By blocking the receptor site, such a chemical may prevent the proper neurotransmitter from reaching its target receptor. In other cases, chemicals attack neurotransmitters in the synapse, destroying them before they can reach the receptors.) While this lock-and-key metaphor applies to all neurotransmitters and psychoactive drugs, it was the basis for one of the great discoveries of modern psychopharmacology: endorphins.

The story begins with the study of opiates – a family of drugs which includes morphine, heroin and opium, all derived from the opium poppy. Although opiates have been used for hundreds of years (notably through the smoking of opium), the basis for their euphoric effects was unknown. As psychopharmacology developed, it became clear that drugs which affect behaviour must do so by affecting neural activity. This suggested that there might be a type of neural receptor which opiates activate. Based on this reasoning, a young researcher named Candace Pert began looking for opiate receptors in the brain. After several failures, she succeeded – the human brain did indeed have opiate receptors. Furthermore, comparative studies found that *many* species had such receptors – all the way down to the hagfish, which has existed essentially unchanged for 350 million years. This raised a new question: why should a 350-million-year-old fish have receptors for a chemical derived from a flower? The only reasonable answer seemed to be that there must be a similar chemical which occurs naturally in the brain! Given that the opiate receptor sites which Pert found were located in regions of the limbic system and brain stem that are associated with pain and emotion, it suggested that the body may produce its own natural painkillers. The race was on to find such chemicals, and within a year, the search was successful. The first discovery was dubbed *enkephalin* (Greek for 'in the head'); shortly after, C. H. Li found

what have become known as **endorphins** (for *endo*genous – 'naturally occurring' – mor*phine* (Villet 1978)). It was quickly recognized that endorphins were not typical neurotransmitters, but were rather small molecules, called peptides. This prompted increased interest in such *neuropeptides* – chemicals which function as both hormones and neurotransmitters (see *Chemical Processes in Behaviour*, above).

endorphin (endogenous – 'naturally occurring' – morphine) a neuropeptide which plays a significant role in pain and mood states.

Subsequent research has found that, as Pert believed, endorphins play a role in pain relief, and may also mediate mood enhancement associated with exercise – so-called 'runner's high' (Hoffman 1997).

The discovery of endorphins is like a detective story – finding clues, making deductions about what they mean and testing hypotheses until the solution is found. It also provides a good model for how drugs are discovered and evaluated today – by examining the molecular shape and matching it with receptor sites in the brain.

Types of Psychoactive Drugs

Advances in psychopharmacology have led to an increasing diversity of psychoactive drugs, and also to more widespread usage. At the same time, the frequency of their use has led to a change in social attitudes, so that drugs are more widely accepted, and in fact may be actively sought (studies suggest well over half of visits to doctors include writing a prescription – in part because patients have come to see drugs as a cure-all). In addition to prescription drugs, there are a number of other drugs which have behavioural effects, but are often overlooked by consumers because of their non-prescription nature. For example, antihistamines, which are commonly used for the sinus problems of allergies, can also cause drowsiness – in fact, one common antihistamine, diphenydramine, is marketed as an allergy medication, and separately as

a non-prescription sleeping aid! Given their pervasive presence in our culture, it is worth examining some commonly encountered drugs and their effects (see Box 2.2 for a summary).

Psychoactive drugs are commonly divided into various categories, according to the general nature of their effects on behaviour (although, as noted previously, such categories are often imprecise). One category often overlooked in daily experience is the **stimulants**. Stimulants

stimulant a drug which increases activation of the CNS and the autonomic nervous system, typically by increasing levels of dopamine; these drugs tend to decrease fatigue, increase physical activity and alertness, diminish hunger, and produce a temporary elevation of mood.

act on both the CNS and the autonomic nervous system (a portion of the peripheral nervous system that controls such functions as heart-rate and breathing, as well as general arousal level); in the CNS, they increase the activity in neurons which use *dopamine* as a neurotransmitter (Baldessarini and Tarzi 1996). (As noted earlier, dopamine affects a number of functions, including motor control and cognitive processes.) These drugs tend to decrease fatigue, increase physical activity and alertness, diminish hunger and produce a temporary elevation of mood. Both *caffeine* and *nicotine* are stimulants, although not as powerful as the prescription drugs known as *amphetamines*. Another stimulant, *cocaine* (often associated with drug abuse), works by blocking the reuptake (reabsorption by the terminals) of dopamine, rather than mimicking its effects (Volkow *et al.* 1997). (See *antidepressants*, below, for discussion of a similar mechanism involving serotonin.)

Box 2.2 Types of Drugs and their Effects

Sometimes drugs in the same category work by affecting the nervous system in different ways.

Type of drug	Mechanism and effects	Examples
Stimulants	Increase CNS activity – particularly by enhancing dopamine activity Increase alertness, suppress appetite, etc.	Caffeine, nicotine, amphetamines, cocaine
Depressants	Reduce CNS activity – particularly by enhancing inhibitory effects of GABA Relaxation, sleepiness, etc.	Alcohol, barbiturates
Anti-anxiety drugs	CNS depressants – by reducing serotonin and norepinephrine effects and increasing GABA activity Lower anxiety; see also Depressants	Benzodiazepines: diazepam (Valium), lorazepam (Ativan), etc.
Antidepressants	MAO inhibitors – stimulate CNS amines (serotonin, norepinephrine, dopamine) by blocking enzyme for their breakdown	Phenezine (Nardil), tranylcypromine (Parnate), etc.
	SSRIs – enhance serotonin activity by blocking reuptake after release	Fluoxetine (Prozac), paroxetine (Paxil), etc.
	Dual-acting – enhance serotonin and norepinephrine activity by blocking reuptake Reduce depressed mood states	Mirtazapine (Remeron)
Hallucinogens	CNS stimulants – various pathways depending on drug Enhance mood and perception; depending on drug and dosage, causes hallucinations	Lysergic acid (LSD), mescaline, MDMA (Ecstasy) – in large doses, cannabis (marijuana) – in large doses

Because stimulants tend to diminish hunger, amphetamines are sometimes prescribed as 'diet pills'. Smokers often experience a related effect when they reduce their smoking: the reduced nicotine level leads to an increase in appetite. Amphetamines are also sometimes prescribed for treating hyperactive children who show unusually high activity levels and an inability to concentrate; for reasons which are not clear, amphetamines seem to calm them down. Beyond these uses, stimulants have very few legitimate applications. They do not really reduce depression, nor are they a proper substitute for sleep when fatigued. Yet their use (and misuse) are widespread – sometimes users are even unaware of taking them, since stimulants like caffeine can be found in many common foods. Caffeine is found not only in coffee, but also in tea, cola and chocolate bars. Children exposed to average amounts of cola and candy may be accustomed to caffeine long before they ever taste coffee. Nicotine, found in cigarettes, is also a stimulant.

Although stimulants like caffeine and nicotine are treated casually in our culture, they nonetheless can cause adverse effects. With prolonged use, the nervous system tends to adapt to the presence of the stimulants. This can result in the phenomenon of *tolerance*, whereby one needs higher and higher doses to maintain the effect. In extreme cases, misuse of drugs can lead to *addiction*, which is determined by the occurrence of symptoms of physical *withdrawal*: when a person is addicted, stopping the drug provokes vomiting, muscle and heart tremors and seizures. (Note that addiction is not limited to stimulants – the pattern can arise with a variety of drugs.) While withdrawal symptoms to caffeine and nicotine are usually relatively mild, abuse of amphetamines or cocaine can be more serious. Chronic high doses of these drugs can lead to marked side effects, including hallucinations, delusions and even a psychosis very similar to paranoid schizophrenia. (This phenomenon is one reason that some researchers believe schizophrenia may be caused by excessive dopamine levels, as will be discussed in Chapter 9.)

Curiously, individuals often confuse stimulants with **depressants**, which reduce CNS activity; in large doses, depressants can cause coma and even death. Among the well-known depressants are alcohol and barbiturates. People often regard alcohol as a stimulant, because in small doses it reduces inhibitions and increases talkativeness. In reality, these effects are due to differential sensitivity to the depressant effects by different parts of the brain. The 'higher' functions of the cortex are the first to be affected, which can lead to diminished self-consciousness and a reduction in learned inhibitions. In large enough quantities, alcohol (like other depressants) is a general anaesthetic, producing loss of consciousness. Over time, large doses of alcohol can also cause severe physiological effects, including memory deficits and liver damage.

depressant a drug which reduces CNS activity, by enhancing the effects of the neurotransmitter GABA; in large doses, depressants can cause coma and even death.

Alcohol seems to enhance the effects of GABA, which is probably the most significant inhibitory neurotransmitter in the brain (see Box 2.1). Not only do about a third of all neurons in the brain have GABA receptors, but GABA can also directly affect axons, changing the threshold for firing. Alcohol's GABA-enhancing effects are similar to those of tranquillizers like Valium (benzodiazepine). This mechanism not only accounts for the anti-anxiety effects of alcohol, but may also explain reports of tolerance and dependence for the benzodiazepines (Smith 1992).

Abuse of alcohol may well be endemic in our culture: it has been estimated that almost 5 per cent of the population in both the USA and Canada have a serious drinking problem, and alcoholism is a problem in virtually all countries (Grant *et al.* 2006; Helzer and Canino 1992). No one is certain whether alcoholism is based on a physiological malfunction, learned drinking patterns, or a combination of the two. There is evidence that it runs in families, but this may mean either that there is a genetic cause, or that the children learn patterns from their parents. In either case, most treatments show only limited rates of success and alcohol may well be society's largest drug problem.

anti-anxiety drug a drug which functions as a CNS depressant, but whose primary behavioural effect is the reduction of anxiety.

The difficulty in creating descriptive categories for drugs is highlighted when one considers **anti-anxiety drugs** or tranquillizers. While their general effect is based on being CNS depressants, they have broader effects than alcohol and other simple depressants.

That is, although they enhance the activity of the inhibitory neurotransmitter GABA, they also reduce activity of stimulatory neurotransmitters (primarily serotonin and to some degree, norepinephrine), which alcohol does not (Langen *et al.* 2002). The most common anti-anxiety drugs are the benzodiazepines, such as Valium or Ativan. As a result of their broader action, benzodiazepines are more effective at reducing anxiety than is alcohol, but this advantage does not come without a cost: a serious problem with these drugs is their tendency to be addictive, with withdrawal symptoms occurring when discontinued after long periods of use. They have also been linked to the occurrence of depression – an effect which is understandable when we look at the nature of antidepressant drugs.

antidepressant a drug which is used to treat clinical depression, primarily by enhancing the activity of the neurotransmitter serotonin.

Antidepressant drugs are used to treat severe clinical depression, which is characterized by low mood state, fatigue and feelings of hopelessness. Early antidepressant drugs, called *MAO inhibitors*, blocked the enzyme monoamine oxidase, an enzyme which breaks down several stimulatory neurotransmitters, including serotonin, norepinephrine and dopamine. Unfortunately, this often created a variety of adverse side effects, which is not surprising given the many ways that these neurotransmitters are used in the brain. More recently, a new class of antidepressants has been developed, called SSRIs (selective serotonin reuptake inhibitors). As the name implies, their effect focuses on neurons which use serotonin. Rather than simply mimicking serotonin, they enhance the effects of serotonin by delaying its reuptake by the terminals of the neurons which released it. Not surprisingly, SSRIs (such as Prozac) tend to have fewer side effects than the MAO inhibitors, since they do not significantly affect the functioning of norepinephrine or dopamine. The difference between the two classes of antidepressants is a good example of how pharmacologists are seeking to develop drugs with more specific effects. Interestingly, recent research suggests that drugs which enhance norepinephrine as well as serotonin (such as mirtazapine) may be more effective than SSRIs, while reducing the side effects associated with MAO inhibitors (Schatzberg 2002). In all likelihood, as our understanding of the processes underlying depression continues to improve, so will the effectiveness of drugs.

The linkage between low levels of serotonin and depression can also help us to understand several other phenomena. For example, it helps explain why benzodiazepines, which reduce anxiety in part by reducing serotonin activity, have been implicated in depression. It also helps to understand the effects of a street drug, MDMA (often called 'Ecstasy' or 'E'). MDMA seems to work by triggering a massive release of serotonin – hence, its primary effect is to stimulate CNS regions involved with mood and perception. Like any illegal drug, its actual composition depends on the producer, so its nature and purity are often uncertain, along with its effects. What is known is that the artificial cascade of serotonin caused by pure MDMA is followed by significant depletion of serotonin, resulting in a short-term 'down' after use. Given that MDMA is the most popular drug among individuals going to clubs (McCambridge *et al.* 2005 report over 90 per cent of clubbers in the UK have used Ecstasy), the possible long-term effects are a serious concern. Increased incidence of depression and possible long-term damage to the nervous system have been raised as risks, with various studies reporting conflicting outcomes (de Win *et al.*, 2004; Parrott 2001; Piper 2007; Roiser *et al.*, 2005). However, it is hard to assess the effects precisely, because club use does not represent a controlled context for dosage or purity; in fact, analyses find that the majority of Ecstasy tablets sold in clubs are tainted by other chemicals, particularly methamphetamine (MA), a more potent stimulant related chemically to MDMA (Parrott 2004). Even in research studies, there are difficulties: A widely publicized article published in *Science*

The world today: **Evaluating the Effects of Street Drugs**

As has been noted, evaluating the effects of drugs is challenging. Even for prescription medications tested in a controlled context, researchers may find it difficult to identify and describe what the effects are. The challenges are even greater when it comes to illegal ('street') drugs like marijuana, cocaine or MDMA (Ecstasy), whose usage does not occur in controlled circumstances, and for which purity and dosage may be very uncertain. Yet given how common the use of drugs like marijuana and Ecstasy is, it is a serious concern to know what the effects of these drugs are. Since doing lab research on humans for these drugs is unethical (one cannot knowingly risk harm for participants), how can we determine what the effects are?

One answer has been offered by a recent study by Quednow *et al.* (2007). The researchers obtained three groups of 19 males, based on self-identified responses to advertisements in local print media: chronic Ecstasy users (individuals who had used MDMA at least 50 times in a year, but any other drugs to a significantly lesser extent), chronic marijuana users (similar standard), and drug-naive individuals. Hence, this was a *quasi-experiment*, based on selecting members of groups according to reported prior drug usage. At the time of testing, all participants had abstained from drug use for at least three days. All participants were given a variety of tasks intended to measure impulsivity (making hasty or rash responses) and decision making. For example, one test was a simulated gambling situation in which participants selected cards from one of four decks, with the goal of accumulating as many points as possible; part of the task was to determine if participants would figure out that the decks differed in the likely reward. The overall results from the tasks indicated that the Ecstasy users were more impulsive and showed impaired decision making compared to the other two groups; the marijuana users did not significantly differ from the control group. Thus, the study suggests that chronic use of MDMA has an impact on cognitive behaviour.

The results are certainly interesting, but unfortunately do not provide unambiguous answers. Like any quasi-experiment, there is a risk of *confounds*, such as the possibility that Ecstasy users are more likely to also use a variety of other drugs than are marijuana users. (The researchers attempted to control for this through selection interviews, but it is impossible to be certain confounds were eliminated.) Also, since selection of the groups depended on self-report, any distortions in reported drug use may also have affected the results. Can you think of any other problems with interpreting the results? What else would you want to know? Given that doing *experiments* on long-term effects is unethical, what should researchers do to explore the effects of street drugs?

found evidence of long-term damage in monkeys given several doses of MDMA (Ricaurte *et al.* 2002). However, the article was subsequently retracted when the researchers realized they had inadvertently used methamphetamine instead of MDMA in the original study (Ricaurte *et al.* 2003)! At present, we have no precise answer to questions about the risks of Ecstasy use – but it seems likely that the level of risk, both short-term and long-term, is certainly greater than zero.

While by no means exhaustive, the preceding discussion should demonstrate that psycho-active drugs, both prescription and non-prescription, are extremely common. Their prevalence often lulls people into thinking they are harmless, yet chronic, casual use of drugs can be a danger in many ways, and as noted, prolonged use can lead to tolerance and addiction. In other cases, side effects may be infrequent but severe (for example, Prozac can severely suppress appetite in some individuals; at one time, its manufacturer considered seeking certification for its use as a diet pill). Another potential problem can arise from the interaction of a drug with other drugs or even certain foods. For example, barbiturates (a depressant) can interact with alcohol (also a depressant) in a *synergistic* manner – that is, the effect of the two together is greater than for either alone. (Marilyn Monroe died from a combination of alcohol and barbiturates.) Synergistic interactions may also occur between drugs and non-drugs, such as food: some cheeses, such as Blue or Roquefort, can be dangerous or even lethal if consumed while taking certain drugs.

Our knowledge of synergistic effects is limited at present, and undiscovered combinations may exist. Unfortunately, casual attitudes towards drugs may cause people to underestimate the possible risks. For the present, the best approach seems to be caution: never take a drug without reason, and then only under a doctor's supervision. Always tell a doctor if you are taking medicines which have been prescribed by another doctor. If you take a drug, watch for drowsiness or other side effects that may impair your ability to deal with your surroundings.

Drugs which affect mood or behaviour are not new, nor are the circumstances that lead people to use them, such as seeking relief from anxiety. However, our understanding of the mechanism of such drugs is growing. The methods of research are becoming more sophisticated, and with them our ability to use drugs as a therapeutic tool. While no amount of research can ever determine social attitudes, ideally such attitudes are based on knowledge. To this end, the next few years offer hope of great strides in our ability to understand the role of drugs in mind–body interactions.

The Split Brain and the Whole Mind

According to the materialist view, consciousness *must have* a physical basis, most probably in the brain. The problem for researchers has been to find a way of identifying it. While research has produced support for the principle of localization of function, it still has not answered the question: where is the mind?

cerebral hemispheres two half spheres, made up of the cortex and underlying structures, which comprise the major portion of the brain.

corpus callosum a wide band of nerve fibres which connect the two hemispheres.

Normally, our experience of the world, reflected in our inner thoughts and feelings, seems unitary – that is, we have only a single consciousness. Yet the structure of the brain, especially the cortex, is basically two symmetrical halves. These halves, made up of the cortex and underlying structures, are called the **cerebral hemispheres**. Connecting the two hemispheres is a wide band of nerve fibres called the **corpus callosum**. Researchers have long known that each hemisphere is basically responsible for the opposite side of the body (for example, your left hemisphere receives sensations from, and gives motor commands to, the right side of your body). Now, if consciousness is really associated with the cortex, then it implies that the unitary nature of our experience and awareness is based on the integration of the two hemispheres. This reasoning led pioneering psychologist Gustav Fechner to speculate, more than 100 years ago, that if the two hemispheres were somehow separated, we would have two separate consciousnesses. Fechner never thought that this could be tested, but time has proven differently.

In the 1950s psychologist Roger Sperry, working with monkeys, suggested that separating the two hemispheres by cutting the fibres of the corpus callosum had no grave effects on behaviour – certainly less than procedures like *frontal lobotomy*. Still, this gave no indication of what might happen in humans. One obvious difference between primates and people is that monkeys do not speak, and Broca had shown that speech was found in only one hemisphere. Consequently, no one was sure what would happen if the hemispheres were separated in a person.

The question was answered in the course of dealing with a more immediate medical problem. In the 1960s, Los Angeles surgeon Philip Vogel was trying to treat patients with a long history of epilepsy. While in many cases epileptics could be treated with anti-seizure drugs, these patients did not respond to drug treatment; consequently, they had major seizures, on average, twice a week. In epilepsy, the random neural activity of a seizure usually starts at a point in one hemisphere and spreads, creating sensory distortions and convulsions. In cases of *grand mal* (French for 'great ill') attacks, the seizure activity spreads from one hemisphere to the other across the bridge provided by the corpus callosum. In such cases, the recurring seizures can disrupt normal life, and even present a life-threatening situation. When all other treatments failed, Vogel tried a new and radical approach: by cutting the fibres of the corpus callosum, he hoped to restrict the seizure activity to one hemisphere, and thus prevent grand mal attacks. While he knew of Sperry's work, and there had been occasional clinical reports of damage to the corpus callosum, no one had ever purposely separated the hemispheres before. Vogel and his patients were venturing into new territory.

Key Thinker: **Roger W. Sperry**

Roger Walcott Sperry (1913–94) was an American neurological researcher who pioneered much of our understanding of hemispheric specialization. His career began relatively slowly, and he received his doctorate in zoology at the University of Chicago at the age of 28. While there, he worked with the biophysicist Paul Weiss, studying how the connections between neurons and muscles are formed. This led to further work on the regeneration of neural connections between the retina and brain in amphibians. While doing this work, he met biologist Norma Dupree, with whom he collaborated; they married in 1949. In 1952, he moved to the California Institute of Technology, ending up as professor emeritus of psychobiology. In 1953, one of his graduate students, Ronald Myers, invented the split-brain procedure, the study of which later led to Sperry's most important discoveries; ironically, Myers's initial role is seldom cited in this regard. They first studied the effects of severing the corpus callosum in cats and primates; however, it was Sperry's later work on epileptic patients, in collaboration with neurosurgeon Joseph Bogen, that eventually led to Sperry sharing the 1981 Nobel Prize in Physiology or Medicine. Sperry's contributions continue to be carried further by his students, including Jerre Levy and Michael Gazzaniga.

Medically, the treatment worked. Not only did it prevent further grand mal attacks, but (for reasons still unclear) it also reduced the frequency of more limited seizures. At the same time, it was desirable to know what negative effects, if any, the surgery had caused. Knowing of Sperry's research, Vogel asked him to collaborate on evaluating the patients. The results were a surprise to all concerned.

Initial observations suggested that the patients were remarkably normal. Everyday actions like walking and eating seemed to occur naturally. However, by a series of ingenious testing procedures, Sperry, Vogel and their associates discovered that, in fact, these individuals had an unusual mental syndrome. As Sperry reported, 'Instead of the normally unified single stream of consciousness, these patients behave in many ways as if they have two independent streams of conscious awareness, one in each hemisphere, each of which is cut off from and out of contact with the mental experience of the other' (Sperry 1968, p. 724). In other words, *two* minds, each functioning separately from the other – Fechner's prediction had been correct! (Ultimately, Sperry's research on the split brain led to his receiving the Nobel Prize in physiology in 1981.)

To assess the effects of the surgery, the researchers had to use techniques whereby information was presented to only one hemisphere. The simplest case involved touch: if the split-brain person were given an object in their *left* hand while blindfolded, the left hand could later pick it out again, by touch, from a selection of several objects. However, if the *right* hand attempted to pick out the article previously held by the left hand, it did no better than chance. In the case of vision, the situation is a bit more complicated, because each eye is connected to *both* hemispheres. The division of visual processing is such that the visual world of each eye is divided in two, so that objects on the *left* side of the visual world (or *visual field*) are seen by the *right* hemisphere, while objects on the *right* side are seen by the *left* hemisphere, regardless of which eye is used (see Figure 2.8). Thus, if a person looks straight ahead and an image briefly appears to the left, only the right hemisphere receives the information. In Sperry's research, this procedure led to an interesting discovery: because only the left hemisphere had language, a split-brain person presented with a word or picture on the left side (conveyed to the right hemisphere) could not say what they had seen! Only the left hemisphere seemed able to talk, while the right was silent (note, of course, that these effects only apply when the corpus callosum has been cut; in a normal individual, there is continual exchange of information between the two hemispheres).

As it turns out, the differences are not quite what they first seemed. The right hemisphere, while usually unable to speak, is not completely ignorant of language. If presented with a word or picture, it can point to a corresponding picture or word. Thus, if the right hemisphere sees the word 'key', the left hand can correctly choose a key. At the same time, the right hemisphere has musical and spatial abilities which seem to be lacking in the left hemisphere. If given geometric figures to copy (such as a circle overlapping a square), the left hand (right hemisphere) does a better job of copying it than does the right hand (left hemisphere). This is particularly striking, since the patients Sperry tested were all right-handed, so in principle one might expect the right hand to be more skilled. For handwriting, the right hand is better; for drawing, it is not. This raises a fascinating problem: since lettering is a type of artistic skill, why is it that the left hand, so superior for other drawing tasks, is poor at reproducing letters and words? So far, this aspect of the split-brain phenomenon has not been fully explored.

Despite the apparent handicap and dual-consciousness which they possess, split-brain individuals manage to cope very well in everyday life. Even tasks requiring motor coordination of the two hemispheres, such as riding a bicycle, can be mastered. Over time, it even seems that indirect methods of communicating between the two sides develop. For example, in one experiment, Sperry flashed either a red or green card to the left visual field (right hemisphere), and then asked the person to name (left hemisphere) the colour. As expected, the left hemisphere, not having seen the colour, did poorly. However, if allowed to reconsider, the person was always correct. What seemed to happen was that the right hemisphere, hearing the spoken response of the left hemisphere, would produce grimaces and other gestures if the answer was wrong. These cues let the left hemisphere know its error, which it then corrected!

Since Sperry's original research, a large number of studies have been done, even though the number of split-brain individuals is quite small (between 1962 and 1968, Vogel operated on a total of nine patients). Overall, the results have supported Sperry's original work, although it is now recognized that the differences between the hemispheres are not absolute (Trevarthen 1987). Still, the research does suggest several things:

1 If the corpus callosum is cut, the two hemispheres function independently, although some sensorimotor information is still transferred between hemispheres by the superior colliculus, another connecting area between the hemispheres (Savazzi *et al.* 2007).

2 Each hemisphere seems to possess consciousness, but without awareness of the other (in one case, a patient, seeing her left hand make a response, exclaimed, 'I didn't do that!').

3 The two hemispheres seem to show different types of specialized abilities, with the left hemisphere usually possessing language, logic and maths skills, and the right hemisphere spatial, musical and arithmetical approximation skills (Funnell *et al.* 2007).

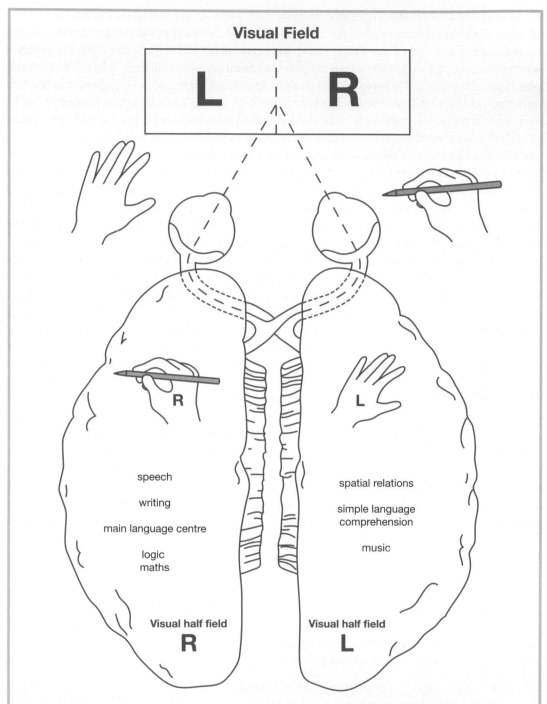

Figure 2.8 Hemispheric Specialization Roger Sperry's work with split brain individuals (note the cut fibres of the corpus callosum between the hemispheres) has helped to identify differences in the functions of the two sides of the brain. (After Sperry 1968)

There is also evidence that there is specialization in terms of emotion, with the left frontal lobe involved in processing positive emotions, and the right frontal lobe involved in negative emotions (Davidson and Irwin 1999).

The Split Brain and the Normal Brain

The striking nature of the split-brain findings makes it tempting to extend the conclusions to normal individuals. At the same time, it must be recognized that severing the corpus callosum is not a natural condition, and normally the two hemispheres communicate freely. Still, research seeking to test these findings in normal individuals does indicate that the two hemispheres tend to become specialized in ways similar to what has been observed in split-brain individuals. For example, clinical cases show that damage to the left hemisphere, whether by disease or trauma, can impair speech. However, one should be careful about over-generalizing. For one thing, it should be noted that in a small percentage of people, primarily left-handers, the pattern of hemispheric specialization is modified or reversed. Also, the degree of specialization for language may depend on what language an individual speaks – language processing may differ for native speakers of Chinese, which uses pictographic characters rather than an alphabet. Research using fMRI imaging demonstrates there is activation in *both* the left and right hemispheres when Chinese speakers read, and the way language is processed in the left hemisphere differs from the pattern for English speakers (Luke *et al.* 2002); and it is not just language which shows variations. While Sperry found that musical ability was normally associated with the right hemisphere, studies indicate that when professional musicians listen to music, the *left* hemisphere is actually more active; in effect, musicians seems to process music as if it were a language (Schlaug *et al.* 1995). Research has also suggested that there may be gender-related differences in the pattern of hemispheric specialization. A variety of studies indicate that language is less lateralized in women (that is, both hemispheres are involved), and that men are superior in spatial tasks (Gazzaniga *et al.* 1998; Kimura 1999; Phillips *et al.* 2001). Hence, while the general notion of hemispheric specialization seems valid, there can be variation in the details.

cerebral dominance the tendency for one hemisphere to be superior for particular functions, as expressed through behaviours like handedness.

One issue that has arisen out of split-brain research is an increased interest in **cerebral dominance** – the tendency for one hemisphere to be superior for particular functions. In most individuals, one hand, foot, eye and ear are usually preferred for many actions – for instance, if standing, we begin walking with the dominant foot. Similarly, if using a camera or telescope, we usually focus with the dominant eye. Such preferences have been noted since ancient times, and the origin of cerebral dominance has caused much speculation among researchers. Evidence suggests that dominance, as seen in preferences for one side, is already developing at birth.

Handedness, which is the most visible indicator of dominance, has often been the focus of social prejudice. In many languages and cultures, being left-handed is viewed negatively. This can be seen in the way we use words: A 'left-handed compliment' is not really a compliment. To be 'right' is to be correct. A suspicious person is 'sinister' (Latin for left-handed), while a skilful person is 'dexterous' (Latin for right-handed). Similarly, a 'gauche' (French for left) remark is in bad taste. These usages reflect a form of cultural bias, and lead to questions about the origin of handedness, and dominance more generally.

Theories of the origin of handedness cover a broad range, including genetic factors, prenatal learning (position within the womb) and congenital brain damage (left-handedness being the result of such damage) (Corballis 1997; Coren 1995; Previc 1991). At present, there is no conclusive evidence for any of these theories, though a relatively recent article provides an interesting link between a genetic factor for handedness and which direction hair spirals on the scalp (Klar 2003). While it is known that dominance is somehow related to hemispheric specialization (for example, stuttering in adults correlates highly with forcing right-hand use on a left-handed child), no one is sure exactly what the connection is. Attempts to alter dominance *do* seem to have some impact on skills like language, but that does not prove that dominance is the source of specialization. In fact, the *pattern* of hemispheric specialization seems much the same in both left- and right-dominant individuals (although left-handers are slightly more likely to show a reversed or mixed pattern of hemispheric specialization). In addition, there is no proven explanation as to why right-handedness (dominant left hemisphere) is the norm across races and cultures (though if Klar's analysis is correct, there is a genetic bias toward right-handedness). Like many aspects of brain function, there are still many unanswered questions about handedness, dominance in general and hemispheric specialization. Even so, most researchers would agree that, despite social prejudices, one should not interfere if a child shows a preference for being left-handed.

The research on the split-brain and cerebral dominance brings us back to our initial questions: is localization of function correct, and does consciousness reside in the brain? The research on split-brain individuals seems to indicate that consciousness involves the cortex, for separating the cerebral hemispheres seems to split consciousness as well. However, since it involves such a large-scale division, it offers us very little information in terms of determining precisely where consciousness resides. After all, the hemispheres each involve cortex, underlying sub-cortical tissue, limbic system structures and so on, down into the brain stem, spinal cord and beyond. To say that the two sides of the body can each have their own consciousness does not tell us what sort of structure produces consciousness. A materialist view which assumes localization of function would argue that we should be able to find some specific neural circuit that represents conscious awareness. At present, no study has found such a circuit; current attempts to do so tend to limit themselves to particular aspects of consciousness, such as visual awareness, attention or mathematical abilities (Blanke *et al.* 2002; Crick and Koch 1992; Funnell *et al.* 2007; Newman 1995). Increasingly, researchers are using tools like fMRI to identify neural patterns associated with specific thoughts (Haynes and Rees 2006), including soft-drink preferences (McClure *et al.* 2004)! So where does this leave us in trying to identify the origin of consciousness?

The lack of evidence for a single circuit representing general awareness has led various researchers to take different points of view. In a book written shortly before his death, Penfield noted the absence of any evidence for the localization of consciousness. Consequently, he concluded that consciousness was not a function of the brain, and he essentially reverted to a form of dualism (Penfield 1975). Sperry, by contrast, simply rejected the idea that consciousness is localized, without abandoning materialism. He viewed consciousness as an *emergent property* of the brain (that is, a phenomenon which emerges from the system working as a whole), and suggested that no study of individual parts will enable us to pin it down (Sperry 1969). This view is supported by a French EEG study which found that the moment of recognition of an ambiguous visual image was marked by synchronized activity across many areas of the brain (Rodriguez *et al.* 1999). Neurologist Antonio Damasio goes even further than Sperry, arguing that the mind is a product of the entire organism, operating as an ensemble (Damasio 1999). In his view, not only the brain must be considered, but also its links to the rest of the body; severing any of these links would also change the mind. Thus, to go back to the 'brain in a bowl' question raised earlier, Damasio would say a brain removed from the body could never function as a normal mind. At present, all these views are ultimately speculative, but current data suggest both that there is localization of some functions, and that the nervous system works as a coherent unity. In this sense, it may well be that the mind is connected to the body – but we may never be able to fully describe the relationship.

Try it Yourself

Are you left- or right-handed? Consider the types of skills that are associated with each hemisphere (for example, language with the left hemisphere, musical ability with the right hemisphere). Do you see any relationship between your own dominant hemisphere and your relative abilities? (Remember, the preferred hand is associated with the opposite hemisphere.) Do you think that it's more likely for artists to be left-handed? Why or why not?

Consider further the popular idea that traditional schooling is primarily 'left hemisphere', with the right hemisphere virtually ignored. Do you think this is true? Does the right hemisphere learn little in school? Why or why not?

The Effects of Mind on Body

'Mind over matter.' The phrase has been used to describe many things, from accomplishing a difficult task to claims of levitation. The most common meaning is to describe how physical reactions are seemingly altered by mental processes. The view that this is paradoxical or impossible can be traced to the dualistic conception of mind and body proposed by Descartes, in which the mind has no physical basis. In this sort of framework, it becomes difficult to imagine how mental states could affect specific body functions. By contrast, in a materialist framework, where mind and body are linked, it becomes easier to conceive of such interactions. 'Mind' and 'brain' may represent different levels of description, but materialism assumes that they have a common physical foundation.

This unified view can help us to understand what would be otherwise inexplicable phenomena. A common example is the reaction to painful stimuli: everyday observation demonstrates that people react differently to similar physical traumas. To one person a trip to the dentist may be terrifying, whereas to another it is no more painful than scratching an itch. Such variations can occur across cultures as well. In western culture, childbirth is usually regarded as an intensely painful experience, but not by members of some other cultures (Melzack 1973). Similarly, the Sherpas of Nepal are noted for their stoic response to the gruelling conditions of mountain-climbing (Clark and Clark 1980). Thus, response to painful stimuli seems to show considerable variation. Pain researcher Ronald Melzack believes that such variations in pain are due to differing cognitive expectations and perceptions, a view supported by clinical research (Haythornthwaite *et al.* 1998). Since cognitive processes (including perception and attitudes) are regarded as functions of the cortex, Melzack's theory says that the effect of expectations on pain response is mediated by cortical influences. Phantom limb phenomena, as mentioned at the beginning of this chapter, may also be the product of the way the person interprets sensory inputs, rather than an automatic response (Melzack 1992). Such phenomena give new meaning to the phrase 'mind over matter', by suggesting that mental states can influence physical functioning and behaviour. In this section, we will consider research related to two issues that highlight these interactions: the effects of stress, and relationships between mental states and health.

Try it Yourself

Does your dentist play music while he or she drills teeth? Why do you think this might be so? If being distracted can reduce our experience of pain, in what sense do you think pain is 'real'?

The Nature of Stress

Like pain, stress is a common human experience. We are all familiar with stressful events: your heart races as you sit down to write a test; or the boss wants to see you now about the last quarter's sales figures; or you go to bed, only to hear the neighbour's stereo blaring away. The pulse-pounding, gut-wrenching sensations that result from such moments are common in modern life. When we recognize the feelings, we may experience the desire to run away to a desert island. Unfortunately, even this may not solve the problem of stress.

According to Hans Selye, the doctor who pioneered stress research, stress is the non-specific response of the body to any demand on it (Selye 1978). Interestingly, what first led Selye to the study of stress was an observation he made as a second-year medical student in 1926. As part of their clinical training, the students encountered patients suffering from a variety of disorders, and Selye noted that 'they all looked sick'. His professors and fellow students laughed at his suggestion that disease, no matter what its nature, could produce certain consistent changes. Some ten years later, as a medical researcher, Selye returned to this question, and named the syndrome 'stress'. The term, borrowed from physics, was meant to refer to the effects of resisting an outside force.

Key Thinker: **Hans Selye**

Hans Selye (1907–82) was born in Vienna, Austria. He was educated in Prague, Paris and Rome, entering medical school when he was 18. He eventually earned three doctorates (MD, PhD and DSc), though primarily he was regarded as an endocrinologist (a doctor specializing in hormone functions). He began his pioneering research in the 1930s, and coined the term 'stress' in a 1936 paper. (Subsequently, lectures in France and Germany led to coining *le stress* and *der Stress*.) World War II led to him moving to Canada, where he became a professor at the University of Montreal and first director of the Institute of Experimental Medicine and Surgery. During the course of his career, he published over 30 books and more than 1500 articles on stress and related subjects. Whereas his first observations of stress-related phenomena (while still a medical student) were greeted with scepticism, over time his research became widely acknowledged, and he was the recipient of many scientific honours, including 43 honorary degrees. After retiring from the University of Montreal, he founded the Canadian Institute of Stress in 1979. He died in Montreal on 16 October 1982.

As Selye noted, stress occurs as a response to a range of circumstances. Biologically, stress reactions evolved as an emergency response intended to prepare an individual for 'fight or flight' – that is, either to defend oneself or try to run away from a threat (essentially the same pattern of reactions can be found in all mammals). In psychological terms, stress is a response of the body to whatever is perceived as an emergency situation. However, not all situations that trigger stress are alike, and under some circumstances what evolved as an adaptive mechanism can be potentially harmful. To understand this, first consider what happens when one experiences stress.

adrenal glands endocrine glands, located just above the kidneys, which play an important role in arousal and stress; the outer layer, the cortex, secretes corticosteroids, and the medulla (the inner core) secretes adrenaline (epinephrine) and noradrenaline (norepinephrine).

A significant link in the body's chain of reactions to stressful situations is the release of hormones by the **adrenal glands**. The adrenal glands, located just above the kidneys, are made up of two portions, the *cortex* or outer covering, and the *medulla* or inner core. When stimulated, the adrenal medulla secretes *adrenaline* (also called epinephrine) and *noradrenaline* (norepinephrine). Each of these hormones plays a role in stress reactions. (As noted earlier, the same chemicals also function as neurotransmitters.)

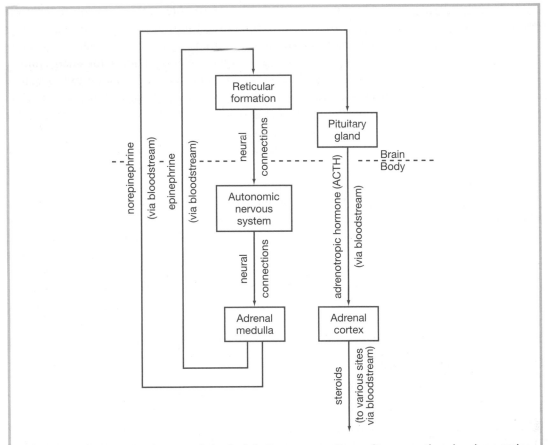

Figure 2.9 A Schematic Diagram of the Body's Response to Stress Stress reactions involve a series of effects involving an interaction of the nervous system and the hormonal system. Note that the response involving epinephrine is a 'closed loop', which tends to be self-maintaining in the absence of offsetting interventions by the parasympathetic division of the autonomic nervous system.

The release of adrenaline into the bloodstream produces reactions in both the brain and the peripheral nervous system. In the brain, it increases activity (particularly in the reticular formation, which controls overall arousal). In turn, the reticular formation sends signals to the autonomic nervous system (a branch of the peripheral nervous system), which shuts off digestion, increases heart rate and raises blood pressure, among other reactions (see Figure 2.9). Since the adrenal glands are among the organs affected by the autonomic nervous system, the overall sequence of responses is a 'closed loop'; the circular nature of the sequence means that the stress reaction produced by adrenaline can be prolonged. Anyone who has been startled or has otherwise experienced sudden stress knows that the racing heartbeat and other signs can linger beyond the moment of stress.

pituitary gland a small gland adjacent to the hypothalamus which regulates many endocrine functions, including growth, and also interacts with the nervous system via hypothalamic connections; in stress, it releases a hormone called ACTH which triggers the release of steroids by the cortex of the adrenal glands; sometimes called 'the master gland' because of its many functions.

As mentioned above, noradrenaline also plays a role in stress reactions, but its function is more indirect. Travelling through the bloodstream, it reaches the brain, where it activates another gland, the **pituitary**, which in turn releases another hormone, ACTH (adreno-corticotropic hormone). ACTH in turn reaches the adrenals, causing the adrenal cortex to produce hormones called steroids. (Note that the adrenal *medulla*, *not* the cortex, produces noradrenaline and adrenaline.)

steroids hormones produced by the cortex of the adrenal glands which are involved in the regulation of water and sugar metabolism, immune system function, and other basic bodily processes; sometimes called 'corticosteroids'.

Steroids (sometimes called 'corticosteroids') play a role in a diverse range of body processes, both at times of stress and in daily living. They are involved in the normal regulation of water and sugar metabolism, including the quick release of sugar for energy under stress. They also affect the immune system, including inflammatory response. Among the most significant of these steroids is *cortisol*; a synthetic form of this steroid, cortisone, is used in medicine for treatment of allergic reactions, arthritis and shock.

While this description may seem to emphasize the role of hormones, and particularly the adrenal glands, the changes associated with stress are actually a complex sequence involving many body systems, as noted above. Selye described the overall pattern as the **general adaptation syndrome** of stress, involving three stages. He called the initial, acute stress response (described above) *alarm*; essentially, it is equivalent to the fight-or-flight response described above. If the stress continues, there is a second stage, *resistance*, where the organism seems to be coping with the stress, and *outward* signs of arousal disappear; internally, increased hormonal production, etc.

general adaptation syndrome a model of stages of stress identified by Hans Selye, ranging from acute stress (alarm) to outward coping (resistance) to finally depletion of bodily resources (exhaustion).

continues. If the situation persists, Selye argued that the final stage, *exhaustion*, may be reached, where the body's resources are depleted; in studies with experimental animals, this has resulted in sickness or death. Autopsies on these animals reveal enlarged adrenal glands, severe ulcers of the stomach, and shrinkage of the thymus gland and lymph nodes, which are involved in the body's immune system.

The stress response originated as a means of coping with physical danger, and its evolutionary survival suggests the mechanism is basically adaptive. However, it also creates two major problems. First, for modern humans the 'danger' may often be psychological rather than physical (for example, pressure to meet a deadline), and hence no physical response is either required or appropriate. This means that one is left with a surge of activity-oriented chemical changes, and no outlet for the energy. Second, as Selye noted, the stress response may carry beyond the moment of crisis, and chronic stress can have negative effects (for either people or animals). Consistent with Selye's early description of the effects of prolonged stress, a wide range of disorders, including heart disease, viral infections, asthma and rheumatoid arthritis, seem to be affected by stress responses (Everly and Lating 2002; Heninger 1995; Krantz *et al.* 2000; O'Leary *et al.* 1997). To a large degree, these effects are related to hormonal changes, particularly the excess production of steroids. For example, elevated levels of cortisol have been associated with both depression and memory problems (Newcomer *et al.* 1999; Pruessner *et al.* 2003; Wolf *et al.* 2001). The effects of cortisol have also been interpreted as the cause of damage to the hippocampus found in MRI studies of individuals suffering from **post-traumatic stress disorder (PTSD)**, a chronic stress-like condition frequently found in trauma victims (Bremner 2003). While researchers are beginning to understand the underlying mechanism of these effects (see *Mental States and Health*), a more immediate question is what triggers chronic stress.

post-traumatic stress disorder (PTSD) a chronic stress-like anxiety disorder that can occur as a result of a terrifying experience, such as being in a car accident or being attacked in wartime.

The pioneer for such studies was a psychiatrist named Thomas Holmes, who in the late 1940s became interested in the effects of major life changes on the health of his patients. He examined the case histories of more than 5000 patients, and developed a 'stress barometer' of life changes now known as the Social Readjustment Rating Scale (see Box 2.3). Later, Dr Richard Rahe used

Box 2.3 *The Holmes–Rahe Social Readjustment Rating Scale*

Stressful experiences can have great impact on a person's ability to function. But what are stressful circumstances, and what types of experience typically cause the greatest stress? A long-term study by Rahe, referred to in the text, attempted to answer these questions by looking at the effects of various events on the probability of becoming ill. Generally, the effects were found to be additive – that is, people who went through more life changes were more likely to get sick. High stress levels seem to impair the body's ability to function.

A look at the table below will show you the estimated stress value of various events. Rahe suggested that if your stress total went above 150 for any 12-month period, you were in a high-risk group, and should heed the storm warnings of the stress barometer.

Rank	Life event	Stress score
1	Death of spouse	100
2	Divorce	75
3	Marital separation	65
4	Jail term	63
5	Death of close family member	63
6	Personal injury or illness	53
7	Marriage	50
8	Fired from job	47
9	Marital reconciliation	45
10	Retirement	45
18	Change to different line of work	36
25	Outstanding personal achievement	28
27	Begin or end school	26
32	Change residence	20
40	Change in eating habits	13
41	Vacation	13
43	Minor violations of the law	11

Adapted from Rahe (1972)

Holmes's work as the basis for a study of 2500 men in the US Navy. Using the stress scale as a predictor of illness over a 12-month period, he found that those who underwent the highest number of life changes suffered nearly twice as many ailments as those in the lowest category (Rahe 1972). Subsequently, the value of life-changes as an indicator of stress has been supported in other studies (for example, Brown and Harris 1989). One study followed laid-off Finnish workers over several months, and found high rates of depression and stress-related illnesses (Viinamaeki *et al.* 1996).

Despite such results, critics have raised a number of problems, the most basic being that the research is correlational, and so cannot prove that the indicated life changes are the causal factor. Beyond that, there are questions about the specific types of events that the scale measures – for example, whether positive changes are as damaging as negative changes, and whether major life changes are really more stressful than encountering many minor hassles (Everly and Lating 2002). The life-change scale continues to be popular (in part because it provides a quick and simple tool for clinicians), but understanding the dynamics of stress requires looking more closely at individual factors. Doing so will also provide some understanding of how to deal with stressful situations.

Coping with Stress

As should be clear, the basic fight-or-flight response that underlies stress has been programmed by our evolutionary history. But what triggers that response? Although Holmes and Rahe focused on life changes as a source of stress, defining what is a **stressor** can in fact be difficult. Life-threatening situations by their nature create stress, but individuals will sometimes react to more minor situations (like a traffic jam) with the same fight-or-flight response. In general, the degree of stress experienced depends not only on the situation, but also on one's perception of the situation and one's mode of response (Endler 1997; Weiten and Lloyd 2003).

stressor any factor which triggers a stress response in an individual.

The individual's interpretation of the situation may in fact be the most important determinant of the effects of 'stressful' situations. As was discussed in Chapter 1, individuals perceive any situation in terms of their own cognitive schemata. For example, a person who has been thinking of making a career change may welcome an offer of early retirement, whereas a person content in their job may be very upset at a similar offer. Similarly, diving into cold water may sound stressful, yet every New Year's Day members of 'polar bear clubs' willingly jump into icy lakes or oceans. Thus, our *cognitive appraisal* of the situation is a key factor in determining whether, and to what degree, we experience a situation as stressful. Because the processes that underlie perception are embedded in the brain, the link between cognitive appraisal and stress is potentially understandable as an interaction of the mind and body.

Psychologists have identified several factors that seem to influence how stressful a situation seems. One classic study looked at everyday sources of stress in urban environments; one factor identified as influencing the impact of stressors is *predictability* (Glass and Singer 1972). For example, people who live near subways or railroad tracks often show no discomfort from the sounds, which tend to occur at fixed times. Visitors, however, may be greatly stressed by what they see as 'unpredictable' noise. A second factor that affects our appraisal of a situation is *perceived control.* That is, having control of the situation (or even *feeling* that you have control even if you don't) can reduce the effects of a stressor. For example, a field experiment done in a nursing home showed that when individuals were given more choices in their daily routine, they experienced less stress (Langer and Rodin 1976). By contrast, a range of studies have shown that when people develop the sense that they have no control of a situation (a phenomenon sometimes called *learned helplessness*), they experience increased stress and depression (Maier and Watkins 1998; Peterson *et al.* 1993). Thus, the way we perceive the situation may be an important factor in reducing our susceptibility to stress.

The third key factor, along with the situation and our perception of it, is the way we try to cope with the situation. Hans Selye distinguished two types of reactions to a stressor: those responses intended to *resist* the situation (*catatoxic* reactions) and those intended to help one *adapt* to the situation (*syntoxic* reactions). If someone cuts in front of you while driving, you may get angry and upset (an aggressive, catatoxic response), or you can laugh and dismiss the other driver's behaviour as foolish (an adaptive, syntoxic response). While Selye suggested that a syntoxic response is often preferable, unfortunately he offered very little direct evidence to support this view.

More recently, researchers have studied differences between *problem-focused* strategies and *emotion-focused* strategies (Lazarus and Folkman 1984). Problem-focused coping attempts to deal directly with the situation, viewing it as a problem to be solved. By contrast, emotion-focused coping concentrates on the individual's internal emotional state, and leads to avoiding the problem, blaming oneself, or engaging in fantasy or wishful thinking as responses to the stressful situation. Unlike Selye's model, Lazarus and Folkman did not suggest that one strategy is always preferable. Instead, they suggested that problem-focused strategies are more likely to be used when the situation is perceived as being controllable – for example, in dealing with work-related stressful situations. By contrast, they argued that emotion-focused coping is likely to occur in dealing with situations that are perceived as not controllable – for example, health problems or a natural disaster (such as one's home being destroyed by a storm). Research suggests that matching of strategy and perceived control does tend to occur, but interestingly, the results do not demonstrate that changing coping strategies necessarily leads to less stress (Zakowski *et al.* 2001). In fact, a recent study indicates that the combination of both forms of coping strategies is most effective in handling stress (Sideridis 2006).

Clearly, a number of factors influence stress, both within the individual and within the situation (see also Box 2.4, discussing the role of culture). While it would be appealing to end this discussion with a precise statement about how to cope with stress, at present, defining an 'optimal' response is not possible. This may reflect the difficulty in defining a stressor, or maybe we need to rethink the nature of stress itself. One researcher, endocrinologist Bruce McEwen, has argued for the concept of 'allostasis', which considers stress within the context of the energy demands of behaviour (McEwen 2002, 2005). McEwen has argued that this concept can explain the relationship between 'normal' behaviour (such as foraging, breeding or migrating) and

Box 2.4 Stress and Culture

Stress, like beauty, often seems to be in the eye of the beholder. As discussed in this chapter, many of the factors that influence our perception of stress are individual. Yet there are also indications that a person's culture plays a significant role in determining what is a stressor. For example, psychologists, sociologists and anthropologists have noted that cultures can often be loosely divided in terms of the culture's value of individualism vs. collectivism. An individualistic culture, such as the USA, emphasizes the rights of the individual above those of the group – a value which promotes the development of independence in its members. A collectivist culture, such as many parts of Asia, values the group (usually the family) and its welfare above the concerns of the private individual. In so doing, the individual is encouraged to develop and maintain strong group ties and responsibilities. Bond (1991) found that people who live in collectivist cultures, such as India, Thailand and China, showed fewer stress-related illnesses than people living in individualistic cultures such as Canada and the USA. It is thought that one reason for this is that in collectivist cultures, there is always a support group for the individual, to help with everything from finding a job and maintaining financial security, to choosing a mate and raising children. (Note that social support is a factor which can reduce stress in any culture, but some cultures place greater emphasis on maintaining support networks.)

There are also cultural variations in the kind of strategies which individuals use to cope with stress. In some cultures, 'escape valves' in the form of emotional outbursts are seen as acceptable. In India, emotional outbursts in family arguments that to an outside observer may seem to be extremely hurtful, in fact typically leave no permanent mark on the family relationships (Laungani 2001). In other cultures, such as some in Africa and Malaysia, 'demonic possession' is used to give people a societally acceptable way of letting out their accumulated frustrations and stresses (Lee and Ackerman 1980). While clearly there are differences in how people in different cultures tend to deal with stress, there is little evidence comparing the effectiveness of these strategies. Emotion-focused strategies may serve the function of reducing autonomic nervous system arousal, thereby helping to reduce stress – but why particular cultures favour different strategies is still an unsolved mystery.

stressful situations; for example, foraging is not normally stressful, but would cause stress when food is scarce. In addition, he has suggested that allostasis can also shed light on factors such as gender differences in stress. The latter point has also been supported by psychologist Shelley Taylor and her colleagues, who suggest that women are more likely than men to engage in nurturing and socializing as ways of coping with stressors (Taylor *et al.* 2000).

Given the variations in the way individuals respond, the most reasonable advice that can be given in terms of coping with stress is that we should:

1 acknowledge how our perceptions influence our reactions;

2 recognize when we are stressed; and

3 develop a range of possible coping responses.

Perhaps the best illustration of successful adaptation was offered by Selye's own behaviour. At the time of writing his last book, he would normally get up at dawn to cycle five miles to his office, and then work until 8 p.m. – and this from a 68-year-old man with two artificial hips!

Try it Yourself

Do you have any major stressors in your life? Illness? Money problems? Problems with family or at work? Other major life challenges? Even if you don't have a major source of stress, we all encounter stress in the form of 'daily hassles' (Weiten and Lloyd 2003). Imagine your day starting like this: you oversleep and realize you will be late for class/work. You jump into the shower and find that there's no hot water. Toweling yourself off, you race to the refrigerator, pull out some milk and gulp it down, only to find that it's sour. You gather your clothes, and discover that you have no clean underwear. As you run out the door, you see your bus pulling away from the stop. And all this in less than an hour! What will the rest of the day bring? Stressors can take many forms, but daily hassles are perhaps the most common (as Buddhist doctrine states, 'life is suffering'!). What can you do to deal with these situations? Can you change them, or change your response? Meditation and relaxation techniques can reduce our stress response, and possibly change the way we perceive frustrating situations; regular exercise is also beneficial. Pursuing one of these options, or even seeing if there is a course in stress reduction available in your community, could provide major benefits in your life.

Mental States and Health

One of the clear implications of research on stress is that our behaviour can affect our health. Since stressors are partly defined by our perceptions, and stress reactions affect the immune system, this points to a link between mental states and physical health. To many people, this is a surprising idea. After all, we have grown up accepting a model of health in which disease processes are due to pathological agents – either invading germs or defective cell processes. Surely such events have nothing to do with laughter or loneliness!

In fact, research today seems to be pointing to a very different conception of health and healing. Consider some of the clues offered in the research considered already: while neural and hormonal pathways appear distinct, the two systems are also highly interrelated. Processes like chronic stress affect both systems – and also affect the immune system. Meditation in some ways appears to be the opposite of stress, with beneficial effects on body processes. While such observations suggest a relationship between mental states and health, they don't adequately explain how mental states could affect the course of disease.

The possibility of mental states affecting health has a long, if unconventional, history. Every doctor can tell stories about patients who have recovered despite an unfavourable prognosis, or conversely, of patients who should have survived, but died. Traditionally, if they spoke of such cases at all, doctors referred to 'the will to live' or used similar phrases. One such case has become well known. In the 1970s, Norman Cousins, the long-time editor of *Saturday Review* magazine in the USA, was diagnosed with Hodgkin's disease, a form of cancer which attacks the immune system. His doctors were pessimistic about the outcome, but Cousins decided that giving up would only hasten his end. So, while treatment (chemotherapy, etc.) was in progress, he embarked on a determined programme to bolster his spirits; perhaps the best-known aspect of his plan involved viewing classic comedy films in his hospital room. In the end, Cousins recovered. Although he was grateful to his doctors for their treatment, he also was convinced that, in the old phrase, laughter is truly the best medicine. As a result, he embarked on a quest both to document this belief, and to understand the processes involved (Cousins 1989).

placebo effect a phenomenon whereby inert substances labelled as drugs (such as a painkiller) produce effects similar to the real drug.

At the time of his recovery, Cousins's ideas were widely dismissed as delusional or at best, a type of **placebo effect,** a phenomenon whereby labelling an inert substance as a drug – for example, a 'painkiller' – produces effects similar to the real drug. Of course, how this occurs is in itself something of a medical puzzle. The experience of pain is itself complex (Melzack and Wall 1982), but research suggests that placebos used to reduce pain do so at least partly by altering the activity in the prefrontal cortex associated with anticipating pain, thereby reducing the overall response to pain (Wager 2005). Interestingly, expectations associated with treatment can also work in reverse (Benedetti *et al.* 2003): when patients received a drug but *thought* they weren't, there was a reduced effect of the drug!

psychoimmunology the study of mental states and their effect on health, as expressed through the functions of the immune system; sometimes referred to as *psychoneuroimmunology*.

Like Norman Cousins's experience, the effects of placebos seem hard to understand for theories which assume mind and body are separate. Over time, as discoveries have been made about the functioning of the immune system, new theories and data have begun to emerge. Today, the study of mental states and their effect on health is referred to as **psychoimmunology** (or sometimes psychoneuroimmunology) (Cohen and Herbert 1996). Just as research led to recognition of the interrelations between the nervous system and the endocrine system, there is also a new awareness of how both of these are related to the functioning of the immune system.

Psychoimmunology is a fast-developing field, and it is impossible to summarize all of the current research, but a few examples can help to clarify the direction in which the field is moving (for general reviews, see Ader 2000; Irwin 2008; Kubo and Chida 2006; Sternberg and Gold 1997). As noted in discussing stress, it has long been known that high stress levels increase the likelihood of disease. The more recent research suggests that a wide range of social-environmental factors may effect health either negatively or positively. Generally, negative interpersonal events, such as the death of a loved one, or marital conflict, have been identified as having a negative effect on health (Maier and Laudenslager 1985; O'Leary *et al.* 1997; Solomon 1990). On the positive side, patients recovering from heart attacks do significantly better if they have a good social support network, or even just have a pet for company (Cousins 1989; Oxman *et al.* 1995). There are also some indications that laughter may be beneficial to health (R. A. Martin 2002). One concern with the available evidence is that most studies are quasi-experiments, since researchers cannot control the life events, but the results suggest that something is happening in terms of a pattern. The question is, how do such psychological and social influences get translated into immune responses?

While Hans Selye correctly noted that chronic stress resulted in a deterioration of the immune system in experimental animals, he did not know the precise mechanism. Today, advances in biochemical techniques are helping to provide answers. In general, the linkage seems to be based on the impact of hormones on the immune system. One of the earliest clues involved the role of *neuropeptides* – particularly the 'natural opiates' called endorphins. As noted earlier, neuropeptides play a role in both the nervous system and as hormones. Endorphins serve as natural painkillers in the brain, and receptors for them have been identified at a number of sites, particularly in the brain stem. Interestingly, studies have also shown that a number of types of immune cells, collectively called monocytes, also have receptors for endorphins – and that the endorphins play a role in regulating the activity of the immune cells (Maier and Laudenslager 1985; Pert 1990). At a higher level, there is evidence for interactions between the hypothalamic/ pituitary/adrenal (HPA) system of the fight-or-flight response and the immune system (Irwin 2008; Kubo and Chida 2006; McEwen and Wingfield 2003; Michelson *et al.* 1995; Sternberg and Gold 1997). While the linkages between the two systems are complex and not yet fully under- stood, it appears that *cortisol* and other steroids play a key role in both. As noted in discussing stress, steroids play an important role in regulating metabolic functions as part of the fight-or- flight response, and also regulate immune function. As a result, situations which promote a chronic stress response also produce inhibition of the immune system. This connection has been supported by research that shows that couples experiencing marital problems show both elevated cortisol levels and poorer health (Kiecolt-Glaser *et al.* 2003; Kiecolt-Glaser and Newton 2001). In addition, there is evidence that the type of coping strategy individuals use to deal with stress affects both cortisol levels and immune system functions (Bosch *et al.* 2001; Creswell *et al.* 2005; Stowell *et al.* 2001).

While many details remain to be clarified, the notion of mental states affecting health can no longer be considered a delusion or fantasy. At the same time, one must be cautious about drawing conclusions based on the available research. While mental states may play a role in health, none of the researchers involved is suggesting abandoning conventional medical treatment. If anything, the implication seems to be that doctor–patient relationships are more important than ever to effective health care. Thus, the traditional 'good bedside manner', downplayed in the focus on new medical technology, becomes once more an important adjunct to medical treatment (Werner and Malterud 2005). At the same time, an important concern has been raised by Marcia Angell, editor of the *New England Journal of Medicine*. Essentially, Angell argues that telling patients (particularly those with terminal illnesses) that their attitudes and behaviour produced their condition can add an unjustified burden of guilt on those already afflicted – especially in the absence of direct evidence (Angell 1985). Cancer, for example, may arise despite 'positive thinking', since other factors are clearly involved (including genetic factors and environmental hazards). Regardless of what future research on psychoimmunology reveals, the multi-faceted nature of health is unlikely to change. What may change, however, is the concept that individuals must be passive in the face of illness.

From the point of view of psychology, the research on psychoimmunology adds a further dimension to our understanding of the relationship between mind and body. In some ways, it brings us full circle back to where we began this chapter. We have seen how processes in the body affect our mental state, and in turn how mental processes can affect the body. Obviously, many questions remain, but the basic assumption of the materialists – that 'mind' and 'body' are different ways of talking about the same thing – seems relatively secure. While we may never be able to do away with one or the other term, research on mind/body issues has led to exciting discoveries about how we function. In the end, it is these advances in our understanding that justify the biological approach.

THE HEREDITARY BASIS OF BEHAVIOUR

While the relationships between mind and body are significant, there is one element of our biological nature that has not been discussed. The human brain is an incredibly complex structure, unparalleled (so far as we know) in the universe. The body, too, with its highly integrated systems, is a wondrous thing. But how did our complex physical structure arise? How do nerve cells grow and develop into the specialized networks that make up the brain? What determines the variability found between individuals – not just in height or eye colour, but also in the brain (Edelman 1992)? To try to answer such questions, we must look at another aspect of the biological approach – the study of *heredity*.

In the 1970s, a group of researchers announced that they had found a genetic pattern associated with criminal behaviour. They had discovered that certain men were born with an extra Y chromosome; individuals with the resulting XYY pattern, the researchers argued, tended to become criminals. This assertion led to great controversy, both among researchers and the general public. If someone could be identified at birth as a potential criminal, advocates argued, they could be closely watched, or even locked up before they could cause harm. Opponents questioned both the evidence and the moral principle of prejudging guilt. Soon, other researchers discovered that many XYY men existed who had no apparent history of criminal actions. Given this and other contrary evidence, the XYY-criminality theory was cast into doubt, and the controversy died (Gould 1981). However, it is significant that, throughout the debate, *no one ever questioned the underlying assumption that behaviour could be inherited*!

The concept of inherited traits has become so widely known and accepted that it is difficult for us to recognize its impact on our thinking. Yet it is little more than 100 years since Charles Darwin suggested that variations could be passed on from one generation to another. 'Like father, like son', people say – but *how much* like, and *why*? Even Darwin, who believed in the phenomenon of inheritance, had no idea how heredity actually functioned.

evolution a theory to account for the development of species diversity by means of variations which are transmitted to offspring by inheritance; Darwin's theory of **natural selection** proposed that variations which enhance adaptability, and thereby enhance survival and reproduction rates, are the most likely to be transmitted.

Darwin's ideas about inheritance between generations were closely linked to another concept: **evolution**. He recognized that variations existed within a species, and believed that such traits could be transmitted from parents to offspring. Traits which enhanced survival and reproduction rates were the most likely to be transmitted; thus, Darwin's principle of **natural selection** as the basis of evolution is sometimes referred to as 'survival of the fittest'. Darwin believed that the same process which produces variations within a species also produces the variations which are ultimately labelled as different species. Thus, all species are ultimately related through the mechanism of evolution. This concept of continuity between species was contentious in Darwin's day (and sometimes still is), but it has significantly influenced the way we view behaviour. For example, one can compare human behaviour and physiology to that of other species as a tool for improving our understanding (chimpanzees, for example, are genetically very similar to humans). This is not to say that chimpanzee studies, or those involving other species, are a substitute for research on humans. Rather, comparisons of similarities and differences can lead us to new questions, and new insights. In a similar vein, paleoanthropologists and evolutionary psychologists study the ancestors of humanity to provide new insights into our own behaviour. Ultimately, the goal of such studies is not to diminish the wonder of human existence, but to understand better and appreciate who and what we are.

These concepts – *heredity* and *evolution* – have been significant in improving our knowledge of human behaviour. As we shall see, the pace of research in genetics in particular has been accelerating tremendously in the past few years, so no account can be fully current. However, an understanding of the foundations and assumptions underlying current research can help us to understand better the significance of what George Beadle, a Nobel laureate in genetics, has called 'the language of life' (Beadle and Beadle 1966).

Basic Mechanisms of Heredity

The word 'genetics' was coined by the English biologist William Bateson. In an article published in 1902, he urged his fellow researchers to look at the causes of inherited resemblances and differences, to understand 'the essential process by which the likeness of the parent is transmitted to the offspring'. At first, Bateson drew little response. For many years, the study of genetics was considered a bit eccentric, being based on taking inventories, raising generations of fruit flies, keeping animal pedigrees, and talking about concepts like 'dominance', 'unit characters' and 'ratios'. At the same time, chemists were working on the chemical structures of enzymes and other organic chemicals. Although it took many years before they realized it, both groups were working on the same problem. Ultimately, the result was the breaking of 'the code of life', embodied in the chemical structure of genes.

What is perhaps most fascinating about the development of genetics is that the early population geneticists (like Bateson) came to a clear understanding of the basic properties of genetic inheritance *without* any knowledge of the underlying biochemistry. In fact, the basic mechanism was identified by an Austrian monk named Gregor Mendel more than *100 years* before anyone actually isolated a gene! The son of a farmer, Mendel became interested in problems of plant hybridization (the crossing of different strains to produce new varieties). Working with garden peas, he set up an experimental plot to see if he could determine some orderly principles underlying the results of hybridization. As it turns out, he was wrong on many details, but correct in the general outline. Mendel discovered that an inherited characteristic passed from parent to offspring. (Mendel, of course, did not know that it was a *chemical* process, but he knew there must be a mechanism.) In any individual, this code is made up of two genes, forming a pair. When reproduction takes place, the gene pair is split, so that one parent contributes only one gene to the offspring; the other member of the offspring's gene pair comes from the other parent. Thus, the offspring carries genetic information from both parents.

gene the basic unit of heredity, made up of sequences of 'building blocks' called amino acids; it is estimated that humans possess about 30,000 different genes, each regulating production of various proteins.

chromosomes thread-like genetic structures composed of double strands of DNA and proteins, containing the genes; in humans, there are 23 pairs of chromosomes.

Today, thanks to the advances made in biochemistry, research in genetics has moved from hypothetical concepts to molecular processes. We now recognize the **gene** as the basic unit of heredity, made up of sequences of building blocks called amino acids. The genes in turn are part of the larger structures called **chromosomes** (see Figure 2.10). Understanding this complex structure has been one of the most remarkable achievements in modern science. Consider this chronology: in 1953, 50 years after Bateson coined the term genetics, the basic structure of chromosomes was deciphered by James Watson and Francis Crick. However, it took almost another *20* years before anyone actually isolated a single gene. As recently as 1990, less than 1 per cent of the total 'string' of 3 billion amino acids in human DNA had been identified. Subsequently, thanks to

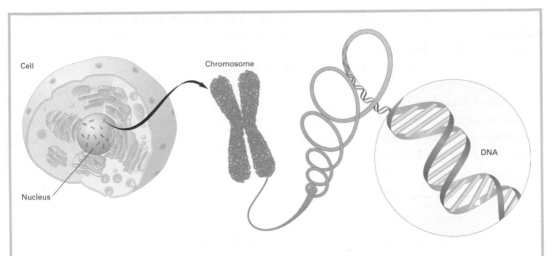

Figure 2.10 Cells, Chromosomes, Genes and DNA Every cell (left) contains a nucleus, which contains a set of chromosomes (middle); the chromosomes in turn are made up of strands of DNA (right). Genes are composed of segments of the chromosomal DNA.

an international research effort called the Human Genome Project, a basic 'map' was completed in 2003, almost exactly 50 years after Watson and Crick's discovery (Collins *et al.* 2003). Because of the techniques used (essentially, cutting up the genetic material, analysing it, and then trying to reassemble it), there are still gaps and limitations. One critical limitation is that no one yet knows precisely how many active genes humans have; most researchers believe there are about 30,000 genes, but some estimates go as high as 75,000. (To give some comparison, about 1600 disease-related genes have been identified, along with a variety of other genes.) Leaving the numbers aside, what does this have to tell us about the origins of behaviour? How does inheritance work, and what is it that is inherited?

As Mendel had hypothesized, genes are the fundamental units of inheritance. However, it turns out that the mechanism of splitting and recombining (which provides for variability) across generations depends on the chromosomes. Composed of double strands of DNA and proteins, chromosomes are the large-scale structures of heredity, containing the genes. In humans, there are 23 pairs of chromosomes, each holding thousands of genes, like pearls on a necklace. Because each of the 23 pairs of chromosomes splits and recombines independently of the others during reproduction, there are 2^{23} possible chromosome combinations from each parent, meaning that genetic recombination provides for almost limitless variety. (With over 8.4 million combinations from a single set of parents, the likelihood of even two siblings having identical sets of chromosomes is very small.) The result is that genetic mechanisms provide a basis for variability, as well as similarity, from parent to offspring.

genotype the genetic code which an individual carries in the DNA of their cells.

unigenic inheritance genetic transmission which is dependent on the action of a single pair of genes; also called Mendelian inheritance, in recognition of Gregor Mendel's pioneering work.

The genetic code which an individual carries in the DNA of their cells is called their **genotype**. Genes function in pairs, and the gene-pair members for particular characteristics (for example, blood type, eye colour) come in several variants, called alleles. Each allele represents the chemical code for a single variation. For example, basic blood types in people are based on three alleles, representing A, B and O. Normally, for a characteristic based on a single gene (i.e., one pair – called **unigenic** or Mendelian **inheritance**), one allele, called the *dominant* allele, will be expressed (that is, active) whenever it occurs in the gene pair. Other alleles will only be expressed (active, and therefore observable in the individual) if both members of the gene pair are the same. Because they are not as influential as the dominant form, these genes are called *recessive* alleles. For eye colour, brown is the dominant form, while blue is recessive (see Figure 2.11). Thus, the observed form of the characteristic depends upon what pairing of dominant and/or recessive alleles of the gene is present. (Note: this description is based on the classical model of unigenic inheritance; while it works very well for the vast majority of cases, research in recent years has indicated ways in which it oversimplifies, and hence occasionally leads to faulty predictions. For the purpose of understanding the basics of heredity, these subtleties are not critical.)

One must distinguish between the genotype, defined by the genes, and the observed characteristics of the individual, called the **phenotype**. One reason for this distinction has already been noted: a person may possess a recessive gene for blue eyes, but it will not be expressed if they also have a dominant gene for brown eyes. In terms of appearance, they would seem no different from a person with two brown eye genes. (Hence, one cannot always determine the genotype simply by observing the phenotypic appearance.)

phenotype the observed characteristics of the individual, based on the combination of genotype and environmental influences.

More importantly, genes only determine a *potential* for a characteristic, which must then be realized through a long sequence of biochemical processes (basically, genes code for the production of proteins, which may in turn affect many basic physiological processes). Along the way, other factors, including environmental influences, may intervene. For example, an individual may be born with PKU (phenylketonuria), a metabolic disorder based on a recessive gene (which differs from the dominant in lacking one amino acid, phenylalanine). If untreated, PKU can result in severe mental retardation. However, appropriate medical treatment and dietary restrictions can compensate if the disorder is detected early, and the individual need never suffer the effects. Depending on the particular characteristic, the amount of environmental influence differs. The genetic code for most aspects of our physical structure is relatively rigid – for instance, dictating the location of the eyes. For traits related to behaviour, such as intelligence, the reverse may be true – environment may play a decisive role. Consequently, one cannot easily generalize about the genetic expression, except to note that the observed characteristics of an individual (the phenotype) are based on a combination of genotype and environmental influences. Because of this, even genetically identical individuals can differ; this was vividly illustrated by a cloned kitten which differed in colouring from its genetically identical 'mother' (Taeyoung *et al.* 2002). For psychologists, the nature of genetic expression is one of the most important aspects of heredity.

To summarize thus far, inheritance of characteristics is based on a chemical code carried by genes, which are themselves carried by the chromosomes. Genes function in pairs, and various forms (alleles) of the gene for a characteristic exist. The recombination of genes from parents to offspring provides a basis for genetic variability within families. Ultimately, though, the observed characteristics of an individual depend on the interaction of genetic and environmental factors. As we will discuss, determining the relative role of these factors in behaviour has been one of the major concerns of psychologists studying heredity.

One other issue needs to be considered in relation to genetic mechanisms: the origin of *new* traits. Although recombination provides for considerable variation, it does not provide for the creation of any new traits. Thus, if heredity functioned only in the way described above, there would be no possibility of evolution. Darwin recognized this, even without knowing anything about the basis of hereditary mechanisms. Hence, along with the normal sequence of biochemical

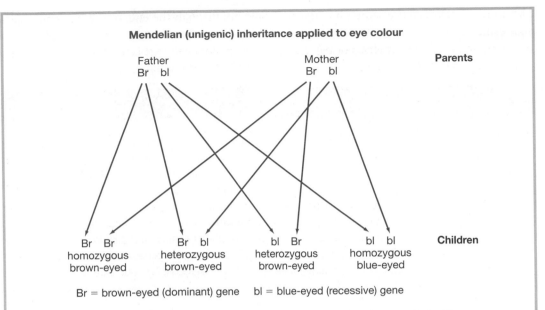

Figure 2.11 Unigenic Inheritance As discussed in the text, observed characteristics like eye colour depend on the individual's genetic make-up, inherited from the parents. If both parents are heterozygous brown-eyed, then the unigenic model says they have a 25 per cent chance of any child being homozygous blue-eyed, as the combinations suggest.

mutation a change in the genetic material of a cell; while rare, mutations can result in new characteristics which may be transmitted to descendants of the original cell.

processes, it is possible for new gene forms, called **mutations**, to occur. Mutations are very rare, happening perhaps once in a million times. However, when they do occur, by whatever random process, a new trait may appear. Again, Darwin was alert to the significance of such events, which he expressed in the principle of *natural selection*: any new trait which offers an advantage in terms of survival will tend to be passed on (because the individual is more likely to survive to reproduce). Conversely, any trait which weakens the ability to survive will normally disappear (if the individual dies before reproducing). Today, this is often referred to as 'survival of the fittest'.

More recently, a second mechanism for genetic variation has been identified: transfer of genes between different species, such as from bacteria to mammals (Amábile-Cuevas and Chicurel 1993; Summers 2006). Whether by mutation or other mechanism, the emergence of new traits due to genetic variation is the basis of evolution, the development of species diversity. From a psychological point of view, this is significant, because it indicates that the development of human characteristics has a long history. The structure of our brain is linked to the structure of the brains of other species. In the same way, hands are related to flippers and wings. Darwin recognized these connections, but also knew that his contemporaries would not be likely to accept them. So, in his first book, *On the Origin of Species,* he carefully avoided any mention of *human* evolution (Darwin 1859). Only in his later writings did he become more explicit.

Heredity, then, is an important key to understanding behaviour. To the extent that it provides the organizational code for the developing embryo, it underlies all that we have talked about in terms of physiological processes. Through evolution, humans have developed the characteristics and abilities that distinguish us from other species. The cortex of our brains, which in many respects seems more highly developed than in other species, has played an important part in those gains. At the same time, the environment, through the effects of experience, has a significant impact on both our biochemistry and our brain. What we are depends on both our genotype and our environment. For psychologists, the major challenge is to understand precisely how these two factors interact.

Try it Yourself

Our increasing understanding of genetics brings with it new dilemmas. For example, it is now possible to determine when an individual has the genes for a serious disorder, such as Huntington's disease (a fatal neurological disorder, which is due to a dominant gene, but is not expressed until the person is in their 40s). If you had the gene for Huntington's disease, would you want to know? Why or why not?

Once we understand how genes function, it will be tempting to try to *control* the process. Consider the implications of the movie *Gattaca,* which portrays a world where parents can select the genetic make-up of their children. Is such a scenario desirable? Would this ensure that a child would be exactly the person the parents desired? Would you want to be able to select the genetic make-up of your child? Would you want to *be* a child whose genetic make-up had been selected by your parents?

Nature and Nurture in Behaviour

Of all the disputes in psychology, perhaps the most contentious concerns the relative importance of heredity and experience. Long before Mendel formed his genetic theory, people had an intuitive belief that something like heredity existed. Plato, for example, talked about knowledge being inborn or 'native' to the person, rather than being acquired through experience. This led to the view of knowledge and behaviour called **nativism**, the belief that characteristics are innate (Weimer 1973).

nativism the philosophical view, held by Plato and others, that knowledge and behaviour are innate in origin.

empiricism the philosophical position, first attributed to John Locke, that all knowledge is based on experience; hence, the basis of the view that behaviour is learned.

However, not everyone has taken this viewpoint. Other thinkers have maintained that all new-born babies are basically alike, and only develop unique characteristics as a result of differing experiences. John Locke, an English philosopher, expressed this view in 1690, saying the mind at birth is like a blank paper, on which experience is gradually written (Locke 1690). This view, which emphasizes the importance of environmental influences, is often called **empiricism**.

The philosophical split between nativism and empiricism has led to arguments about the relative importance of heredity (nature) and environmental factors (nurture) in various aspects of human functioning. Advances in our knowledge of genetics have made it possible to identify specific genes related to a variety of disorders, such as Huntington's disease and Tay-Sachs disease (both are fatal disorders which affect the nervous system). With behaviour, the situation is more complex, in part because there may not be a simple equivalence between genes and behaviour. That is, genes typically produce a variety of proteins, which may affect the body in diverse ways; similarly, most behavioural traits are probably influenced by a variety of genes, rather than a single gene as in the diseases mentioned above. Intelligence, for example, is a characteristic for which the relative contributions of nature and nurture are still being assessed. Similarly, the role of heredity in mental disorders like schizophrenia is still not well understood. With such complex aspects of behaviour, the techniques involved in molecular genetics may be of limited help for some time to come. Consequently, the study of genetic influences on behaviour typically involves methods associated with traditional population genetics – tracing observed traits among related individuals.

Ideally, one would like to have total control of both genetic and environmental factors, so that they could be studied experimentally. Although this is impossible both technically and ethically, one can often approximate the ideal by doing **concordance** (literally, 'agreement') studies to examine the characteristics of individuals whose genetic relationship is known. In these studies, *identical twins* are the preferred subjects, because they come from the same fertilized egg, and therefore have the same genetic make-up. (*Fraternal twins*, by contrast, are conceived at the same time, but develop from separately fertilized eggs, and are genetically no more alike than any two siblings.) At a basic level, the logic of concordance studies is easy to understand: because of the similar genetic make-up of identical twins, if a particular trait is controlled by the *genes*, then the twins should develop similarly, whether they are raised together or in different settings. On the other hand, if *environment* plays the major role in a trait, then the degree of similarity between identical twins should depend on how they were raised – if raised together in the same family, they should show some similarities, as do any siblings. However, if raised *apart* from each other (for example, in separate adoptive families), identical twins should be more like members of their adoptive families than each other. Concordance studies can also involve other genetic relationships, such as fraternal twins or other siblings, or parent–child comparisons. In each case, the goal is to measure behavioural similarities in accordance with what would be expected based on the degree of genetic similarity. (For example, on average, any child shares 50 per cent of their genes with each parent, as do siblings; a grandparent and grandchild share 25 per cent of their genes on average.)

concordance a technique for studying inheritance by examining characteristics of individuals whose genetic relationship is known.

Unfortunately, although the concept of concordance is fairly straightforward, the methodology is not as clear-cut as it may seem. Although identical twins are the preferred group, such twins are quite rare, and finding cases where they have been separated at an early age (due to parental death, marital break-ups, etc.) is rarer still. In addition, the fact of separation may make it difficult for researchers to locate both twins at a later time. (In some cases of separation in infancy followed by adoption, the children are not informed that they have a twin.) When separated twins *are* located, the degree of separation can be hard to assess. In one case, a researcher described twins as 'separated' who had been separated in name only – for example, one raised by the parents, and one by a maiden aunt who lived 100 yards away (Shields 1962). Determining early history is a crucial factor to the validity of concordance studies, because when twins actually have contact despite living under different roofs, it cannot be claimed that the environments are truly different. Even when twins are separated at birth and raised separately, they still share the same prenatal environment in the mother's womb (and for this reason, fraternal twins tend to be more alike than other siblings, since they are conceived and born at the same time – but this reflects an *environmental* influence, not heredity). Consequently, it is a practical impossibility to find identical twins who have grown up in completely different environments, and assumptions about twins reared apart may overestimate the contribution of heredity to observed similarities.

At the other end of the scale is the idea of studying two individuals (regardless of genotype) who have grown up in identical environments. Unfortunately, this is equally tricky. Twins raised in the same family appear, superficially, to meet this criterion because both prenatal and postnatal circumstances are shared. However, even when two children grow up in the same family, there is no guarantee that they will have identical experiences, or be treated in exactly the same way. This becomes especially clear when one considers fraternal twins of different sexes. Regardless of their shared prenatal environment, they are likely to encounter increasingly different circumstances as time goes on, due to social factors (for a discussion of current research results, see Chapter 7).

Apart from the methodological difficulties, concordance studies have sometimes oversimplified the issue (much like early philosophers did) by assuming that behaviour is due to heredity or environment. Over time, both psychological and genetic research has led to a growing recognition that the picture is more complex: genetic predispositions can lead people to make changes in their environment, and the environment can trigger genes to turn on or off. As a result, most psychologists today accept an *interactionist* view, which suggests that genetic and environmental influences are interwoven in determining the final shape of behaviour (Denenberg 2000). In this sense, the answer to the question, 'Is it nature or nurture?' is actually, 'Both.'

Try it Yourself

In the hectic modern world, we sometimes wish we could be in two places at once. This theme is explored in the movie *Multiplicity*, which focuses on a man who seeks to give himself some extra time by having himself cloned; not surprisingly, he runs into some difficulties. Suppose that scientists created a clone (genetic duplicate) of you. Would you expect them to be identical to you when grown? What does your response tell you about your own view of the nature/nurture issue? Given that even identical twins show some differences in both behavioural and physical characteristics, how would you feel about another individual who was identical to you in *every* respect?

Evolution and Behaviour

While it can be difficult to determine precisely how much heredity influences behaviour, there is little doubt that it plays a significant role in what we are. However, the mechanism of heredity applies not just to the transmission of characteristics from parents to children, but to the whole process of evolution described by Darwin. What we are as a species (and therefore as individuals) is influenced by our evolutionary history, and our heredity provides clear links to that history. For example, there is an approximately 99 per cent overlap in the genetic material of people and chimpanzees. The 1 per cent difference is obviously significant (for example, in the development of language areas in the cortex), but the implication is that we share a great deal of our nature with other species. This concept, which flows naturally from both Darwin's theory and basic data about genetics, has led to the development of a new sub-area in psychology and biology, called **evolutionary psychology**.

evolutionary psychology the application of evolutionary principles to the understanding of behaviour.

Evolutionary psychology attempts to apply the principles of evolution in order to enhance our understanding of behaviour. In many ways, it traces its origin to the ideas of a Harvard University biologist, E. O. Wilson. Wilson, whose specialty is the study of ants, wrote a book advocating the application of evolutionary principles gleaned from the study of other species to human social behaviour (Wilson 1975). He called this approach, and his text, *sociobiology*. Wilson's ideas were highly original, and also controversial, and that sense of controversy is still evident today in discussions of evolutionary psychology.

According to its advocates, both the body and the brain evolved in response to the pressures of natural selection; therefore, if a functional capacity exists in humans today, it must be because at some stage it conveyed a survival advantage (Barkow *et al.* 1992; Buss 1995; Derksen 2007). They then attempt to analyse this sequence in reverse, by identifying a brain structure or behaviour, and then attempting to explain its development in a manner consistent with evolutionary principles. Sometimes, this process can be very useful, as when visual researcher Jerome Lettvin used ecologically relevant stimuli (bugs, stems, etc.) to understand visual processing in a frog's eye (Lettvin *et al.* 1959). Lettvin reasoned that a frog's eye evolved to adapt to its environment, and that therefore such stimuli would probably provide a better understanding of functioning than would arbitrary stimuli like spots of light or simple lines. The resulting study, considered a classic, was both insightful and highly influential. In a similar vein, the idea that parts of the brain evolved at different rates, and in response to differing demands, is proving useful in our attempts to understand brain functions. For example, LeDoux has argued that because the brain structures involved in emotion evolved before the cortex, we should not assume that the cognitive (conscious) aspects of emotional experience provide a full picture of the role of emotions in our survival (LeDoux 1995).

Thus, evolutionary theory provides a useful point of reference as we strive to enhance our understanding of the brain. As Nobel laureate Gerald Edelman notes, we need to recognize that the nervous system has an evolutionary history which is relevant to its current structure and functioning (Edelman 1992). Yet there remains a significant gap between acknowledging that the brain has evolved, and determining the specific ways in which evolutionary theorizing can explain behaviour. For instance, Wilson has tried to argue that morality has an evolutionary basis, even though he admits that we lack the evidence to prove this assertion (Wilson 1998). In addition, researchers have attempted to explain intelligence and personality differences among people by using principles of evolutionary theory, although their proposals are only theoretical (Penke *et al.* 2007).

One area that has been hotly debated is the relevance of evolutionary interpretations of gender. It seems obvious that differences exist between men and women – for example, men are typically larger and stronger, and women tend to live longer. Does this mean there is an evolutionary reason for these differences, and therefore that gender differences can be understood by trying to interpret the survival value of these differences? Evolutionary psychologists say yes, and have used this notion to interpret many aspects of gender-related behaviour, particularly with regards to mate selection. For example, it is argued that men are by nature polygamous, because they are capable of impregnating multiple women over a short period of time, thereby increasing the likely survival rate for their genes. (Remember, natural selection says that traits evolve because they carry a survival advantage.) Women, it is argued, are by nature monogamous, because they must invest a great deal, both during pregnancy and after birth, to ensure that their child (and therefore their genes) survive. Whether one finds this reasoning plausible or not, the real question becomes, how can we evaluate it in a scientific way?

One basic problem is that the interpretations (like most ideas in evolutionary psychology) are essentially correlational and *post hoc* (that is, applied after the events they are trying to explain have already occurred). As such, they don't easily allow for the predictive evaluations which most researchers favour. (Recall the discussions about experiments vs. other research methods in Chapter 1.) This is a serious concern, and has led evolutionary psychologists to seek possible experimental tests. One example relates to the concept of *paternity uncertainty*. According to this theory, men are inherently less able to determine if a child carries their genes than women (since in a normal pregnancy the mother always knows that the egg has her genes, but the sperm may or may not be from the claimed father). Hence, evolutionary psychologists have argued that male forebears should be less willing to invest resources in children than are females. For example, a paternal grandfather cannot be certain that his son really is genetically related, and that man in turn cannot be certain his child is really his own. By contrast, a maternal grandmother is completely certain, because she knows her daughter carries her genes, and her daughter knows her own child carries her own genes (and therefore half of the grandmother's as well) (see Figure 2.12).

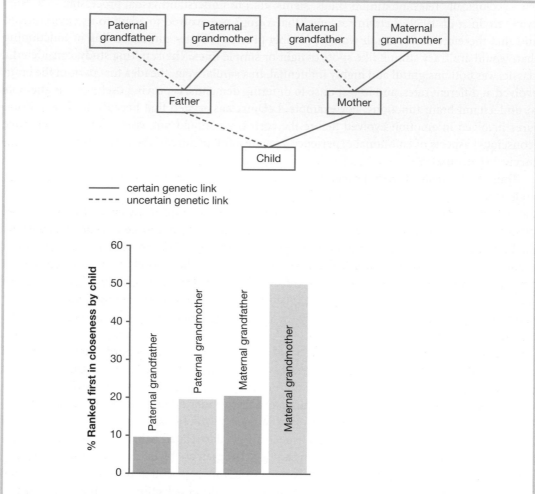

Figure 2.12 Certainty of Genetic Relatedness and Emotional Closeness Retrospective ratings by adults of which grandparent was emotionally closest to them in childhood reveal a pattern consistent with a model based on certainty of genetic relatedness. (Data from Euler and Weitzel 1996)

Drawing on this reasoning, German researchers did a study examining the emotional closeness between grandparents and their grandchildren; as predicted, emotional closeness was consistent with degree of genetic certainty (Euler and Weitzel 1996). This study is interesting not simply for the clear pattern of the results, but also because the outcome is one that most people would find very unexpected. Although technically the research is only a quasi-experiment, it is worth noting that other factors, like where grandparents lived, their age, and availability of other grandparents, did not show any patterns. Thus, it is an example of a study that not only is quite consistent with the evolutionary view, but one where alternative explanations are not obvious. (One factor that cannot be ruled out is the role of culture, since only German families were considered.)

At present, there is no clear consensus about the value of evolutionary psychology. Its advocates appear correct in suggesting that evolution has influenced what we are. The problem, though, is that making retrospective interpretations is fraught with many perils. As with any correlational research, alternative explanations are almost always possible, and observed patterns do not prove a causal link. This difficulty was noted by Stephen Jay Gould, an American evolutionary theorist who was a frequent critic of evolutionary psychology. Gould argued that as structures evolve, their function can also evolve – a process he called *exaptation*. This type of change can then make it difficult to apply natural selection retrospectively as a means of explaining the current function. For example, Gould demonstrated that small wings would have had no advantage for flight, but would be very useful for regulating body temperature; only later, as they became larger, would their potential for flying emerge (Gould and Vrba 1981). Thus, one could propose that wings evolved in order to permit flying – but one would be wrong! Similarly, we cannot be certain that evolutionary explanations of behaviour are necessarily correct, even when they appear plausible.

The limitations of research in evolutionary psychology are particularly evident when it comes to issues related to gender and sexual behaviour, which are often based on arguments about sexual selection (reproductive success). (Remember that evolutionary theory explains the origin of characteristics in terms of making transfer of the underlying genes more likely.) For example, sexual selection has been used to explain the adaptive value of pretty faces and symmetrical bodies, and even traits like sympathy and fidelity (Miller 2000). While some of the interpretations may elicit scepticism, consider the more extreme assertion that rape is an evolutionary adaptation in human males (Thornhill and Palmer 2000). Using insect data to extrapolate to a behaviour that occurs in only a minority of men seems to place a heavy burden on evolutionary principles. Not surprisingly, Thornhill and Palmer's book has drawn criticism (Segal 2001), and may actually tend to discredit more serious work (Roughgarden 2005). At best, attempts to explain gender-related behaviours in evolutionary terms remain controversial (Buller 2005; de Waal 2002; Segal 2001).

Controversy, of course, is not always bad, and evolutionary psychology may be of value precisely because it is provocative. As Frans de Waal, a noted primate researcher, has commented, psychology needs to move beyond simple polarities like mind vs. brain, or nature vs. nurture, and evolutionary theories challenge accepted notions about behaviour (de Waal 2002). In that sense, the value of evolutionary psychology may lie in how it reshapes other types of research by suggesting new questions (as in the study of vision or emotion, as noted above), rather than in the specific explanations it provides. In the short run, it seems likely that the debates between its advocates and critics will continue.

CONCLUSION

The biological approach is oriented towards understanding the physiological and genetic basis of our behaviour. Within psychology, it is the only approach which tries to explain behaviour in terms of the workings of the physical system. By contrast, consider psychoanalysis (see Chapter 5). Although Freud was trained in neurology, and believed that ultimately the system was biologically based, psychoanalysis uses concepts which are purely psychological, not physiological. Behaviourism (see Chapter 3) is even more extreme, regarding the body as a 'black box' whose workings are neither known nor relevant to explaining the relationships between stimuli and behaviour. Hence, the biological approach is alone in emphasizing the physical system.

The biological approach, by its nature, focuses on the internal processes associated with physiology and genetics. As important as these processes are in understanding behaviour, they are not the only source of influences. Each individual's behaviour represents a unique combination of genetic factors (*heredity*) and life experiences (*environment*). While the biological approach acknowledges the role of environmental factors such as stressors, it does not place primary emphasis on these factors, or the impact they can have on behaviour. Rather, the study of environmental influences is the focus of other approaches, such as behaviourism.

Over 200 years ago, Julien de La Mettrie made the assumption that the mind has its physical basis in the brain. In the time since, this concept of *materialism* has gained increasing acceptance. Today, as our understanding of physiological processes increases, it seems more and more evident that mind and body *are* fundamentally linked. This is not to suggest that all the questions, such as the nature of consciousness, have been fully answered; in part, mind and brain may represent different levels of description, and the issue may never be completely reconciled. But our knowledge is increasing, and perhaps most significantly, the insights are being applied – in medicine, in business and in everyday activities. The concept of *stress* has become widely known, as have methods for coping with it. The use of *psychoactive drugs* has radically altered the treatment of mental disorders, with the number of hospitalized patients in the USA being more than halved between 1955 and 1971. Advances in areas like *psychoimmunology* may have even greater impact in the future.

At the same time, problems remain. One of the greatest challenges concerns the complexity of the physiological system. There are approximately 10 *billion* neurons in the cortex of the brain alone, which are interconnected in manifold ways. In addition, there are countless chemical interactions involving *neurotransmitters*, *hormones* and *neuropeptides* – plus environmental influences. This complexity makes achieving a complete understanding of the processes which affect behaviour a daunting goal. Even on a more limited scale, the ways in which factors interact make it difficult to make specific statements about one factor (for example, stress as a cause of heart attacks) in the absence of knowledge about other factors (for example, exercise and family history). Similarly, there is a growing awareness that what we are reflects in part our evolutionary history as a species, and this, too, is influencing the kinds of questions asked. All of these factors point to the reality that the picture we have is not yet complete – but that is characteristic of science, and it is likely that missing details will continue to be filled in as research continues.

Putting It All Together – Biological Approach

Given the circumstances of his life, and the difficulties he is experiencing, it is evident that Sam (see Chapter 1) is feeling significant stress. When confronted with a heavy workload, the perceived need to be successful, and his unrequited affection for Vanessa, Sam initially experiences the short-term arousal triggered by stressors – what Selye would call the alarm stage of the general adaptation syndrome. After this initial reaction, which is mediated by Sam's sympathetic nervous system, his parasympathetic nervous system seeks to moderate his body's reactions, moving arousal back towards equilibrium. However, given the continuing pressures, Sam enters the resistance stage, where many aspects of arousal remain somewhat elevated. This is a deceptive stage, because the individual tends to feel that they are functioning well, not knowing that the body is still at a higher than optimal arousal level that cannot be sustained without significant adverse effects. Some of Sam's procrastinating activities, like socializing with his friends, may help to reduce his physiological arousal – an emotion-focused strategy. However, because procrastinating doesn't address the actual stressors, this strategy is not completely successful; in this sense, a problem-focused strategy would probably be more effective, both for dealing with his academic workload and for making an approach to Vanessa.

As discussed in the chapter, prolonged stress affects the immune system, and Sam's flu is indicative of this type of effect. Feelings of fatigue can also be a result of the negative metabolic changes stress can produce.

Sam is feeling badly about himself, which may indicate that he is becoming depressed. Stressful life events are often related to the onset of depression. No one is completely sure how this works, but evidence is accumulating that the hormones involved in a stress reaction (particularly steroids) affect the neurotransmitters serotonin and norepinephrine in the brain. The continued activity of these hormones may atrophy neurons in those parts of the brain that contribute to the experience and regulation of emotions (Brown and Barlow 2001).

Consulting a medical specialist might lead to Sam being prescribed an antidepressant and/ or anti-anxiety drug, which might help offset some of the biochemical consequences of stress. However, it may be more useful to consider the factors causing Sam's stress. Since many of the underlying circumstances are unlikely to change in the short term, he needs to re-evaluate his situation, and look for more productive ways of dealing with it, as the chapter discusses.

CHAPTER SUMMARY

- The biological approach is based on the assumption of *materialism*, which asserts that all behaviour has a physiological basis.
- The two primary concerns of the biological approach are the workings of the nervous system, and the role of heredity in behaviour.
- The nervous system is composed of billions of individual nerve cells called *neurons*; the most significant component of the nervous system is the *brain*.
- Perhaps the most challenging question in the study of the brain is the understanding of the nature of consciousness, and the relationship between the *mind* and the brain.
- Various techniques have been used to study the workings of the brain, including *case studies*, electrical recording (*EEG*) and stimulation (*ESB*), and computerized imaging techniques (*CAT*, *PET* and *MRI* scans). Chemical processes have been explored by looking at the role of *neurotransmitters*, *hormones* and *neuropeptides*.
- The effects of the body on the mind have been studied in various ways, including the study of psychoactive *drugs*, and the impact of severing the corpus callosum (*split brain*).
- The influence of mental processes on the body has been examined in terms of the effects of stress; more recently, researchers have begun to look at how mental states affect the immune system (*psychoimmunology*).
- The study of *heredity* involves both the direct study of genes and how they function, and also looking at interactions between heredity and environment by the study of twins and other groups who have an identifiable genetic relationship (*concordance*).
- *Evolutionary psychology* applies the principles of evolution to gain insight into the way selection pressures have influenced behaviour.

❶ Key terms and concepts

materialism
neuron
synapse
nerve impulse
neurotransmitters
punding
central nervous system (CNS)
cortex
limbic system
brain stem
endocrine glands
hormone
neuropeptide
psychoactive drug
electrical stimulation of the brain (ESB)

cerebral dominance
stress
stressor
post-traumatic stress disorder
psychoimmunology
heredity
gene
chromosome
genotype
phenotype
nativism
empiricism
concordance
evolutionary psychology

Test yourself questions

1 How do neurotransmitters get from the end of one neuron to another neuron?
2 Describe three computerized imaging techniques used in studying brain activity.
3 What is a 'split brain'? How does studying this add to our knowledge of how the brain works?
4 What effects does stress have on health?

Online
Learning Centre

When you have read this chapter, log onto the Online Learning Centre website at
www.openup.co.uk/glassman where you will find answers to these Test Yourself questions and
suggested answers to the Try it Yourself activities, plus many more learning resources to help
you study psychology.

Suggestions for Further Reading

- **Colin Blakemore's** *Mechanics of the Mind* (1977) provides a very readable and entertaining history of research on the brain. For a more current overview, see **Gazzaniga** *et al.*'s *Cognitive Neuroscience: The Biology of the Mind* (1998). To gain an appreciation of the complexities which doctors and researchers face, read *The Man Who Mistook His Wife for a Hat*, by **Oliver Sacks** (1985), a neurologist who is both knowledgeable and wise.

- Two interesting, if idiosyncratic, views of the relations between the brain and behaviour are *Descartes' Error: Emotion, Reason and the Human Brain*, by neurologist **Antonio Damasio** (2005), and *Bright Air, Brilliant Fire*, by Nobel biologist **Gerald Edelman** (1992). Damasio offers a new interpretation of emotions and cognition, while Edelman discusses how physiology and genetics are converging in their understanding of the nervous system.

- For a fascinating and lavishly illustrated account of how techniques for viewing the brain have advanced our understanding, read **Rita Carter's** *Mapping the Mind* (1998).

- *The Stress of Life* (1976) is probably the best of **Selye's** accounts of stress intended for the general reader. For a current review of stress and techniques for dealing with it, consider **Jerrold Greenberg's** *Comprehensive Stress Management* (2006).

- For readers interested in the fast-developing area of psychoimmunology, a recent, though technical, overview is provided by **Kiecolt-Glaser** *et al.*'s *Emotions, Morbidity, and Mortality* (2002). Those seeking a simpler account may prefer **Norman Cousins's** *Head First: The Biology of Hope* (1989), or **Bill Moyers's** *Healing and the Mind* (1993), which was written to accompany a PBS television series.

- The excitement and challenge of our increasing knowledge of genetics and behaviour are knowledgeably presented in **Plomin** *et al.*'s *Behavioral Genetics in the Postgenomic Era* (2003).

- **Geoffrey Miller's** *The Mating Mind* (2000) provides a lucid overview of how evolutionary psychology is challenging traditional ideas about human behaviour. For a readable critique, try **Anne Innis Dagg's** *'Love of Shopping' is Not a Gene: Problems with Darwinian Psychology* (2004).

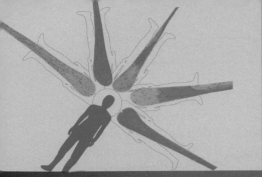

Chapter 3

The Behaviourist Approach

LEARNING OBJECTIVES

In this chapter, the objectives are to learn:

- ☑ the basic assumptions of behaviourism
- ☑ the nature of stimuli and responses
- ☑ the principles of classical conditioning, including
  - unconditioned stimulus and response
  - conditioned stimulus and response
- ☑ the phenomena of classical conditioning, including
  - stimulus generalization and discrimination
  - extinction and spontaneous recovery
  - higher order conditioning
- ☑ the applications of classical conditioning, including
  - conditioned emotional responses
  - conditioned drug and immune responses
- ☑ the principles of operant conditioning, including
  - reinforcers and reinforcement
  - contingencies of reinforcement
  - schedules of reinforcement
- ☑ the phenomena of operant conditioning, including
  - shaping
  - extinction
  - discriminative stimuli
  - non-contingent reinforcement
- ☑ the applications and implications of conditioning, including
  - aversive control of behaviour
  - the interrelationships of classical and operant conditioning
  - autonomic conditioning and biofeedback
  - biological constraints on learning

MIND DOESN'T MATTER

One of the basic themes of this book is that behaviour can often be understood in different ways, represented by the five approaches. As we will see in this chapter, the behaviourists emphasize links between the environment and behaviour. In doing so, they tend to ignore both physiological processes and mental events, even in circumstances that might invite such interpretations, as in an example reported by a psychologist named Israel Goldiamond (1973).

As the result of a car accident, Goldiamond spent several months in hospital undergoing treatment for a spinal injury. At one point, he shared a room with a man who had suffered brain damage. This patient was often disoriented, urinating on walls and muttering, 'What the hell am I doing in Panama?' (He wasn't.)

Thus far, this story appears unremarkable – after all, Chapter 2 explores how the brain controls behaviour. Yet, rather than focusing on the brain damage, Goldiamond examined the influence of the environment on the man's behaviour. He noted, for example, that the man did not act oddly in the hospital cafeteria – a fact which the staff had overlooked. Goldiamond accounted for this by noting that the features of cafeterias are fairly universal, while those of a rehabilitation hospital are not familiar to most people. Hence, the man was only disoriented when he was in an unfamiliar setting. Furthermore, the hospital was located on a large lake, and the patient's room overlooked a naval pier – perhaps accounting for his questions about Panama. Goldiamond suggested that the man's urinating inappropriately could be dealt with by rewarding him with cigarettes for urinating properly – in effect, controlling the behaviour by means of an external incentive. As anticipated, the technique worked.

The point of this story is to show that looking at the brain is not always the best way to understand behaviour. Goldiamond, like other behaviourists, preferred to look at the role that the environment plays in behaviour. There is no question that the man in the story had suffered brain damage. But it is equally clear that his behaviour could not be fully understood by looking *only* at the brain damage. In one sense, by placing such a heavy emphasis on *internal* events, the biological approach tends to give too little attention to the *external* context of behaviour – that is, the environment in which behaviour occurs. In this chapter, we will consider the role of environmental influences on behaviour, as seen from the behaviourist perspective.

INTRODUCTION

The *behaviourist approach* emphasizes the role of environmental stimuli in determining the way we act. In large measure, this means focusing on **learning** – changes in behaviour which occur

---
learning a change in behaviour which occurs as the result of experience.

---

as the result of experience. (By emphasizing experience, behaviourists exclude changes due to fatigue, injury or drug effects.) Behaviourism has added considerably to our understanding of learning through the study of what is called *classical* and *operant conditioning*. Before examining what has been discovered, let us look at the basic assumptions and methods which distinguish behaviourism from the other approaches.

As with all of the approaches, the choice of focus is one of the factors which gives behaviourism its uniqueness. In this case, the behaviourist approach is commonly distinguished by its emphasis on the relationship between observable behaviour (*responses*) and environmental events (*stimuli*). Consider the simple interaction involved when a child reaches out towards a glowing fire, and then quickly draws back from the heat: first, the stimulus of the sparkling flame attracts their attention, so that they move their hand forward (stimulus of fire leads to response of reaching). Then, the heat of the fire leads to a reflexive withdrawal (stimulus of heat leads to withdrawal response). This, in turn, might lead the child to throw water on the fire, or take some other action. Thus, from the behaviourist perspective, human experience can be understood in terms of the interrelations between stimuli and responses.

Basic Assumptions of Behaviourism

Like other approaches, the behaviourist approach is defined not only by the kinds of data it emphasizes, but also in terms of its basic assumptions, which are closely related to its historical origins. At the turn of the twentieth century, psychologists tended to focus on either the experimental study of physiological processes, or the introspective analysis of experience (see Chapter 1 for a review). Physiological research was hampered by the limited technology available for studying the brain (for example, not even X-rays or EEGs existed), and introspectionism was proving limited due to problems of subjectivity in describing sensory experience. Consequently, both had serious limitations. As an alternative, William James argued that psychologists should focus on how behaviour relates to its purpose (called *functionalism*), but he was often better at framing the issues than at doing research to solve them. Thus, none of the available methods was achieving unequivocal success. It was against this backdrop that behaviourism arose. (It should be noted that 'behaviourism', like other approaches, can refer to a number of theories, each with some unique aspects. Nonetheless, it is possible to identify some common elements within the approach.)

While the temptation in discussing the behaviourist approach is to emphasize the type of data collected (the observable behaviours which give the approach its name), doing so ignores the broader assumptions which underlie the approach.

The most fundamental of the basic principles in behaviorism is the concept of parsimony. Sometimes called 'Occam's razor' after the English philosopher who first proposed it, **parsimony** favours seeking the simplest possible explanation for any event. If, for example, one can explain a person's eating a pastry without referring to a non-observable concept like 'hunger' or 'oral personality', then parsimony says one should avoid using such concepts. Behaviourists reacted against introspectionism in part because it seemed to invoke too many vague concepts, and thereby lacked parsimony. Instead, behaviourism focused on the use of *operational definitions* (defining concepts in terms of observable events) – and this led naturally to the focus on 'stimuli' and 'responses' (for further discussion of operational definitions, refer back to Chapter 1).

> **parsimony** in the philosophy of science, the principle that one should always seek the simplest possible explanation for any event.

The second basic assumption of the behaviourist approach relates to the basis of behavioural change. Like functionalism, behaviourism tries to understand the conditions under which behaviour occurs. When does a particular behaviour occur? What conditions lead to it? What changes in the environment result from it? Since relatively few behaviours in human beings are genetically programmed, this leads to a focus on the role of experience, which is expressed through learning. It is easy to say that the way we act depends on our past experiences, but just *how* does learning occur? Since the time of Aristotle, the basic explanation has been that we learn by *association* – that is, by forming connections between ideas and/or events. For example, if the sound of an electric can opener leads a dog to run to the kitchen, we can speculate that the dog has formed an association between the sound of the can opener and being fed (canned food!). This concept of

associationism, which was also favoured by such English philosophers as David Hume and J. S. Mill, has had a fundamental influence on psychology, particularly for the behaviourists. As we shall see, behaviourist theories are essentially theories of how associations are formed.

associationism the doctrine, supported by Aristotle, Hume and others, that mental processes, particularly learning, are based on forming connections between ideas and/ or events.

Taken together, parsimony and associationism formed the foundation from which behaviourism arose. Exactly how, and what the result has been for our understanding of psychology, will form the substance of this chapter.

The Pioneers of Behaviourism

Just over 100 years ago, an American named Edwin L. Thorndike was studying for his PhD in the newly-formed psychology department at Columbia University (he started at Harvard, under William James, but transferred for financial reasons). For his research, he studied problem solving in animals, using a series of puzzle-like tasks (such as confining a cat in a box, from which it could release itself by pressing against a lever). His dissertation, published in 1898, had the rather cognitive-sounding title of *Animal Intelligence* (Thorndike 1898).

law of effect a principle of learning developed by Edwin Thorndike, stating that any response which leads to a satisfying outcome for the organism is likely to be repeated, and any response which leads to an unpleasant outcome is not likely to be repeated.

Despite the title, Thorndike's research was basically concerned with trying to analyse the conditions under which animals changed their behaviour – that is, *learned*. In doing so, he focused on the relationship between a response and its consequences, resulting in what he called 'the law of effect'. Basically, the **law of effect** said that any response which leads to an outcome that the organism finds satisfying is likely to be repeated, and any response which leads to an unpleasant outcome is not likely to be repeated. This was a form of associationism, in that the organism (animal, person) was seen as making a connection between a response and its consequences. (This is technically called association by *contiguity*, in that it assumes the response and consequence must be closely linked in time and space.) While basically unoriginal – the idea that individuals respond to reward and punishment extends back to the ancient Greeks – Thorndike's version could be said to differ in that *it was supported by experimental data* (Robinson 1979). By framing the issue in experimental (and therefore scientific) terms, Thorndike paved the way for the behaviourist approach.

Key Thinker: **Edwin Lynn Thorndike**

Edwin Lynn Thorndike (1874–1949) was born in Williamsburg, a small town in western Massachusetts. After receiving his bachelor's degree from Wesleyan University, he went to Harvard University to study psychology under William James, but was forced to transfer to Columbia University because of financial difficulties. In the newly-formed psychology department at Columbia, he studied under James McKeen Cattell, one of the most influential early American psychologists. For his research, he studied problem solving in animals, using a series of puzzle-like tasks (e.g., confining a cat in a box, from which it could release itself by pressing against a lever). His dissertation, published in 1898, had the rather cognitive-sounding title, *Animal Intelligence*. Thorndike is probably best known today for his 'law of effect', which foreshadowed Skinner's concept of reinforcement as a description of the role of consequences in learning. From 1899 he taught at Teachers College at Columbia, where he wrote prolifically on education as well as psychology. He died in New York at the age of 75.

Thorndike's law of effect, while significant, was not without problems; a key difficulty was that it was vague about what made something 'satisfying'. One way to resolve this might be to seek physiologically-oriented mechanisms for 'satisfaction'. However, given turn-of-the-century knowledge of physiology, this often required resorting to non-observable concepts, which violated the principle of *parsimony*. A more radical approach, pioneered by John B. Watson, was to pare theorizing to the bone, restricting theoretical descriptions to factors which could be directly observed and measured.

John B. Watson was both gifted and provocative. As a student at the University of Chicago, he initially trained in introspectionism, but found its approach to psychology excessively vague, especially in its emphasis on mental processes. He began working with animals, and completed his PhD in three years – at that time being the youngest such graduate from the university. After teaching for only four years at Chicago, he was offered a full professorship at Johns Hopkins, and shortly after became chair of the psychology department there – an example of remarkable career advancement!

Watson can only be described as zealous in promoting his ideas. Reading his major work (*Behaviorism* 1930) today, one is struck by the scorn he heaps on William James and others, and by his willingness to test his ideas whenever possible (even using his own children). Confident that he was correct, he was willing to extend his claims even when he lacked experimental support, as in his famous remark, 'Give me a dozen healthy infants, well-formed, and my own specified world to bring them up in and I'll guarantee to take any one at random and train him to become any type of specialist I might select – doctor, lawyer, artist, merchant-chief and yes, even beggar-man and thief, regardless of his talents, penchants, tendencies, abilities, vocations, and race of his ancestors.' What is often omitted in this quotation is the statement which follows it: '*I am going beyond my facts and I admit it, but so have the advocates of the contrary* and they have been doing it for thousands of years' (Watson 1930, p. 104; emphasis added). Clearly, Watson did not shirk from confrontation in pursuing his ideas.

Key Thinker: **John Broadus Watson**

John Broadus Watson (1878–1958) was the founder of behaviourism. Educated in a one-room schoolhouse in the American farm belt (like many of his era), he went on to complete his PhD at the University of Chicago. After a brief exploration of the introspectionist approach, he continued under John Dewey and James Angell, two of the pioneers of the function-alist approach. Watson was both gifted and outspoken – two characteristics which played a major role in his career. He completed his PhD in only three years and began teaching at the university; four years later, he was offered a full professorship in psychology at Johns Hopkins University, and shortly after became chairman of the department. In 1913 he began publishing the first of a series of publications which outlined his behaviourist approach, which quickly gained him both fame and notoriety – his statement about shaping a healthy infant in any way desired (quoted in the text) is characteristic of his assertive style. While at Johns Hopkins, he met graduate student Rosalie Rayner, who became his second wife. After collaborating with Rayner on the case of 'little Albert', Watson became interested in human sexual behaviour; his activities in this regard (including participant observation) did not sit well with the prevailing moral views, and he was finally dismissed. At this point, he took a job with the J. Walter Thompson advertising firm. Not surprisingly, he did well in his new role, embarking on studies of consumer behaviour, writing psychology articles for the general public, and becoming a vice-president of the advertising firm in fewer than four years. Thus, Watson not only founded an entire approach to psychology, but perhaps was also the first psychologist to apply psycho-logical theory to advertising and marketing! He died in New York at the age of 80.

Watson's writings and ideas were a lever that moved the world. In the following decades, until the mid-1950s, behaviourism became the dominant force in psychology, particularly in North America. The irony is that while the general approach became highly influential, most researchers never accepted Watson's extreme position, which is sometimes called *radical behaviourism*. Even B. F. Skinner, the spiritual heir to Watson's work, has commented, 'A shortage of facts is always a problem in a new science, but in Watson's aggressive program in a field as vast as human behaviour it was especially damaging' (Skinner 1974, p. 6). The greatest impact of Watson's ideas can be traced to three central elements:

1 the emphasis on observable responses and environmental stimuli;

2 the rejection of mentalistic concepts not grounded in direct observation; and

3 the focus on learning and experience as central to the understanding of human behaviour.

Some 70 years of research, both basic and applied, has demonstrated that in many ways, we are indeed what we learn.

Behaviourism, as already noted, has many variants; indeed, some would say it is more appropriate to speak of the behaviouristic approach than the behaviourist approach. Even E. C. Tolman, often regarded as one of the founders of the *cognitive* approach, considered himself a 'behaviourist' (Tolman 1932). However, what all behaviourists share is an interest in how behaviour is learned, and an emphasis on explanations based on observable events. In this chapter, we will see how this approach has been applied to a variety of situations. (Note that today, research which focuses on the relationship between environmental factors and behaviour is sometimes described as 'behavioural' – but this is a more general term than *behaviourism*.)

Try it Yourself

In everyday life, we all try to make sense of the behaviours we see in ourselves and others – but often we violate behaviourist principles by going beyond what is observable. For example, consider this scenario: you good-naturedly tease a friend about forgetting her wallet at home, and she snaps at you to mind your own business. You may think, 'She's feeling upset – she must have had a fight with her boyfriend.' This explanation, however, violates the basic assumptions of behaviourism: it explains your friend's behaviour in terms of something you can't see (her being upset with her boyfriend), while it neglects the role of observable events (her comment immediately followed your teasing). If you look at your friend's behaviour the way Watson recommended, you might conclude that her remark was in fact a reaction to your teasing. With the first explanation, you might disregard your own behaviour and instead focus on her (presumed) anger at her boyfriend. With the more behaviourist explanation, you might conclude that teasing a friend isn't always a good idea. The point here is that the behaviourist approach leads you to focus on observable aspects of the situation, and that can change your interpretation. Look at the following situations: are the interpretations you make using behaviourist principles the same or different from what you would normally conclude?

- A toddler hits another child in a school playground.
- A driver 'tailgates' your vehicle while driving on a highway.
- A classmate you encounter in the library offers to buy you a coffee.

Stimuli and Responses

Behaviourism, by focusing on *observable* events, sets its own limits on what can be studied. Thoughts, feelings and other inner mental states cannot be studied empirically, and so have no place in behaviourist theory. Genetic variation, while presumably contributing to differences among individuals, is also ignored, because traditionally it was not measurable (and is still largely inaccessible). By contrast, environmental conditions are relatively easy to measure and study.

Taken as a whole, the environment involves colours, shapes, smells, sounds and many other characteristics. Obviously, it is impossible in an everyday setting to measure every element of a typical environment. However, in most cases, this would be unnecessary, because there are many environmental elements that typically do not seem to enter our awareness, and consequently have little impact. (Recall the discussion of perceptual processes in Chapter 1.) Nonetheless, behaviourists recognize that in order to study environmental influences on behaviour, one must be able to rigorously define the environmental characteristics involved in a situation. In practice, this means that research often involves limiting the complexity of the environment, particularly in laboratory studies. It also means that one must be able to define terms clearly. With regard to the environment, sights, sounds and smells are all considered examples of stimuli. A **stimulus** (often abbreviated as **S**) is any event, situation, object or factor that is measurable and which may affect behaviour. Simple examples could include a red triangle, the ticking of a watch or a pinprick.

stimulus in general, any event, situation, object or factor that may affect behaviour; for the behaviourists, a measurable change in the environment.

For a behaviourist, an important element in understanding a particular behaviour is to identify the stimulus (or stimuli) involved. From the examples above, this would seem to be a fairly straightforward task. In reality, however, it can sometimes be quite difficult to define which environmental elements are involved as stimuli in a specific situation. For example, a mother approaches her 2-month-old infant, and the baby smiles. The mother seems to be the stimulus which elicits the baby's smiling. But is it the mother as a whole, or her face, or her expression, or her smell, or her touch, or some combination of these and other elements to which the baby is actually responding? In research, it would be necessary to identify the actual stimulus elements in order to understand the situation properly. (In this regard, the desire for *operational definitions* of terms, including 'stimulus', becomes understandable as a means of avoiding ambiguity.)

Similarly, it is necessary to describe clearly the behaviour being studied. Normally, the behaviour which is measured is called the **response** (often abbreviated as **R**). Again, this may seem very simple at first glance. For example, a person sits at a table, eating. 'Eating' is obviously a response; however, a moment's thought will show that there can be tremendous variations in the behaviour described as eating. A finicky child may pick reluctantly at a disliked vegetable. A hungry person may ravenously devour a favourite dish. While both are eating, there is clearly a large difference in their behaviour. Consequently, researchers must be careful to describe a response in terms that are meaningful to the situation. Often this will require specifying the rate, intensity and/or other characteristics of the response.

response in general, any reaction to a stimulus, whether overt or mental; for the behaviourists, a measurable change in behaviour.

One of the distinctions among responses that became evident to the early behaviourists was a distinction between reflexes and voluntary actions. **Reflexes** are unlearned responses that can be triggered by specific environmental stimuli. Examples of human reflexes include withdrawing the hand from a hot surface, or a baby's sucking on an

reflex an unlearned response that can be triggered by specific environmental stimuli, such as a baby's sucking on an object placed in the mouth.

voluntary response a response which is controlled by the individual (i.e., emitted) rather than being triggered (elicited) by specific stimuli the way reflexes are.

object placed in the mouth. By contrast, **voluntary responses** are emitted – that is, they are not triggered by stimuli in the way reflexes are; typically, they involve more complicated actions, which often require extensive practice. Thorndike, for example, in his studies of problem solving by animals, was looking at voluntary responses, and he found it took repeated trials for learning to occur. Voluntary behaviour can span a tremendous range, from simple actions like learning to use a fork, to complex behaviours like speaking a new language. Such differences led early behaviourists to the separate study of reflexes and voluntary responses. As we shall see, they discovered that the principles of learning seem to differ for the two types of behaviour. As we will also consider later in the chapter, the actual differences between the two types may be smaller than they initially appear.

CLASSICAL CONDITIONING

At the turn of the twentieth century, a Russian physiologist named Ivan Pavlov was engaged in a long-term project to understand the process of digestion. Beginning in 1879 and working primarily with dogs, his work earned him the Nobel Prize in 1904 (Windholz 1997). But some time around 1902, he noticed a phenomenon which was to lead him in a new and unexpected direction. In order to study digestion, Pavlov measured a number of factors, including how much a dog salivated when it was given food. Then one day he noticed a phenomenon he labelled 'psychic salivation' – a dog would salivate before it was actually given food. Since Pavlov believed that digestion involved a series of reflexes, he set out to determine what controlled this antici-

classical conditioning the study of learning which involves reflex responses, in which a neutral stimulus comes to elicit an existing reflex response.

patory response. What he discovered became the basis for what is now commonly called **classical conditioning** – the study of learning which involves reflex responses. Essentially, classical conditioning explores how a new stimulus can come to elicit an existing reflex response due to learning.

Key Thinker: **Ivan Petrovich Pavlov**

Ivan Petrovich Pavlov (1849 – 1936) was a Russian physiologist who pioneered the study of classical conditioning. Born in Ryazan, Russia, he initially began seminary studies, but then changed to St Petersburg University, where he graduated in natural science, and subsequently received his doctorate in physiology from the Military Medical Academy. After a few years spent in Germany, he went on to become a professor at the Military Medical Academy. His work on the physiology of digestion, begun in 1879, earned him the Nobel Prize in 1904. He first became aware of reflexes by reading Sechenov's work while still at seminary, but his own research on what became known as classical conditioning did not begin until about 1902. At this time, while still studying digestion in dogs, he noticed what he called 'psychic salivation' – a dog would salivate before it was actually given food. Since Pavlov believed that digestion involved a series of reflexes, he set out to determine what controlled this anticipatory response. Ultimately, his work on conditioning overshadowed the research which had earned him the Nobel Prize. He continued to be intellectually active, forming a genetics institute only a few years before his death at the age of 87.

Pavlov's original studies have become so well known as to be the object of jokes (like the psychologist who salivates when he hears the name 'Pavlov'!). In simple outline, Pavlov found that by ringing a bell and then immediately giving the dog some food, the bell came to evoke the same response as the food itself – salivation. To understand why this is remarkable, we need to consider the elements of the situation more closely. As Pavlov's lengthy studies of digestion showed, salivating at the presence of food is a basic neural reflex that requires no learning. For example, if you put a piece of chocolate in your mouth, you will salivate. A light shone in the eye will cause the pupil to contract. Reflex responses like these (and they exist in species from worms to humans) are referred to in classical conditioning as **unconditioned responses**. For any reflex, there is some stimulus which will trigger (*elicit*) the response (for example, food for salivating, light for pupil contraction); the stimulus which elicits an unconditioned response is called an **unconditioned stimulus**. Since 'conditioned' refers to *learned*, the term refers to the unlearned nature of reflexes. (Pavlov of course wrote in Russian, and actually used the term 'unconditional', but an early English translator erred, and the mistake has remained.)

If reflexes are unlearned, then what is the learning that occurs in classical conditioning? Pavlov noted that the learning is based on forming a connection between stimuli – in the dog's case, between the bell and the food. Ringing the bell initially had no effect on salivation – that is, with respect to the response of salivation, it was a **neutral stimulus**. (To be a stimulus, an environmental element must be something which the organism is aware of; normally this is demonstrated by the stimulus arousing attention, called an *orienting response*.) After repeated pairings with the food placed in the dog's mouth, the sound of the bell came to elicit drooling. At this point, the sound has become a **conditioned stimulus**, and the salivating which results is called a **conditioned response** (to distinguish it from the response to food alone, see Figure 3.1). Essentially, the conditioned stimulus has become *associated* with the occurrence of food (Pavlov 1927).

unconditioned response in classical conditioning, a reflexive response produced by a specific stimulus, such as pupil contraction to bright light.

unconditioned stimulus in classical conditioning, a stimulus which elicits a reflexive (unconditioned) response.

neutral stimulus in classical conditioning, a stimulus which initially produces no specific response other than provoking attention; as conditioning proceeds, the neutral stimulus becomes a conditioned stimulus.

conditioned stimulus in classical conditioning, a stimulus which by repeated pairings with an unconditioned stimulus comes to elicit a conditioned response.

conditioned response in classical conditioning, a response to a previously neutral stimulus which has become a conditioned stimulus by repeated pairing with an unconditioned stimulus.

In order to appreciate the significance of classical conditioning, we must examine its characteristics more closely. Since the response involved is essentially a pre-existing reflex, the learning which occurs does *not* involve a new response; instead, it consists of forming a connection (*association*) between two stimuli (the CS and UCS). In order for optimal conditioning to occur, the conditioned stimulus (CS) must occur a second or so before the unconditioned stimulus (UCS). If the two occur simultaneously, conditioning may occur, but is typically weaker. If the CS is presented *after* the UCS (sometimes called *backward conditioning*), then *no* learning occurs. What this tells us is that conditioning is closely linked to the ability of the CS to serve as a signal that the UCS is going to occur. This is further demonstrated by studies which show that conditioning is only likely when the CS *reliably* predicts the occurrence of the UCS (Rescorla 2000). In some sense, what makes classical conditioning a valuable process for the organism is the fact that *it allows one to anticipate environmental events*. This notion that classical conditioning helps in adapting to the environment is supported by research on a phenomenon called *blocking*. If a new stimulus is presented simultaneously with an existing CS, conditioning to the new stimulus does not occur, because the original CS is *already* an adequate signal (Kamin 1969). Flashing a light to signal food is unnecessary, if a bell already serves that purpose. Conditioning, then, seems to

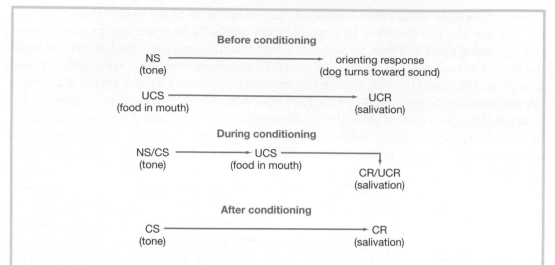

Before conditioning

NS ⟶ orienting response
(tone) (dog turns toward sound)

UCS ⟶ UCR
(food in mouth) (salivation)

During conditioning

NS/CS ⟶ UCS ⟶
(tone) (food in mouth)

CR/UCR
(salivation)

After conditioning

CS ⟶ CR
(tone) (salivation)

Figure 3.1 The Basic Classical Conditioning Procedure In classical conditioning, repeated pairing of a neutral stimulus (NS) with an unconditioned stimulus (UCS) results in conditioning, whereby the NS becomes conditioned (CS) to elicit the same type of response as the UCS did.

occur because such learning is often adaptive, enabling individuals to deal with the world more effectively.

Classical conditioning has been demonstrated in a wide variety of species, from worms to birds to primates. Thus, it appears to be a very fundamental form of learning. But given that much of human behaviour does not depend on reflex responses, it might seem that classical conditioning is of little significance in people. In fact, the reality seems to be just the opposite: examples of classical conditioning seem pervasive in our lives. For example, we respond to stimuli associated with food – smells, pictures in advertisements, words like 'chocolate cake' – in much the way that Pavlov's dogs reacted to the bell: by increased digestive activity. In these cases, the food cues, having been associated with food itself (the UCS), are conditioned stimuli. Such food cues are among the most reliable of conditioned stimuli, because the sight and smell of food always precede the actual eating of it. In movies, directors will use sounds to enhance the emotional content of the story. For example, a particular theme may precede the repeated appearances of the villain in a horror movie; viewers then come to associate the theme to the moments of mayhem that follow. (Of course, film images of violence are *themselves* conditioned stimuli, associated with past experiences of actual injury (UCS). This relates to the process of *higher order conditioning*, which we will discuss later in the chapter.) Many people, when showering, develop a conditioned response of anxiety to the sound of a toilet flushing (CS), since

Try it Yourself

Pick up any magazine and look at the advertisements. You will probably see that in each advertisement, the product is displayed along with one or more attractive models. Given the basic principles of classical conditioning, why might this be so? Do you find the advertisements using attractive models to be more compelling than those that do not? Is that because you are focusing on the product or on the model? What about political advertising: although 'sex appeal' may not be used in the same way, do political ads seem to make use of classical conditioning principles? How?

it often results in a sudden increase in the temperature of the water (UCS)! Classical conditioning is thus a flexible process which allows us to anticipate biologically significant events (UCSs) by making an association to stimuli (CSs) which precede them.

Classical Conditioning Phenomena
Stimulus Generalization and Discrimination

Having established the basic elements of classical conditioning, Pavlov (and later, others) began to explore some variations of the original situation. One subject that interested him was the element of stimulus novelty: what would happen if a new stimulus was presented as a CS? Tests with unrelated stimuli quickly established that a neutral stimulus will not elicit a response which has been conditioned to a different stimulus (for example, flashing a light will not elicit a CR if the previous CS was the sound of a bell). However, what would happen if a stimulus similar to the CS were used (such as a different bell)? Tests of this type revealed a new phenomenon, called **stimulus generalization**: stimuli similar to the original CS would tend to elicit the same CR. Research has shown that the degree of response is related to the degree of similarity between the new stimulus and the original CS (see Figure 3.2).

stimulus generalization in classical conditioning, the tendency to produce a CR to both the original CS and to stimuli which are similar to it in some way.

This may not seem like a very surprising result, but it is very profound in its implications. In everyday life, we seldom encounter the same precise situation twice. For example, the traffic pattern on a road is never identical on two occasions, requiring us to pay attention each time we drive the same route. Even people change, as they wear different clothes, change their hair style, etc. Given this reality, it is generally desirable to be able to ignore these minor variations – in other words, to generalize across basically similar stimuli. This is precisely what the studies

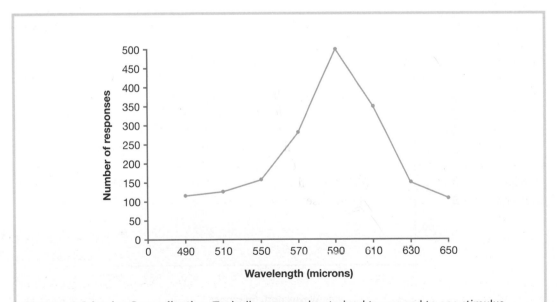

Figure 3.2 Stimulus Generalization Typically, an organism trained to respond to one stimulus will respond in the same way to stimuli which are perceived as similar. In the example, varying the wavelength (colour) from the original greenish stimulus leads to responding which decreases as the test stimuli become less similar. (These data, averaged from Peterson 1962, actually refer to operant conditioning of pigeons, but the basic phenomenon is the same in classical conditioning.)

of stimulus generalization in classical conditioning demonstrate. In practical terms, stimulus generalization results in responding to *a whole class of related stimuli*, after initial learning with a single stimulus. A child who has learned to withdraw after touching a glowing burner on a gas stove will tend to generalize this withdrawal to other stimuli that are similarly bright and hot – electric burners, open fires, etc. In this sense, stimulus generalization can enable organisms to adapt better to their environment – though it may not always be adaptive. For example, stimulus generalization has been noted in how people respond to brand names for products (Till and Priluck 2000). After using conditioning to establish favourable attitudes to imaginary brands, the researchers found that ratings carried over to products with the same brand in a different category. Hence, companies can 'build on the brand name' to market new products!

How, exactly, can we define or measure 'similarity'? Ideally, we should have some general procedure, operationally defined, to measure similarity for any stimuli. Considerable attention has been given to this problem, but as yet there is no universal standard to determine similarity. Lacking a clear general definition, one must resort to defining similarity by observing the outcome of experimental tests. Thus, if two stimuli elicit essentially identical results, they are highly similar; if CS_1 produces a strong conditioned response, but CS_2 elicits only a weak response, then they are not very similar.

The fact that there is no reliable way to predefine similarity may seem a serious weakness, but in fact it may actually tell us something about the nature of stimulus generalization. The typical experiment produces results like those in Figure 3.2, where response intensity drops off as the difference between stimuli increases. However, this is not the only possible outcome. Depending on experience during and prior to training, results can vary significantly. For example, when two stimuli are randomly mixed as the CS during training, generalization is basically equal to both stimuli (Grice and Hunter 1964). Even more interesting are the implications of experiments on stimulus generalization where the environment of the animals has been carefully controlled

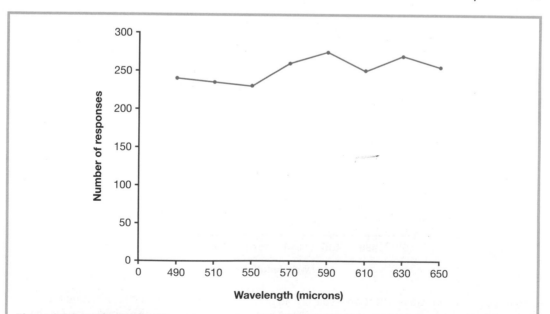

Figure 3.3 Pure Generalization When pigeons were raised under monochromatic light, testing for stimulus generalization with other colours of light yielded essentially no differences in responding – in effect, the animals generalized to any colour of light. (Data averaged from Peterson 1962)

prior to conditioning. For example, if pigeons are reared from birth with only yellow light for illumination, and then a coloured light is used as the CS, the pigeons will respond *equally* to *any* colour of light (Peterson 1962) (see Figure 3.3). In this situation, it seems that the absence of prior experience with colour as a stimulus characteristic leads to regarding all colours as similar. Babies show a somewhat comparable response, in that initially they smile at anyone who smiles at them, whether parent or stranger. Thus, it seems that the initial tendency of an organism is to generalize when encountering a new situation. (As a perceptual characteristic, this may also relate to such behaviours as *stereotyping*, which involve generalizing based on group membership.)

Why, then, do most experiments show the gradients seen in the first example? The answer seems to lie with another phenomenon which Pavlov studied. He noted that a dog conditioned to salivate to the presentation of a black square (CS) also salivated at the sight of a grey square – an example of stimulus generalization. Pavlov then ran a series of trials during which the black square was always followed by food (UCS), but the grey square was never followed by food. After a number of such trials, the dog reliably salivated to the black square, but no longer did when presented with the grey square. This was a demonstration of **stimulus discrimination**, whereby the organism is conditioned to *distinguish* between two stimuli (see Figure 3.4). Pavlov subsequently demonstrated that such discriminations can be remarkably precise, if training is continued with stimuli which become progressively more alike. What is notable is that *stimulus discrimination always requires training* – in the *absence* of such training, organisms tend to *generalize*.

stimulus discrimination in classical conditioning, selective responding to the CS, but not to stimuli which are similar in some way as a result of training.

If we then reconsider the puzzle of generalization gradients, what seems to emerge is the implication that 'typical' gradients reflect a *combination* of generalization and discrimination. In the everyday world, organisms learn that stimulus variations sometimes are significant, and sometimes are not. Pigeons, for example, may use their colour vision to determine when berries

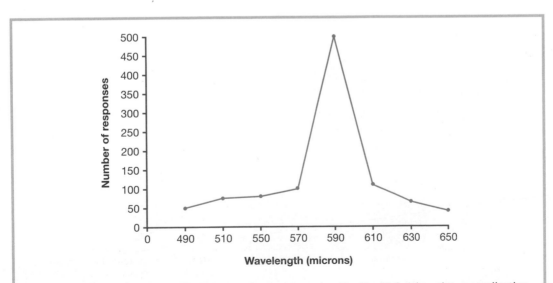

Figure 3.4 Stimulus Discrimination When pigeons are trained in discrimination, the generalization gradient becomes much steeper (compare to Figure 3.2). Taken with the two previous graphs, this suggests that a 'typical' generalization response actually reflects a degree of discrimination, unlike the pure generalization produced when there has been no prior experience of stimulus variation (Figure 3.3).

are ripe or not, but not to distinguish between berries and seeds. Typically, the smaller the colour difference, the less significant it would be. Only when they have *no prior experience* with colour variations (as in the unusual experiment described above) will they totally ignore colour differences. According to this analysis, trying to determine a universal standard of similarity is a hopeless task, since organisms will show varying response patterns depending on their past experience. In other words, learning based on classical conditioning is a cumulative process, with present behaviour being influenced by prior conditioning experiences.

While *what* we discriminate may depend on past experience, the *capacity* to discriminate seems to be inborn, and can often be crucial to adaptation. For instance, detecting the difference between food which is safe or spoiled often depends on discriminating particular odour cues. Some occupations are closed to individuals with colour blindness, because job performance requires discrimination based on colour (for example, certain types of electrical work, where wires are colour coded). Thus, in some circumstances, lacking the capacity to discriminate could seriously reduce our capacity to adapt, or even survive.

Extinction and Spontaneous Recovery

We have seen how classical conditioning, combined with stimulus generalization and discrimination, can lead to learning which is often highly adaptive. However, we have not said anything about how long the effects of conditioning last, or what happens if a conditioned response is *not* adaptive. A Russian researcher, W. H. Gantt, has commented on the possibility that conditioned responses, being persistent once formed, can turn an individual into 'a museum of antiquities' as time goes on. Many reactions would be based on particular past situations, and consequently might be either no longer useful, or even detrimental (Gantt 1966). For example, a person who broke an arm might continue to favour it (because of the pain associated with the original injury) long after healing had been completed. This would represent a form of persistent classical condi-

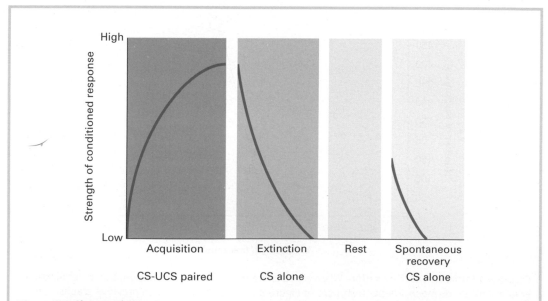

Figure 3.5 Changes in the Strength of a Conditioned Response As seen in the graphs, the strength of a conditioned response increases during acquisition, but drops dramatically during extinction; with the passage of time (represented by the rest interval), a previously extinguished response may reoccur (spontaneous recovery), but tends to be weak, and to extinguish relatively rapidly.

tioning which, as Gantt suggested, would be maladaptive. Clearly, if *all* conditioning persists indefinitely, then inappropriate responses become a serious possibility.

In part because of this possibility, Pavlov was also interested in the degree of permanence of classical conditioning. In order to test the limits, Pavlov and his colleagues first conditioned a dog to salivate at the sound of a bell. Once the response was well established (by pairing the sound of the bell with a UCS of food placed in the dog's mouth), they continued to ring the bell, but no longer provided food. Under these conditions, the conditioned response (salivating) became weaker and weaker, and eventually ceased altogether. Pavlov referred to this cessation of responding when the CS is presented repeatedly *without* being paired with the UCS as **extinction**. Thus, extinction seems to suggest that what can be learned can be unlearned, and that conditioned responses are not necessarily permanent.

extinction in classical conditioning, the cessation of responding when the CS is presented repeatedly without being paired with the UCS.

However, this conclusion is not as straightforward as it seems. First, one should distinguish between active training in extinction, such as Pavlov used, and the persistence of conditioned responses in the absence of such training. Potentially, without active extinction, a conditioned response may simply remain dormant until the person encounters the CS again. For example, a fear response associated with the sound of a dentist's drill may persist despite lengthy intervals between visits, because no extinction training occurs. The effectiveness of extinction also depends on the *type* of conditioned response. Work by Gantt and others has indicated that internal responses like heart rate and blood pressure changes, which are frequently associated with stressful or emotional stimulus situations, are more persistent than simple muscle responses like withdrawing from a hot surface, or positive associations like salivation to food cues. This has implications for the conditioning of emotions, as we will see below.

Given that extinction occurs, one might ask what effect the passage of time will have on it. One might assume that the effects of extinction in 'erasing' the original conditioning would be as long-lasting as conditioning itself is in the absence of extinction. However, this is not really the case. Pavlov found that if he waited several hours after extinguishing salivation to the bell, ringing the bell tended to elicit the conditioned response again. While the response was weaker than when originally learned, and could in turn be re-extinguished, the most striking point was that it reoccurred *at all*. Pavlov called this return of the conditioned response **spontaneous recovery**, which is defined as the restoration of the response when the CS is presented after some time has elapsed since extinction training (see Figure 3.5). Spontaneous recovery of extinguished responses has been well demonstrated in a variety of species, sometimes after long time periods. This implies that, in terms of conditioning, what we learn is never really forgotten, but at best is simply overlaid with different experience. Instances where old fears re-emerge long after we thought we had conquered them (for example, fear of public speaking, fear of doctors, etc.) may reflect the enduring nature of conditioned behaviour. The results of research on extinction and spontaneous recovery suggest that conditioning is a 'one way street', whereby conditioned behaviour can be modified, but no conditioning is ever simply erased. Instead, extinction, and even new learning, are overlaid on earlier learning (Rescorla 2001).

spontaneous recovery in classical conditioning, the reoccurrence of the CR when the CS is presented after some time has elapsed since extinction training.

Higher Order Conditioning

We have seen that the principles of classical conditioning provide a mechanism whereby new stimuli can come to elicit a reflex response. Typically, the conditioned stimulus serves as a signal allowing anticipation of the UCS, which can be helpful to the organism. Sometimes, the sequence involves stimuli like food or water, which are beneficial to the individual. In other cases, the CS may signal something harmful, like heat or electric shock (for example, farm animals typically develop a fear of electric fences after a single experience of getting shocked). However, sometimes we encounter situations where the conditioned stimulus seems to have no direct connection to an unconditioned stimulus. For example, a child hears the word 'cake' and begins to salivate. How can this arise from the processes we have discussed?

Pavlov proposed a possible mechanism for such remote associations in terms of what he called **higher order conditioning**, where a previously established conditioned stimulus is used as if it were an unconditioned stimulus to create conditioning to a new stimulus. While the description may seem complex, the process itself is easy to grasp. In Pavlov's original experiment, he first trained a dog to salivate to the sound of a buzzer (CS_1), using food as a UCS. Once conditioning was established, he introduced a new stimulus, a black square, which was repeatedly paired with the sound of the buzzer (but not food). After several such pairings, presenting the black square alone tended to elicit salivation (see Figure 3.6). Not surprisingly, the effect was rather weak, since each trial also functioned as extinction training for the original buzzer–food association. Pavlov called such conditioning *second order* conditioning, and tried to extend the sequence by using the black square as if it were a UCS, and attempting to link a new stimulus (*third order* conditioning). He found this was not possible when food was the UCS; however, he was able to create third order conditioning when conditioning leg withdrawal, with electric shock as the UCS. (This result may actually tell us more about the significance of aversive stimuli like electric shock than it does about higher order conditioning as such. As with extinction effects, the distinguishing element may be the use of stimuli associated with stress or negative emotions.)

> **higher order conditioning** a form of classical conditioning in which a previously established conditioned stimulus is used as if it were an unconditioned stimulus to create conditioning to a new stimulus.

Dogs, of course, are not exactly like people, and the everyday world is not exactly like the laboratory. Without the controlled conditions of a laboratory, it can be difficult to prove the existence of higher order conditioning, but many researchers believe that analogues exist in human behaviour. For example, it is likely that the child who salivates to the word 'cake' has previously developed a conditioned response of salivating to the sight of cake (the original CS). Then, in the process of learning to talk, the word 'cake' became associated to the sight of the object it described; by repeatedly pairing word to the sight of cake, higher order conditioning became established.

It is tempting, certainly, to speculate on how language learning may be closely linked to higher order conditioning. Parents sometimes will verbalize (for example, 'that's bad!') while physically punishing a child; it is easy to understand how 'that's bad!' would then come to evoke fear and withdrawal, almost like a physical blow. If later, receiving a poor grade on a school report card leads to 'that's bad!', a poor grade could itself become a conditioned stimulus for fear and withdrawal. Precisely how significant this process is in everyday life, no one really knows. At the very least, we know that words *do* elicit emotional reactions, and such reactions are consistent with higher order conditioning. Rather than speculating further on this issue, let us examine some of the evidence for classical conditioning processes in everyday behaviour.

Applications of Classical Conditioning

While deceptively simple at first glance, classical conditioning seems to be a potent process for learning in a wide variety of species. In humans, salivation to food cues, fear arousal in the

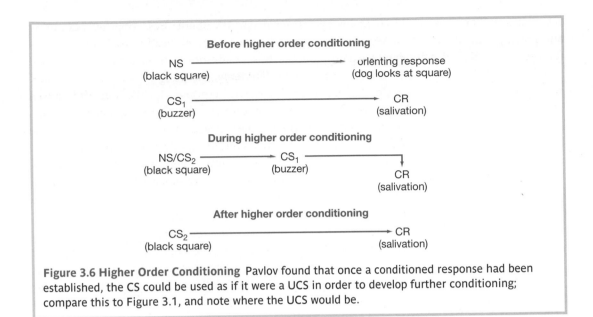

Before higher order conditioning

NS ⟶ orienting response
(black square)   (dog looks at square)

CS₁ ⟶ CR
(buzzer)   (salivation)

During higher order conditioning

NS/CS₂ ⟶ CS₁ ⟶
(black square)   (buzzer)   ↓ CR
(salivation)

After higher order conditioning

CS₂ ⟶ CR
(black square)   (salivation)

Figure 3.6 Higher Order Conditioning Pavlov found that once a conditioned response had been established, the CS could be used as if it were a UCS in order to develop further conditioning; compare this to Figure 3.1, and note where the UCS would be.

shower when the sound of a toilet flushing occurs, and a wide range of other instances show how many types of stimuli can come to elicit reflex responses. Sometimes, time itself can be a conditioned stimulus. For example, most pet owners notice that their pets are sensitive to the timing of daily routines, ranging from meal times to when a particular family member comes home. Since mammals (and a range of other species) have an internal biological clock, time of day can be an unseen stimulus for various responses, including hunger pangs. If you normally eat meals at a particular time of day, you have likely noticed that your stomach becomes active when that time approaches. This conditioned response enables your body to correctly anticipate the arrival of food (provided you don't skip a meal!). While these examples illustrate classical conditioning, note that some involve more than simply *motor reflexes*. To understand this more clearly, let us look at some other areas where the role of classical conditioning has been explored.

Conditioned Emotional Responses

Pavlov's work on classical conditioning became known relatively quickly – perhaps because he was already famous for his work on digestion. (By contrast, an American named Louis Twitmeyer, who discovered the same phenomenon almost simultaneously with Pavlov, died essentially unrecognized.) Among those who saw the importance of this new paradigm was John B. Watson, who saw in Pavlov's work a model for the behaviourist methodology he was trying to foster. One area where he saw potential was in the study of emotions, which had previously been the domain of the introspectionists. The introspectionists studied emotions, like other aspects of experience, by trying to describe the mental states involved. Watson instead believed that emotions represented observable responses, and proceeded to study the issue by attempting to create emotional responses experimentally. While he used a number of subjects, including his own children, the best-known case was a study done with Rosalie Rayner, using a toddler identified as Albert (Watson and Rayner 1920).

Albert was an 11-month-old boy who had been admitted to hospital for reasons unrelated to Watson's research. Watson initially observed Albert at play, and tested his responses to various stimulus objects, including blocks, a ball of cotton, some furry material and a white rat. The boy, like most children of his age, seemed curious about these objects, examining and playing with them. Then, Watson and Rayner began to systematically associate the white rat with the noise of a loud metal gong. On the first conditioning trial, Albert approached the animal without fear. Suddenly, the gong sounded behind him. The loud noise elicited a startle response (UCR), and also caused Albert to begin crying. Three times, the same sequence of events was repeated. Each time, Albert began crying at the sound of the gong. After a total of seven conditioning trials on two occasions, the white rat was presented without ringing the gong – and Albert began crying. Thus, a fear reaction had been classically conditioned to the rat, which previously had been a neutral stimulus. Watson called this fear a **conditioned emotional response**.

conditioned emotional response an emotional response such as fear which is established through classical conditioning.

About a week later, Watson and Rayner returned to test Albert again. This time, the experimenters showed Albert the objects from the original session. The toddler continued to show interest in the blocks and several masks. However, certain objects – balls of cotton, a white fur coat and a Santa Claus mask with a white beard – elicited the same crying and withdrawal as the white rat. In terms of classical conditioning, Albert had *generalized* his response to any white, fluffy stimulus!

Having established that fear could be classically conditioned, Watson and Rayner then sought to eliminate the fear response. To accomplish this, they used Pavlov's extinction procedure – presenting the white rat without pairing it with the sound of the gong. They tried this several times over a three-week period, but found that, contrary to their expectations, the fear did not extinguish. Unfortunately, before they could pursue the matter further, Albert was discharged from the hospital, ending the test.

With hindsight, we can recognize two factors that contributed to the failure of extinction. One is the fact that fear responses, like various other responses of the autonomic nervous system, are hard to extinguish (Gantt 1966). (Recall Pavlov's experiences with higher order conditioning – the conditioned fear produced by electric shock may account for his success in conditioning leg withdrawal to shock, but not salivation to food.) In addition, the occurrence of stimulus generalization, which is common for fear responses, tends to make extinction difficult, since a whole *range* of stimuli must be extinguished. Today, other techniques have been developed to deal with conditioned fear responses, since extinction training has such limited impact (see Chapter 9 for a discussion of such techniques, including *systematic desensitization*).

Before continuing our discussion of conditioned emotional responses, it is appropriate to consider the ethics of Watson and Rayner's study. Not surprisingly, they have been frequently criticized for the questionable ethics and potential harm of their test. Without attempting to second-guess past actions, it should be noted that the intent was not to permanently harm Albert; at the outset, Watson believed both conditioning *and* extinction would be successful. At the same time, it is clear that the procedure involved suffering for Albert, and it is unlikely that such a test would pass current ethical standards. (For a follow-up discussion of this study, see Harris 1979).

Watson and Rayner's demonstration, however questionable ethically, served to illustrate that emotional responses like fear could at least potentially arise from classical conditioning. In fact, most behaviourists would argue that phobias (a clinical category for irrational fears) can best be understood as conditioned emotional responses. Thus, anything from the fear of water to the fear of dogs could result from a traumatic episode in which the stimulus (water, dogs, etc.) was associated with a pain-evoking event.

However, human emotions extend well beyond fear. Could other emotions also be classically conditioned? Behaviourists would assert not only that such conditioning can happen, but also that it is responsible for most of the emotional richness of our lives. A new-born infant may instinctively respond to contact with the mother's body, but later this pleasurable response becomes associated to the mother's face, and still later to objects in the home, and maybe even to the home itself. Individuals who experience pleasure at hearing a favourite old song are experiencing emotions which have become associated to the conditioned stimulus of the music. Even when we go to the movies, conditioning is involved (probably through a higher order process) in our responses to heroes, villains and a variety of plot situations.

Words may even be the most refined of stimuli in terms of emotional conditioning. Words have a literal meaning and an emotional meaning; what is curious is that the two often do not correspond. For example, terms of endearment may range from the silly to the meaningless – 'little cabbage' or 'snuggie-poo'. Even more interesting is the emotional response to profanity. Generally, what are considered 'dirty words' varies from language to language – in English, most forbidden words relate to sexuality; in French, they usually relate to religion. Such differences relate not to the literal meaning of the words, but to the emotional significance of sexuality and religion in the respective cultures. When Shakespeare noted that 'a rose by any other name would smell as sweet', he recognized that the word is only a label – and labels depend on learning for their meaning. Without classical conditioning, it is likely that all language would be emotionally meaningless!

Try it Yourself

- When I (MH) was 3, a robin, protecting its nest, pecked me on the head. To this day, I have a fear of birds. How would Pavlov explain this? What were the UCS and the UCR? What are the CS and the CR today? How can you explain the fact that I have no fear of penguins or hummingbirds?

- *Jaws* is a classic movie depicting a huge shark killing swimmers in an Atlantic seaside town. When the movie first came out, many people who saw it became afraid to go swimming, even though they had never been attacked by even a small fish when swimming previously. How would classical conditioning principles explain this?

- Can you identify one fear which you feel affects you significantly? Can you recall a traumatic event that produced the fear (for example, a fear of dogs resulting from having been bitten as a child)? If not, do you think this invalidates the idea that phobias are based on conditioning?

Conditioned Drug and Immune Responses

As discussed in relation to the biological approach to psychology, the human body is a highly integrated system, involving neural, hormonal and immunological activity. Although we have not discussed the possible physiological mechanisms underlying classical conditioning, Pavlov believed that the mechanism was neural. Assuming this is true (and the available evidence supports this idea), one might still ask whether conditioning can influence other bodily processes, such as the response to drugs or disease. The exploration of such possibilities represents perhaps the most exciting area of conditioning research today.

Pavlov himself was interested in how drug reactions might be classically conditioned. In one study, the sound of a tone was repeatedly paired with a drug which induced vomiting (UCS); after several trials, the dog began to vomit at the sound of the tone alone. Similarly, diabetics taking insulin by injection sometimes show decreased glucose levels to cues associated with the injection (Stockhorst *et al.* 2004). This suggests that stimuli present when a drug is administered may acquire the power to induce the drug's effects.

Interestingly, other work has suggested that with some drugs the conditioned response is the *opposite* to the primary effect of the drug itself. For example, rats were conditioned by giving injections of morphine in a specific environment. While morphine normally reduces sensitivity to painful stimuli, the rats after conditioning showed *increased* sensitivity to pain when placed in the conditioning context (Siegel 1976). This phenomenon of conditioning associated with drug use has been proposed as the basis of *tolerance* effects for addictive drugs, whereby repeated usage leads to lower response to the drug (MacRae *et al.* 1987; McDonald and Siegel 2004). Sometimes the cues involved are based on the location; for example, being in a pub can trigger both cigarette cravings and cardiac changes in smokers (Lazev *et al.* 1999). Internal bodily cues may also serve as conditioned stimuli. Thus, the physiological state or even the emotional state (such as anxiety) of the individual prior to using may trigger the desire for an addictive drug (Siegel 2005).

Why would conditioning mimic the effects of some drugs, and counteract others? At present we don't have a complete explanation, but the result seems to depend on the type of drug, and the body's response to it. For some drugs, like the vomiting agent used by Pavlov, the body reacts by showing a strong reaction, which gradually diminishes as the drug dissipates. By contrast, certain drugs, such as morphine, interact with the body's natural mechanisms for maintaining equilibrium (called *homeostasis*). In these cases, there is an initial reaction triggered by the drug, which is then followed by an opposite reaction, triggered by the body's homeostatic mechanisms. As a result, the conditioned stimulus becomes associated with the second reaction – which is opposite to that of the drug itself. Such *compensatory conditioned responses* have even been implicated in drug addiction fatalities: when drug addicts take drugs in an unfamiliar location (which doesn't trigger the offsetting conditioned response), the result can be an accidental (sometimes fatal) overdose (Siegel and Ramos 2002).

While drugs seem to interact with the body's own equilibrium processes, what about the immune system? Can classical conditioning affect the way our body reacts to disease? Research suggests this may be a real possibility. In one study, rats were given saccharin-sweetened water at the same time that they were injected with cyclosporine, a drug which inhibits immune system response. After several such pairings, tests showed that the taste of saccharin alone was able to suppress the immune system of the rats (Ader and Cohen 1975). Other studies have shown similar effects (see Ader and Cohen 1985). These studies imply that stimuli associated with low points of immune system functioning (for example, gifts received during a major illness, or objects associated with the death of a loved one) may continue to impair immune response at later times. Conversely, researchers have also been able to use conditioning to *enhance* immune system response (Alvarez-Borda *et al.* 1995; Gorcynski *et al.* 1982). While the practical implications have yet to be adequately tested, it may well turn out that conditioning effects can influence our long-term health (Ader 2003).

Research on conditioned emotional responses and drug/immune effects indicates that Pavlov's basic paradigm is still providing us with new insights on behaviour. The significance of classical conditioning is easily underestimated, since involuntary responses are often overlooked in our daily experience; this is partly because they *are* involuntary, and operate with no conscious intervention. Equally, conscious attempts at controlling reflexes have minimal success – as those who recognize that their fear responses are irrational can testify. While we cannot say at present that all issues related to classical conditioning have been resolved, neither have we reached the limit in terms of finding new applications and insights.

OPERANT CONDITIONING

As important as classical conditioning is, it must be recognized that it only deals with how new stimuli come to control existing involuntary responses. While reflexes and the 'gut-level' responses associated with emotions play a significant role in our everyday experience, most of our behaviour is self-generated, or *voluntary*. Behaviours like driving a car, working at a computer or calling a friend on the telephone are not elicited by conditioned stimuli. Instead,

operant conditioning in the behaviourist approach, the form of learning concerned with changes in emitted responses (voluntary behaviour) as a function of their consequences.

they are *emitted* – that is, generated by the individual as a way of influencing the surrounding environment. In order to understand the dynamics of such behaviour, we need to consider a different approach to learning. This approach, called **operant conditioning**, deals with how voluntary (emitted) responses change over time as a function of their consequences. For example, if Johnny climbs a tree (voluntary response) and gets hurt (consequence), he may not climb the tree thereafter.

To understand the origins of operant conditioning, we need to go back to the work of Edwin Thorndike. Although Thorndike was studying animal behaviour and learning at roughly the same time as Pavlov, his approach was very different. Whereas Pavlov began with an interest in digestion and then became interested in conditioning, Thorndike was initially interested in problem solving and intelligence. Consequently, instead of focusing on simple reflexes, Thorndike studied situations where an animal was actively interacting with its environment. In a typical experiment, a cat was confined in a 'puzzle box', a cage-like structure from which it could free itself by pressing a lever. As any cat owner can testify, cats generally dislike confinement; hence the cats were typically eager to escape. However, Thorndike increased the incentive by depriving the animals of food prior to testing, and then placing food outside the puzzle box, where it was visible to the cat. Not surprisingly, the cats learned to press the lever, thereby escaping and obtaining the food (Thorndike 1898; see Figure 3.7).

Two primary conclusions emerged from Thorndike's work. The first was that if one measured *how long* it took a cat to escape, the time gradually declined with repeated trials. This improvement in performance represented a change in behaviour as a result of experience – in other words, *learning*. The other major conclusion concerned the relationship between the cat's behaviour and its consequences. Both escape and obtaining food appeared to be desirable to the cats, leading Thorndike to conclude that the satisfying outcome was what led to the behaviour being repeated. By contrast, flailing at the walls of the box, and other behaviours which did not lead to escape, declined. From observations like this, Thorndike formulated his *law of effect*: behaviour which leads to a satisfying outcome tends to be repeated, while behaviour that leads to an unsatisfactory outcome is unlikely to be repeated. Note that the law of effect makes no reference to reducing hunger, desire to escape or other mentalistic concepts. The observational nature of the principle was one of the factors which attracted the attention of Watson and later behaviourists.

Thorndike's research laid the foundation for the study of non-reflex behaviour. By emphasizing the connection between an action and its outcome, his law of effect provided a framework for studying such behaviour. In Thorndike's system, responses are initiated by the organism as part of dealing with its surroundings, not as a reflex triggered by an environmental stimulus. Depending on the consequences, a particular behaviour might or might not be repeated in the future. For example, a child who draws a picture and presents it to Mum may receive praise; this will encourage the child to draw more pictures in the future. On the other hand, if the child takes a cookie without permission and is scolded, they are less likely to try this again. In its simplest form, the law of effect reaffirms what might be considered 'common sense'. At the same time, by suggesting a simple framework for the study of non-reflex behaviours, it fits well with the developing behaviourist approach. Yet, while Thorndike's work was acknowledged by Watson, and stimulated a variety of subsequent research, it did not result in a coherent system comparable to Pavlov's paradigm until the work of B. F. Skinner in the 1930s.

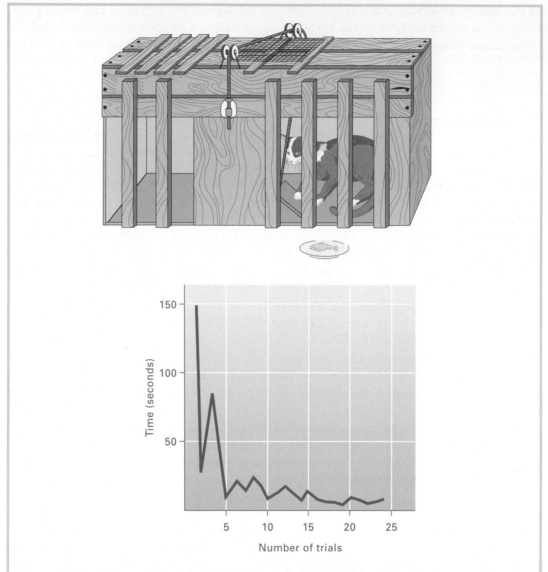

Figure 3.7 Thorndike and the Law of Effect Thorndike explored learning by placing cats in a box like that shown here; pressing on the pedal activated a mechanism which allowed the cat to get out of the box. As shown by the graph, over several trials, the cat learned to escape much more quickly; Thorndike explained this by saying behaviour changed as a result of the desirable consequence of escape.

Skinner and Operant Conditioning

Within behaviourism, B. F. Skinner occupies a position of influence equal to, and in some ways greater than, that of John B. Watson. As the pioneer of operant conditioning, he almost single-handedly created a framework for the study of learned behaviour. Skinner's contributions are significant in terms both of research methods and conceptual analysis. To understand this, we need to consider the origins of his work.

Try it Yourself

'Satisfaction', like beauty, is in the eye of the beholder. We all differ in terms of what we consider to be satisfying, and sometimes what other people find satisfying surprises us. Consider, for example, the foods you like to eat and the clothes you like to wear. Clearly your preferences are not those of everyone else. Make a list of some things you would find 'satisfying' and some that you would find 'unsatisfying'. Ask a friend to do the same and compare your lists. Since friends often become friends because of their commonalities in what they enjoy, you will probably find many commonalities on your two lists. But you will undoubtedly find many differences. Ask an older person, a parent or grandparent perhaps, to make up a list as well. There are probably fewer commonalities between this list and the lists of you and your friend, and many of the differences reflect the age/generational differences between the list-makers. Keep the differences in lists in mind the next time you buy a gift for someone: we often select a gift thinking of what *we* would find satisfying instead of what the *recipient* would find satisfying!

While training as a graduate student at Harvard, Skinner was doing studies of animal behaviour somewhat similar to Thorndike's. Influenced by Watson, he found himself frustrated that so much of the vocabulary of psychology seemed clouded by the ambiguities of everyday language. In particular, he felt that terms referring to mental states (for example, 'drive', 'belief', 'intent') were both vague and unnecessary to the understanding of behaviour. For Skinner, the inner workings of the mind (and the body) were a 'black box', inaccessible to direct observation. This point of view was shared by all behaviourists, but Skinner went further, arguing that even if thoughts and other mental states *could* be studied, they would have no real value in explaining behaviour. Instead, the environment in which a response occurs, the response itself, and the response's consequence are all that are necessary to understand behaviour. By insisting that mental states are both inaccessible to study *and irrelevant to understanding behaviour*, Skinner was advocating a point of view which has come to be called **radical behaviourism**.

radical behaviourism a position adopted by Watson and Skinner which argues that mental states are both inaccessible to scientific study and irrelevant to understanding behaviour.

Given his concerns about amibiguities in language, one of Skinner's first goals was to develop new terms for describing and analysing behaviour. He began by coining the term *operant conditioning* to replace Thorndike's 'instrumental learning'; similarly, he renamed classical conditioning as 'respondent conditioning'. He referred to emitted behaviours as operant responses, arguing that 'voluntary behaviour' implies undesirable notions about free will. By developing this new vocabulary, he attempted to purge the study of behaviour of all excess conceptual baggage (Skinner 1987). (Skinner even went so far as to say radical behaviourism is not a part of psychology, but rather an approach to understanding certain issues both inside and outside psychology.) Operant conditioning has in fact become established as a major form of behaviourism, as we shall see. While Skinner often argued that his approach is pragmatic, not theoretical (Skinner 1950), his critics have disagreed. In fact, Skinner's framework is generally regarded as a *meta-theory* – that is, a theory about what makes a good theory of behaviour. In this sense, the apparent simplicity of his ideas can sometimes be deceptive.

Key Thinker: **Burrhus Frederic Skinner**

Burrhus Frederic Skinner (1904–90) is probably the best-known American behaviourist, and the founder of operant conditioning. His early years were rather peripatetic – educated at Hamilton College and then Harvard (receiving his PhD in 1931), he taught at the University of Minnesota and Indiana University. During World War II, he did research with a military flavour, including a programme designed to teach pigeons to direct missiles to targets while flying in the nose-cone; the technique was never implemented. In 1947 he returned to Harvard to deliver the annual William James Lectures; in 1948 he was appointed as a full professor at Harvard. Skinner's development of operant conditioning began while training as a graduate student at Harvard. Although his initial work on animal behaviour was somewhat similar to Thorndike's, he became influenced by Watson's ideas, and began a systematic attempt to purge psychology of mentalistic concepts and language. While his theories have remained controversial, the practical applications of operant conditioning have been widespead. Skinner died in Cambridge, Massachusetts, in 1990.

A second key aspect is the interaction between the *concepts* of operant conditioning and the *procedures* used – that is, the methods of observing and measuring behaviour. As a graduate student doing research with rats, Skinner found that the typical learning tasks, like mazes or Thorndike's puzzle boxes, required extensive labour. For each trial, the researcher had to put the animal in the box, record behaviour, retrieve the animal after the trial, etc. In order to simplify this process, Skinner developed an apparatus which would allow running continuous trials, with behaviour automatically recorded. He called this apparatus (which resembled a small box with a lever within) an 'auto-environmental chamber', but it became known (to Skinner's lasting dismay) as a Skinner box! While it accomplished Skinner's basic goal of automating Thorndike's approach, it also led to other consequences. The most notable of these involves the way behaviour was measured. Since pressing the lever in the Skinner box could be considered analogous to the cat pressing the lever in Thorndike's puzzle box, counting the number of presses (that is, the frequency of response) became the standard measure of operant learning. In some respects, this is unfortunate, since it has led to operant conditioning mostly considering *only* the frequency of behaviour; as a result, aspects of behaviour such as intensity, duration or quality of responses have been largely ignored. (Consider, for example, the many different aspects of a response like hitting a tennis ball – especially if one is comparing an amateur and a pro player!) While the focus on frequency was a practical consideration, it eventually became part of the overall conceptual framework as well.

Although research based on analysing the frequency of behaviour has often been highly productive, it should be noted that in everyday life, frequency is not always the most meaningful aspect of behaviour. (For example, should we judge the quality of an artist by *how many* works they create, or should we look at the *content* of their work?) Thus, operant conditioning, while claiming to be a pragmatic analysis unencumbered by theory, in fact has evolved out of a unique set of assumptions about both theory and methodology. As with other approaches to psychology, recognizing the foundations of behaviourism should help in comprehending where it has led in the understanding of behaviour.

Reinforcers and Reinforcement

One of the first issues which Skinner attempted to address was Thorndike's law of effect. While it is intuitively obvious that a response which leads to a satisfying consequence is likely to be repeated, Skinner was bothered by the vagueness of 'satisfying'. To avoid this, he coined a new term, 'reinforcer'. A **reinforcer** is a stimulus which, when it follows a response, results in a change in the probability of the response recurring. Thus, unlike notions of satisfaction, a reinforcer becomes an *observable environmental event*. **Reinforcement** is the process by which a reinforcer *increases* the probability of a response. (Note that in talking about probabilities, one is implicitly describing how *often* a response occurs – i.e., frequency.)

reinforcer in operant conditioning, a stimulus which, when it follows a response, alters the probability of the response recurring.

reinforcement in operant conditioning, the process by which a reinforcer increases the probability of a response.

The most basic reinforcers are those which are related to survival, such as food or water. Such reinforcers are described as **primary reinforcers**, since they have an innate biological significance. For example, a baby cries because it is hungry. When it receives food, this serves as a reinforcer for the response of crying. As a result of this reinforcement process, the baby is more likely to cry the next time it is hungry. (Hunger, of course, is a reference to an internal state which can't be directly observed. To avoid such terms, Skinner would talk about the length of time since the baby was last fed. Any parent who has monitored a baby's feeding schedule can testify that this is a reasonably accurate gauge of hunger!) While food and water are the most common primary reinforcers, many other items (including clothing when it's cold, air to breathe, and drugs such as nicotine or opiates) also seem to function as primary reinforcers. Note that primary reinforcers also typically elicit some form of reflex response – that is, they are *also* unconditioned reinforcers, in terms of classical conditioning. Food, for example, is a positive primary reinforcer, but also elicits salivation. This dual nature underlines the fact that primary reinforcers seem to have direct biological significance.

primary reinforcer in operant conditioning, a stimulus whose capacity to act as a reinforcer is based on an innate biological significance, such as food, water or electric shock.

By contrast, there are a large number of environmental events which seem to act as reinforcers, but are not based on biological survival. For example, attention, praise, money and trophies can all act as reinforcers. Reinforcing stimuli like these are described as **conditioned reinforcers**. As the name suggests, conditioned reinforcers are stimuli which assume reinforcing properties because they have been reliably associated with a primary reinforcer (this is actually a form of classical conditioning, with the conditioned reinforcer and primary reinforcer related as CS and UCS, respectively). For example, Skinner has argued that attention becomes a conditioned reinforcer in early infancy because

conditioned reinforcer in operant conditioning, stimuli which act as reinforcers but are not based on biological survival, such as praise, money or criticism.

it precedes (and is therefore associated with) receiving primary reinforcers: the baby cries, an adult gives attention by coming to see what is wrong, and then the adult provides a primary reinforcer like food or a dry nappy. A young child may receive praise for a particular action, and receive a cookie; soon, praise itself becomes a reinforcer, because it is associated with the cookie. Later, other conditioned reinforcers may develop as stimuli are paired with existing conditioned reinforcers. For example, the adult often smiles while giving praise to the child, and the smile alone becomes reinforcing on its own. (Recall how higher order conditioning allows new stimuli to become linked to existing conditioned stimuli.) Since conditioned reinforcers are based on learning, not innate factors, the potential range of such reinforcers is virtually unlimited. Perhaps the most powerful conditioned reinforcer in our society is money, which can be used to obtain a wide range of other reinforcers, both primary and conditioned.

Reinforcement, the process of increasing the frequency of a response by means of a reinforcer, is at once both simple and subtle. One element which is important for proper reinforcement is contiguity – that is, the reinforcer should immediately follow the response. If a child does something desirable, then praise should be given *immediately*; if not, one runs the risk that the reinforcer will influence a subsequent response. For example, 2-year-old Johnny uses the toilet instead of wetting his pants. Half an hour later, Johnny's mother realizes what has happened, and praises Johnny – who is now engaged in pulling books out of the bookcase. In this situation, the positive reinforcer is unlikely to be strongly associated with going to the toilet, and may in fact reinforce the less desirable current behaviour! Parents sometimes misunderstand the significance of contiguity, but it is a powerful factor in operant conditioning. When the wrong response is reinforced, the tendency is to assume that the principles don't work. But Skinner once commented that if an experiment doesn't turn out the way we expect, there is a temptation to tell the animal, 'Behave properly!' However, in such cases, the animal *always* behaves – the error is in our understanding (Skinner 1967).

The world today: **Video Games**

In the past 20 years, a new form of entertainment has entered our lives: video games. Some people say they are good, and some say they are bad. Good or bad (and there may be elements of each), there is no question that many people are spending hours each day playing these games, some even to the extent where they seem to be addicted. Why do people spend so much time on these games? Skinner would answer, 'Well, obviously, they are being reinforced for playing.' By Skinner's definition of positive reinforcement, it *is* obvious: positive reinforcement increases the behaviour. And video games are highly reinforcing. In the first place, for most video games, feedback (which in itself is reinforcing) comes immediately: information that one has responded correctly comes immediately after the response and is often accompanied by points, flashes of light, screen congratulations, advancement to a higher level of game-playing, etc. The feedback is not the only reinforcing part of video games, however. As in any other situation, what is reinforcing to one person may not be reinforcing to another. For example, reinforcement for successful playing may be the admiration of peers, mastering the game, achieving a 'personal best', and so on. Richard Wood and his colleagues (2004) (some of whom are 'gamers' themselves) conducted an online survey of 382 university students who played a variety of video games, asking them about what they found important (i.e., reinforcing) in the structure of various games. Here is what they found:

- Good quality, realistic sound and graphics were important for both males and females, although the exact form of the graphics in particular revealed gender differences. Males prefer realistic graphics with competitive, action-based, fast-moving events, such as simulated battles and sports contests, while females prefer gentler, cartoon-like graphics with fantasy-based themes.

- The ability to compete with or form alliances with other players online was considered important/ reinforcing for males, although less so for females. (Can you speculate on why this might be?)

- Both males and females found the ability to get into the game and to advance in the game quickly to be important.

Not surprisingly, success at playing video games makes people feel good and induces them to play more (Chumbley and Griffiths 2006). No wonder it's so easy to get hooked!

Misunderstanding how reinforcement works can lead to difficulties in trying to change behaviour. In everyday life, people tend to invoke rationalizations for failing to change, particularly when it comes to bad habits. A would-be dieter, or a heavy smoker, might say, 'I lack willpower.' Skinner would argue that such phrases have no real explanatory value, and in fact obscure the actual dynamics of the situation. A smoker, for example, may worry that they will develop lung cancer some years hence, and thus wishes to quit. When the attempt fails, the person concludes that it is because of personal weakness. In fact, they are ignoring the actual reinforcers – the nicotine, the conditioned reinforcement of smoking being associated with enjoyable moments, possibly peer approval, and so forth. Compared to these *immediate* reinforcers for the act of smoking, the perceived value of better health some time *in the future* has much less effect on the response of quitting. Thus, both *what* the reinforcers are, and *when* they are received, is crucial to understanding the dynamics of behaviour. For example, the reinforcing value of video games is discussed in *The World Today: Video Games.*

As noted previously, reinforcers are stimuli that alter the probability of a behaviour. While this is correct, it should be noted that, thus far, we have been talking as if all reinforcers are desirable things. However, just as Thorndike distinguished between 'satisfying consequences' and 'unsatisfying consequences', Skinner recognized that not all reinforcers are alike. In fact, the examples we have been discussing all represent **positive reinforcers**, which Skinner defined, not by intuitive notions of satisfaction, but by the effect on behaviour: if a reinforcer which follows a response makes that response more likely in the future, it is a positive reinforcer. In everyday terms, a positive reinforcer is similar to what is often called a 'reward' – but of course, Skinner would reject such words as being too imprecise for scientific purposes. By contrast, a reinforcer which makes the behaviour *less* likely in the future Skinner called a **negative reinforcer**. This would be equivalent to Thorndike's dissatisfying consequences; in everyday terms, something unpleasant or aversive. (Note: some researchers refer to 'punishers' instead of 'negative reinforcers'; however, this discussion will follow Skinner's usage.) Like positive reinforcers, negative reinforcers can be either primary or conditioned: negative primary reinforcers are consequences which cause harm or threaten survival, such as a physical blow or electric shock. Negative reinforcers may also be conditioned, by being associated with negative primary reinforcers. For example, a child may learn to associate criticism or the word

positive reinforcer in operant conditioning, a stimulus which, when it follows a response, serves to increase the probability of the response in the future.

negative reinforcer in operant conditioning, an aversive stimulus which, when it follows a response, serves to decrease the probability of the response in the future.

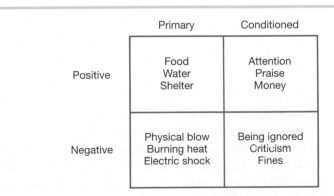

	Primary	Conditioned
Positive	Food Water Shelter	Attention Praise Money
Negative	Physical blow Burning heat Electric shock	Being ignored Criticism Fines

Figure 3.8 Types of Reinforcers Both positive and negative reinforcers can be either primary or conditioned, as the chart shows. Note that the reinforcers mentioned are examples, not a complete list of possibilities; Skinner would also argue that defining any reinforcer can only be done with reference to a specific situation!

'bad' with being hit; criticism then becomes a negative conditioned reinforcer. (For an overview of the various types of reinforcers, see Figure 3.8.)

At first glance, talking about positive and negative reinforcers may not seem much different from Thorndike's satisfying and unsatisfying consequences. Indeed, some critics have suggested that both the law of effect and the definition of a reinforcer are circular, since we cannot determine the value of a stimulus until we observe how it affects behaviour. For example, we only know something is a positive reinforcer when we see that it results in an increase in the probability of behaviour. This issue is still a source of debate, but it should be noted that Skinner went much further than Thorndike in analysing how the relationship between a response and a reinforcer affects behaviour, as we will see in the next section.

Contingencies of Reinforcement

In general, operant responses are freely produced by the individual, but the likelihood of making a response is determined by its consequences on previous occasions. For example, if Tim is given a cookie for having finished his peas at dinner, he is likely to eat his peas in the future. Thus, there is a relationship between the behaviour (the response of eating peas) and its consequence (the cookie as positive reinforcer). In Skinner's terminology, the relationship between a response and a reinforcer is called the **contingency of reinforcement**. (A 'contingency' describes how something depends on another event.) As he realized, identifying the contingency is a powerful tool for understanding changes in behaviour.

contingency of reinforcement in operant conditioning, a description of the relationship between a response and a reinforcer.

One type of contingency is *reinforcement*, as already mentioned. Reinforcement *always* results in an *increase* in the likelihood of a response. In the example above, it is easy to recognize that a biscuit is a positive reinforcer, and that the likelihood of eating peas will increase. Thus, when a response is followed immediately by a positive reinforcer, the response becomes more likely; Skinner called this process **positive reinforcement**, because it is reinforcement using a positive reinforcer.

positive reinforcement in operant conditioning, a process of increasing the probability of a response by immediately following the response with a desirable stimulus (a positive reinforcer).

A second possible contingency is when a response is immediately followed by a *negative* reinforcer. Since this represents an aversive consequence, do you think that it would make the response more likely in the future? Obviously, the answer is no – in fact, the response would become *less* likely. For example, 3-year-old Sally pokes a pin in an electric outlet and receives a shock. In the future, Sally is not likely to repeat this action! Since the probability of the response does not increase, this cannot be termed a case of *reinforcement*. In everyday life, one would likely call it 'punishment' – and that is the term used in operant conditioning as well. (It is one of the rare instances where Skinner adopted a term with obvious everyday meaning!) He defined **punishment** as a process whereby a response is followed by a *negative reinforcer*, which results in a decrease in the probability of the response.

punishment in operant conditioning, a process whereby a response is followed by a negative reinforcer, which results in a decrease in the probability of the response.

The distinction between positive reinforcement and punishment goes to the heart of Skinner's framework. In order to understand the dynamics of learning, one must be able to identify the contingency which is involved. For example, parents and teachers often react to a child who is misbehaving by scolding the child. The intent, of course, is to decrease the undesirable behaviour – that is, to use *punishment*. What sometimes happens, however, is that the child continues to misbehave, and may even become more disruptive. The frustrated adult exclaims, 'I don't know what's wrong with Johnny! The more I punish him, the worse he behaves!' Skinner would respond by looking at the situation from the child's point of view (since the child is the one receiving a reinforcer). Given that the disruptive behaviour *increases*, Skinner would say that obviously the child is receiving reinforcement, and so the reinforcer (scolding) is actually a positive reinforcer for the child! At first glance, this may seem silly, but in fact, scolding requires paying attention to the child – and attention is a powerful positive reinforcer, especially for a child who feels neglected. What typically happens is that a busy adult ignores the child who plays quietly, but immediately responds to misbehaviour; so, in order to get attention, the child misbehaves more and more. The moral of this example is that the *organism* (i.e., the child) determines the significance of the reinforcer, *not* the environment which delivers the reinforcer (the adult, in this case).

Reinforcement and punishment represent the most common contingencies in operant conditioning – they are roughly equivalent to the old notion of using 'the carrot and the stick' to train a mule. However, reinforcers can also be related to behaviour in other, more indirect, ways. For example, it is also possible to produce an increase in behaviour by *terminating* or *withholding* a negative reinforcer (an aversive stimulus); this process is called **negative reinforcement**. For example, a teenager is nagged by a parent to clean up a messy bedroom. In this situation, the nagging is unpleasant – a negative reinforcer. When the teenager eventually (albeit reluctantly) cleans up the room, the parent stops nagging. If we look at this from the viewpoint of operant conditioning, the desired response is cleaning up the room. As long as the response is *not* made, a negative reinforcer is presented (the nagging). When the response is finally made, the negative reinforcer ceases!

negative reinforcement in operant conditioning, a process for increasing the probability of a response in which a response immediately leads to termination or withholding of an aversive stimulus (negative reinforcer); note that since the response increases in frequency, it is not equivalent to punishment.

In the example just given, the teenager reacts to eliminate the nagging – that is, to escape from an existing negative reinforcer. In the future, they might respond at the first hint of parental displeasure, before the nagging actually begins. In this case, they would be responding before the reinforcer is given, in order to *avoid* it. (In this case, making the response leads to the withholding of the negative reinforcer.) Thus, negative reinforcement actually has two variations, *escape* and *avoidance*. Normally, initial learning requires presenting the negative reinforcer until the response is made (that is, escape); later, the individual anticipates the sequence, and responds before the negative reinforcer is presented (that is, avoidance). Experiencing a 'sigh of relief' after getting out of an unpleasant situation (such as leaving the dentist's office) is characteristic of *escape*. Similarly, the anticipatory fear that you feel in some situations (for instance, if a large, unkempt stranger approaches you on an isolated street) can trigger a response (such as crossing to the other side of the street) in order to *avoid* an anticipated unpleasant situation (a confrontation with a hostile stranger).

If you review the foregoing discussion of contingencies, it may occur to you that there is a fourth possibility, based on terminating or withholding a positive reinforcer. How would you react if your behaviour led to losing a positive reinforcer? For example, a teenager comes home very late, and loses their driving privileges as a result. As you can imagine, when a response leads to terminating or withholding a positive reinforcer, the behaviour becomes less likely. (This contingency is generally called **omission**, or sometimes 'positive punishment'). Thus, the effects of omission, in terms of reducing the likelihood of a response, are similar to the effects of punishment (see Figure 3.9 for a summary of the four contingencies).

omission in operant conditioning, a process whereby a response is followed by terminating or withholding a positive reinforcer, which results in a decrease in the probability of the response.

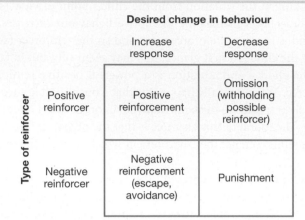

Figure 3.9 Contingencies of Reinforcement Skinner argues that in order to understand how operant responses change, one must look at both the type of reinforcer, and its relationship to the response. (See text for definitions of forms of reinforcement.)

To recap what has been said about the process of reinforcement, one can understand the dynamics of behaviour by identifying the *contingency of reinforcement* involved. To do so, one must identify the response and the reinforcer, *and* how they are related. In doing so, one must remember that the value of the reinforcer is determined by the organism, not the environment. An example might help to clarify this.

Imagine that you are offered a chocolate milkshake if you will sing a song. Assuming you like milkshakes, you will likely sing; thus, the milkshake is a positive reinforcer. Based on your rousing performance, you are offered a second shake if you sing another song. You do so, but drink the second shake more slowly. When you finish, you are offered a third shake for another song. At this point, the prospect of consuming another milkshake is very unappealing, and you refuse to sing. Thus, what started out as a *positive* reinforcer has now become a *negative* reinforcer. The shakes haven't changed, but their value to the organism has – and that is the crucial point. In order to understand behaviour, one must look at how the behaviour changes in order to identify the contingency involved. As Skinner said, the organism always behaves, it is our understanding that is sometimes wrong.

Try it Yourself

In order to understand the contingencies of operant behaviour more fully, consider the following situations:

■ You have worked very hard and your employer wants you to keep on working hard. How might he or she do this? Would you prefer a raise in pay, or movement to a better office where there is less noise and fewer distractions? Would both be positive reinforcers for you, even if differing in value? If one was actually a negative reinforcer, how would this affect your working?

■ Unthinkingly, you said something that hurt your friend's feelings. Your friend now has certain options. For example, they may respond angrily to you, or they may stop speaking to you for some period of time. With both of these options, you might learn to stop hurting your friend's feelings (i.e., this behaviour would decrease). Are they the same contingency? Which would you prefer? Why?

Operant Conditioning Phenomena
Shaping and the Learning Process

In all the examples we have discussed, the reinforcer was used to alter the likelihood of an existing response. While this shows the power of reinforcement, it also poses a problem. Since one cannot reinforce a response that doesn't occur at all, how do new behaviours arise? And how can operant principles explain the development of complex behaviours? For example, how does a child learn to walk, or an adult learn to play the piano? One factor to recognize is that complex behaviours do not suddenly emerge fully formed. Instead, they tend to be formed out of a series of simpler behaviours, which can then be combined. A child learns to crawl, and to pull itself upright, before taking its first steps. Piano playing involves a whole set of responses, from learning how to position the hands and body at the piano, to identifying written musical notes, to controlling the pedals while playing. Thus, complex behaviours can be thought of as a series of simpler responses that are combined as a sequence, which is then treated as a single response in terms of getting reinforcement.

While this description can account for complex responses, it still doesn't explain how new responses arise. Skinner explained variability and originality as forms of 'behavioural drift'. That is, operant behaviour, in the absence of reinforcement for a specific response, tends to vary somewhat over time. Much of this variation is simply random, but the fact that drift occurs means that sometimes new responses will occur – and therefore may be reinforced. This means that desired new behaviours can be encouraged through a process called shaping.

shaping in operant conditioning, the process of guiding the acquisition of a new response by reinforcing successive approximations to the desired response.

Shaping is defined as the process of reinforcing *successive approximations* to a desired response. The process assumes that someone (an experimenter, a parent, etc.) has in mind a behavioural goal, and can control the delivery of a reinforcer accordingly. For example, most operant research involves animals (such as a white rat) pressing a lever in a Skinner box. While rats are capable of pressing a lever, it is not a natural response in the wild. Consequently, the rat must be shaped to acquire the response. (As graduate students working as lab assistants, we had many experiences of doing such training.) Typically, when one places an untrained rat in the Skinner box, it begins to explore this new environment, looking around and sniffing at everything. In one corner of the chamber, there is a food dispenser which can deliver pellets of dry food. At first, one simply dispenses pellets, one at a time, until the rat associates the click of the mechanism with arrival of a food pellet. Once this pattern is established, a food pellet is given only when the rat turns towards the lever (a first approximation to the desired response of pressing the bar). After eating, the rat will likely turn back towards the lever. If it moves closer, or lifts a paw towards the lever (a closer approximation to the desired response), another pellet is given. Finally, the pellet is only given when the rat actually presses the lever – and at this point, the desired shaping has been achieved.

Shaping is a simple concept, but very powerful. Although they might not use the terms of operant conditioning, generations of animal trainers have applied the same principle in their work. There is even a story, probably apocryphal, about a class of psychology students who shaped their professor to stand in the corner. The students used writing in their notebooks as the reinforcer (professors tend to find this reinforcing, since it implies both paying attention and being interested). Whenever the professor, who tended to walk about, moved towards one corner, the students all wrote furiously. When he moved in the opposite direction, they all put down their pens. By the end of the class, the story goes, the poor professor was wedged into the corner!

The process of shaping has also been applied to more serious purposes, including assisting children with language learning and helping accident victims to reacquire basic skills. Anyone who has watched trained animals perform, whether at a circus or in a movie, has also witnessed the power of shaping. Having said this, it is also worth noting that shaping is easier to grasp as a concept than to apply in practice. I (WG) can still recall my first attempts to shape a rat to press the lever in a Skinner box – it took nearly an hour. Later, after gaining more experience, I could typically do it in 15 minutes! The difference was one of judgement and timing – deciding when a new approximation was good enough to merit a reinforcer. If I rewarded too often, the rat spent more time eating than learning; if I rewarded too infrequently, the rat lost interest, or seemed to forget what the last reinforced response had been. In this sense, shaping, while clearly consistent with operant principles, is not simply a mechanical process.

Extinction

Shaping uses the variability inherent in responding in order to produce a desired response. Once a response occurs, it can be reinforced, as we have seen. But what happens if the reinforcement is discontinued? Consider a rat that has been reinforced with a food pellet each time it presses the lever, or a child that has been praised each time they pick up their toys. If the situation changes so that reinforcers are no longer given, what will the organism do? An intuitive answer, which is supported by research, would be that the behaviour might continue for a short time, but once it is recognized that reinforcers are no longer forthcoming, the behaviour will decrease in probability. This drop in responding when reinforcement is discontinued is called **extinction**. (One can see a parallel to extinction in classical conditioning, where the CR disappears when the CS is no longer paired with the UCS.) Note that while both extinction and punishment in operant conditioning produce decreases in responding, they do so in very different ways: extinction can be considered a passive process, in that it diminishes the value of the response by eliminating the reinforcer which supported it. Punishment, on the other hand, uses an aversive stimulus to actively suppress the (undesired) behaviour.

extinction in operant conditioning, a drop in responding when reinforcement is discontinued.

One implication of extinction seems to be that, in order to be effective, reinforcement must be continuously given for every response. Unfortunately, this seldom occurs in the real world. Students study regularly, but receive reinforcement only after the occasional test. People go to work every day, but may be paid only weekly or even monthly. How, then, can operant conditioning be said to apply to such behaviours?

Schedules of Reinforcement

Early in his research, Skinner recognized that in everyday life we rarely experience either true extinction (no reinforcement at all) or **continuous reinforcement** (every response reinforced). Instead, what we tend to encounter is something in between – some responses get reinforced, and some don't. Skinner coined the term **partial reinforcement** to describe situations where reinforcement is given only intermittently. In order to understand what happens under such circumstances, he began a series of studies looking at various forms of partial reinforcement. In order to distinguish various types of intermittent reinforcement, Skinner coined the term **schedules of reinforcement** (see Ferster and Skinner 1957). In general, a reinforcement schedule describes when a reinforcer is given, in much the same way that a train schedule describes when a train departs.

continuous reinforcement in operant conditioning, a reinforcement schedule in which every response is followed by a reinforcer; equivalent to a FR 1 schedule.

partial reinforcement in operant conditioning, a contingency of reinforcement in which reinforcement does not follow every response.

schedule of reinforcement in operant conditioning, a description of the conditions which determine when a response will be followed by a reinforcer.

The most straightforward schedule, of course, is continuous reinforcement, since every response receives a reinforcer. By contrast, partial reinforcement can occur under an essentially infinite number of variations. However, a surprising variety of situations can be described in one of two ways: according to the number of responses made before a reinforcer is given, or the amount of time that elapses between reinforcers. Schedules which depend on the number of responses made are called *ratio schedules*; those which are time-dependent are called *interval schedules*. In addition, such schedules may be very regular (for example, every third response, every 15 seconds), or somewhat unpredictable. Regular schedules are called *fixed schedules*, while those which are more unpredictable are called *variable schedules*. Let us look at the different types more closely in order to see how they affect behaviour.

fixed ratio schedule in operant conditioning, a reinforcement contingency defined by the number of responses the organism must make in order to get a reinforcer; the ratio is measured as FR *x*, where *x* is the required number of responses.

Fixed ratio schedules are the simplest to understand: the ratio is measured as FR *x*, where *x* is the number of responses the organism must make in order to get a reinforcer. (Continuous reinforcement is actually equivalent to FR 1, since each response leads to a reinforcer.) Thus, FR 5 means that every fifth response would receive a reinforcer (see Figure 3.10a). In everyday life, this is analogous to piecework, where a person will be paid according to the number of responses made. An example might be a seamstress: each shirt may have seven buttons to be sewn, and completing a shirt earns $1; this would be FR 7. Skinner found in his experiments that increasing the ratio tended to increase the rate of responding; the animals sought to maintain the total amount of reinforcement received, regardless of the schedule (in the same way that a seamstress might try to work faster if the rate of pay per shirt declined; the faster the seamstress works, the more shirts she completes and she is able to maintain her previous rate of pay). In the laboratory, pigeons would peck at a key 50 times or more to get one reinforcer! Eventually, however, as fixed ratios increase, behaviour slows, and may even cease. Essentially, if the ratio is too high, the organism reacts as if it were an extinction situation (for example, if it takes 150 responses to produce one reinforcer, it may seem as though reinforcement has ceased!).

Interestingly, when the ratio is made less predictable, performance tends to be better. A **variable ratio schedule** is defined in terms of the *average* number of responses required to receive a reinforcer (for example, VR 10 means on average every tenth response is reinforced) (see Figure 3.10b). This means that the ratio is predictable in the long run, but in the short run the number of responses required varies. This is much like a slot machine, which pays out on a predefined percentage of plays – but one cannot predict precisely when the next pay-out will be. This analogy actually works surprisingly well, for animals on variable ratio schedules tend to perform very steadily, much like the gambler who plays a slot machine for hours, hoping that the next play will be the big pay-out. In both cases, the fact that reinforcement occasionally occurs after only a few responses tends to maintain the behaviour over the sequences when no reinforcement occurs. Many other activities also seem to be based on variable ratio reinforcement. In sales jobs, for example, a sales agent might have to make a varying number of client contacts before closing a sale; even so, the occasional sale sustains the behaviour. Sport fishermen typically don't succeed on every outing, and cannot predict when they will catch a 'big one'; even so, they continue to try, knowing the next outing may lead to success. Thus, while both variable and fixed ratios tend to produce very steady responding, variable schedules are slightly better overall.

variable ratio schedule in operant conditioning, a reinforcement contingency defined in terms of the average number of responses required to receive a reinforcer; thus, VR 8 means that on average every eighth response is reinforced.

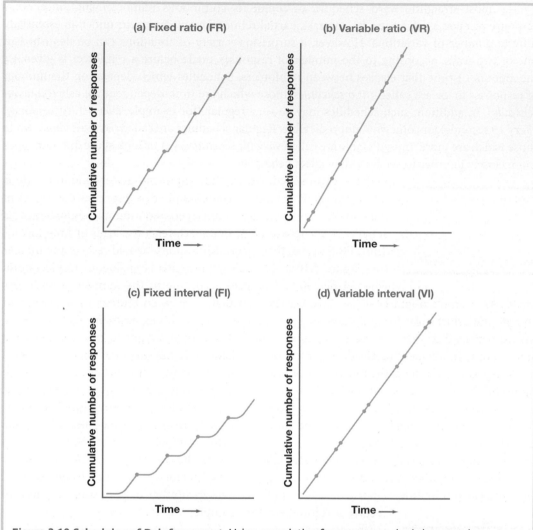

Figure 3.10 Schedules of Reinforcement Using cumulative frequency graphs (where total responses are counted), one can see the differences in response patterns using different types of schedules. Note in particular the lag in responding after a reinforcer (shown by dots) under fixed interval schedules, and the relatively fast response rates (steep curve) under variable ratio.

fixed interval schedule in operant conditioning, a reinforcement contingency defined by the amount of time that must pass since the previous reinforcer was given, before a response will receive a reinforcer; thus FI 5 min. means a fixed interval of five minutes.

In ratio schedules, since getting a reinforcer depends on making the specified number of responses, performance tends to occur at a relatively high rate. The situation is somewhat different with *interval* schedules, where time is the crucial factor. In a **fixed interval schedule**, a timer determines how long it has been since the previous reinforcer was given, and only a response made *after* the required time interval has elapsed will receive a reinforcer (of course, if no response at all is made, no reinforcer is given). Thus, in a FI 15 sec. schedule, at least 15 seconds must pass between delivery of reinforcers (assuming a response is made at the end of the required interval, see Figure 3.10c).

It may seem odd to consider reinforcement as being time-dependent, but in fact there are many situations where this type of schedule applies. For example, if you are waiting for a bus on a rainy day, you must go out at the appropriate time in order to get the bus. It does not matter how often you go out to check (i.e., make multiple responses) – only going out at the *appropriate* time will get reinforced (by actually getting the bus). Another example is the administering of painkillers in hospitals. In many cases, a patient will only receive medication for pain (the reinforcer) if they request it (the response). However, to avoid overdoses, the medication will only be given after a certain time interval since the previous dose, such as four hours (the fixed interval); any requests made before this time has passed will be ignored. Work which is paid on an hourly rate rather than piecework basis may also be considered a type of interval schedule. In this situation, there is an assumption by employers that responses are being made (i.e., that work is being done), but technically the response which is reinforced is being present at work! (You get paid according to how many hours you work, not the number of things you accomplish.) Thus, fixed interval schedules are actually a fairly common form of reinforcement.

One special characteristic of fixed interval schedules is that they only *require* a single response in order to receive reinforcement, provided the required time interval has elapsed. The result is that fixed interval schedules tend to produce rather low rates of responding compared to ratio schedules. In fact, even in laboratory studies with animals, as the animal becomes familiar with the situation, one finds a distinctive pattern emerges. Typically, few responses are made immediately after a reinforcer is delivered. Instead, there is a lull, and then a few tentative responses, and finally a brief surge in responding clustered near the end of the time interval. Essentially, the organism comes to recognize that premature responses are wasted, and tries to determine the end of the time interval. (While not as precise as a real clock, most species have a biological clock which provides a sense of time.) On a cumulative record of responses, this clustering of responses produces a distinctive 'scallop' in the graph (see Figure 3.10c). An inventive demonstration of this phenomenon is a study by Weisberg and Waldrop (1972), which found that the number of bills passed in sessions of the US Congress showed this FI scallop – the closer it was to the end of a session, the more bills were passed!

If the intention is to encourage steady responding, a fixed interval schedule is inappropriate, because of the clustering of responses which it produces. Given this difficulty, is there any time-based alternative schedule that can remedy this problem? The answer is yes; the trick is to vary the time interval. In a **variable interval schedule**, the schedule is defined in terms of the average time interval required over the long term, much as a variable ratio is defined by an average number of responses required. Thus, on a VI 15 sec. schedule, one interval might be only 5 seconds, the interval after another reinforcer might be 20 seconds, and so on – only over a long period would the average duration be 15 seconds (see Figure 3.10d). From the point of view of the organism being reinforced, this variability means that the availability of a reinforcer is no longer predictable; consequently, the only way to determine if the interval has elapsed is to make a response. The result is that variable interval schedules result in steady behaviour – albeit at much lower rates than ratio schedules. Since the schedule is still time-based, very fast response rates don't accelerate the process of getting a reinforcer; instead, the purpose of responding regularly is simply to check if a reinforcer is available.

variable interval schedule in operant conditioning, a reinforcement contingency defined by the average time interval which must elapse since the last reinforcer before a response will be reinforced; thus, on a VI 15 sec. schedule, over a long period the average duration would be 15 seconds.

An example which provides an analogy may help clarify the nature of behaviour under variable interval schedules. Imagine someone who works as a quality control inspector on an assembly line; the person's role is to watch items as they pass by, and pick out any which appear defective. In this situation, a person who ignores the task (for example, to read a newspaper) may not be detected for several months, until complaints about defective products are received from customers. Consequently, the foreman checks the person every two hours, on the hour. Since this is equivalent to a fixed interval schedule, a person intent on bunking off could simply begin working just before the foreman arrives, and then return to loafing after the foreman leaves (this is equivalent to a fixed interval scallop). In order to avoid this, the foreman varies the time of his visits – in effect, a variable interval schedule. Now, since the visits are unpredictable, the worker must work steadily, or run the risk of being caught unexpectedly. The result would be typical of behaviour under variable interval schedules – steady responding! (Compared to variable ratio schedules, where there is a direct incentive for fast responding, variable interval schedules tend to produce slow but steady response rates.)

While these four types of schedules are only a small sample of the possible types of partial reinforcement, they show that intermittent reinforcement can be used to sustain behaviour, and that the behaviour tends to reflect the specific requirements of the schedule. In this sense, both people and animals are adept at recognizing the demands of their environment and adjusting their responses to fit the situation. Beyond that, it is worth noting some other characteristics of behaviour using partial reinforcement. The most obvious difference between continuous and partial reinforcement is that under partial reinforcement, an organism does more work to get a reinforcer. This gap increases as the size of the ratio or length of the interval increases. One might expect that this 'more work, less pay' regimen would result in resistance (reduced responding), yet behaviour tends to occur at a *higher* rate with partial reinforcement than with continuous (except with very high fixed ratios, as discussed previously). In addition, variable schedules (ratio *or* interval) tend to produce greater response rates than equivalent fixed schedules. Overall, variable ratio schedules seem to be the most effective in maintaining high rates of behaviour. Skinner, of course, would never speculate about *why* this occurs, since that would require discussing non-observable events. Still, the dynamics may involve the fact that primary reinforcers have survival value, and organisms must meet their survival needs, regardless of the effort involved. Early hunters, for example, likely received only partial reinforcement for their efforts, and still had to persist in hunting when game was scarce. Studies of foraging behaviour have in fact led to the suggestion that animals (and presumably people) look at long-term costs, as well as the immediate consequences, when seeking food (Collier *et al.* 1997).

Since partial reinforcement tends to produce higher rates of responding than continuous reinforcement, what happens under extinction conditions (when no reinforcement at all is given)? Generally speaking, *behaviour acquired under partial reinforcement is much more persistent than behaviour acquired under continuous reinforcement.* The standard measure is to count how many responses are made once reinforcers are no longer available; this is called 'resistance to extinction', where a larger number reflects more persistent behaviour. Interestingly, one finds that resistance to extinction roughly parallels the hierarchy found when reinforcement is available; that is, variable schedules are more resistant to extinction than fixed schedules. One example of this is gambling, which tends to produce very persistent behaviour, in spite of the fact that individuals are assured of losing in the long run (for example, slot machines, roulette and craps all fit this description). Again, Skinner does not speculate as to *why* this is true, but a number of researchers have noted that the change in contingency (from reinforcement to extinction) is simply harder to detect with partial reinforcement. That is, with continuous reinforcement, it is immediately obvious if reinforcement ceases, since a reinforcer should follow every response.

By contrast, with any form of partial reinforcement, the organism has learned (expects) to make responses that go unreinforced; the more variable the schedule, the longer it would take to determine that reinforcement has definitely ceased. Consider an analogy: if you play a slot machine for some time without winning, when would you conclude that the machine was broken or crooked, as opposed to your simply being on a losing streak? In a study with children who used machines that either paid out every time or on a variable ratio, a change to extinction was quickly recognized by the first group, while the second group continued playing for lengthy periods without ever winning (Lewis 1952). Thus, partial reinforcement produces higher rates of responding during reinforcement, and greater persistence during extinction.

Discriminative Stimuli

At this point, it should be clear that contingencies of reinforcement are very diverse, and that individuals seem to be capable of adapting to the requirements of different situations. But how do they *know* what the requirements are in a particular situation? Consider a simple example: 5-year-old Manny likes to eat spaghetti with his fingers. His mother dislikes this behaviour, and slaps his hand when she catches him eating that way. By contrast, his father is relatively indifferent to the behaviour, neither scolding nor praising it. Thus, depending upon who is present, the consequences of Manny's behaviour differ significantly. Obviously, Manny is likely to make the connection between who is present and what consequence occurs, and adapt his behaviour accordingly – eating with his fork when his mother is present, but using his fingers when his father is present! In this situation, the parents are **discriminative stimuli** – stimuli which signal the contingency of reinforcement available. In the above case, Manny's mother is a stimulus which signals *punishment* for eating with his fingers, while Manny's father signals *positive reinforcement* (i.e., Manny presumably eats with fingers because it is reinforcing). In general, discriminative stimuli arise when elements of the environment are associated with a particular contingency.

discriminative stimulus in operant conditioning, a stimulus which signals the contingency of reinforcement available.

In principle, it is possible for any contingency to become associated with a discriminative stimulus. Researchers have found, for example, that rats will use discriminative stimuli to decide when to press a bar – pressing it when the contingency is highly reinforcing (continuous reinforcement), and not responding when the contingency is not reinforcing (extinction). In another case, pigeons were trained to discriminate between cubist paintings by Picasso and impressionist paintings by Monet (Watanabe *et al.* 1995)! In everyday life, we all make distinctions based on the perceived contingency in the situation. For example, most people will exceed the speed limit when no police are visible (in which case speeding is not punished), but will immediately slow down when a police car is spotted (a discriminative stimulus that speeding will be punished). Children may react differently with each parent, as in the case of Manny, above. We act differently at a party than at work, because the situation signals that different behaviours will be rewarded in each case. Thus, discriminative stimuli, by indicating the potential consequences of behaviour, tend to influence the responses we make. The behaviour is still operant, not reflex – it is up to the individual what response is produced. For example, some people would rather park a car illegally and risk a ticket, than use a car park where it is certain they must pay a fee. Our capacity to recognize discriminative stimuli, and to modify our response, makes it easier to adapt to a changing environment.

Non-contingent Reinforcement

In all of the situations we have been examining, there has been a clearly identified relationship between a response and a reinforcer, described by the contingency. Depending on the type of contingency, behaviour increases or decreases systematically. But is this really a fair description of what happens in the real world? Is reinforcement always clearly dependent on behaviour, or do consequences sometimes occur randomly? Most people would quickly grant that some events in life are random, at least in terms of our ability to control them through our actions. That means that sometimes reinforcement is also random. For example, if you find money on the pavement, is it likely a result of someone seeking to reinforce you? And if it is actually a chance event, can we say anything about how organisms react to such random consequences?

Skinner considered this question, and described such random consequences in terms of **non-contingent reinforcement**, which means that the presence of the reinforcer is unrelated to the occurrence of the response. Using pigeons as subjects, Skinner did some inventive studies of the issue. In the typical situation, a pigeon that was already familiar with a Skinner box apparatus would be placed in a chamber, and a timer would provide a food pellet every 15 seconds, regardless of what the pigeon did. (Note that since *no* responses are required, this is *not* the same as a fixed interval schedule; in the extreme case, if the pigeon went to sleep, the feeder would still keep dropping food pellets!) After a period of time, Skinner and another observer would return to see what was happening. According to his description (Skinner 1948a), six out of eight pigeons had developed elaborate, stereotyped response sequences. Since these behaviours actually had no effect on the availability of reinforcement, Skinner called such behaviours 'superstitious'. All that was happening, he argued, was that responses were reinforced *by coincidence*, and then the organism maintained the response that was reinforced.

non-contingent reinforcement in operant conditioning, a situation where reinforcers sometimes occur independently of any specific response; chance forms of reinforcement.

Skinner went on to suggest that non-contingent reinforcement has similar effects on people. Superstitious behaviours seem to arise in situations where behaviour is only inconsistently reinforced, and where the behaviour has no real influence on the outcome (note that this is *not* the same as partial reinforcement, where the behaviour *does* influence the outcome). For example, many people have particular rituals for trying to make elevator doors close – tapping the edge of the door, holding the 'close' button, even jumping to momentarily increase the load on the elevator! Unfortunately, most modern elevators operate on a programmed cycle, and so people are really acting like Skinner's pigeons, engaging in a ritual which makes the time go by. Similarly, many sports rituals, like having a lucky shirt, seem to be based on superstitious behaviour.

The idea that superstitious behaviour can develop due to non-contingent reinforcement has been demonstrated experimentally – though, interestingly, not every participant developed a superstitious ritual (Ono 1987). Also, it may be that people are more likely to develop superstitions when trying to avoid negative reinforcers than when trying to obtain desirable outcomes

Try it Yourself

Do you feel uneasy if you break a mirror, half-expecting to have seven years of bad luck? Do you avoid walking under ladders? Do you always take your 'lucky pen' with you when you write a test or examination? Can you think of an instance of superstitious behaviour in everyday life (for example, your own behaviour, or someone you know)? Can you identify the reinforcer that seems related to the behaviour? Can you tell whether it is contingent or non-contingent? Is it possible that performing the superstitious behaviour makes you feel better and more confident, and that this is what actually contributes to a positive outcome? Does that seem to support or contradict Skinner's interpretation of superstitious behaviour?

(Aeschleman *et al.* 2003). That is, people are more superstitious about trying to 'ward off bad luck' than about trying to 'attract good luck'. At the very least, non-contingent reinforcement shows how sensitive organisms are to environmental consequences.

APPLICATIONS AND IMPLICATIONS OF CONDITIONING

One of the striking things about behaviourism is the strong pragmatic element which underlies it. Behaviourists are typically very interested not only in trying to understand behaviour, but in

behaviour modification the application of conditioning techniques to altering human behaviour, particularly those behaviours identified as abnormal.

applying their understanding in the real world. Watson's claim about raising children, cited at the start of this chapter, is one example of this impulse. Skinner was often outspoken concerning his ideas for reshaping society, including writing a utopian novel, *Walden Two* (Skinner 1948b). In more limited ways, behaviourist methods have been applied to many aspects of human behaviour; these applications

are commonly referred to as **behaviour modification**. While more specifics about the application of conditioning principles to therapy will be given in Chapter 9, it is appropriate to consider here some general issues related to conditioning.

Negative Reinforcers and the Aversive Control of Operant Behaviour

As Thorndike noted, not all behavioural outcomes are alike. While positive reinforcers like praise or money are welcomed by individuals, negative reinforcers like criticism or physical punishment are unpleasant. Therefore, positive reinforcement is more appealing as a means of modifying behaviour than are punishment and negative reinforcement, which depend on the use of negative reinforcers. Although Skinner would shun descriptions like 'positive reinforcement is more appealing' as being vague and subjective, researchers have found a number of ways to examine the differences between the use of positive and negative reinforcers.

The use of negative reinforcers is often referred to as *aversive control of behaviour*, because of the way organisms react to negative reinforcers. As noted previously, there are two ways in which aversive control is used: *punishment* is used to reduce the frequency of a response, whereas *negative reinforcement* is used to increase a response (that is, the response leads to escaping or avoiding the negative reinforcer).

Punishment is probably the most used, and misunderstood, method of dealing with undesirable behaviour. Parents resort to scolding when disciplining their children. Employers will criticize or threaten hapless employees. Even our legal system is based on punishment for breaking society's rules. Unfortunately, punishment has several limitations, which are worth noting.

contiguity in operant conditioning, the principle that a reinforcer must occur immediately after a response in order for learning to occur.

First, as with *any* operant reinforcement, the use of punishment depends on **contiguity** between the response and the reinforcer – for effective learning, the reinforcer must immediately follow the response. Punishment which is delayed will be ineffective in controlling the response, or worse, may become associated with a

different response. For example, 5-year-old Sarah breaks a plate, and then later tells her mother what happened. The mother, upset about the broken plate, scolds Sarah – but in fact this negative reinforcer will tend to be associated with *telling* about the accident, *not* breaking the plate. In the future, Sarah may still break things, but may not be forthcoming about admitting it! In the same way, imagine if your dog soiled the carpet, and two hours later, when you discovered the damage, you yelled at the dog, who was now quietly resting on his blanket. Ignoring the importance of contiguity can seriously hamper the effectiveness of punishment. (Similarly, one might note that our legal system, with its typically long delays between crime and punishment, is also poorly designed in terms of contiguity.)

A second limitation of punishment is that it tends to encourage avoidance behaviours. A child in school may be scolded by a teacher for giving a wrong answer. Obviously, the teacher's intention is to get the child to study harder, and thereby give more correct answers, but the real result may be rather different. The child may refuse to answer at all, or even skip the classes taught by that teacher. Because of classical conditioning, any stimulus associated with a negative reinforcer (the teacher, the classroom) may itself become aversive, and trigger avoidance. The avoidance responses may be directed at the situation, or simply at finding ways to avoid the negative reinforcer itself. A criminal with a history of robbing banks was once confronted by a prison official, who asked, 'After all these years, don't you know robbing banks is wrong?' The criminal's response was, 'Actually, I don't see anything wrong with robbing banks; it's getting caught that I don't like!' Research by criminologists has indicated that most people obey laws because they feel it is the right thing to do (feeling virtuous can be a form of positive reinforcement); it is only a minority of people (mostly criminals) who focus on the punishments for transgressing. As anyone aware of crime statistics knows, having laws which specify punishments for criminal acts does not in itself deter criminal behaviour, since those so inclined will simply seek to avoid getting caught.

This issue of punishment encouraging avoidance is a major concern, because punishment tends to *suppress* behaviour, not *extinguish* it. Any operant response occurs because there is some reinforcer supporting it; applying punishment to suppress the response simply pits one reinforcer against the other. Worse, whereas positive reinforcement can be highly effective with only partial reinforcement, *punishment must be continuous in order to suppress behaviour effectively*. Thus, in situations where it is possible to avoid the punishment even occasionally, punishment will not be fully effective in suppressing the undesired response. (Consider what this means in terms of our legal system, where arrest and conviction rates rarely approach 100 per cent.) Instead, it would be better to identify the factor which encourages the undesirable behaviour, and try to alter the environment to eliminate that positive reinforcer (Lerman and Vorndran 2002). For example, children sometimes misbehave because it quickly draws parental attention (a positive reinforcer); to a child starved for attention, the scolding which may follow is less significant than the attention. The result is an increase in disruptive behaviour, followed by more attention (and scolding), etc. The way out of this may be for the parents to *ignore* (extinguish) misbehaviour, and *also* attempt to offer attention when the child is playing quietly or otherwise desirably engaged. (In cases like this, the reinforcing of appropriate behaviour is as important as the extinguishing of undesirable behaviour.)

Because of the way the contingency operates, negative reinforcement is often more effective than punishment as a form of aversive control. Since the focus is on *increasing* a desired response, one does not encounter the problems of suppression associated with punishment. In addition, the acquired fear which can lead to escaping or avoiding the punishment situation, in negative reinforcement tends to *sustain* the desired behaviour. For example, a child may refuse to dress for school, whereupon the parent scowls, and begins yelling at the child, who finally gets dressed. In the future, a scowl may be sufficient to induce the child to dress. Because it is designed to increase a response, not suppress it, negative reinforcement is probably preferable to the use of punishment. In addition, because making the desired response is directly linked to removal of the aversive stimulus, negative reinforcement is more effective than punishment in signalling the desired behaviour (punishment simply indicates what is *not* desired, nothing about what is desired).

Unfortunately, there is one consequence of aversive control which is associated with *any* use of negative reinforcers. By their nature, negative reinforcers represent aversive stimuli, and no organism readily tolerates such events. The use of aversive control therefore tends to promote anxiety, resentment and even aggression, in addition to the problems identified above (Azrin and Holz 1966; Berkowitz 1983). This means that depending on aversive control to regulate behaviour is going to produce a whole range of secondary problems, which may even be less desirable than the original behaviour.

Because of the difficulties outlined above, behaviourists would say that the use of aversive stimuli, in any form, should never be a preferred choice. Despite this, it is clear that punishment is still frequently used, by parents, and by society (Gershoff 2002; Lerman and Vorndran 2002). By contrast, Skinner once suggested that a well-designed society would depend on a combination of positive reinforcement (for desired behaviours) and extinction (for undesired behaviours), not aversive control (Skinner 1948b). It is unlikely that we will ever achieve Skinner's ideal of a punishment-free society – as Vollmer (2002) has noted, aversive outcomes happen, and sometimes they have nothing to do with social interaction (for example, turning the wrong knob on the shower, or slipping on a patch of ice). Nonetheless, better recognition of both the limitations of aversive stimuli and the alternatives to their use is potentially worthwhile.

Try it Yourself

My (MH) adult niece relates the story of being a physically small child of 8, and being tormented one winter by several children who were younger than she, but physically much larger. One day, when returning home from school, the younger children chased her, pelting her with rocks covered with snow. Unable to outrun her tormentors, she threw some snow at their feet to try to keep them at a distance. The next day, she told her teacher about the episode, and was severely reprimanded and punished for having 'thrown snowballs at younger children'. My niece still flushes with resentment when she recounts the story and says, 'Even today, I don't know what it was I was supposed to do!' Given what you know about ways that learning principles can be used to modify behaviour, what do you think she should have done? What should the teacher have done? How can learning principles best be used to modify the behaviour of bullying children?

Interrelationships of Classical and Operant Conditioning

For most of this chapter, we have been discussing classical and operant conditioning as if they were totally separate aspects of behaviour. However, it should not be surprising to find that there are interconnections between the two: after all, organisms are constantly producing *many* responses, both reflex and operant. In this sense, the distinction between the two types of learning is partly a way of simplifying the analysis of behaviour, by breaking it into reflex and operant components. In the real world, both processes can be occurring simultaneously. One striking example of this is *negative reinforcement*. You may recall that negative reinforcement utilizes a negative reinforcer in order to increase the probability of a response. One form of this is escape, where a negative reinforcer is presented, and is only removed after the organism makes the desired response. In this circumstance, the removal of the aversive stimulus is effectively like a reward, so the behaviour becomes more likely (hence, reinforcement). For example, a dog given a mild shock through an electrified floor grid will learn to jump to another chamber to escape the shock. Now, if a light flashes before the start of the shock, the dog will soon anticipate the shock, and jump before the shock begins. This becomes *avoidance* – the dog is jumping in order to avoid the negative reinforcer. This leads to an interesting problem: since the dog jumps before the shock, there is no longer any experience of the original reinforcer – a circumstance that would lead to *extinction* of the response if one were looking at positive reinforcement. So why does the dog keep jumping each time the light goes on? The light, of course, has become a discriminative stimulus, enabling the dog to respond before the shock occurs. Still, why should the dog persist in jumping without at least an occasional experience of shock? The answer seems to be that, through classical conditioning, the light has become a CS associated with the UCS of shock – which is a perfect scenario for creating a conditioned fear. Thus, the dog continues to jump, not to *avoid* the *shock*, but to *escape* from the feared *light*! (Mowrer 1956; Rescorla and Solomon 1967).

Recognizing that the two processes (operant and classical conditioning) are occurring together also adds to our understanding of conditioned fears. Watson, in his demonstration with little Albert, discovered that conditioned fears do not readily extinguish. The reason for this seems to be that the feared stimulus (the CS) *also* triggers operant escape behaviour. This escape response removes the individual from the situation *before* there is an opportunity to determine if the UCS will follow or not – thereby preventing the conditions necessary for extinction. (The same mixture of classical and operant responses happens in the shower when we hear the toilet flush: while we *fear* the sound, we also tend to *jump* away from the water spray to avoid being scalded.) The fact that fear stimuli can evoke an operant response is a very significant point in terms of those everyday fears, which are called phobias. If, as Watson argued, such fears are based on classical conditioning, then it is also likely that the fears persist long after the original experience, because we *avoid* the situations that *elicit* the fear. As a result, there is no opportunity to find out if our fear is realistic or not. For example, a person who is afraid of flying will be reluctant to fly, and therefore has no chance to find out that flying is safe, and that there is nothing to fear. In essence, until we face the fear situation, there is no opportunity to extinguish the fear response.

Another type of interaction can occur in which conditioned behaviours are also sustained by reinforcement. For example, a phobia may arise through classical conditioning, but the individual may also be positively reinforced by attention and sympathy from other people. In such circumstances, the individual may be unlikely to try to change.

Try it Yourself

If you have a phobia or fear yourself, how do you cope with it? If you tend to avoid the fear-arousing situation, do you think this reaction is adaptive for you in the long run? For example, many students with a fear of public speaking avoid taking courses in which they will be required to give oral presentations. Can you suggest a technique based on learning principles that might help in dealing with such fears?

Autonomic Conditioning and Biofeedback

Consider the following proposal: we will give you $20 if you raise the temperature of your left hand while simultaneously lowering the temperature of your right hand. Short of getting a blanket and ice pack, this may seem like an impossible goal. After all, body temperature is an involuntary (reflex) function. How could we expect to control it with a reinforcer like money? At one time, psychologists would have agreed that such a task was impossible – after all, reflexes are the domain of classical conditioning, not operant conditioning. Even the evidence that shows the two types of learning can occur together (as in avoidance learning) does not challenge the fundamental distinction of reflex vs. operant responses. In fact, however, we now recognize that the boundaries are more ambiguous than the traditional view suggests.

The change was triggered by the work of Neal Miller, a noted researcher in the field of learning, and Leo DiCara, then a graduate student working with Miller. Miller and DiCara wondered if it would be possible to use operant reinforcement with so-called involuntary responses. Although this seemed far-fetched, data on phenomena like meditation suggested that under some circumstances individuals *could* deliberately alter these responses. While the details of the original procedures were rather complex (involving partially paralysed rats, with electrical stimulation of the brain as a positive reinforcer), the implications of the results were quickly apparent: involuntary responses *could* be operantly controlled!

Key Thinker: **Neal Miller**

Neal Miller (1909 – 2002) contributed to many aspects of psychology over a lengthy career. Born in Milwaukee, Wisconsin, the son of a psychologist, Miller got his BS at the University of Washington in 1931, an MS at Stanford a year later, and a PhD in psychology from Yale in 1935. Miller then spent a year as a research fellow at the Institute of Psychoanalysis in Vienna. Though he began as a Freudian, Miller gradually became interested in focusing on more measurable aspects of behaviour. Over the course of his career, he worked on developing selection procedures for aircrew during World War II, collaborated with John Dollard on a behaviourist translation of Freudian concepts, and did pioneering work in learning and neuroscience. Perhaps the most significant of his contributions stemmed from his work on autonomic conditioning. While the breakthrough studies were done with his student Leo DiCara, the foundation of this work went back to Miller's interests in motivation, behaviour and the brain, starting in the 1930s. The work of DiCara and Miller was initially greeted with scepticism by many, but biofeedback procedures are now a standard form of medical treatment. From his early Freudian days, Miller had evolved into a rigorous researcher whose contributions, particularly in learning, were recognized by many awards, including the presidency of the APA in 1961. Miller remained active throughout his career, in later years serving on the APA Board of Scientific Affairs. He died in March 2002, at the age of 92.

autonomic conditioning (also called 'learned operant control of autonomic responses') the conditioning of changes in autonomic (involuntary) responses (such as heart rate or blood pressure) by means of operant reinforcement.

Miller described the process as 'learned operant control of autonomic responses', or **autonomic conditioning** (Miller 1969). By providing reinforcement which was based on changes in autonomic (involuntary) responses, it was possible to alter behaviours such as heart rate, blood pressure – even the temperature of various limbs (by changes in blood flow). To understand what is involved in autonomic conditioning, it is necessary to consider how operant responses normally function. For all voluntary muscle movements, our brain receives information, called *proprioceptive feedback*, about the execution of the movement. It is proprioceptive feedback which tells you the position of your arm even when your eyes are closed, for example. But for involuntary functions (involving the autonomic nervous system), there is little or no proprioceptive feedback. Consequently, there is typically no direct awareness of autonomic responses like blood pressure. To circumvent this limitation, DiCara and Miller used sophisticated equipment to monitor these hidden processes, and thus determine when to deliver a reinforcer. Since most autonomic functions show natural fluctuations (for example, heart rate varies slightly even when sitting), the procedure amounted to a process of shaping a desired response.

biofeedback a general term for applications of the process of autonomic conditioning; the name refers to the fact that in humans reinforcement is based on providing an individual with information (feedback) about physiological processes (bio) which are normally not observable.

Thus, the essential element of autonomic conditioning is the ability to measure the response. While the recording of physiological activity dates back to the 1930s, using such techniques in the context of operant conditioning is much more recent. Today, applications of the process are frequently referred to as **biofeedback**, since the process provides an individual with information (feedback) about physiological processes (bio) which are normally not observable (see Mercer 1986).

Basically, any biofeedback procedure requires equipment to monitor the response of interest, and a means of conveying information to the individual about changes in their response (unlike the original animal studies, in applications with people, informational feedback is often a sufficient reinforcer). For example, if one is interested in muscle relaxation, one would use a device called an EMG (electromyograph), which measures the electrical activity in the motor neurons which control the muscles. If the heart is of interest, one would use an ECG (electrocardiograph), and so on. The means of providing feedback might be a buzzer, or a light which flashes, when the desired response occurs (see Figure 3.11).

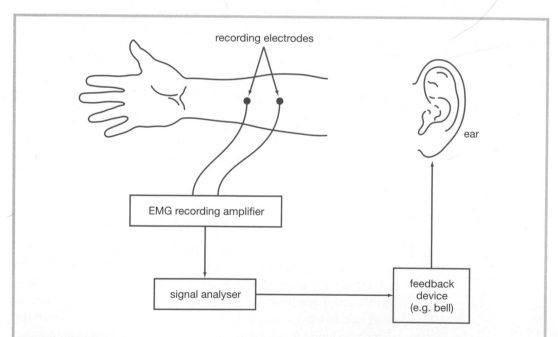

Figure 3.11 Biofeedback Basically the procedure for biofeedback requires some means of monitoring the physiological response (in this case a muscle twitch, recorded using an electromyograph), and a means of making the individual aware of changes that occur (in this case, a bell that rings whenever the target muscle twitches). Using this type of procedure, while monitoring several muscles with several bells, subjects actually can learn to play tunes!

The most significant applications of biofeedback are for medical treatment. It has proved very effective for the relaxation of voluntary muscles (for example, arms, legs, neck), which is often utilized for tension control. In fact, Grazzi (2007) reports that biofeedback treatment of migraine and tension headaches is just as effective as treatment with medication, with the advantage that biofeedback does not entail side effects or complications, as is often the case with medication. Biofeedback has also proved moderately effective for reducing hypertension (high blood pressure), and for regulating the rhythm of the heart, but not very effective for reducing overall heart rate (McGrady 1996). One of the more interesting uses has been to train individuals to control epileptic seizures, by teaching them to produce a brain-wave pattern which seems to inhibit seizure activity (Sterman 1978). Biofeedback has also been successfully used to help people with physiologically-based behavioural disorders, such as voice disorders related to the removal of the larynx. In this situation, biofeedback has been found to be effective in helping people improve the quality of their voice and their voice performance, and thereby the quality of their lives (Maryn *et al.* 2006).

From a more theoretical point of view, autonomic conditioning demonstrates that the processes of classical and operant conditioning are more closely intertwined than was once believed. While it does *not* imply that Pavlov was wrong about the formation of CS–UCS associations, it raises questions about the definition of operant behaviour. Skinner originally defined operants as emitted responses, in contrast to elicited reflexes. This made sense, in view of how such responses can be used to alter one's environment. Now, however, it seems that operant conditioning can be applied to almost any response, *provided that there is a clear contingency of reinforcement* (i.e., connection to consequences). Clearly, this would suggest a widening of the boundaries for operant behaviour. Thus, the study of autonomic conditioning has opened up new areas for operant research. Ironically, at just about the time that research on autonomic conditioning was broadening the boundaries, other research was suggesting new limitations of operant learning.

Before leaving the topic of autonomic conditioning, there is a sad side-note to the original discovery that bears mentioning. The initial study by DiCara and Miller was very complex, as noted. When it was first reported, it was viewed as so remarkable and unexpected that other researchers immediately set out to duplicate the results – and failed. Miller himself eventually tried, and also could not reproduce the original findings. While no one today doubts that

Try it Yourself

While you probably don't have access to a machine that will measure and signal changes in your autonomic arousal, you can still try to control some of your autonomic responses yourself. Lie down comfortably and imagine that you are on the beach or in a meadow. Imagine the sun streaming down, warming your whole body. Imagine that your stomach is becoming very warm with the sunlight. After a few minutes of imagining this, many people feel an actual warmth in their abdominal region. In fact, this is a popular technique in physical relaxation training that is often used for stress management. Try it a few times. Does your stomach feel warm? Do you feel more relaxed? Do you think this effect might be enhanced if a machine told you when your surface body temperature was increasing?

If you know anyone who has had biofeedback, talk to them about their experiences. Would you consider biofeedback in preference to medication if you experienced severe headaches? Why or why not?

autonomic conditioning is a real phenomenon, and Miller maintained that there was no evidence of fraud in DiCara's work, the younger researcher was discredited by the controversy. Today, the original study goes largely uncited, and DiCara has become a forgotten pioneer. In science, reputation can sometimes make or break a career.

Biological Constraints on Learning

When most people read about conditioning processes for the first time, one of the first things to strike them is the apparent artificiality of the experimental situations. After all, what does a ringing bell, or manipulating a lever, have to do with an animal obtaining food in the real world? What can the study of such arbitrary acts tell us about ordinary behaviour? In fact, the situations *are* rather artificial, and deliberately so. Behaviourists would argue that laboratory environments provide a high degree of experimental control, and behaviour is still behaviour, in the lab or out. Consequently, many would see the success of their methods as demonstrating just how powerful the basic principles are. However, as with all research, there are inevitably assumptions made when one generalizes from the laboratory to the real world.

equipotentiality premise an assumption made by some behaviourists which states that the principles of conditioning should apply equally to all behaviour, in any species.

One of the assumptions commonly made is called the **equipotentiality premise**. Essentially, this premise says that the principles of conditioning should apply to any response, and any species. (Interestingly, Skinner himself never endorsed such generalizations. He might be willing to generalize from observations of one pigeon to another, but would hesitate to generalize from one species to another.) For many years, studies of a wide variety of species in the laboratory seemed to demonstrate that the equipotentiality premise was correct.

ethology the study of the behaviour of animals in their natural environments.

species-specific behaviour behaviours which are characteristic of all members of a particular species; these response patterns (sometimes popularly called 'instincts') apply to behaviours such as mating, finding food, defence and raising offspring.

However, quite independently of behaviourism, other researchers, coming from a tradition of biology rather than psychology, have studied the behaviour of animals in their natural environments. This approach is called **ethology**. The founder of ethology is often regarded as Konrad Lorenz, a German researcher who did pioneering studies of species ranging from fish to wolves (Lorenz 1967). Ethologists like Lorenz have tended to study **species-specific behaviours** – behaviours which are characteristic of all members of a particular species. These response patterns (sometimes popularly called 'instincts') apply to behaviours such as mating, finding food, defence and raising offspring. Typically, the behaviours seem to be genetically shaped, but also responsive to environmental demands. For example, the young of many species identify their parents through a process called *imprinting*, whereby they attach themselves shortly after birth to the nearest moving stimulus. (Lorenz at one point had a group of ducklings who followed him around as though he were their mother!) Unlike simple reflexes, species-specific behaviour can involve complex sequences of responses, such as the ritual fighting in some species of tropical fish.

For many years, ethologists and behaviourists pursued their interests separately, but in recent years there has been increasing dialogue between the approaches. One of the prime areas of interest has been the interaction of hereditary and environmental influences on learning. The ethologists have tended to assume that much of behaviour is governed by the genetic make-up of a species, while many behaviourists have viewed behaviour as completely malleable, based on the principles of conditioning. As with many such issues, the truth seems to be something in between: environmental circumstances affect the expression of many species-specific behaviours, and biological constraints limit the process of learning. Contrary to the equipotentiality premise,

critical period in development, the concept that there are optimal periods for the learning of certain behaviours.

not all learning is the same. Some behaviours are easier to acquire than others (for example, learning to clap your hands is easier than rubbing your stomach and tapping your head simultaneously). Also, some behaviours appear to be learned best at particular times during development, called **critical periods**. For instance, a child who is not exposed to language prior to the age of 6 will generally have great difficulty learning to speak later.

One way to make sense of these variations in ease of learning is the preparedness dimension developed by Martin Seligman (Seligman 1970). **Preparedness** refers to the degree to which physiological structure influences the occurrence of behaviour (see Figure 3.12). Some behaviours seem to develop with little or no specific experience required; and Seligman refers to these as *prepared* behaviours, because the organism seems physiologically structured to produce the behaviour. Species-specific behaviours would belong to this category; the pouncing behaviour of cats is an example – cats

preparedness a concept developed by Martin Seligman to describe the degree to which physiological structure influences the occurrence of behaviour.

don't have to be taught to pounce! Dogs, by contrast, do not have a preprogrammed pounce response; instead, pouncing must be learned. In the same way, most human behaviour does not stem from 'pre-wired' origins. For example, while we are capable of the balance and coordination required to ride a bicycle, the specific responses involved are not inborn, but must be learned. Seligman refers to behaviours which must be acquired through experience as *unprepared*, since there is no hereditary predisposition involved. At the other extreme, there are some types of complex patterns of behaviour that we find very difficult, if not impossible, to acquire. In these cases, it seems that the physiological structure is not intended to cope with these situations. Seligman says that we are *contraprepared* to acquire such behaviour patterns. For instance, cats are prepared to lick themselves after eating, but they are contraprepared to use licking as an operant response to obtain food. Their physiology is structured for a 'food, then lick' sequence, not 'lick, then food'. (Rats, which have no 'food, then lick' predisposition, *can* use licking as an operant response for food.)

Traditionally, behaviourists focused on those response patterns which depend on learning (that is, unprepared behaviours). In doing so, they developed the view that all behaviour was alike, as expressed by the equipotentiality premise. As time went on, however, evidence arose that called this concept into question. While unlearned species-specific behaviours are clearly prepared, there are other behaviours which are learned so quickly as to seem prepared as well. One example concerns food-avoidance learning: Food preferences are well known in both people and animals – but what leads to rejecting a particular food? (See Box 3.1 for why we prefer certain foods.)

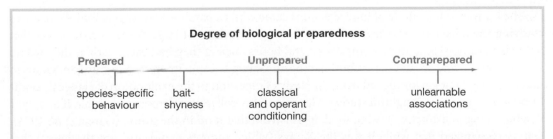

Figure 3.12 Seligman's Preparedness Continuum Martin Seligman has suggested that not all responses are the same, and that various behaviours can be understood in terms of how physiological factors prepare us to learn easily (prepared) or not at all (contraprepared).

Box 3.1 *Taste Preferences: Experience and Culture*

People in all cultures learn to salivate in anticipation of tasty food, but what do they find tasty? Does experience determine what appeals, or are there genetic differences? Certain aspects of taste, such as our capacity to detect differences in sweetness and saltiness, appear to be innate (Laing *et al.* 1993). However, how much sweetness or saltiness we *prefer* in our food seems to be the result of past experiences with food. For example, foods in both Syrian and New Orleans Cajun cooking tend to be highly salted. It is no wonder, then, that people who grew up with these types of food find Swedish cooking (which uses little salt) to be bland and tasteless (Beauchamp 1987).

As Garcia's work on bait-shyness demonstrated, there is an adaptive value to developing an aversion to the taste of something which makes you sick. But why do people show differences in what they prefer? Research on the origins of taste preferences suggests that they are based on traditional classical and operant conditioning, not biological predispositions. Infants, for example, will make active food choices based on what they like and dislike; in operant terms, different tastes differ in their reinforcing value (Mennella and Beauchamp 1997). Interestingly, however, these preferences seem to be influenced by exposure to flavours in the mother's breast milk, and even in the amniotic fluid prenatally – in other words, the infant comes to like the flavours of food the mother eats! Essentially, a process of classical conditioning is going on, whereby the flavours are associated with the nourishment of the food, but also with positive emotions elicited by contact with the mother during feeding. (Studies of contact comfort would imply that similar emotional conditioning would occur with bottle feeding – but, of course, the caregiver's diet would not affect the flavour of the milk!)

The effects of reinforcement on taste preferences are clear in many cases, too. As discussed in the chapter, food is an important reinforcer, and caregivers not only use food as a positive reinforcer (for example, a sweet as a reward), but also will typically encourage children to eat less attractive foods (for example, vegetables) by using praise, encouragement and other reinforcers. (A friend recalls as a child not being allowed to leave the table until his plate was empty!) Eating is also a social activity, and most people grow up associating certain foods with loved ones (for example, Grandma's special soup) and special occasions (for example, holiday desserts). These foods then tend to elicit emotions of well-being and happiness, due to classical conditioning. This is why we regard some foods as 'comfort foods'.

While food preferences depend on the individual's experience, culture also plays a role, producing commonalities within a culture and differences between cultures. Thus, in Toronto, one restaurant lists the heading of 'Comfort Foods' on its menu, with offerings such as macaroni and cheese, and chicken noodle soup. In Newfoundland, cod tongues might evoke similar appeal. In China, monkey brains were traditionally considered a delicacy, while on the prairies of Canada some people would feel the same way about the testicles of a bull. Whether one prefers potatoes, pasta, couscous or rice with meals likely reflects one's cultural background. In the end, what we choose to eat may not determine who we are, but it says a lot about our past experience!

The answer to the puzzle of food aversions came while a psychologist named John Garcia was studying the effects of exposure to X-rays. Among the effects of large doses of X-rays was that animals became sick to their stomachs several hours later; if they had eaten earlier, they would subsequently avoid whatever the food had been. Garcia became interested in this behaviour, in much the way that Pavlov moved from the study of digestion to the exploration of classical conditioning. In a series of insightful studies, Garcia and his colleagues demonstrated that if a rat gets ill after eating a distinctive-tasting food, it will avoid that food in the future (Garcia *et al.* 1974). Garcia recognized that while it was the X-rays (which the rats could not directly detect) that produced the sickness, the rats associated it with the *food* instead. Garcia called this behaviour *bait-shyness* (based on fishermen's belief that a fish nearly hooked on a particular bait won't strike it again).

To understand the bait-shyness effect, imagine a person who, while coming down with the stomach flu, happens to go out for dinner and eats something out of the ordinary (for example, curried chicken). Later, they feel sick because of the flu – but the next time they order curried chicken, the reaction of nausea reoccurs. Subsequent research, as well as anecdotal evidence, has confirmed that this phenomenon is genuine. For example, cancer patients often develop a wide range of food aversions as a result of the nausea produced by chemotherapy (Bernstein 1991).

The exploration of bait-shyness led to the conclusion that many species, including man, have developed in such a way that getting sick is very readily associated with the last food eaten (Logue 1988). The link between food and sickness often occurs after a single experience, despite the long delay between eating and getting sick. This long delay violates the basic behaviourist principle of *contiguity* – imagine trying to teach a rat to press a bar by giving it a positive reinforcer several hours after it makes the correct response! Garcia suggested that this capacity to learn even with long delays between eating and the consequence evolved because it was adaptive: an animal which ate something harmful would do well to avoid it in the future. Through mutation and natural selection, a neural mechanism was created to link taste with stomach upset. Thus, bait-shyness represents a form of prepared behaviour.

Over time, research has shown that food-avoidance learning is only one example of such prepared behaviours. For example, migratory birds are biologically predisposed to learn landmarks on their route (Shettleworth 1972). It has also been suggested that some types of human fears are more easily conditioned than others. Consider fear of the dark: humans are basically daytime creatures. To our ancestors, who depended (as we still do) on vision more than smell or hearing, the night world of darkness was a place of invisible dangers. Consequently, natural selection may have 'prepared' us to be afraid of the dark. (Note this does not mean that *all* people automatically have a strong fear of the dark; it simply implies that very little experience is needed to *develop* such a fear.)

Studies of classically-conditioned fears suggest that not all stimuli are equally likely to elicit conditioned fear responses. A few years after Watson's study of little Albert, another researcher found that an infant could be conditioned to fear a rat, but not wooden blocks or pieces of cloth (Bregman 1934). More recently, studies with adults have shown that fear is more easily conditioned to pictures of snakes or spiders than to pictures of flowers or houses (Ohman 1986; Ohman and Soares 1998). One way of interpreting such differences in the frequency of occurrence of different phobias is to assume that some fears (like snakes and spiders) are biologically prepared. This would make sense in evolutionary terms, since being fearful of creatures which are potentially poisonous or otherwise dangerous can be seen as adaptive. While other factors (such as cultural influences) could also be involved, evidence that other primates are similarly predisposed to fear snakes supports the evolutionary interpretation (Ohman and Mineka 2003).

It is harder to evaluate the possibility of there being *contraprepared* behaviours in humans. One of the difficulties is that, by definition, what is contraprepared is unlearnable. So, if there is some behavioural pattern that we cannot learn, would we even be able to recognize it? Thus far, no one has identified a clear example of contrapreparedness in people, despite many known examples in other species (such as the lick-then-food sequence in cats). Since there is no logical necessity that states that there must be such behaviours in humans, the absence of examples tells us little. So, at present, the issue is unresolved.

Overall, there seems little doubt that genetic and physiological factors play a role in human behaviour. However, such factors do not seem to play as significant a role in human activity as they do in many other species. This is indicated in part by the long infancy/childhood of human development; whereas many animals may be fully developed at birth, human infants require care and assistance longer than any other species. While this is a disadvantage in terms of survival, it allows for maximum flexibility of behaviour, based on experience (Bjorklund 1997). Learning takes time, and with time, the helplessness of the infant becomes the diverse and complex behaviour of the adult.

The study of biological constraints, by both ethologists and behaviourists, has enriched our understanding of behaviour, even as it has limited the range of application of conditioning principles. One of the significant lessons seems to be a recognition of the limitations of laboratory research. Whenever one enters the laboratory to study behaviour, one trades the advantages of control for the disadvantages of an artificial situation. It is well recognized that people often react differently when they know they are being studied (see Chapter 1), and even with animals, the laboratory setting may give a distorted perspective. This is not to say that the years of research on operant and classical conditioning are invalid; indeed, both frameworks have added a great deal to our understanding. However, just as each approach to psychology has its limits, so too it seems that a full understanding of behaviour cannot come from the laboratory alone. By exploring biological constraints, it can be argued that behaviourists have enriched their approach, rather than weakened it.

Try it Yourself

Have you ever developed a sudden aversion to a particular food? Do you recall the circumstances? Does Garcia's work on bait-shyness help you to understand your own taste preferences? In what ways?

CONCLUSION

The behaviourist approach is rooted in the assumption that science must be based on the study of observable events. In terms of behaviour, this means looking at the interactions between an organism and its environment. In adopting this stance, behaviourists forgo attempts to study consciousness and internal subjective states. As Skinner has pointed out, behaviourism is a method of analysis rather than simply a theory (Skinner 1987). Critics say that treating the organism like a 'black box' means that one ignores the mental processes that are central to human behaviour. Skinner says that such events are scientifically unknowable, and in any case, do not *cause* behaviour: thinking about something before doing it is simply correlated with the observable behaviour. For example, if a Freudian theorist suggests that adult behaviour can best be understood by looking at childhood experiences, Skinner agrees – but suggests that the connections are based on the reinforcement history of the person, not some vague concept of 'conflicts between id and ego'.

Ultimately, the best criterion for judging any approach, including behaviourism, is not our theoretical preference, but the extent to which it helps us to make sense of behaviour. While many have criticized the restrictions of behaviourism, the reality is that the study of classical and operant conditioning has added to our overall understanding in psychology. The appeal of behaviourism is reflected in the fact that for many years it was the dominant force in North American psychology. It is interesting, and in some ways ironic, that behaviourism has influenced the attitudes and methods of many psychologists, and has even contributed to the success of the cognitive approach. For example, Edward Tolman, regarded as one of the founders of the cognitive approach, considered himself a behaviourist – though not a radical behaviourist like Skinner. In addition, the study of many cognitive issues, such as observational learning (imitation) and the use of hypotheses in problem solving, began with similar behaviourist studies of animals. Where the introspectionists failed in their attempts to make sense out of mental processes, the behaviourists have pointed the way to new possibilities for a scientific psychology of the mind. More broadly, while radical behaviourism is no longer very influential, there is an active interest in exploring environmental influences on behaviour – what is sometimes called 'behavioural' psychology.

Although the behaviourist approach has contributed significantly to our understanding of behaviour and has led to some highly effective therapies for some behavioural disorders, it no longer occupies the pre-eminent position it once did within psychology. In part, this reflects changes in the discipline, and in part, the limitations of the approach. One major weakness is that research by ethologists and others has shown that the principles of conditioning are not as universal as was once asserted. This failure of the 'equipotentiality premise' restricts the generality of behaviourist principles in important ways. Beyond that, interest in mental processes has not diminished simply because the behaviourists have refused to address the issues. Instead, researchers have found new ways to study mental processes, resulting in new interest in the cognitive approach – as we shall see in Chapter 4.

Putting It All Together – Behaviourist Approach

There are several ways in which the behaviourist approach can shed light on Sam's behaviour. First, it seems likely that he had developed a conditioned fear to writing tests. Given that Sam was always a student who had to work hard to attain good marks, through classical conditioning, he probably came to associate schoolwork with anxiety. While the case study does not specify the circumstances, it is likely that on one or more previous occasions, Sam did badly on tests. The poor grade was likely associated with scolding or disapproval from his parents, or embarrassment from friends (UCS). The fear and anxiety produced (UCR) by these stimuli then became associated with the test situation, so that now a test is a CS for anxiety (CR). (Note that this process may reflect higher order conditioning, in that the anxiety/fear produced by criticism was likely itself acquired through prior conditioning.) Similarly, Sam may have had experiences in which bright, independent girls rejected him (UCS). The anxiety of embarrassment he felt (UCR) became associated with bright, independent girls, so now, even though he is attracted to Vanessa, she is a CS for anxiety (CR).

Sam's procrastination represents a form of operant conditioning. Because his schoolwork is highly aversive (conditioned negative reinforcer), he avoids it by procrastinating. Since procrastinating produces removal of the aversive stimulus, this is negative reinforcement, so he continues to avoid doing his schoolwork. At the same time, socializing with his friends, doing household chores and watching TV have some positive reinforcement value, even though this may be limited by the guilt he feels (a negative reinforcer) while engaging in these pastimes. Note that the reinforcement for procrastinating is immediate, as opposed to the delayed reinforcement he would get from completing his schoolwork (for example, passing his courses), so it has greater strength. The books in this situation represent a discriminative stimulus – as noted in the chapter, behaviour under a contingency of negative reinforcement usually begins as escape (for example, from the anxiety associated with poor school results) and progresses to avoidance of the discriminative stimulus (the books) which signals that negative reinforcer. (It is also worth noting that in this situation, Sam's behaviour is being affected by several types of reinforcers and contingencies of reinforcement. In the real world, behaviour is seldom as simple as in laboratory situations.)

Despite his obvious struggle with anxiety and procrastination, Sam has managed to pass his courses in the past, so he has received some positive reinforcement for being in school. Because he does not seem to enjoy the process of studying, it appears that the main reinforcers for his school behaviour are his grades. Given that his academic success does not appear to have been consistent, and the reinforcers (passing grades) only intermittent, this represents a form of VR schedule. Thus, despite the limitations of his last-minute techniques, he is being positively reinforced for continuing this pattern of behaviour. (As noted in the chapter, a VR schedule is highly resistant to extinction.)

Sam seems to generalize his behaviour to all his school subjects, but the chances are he shows discrimination in his procrastinating by recognizing that not studying just before work is due will result in an immediate negative reinforcer (a failing grade) – that is, the due date is a discriminative stimulus for a change in contingency.

Vanessa is presently a friend of Sam's, so she provides a positive reinforcer for him, as he does for her. He is not sure, however, whether this positive response of hers would generalize to a more romantic relationship, or whether she would discriminate between Sam the friend and Sam the lover. He fears that Sam the lover would receive negative reinforcers from her, so he shows discrimination in his behaviour – he demonstrates only the behaviour guaranteed to bring him a positive reinforcer and does not ask her on a date. That is, he avoids the possibility of anxiety through rejection.

Behaviourists would say that Sam, like all individuals, has a complex history of past learning. But to deal with his anxiety and both his academic procrastination and his avoidance of a romantic overture to Vanessa, it is more important to focus on changing his current behaviour by means of behaviour modification.

CHAPTER SUMMARY

- The behaviourist approach emphasizes the study of *observable responses*, and rejects attempts to study internal processes like thinking.

- In doing so, behaviourists focus on *learning* as the primary factor in explaining changes in behaviour. Depending on the type of response, this involves either *classical conditioning* or *operant conditioning*.

- Classical conditioning is concerned with how *conditioned stimuli* come to elicit *conditioned responses* – reflex responses which are normally elicited by *unconditioned stimuli*.

- Classical conditioning can be applied to a number of aspects of human behaviour, including *emotional responses* like fears, and even activity of the *immune system*.

- Operant conditioning is concerned with how the probability of a *voluntary* 'operant' *response* changes as a function of the environmental consequences (*reinforcer*) which follow the response.

- This process of *reinforcement* can be analysed in terms of the *type of reinforcer*, the *contingency of reinforcement* and the *schedule of reinforcement*.

- The application of operant conditioning to everyday behaviour is commonly called *behaviour modification*; related research includes the effects of *aversive control* and methods of altering behaviour by *biofeedback*, among other uses.
- Recent research has indicated that while conceptually distinct, classical and operant conditioning are interrelated in actual behaviour. In addition, research on *biological constraints on learning* has suggested that there are limits to the generality of conditioning principles, as illustrated by the concept of *preparedness*.

❸ Key terms and concepts

learning
law of effect
classical conditioning
unconditioned response
unconditioned stimulus
conditioned stimulus
conditioned response
stimulus generalization
stimulus discrimination
extinction (classical)
spontaneous recovery
higher order conditioning
conditioned emotional response
operant conditioning
reinforcer
reinforcement
primary reinforcer
conditioned reinforcer
positive reinforcer

negative reinforcer
positive reinforcement
punishment
negative reinforcement
omission
shaping
extinction (operant)
continuous reinforcement
partial reinforcement
schedules of reinforcement
interval schedules
ratio schedules
discriminative stimulus
behaviour modification
aversive control
biofeedback
species-specific behaviour
preparedness

Online
Learning Centre

When you have read this chapter, log onto the Online Learning Centre website at
www.openup.co.uk/glassman where you will find answers to these Test Yourself questions and suggested answers to the Try it Yourself activities, plus many more learning resources to help you study psychology.

Test yourself questions

1 What is the meaning of the following terms?
   unconditioned stimulus
   conditioned stimulus
   unconditioned response
   conditioned response
   conditioned emotional response
2 What are the differences and similarities between classical and operant conditioning?
3 Why is punishment not recommended in reducing misbehaviour in children?
4 How does biology constrain learning?

Suggestions for Further Reading

- For the reader interested in a more detailed discussion of the principles of learning (both classical and operant), **Chance's** *Learning and Behavior* (2008) is a very readable account. For an assessment of the impact of behaviourism, see **Kunkel's** (1996) article.

- **B. F. Skinner** has maintained a distinctive position within behaviourism, not least for his outspoken comments on changing society. One of his clearest presentations of his views on society is *Beyond Freedom and Dignity* (1971).

- One significant influence of behaviourism has been the practical application of conditioning principles to everyday behaviour. **Martin and Pear's** *Behavior Modification: What It Is and How to Do It* (2006) provides a good overview of such applications. For a more specific discussion of the use of biofeedback techniques in clinical applications, see *Biofeedback: A Practitioner's Guide* (2005), edited by **Schwartz and Andrasik**.

- For an account which shows how the ethological approach differs from laboratory studies of behaviour, **Jane Goodall's** *Through a Window* (1990) provides a highly readable beginning.

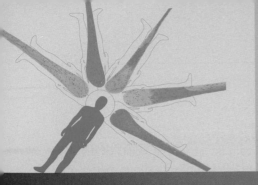

Chapter **4**

The Cognitive Approach

LEARNING OBJECTIVES

In this chapter, the objectives are to learn:

☑ the role of mediational processes in the cognitive approach

☑ the relationship between perception and cognition

☑ the stage model of memory, including
  • sensory memory
  • short-term memory
  • long-term memory

☑ concepts of encoding and storage in memory, including
  • rehearsal in STM
  • procedural, episodic and semantic long-term memory

☑ the nature of forgetting in memory, including
  • decay
  • displacement
  • interference and context-based retrieval in LTM

☑ the role of reconstruction in memory

☑ methods of improving memory

☑ models and techiques for problem solving

☑ how creativity is used in problem solving

☑ how people acquire problem solving skills

☑ how people learn language

☑ the relationship between thinking and language

☑ how thinking processes affect other aspects of behaviour, including
  • modifying attitudes through cognitive dissonance
  • the role of attribution theory in everyday behaviour
  • the relationship between cognition and emotion

THOUGHT AND ACTION

At the turn of the last century, a young physicist was working as a clerk in the Swiss patent office. In his spare time, he pursued his interest in theoretical physics. Like other physicists of the day, he was puzzled by discoveries which seemed to challenge long-held notions about matter and energy. For one thing, the speed of light seem to be a constant throughout the universe, but no one could explain why. Then, the young clerk tried reversing the problem, suggesting one *assume* that the speed of light was constant. Having made this shift, many aspects of the problem fell into place. Most of his older colleagues were perplexed and even outraged; after all, the proposal contradicted all of their previous training. In the end, his solution was accepted, and his work triggered significant changes in science and the world. The theory is now called the special theory of relativity, and the young clerk was Albert Einstein.

Today, all college physics students, and many others, have a basic grasp of Einstein's insights, expressed as $E = mc^2$. It is one of the marvels of great ideas that, once formulated, they can be readily understood by many. Yet the first formulation of a solution is often elusive; even many of Einstein's colleagues had difficulty grasping it. What leads to such insights? How do we develop new solutions to old problems?

Consider a simpler example of problem solving: a young child is given a problem in which pointing to a star leads to getting candy as a reinforcer, but pointing to a circle does not. Gradually, the child becomes consistent in choosing the star. However, once they have learned this discrimination, they are given a new problem, involving a square and a triangle. On this problem, the child is consistently correct by the second trial. (On the first trial, of course, they must guess.) On other problems with new shapes, the child continues to perform consistently well. Behaviourists would describe the task as learning to respond to a discriminative stimulus (the shape), a process which requires trial and error learning. Yet in this situation, the child seems to develop a *rule* for making choices, rather than simply being reinforced for a particular response. Can conditioning adequately explain such complex behaviour?

Or consider this: if you have developed a skill, such as playing a piano, does the skill disappear if there is no piano present? Is *knowing* something the same as *doing* something?

To the behaviourists, all human activity can be described in terms of responses to environmental cues. Behaviour, defined as observable responses, is based on conditioned reflexes, reinforcement and other simple processes. By its nature, this approach tends to deny that anything happening *within* the person is significant. Memories, thoughts and feelings are seen as irrelevant to science – and therefore meaningless. Expressed in these terms, all of the above examples become virtually impossible to understand.

As the above examples illustrate, much of our behaviour involves not simply actions, but mental processes such as perception, memory, problem solving and language. While these processes cannot be directly observed, that does not seem sufficient reason to ignore their existence, or the ways in which they affect behaviour. Consequently, the *cognitive approach* is concerned with understanding the thinking processes that underlie our actions.

INTRODUCTION

Unlike the behaviourists, cognitive psychologists believe that one cannot fully explain behaviour in terms of stimulus–response connections (the child learning a 'rule' for discrimination problems, described above, is one example). Instead, the cognitive approach sees events within

mediator a process or event within the individual which comes between a stimulus and a response.

the person as being at least as important as environmental stimuli in the understanding of behaviour. These internal events are described as mediational processes or **mediators**, because they come between the stimulus and the response. Thinking processes like memory, problem solving and language are all based on mediators.

This emphasis on mediating processes, and the way they are defined, is central to the cognitive approach. However, the nature of these mediators is also important. Mediational processes are defined functionally – that is, with reference to how behaviour is altered. Mediators are therefore *conceptual* – for example, describing the process of memory without concern for its physical basis (by contrast, the biological approach also deals with mediational processes, but they are defined *physiologically*, not conceptually – for example, looking at how the visual cortex is involved in perception). Hence, the cognitive approach is distinct in terms of what it studies, and the basis of the concepts used.

The development of the cognitive approach is closely related to behaviourism, since in part it developed as a reaction against the behaviourists' emphasis on external events. By the time Watson published the first edition of *Behaviourism* in 1924, he felt that his approach was gaining ground against the ambiguities of introspectionism. Yet at virtually the same point in time, the seeds for a new alternative were being sown, as shown by two other books which appeared. The first was by a young German researcher named Wolfgang Kohler, called *The Mentality of Apes* (Kohler 1925). In this book he reported observations which suggested that animals could show behaviour which was *insightful*, and he rejected behaviourism in favour of an approach called Gestalt psychology. The other challenge to behaviourism came from someone who actually called himself a behaviourist. In 1932, E. C. Tolman published a book called *Purposive Behavior in Animals and Man* (Tolman 1932). In this book, he described research which was difficult to explain in terms of traditional behaviourism. Instead of associations between stimuli and responses, Tolman talked about learning as based on relationships among stimuli, referred to as forming **cognitive maps**. In addition, he argued that learning and responding are not the same, and that it is possible to learn without showing a correct response. Taken together, the work of Kohler and Tolman raised basic questions about the validity of behaviourism, and laid the foundations for what has become the cognitive approach. To see how, let us briefly examine each man's work more closely.

cognitive map Tolman's term for the mental representation of learned relationships among stimuli.

While early behaviourists saw learning as basically a matter of trial and error, Kohler argued that we tend to *organize* experience in particular ways. This is illustrated by the phenomenon Kohler called **insight**. This is a sudden change in the way one organizes a problem situation, typically characterized by a change in behaviour from random responding to rule-based responding. For example, a child solving discrimination problems can show insight, as mentioned above. In general, insight can be described as forming an appropriate *schema* (or, to use Kohler's term, **mental set**) for a particular situation.

insight a sudden change in the way one organizes a problem situation; typically this is characterized by a change in behaviour from random responding to rule-based responding.
mental set in Gestalt theory, the cognitive schema an individual uses to organize their perception of a particular situation, such as a problem.

One of the most famous examples of Kohler's work on insight involved an ape named Sultan. Kohler gave Sultan a series of related problems, in which he had to use a stick to reach for a banana which was placed outside his cage, out of arm's reach. After solving such problems on several occasions, Sultan was then presented with a stick which was not long enough to reach the banana. However, outside the cage was a longer stick. After several unsuccessful tries, Sultan threw down the short stick in evident frustration, and retreated to the corner of his cage. A little while later, he suddenly went over to the short stick, used it to reach the other, longer stick, and with the new stick, reached the banana! As Kohler noted, there was no gradual sequence, as one might expect with shaping, nor did it seem to be the result of trial and error. Instead, there was a sudden change in the way Sultan organized the elements – insight. Kohler's work thus created a shift away from looking at all behaviour as trial and error, towards examining the internal organizing processes that mediate behaviour.

Key Thinker: **Wolfgang Kohler**

Wolfgang Kohler (1887 – 1967) was a founder of Gestalt theory. Born in Tallinn, Estonia, he was educated in Germany, attending the universities of Tübingen, Frankfurt and Berlin (where he received his doctorate). While at Frankfurt, he met Max Wertheimer and Kurt Koffka, who also contributed to the development of Gestalt theory. In 1913, Kohler went to Tenerife in the Canary Islands as director of a lab studying the apes residing on the island; in what became an act of serendipity, he was stranded there for the duration of World War I, unable to leave until 1919. During this period, his studies with the apes led him to a view of problem solving as an active process of insight, unlike the trial and error viewpoint advocated by Tolman. Eventually, this work became an important influence on Gestalt theory, which Kohler promoted as a professor at the University of Berlin (he was made chair in psychology in 1921). In 1934 he travelled to the USA to deliver the annual William James Lectures at Harvard; aware of Hitler's rise to power in Germany, he accepted an appointment at Swarthmore University in Pennsylvania, where he remained almost until his death at the age of 80.

Kohler talked about internal organizing principles, a subject which behaviourists avoided. By contrast, Tolman regarded himself as a behaviourist, in that his data were strictly based on observations of stimuli and responses. But the problems he examined were very embarrassing to the traditional behaviourists of his day. For instance, behaviourists argued that unless there was a change in behaviour (performance of a new response), no learning had taken place. Tolman demonstrated that animals may learn the pattern of a maze, forming a *cognitive map*, and yet not perform correctly until a reward is given. This **latent learning**, being unobservable as it occurred, suggested that learning is distinct from the performance of a behaviour. In another study, rats explored mazes which had several paths of varying length, all leading to the end; later, if the shortest path to reach food at the goal was blocked, the rats chose the second shortest route, rather than choosing randomly. This is similar to a person who finds his normal driving route blocked by construction, and quickly selects the most reasonable alternate route. In both the rat and person, this seems to require a knowledge of how locations are connected, rather than mechanical repetition of a shaped sequence of responses. Thus, Tolman's theory ultimately emphasized the importance of mediational processes.

latent learning a term used by Tolman to describe situations in which learning is distinct from the performance of a behaviour.

Both Kohler and Tolman had an important influence in laying the foundation of the cognitive approach. Yet despite their early role, neither has many direct followers today. This does not mean that the cognitive approach is not important (if anything, its influence has grown in recent years). Rather, it means that the impact of these pioneers is diffuse, and sometimes not directly recognized. To a large extent, the coherence of the cognitive approach is not based on a single theory or researcher, but rather on the underlying assumptions about behaviour, and the central focus given to internal mental processes. Hence, various elements of the approach have been transformed or used piecemeal by researchers of various outlooks. Still, much of the basis of current work can be traced back to the influence of Kohler and Tolman.

Key Thinker: **Edward Chace Tolman**

Edward Chace Tolman (1886–1959) was born in Newton, Massachusetts. He received his bachelor's degree from MIT, and his doctorate in psychology from Harvard in 1915. Tolman spent almost his entire career at the University of California at Berkeley. While he considered himself a behaviourist, and his own research was done almost entirely with rats, Tolman's work bears little resemblance to the radical behaviourists, such as Watson and Skinner. A contemporary of Watson, he rejected the emphasis on reflexes and trial and error learning which were central to Watson's views. Instead, he developed a concept of 'purposive behaviourism', which emphasized the distinction between learning and performance (as seen in latent learning), and viewed learning in terms of the formation of 'hypotheses' and 'cognitive maps'. Both by showing the weaknesses of radical behaviourism, and by proposing concepts which acknowledged the existence of mediational processes, Tolman helped lay the foundations for the cognitive approach. He was 73 when he died – just a few years before the blossoming of the cognitive approach in the 1960s.

Since no single theorist has dominated the cognitive approach in the way that Skinner has operant conditioning or Freud has psychoanalysis, there has been a greater exchange with other approaches, both within and outside psychology. As a result, today one can encounter a cognitive theory of emotion, or social behaviour, or even cognitive behaviour modification. At the same time, cognitive psychologists have borrowed from other fields, including computer science and physiology. In fact, some even refer to 'cognitive science' as a hybrid discipline, incorporating elements of psychology, linguistics, computer science and physiology!

One reason for this broad interchange is the tendency of psychologists to seek new models. Analogies and metaphors have long played a role in scientific thinking, in the desire to describe problems in new ways. In the seventeenth century, Descartes talked about hydraulically-operated statues in the Tuileries Gardens in Paris as a model for the physiology of body movements. At the turn of the last century, psychologists compared the brain (as a network of stimulus–response connections) to a telephone switchboard. Today, computers play a large role in our lives, and psychologists have borrowed from the language of computer technology, in the form of 'information processing' models. Each analogy has benefits and limitations, but the use of such models to aid our understanding is a well-established practice.

Consciously or not, those who use information-processing descriptions fall within the tradition of Kohler and Tolman. **Information processing** refers to the intervening events (mediators) which come between input (stimulus) and output (response) of the system (person). In a computer, one cannot predict the output from the input without knowing something about what is going on within the computer. In the same way, a person's behaviour cannot be understood solely by looking at environmental stimuli. There is a further parallel in that the computer model emphasizes the

information processing a term borrowed from computer science by cognitive psychologists to describe the mental functions which occur between stimulus and response.

concept of *processing* of information, by which we mean that the output represents a qualitative change in the input, such as combination, analysis or comparison of input data. This element of active transformation is also seen in Kohler's emphasis on insight as creative, and Tolman's view of cognitive maps as going beyond mere repetitions of previous responses. Thus, information processing models fit very comfortably within the cognitive approach.

In this chapter, we will look at several aspects of behaviour from the cognitive viewpoint. The most general concern is simply trying to understand how we behave. Generally, cognitive researchers have focused on questions concerning how we remember, why we forget, what leads to effective solutions to problems, and related questions. This emphasis on thinking processes (memory, problem solving, decision making, language) is natural, given that the word 'cognitive' refers to thinking. (See Green 1996 for a history of how the term has been used by psychologists and philosophers.) At the same time, the scope of the cognitive approach has broadened in recent years, and even includes such 'irrational' aspects of behaviour as emotions. Whatever the topic, the key elements of the cognitive approach remain the same:

1 processes within the person are considered central to understanding behaviour; and
2 these mediating processes operate in an organized and systematic way, not by trial and error.

PERCEPTION AND COGNITION

Traditionally, psychologists tried to separate the process of perceiving from thinking – that is, to separate perception and cognition. Perception was used to refer to the receiving of sensory inputs, while cognition referred to mental processes. However, over time, it has come to be recognized that the distinction is hard to maintain. For example, perceiving involves recognizing a stimulus – and recognition of something as familiar requires making use of memory (a cognitive process). In the same way, thinking does not occur in the absence of something to think about, and much of the content of thought relates to present and past sensory stimuli. Hence, while clearly not synonyms, perception and cognition are also not totally distinct terms (Robinson 1979).

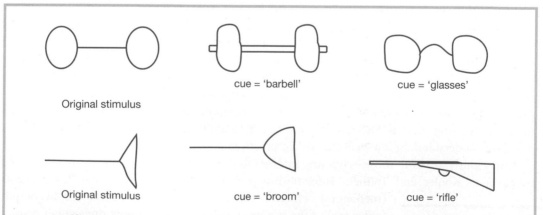

Figure 4.1 Closure in Perception and Memory The Gestalt concept of closure suggests we distort perception based on what we expect to see; as shown in these examples, the same applies to memory. (Adapted from Carmichael *et al*. 1932)

One example of this overlap is Gestalt theory, as developed by Kohler and others. Gestalt theory is a theory of perception as well as cognition. For instance, memory for stimuli is related to how they are perceived. In a classic study by Carmichael and his colleagues, subjects were given simple line figures to remember, along with a word cue (Carmichael *et al.* 1932). Later, they were asked to draw each figure when given the appropriate cue. The crucial variable was the word cue used. For example, one figure consisted of a short horizontal line, terminated at each end by a circle. The verbal cue given to different subjects was either 'glasses' or 'barbell'. Later, the drawings produced tended to be distorted in ways that reflected the word cue (for example, by adding extensions for 'glasses', or changing the line to a solid bar for 'barbell') (see Figure 4.1). This study, while complicated by the problem of interpreting participants' drawings for accuracy, is consistent with a number of Gestalt studies which suggest that perception and memory are interrelated. In the first chapter, we noted how perception is best conceived as an active process of interpreting the environment; the interpretations we make are influenced by our mental schemata, which in turn are shaped by our experiences. This model of the perceptual process is similar to Gestalt theory, which sees perception as based on a number of internal organizing principles. While it is beyond the scope of this chapter to provide a full overview of Gestalt theory, we will touch upon various aspects related to memory and problem solving. For the present, it is worth noting that the cognitive processes we will discuss are in fact closely linked to the process of perceiving.

Try it Yourself

The analogy of the mind to a computer is a popular one today. In what ways do you see the comparison as reasonable? In what ways do you feel the analogy is not appropriate? For example, do you see current computers as actually capable of thinking?

Imagine a science fiction universe in which part of the population was made up of mechanical people (androids) whose minds were, in fact, computers. Could you tell the difference between these androids and biological people? How could you tell? What sort of tests might you employ to determine which people are androids and which are biological?

LEARNING AND MEMORY

Learning as Information Gathering

While behaviourists talk about learning as changes in responses, the cognitive approach focuses on the knowledge which guides those responses. In terms of the information processing model, learning is based on *gathering information*. 'Information' can be any meaningful data. In everyday life, we gather, and store in memory for later use, everything from the names of new business contacts to the location of the washroom in our favourite restaurant. (There is no requirement that what we store has to be 'significant'.) In the process, we all accumulate vast amounts of seemingly useless information. For instance, what does WWW stand for? What were the first names of The Beatles? What did you have for dinner last night?

At first glance, the gathering and storage of information may seem less efficient as a learning system than the behaviourist notion of associations between stimuli and responses. But learning through information gathering has one great advantage: flexibility. Tolman's concept of cognitive maps illustrates this clearly. For example, if your route to work is represented by a mental map of the city, not a fixed series of responses, then you can detour to go to the dry cleaner, take an alternate route when traffic is bad, and so on. Information which was previously not reflected in behaviour thus becomes significant as the situation is altered (for example, knowing that a particular street is one-way affects your choice of alternative routes). Tolman would call this a form of *latent learning*.

learning in cognitive psychology, the process of gathering information and organizing it into mental schemata.

For the cognitive psychologist, **learning** involves both gathering information and organizing it into mental schemata. In this sense, the way we select and use the information is what determines the relationship between any stimulus and response. Consider again the example of the traffic jam: the stimuli could include your present location, the time of day, the density of traffic and awareness of your goal. Making a detour involves several types of mediators: your knowledge of the street layout (a cognitive map), information from past experiences about where traffic is likely to be lighter (memory) and motivational preferences (such as a short route through slow-moving traffic, or a longer route by an expressway). As plausible as this description may seem, it also raises several questions. How did you develop a cognitive map of the city originally? How do you recall past experiences about traffic patterns, especially if the information didn't seem important at the time? And how did you decide the best route, given all of the information? Let us begin by considering the question of how we remember things.

Memory as the Retention of Learning

Effective behaviour often depends on remembering information at the right time. In cognitive terms, **memory** can be defined as the retention and use of prior learning. Memory is a mediator of behaviour because, through memory, past experiences influence what we currently do. However, there are several ways in which this information about the past can be used.

memory the retention and use of prior learning.
recall in memory, the active retrieval of information.
recognition in memory, the process of identifying presented information as familiar.
relearning in memory, an improvement in performance which occurs by reviewing, despite the inability to recall or recognize the information.
priming a phenomenon whereby a thought or memory increases the activation of associated thoughts or memories (the term is analogous to 'priming a pump' by using a small quantity of water to enhance the flow of water).

Usually, we simply remember information as we need it. This is called **recall**, the active retrieval of information. Answering any of the 'trivia' questions in the previous section would involve recall. Sometimes, however, we can't recall something, but are able to recognize it as correct if it is presented to us. For instance, does A-OK refer to the name of a ranch, teen slang or astronauts' jargon? This process of identifying information as familiar is called **recognition**. Multiple-choice tests of memory are based on testing recognition, not recall. (What sort of examination would test recall?) Both recall and recognition involve a conscious effort to remember the information (sometimes called 'explicit memory'). There are also circumstances where information has been retained, yet we are not consciously aware that this is the case. In such situations, we may not be able to recognize something, yet on reviewing it, it quickly seems familiar. For example, a person who hasn't spoken a foreign language for several years adapts more quickly than a first-time learner. This type of improvement by reviewing is called **relearning**, and is sometimes referred to as 'implicit memory'. Another form of implicit memory is **priming**, where prior exposure to information affects later ability to recall something related. Thus, if we see the word 'hot' we find it easier to supply the missing letters in 'c_ _d' and form the word 'cold'; if we see the word 'ace', however, we are more likely to form the word 'card' (as we will discuss in Chapter 8, priming has been implicated in social behaviour as well as memory). Hence, there can be some memory of a prior experience, even when we are unable to recall or recognize the information.

Remembering, then, can take many forms. Although it is easy to say that memory refers to the storage of information, that definition does not tell us very much. To understand how memory functions, we must look more closely at its characteristics. First, though, try to answer the following questions. What colour was the house you grew up in? Was your first teacher a man or a woman? Can you recall the teacher's name? These questions may sound like further trivia items, but with a difference. Virtually everyone could answer at least the first two questions. Yet for most readers, those events occurred at least 15 years ago, and possibly much longer. Such recall is not unusual; many people have recalled personal experiences which happened 60 or 80 years earlier. So, we might say that memory is permanent – or at least potentially permanent, since we do seem to forget some things.

Forgetting can be both frustrating and puzzling, given that we can be so good at remembering. In fact, though, not all memory is alike; to understand this, let us take another example. Have you ever looked up a phone number, found it busy on dialling, and then had to look it up again to dial a minute later? Or have you ever been introduced to someone, and then not been able to remember their name at the end of the conversation? Often we forget information almost immediately after we encounter it. How can we forget something which happened 30 seconds ago, and yet remember something from many years ago? To understand these variations, we need to consider what is known about how memory functions.

A Basic Model of Memory

The information processing approach has led to a model of memory which is based on a computer analogy. Since many researchers have contributed to the development of this model, it is frequently discussed in generic terms (see Atkinson and Shiffrin 1968; Waugh and Norman 1965). This model views memory as consisting of a series of distinct stages, each with its own special characteristics (see Figure 4.2). Like most analogies, this model has limitations (see Logie 1996; Nairne 2002), but is useful for organizing the basic features of memory.

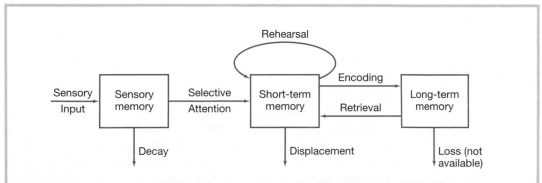

Figure 4.2 A General Model of Memory We tend to view memory as consisting of a number of stages, which are linked by processes like selective attention; one of the first models of this type was proposed by Atkinson and Shiffrin (1968).

sensory memory a modality-specific transient form of memory which serves as a buffer between the senses and short-term memory.

Information which we gather must be acquired through our senses, and research has demonstrated that there is a distinctive form of **sensory memory** for each sense modality (such as vision and hearing). Typically, however, this form of retention is very transient, and serves primarily as a sort of buffer between the senses and our true memory. Extensive work has been done on the nature of the various forms of sensory memory, especially for vision and hearing. Each sense mode turns out to have rather specific differences (for example, visual sensory memory lasts less than a second, but auditory sensory memory can last up to three or four seconds.) However, for our purposes, it is what happens *after* sensory memory that is most significant, so we will not provide further detail here. (For more information, see Sperling 1960; Crowder and Morton 1969.)

Since we are continually bombarded by sensory stimuli, we must focus selectively on those elements which are likely to be most significant. This selection occurs through the perceptual process of **attention**, as mentioned in Chapter 1. Because sensory memory functions at a level *before* the filtering of attention takes place, it is sometimes referred to as being *pre-attentive*; in general, the evidence suggests that stimuli have no enduring influence on us unless we pay attention to them. Attention limits our conscious awareness to a small portion of our moment-to-moment environment. What we focus on can be influenced either by deliberate choice or by a particularly compelling stimulus (for example, a sudden loud noise while you are studying). This capacity to redirect our attention enables us to shift from one sense mode to another, or even to focus on particular stimuli within one sense mode. A good example of this is the so-called *cocktail party effect*: in a crowded room, you can shift your attention from talking to a person in front of you to suddenly listening to another conversation taking place behind you – without even shifting your head! Attention thus selects the information which becomes available to memory.

attention the process of selectively focusing on particular stimulus elements, typically those deemed most significant.

Determining the precise limits on attention (in terms of both the capacity to process information and the ability to switch between sources) is complex, and has both theoretical and practical significance. For example, there is an ongoing concern about the extent to which using a mobile phone while driving affects one's ability to attend to traffic conditions. Answering the question is challenging, with various studies using either lab-based simulators, real-world testing or statistical analyses of accidents. Overall, the results indicate that using a mobile phone while driving *does* impair attention and driving performance (Royal Society for the Prevention of Accidents 2004), with some lab studies showing an impairment roughly comparable to driving while drunk (Strayer and Drews 2007).

short-term memory (STM) the component of memory which handles retention over relatively brief intervals of up to approximately 15 seconds.
long-term memory (LTM) the component of memory which is involved with retention over relatively long periods (hours, days, weeks or longer).

While we talk about memory in everyday life as a single process, the evidence suggests that it is more meaningful to consider it as two separate stages. **Short-term memory (STM)** refers to retention over relatively brief intervals – usually 15 seconds or so. By contrast, **long-term memory (LTM)** refers to retention over relatively long periods – hours, days, weeks or longer. The general model assumes that the two types of retention reflect different processes. Since both represent mediating processes that cannot be directly observed, it is worth considering the evidence which is used to support this view.

One type of evidence has already been noted: *duration*. LTM is potentially permanent, while STM is very limited. As noted already, there is a great deal of evidence suggesting people can remember information for decades or more (Bahrick and Hall 1991). By contrast, information held in STM will normally be lost after several seconds, unless it is transferred to LTM (how this might happen will be discussed later) or rehearsed (that is, repeated over and over). For example, have you ever found yourself rehearsing a phone number as you dial? As we will discuss, such repetition is actually a poor way to ensure information is retained in LTM – thus, it is more useful for looking up phone numbers than as a study strategy for an exam!

There is another important distinction between STM and LTM, that of *capacity*. STM is very limited in the amount of information it can retain. In order to see this, try the following test: In Box 4.1, you will find a string of letters. Read through them once, then turn the page over and immediately try to recall them in the correct order. Then, check your accuracy. Only those letters which are correct, and are in the correct sequence, should be counted as correct. If you remembered about seven letters, you are average. Nine or more letters would be very unusual.

chunk the basic measure of STM capacity, representing a meaningful unit, such as random letters, numbers or words.

Now, consider how long you had to retain the letters before writing them down: perhaps four seconds? Yet, on average, people forget about one-third of the letters (assuming ten altogether). Increasing the original number of letters would lower your percentage, for the number seven, not two-thirds, appears to be the best measure of STM capacity, which is often described as being 7 ± 2 meaningful items, or **chunks**. That is, STM appears to be limited to between five and nine independent items, such as random letters, numbers or words (Miller 1956). Phone numbers, because they have familiar three-digit exchanges, are not really seven independent items. Similarly, letters that spell a word are neither independent nor random, and are therefore easier to remember. Attempts to remember longer sequences of items usually result in greater forgetting of the earlier items, due to the limited capacity of STM.

Box 4.1 *A Test of Short-term Memory*

To test your short-term memory, follow the instructions in the box.
To test your STM capacity, read through the list of letters below. Read the list slowly, but only once. Immediately after reading the last letter, try to write down the entire sequence in the correct order.

L R X D V C M Q B N

For scoring, give yourself credit only for letters in the correct order, not counting reversals, omissions or other errors. Typical recall would be about seven correct.

Try it Yourself

To better understand how STM and LTM differ, first review Box 4.1 on STM, then consider the following questions on LTM.

What is your oldest distinct memory? What was the situation? How long ago did the event occur? What details do you remember? How confident are you that your recall of this memory is accurate? Is there other information that you have known for a long time but don't remember when or where you learned it? How do those memories differ from STM?

LTM, on the other hand, appears to be practically unlimited in capacity. At the very least, there is no documented case of someone 'running out of memory space'. You may have encountered speculations about the capacity of the human brain, and statements such as, 'Einstein only used 40 per cent of his brain capacity.' While provocative, such statements must be taken lightly, since at best they are crude estimates. The problem is that we still know very little about how information is stored in the nervous system, and consequently any estimate of capacity is purely guesswork.

Encoding and Storage in Memory

encoding the processing of stimulus information for retention in memory.
storage the retention of information in memory.

The issue of how much information LTM can hold raises two basic questions: what determines what we remember, and how is it retained? Cognitive psychologists refer to the underlying processes as **encoding** and **storage**. While storage is clearly related to LTM, encoding is more closely related to the workings of STM.

STM

In the general model of memory that we have been looking at, STM has been represented as simply a transient storage system. In fact, it seems to have a much more complex role, in terms of processing new stimulus information, but also interacting with LTM when we need to retrieve information. For this reason, some researchers prefer to call STM 'working memory' (Baddeley 1992; Logie 1996; Repovš and Baddeley 2006). Essentially, STM works as both a buffer to hold limited amounts of information (called 'immediate memory'), and as a processing system to manipulate information in various ways (working memory).

As already noted, information in STM must be actively maintained in order to be retained for very long. When dealing with verbal information, often we simply repeat the information; this type of rote repetition is called **maintenance rehearsal** (Craik and Lockhart 1972). We are often subjectively aware of this rehearsal as a form of talking to ourselves. Research suggests that even when rehearsal is silent, the coding of verbal information in STM is normally *acoustic* (based on speech sounds): speech muscles in the larynx are active, and errors made are typically related to the sound of the items (Glassman 1972). An analogy to this process is the game of Gossip, in which a message is whispered from person to person in a group. By the end, 'Diane, be quiet' may become 'I am on a diet'! In the same way, errors in STM often involve words which sound alike.

maintenance rehearsal the retention of material in STM by means of rote repetition.

The nature of rehearsal is also relevant to STM's other role, which is to provide for the transfer of information into LTM. With maintenance rehearsal, repetition leads to information re-entering STM, and each entry into STM seems to make it more probable that the information will be stored in LTM (note, however, that repetition could also be aloud or occur over a long time period, etc.). While this type of 'recycling' is useful for immediate retention, it is less effective for maximizing later recall. The reason for this seems related to one of the basic purposes of encoding, which is to *structure* the information in a way that will assist later retrieval. To understand this, consider an analogy: imagine a library having hundreds of thousands of books but no cataloguing system – how could one find a particular book? Similarly, LTM, with its vast capacity, must process information in some way that makes it possible to locate it later – that is, effective encoding must involve more than simply repetition.

elaborative rehearsal the active process-ing of items in STM in order to code the information for LTM; material may be processed in various ways, ranging from an emphasis on sensory characteristics (visual appearance, sound) to a focus on the semantic content (meaning) of information.

What is the alternative to maintenance rehearsal for encoding? Craik and Lockhart have described it as **elaborative rehearsal**, which involves manipulating the stimulus information in some way (Craik 2002; Craik and Lockhart 1972). The processing may take many forms, ranging from an emphasis on sensory characteristics (visual appearance, sound) to a focus on the semantic content (meaning) of information. An emphasis on *sound* might lead to noting what words rhyme with a given word. Emphasizing *meaning* can involve, for example, extracting the gist of a speech, without remembering the specific words used. Overall, the evidence indicates that the more one elaborates the material (such as focusing on meaning), the more effective the encoding will be for later retrieval. Unfortunately, because of the limitations of STM, there is a trade-off between processing (working memory) and retention (immediate memory), as noted above. This means that the more processing we do, the fewer the chunks of information we can simultane-ously retain. Because of the constraints this imposes, the type of processing used for encoding can vary. Processing the meaning of information (called 'semantic' encoding') is generally the most effective for enhancing later recall, but is also the most demanding in terms of cognitive resources. As a result, individuals will sometimes resort to faster, but more superficial, forms of coding (for example, sound or appearance), or even simply use maintenance rehearsal. Thus, the effectiveness of encoding is an important element in determining our ability to remember infor-mation later, but not all types of encoding are equally useful.

While much of the information that we deal with is verbal, what happens when we encounter information which is visual? Although it is often possible to extract verbal meaning from visual stimuli (for example, the word 'STOP' rather than the colour and shape of a traffic sign), it has been argued that we can also process information visually (Paivio 1971). One type of evidence is derived from studies which indicate that people handle visual information in memory in much the same way that they process direct visual inputs. For example, in one innovative study, subjects were asked to make comparisons of pairs of three-dimensional shapes, to decide if they repre-sented the same shape seen from different angles, or two different shapes (Shepard and Metzler 1971). The time required to compare the shapes correlated with the amount of rotation required to match the orientation of the two shapes; this implied that subjects were using something analogous to a visual image. Without directly proving that the information is represented in memory as an image, the results do suggest that people perform certain memory tasks in ways that are consistent with a visual representation. Interestingly, STM seems capable of handling verbal and visual information more or less independently (Logie 1996).

LTM

procedural memory that component of LTM which stores 'how-to' information, such as how to play a musical instrument or solve a puzzle.
semantic memory the component of LTM which involves general knowledge of the world.
episodic memory the portion of LTM which contains personal experiences, organized according to where and when events happened, such as what happened on your last birthday.

The importance of encoding highlights one of the most significant aspects of LTM, which is the fact that information is retained in an *organized* way, not simply as randomly deposited items. In essence, it is more like a cross-referenced card catalogue than a junk box. As we seek to understand the nature of the underlying structure, it is becoming clear that retention in LTM is related both to the type of information and how it is encoded. In fact, it seems that there are several different types of LTM, which independently process and store different forms of information. Canadian psychologist Endel Tulving, one of the pioneers of this view, has argued that there are three distinct forms of long-term memory: procedural, semantic and episodic (Tulving 1985). **Procedural memory** stores 'how-to' information, such as how to play a piano or cook a turkey. **Semantic memory** involves general knowledge of the world, such as knowing the capital of Japan, or the temperature at which ice melts. **Episodic memory** contains personal experiences, organized according to where and when events happened, such as what happened on your last birthday. Tulving believes the three systems function independently, a view which is supported by a variety of research, including fMRI scans and studies of various types of brain damage (Tulving 2002; Rosenbaum *et al.* 2005; Wheeler *et al.* 1997). For example, it is possible for a patient with brain damage to learn how to solve a puzzle (procedural), and yet not be able to recall having seen it before (episodic). In the same way, a patient may learn a specific fact (semantic), and not know when they learned it (episodic). Equally fascinating, though more difficult to interpret, are case studies of *dissociative amnesia* (van der Hart and Nijenhuis 2001). In such cases, individuals suffer memory loss, typically as a result of stress or traumatic events. Episodic memory is almost always affected, with semantic and procedural more likely to remain intact. Tulving believes that episodic memory (which is closely involved with our sense of self-identity) is the most recent form of memory in terms of evolutionary development, and consequently is the most vulnerable to traumatic damage – as case studies support. By contrast, procedural memory is likely the oldest form of memory, and the most resistant to damage (see Figure 4.3).

While there is growing evidence for difference storage systems in LTM, understanding exactly *what* is stored is a challenging question. Although recall can be readily measured, coding and storage are not directly observable, and must be inferred. In fact, the nature of storage is one issue where the computer analogy may be misleading. In a computer, LTM would be analogous to a storage device like a hard disk. Information is stored as a series of bytes in specific locations on the disk, and a directory list indicates which locations contain a particular piece of information (for example, a file). In essence, this system is like a huge series of postal boxes or cubicles, with

		Characteristics	
Type of memory	Content	Organization	Retrieval process
Episodic memory	Events, experiences	Time-based	Deliberate (high effort)
Semantic memory	Facts, concepts	Cognitive schemata	Deliberate (low effort)
Procedural memory	Actions, processes	Activities	Automatic

Figure 4.3 Episodic, Semantic and Procedural Memory The three aspects of long-term memory differ in many of their characteristics.

one item in each container. By contrast, LTM seems to be distributed rather than localized, with information represented by patterns of connections. In this sense, a better analogy might be patterns created on a computer monitor: the same pixels (neurons) can be used to represent an infinite number of images. Even this analogy may prove misleading, since we still know little about the physical basis of memory storage. Nonetheless, cognitive research has identified at least two descriptive mechanisms for how patterns of connections might be formed.

The traditional view of connections in LTM is based on *associationism*. Just as learning can be seen as a process of forming ties between a stimulus and a response, so memory is seen as forming ties between new experiences and prior knowledge. These ties, called associations, are typically a result of repetition. For example, maintenance rehearsal allows information to re-enter STM, and each entry makes it more probable that the information will enter LTM. In this situation, it is impossible to predict what type of association, if any, will be formed to mediate between a stimulus and prior knowledge. In other cases, an association may be created based on stimulus aspects that have meaning. For instance, to remember the name of someone you meet, you may associate the name with some aspect of their appearance (for example, Bob has a beard, Susan is short).

free association a technique originated by Freud for studying the mind, based on asking a person to simply say whatever words floated into their mind, and then looking for patterns.
repression in Freud's theory, a defence mechanism in which impulses, memories or ideas are forcibly blocked from the conscious mind.

Sigmund Freud recognized the significance of associations as a tool in psychoanalysis: by using **free association** (that is, asking the person to simply say whatever words floated into their mind), he looked for patterns that might reveal their inner conflicts. In Freud's view, such conflicts could produce a type of forgetting called **repression**. Consider an example: a teaching colleague separated from his wife, named Barbara. Shortly after, he met a former student on the street. He remembered having taught the girl, what course she had taken and even her final grade, but not her name. When he asked her, it was, of course, Barbara! The association of names evoked an unpleasant event for our colleague, leading to a memory failure. (The validity of repression as a memory phenomenon has been the subject of prolonged controversy. See the discussion of repressed memories in Chapter 5.)

One need not turn to psychoanalysis to recognize that associations can seem obscure, yet still be based on an organizing structure. For example, conversations at a party may wander over many topics, yet if you trace back carefully, you can always find the links between topics. The reality is that the mind (including memory) does not seem to function as a random structure.

cue-dependent coding the concept that all information is stored in memory as a set of relationships called the context; remembering is seen as dependent on restoring the cues which formed the original context.

An alternative to the associationist view exists, and it may be both closer to reality and easier to apply in improving memory performance. According to the concept of **cue-dependent coding**, all information is stored in memory as a set of relationships which are called the *context*. Remembering is dependent on restoring the cues which formed the original context (Tulving 1974). When meeting someone on the street who seems familiar, you may try to recall *where* you met them, or *who* you were with, or *when* it was, since these are all potential parts of the context of the original encounter. Similarly, hearing an old song may bring back a flood of memories related to the situation in which you first heard the song. In this case, the song provides the cues for remembering the events. Even internal body states may provide context cues: an athlete, recalling a performance, may make movements of the same muscles originally used.

While there is evidence for cue-based encoding in both episodic and semantic memory, not surprisingly, the types of cues may differ in the two cases. Semantic memory, being based on the meaning of information, tends to be structured in logical and conceptual ways (for example, 'apples' would be related to 'fruits'; a geometry theorem may be related to other maths information). By contrast, episodic memory is situational in nature, and hence coding reflects the context of when, where and what happened. Just as one can ask why particular associations are formed, one may ask what determines the contextual coding of a specific memory. Unfortunately, there is no absolute answer to this, since it is possible that different individuals develop different organizational structures over time.

Culture can also influence individuals' organizational structures, and consequently the relevance of particular cues for encoding. For example, a study compared Australian Aboriginal women and American women for recall of a story about a sick child (Steffensen and Calker 1982). The researchers found that the Australians remembered more accurately when the story involved native medicine, and the Americans remembered more accurately when the story involved western medicine. Encoding, and subsequent recall, are better when the context is relevant to an individual's experience.

In some ways, the concepts of cue-dependent coding and associationism are complementary. Associations seem useful for explaining the benefits of rote repetition (maintenance rehearsal), while coding for context can be related to the value of elaborative rehearsal. However, as with any competing theories, there are also important areas of difference. One area where differences emerge is in how the two views deal with forgetting.

Try it Yourself

Various types of brain damage, such as Alzheimer's disease, can disrupt the capacity to form new long-term memories. (The movie *50 First Dates* revolves around a woman like this, whose suitor had to try to win her afresh every day!) Imagine that your capacity to form new long-term memories was gone. What would be the most important effects? How would it affect your schooling or job? What about personal relationships? Daily tasks like running errands? Would you rather lose new episodic memories or semantic memories?

Forgetting

The failure to remember, or *forgetting*, is perhaps the most salient aspect of memory for most people. When we succeed at remembering something, we tend to take the act for granted. When we *can't* remember, we get irritated and frustrated, and are eager to find ways to remedy the situation. While no panaceas exist, understanding *why* forgetting occurs is important to knowing what one can do to make forgetting less likely to occur.

As noted previously, the first stage of memory is sensory memory. Since the sensory stores serve primarily to provide an input channel, it should not be surprising to learn that the information held in sensory storage is very transient. Unless selected by attention for transfer to short-term memory, the contents of sensory memory are quickly lost. The spontaneous loss of information from sensory memory is described as **decay**, to note its time-related character (Cheour *et al.* 2002; Lu *et al.* 2005; Neath and Suprenant 2003). Other than selecting information by means of attention, there is very little one can do to influence sensory memory.

decay in memory, the spontaneous loss of information with the passage of time.

Forgetting in STM

STM is a more complex system than sensory memory, because it is used both to process incoming information and to retrieve material from LTM. At first glance, STM seems ill-designed for such a weighty role, since it has limited duration and limited capacity. Because information passing

displacement in memory, forgetting due to new incoming information pushing out the previous contents.

through STM leaves no permanent impression, one might think that its limited duration is directly responsible for forgetting. Instead, forgetting in STM seems to be related to its limited capacity: new incoming information tends to push out the previous contents. This **displacement** of information is the basic cause of forgetting in STM.

Since the capacity of STM is fixed, one cannot really reduce displacement. On the other hand, awareness of displacement *does* imply that in order to remember important material, you should avoid distractions. Have you ever been talking about something, been interrupted, and then been unable to recall the point where you left off? In this situation, an interruption leads to displacement of the previous words spoken. Similarly, forgetting a phone number you've just looked up involves forgetting by displacement.

While the basic capacity of STM does not seem alterable, we can improve the *use* of STM by better encoding of information. As noted earlier, the capacity of STM is about 7 ± 2 *chunks*. A chunk may be a letter in a random series (as in Box 4.1), a word (as in an item on a grocery list) or a whole concept (as in the key points of a speech). In general, a chunk represents a unit of information that is meaningful to the individual. This means that one can increase the *effective* capacity of STM by recoding information into larger chunks whenever possible. Consider a grocery list: by grouping items into *categories* (for example, fruits, meats, canned goods), you can focus on remembering the categories. Then, each time you think of a category, the individual items will be easier to recall. The effect of categories on improving learning and recall has been well established in research (for example, Strand 1975). Another approach is to convert meaningless items into meaningful chunks (that is, *recoding* the information). Telephone numbers are one example: at one time, everyone learned the initial numbers as the name of an exchange (for example, Cherry stood for CH, or 24). Today, the telephone company officially avoids these names, but using letter equivalents can still be helpful. For example, a Canadian bank advertises its telephone number as 980-CIBC (the letters of the bank's name). You may be able to make similar codes for numbers that you need to remember.

As with many activities, practice makes such recoding easier to accomplish. In one well-known study, a student given long sequences of random numbers learned, over several months, to recode them as chunks, and then as chunks-made-up-of-chunks. Over time, he was able to increase his performance to the point that he could recall sequences of *80 digits* correctly after one presentation (Ericsson and Chase 1982)! This feat was a function of developing efficient codes, not somehow stretching capacity by extensive use – in fact, when tested with random *letter* strings at the end of the experiment, his performance was only average. Similarly, a man who could recall telephone numbers by efficient chunking (in one case, remembering numbers for 15,000 hotels!), was only average for recall of complex stories (Wilding and Valentine 1994). As we will discuss later, such recoding techniques are one example of memory aids called *mnemonic devices*.

The use of recoding to enhance chunking compensates for the limited capacity of STM. However, it would be wrong to believe that chunking occurs independently of LTM (Nairne 2002). Clearly, the use of any coding method involves drawing on past experience which is stored in LTM. In fact, it can be argued that the *real* function of chunking or other coding is to increase transfer into LTM – that is, recoding represents a form of elaborative rehearsal. To understand this, let us consider forgetting in LTM.

Forgetting in LTM

The first point to note is that not everything blamed on 'forgetting' really is a failure to remember. In order to be remembered, information must first *reach* LTM. Simply being exposed to something does not guarantee that we will retain it, since there is filtering by attention prior to STM. In addition, as we have seen, not everything which reaches STM is transferred to LTM. In both of these circumstances, one cannot really speak of 'forgetting' that which never entered LTM! Having said that, it is still clear that there are circumstances which reflect genuine forgetting. Since capacity in LTM appears to be unlimited in any practical sense, clearly forgetting cannot be based on displacement. And despite the limitations on what reaches LTM, information which does enter LTM may potentially be available for the rest of our lives. Given this picture of a permanent system, unlimited in capacity, it may seem puzzling that we ever fail to remember.

interference according to associationism, competition between items which can hamper learning and produce forgetting.

The traditional explanation offered by associationism is **interference**, or competition between various items of information. The concept of interference implies that as our store of information grows, it becomes harder and harder to uniquely identify a piece of information (much like trying to locate a particular book on your bookshelf: if you only have five books, the task is easy, but if you have 500 books, the task is much harder). In terms of associationism, the associations for a particular item may overlap those for similar items. ('Was it *last* summer that I met Larry in Boston, or when I was there two years ago?') As time goes on, we experience a running together of past experience, and a consequent loss of details, due to interference. If there are too many competing associations, you may end up unable to remember the desired information.

Interference takes two basic forms, which differ in terms of the time relationship between competing responses. The first form is **retroactive** (acting backwards) **interference**, which involves the effect of recent experiences making it more difficult to recall something learned earlier (see Figure 4.4a). One classic experiment concerned testing recall for two groups of people; one group went to sleep after the original learning session, and the other went about their daily activities (Jenkins and Dallenbach 1924).

retroactive interference in memory, a form of interference in which recent experiences make it difficult to recall something learned earlier.

When both groups were tested after the same interval of time had passed, the sleep group showed better recall. Why? Because daily experiences created more interference than did sleeping! Students often experience retroactive interference when they find that, for example, this semester's physics has interfered with remembering last semester's biology. Similarly, retroactive interference can occur at work when a person changes job responsibilities. The programmer who becomes a supervisor may get rusty at programming skills. In each case, recent experiences and the associations they create can interfere with recall of earlier experiences, particularly if there is some overlap of associations.

proactive interference in memory, a form of interference in which prior experiences make learning and recall of subsequent experiences difficult.

The other form of interference, called **proactive** (acting forwards) **interference**, concerns the effect of prior experiences making learning and recall of subsequent experiences more difficult (see Figure 4.4b). At first glance, this may seem rather odd – how can old memories disrupt something more recent? The reason, according to interference theory, is that interactions among associations are not directional with respect to time. Consequently, it is just as possible for old information to interfere with new information as vice versa. Interestingly, researchers were slow to recognize the possibility of proactive interference, despite existing evidence of the phenomenon. For example, William James, after spending time learning large amounts of material, found that learning was *slower* than it had been initially – a clear sign of proactive interference from the previous material learned. In everyday life, proactive interference is most likely to arise when two situations show some similarities. For instance, car drivers travel either on the right or the left side of the road, depending on the country. The side makes no difference when one is first learning to drive, as the task is completely new. But an experienced driver may experience great difficulty in changing if visiting a country where it is opposite – the prior learning interferes with behaviour in the new situation. Part of the reason that people are slow to change their attitudes, or learn new technology, as they get older may be due to proactive interference from what they already know. Thus, it may be that proactive interference is more significant in the long run than is retroactive interference.

Tulving has suggested that interference may be more significant for episodic memory than for semantic memory (Tulving 1986). Since episodic memory tracks the 'where and when' of our lives, it would be vulnerable to interference, given the continual flow of new experiences. As a trivial example, try to recall what you had for lunch three weeks ago today – remembering is difficult due to the interference from other lunches, both more recent and more distant. By contrast, semantic memory, based on meaning, forms associations based on existing logical concepts, rather than physical context. Consequently, it should be less sensitive to variations in external context. At present, the available research seems to support this interpretation (see for example, Enmarker 2004).

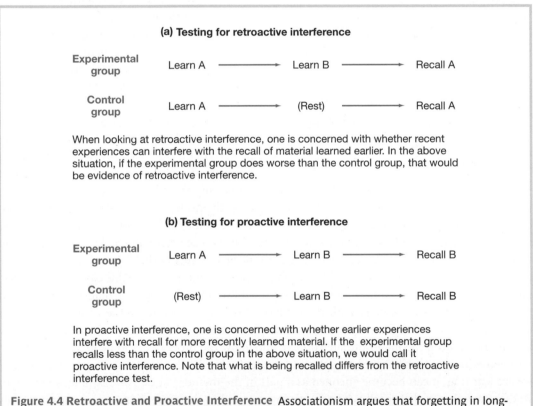

(a) Testing for retroactive interference

Experimental group Learn A ⟶ Learn B ⟶ Recall A

Control group Learn A ⟶ (Rest) ⟶ Recall A

When looking at retroactive interference, one is concerned with whether recent experiences can interfere with the recall of material learned earlier. In the above situation, if the experimental group does worse than the control group, that would be evidence of retroactive interference.

(b) Testing for proactive interference

Experimental group Learn A ⟶ Learn B ⟶ Recall B

Control group (Rest) ⟶ Learn B ⟶ Recall B

In proactive interference, one is concerned with whether earlier experiences interfere with recall for more recently learned material. If the experimental group recalls less than the control group in the above situation, we would call it proactive interference. Note that what is being recalled differs from the retroactive interference test.

Figure 4.4 Retroactive and Proactive Interference Associationism argues that forgetting in long-term memory is based on competing associations, particularly in terms of when information was learned. Retroactive and proactive interference represent the two basic forms of interference.

unlearning an alternative interpretation of the interference theory of memory which holds that the build-up of interference can lead to the breaking of associations, and therefore the destruction of memories.

The precise nature of interference is not fully understood. As already noted, the common view is that similar associations produce competition among responses. An alternative view holds that the build-up of interference can lead to the actual destruction of memories; this notion is referred to as **unlearning**. Basically, unlearning implies that amid the tangles of associations, some ties are broken. While various attempts have been made to test this idea, the evidence favouring it is rather limited (for example, Shiu and Chan 2006). Unfortunately, there is no way to know for certain that something forgotten is truly gone for ever. In fact, it may make more sense to assume the opposite – that memories are permanently stored (assuming no physical damage to the brain). Consider the following situation: suppose someone tries to recall something, and, despite every conceivable attempt, cannot remember it. Then, a short time after they have given up, the desired information mysteriously floats into consciousness. This effect is familiar to most people, but how can interference theory account for it? Clearly, the information was not permanently lost, so it is not a case of unlearning. While one could conceive of changes in associations, such a spontaneous change in a short period of time would seem little short of miraculous. Hence, spontaneous recall after forgetting poses a serious challenge to interference theory.

As noted previously, the alternative to associationism is *cue-dependent coding*. According to this view, remembering depends on restoring the appropriate context, in terms of the cues present at the time of learning. If you do not remember something at a particular moment, it does not mean that the information is destroyed (referred to as a lack of **availability**). Rather, the information may not be retrievable, given the cues used to search for the information (that is, it is not **accessible**). Since LTM appears to be largely permanent, most forgetting should be due to problems of accessibility rather than availability. Forgetting due to a failure to retrieve the desired information is called **context-dependent forgetting**.

availability in memory, the principle that remembering is determined by whether the information exists in LTM or not; forgetting implies that the information is destroyed.
accessibility in LTM, the principle that remembering and forgetting are dependent on effective retrieval; without the proper cues, information which exists in LTM may not be accessible.
context-dependent forgetting failure to retrieve information from LTM due to the absence of appropriate contextual cues.

The concept of context-dependent forgetting suggests that generally we fail to remember because the cues we use to aid retrieval are inappropriate. For example, a friend once told me (WEG) of having met a Nobel laureate in physics at a party the previous night. When I asked the physicist's name, my friend could not recall, except to say the last name began with the letter P. He strove to remember, but it was not until a few days later that he told me the name: Dirac. 'Dirac?' I asked. 'But you told me it began with P!' 'Yes, I know,' he replied. 'But you see, his name is Paul Dirac, and on his name badge it said "P. Dirac". All I could think of was seeing that letter P, until the name popped into my head this morning!' By emphasizing the wrong cue – in this case, seeking a last name beginning with P – it is possible to block retrieval of the desired information. Similarly, in trying to remember someone's name, if you place a previous encounter in the wrong context (for example, at work, rather than at a party), you may block retrieval of the name. By relaxing, it may be possible to drop the inappropriate context, and allow the proper cues to be generated.

Even when we don't regard the physical context (that is, the location) as relevant to what we are learning, it can become encoded as a part of the memory cues. For example, a variety of studies have shown that recall is best if people are tested in the same room where learning takes place. In one unusual variation of this technique, scuba divers learned information either above or underwater and were subsequently tested on the information in the same or the alternate environment as their learning. As expected, changing environments between learning and testing impaired memory: scuba divers who learned the information while underwater remembered the information better when they were tested underwater than when they were tested on dry land, and those who had learned the information on dry land remembered it better in that location than when they were tested underwater (Godden and Baddeley 1975). Context-dependent forgetting may apply more strongly to episodic than semantic memory, as with interference effects. Nonetheless, one implication is that it might be beneficial to study where one will be writing an exam!

Normally, we think of 'context' as being our physical surroundings. But part of the context is actually internal – the thoughts, feelings and state of mind that are part of our moment-to-moment experience. The changes in context associated with physical and mental state are often referred to as *state-dependent coding*, to distinguish these cues from those related to the external environment. Forgetting related to these internal cues is therefore referred to as **state-dependent forgetting**. Many students have experienced the frustration of studying hard, then blanking out while writing a test – only to have the information come flooding back shortly after leaving the test. This effect can be explained in terms of state-dependent forgetting. If a student is relaxed while studying, but anxious during a test, the change in mental state makes recall difficult. After the test, anxiety is reduced – and the answers become accessible once more.

state-dependent forgetting forgetting related to changes in context associated with internal cues of physical and mental state, as opposed to the context defined by the external environment.

Clearly, performance while highly anxious can lead to an inaccurate impression of what is known. To reduce this state-dependent forgetting, one must make the study and test circumstances more alike – either by learning to relax during tests, or possibly becoming anxious while studying! Since anxiety can hamper performance in other ways, obviously the former is the preferred solution. Another example of state-dependent forgetting occurs with drugs. A person who is drinking alcohol may not be able to remember where they left their wallet while sober, but remember the location when sober again; a user of cocaine may later be unable to remember what happened while 'high', and so on. Such effects have been found in many studies with animals, and they appear to occur in varying degrees in people, depending on the dosage and other factors.

The effects of variations in context should not be underestimated. Successive changes in context can make it difficult to reinstate a particular context. This may be one reason that information which is not used for a long period can be difficult to recall (for example, foreign language skills). Often in this situation, attempts at *relearning* (such as refresher courses) will quickly restore the context, and hence increase access to the information. Thus, providing refresher courses is highly desirable for seldom-used job skills. One example of this is the requirement in Canada for annual training in cardiac resuscitation (CPR) by all medical staff.

Context-dependent forgetting also helps to explain the typical differences found between memory performance involving recall versus recognition. Characteristically, people find it easier to recognize something as familiar than to remember something spontaneously – in other words, recognition is usually easier than free recall. This can be explained in terms of more cues being provided in the recognition situation (in fact, the information itself is given, so it only needs to be compared to what is already in memory). With unstructured recall, there is little contextual support to aid access (perhaps explaining why most students prefer multiple-choice tests to essay exams).

At the same time, the superiority of recognition depends on the context. Most people have had the experience of spotting someone familiar down the street, only to discover as they approach that it is actually a stranger. This is an example of **false recognition**, whereby the presence of familiar cues (such as hairstyle, colour of jacket, etc.) leads one to believe the stimulus matches an item in memory. This effect is more than anecdotal, having been demonstrated in a number of experimental studies. What is more

false recognition a form of memory error whereby the presence of familiar cues leads one to believe the stimulus matches a previously experienced stimulus.

interesting is that studies have also shown that individuals can fail to recognize something they have just recalled – that is, sometimes recall is *better* than recognition! In the classic study, students learned a list of words until they could recall the list perfectly (Tulving and Thompson 1971). Then, the students were given a longer list, which included some of the previously-recalled words. By changing the context of surrounding items, the experimenters fooled subjects into ignoring words they had just recognized. For example, steel, iron and copper appeared in the original list; on the recognition task, the items broom, stove and iron appeared. Given the different context, subjects failed to recognize 'iron' as one of the words they had learned. Thus, context-dependent forgetting seems to account for a wide variety of memory phenomena.

Try it Yourself

Have you ever chosen an answer on a multiple-choice test, been confident you were correct, and then afterwards discovered you were wrong? Can you explain this in terms of context-dependent coding? Has the same thing ever happened on an essay test? What can you say about this?

As discussed in the chapter, whether or not we forget is heavily influenced by what happens while we're learning (i.e., during encoding). What is your environment like when you study? Many students study while lying on their beds with music playing. Knowing what you know about context-dependent coding, do you think this is a good idea? What would be the best setting for studying? What can you do to make your own environment optimal for studying?

Memory as Reconstruction

Forgetting can certainly be frustrating, especially when we sense that the information is available, but we cannot retrieve it. Ironically, the emphasis on forgetting as a failure of retrieval tends to create the impression that memory storage is static and unchanging. Yet this interpretation,

reconstruction in memory, the process of remembering by actively creating a whole out of partial information.

with its implication that retrieval is a neutral process of locating the correct item, may not be correct. Although there is little evidence to support unlearning, as previously discussed, it can be argued that remembering is not simply passive retrieval. Instead, it may involve **reconstruction** – that is, creating a whole out of partial information.

The view that remembering is somehow creative was supported by Gestalt theorists, who saw perception and memory as closely linked (see *Perception and Cognition*, earlier in this chapter). Context not only provides cues for retrieval, but allows us to create information to fill gaps in our recall. For example, if you hear a funny joke, and then later retell it, it is unlikely that you will use exactly the same words as the person who told you the joke originally. Instead, you will remember the outline of the story, including crucial elements like the punchline, and then *fill in* the rest, using both your knowledge of the joke and your general knowledge of language and the world to make the joke work. Since semantic memory stores meanings, not the original words, it is inevitable that one will reconstruct, not retrieve, most of the details of the joke. (Those who don't remember jokes likely ignore crucial elements, such as noting whether the punchline depends on a particular play on words.)

The idea that *all* recall involves reconstruction as well as retrieval was supported by a classic study by British psychologist Frederick Bartlett. Bartlett read a story based on a Native American legend to his subjects, and then later asked them to retell it from memory (Bartlett 1932). The study found several interesting results. While the subjects tried to be faithful to the story, minor details tended to be forgotten. In addition, points which were central to the storyline were sometimes exaggerated. Most interestingly, Bartlett found that his subjects (British university students) tended to *change* details which, although consistent with Native American beliefs (for example, the role of spirits), were not consistent with the students' own beliefs. Typically, the subjects were unaware of making such changes – they were simply trying to reconstruct the story in a way that made sense to them.

The basic phenomenon of reconstruction has been well supported by subsequent research (for example, Ahlberg and Sharps 2002; Gerrie *et al.* 2006; Marsh 2007; Roediger *et al.* 2000), and it seems likely that whenever we recall, there is a potential risk of distorting what we experienced. One ironic indication of this involves how people describe Bartlett's original study: two researchers, rereading Bartlett's study, noted that it provided examples of highly accurate recall, as well as the types of distortions discussed above – but most citations mention only the distortions. In essence, summaries of Bartlett's study have produced the same oversimplifications he saw in his participants (Ost and Costall 2002)!

Eyewitness Testimony

The idea that memories are reconstructed rather than simply retrieved has aroused concern in the legal system. After all, if memory for events can be altered by reconstruction, what does this say about the accuracy of eyewitness testimony? Our culture, especially our legal system, tends to place great value on personal testimony when trying to analyse events. 'Seeing is believing' says the old proverb, even though we know perception is not always accurate (see Chapter 1). In much the same way, we tend to assume that testimony about past events will somehow be free from distortion or error. Unfortunately, our understanding of memory, particularly the role of reconstruction, suggests that errors are quite possible.

One of the pioneers in exploring this issue is American researcher Elizabeth Loftus, who has done a number of experiments involving the basic elements of courtroom testimony (Loftus and Hoffman 1989). In one case, individuals first watched a tape of an auto accident. Later, they were questioned about what had happened, in much the way that courtroom witnesses are. During this interrogation, the questioner sometimes asked how fast the cars were going when they *hit*, or else how fast they were going when they *smashed into* each other. When 'smashed into' was used in the question, estimates of speed tended to be higher. What's more, when later asked about broken glass at the scene (there was none in the tape), individuals who heard the 'smashed into' phrasing were more likely to report having seen broken glass! Loftus argues that studies like this call into question the reliability of eyewitness testimony, since the wording of questions can influence both witnesses' interpretations (for example, speed estimates) and even their subsequent recall (for example, seeing broken glass when there was none – in other experiments, individuals have been influenced to 'recall' stop signs that were not present, and similar details).

Loftus believes that the person's memory for the events is actually altered by these manipulations. Other researchers have questioned this interpretation, arguing that misleading subjects simply leads them to question their original memories (McCloskey and Zaragoza 1985). In effect, it would be like Loftus's subjects thinking, 'Well, if she's mentioning broken glass, I guess there *was* broken glass.' At present, whether the original memories are altered or not, it is clear that there is a potential for witnesses to make errors in reporting the original events.

Similar problems arise with eyewitness identifications of suspects. In a typical police line-up, witnesses might readily assume that the criminal is one of the individuals in the line-up; in effect, choosing becomes equivalent to guessing at a multiple-choice test. However, like multiple-choice tests, the accuracy of the choice depends on how similar the alternatives are; in addition, accuracy of eyewitness identification can be affected by the instructions given, the behaviour of the officer conducting the line-up, and other factors (Wells and Olson 2003; Wells *et al.* 2006). Such factors can lead witnesses to feel confident of their choice even if the person identified is not the true criminal. Mistaken identifications were documented in the real world throughout the twentieth century, and have been identified as the primary reason for false convictions of innocent people (US National Institute of Justice 1996). In one case, because of apparent similarities in appearance and demeanor, a priest was falsely charged with bank robbery (Loftus and Ketcham 1991)!

While memories of eyewitnesses may be inherently imperfect, the interview process itself is also a source of potential distortions. For example, experimental data suggest that investigators, as authority figures, may trigger false memories if witnesses feel pressured to comply (Roper and Shewan 2002; Wells *et al.* 2006). In addition, research indicates that when witnesses are given supportive feedback after making an identification (as often happens in the real world), it can further distort memory. Witnesses given favourable feedback are more likely to report having felt very confident when making their original judgement, and also to recall details not part of the original event (Wells and Bradfield 1998). Thus, whether in a courtroom or not, what witnesses recall may be influenced by the context and by what others say and do.

While certainly raising concerns about how witnesses are questioned, the research does not answer the basic question of how memories are changed by misleading questions. That is, does the original memory of the event get altered, or only the response at time of recall? Given that recall is nearly always a combination of retrieval and reconstruction, there may be no possible experiment that can tell us conclusively whether what is retrieved can be modified. Yet, while research may not end the debates about eyewitness testimony, it is probable that increased understanding of how memory functions may allow the police and the courts to perform their functions more effectively.

Try it Yourself

The idea that memories are reconstructed (rather than static, like papers in a file folder) has a number of interesting implications. For example, think about events in your early childhood. Do you really remember them, or are you 'remembering' something based on anecdotes that you have heard repeatedly from your parents and other family members? How can you tell the difference? Are you sure?

Reconstruction also raises the possibility that we distort memories of earlier events to fit our later knowledge (Blank and Nestler 2007; Erdfelder and Brandt 2007). This *hindsight bias* is expressed in the phrase, 'hindsight has 20–20 vision'. For example, sports fans will often dissect a disappointing game, focusing on elements that seemed insignificant during the game itself, in order to 'explain' the outcome. Have you ever had the experience of looking back on a situation and thinking 'I should have seen that!'? Was there really something you overlooked, or is this hindsight bias at work? Is there a simple way to decide?

Improving Memory

Clearly, the greatest memory concern for most people is forgetting. Despite advances in our understanding, it may be small consolation to know that something is temporarily inaccessible rather than gone for ever. There is no magic potion for improving memory, but there are techniques which can make memory more effective. The study and use of such memory aids is called **mnemonics** (from the Greek for 'memory'). The origin of mnemonics is credited to a Greek poet named Simonides. By a strange sequence of events,

mnemonics the study and use of techniques for improving memory (from the Greek for 'memory').

Simonides was the only survivor when the roof of a banquet hall collapsed. The bodies were so mangled that mourning relatives could not identify them for burial. However, by remembering the seating arrangement, Simonides was able to identify each body. Impressed with his own feat, he began a systematic study of techniques for aiding memory (Yates 1966). Today, a number of mnemonic devices, or memory aids, are known.

One of the most basic ways to improve memory is by *concentration*. Too often, memory failure is blamed for what is really a lack of attention. For example, many people report difficulty in learning names. When introduced to someone, they are not focusing on the name, but instead worrying about the impression they're making, what to talk about, or some other concern. The result is that the name, never having been processed, is not available (not in memory) later on. By focusing on the name during the introduction, you facilitate storage, and consequently later recall. One memory expert used to advise, 'Look at the person, listen to the name, repeat it in your mind, and then say the name when you shake hands.' Concentration can be helpful for many learning situations – too often, students study by casually glancing at the page, rather than reading carefully and thinking about the material.

Organization is another important element in improving memory. Taking the time to organize material which you wish to remember can improve retrieval by providing a natural context and set of retrieval cues. For example, outlining the contents of a chapter in a textbook can help show how various concepts are related to each other. Creating a time line for events in a history course can provide both a visual and verbal structure for remembering. Even if material has no natural structure, it is possible to create one artificially by recoding the information in some way (see below). Interestingly, research indicates that when students begin learning a new subject, the information tends to be learned as isolated experiences in episodic memory; as learning progresses and the students develop an organizational schema, the information becomes more readily retained in semantic memory (Herbert and Burt 2004). Hence, a deliberate focus on organizing information is likely to be beneficial.

One unusual technique which can be used even with non-organized material is called the *method of loci* (*loci* is Latin for 'places'). This was the technique used by Simonides, and later recommended by Cicero, a Roman noted as an excellent speaker. Orators like Cicero would mentally 'place' key points of a planned speech in various locations around the assembly hall. By looking around the room in sequence, they would recall the desired points of their speech. Although it may seem a strange notion, the method of loci is quite effective, even with minimal practice. (To try your own hand at this, look at the exercise in Figure 4.5.) A variant of the method of loci can also be used to remember tasks you wish to do in the future, such as calling a friend when you get home. By vividly associating the task with some routine action, such as taking off your coat, you are reminded of the task when you reach home. In this example, the visualized action provides the cue for recalling the task. By appropriate choice of key action, you can jog your memory at almost any point in the day's routine. Such techniques work by creating vivid and distinctive associations between new information (the task) and prior knowledge (about daily routine); by doing so, the technique minimizes interference. At the same time, the cues used in these techniques also make effective use of context.

Mnemonic techniques like the method of loci can be helpful by providing prearranged cues for recall. But for non-meaningful material, such as long lists of dates or terms, *recoding* into a more meaningful form may be more effective. As mentioned earlier, there are various ways to encode information, but the general goal is to make meaningful chunks. For example, generations of medical students have spent many hours memorizing the body's parts. The sequence of cranial nerves was made easier to remember by the nameless wit who recoded them into, 'On old Olympus' tallest top, a Finn and German vault and hop.' The purpose of the low poetry lies in the first letter of

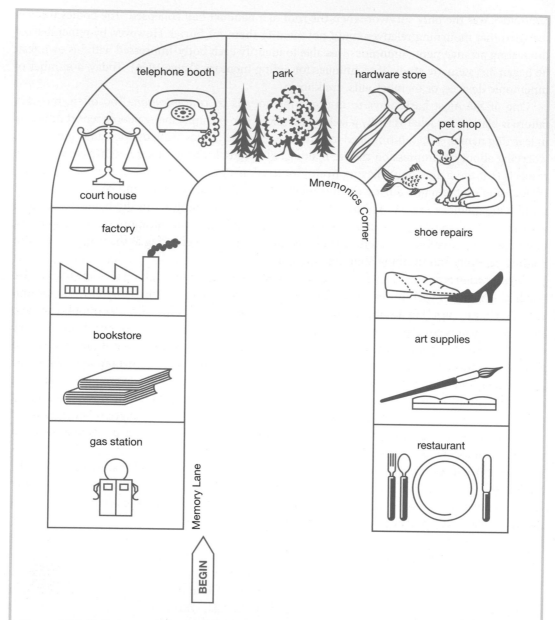

Figure 4.5 A Walk Down Memory Lane If you want to see how mnemonic techniques like the method of loci work, use the 'map' with the following list of words. Take about five seconds for each word, trying to form a mental link to each location in sequence; when you get to the end of the map, go back and start again – hence, you will end up with two words for each location. Then, use the map to trigger your recall of the words. On average, most people get about 17 words correct! Word list: voice, dollar, lake, soldier, library, plant, train, symphony, cup, game, desert, hat, turtle, sofa, moon, wasp, frame, home, elbow, speaker, shovel, pillow.

each word, which is also the first letter for a nerve, in proper sequence. This type of recoding, which creates a sentence or similar verbal structure as a cue, is called the *narrative technique*.

Another form of recoding creates a cue by making a word out of the first letters of a set of words. For example, 'Roy G. Biv' is a name cue for remembering the colours of the rainbow (red, orange, yellow, etc.). Such made-up words are called *acronyms*. The US army (which seems to love such creations), has added snafu (situation normal: all fouled up) to our language, as well as GP (general purpose vehicle) and many other terms. (Note that the phonetic spelling 'jeep' was later trademarked by an enterprising ex-GI – that is, *general infantry!*)

The most general form of recoding is *elaboration*. This involves any form of recoding which adds to the information in some way which makes it meaningful and/or distinctive. One example is the use of *rhymes*. 'Thirty days hath September' is the beginning of a rhyme to remember the number of days in each month. 'I before E except after C, or when sounded as "ay", as in neighbour and weigh' is a rhyme which provides assistance with spelling rules. Sometimes *unique recodings* can be particularly useful. At one time, my (WEG) postal code was M6C 1X1; I eventually remembered this by noting that 6C sounds like 'sexy', and that one times (X) one equals one, and then recoding it as 'my sexy one'!

Whatever the form, mnemonic techniques function by creating meaningful connections for information which has no natural structure. This has several advantages: stronger associations, forming larger chunks, and creating a distinctive context for retrieval. While it might seem that these techniques, especially elaboration, increase memory demands, remember that the problem in LTM is not storage capacity, but retrieval. Although mnemonic techniques add to the information to be retained, they also make access for retrieval easier. The only limits to the use of such methods seem to lie in one's willingness to use them, and possibly in one's creative abilities (see Box 4.2 for a summary).

While practising mnemonic techniques can lead to more efficient coding, there is little one can do to make memory infallible. Unfortunately, the very factors that make memory efficient (for example, using context to stimulate retrieval) also create the conditions for errors (for example, false recognition). Hence, we must all muddle along, forgetting at least *some* of what we'd like to remember. Lest you find this disappointing, it might be worth considering the consequences of never forgetting: all of life's traumas would remain vividly intact, as would every bit of trivial information, such as grocery lists from ten years ago. Overall, our memory system seems to strike a reasonable balance of benefits and limitations. In any case, in life the crucial factor is usually not how much information one has, but what one does with it.

Box 4.2 *Maximizing Use of Memory*

Most of us experience memory failures at one time or another. Indeed, sometimes it seems the likelihood of forgetting increases with the importance of remembering! What can one do? The following represents a brief guide to some techniques for improving memory. For more detailed information, refer to the accompanying text.

Names – concentrate when introduced; don't let your mind wander as the name is being given. Repeat it silently. If there are couples, mentally link their names. Note the face – often you can make an association between the name and some physical feature (for example, 'Tom is tall').

Phone numbers – the trick is to make the number meaningful, or at least familiar. Is there a sequence (for example, 1357) or other cue (for example, 1293 is 'Dec. '93')? Failing that, repeat the number several times, each time saying the person's name.

Aids to learning
1 Distribute learning time – cramming is not effective (*unless* you only want to recall the material for an hour or two after study).

2 Make the connection – look for links between the current information and what you already know. This may involve finding *similarities* ('how is managing staff like dealing with customers?') or forming *unique associations* ('This is Tom Gordon, whose wife's name is the same as my sister's').

Aids to remembering

1 Use context cues – they can help both by organizing information while learning (making connections) and for remembering (for example, using method of loci when giving a speech).
2 Use mnemonic devices – rhymes, acronyms, stories and other techniques can help structure material, which aids both initial learning and also minimizes the chance of omitting items during recall.
3 Relax – anxiety tends to create state-dependent forgetting (blanking), and increases the chances of fixating on the wrong context. If you start with the wrong context, the more you try, the less likely you are to remember. Overall, relaxation is surprisingly important for effective recall.

While none of these tips represents a cure-all, our memory works best when we act in ways which recognize its basic characteristics.

Try it Yourself

One obvious application for our understanding of memory is in studying. The following recommendations have been derived from memory research (Hadad and Reed 2007). Try them to enhance your own memory on tests and examinations.

1 Find an environment for studying where distractions are minimal. This will increase your attention to important concepts.

2 After a lecture, review your notes, and consider rewriting them into condensed study notes. This will both increase your attention and serve as rehearsal. Reviewing will also help you to see relationships between concepts, thereby aiding in organization.

3 Organize material in your study notes to see how concepts relate to each other and to your already-existing knowledge. This further elaboration of material will aid in retention and later retrieval of information.

4 When studying, ask yourself questions about the material. Try to imagine what questions might be asked on a test and answer them. This increases organization and facilitates retrieval.

5 When you need to study many different topics or subjects, study those that are most different closest in time (for example, study biology and French in the same evening, not French and Spanish). This will reduce interference.

6 Categorize information in your study notes (for example, 'Types of memory'). This will reduce interference and increase the likelihood that information stored will be cued in questions on a test.

7 Use mnemonic techniques. These will help to elaborate on the topic, providing greater organization and a hook for memory.

8 Finally, get a good night's sleep the night before a test, since memory is consolidated during sleep; sleep deprivation results in less recall of information (Huber 2007).

PROBLEM SOLVING

In many situations, the value of retaining information lies simply in being able to recall it when needed – for example, phone numbers are a tool for communication. In other situations, information stored in our memory is used instead to help make sense of the situation, and to overcome obstacles. For example, a person planning a trip from New York to Toronto will be aided by knowing the distance, highway routes, plane schedules, relative cost by car and plane, and so on. Each piece of information is of little value in itself, but is simply an input to the process of choosing the best travel arrangements.

When we are faced with a complex situation like this, the information in memory mediates decisions about what response is most appropriate for the situation. In this sense, memory is the basis of the cognitive maps Tolman described. As Tolman argued, cognitive maps allow the organism to choose different responses at different times. In fact, those situations that we call problems nearly always require a response we haven't tried before. Thus, how well we cope with a problem can depend on the information we have in our cognitive map of the situation (or more broadly, our relevant schemata).

Generally speaking, **problem solving** refers to a process for overcoming obstacles that interfere with reaching a desired goal. That is, a problem is a situation in which we face some sort of obstacle. The challenge becomes one of finding a way to remove the obstacle. Apart from the information about the situation which we have stored in memory, our effectiveness in problem solving often depends on how we approach the situation. Problem solving is a type of skill, and like all skills, it can benefit from training and practice. Unfortunately, the teaching of such skills has been sadly neglected in our society, even though research on problem solving has a history which extends back to the work of Kohler in the 1920s, and even earlier work by Thorndike.

problem solving the process of determining appropriate actions in order to overcome obstacles that interfere with reaching a desired goal.

Defining Problems

Over time, a great deal has been learned about the process of problem solving, and what factors contribute to effective performance. One key finding is that good problem solvers tend to approach the situation systematically, rather than haphazardly. To understand this, it is helpful to consider the general process that people go through in solving a problem.

Stages of Problem Solving

While various researchers have developed slightly different models to describe problem solving, they all generally include three basic stages:

1 defining the problem;
2 developing possible solutions;
3 selecting and evaluating the best solution.

incubation in the Gestalt model of problem solving, a process of ceasing to actively work on a problem, in order to modify one's mental set.

(Gestalt theorists have also talked about a sub-stage of stage 2, called **incubation**, where one temporarily abandons conscious efforts to solve the problem.)

Defining the problem has several aspects. First, one must recognize that a problem exists in order to solve it. Second, the *way* one defines the problem can influence attempts to solve it. In general, it is important to develop a clear and appropriate representation of a problem. Overly broad statements can hinder by their vagueness. For instance, asking 'How can we end air pollution?' does not point towards any specific solutions. On the other hand, overly specific descriptions can hinder problem solving by restricting possible options. For example, asking 'What is the best way to get sulphur dioxide *out* of the air?' may inhibit considering the option of reducing the amount going *into* the air (since it is mainly a product of auto exhaust fumes). As Edward deBono, a well-known British psychologist, has said, a definition is sufficient 'as soon as it allows one to do something about a situation' (deBono 1976).

The second stage of problem solving is *developing possible solutions*. The process of generating solutions often gives people trouble, and one should try to list as many options as possible, rather than just looking for 'the right one'. Studies have shown that when people fail to solve problems, it is often because their set of possible options was too narrow (i.e., they did not include the correct solution as a possibility). Another tendency is to prematurely evaluate possible solutions before exploring the full range of possibilities – this sort of impulsiveness also works against effective performance. Properly, one should try to keep solution generation distinct from evaluation (that is, keep stage 2 separate from stage 3). Later in this section, we will consider a variety of techniques to aid in the process of developing solutions.

The third stage, *selecting and evaluating the best solution*, has different characteristics depending on the problem. Some problems (for instance, many mathematics problems) have only a single solution, so evaluation simply involves checking that the chosen solution is correct. Other problems do not have a single ideal solution. In these cases, choosing the best solution depends on what criteria one selects. For example, in 1960 many people saw nuclear reactors as a means to cheap energy production, but today there is concern with the disposal of nuclear fuel wastes. Thus, the best solution from one point of view (or at one time) may not be the best from another. Among the factors to consider in selecting the best solution might be: What are the relative advantages of each solution? Which aspect of the problem is the most important to solve? Are new problems created by the proposed solution? As seen in the example of nuclear energy, it is possible that different people will prefer different solutions based on the weights they each give to different factors.

Unfortunately, the way people evaluate options can be influenced by a variety of biases which seem to be very prevalent in human thinking. Among the first to explore these biases in decision making were Daniel Kahneman and Amos Tversky (Kahneman and Tversky 2000). For example, when evaluating potential gains, individuals tend to avoid risks, but when evaluating potential losses, individuals tend to make risky choices. Thus, a person might prefer a certain gain of $10 to a 1 in 5 chance of winning $50, but would pick a 1 in 5 risk of losing $50 to a sure loss of $10 – yet 'rationally', all four options have an equal value! Such 'framing effects' affect our evaluations of problem solutions as well as many other kinds of decisions; for their work, Kahneman received the Nobel Prize in Economics in 2002. (Tversky had died in 1996, and was therefore ineligible.)

Types of Problems

Not all problems are alike in their structure. Various systems have been proposed to distinguish problem types, but one useful approach is to characterize the problem according to the type of goal. Many problems that we face in everyday life are **convergent** – that is, they have a single solution, and everything leads towards that solution (Guilford 1967). For example, calculating the cost of a $10,000 loan at 6 per cent over two years has only a single solution. Sometimes, problems with only one solution

convergent problem a problem which has a single solution, and all elements lead toward that solution; also called closed-end or well-defined problems.

are called *closed-end* or *well-defined* problems; by whatever label, such problems are frequently used in studies of problem solving because they are easy to evaluate.

Convergent problems have a single best solution, and all the information ultimately points towards it. **Divergent problems**, on the other hand, do not have a single optimal solution, except according to the criteria one may adopt. For example, asking 'How can I design the perfect car?' depends on your definition of 'perfect'. Similarly, dealing with a problem like air pollution could have many solutions, each differing in cost, complexity and other elements.

> **divergent problem** a problem which does not have a single optimal solution, except according to the criteria one may adopt; rather, the problem tends to lead in several different directions; equivalent to an ill-defined problem.

In this sense, the distinction between convergent and divergent problems is less in the means of developing solutions (stage 2) than in the means of evaluation (stage 3). Since convergent problems have only a single solution, stage 3 consists of making sure the solution is correct. (How many times have you made mistakes which would have been easily caught if you had taken the time to check your work?) With divergent problems, it becomes necessary to identify the criteria for an acceptable solution, and then apply these criteria to the available solution options. For example, in business, most decisions must involve cost factors, and possibly degree of risk. A promising new manufacturing technique which could potentially save money may be considered a poor solution, if there is a concern that it may not work in real production. Thus, the process of evaluation becomes very significant in dealing with divergent problems.

Models of Problem Solving

As discussed in the introduction to this chapter, the cognitive approach has been influenced by both Gestalt theory and information processing. To understand more clearly how this applies to problem solving, let us briefly examine each framework.

Gestalt Theory

Wolfgang Kohler and the other early Gestalt psychologists did extensive studies of problem solving as well as perception. As described earlier, some of Kohler's most famous studies were done with chimpanzees. Interestingly, this work was largely a product of necessity: he was stranded on the island of Tenerife during World War I, which led to his intensive studies of the chimps living on the island (Gardner 1985). In a sense, his studies of problem solving emerged as the solution to the problem of what to do with his time! The Gestalt approach to psychology was based on the premise that behaviour is based on organized structures, and is not simply a collection of stimulus elements. For example, a melody is perceived as a particular unity – a 'Gestalt' – which is independent of the notes (transposing to another key will still preserve the melody).

Similarly, Gestalt psychologists viewed problem solving as a process of changing one's perception of a situation in order to arrive at a solution. This involved a restructuring of the elements in that sudden, spontaneous way called *insight*. Hence, the goal of Gestalt psychology was to understand what creates a particular perception of a situation, described as a mental set. (In this context, the term is roughly equivalent to the more modern term schema, as defined in Chapter 1.) Thinking was seen as productive and creative, rather than a mechanical process of trial and error.

In general, the Gestalt researchers were concerned with the organizational characteristics that influence how we perceive, and therefore solve, a problem. In order to solve a problem, one must organize the information in an appropriate way – that is, one must form the right mental set. To study this process, Gestalt psychologists developed a number of intriguing convergent

persistence of set a phenomenon in problem solving, identified by Gestalt psychologists, in which a mental set developed in a previous problem is maintained even though it is no longer appropriate, and tends to interfere with solving a current problem.

problems. For example, consider the problems in Box 4.3. Once you have figured out the first problem, you can apply the same technique (mental set) to problems 2 to 5. However, you will find the sixth problem impossible to do in this way. This illustrates a hazard called **persistence of set**. The mental set developed in the first problem is no longer appropriate, and tends to interfere with solving the last problem.

Box 4.3 Persistence of Set in Problem Solving

Gestalt theorists state that in solving problems we develop a mental set; if this set is not appropriate for a particular problem, we can get stuck. In the problems below, what happens when you get to problem 6? (Adapted from Luchins 1942)

Water Jug Problems
In each problem, the goal is to use the empty jugs as measures to obtain the desired amount of water. For example, in the sample problem, one would fill jug A, and then use its contents to fill jug B three times (discarding the amount in B each time). One would then have the desired amount remaining in jug A.

Problem	Empty jugs available			Amount desired
	A	B	C	
Sample	29	3		20
1	21	127	3	100
2	14	163	25	99
3	18	43	10	5
4	9	42	6	21
5	20	59	4	31
6	24	49	4	20

This phenomenon is very common, and accounts for many cases of failure in problem solving. In everyday life, it can be the source of a variety of difficulties. For example, while travelling in the UK, I (WEG) once found myself driving on the wrong side of the road, because my prior driving experience was in North America. Persistence of set was also evident when, in the early 1990s, IBM initially failed to recognize the surging demand for personal computers. One could argue that company executives were slow to recognize the shift from mainframe to personal computers, because they had been successful in selling mainframe systems for so long. However, before concluding that mental sets are always negative, you should note that sets also make it possible for us to recognize, and solve quickly, the many problems for which our existing mental sets are appropriate. It is simply that you need to be flexible, particularly if a particular approach to a problem is unsuccessful.

functional fixedness in Gestalt theory, perceiving an object as having only one use.

A related phenomenon which Gestalt researchers identified is **functional fixedness**, which refers to perceiving an object as having only one use. For example, a person moving boxes of belongings into an apartment building may feel frustrated that the front door has no doorstop to keep it open – never realizing that one of the boxes could be used for this purpose! Similarly, many people fail to realize that a coin or knife blade can be used as a screwdriver in an emergency. Obviously, functional fixedness reflects a perceptual rigidity, much like persistence of set.

recentring in Gestalt theory, developing an alternate mental set for a situation, such as when trying to solve a problem.

The first step in avoiding these difficulties is to be aware of the danger. Beyond that, the Gestalt answer to these difficulties was **recentring**, which is developing an alternate mental set for a problem. Sometimes it helps to disengage from the problem, which is one of the functions of *incubation*. The Gestalt theorists believed that a spontaneous restructuring of set was more likely to occur if one ceased active effort when the existing set didn't work. Sultan solving the two-stick problem (described at the beginning of this chapter) shows the effects of incubation. Sometimes, overfamiliarity with a problem inhibits original thinking and recentring. The development of the theory of relativity is an example: since classical Newtonian theory worked well for many physical phenomena, established physicists were reluctant to abandon it. Einstein, as a young physicist, felt no such commitment to the old theory, which made it easier to envision a new approach. (And yet, research indicates that older adults, far from becoming rigid in their thinking, are more flexible in approaching problems, perhaps due to the greater life experience they have which has taught them that problems can be conceptualized in a multitude of ways (Blanchard-Fields 2007)).

In the end, Gestalt theory has some significant limitations. For one thing, its descriptions are rather general, and therefore sometimes difficult to evaluate. More significantly, some of the ideas which the Gestalt researchers developed were incorrect (for example, ideas about how perception is organized in the brain). Nonetheless, by their observations, and the questions raised, they set the stage for later research on cognitive processes.

Problem Solving as Information Processing

Today, the greatest influence on the study of problem solving is information processing. While many researchers have been involved in the development of this paradigm, among the early pioneers were Allen Newell and Herbert Simon (Simon made contributions in several fields, and received the Nobel Prize in Economics in 1978). In the 1950s, they began working on computer programs which could simulate human thinking processes – foreshadowing what has become known as 'artificial intelligence'. Newell and Simon developed a program called Logic Theorist which was able to do mathematical proofs – the first such result by a computer. Rather than using uninsightful 'brute force' procedures, Logic Theorist worked by using rules which Newell and Simon saw as analogous to human problem solving. Later, they began work on a program that could do other forms of problems (Newell *et al.* 1958; Newell and Simon 1972).

One of the influential aspects of their work was the emphasis on studying the actual problem solving behaviour of people. To do so, Newell and Simon would ask individuals what they were doing and thinking as they worked on problems. In some cases, they asked the individuals to think out loud, creating what have become known as **think-aloud protocols**.

think-aloud protocols a transcript of the comments made when an individual is asked to describe their thoughts and behaviour while working on a task such as problem solving.

Since the researchers came from a non-psychological tradition, they felt no qualms about taking such verbal reports seriously – in direct contradiction to behaviourist methods. Subsequently, a variety of studies, including work by Levine (1976), have demonstrated that verbal reports can be correlated with actual behaviour, validating the use of thinking-aloud procedures. Today, the technique is used in many contexts, including usability studies looking at problems with computer software (Van Den Haak *et al.* 2003).

Key Thinker: Herbert Alexander Simon

Herbert Alexander Simon (1916–2001) was born in Milwaukee, Wisconsin, on 15 June 1916. His father, an electrical engineer, had come to the USA in 1903 from Germany, while his mother, an accomplished pianist, was a third-generation American. Even in high school, he was interested in the social sciences, especially psychology and economics. He received his BSc in economics and political science from the University of Chicago in 1936, and his PhD from Chicago three years later. In 1949 Simon moved to Carnegie-Mellon Institute in Pittsburgh to help develop a graduate programme that would combine business education with economics and behavioural science, later becoming a professor of psychology. It was at Carnegie-Mellon that he made major breakthroughs in both economics and psychology. In studying decision making, he rejected the traditional economic notion that people are purely rational, instead arguing for models (based on behavioural data) which said that people seek satisfactory choices rather than ideal ones. Similarly, his interest in developing computer models for business processes led to his collaboration with Allan Newell on problem solving. Admired by his peers for both his eclectic interests and his personal warmth, in 1978 Simon won the Nobel Prize in economics 'for pioneering research into the decision making process'. Simon remained active into his eighties, publishing and collaborating until shortly before his death in 2001, at the age of 84.

initial state in problem solving, the situation at the outset of a problem, including any existing constraints (such as time limits or restrictions on permitted actions).
goal state in problem solving, the desired outcome of a problem.
operator in problem solving, one of the actions permitted in order to solve a problem.

Beyond the impact of their procedures, Newell and Simon also generated an analysis of problem solving which has subsequently influenced cognitive research. In essence, they argued that effective problem solving requires a clear representation of the problem. In simplest form, this means that one must know the situation at the outset (the **initial state**), the desired outcome (the **goal state**) and the available options to solve the problem (the **operators**). For example, to solve a multiplication problem, one must know what the starting numbers are (the initial state), what a product is (the goal) and the rules for doing multiplication (the operators). In suggesting a common framework for describing any problem, the information-processing approach represented by the work of Newell and Simon has had a significant influence on our current understanding of problem solving.

Algorithms

The need for systematic methods of solving problems is very apparent in computer applications. Computers, by their design, are not well suited to handling situations which involve any form of ambiguity. At the same time, their speed enables them to carry out sequences of actions very quickly. These characteristics have led to particular interest in an area of mathematical logic called algorithms. Basically, an **algorithm** is a procedure which always enables one to solve a particular type of problem.

algorithm a procedure for problem solving which, when used appropriately, always leads to the solution of a particular type of problem.

The most basic type of algorithm is *systematic search*, which involves identifying all possible solution options, and then systematically testing them in sequence. For example, suppose you didn't know the combination on a lock which has a dial with 40 numbers, and uses a three number combination. That means that the total number of possibilities is 40 × 40 × 40 = 64,000! If one began testing these in sequence, never trying the same combination twice, then on average it would take 32,000 tries to get the correct number (one might get lucky and find it sooner, or be unlucky and find it only after 63,999 tries!). Clearly, this would be a tedious process for a person; even for a computer, it is not always practical, as the number of trials required grows exponentially as the number of digits on the dial increases (for example, with 60 numbers, the total is 216,000!).

Thus, systematic search is a useful algorithm, but it does have limitations. As noted in the combination lock problem, it becomes cumbersome for problems with many possible solutions. Ideally, one would like to find a solution which is more efficient than this (and therefore remains practical even if the number of possible solutions increases significantly). Another example may help clarify this point: suppose there is a tennis tournament, with 101 players competing. If the tournament is based on elimination matches, what is the minimum number of matches necessary? One algorithm, equivalent to systematic search, is to list all the necessary rounds, providing for 'bys' when there is an odd number of players. A shorter algorithm is possible, however: by definition, every player except one (the final winner) must lose once and only once. Thus, the minimum number of matches equals 101–1, or 100 matches! Obviously, efficient algorithms are quite desirable. Unfortunately, for some problems only inefficient algorithms (like systematic search) are known, and for large problems this approach would tax even a computer.

It is also worth noting that in order to solve a problem, an algorithm must be appropriate for the problem. For example, using the operations for division when the goal is to obtain the product (multiplication) would lead to a wrong answer. In everyday life, we often use devices that have algorithms built in – but if the original designer made an error in writing the algorithm, the device will make mistakes (in one case, an X-ray machine with a faulty algorithm gave patients excessive doses, and staff didn't realize this for months). For situations where no appropriate algorithm exists, other strategies must be used.

Heuristics

The primary alternative to algorithms is the use of **heuristics**, or guides to thinking. Instead of a specific set of steps or rules, heuristics use metaphors, analogies and other intuitive techniques.

Unfortunately, heuristics are only guidelines, and unlike algorithms, do not guarantee finding a correct solution. For example, with the salesman's map problem, the salesman is given the assignment of visiting a number of cities to make sales. The question is, in what order should the salesman visit the cities in order to produce the shortest overall route? A heuristic which gives a *reasonable* solution (but not necessarily the optimum) is to go to the nearest new city next. Or, consider the heuristic for fixing a stalled car that a mechanic once stated: 'A car needs gas and it needs a spark. If one is OK, check the other.' Obviously, such a rule is better than nothing, but equally obviously, it doesn't provide very specific guidance. This is typical of the nature of heuristics.

> **heuristic** a guide to thinking in problem solving, heuristics provide informal strategies which are usually better than random search, but less effective than algorithms.

A number of general heuristics have been identified which can be used for a variety of problems. It is not possible to discuss them all in detail here, but the following list indicates some common possibilities:

- *Working backwards* involves backtracking from the goal to one's current situation. It is often used in situations where reversing the problem reduces the range of possible choices. For instance, when you misplace something, you might retrace your steps from the last point at

Box 4.4 Cultural Values in Problem Solving
Cultures differ in the processes they prefer to use in solving problems.

As discussed in the chapter, the information processing model emphasizes rational analysis for solving problems, with an emphasis on techniques for quickly arriving at a solution. Culturally, this orientation fits well with the kinds of mental attributes which are normally valued by contemporary western societies. For example, we tend to admire someone who is independent and quick-thinking. But these characteristics are not universally valued. For example, Serpell (1993) found that agricultural African societies valued looking at the problem in the context of the whole society, noting its impact on various features of life. Problems were approached by the group, rather than by individuals, and the preferred problem solving style involved group discussion. In most situations, speed in arriving at a solution was not a vital issue; instead, speed might be equated with rashness. (Although Serpell did not examine this issue, one might expect that these characteristics would be particularly appropriate for solving divergent problems.)

Similarly, Ross (1996) discusses what he calls the 'Conservation Withdrawal Tactic' traditionally used by the Cree and Ojibway in Canada. These groups historically lived in wilderness areas and faced many hardships; in these circumstances, they would rarely get a second chance at solving problems. Consequently, these Native people value taking time to reflect on a problem and mentally walk through possible solutions before any action is taken. Unfortunately, when these people move into the dominant urban culture in Canada, the characteristics of deliberation and reflection are sometimes wrongly interpreted as a lack of intelligence. Though western culture may encourage us differently, quick assessments – whether of a problem or the person solving it – are not always appropriate.

Try it Yourself

Using problem solving techniques can be very useful in everyday life. For instance, if you need to write a 20-page essay on an unfamiliar topic, the technique of *creating sub-goals* can be helpful in dealing with the task. Using the technique may look like this:

1 identify clearly what the assignment involves;

2 identify the specific topic which will be the focus of the essay;

3 find information (for example, books and articles from the library) related to the topic;

4 organize the information, making notes where needed;

5 write an outline of the essay, identifying how the information will fit;

6 write the introduction to the essay.

And so on.... Accomplishing each step and crossing it off this list breaks a large task into small, manageable parts – and completing each part can be reinforcing!

Now consider the following problems: in each case, what algorithm or heuristic would you use to make problem solving easier?

■ You want to buy a T-shirt as a gift, but you don't know the person's size.

■ You want to find a misplaced CD, and know it's somewhere in your home, because you played it yesterday.

■ You're trying to explain how to bake a cake to someone familiar with chemistry.

which you had the item (in this case, by starting from a point when you still had the item and then checking the places you know you went thereafter, you limit the possible places to be checked).

- *Creating sub-goals* is designed to break the problem into smaller, more manageable problems. For example, asking 'how can we end pollution?' can be broken down into types of pollution (air, water, etc.) or sources of pollution (industry, motor vehicles, homes, etc.). Once one has identified some sub-goals, one then tries to deal with them individually. (Note that in this example there is more than one way to divide the problem; this vagueness is characteristic of heuristics.)

- *Using metaphors and analogies* involves looking for similarities between seemingly different contexts. For example, asking how a camera is like the human eye has led to automatic focusing and automatic exposure systems for cameras.

In the end, no single technique will prove useful in all situations – a reality recognized in most cultures (see Box 4.4). Furthermore, it is worth remembering the perils of persistence of set and functional fixedness, identified by Gestalt theorists. The wider the range of techniques one can call on in trying to solve a problem, the less likely it is that these difficulties will occur.

Creativity in Problem Solving

For the average person, 'creativity' likely inspires thoughts of artists, writers or musicians, who may be creative in terms of artistic expression. Yet it is also possible to be creative when dealing with problems; indeed, many inventions have been the result of creativity in handling a technical problem (the discovery of the light bulb and integrated circuit are two examples). To address this, researchers often define **creativity** as the production of something which has two characteristics: *uniqueness* and *utility*. Uniqueness is significant, because an idea which occurs to everyone is not regarded as creative (for example, suggesting that wheels should be round instead of square is not creative). On the other hand, unique ideas must also be useful for solving a problem (for example, wearing clothes made out of spaghetti would be unique, but not very practical). As Edward deBono has commented, a creative idea is just a new idea that works (deBono 1976).

creativity the capacity to produce something which is both unique and useful.

DeBono uses the term 'lateral thinking' to describe creativity, in contrast to the relatively rigid patterns of logical analysis (linear thinking). In some ways, his ideas are reminiscent of Gestalt theory. For example, he notes that rigid thinking can take several forms, from failure to recognize that an old solution is no longer appropriate, to arrogant attachment to one's own ideas. To aid recentring, he promotes the value of humour, provocativeness (especially in what-if scenarios) and novelty. While his writings are highly entertaining ('if you cannot imagine any alternatives, it is easy to be convinced that the only one you have is absolutely right'), his approach tends to favour descriptive models over rigorous research.

Guilford, like deBono, believed that creativity involves a different mode of thinking, which he called 'divergent thinking' (Guilford 1967). This process is manifested in solving divergent problems, in which the search for solutions tends to lead in several different directions. Divergent problems are also creative in the sense that they have many possible solutions, not all of which will be equivalent in either originality or practicality. Hence, solving a divergent problem requires selecting the best solution.

Unfortunately, as we saw, defining 'best' can be rather ambiguous. The evaluation of the best solution often involves judgements of value (either personal or social). For example, in our culture we tend to value a businessman who develops a new marketing strategy for a product more than we value a mother who invents an activity to keep a 3-year-old amused. Similarly, social attitudes towards creativity seem to value quantity over quality, and to emphasize the number of ideas generated as a primary indicator of creativity. (Even Guilford was guilty of this simplification, since one of his tests of creativity simply counts how many different uses one can imagine for a common object, like a brick.) We may value highly the person who generates five ideas, none of which are effective, rather than the person who describes only one, because they have already recognized that the other four ideas were not workable! (Sometimes, being creative means knowing when something isn't a solution as well as when it *is*.)

As one might expect, the issue of what sort of creativity is valued tends to arise when looking at different cultures. For example, researchers have argued that in India, creativity associated with spirituality is highly valued, and that Arab cultures favour verbal creativity over pictorial, due to Islamic restrictions on representational art (Bhawuk 2003; Mari and Karayanni 1982). However, making generalizations can be difficult, because cultures may be similar in some ways, and different in others. For example, several studies suggest that both the creation and evaluation of artistic works are similar for European-American and Chinese cultures (Chen *et al.* 2002; Niu and Sternberg 2001; Rostan *et al.* 2002). However, there appear to be differences between these cultures in creative performance on divergent problems (Niu and Sternberg 2002).

In the end, assessments of value are more ambiguous than judgements of uniqueness or practicality. While there is no simple resolution to this issue, it does indicate that evaluation is crucial in solving divergent problems, and possibly in creativity more generally.

The Formation of Problem Solving Skills

Good problem solvers often make use of many of the techniques that we have been discussing, even when they have not been formally trained in problem solving. Other people seem to flounder when given any type of unfamiliar problem. Since research suggests that problem solving is a matter of acquired skills, not general intellect, it leads us to a question: how do people learn the process of solving problems? What makes some people more 'insightful'?

Gestalt theory refers to a *mental set* as the way one perceives a particular situation, including a problem. Insight triggers a shift in mental set, so that one's perceptions are rearranged in a more appropriate way. The question is, *how* does this occur? One of the difficulties with the Gestalt approach is its tendency to be primarily descriptive. Kohler's concept of insight really only describes the end result, not how one arrives at it. Similarly, the description of incubation does not explain why it is sometimes effective, and sometimes not. These and other aspects of the problem solving process were left to other researchers to examine – ironically, some of whom began, like Tolman, within the behaviourist approach.

In the late 1940s, an American psychologist named Harry Harlow discovered a phenomenon which he called 'learning to learn'. Working with primates, he found that problem solving behaviour (such as choosing which of two symbols marked the location of a food reward) was initially trial and error, much as a behaviourist would expect (Harlow 1949). However, given experience with many problems of the same type, the animals would develop a 'set' which enabled them to deal with new problems in an insightful way. Harlow called these learned strategies **learning sets**. (In essence, Harlow's term has the same meaning as the Gestalt concept of *mental*

learning set a learned strategy or set which enables the individual to deal efficiently with problems of the same type; similar in meaning to the Gestalt concept of mental set, except it emphasizes that the set develops as the result of experience.

set, except it emphasizes that the set develops as the result of experience, not as spontaneous insight.)

Harlow's work not only provided a mechanism for explaining Gestalt concepts; it was also instrumental in moving psychology from a behaviouristic to a cognitive view of learning (Rumbaugh 1997). Later research has shown that young children, and even adults, develop similar learning sets from experience (Levine 1976). For example, the story of the child solving problems involving different shapes, presented at the beginning of this chapter, illustrates the formation of a learning set. In this case, the child quickly learns a strategy called 'win-stay, lose-shift'. That is, if the first shape you pick is correct, stay with it; if you choose incorrectly the first time, then this tells you the other shape is the correct one, and should be chosen thereafter. At a more complex level, it can be argued that students in school learn how to learn by learning to select what is most important when studying, by identifying cues to test questions from lecture content, and so on. In this sense, education is a type of problem solving, not simply a passive intake of information. Recognizing this, and teaching students to focus on such strategies, have been shown to improve school performance, even for students with learning disabilities (Hudson 1996). Regardless of the situation, Harlow's work implies that effective problem solving depends on appropriate past experience – not to know the answer, but to know how to get the answer. Insight comes, not out of the blue, but to those who are prepared.

Research on the formation of learning sets has helped to clarify the role of experience in the development of problem solving skills. While adult behaviour is usually insightful in terms of the use of strategies, it is based on a foundation of early trial and error experience. In this sense, Kohler's emphasis on insight as distinct from trial and error appears to be wrong. In the end, though, there is little doubt that cognitive research has increased our understanding of problem solving in ways that have practical benefit.

LANGUAGE

While animals like chimpanzees have demonstrated some ability in problem solving, there is little doubt that people are more capable of dealing with complex problems. We can do so largely because we know so much, which in turn is partly due to our ability to learn from experience, and store that knowledge in memory in an organized way. But another important element is our ability to communicate with each other, and thereby benefit from the experiences of others (reading a textbook like this one is a clear example!). Without language, we would be mostly restricted to learning from personal experience, and there is little doubt that our lives would be the poorer for it.

In many ways, language is a paradox: we learn to use it as a child with very little difficulty, yet as an adult find learning a second language a major challenge. We can use it to understand other people, yet we have very little understanding of the process itself! Psychologists, linguists, philosophers and others have all examined language, but at present there are many unresolved questions.

language a system of communication based on symbols or gestures which can vary across individuals and allow for new forms and meanings.

To start with, not everyone agrees on what language is. It is clear that language serves as a communication method and as a symbol system, but not every form of communication is considered language. For example, the innately determined threat gestures used by baboons to warn away rivals are signals, but not language. In order to qualify as **language**, most researchers would say that the symbols or gestures used for communicating must show *variety* within the species, and must be *open-ended* (that is, allow for new forms and meanings). Baboon gestures show neither of these characteristics, and so would not be considered a true language. Variety is important, in that it implies the influence of learning, and also that symbols are somewhat arbitrary – that is, the same meaning could be communicated using different elements. Interestingly, birdsong is somewhat like language in that it is dependent on learning, and shows intra-species variation, including regional 'dialects' (Marler 1970). However, it is not clear whether birdsong can be considered an open-ended symbol system, as the definition of language requires. For our purposes, we will focus on the role of human language in communication and thinking.

The existence of language is such an obvious human characteristic that even the behaviourists could not ignore it. Traditionally, they have tried to explain it in terms of complex patterns of reinforcers and stimulus-response sequences (Skinner 1957). Beyond accounting for spoken language, the behaviourists showed little interest in its role in thinking, as befits their general point of view. Watson saw thinking as simply muscle movements reduced to small, unobserved twitches; Pavlov saw thought as the product of a 'second signal system', operating in parallel with the process of conditioning. Unfortunately, the behaviourist view of language and thought is challenged by the data. While there is evidence that muscle activity often occurs along with thinking (for example, deaf individuals who know sign language show activity in hand muscles while engaging in problem solving), the evidence regarding thinking as *only* muscle activity is mostly negative. As we will see, there are also other problems with the behaviourist view of language.

By contrast, cognitive researchers see language as a symbol system which can mediate a variety of thinking processes, and which is not dependent on muscle twitches. In addition, the cognitive approach views our use of language as based on innate capacities, not simply reinforced responses. To understand the reasons for this viewpoint, we need to consider how we learn to use language.

Language Learning

We all learn to use language, but typically show little concern about how we learn. Children absorb the vocabulary and basic grammar of their mother tongue long before it is formally taught in school. Yet, when closely examined, early language learning is a remarkable process. At about 6 months of age, a baby will begin *babbling*, producing a wide variety of speech sounds, only some of which will later be used in their first language. Later on, it is difficult to reacquire those sounds which are lost. For example, native French speakers have trouble with the 'th' sound in English; similarly, English speakers have trouble with 'û' in French. Interestingly, research shows that a similar process of social feedback tells both children and baby birds which sounds are important (Goldstein *et al.* 2003). At about 1 year of age, the first words appear. By about 1½ to 2 years, the child produces two-word 'sentences'. These phrases were called *telegraphic speech* by early researchers, but we now recognize that there is considerable complexity in the production and use of these 'simple' phrases. Some examples of telegraphic speech are clear even out of context – for instance, 'that red' for 'that is red', or 'see mummy' for 'I see mummy'. In other cases, what seems meaningless when considered out of context is nonetheless understandable in context. For example, a child, seeing a ball near the mother, may say 'Mummy throw'. (It is worth noting that in some cases adult language is also unclear when taken out of context!) By the age of 2, the typical child produces about two dozen two-word sentences. From this time on, the growth of language skills is explosive, so that at age 3 the average child knows almost 1000 words, and this figure may *double* in the ensuing year (Moskowitz 1978). As an adult, it has been estimated that the average person knows over 100,000 words, though only a small fraction of these may be

Box 4.5 *Stages of Language Development*

The sequence of stages seems to be universal, though the timing can vary somewhat across individuals and even cultures.

Stage	Age	Description of language skills
Babbling	6 months – 1 year	Babies begin by producing all the phonemes found in human language
First words	1 – 1½ years	First words, using phonemes in the language spoken by those around child
Telegraphic speech	1½ – 2 years	Two-word sentences, typically combining a noun and verb or adjective and noun (for example, 'Mommy gone')
Acquiring grammar	2 – 4 years	Learning prepositions, verb forms and other rules; at first, child tends to over-generalize forms (for example, 'I goed')
Competent speech	4 – 5 years	Uses full sentences with conventional grammar, though with less complex structure than adults

used regularly (see Box 4.5 for a summary and Figure 4.6 for children's acquisition of language rules).

The rapid development of language skills poses several difficulties for a behaviourist interpretation of language. First, acquisition seems to occur too quickly and too consistently to be based simply on trial and error. Second, there is evidence that we are best prepared to learn language at the time children normally do. If this 'critical period' is passed, it may be difficult or impossible to learn normal language skills later. (Incidents of children raised in isolation support this view, as do cases of children with correctable hearing deficits which are not recognized until age 4 or 5, which is already past the point when language learning normally begins.) Third, individuals seem to have less difficulty learning a second language as children than as adults (McDonald 1997). All of these factors suggest that language learning is based on some innate capacities which are tied to early development.

The best-known advocate for language as an innate capacity is Noam Chomsky, a linguist at Massachusetts Institute of Technology (MIT) (Chomsky 1972, 2002; Hauser *et al.* 2002). Chomsky argues that human language is based on innate grammatical rules, which are part of what he calls a *language acquisition device* ('device' here means a hypothetical mechanism, without specifying a physical basis). Chomsky's position has gained many supporters. Roger Brown, a cognitive psychologist who is interested in both language and child development, favours the notion of internal rules. After reviewing studies of 12 different languages, he feels that the evidence is compelling (Brown 1973). Steven Pinker, a colleague of Chomsky at MIT, goes so far as to call language an 'instinct' (Pinker 1994).

The possibility that language is based on innate capacities is hardly disturbing to a cognitive psychologist. After all, such capacities would represent a form of mediating process for language learning, and hence are consistent with the general assumptions of the cognitive approach (unlike the behaviourists or the biological approach, cognitive psychologists have no firm position on nature vs. nurture). The Gestalt psychologists, in particular, would find this view comfortable, since they saw many organizing principles as being innate. At the same time, there is a risk in describing language capacity as innate. For one thing, there is a variety of evidence suggesting that learning plays an important role in the development of language. For example, children practise their language skills extensively – spending perhaps 10,000 hours speaking by age 6 (Anderson 1995). Furthermore, there is great variability among human languages and across individuals, and the notion of innate capacities does not address these details (Harley 1995).

The issue of variability is particularly interesting for second language learning. As noted above, there seem to be advantages to learning a second language in early childhood rather than in later life (Hakuta *et al.* 2003; Oh *et al.* 2003). While this does not necessarily prove that there is a *critical period* for *second* language acquisition (vs. learning language at all), it does pose an interesting problem: how does an infant exposed to multiple languages separate them? Since feedback is important to identifying speech sounds in babbling, one might think that adults teach the infant to separate languages. Instead, it appears that infants actually use language features like rhythm to tell one language from another (Jusczyk 2002). Thus, a French-speaking infant can distinguish English from Japanese on the basis of differences in the rhythm! Hence, language learning, even for multiple languages, represents a mix of innate skills with specific experiences.

Despite the appeal of arguments for innate language skills, one must remember that placing an emphasis on innateness does not eliminate the need to *explain* the process. Saying that 'it's part of human nature to use language', even if true, tells us very little about our use of language – or any apparent usage by other species.

Of Apes and Language

The question of language capacity in other species has become a controversial area in recent years. Researchers have long speculated on the possibility of teaching human language to another species, usually primates like chimpanzees. Starting in the 1920s, several teams of researchers attempted to teach chimps to speak, often by rearing them as if they were human children. Then, in the mid-1960s, a husband and wife team of psychologists, Allen and Beatrice Gardner, tried a new approach (Gardner and Gardner 1969). Reasoning that it might be an inability to *speak*, not an inability to *use language*, that led to previous failures, the Gardners decided to try sign language. Using a modified form of ASL (a sign language used by many deaf individuals in the USA), they began training a female chimp named Washoe. To their surprise as well as satisfaction, Washoe began using signs proficiently, albeit with a limited vocabulary.

The first published reports set off an intense controversy in both psychology and linguistics, mostly about what constitutes true language. A rash of studies followed, some using the methods of the Gardners, and some using other methods (including having primates interacting with a computer). Apart from chimpanzees, there have also been studies with gorillas, orang-utans and dolphins. The debate generated by these studies has been considerable. Some theorists say the use of ASL and other symbol systems shows that chimps have basically the same type of language capacity that we have. Other researchers argue that there may be only a very superficial similarity in language potential between humans and other primates (Weiss and Newport 2006). Herb Terrace, a behaviourist, has questioned whether the chimps really show awareness of syntax (use of word order to convey meaning), and has also noted the relatively limited vocabulary of the animals (Terrace *et al.* 1979). It is impossible to discuss every study in detail, but it should be noted that some researchers have found evidence for both syntax and creation of new 'words' (Premack 1983). Even more interesting is the evidence that ASL-trained chimps spontaneously

This is a wug.

Now there is another one.
There are two of them.
There are two _____ .

Figure 4.6 Children's Learning of Language Rules One of the basic aspects of language learning is the acquisition of rules, such as how to form plural nouns. As shown in the figure, a classic study by Jean Berko (1958) tested pre-school and grade 1 children for their understanding of this rule.

teach signing to other chimps (Fouts *et al.* 1983). Similarly, a bonobo (another type of primate) named Kanzi observed his mother being trained to use symbols via a keyboard for his first two years of life. Though he had not himself been trained, Kanzi spontaneously began using the keyboard appropriately at age 2, when his mother was relocated (Rumbaugh 1992).

At present, it seems that the controversy is still unresolved, with each side finding some data which support their viewpoint. However, we should be wary of defining language in such a way that only human behaviour would qualify. For example, the limited vocabulary of chimps does not seem a sufficient reason to discount their behaviour as language. Similarly, judgements of creativity seem ambiguous: while it is true that no chimp has produced the equivalent of Shakespeare, few humans do, either. In this regard, it is interesting that a gorilla named Koko has shown an interest in poetry, and has commented on the death of a kitten in surprising ways (Patterson and Linden 1981; Stone 1988). Communication can range from the mundane to the extraordinary, and it is likely that the study of language-related behaviour in other species will help us to achieve a better understanding of our own linguistic accomplishments. Indeed, recent studies suggest that primates have some crucial innate skills associated with language (matching sounds to facial expressions, much as hearing-impaired 'sight-readers' do; detecting differences in speech rhythms) (Tincoff *et al.* 2005; Zuberbühler 2005; Weiss and Newport 2006). In addition, there is evidence that the limitations on chimps' language skills may be due to the same defective gene found in people with severe language problems (Corballis 2004; Enard *et al.* 2002; Ghazanfar and Logothetis 2003). In the end, the more we study the language skills of other species, the more we may learn about our own language capacity.

Language and Thinking

The study of language raises questions about the relationship of language to thinking. Is all thinking based on words? Do the words we use influence the way we think? In many ways, these questions are much deeper than simply asking if thinking consists of muscle twitches. Thinking processes are central to the cognitive approach, and it is obviously desirable to understand what the basis of thinking is. At one time, it was assumed that all thinking was verbal, in much the way that memory researchers thought all memory was verbal. One consequence of this view was the tendency to assume that infants, lacking language, could not think. More recently, ingenious experiments have shown that infants are capable of thinking (see discussion in Chapter 7). In addition, research on visual imagery and memory, as discussed earlier, suggests that not all thinking is verbal, even in adults. Yet, few would disagree that the *primary* mode of thinking for most individuals is verbal. And if this is so, then how do the words we use affect the way we think?

One answer to this question was proposed some years ago by Benjamin Whorf, a specialist in Native American languages. Whorf argued that the way a language is structured influences the way that individuals perceive, and think about, the world (Whorf 1956). (This has been popularized in the phrase, 'language shapes thought'.) Essentially, Whorf argued that the way we think depends on the words available to us. He based this on the observation that various Native American languages had very different vocabularies, and that it was often nearly impossible to translate from one language to another. One example concerns the fact that the Inuit have many words for different kinds of snow, but the Navajo have only one. Whorf took the strong position that such differences not only affect thinking and communication, but that they also affect perception. That is, he believed that Inuit actually *see* snow differently from other people (such as Navajos).

This view, sometimes called the *Whorfian hypothesis*, has been the subject of extensive research and debate. At the level of perception, the evidence has been mostly negative; for example, despite variations in colour names across languages, people tend to discriminate colours in similar ways (Rosch 1973). However, the milder form, that language can influence the categories used in thinking, is still an open question. Certainly it is true that concepts can be easier to express when there is a specific word available, as opposed to a lengthy description. This is evident in the tendency of English (and other languages) to incorporate foreign words. For example, 'ennui' (borrowed from French) conveys a meaning which is subtly different from 'boredom'. At the same time, the fact that a single word does not exist does not necessarily mean that a concept cannot be expressed in some indirect way.

Since questions of vocabulary seem indecisive in judging Whorf's hypothesis, it is more interesting to consider areas where thinking interacts with the *structure* of a language. For example, consider forms of address: in English, we use the word 'you' to refer to someone we are speaking to, without regard to our social relationship to the person. Other languages, including French, German and Japanese, use different forms depending on the social relationship (for example, *vous* or *tu* in French). Hence, in these languages, addressing someone requires considering what our relationship is to them. Another example concerns counterfactual statements. In English, we frequently express ideas which are contrary to fact – for example, after Derek has a car accident, we might say, 'if he hadn't been drinking, he wouldn't have had an accident.' By contrast, Cantonese Chinese does not have a ready means of producing such statements; instead, individuals are likely to simply say, 'Derek had an accident because he was drinking.' Based on this linguistic difference, one researcher found that Chinese speakers had more difficulty than American English speakers in understanding arguments involving counterfactual statements

(Bloom 1981). Differences have also been found across languages in how people specify object locations, and relationships among objects (Majid *et al.* 2004). For example, speakers of English or Japanese use a person-centric perspective, vs. a landmark-based perspective in Mayan. Thus, in English one might say, 'the cup is to the right of the fork'; a Mayan speaker might say the equivalent of 'the cup is on the side of the fork that is towards the village-square' (Li and Gleitman 2002).

Despite such apparent differences across cultures, Lila Gleitman and her colleagues have done a number of studies which suggest that language poses few real constraints on thinking (Li and Gleitman 2002; Papafragou *et al.* 2002). For example, comparisons of native English and Greek speakers found little difference across languages in remembering or describing events involving motion, for either children or adults. Similarly, Gleitman argues that the language patterns found for spatial relationships reflect a 'culturally shared fashion of speaking', not a fundamental cognitive difference. In Gleitman's view, cultural habits, not basic cognitions, may account for many linguistic differences. Or, as Price and Crapo (2002) suggest, rather than telling us how people think, language may tell us about what is important in their daily lives. This interpretation may undermine Whorf's view, but may help us better understand others – for example, by explaining the way that non-native speakers of our own language express themselves.

At present, the strong version of Whorf's theory seems incorrect, but the debate concerning a milder version is inconclusive. To the extent that differences across languages exist (whether inevitable or just habitual), they leave us with a number of intriguing questions. At what point, one might wonder, do such differences in expression lead to different ways of thinking? On the other hand, does the way we think lead to changes in the language we use? For example, one might speculate that our experience of the world has been changed by concepts like Einstein's theory of relativity, with its suggestion that frameworks of perception are always relative. Whorf may have been too extreme in his position, but the issues he raised are likely to be with us for a long time to come.

The relationship between language and thinking is complex and subtle. Certainly, language is the primary symbol system used in thinking, and the specifics of a language can probably influence the way we organize information. Beyond that, there is much that we do not know about language, *including* precisely how it affects our thinking. Words let us think about the world, and communicate those thoughts to each other. At some level, that process is as wondrous as the latest technology. Future research may help us to understand the process better, but it is unlikely to rob language of the capacity to amaze.

Try it Yourself

Do you speak a second language? If so, you might explore Whorf's hypothesis by thinking about your experiences. Do you notice any ways in which your thinking changes when you switch languages? Are there ideas or feelings you would have trouble expressing in your second language? Is that because of your own lack of fluency, or does the language itself matter? Ask any friends of yours who speak other languages about their experiences; do the results support or contradict Whorf's hypothesis?

THE COGNITIVE VIEWPOINT IN OTHER AREAS

Cognitive psychologists have been active in studying all aspects of thinking, as indicated above. In focusing on these topics, one should not lose sight of the basic viewpoint of the cognitive approach: it is not that thinking processes like memory are the most significant aspect of behaviour, but rather that mediational processes of *some* kind underlie *all* behaviour. As noted in the introduction of this chapter, this approach can be applied to understanding many other aspects of behaviour. For example, early Gestalt psychologists were as interested in perception as in problem solving. Today, one can see cognitive influences in the study of development (as in the work of Jean Piaget, Jerome Bruner and others), computer science (in the area of artificial intelligence), and even applications of behaviourism (where psychologists like Donald Meichenbaum are advocating 'cognitive behaviour modification'). (Some of these topics will be discussed in later chapters.)

Given the many dimensions of human behaviour, it should not be surprising that cognitive interpretations are applied to many aspects of behaviour other than thinking processes. In discussing these areas, the underlying assumptions are the same – there are mediational processes (mental events) which underlie behaviour, and these processes provide an organizational structure for guiding behaviour. At the same time, the specific models used have often developed independently of either Gestalt or information-processing influences. Regardless of origin, the resulting models are characteristically cognitive in nature, as we shall see.

Attitudes and Cognitive Dissonance

One area where the cognitive approach has been particularly significant is social psychology. In this case, the influence is probably direct, owing to the work of Kurt Lewin, an early Gestalt psychologist who wrote extensively about social behaviour (Lewin 1948). Social psychology is concerned with the ways in which behaviour is influenced by social interactions. While this covers a broad territory, one of the primary interests has been **social cognition**, the mental processes involved in the way people perceive and react to social situations. We will look at two aspects of social cognition, beginning with the study of attitudes.

social cognition the mental processes involved in the way people perceive and react to social situations.
attitude a personal belief of an evaluative nature, such as good or bad, likeable or not likeable, which influences our reactions towards people or things.

Attitudes represent personal beliefs of an evaluative nature, such as good or bad, likeable or not likeable. Traditionally, attitudes are regarded by researchers as having three components: the belief itself (cognitive component), the feelings associated with it (emotional component) and the resulting actions (behavioural component). For example, someone may believe smoking is harmful, get angry when someone is smoking near them and boycott a restaurant which allows smoking.

Attitudes are of practical as well as theoretical interest, since they involve such basic concerns as attraction and prejudice. Understanding who likes/hates whom, and why, requires an understanding of how attitudes are formed, and how they are altered. While it is not possible to provide a full exploration of attitudes in this section, we will look at one approach to the study of what leads us to change our attitudes.

cognitive dissonance in Festinger's theory, a state of tension created when there are conflicts between an individual's behaviour and beliefs, or between two beliefs.

One of the best known theories of attitude change is the *theory of cognitive dissonance* developed by Leon Festinger (Festinger 1957). According to Festinger, we all seek to behave in a self-consistent manner. That is, our actions should fit with both our words and our attitudes. What happens, however, if our actions don't fit our beliefs, or two beliefs conflict? Festinger argued that whenever there are conflicts of this type, we experience a tension which he called **cognitive dissonance**. For example, suppose you hate the hustle and bustle of New York City, but have good friends who live there whom you want to see. This creates a conflict between your attitude towards New York and your attitude towards your friends, resulting in dissonance. Festinger's theory deals with the nature of such conflicts, and how we resolve them.

One possibility is to change your attitudes to make them consistent with your actions. In the example given, you could decide New York isn't so bad, and go, or you could decide you really don't care that much about your friends, and not go. In either case, one of your attitudes would change to become consistent with your actions. Or, you could persuade your friends to come to visit you. In this case, your attitudes remain firm, but the conflict is resolved by adding a new factor. This is analogous to a smoking colleague who once commented, 'Sure, I know smoking causes cancer, but I'd be miserable if I *didn't* smoke!' In effect, the belief that life would be miserable without smoking is invoked to resolve the conflict between the belief that smoking causes cancer and the desire not to get cancer. This example is not purely anecdotal: research indicates that smokers use arguments very much like this to justify their continuing the habit (Oakes *et al.* 2004; Peretti-Watel *et al.* 2007). Dissonance theory says that conflict (dissonance) can lead to changes in attitudes or actions; if attitudes are changed, usually the weakest belief is the one to be changed.

Dissonance reduction seems to be a common occurrence. Consider the following example: have you ever waited outside for a movie in the middle of winter, possibly for an hour or more? What was your reaction to the movie afterwards? According to dissonance theory, you very likely thought the movie was good, since it would arouse dissonance to think you suffered outside for a terrible film! In a laboratory analogy to this situation, Festinger paid participants either $1 or $20 to take part in a purposely dull experiment (Festinger and Carlsmith 1959). (It should be noted that $20 was a considerable sum of money in 1959!) They were then requested to tell the next 'participant' that the task was enjoyable. When subsequently asked to *honestly* evaluate the task, those paid $1 rated it much more positively than those paid $20. In effect, lying by telling someone else the task was boring created more dissonance for those paid only $1 than for the better-paid subjects; this led to the poorly-paid subjects actually revising their evaluation of the task in a positive way!

Dissonance theory has generated tremendous amounts of research in social psychology (see Harmon-Jones and Mills 1999). Partly this is because the issues it raises are interesting, and partly because of apparent weaknesses in the theory. One weakness is that the theory does not predict precisely what will happen in a particular situation. For example, a smoker confronted by evidence that links smoking to cancer may react in several ways: he may quit smoking (thereby changing actions); he may reject the evidence as being only correlational (rejecting one belief); or he may justify the discrepancy in some other way, as in the earlier example of the smoker who introduced an additional belief about the consequences of quitting. Festinger himself suggested that we tend to ignore information which creates conflict, a phenomenon called *selective exposure*. While some evidence suggests that this can occur (for example, Frey 1986), a review of a wide range of studies of attitudes suggests the links between attitudes and behaviour are often hard to predict (Kraus 1995).

A second issue concerns how widespread dissonance reactions are in daily life. While it is possible to produce supporting anecdotes, the evidence suggests that not all conflicts produce dissonance. For instance, a person *forced* to do something inconsistent with their beliefs will usually not experience dissonance. (This may explain why the people who were paid $20 in the Festinger and Carlsmith experiment felt no dissonance about telling someone else the task was enjoyable – the money could be seen as the factor 'forcing' them to lie.) Generally, dissonance is most likely to occur when someone *voluntarily* does something which is inconsistent with their attitudes (thus, being paid only $1 was a poor incentive to lie, which created dissonance). Dissonance is also likely to be greater if the situation involves the person's sense of self-esteem, as when a 'nice' person does something cruel (Aronson 2000).

Although clearly not the final word on the subject of attitude change, Festinger's theory shows the influence of the cognitive approach in both name and substance. As a theory of social behaviour, it clearly states that mediating processes are important in understanding how people act. Contrary to behaviourist notions, the stimulus situation alone is insufficient to explain social behaviour. Rather, one must consider internal constructs and processes like attitudes and dissonance reduction. In this and other ways, the cognitive approach plays an important role in understanding social behaviour, and has even been used to help understand serious social problems such as terrorism (see *The World Today: Terrorism and Cognitive Dissonance*).

The world today: **Terrorism and Cognitive Dissonance**

Terrorism is of great concern in the world today, and to many of us, not understandable. Most particularly, what causes a peaceful, non-violent person to adopt terrorist tactics? Maikovich (2005) believes that at least part of the explanation can be found by using the principles of cognitive dissonance. The process is gradual, she says. First, the non-violent person finds that non-violent tactics do not achieve the goals that they want. At this point, there are two dissonant cognitions: 'I want this goal' and 'My preferred methods don't work'. Most people resolve the dissonance by strengthening their commitment to their preferred peaceful methods, but for some, dissonance is reduced by exploring alternative methods.

In the next step, the non-violent person makes a connection with an organization or group that sometimes uses violence to achieve its ends. Such groups are typically hierarchical, so the peaceful person enters at the lowest rung, a status which allows them to participate in only the most menial tasks, such as preparing meals for others. Gradually, they are trusted with more responsibilities and may take part in actions that are only slightly violent, such as writing graffiti. Again, at this point, many people leave rather than participate in any form of aggression, but some stay, now with the dissonant cognitions 'I believe in peaceful means' and 'I committed an act of aggression'. This can be resolved by adding consonant elements to 'I committed aggression': these elements could be in the form of 'The aggression wasn't too bad' or 'Some aggression is justified'. After having committed an act of aggression, the new member may be asked to participate in acts of increasing violence. At each step, the dissonance between the cognition of 'I believe in peaceful means' and 'I am committing violence' may be reduced by strengthening the cognition that 'Violence is justified'.

When a person holds a belief and is persuaded to perform an action that is not consonant with that belief, it is generally easier to reduce the dissonance by changing the cognition, since the action cannot be undone. In a gradual fashion, then, as increasingly violent acts are committed, the belief in non-violence may be reduced in strength and changed to 'I believe in peaceful methods when they have a chance of working, but in this situation they won't work, so violence is the only recourse'.

Maikovich does not believe that this is the whole answer to the question of why formerly peaceful people become terrorists, but she does believe that it helps us to understand some of the complexity of the situation.

Attribution Theory

A second area of social cognition which has been influenced by the cognitive approach is the process by which we interpret the causes of behaviour – our own, and that of other people. The inferences we make about the causes of behaviour are called *attributions*, and the model used to explain the interpretations we make is called **attribution theory**. As Fritz Heider, the founder of attribution theory, said, we are all 'psychologists', in that we all try to make sense out of people's actions (Heider 1958). Heider, like Lewin a Gestalt psychologist, suggested that we tend to interpret behaviour in terms of *internal* (personal) and/or *external* (situational) factors. For example, if you see someone frowning, you may decide they are angry, and speculate about the source of their anger. Depending on the circumstances and the information you have, you may attribute it to internal factors, such as the person having a hostile nature, or you may attribute it to something in the external situation, such as the person having received bad news.

attribution theory a theory dealing with the inferences we make about the causes of our own behaviour, and that of other people; the interpretations made are called attributions.

Trying to understand why someone is acting in a particular way can obviously be useful – assuming our interpretations are accurate. Given that we often have incomplete information, however, errors are also quite possible. As a result, researchers studying attributions have been interested in the types of errors that people make, particularly those that might represent a consistent tendency, or *bias*. One such error, called the **fundamental attribution error**, is the tendency to underestimate the importance of situational influences, and overestimate the importance of internal factors in interpreting other people's behaviour. Thus, if we encounter a sales clerk who is unhelpful, we are likely to assume that the person is unfriendly, rather than consider whether the working conditions or other situational factors might be responsible (for example, the person may have sore feet after standing for several hours). Similarly, it has been suggested that people find the results of Milgram's study of obedience (discussed in Chapter 1) surprising, because it emphasizes that, contrary to our intuitions, situational factors are often more powerful than internal factors (Ross 2001).

fundamental attribution error the tendency to underestimate the importance of situational influences, and overestimate the importance of internal factors in interpreting the causes of people's behaviour.

The fundamental attribution error suggests there is a basic bias in the way we perceive other people. However, attribution theory also applies to the way we interpret our own behaviour. Not surprisingly, there is evidence that errors can also occur in this context; one such error identified by researchers is called the **self-serving bias**. The self-serving bias reflects a desire to see ourselves in the best possible light; in practice, it is expressed as a tendency to attribute our successes to personal factors (that is, our own ability), but blame our failures on situational factors (for example, distraction, lack of time). Thus, if Marie does well on a test, she may say it is because she studied hard, but if she does badly, she may complain that the test was unfair. The end result is a distortion of Marie's self-image in a favourable way.

self-serving bias the tendency to distort our assessment of our own behaviour, by attributing our successes to personal factors, and our failures to situational factors

Attribution theory suggests that such biases are important, because they reflect a source of distortion in the mental schemata that guide our perceptions and behaviour. Unfortunately, the theory is less clear in explaining how these biases arise. One view is that they reflect basic types of cognitive errors, such as the tendency not to seek out information inconsistent with our beliefs (Nisbett and Ross 1980). Others argue that errors like the self-serving bias help preserve our self-esteem, and thus have a motivational basis (Taylor and Brown 1988). Both of these interpretations would suggest that the biases are fundamental human traits, and therefore should occur universally.

Unfortunately, the data from cross-cultural studies reveal a more complex picture. For example, studies in India (Miller 1984) and Japan (Weisz *et al.* 1984) reveal that in both cultures, the internal bias associated with the fundamental attribution error is far less common than in western societies. Similarly, when made aware of situational factors, Thai students are more likely to overcome the fundamental attribution error than are Belgian students (Geeraert and Yzerbyt 2007). The self-serving bias is also less common among Japanese students than among American students (Kashima and Triandis 1986). In attempting to explain results like these, several researchers have suggested that the differences relate to a broader cultural emphasis on the individual in western societies, as compared to a more collective social orientation in Asian societies (Geeraert and Yzerbyt 2007; Moghaddam *et al.* 1993; Ross 2001). At the same time, in both individualistic and collectivist cultures, the degree to which the fundamental attribution error does or does not occur can be influenced by the specific circumstances (Fein 2001; Miyamoto and Kitayama 2002).

In one sense, the finding that attributions can differ across culture is important, since it reminds us that we should be careful about assuming that particular social cognitions are universal. Instead, it seems that the types of attributions we make can be influenced by various factors, including the culture we live in. At the same time, this view does not undermine the basic premise of attribution theory, which is that people continually make interpretations of both their own behaviour, and that of others. As Heider said, we all want to make sense of how people act. As such, the research on attribution theory, including the cross-cultural data, reinforces the idea that our cognitive schemata are an important factor in our behaviour.

Try it Yourself

Have you ever felt judged unfairly because someone attributed your behaviour to your personality instead of taking into account the situation you were in? Were there times in childhood, for example, when an adult punished you and you strove to explain that the situation was the determiner of your actions, not your character? Did the adult listen to you? Knowing about the fundamental attribution error, can you think of any situations when, on reflection, you wonder if you misjudged someone because you did not fully consider the context of the event? (Don't worry – we have all done this at one time or another!) What about the role of culture? Do you think the way you perceive people reflects your cultural upbringing? In what ways?

Cognition and Emotions

We are all aware of the varied nature of emotions. Fear, anger, sadness and joy are all part of everyone's experience. Yet understanding how emotions arise, and how we interpret them, is a more difficult matter. In part, we know that emotions are based on physiological factors, such as changes in heart rate, breathing and blood pressure. These changes, which are referred to as changes in physiological *arousal*, are easy to recognize subjectively, at least in the extremes. But it is less clear that arousal alone can account for the *variety* of emotions that we experience. For example, try listing some of the physiological changes you experience when you're very angry and when you're very happy. If you think carefully, you'll probably note significant overlap in the two cases. (Heart and breathing rates accelerate, etc.) If two such different emotions share a number of physiological characteristics, then can arousal alone account for different emotions? And what role does thinking play in our emotions?

The earliest modern theory of emotion goes back to William James, who argued that our physiological response is what determines our emotional state. Thus, as he famously put it, 'we are afraid because we run, not we run because we are afraid'! James's view was provocative and has been challenged in various ways (see Lang 1994). From the perspective of the cognitive approach, it can be argued that James placed too much emphasis on physiological arousal, and too little on the role of cognitive processes. While arousal is a significant aspect of emotion, there is a variety of research which indicates that our interpretation of the situation influences our emotions.

The first study to suggest a role for cognitive interpretation was a well-known experiment by Stanley Schachter and Jerome Singer (1962). Essentially, Schachter and Singer argued that people tended to look at the situation for clues to their emotional state (that is, using external rather than internal attribution). Depending on the social situation that the researchers manipulated, subjects interpreted their arousal (produced by an injection of adrenaline) as either happiness or anger. The results of the Schachter and Singer study suggested two main conclusions. First, physiological arousal is not always interpreted as indicating emotion. For example, someone who has just run to catch a bus will experience arousal, but will not attribute it to emotion. Second, when arousal is seen as due to an emotional state, our cognitive interpretation of the situation determines how we define the emotion. Thus, a state of tension might be interpreted as anxiety while writing a test, but as anger if one is waiting in a check-out line. While the original Schachter and Singer study has been challenged in various ways (see Levanthal and Tomarken 1986), it was influential in suggesting that attributional processes play a role in our emotions.

This idea that cognitive interpretations influence our emotions has been taken a step further by Richard Lazarus, in terms of what he calls **cognitive appraisal theory** (Lazarus 1993; Roseman *et al.* 1996). Lazarus argues that our emotions are a result of our appraisal of the situation we are in, in terms of how we see its effect on our current well-being or future goals. For example, if we perceive that we are being unfairly punished, we will feel anger; if a friend insults us in a way that we interpret as a joke, we will laugh.

cognitive appraisal theory a theory of emotion which argues that our emotional state is based on our assessment of the situation and its significance to our well-being.

The cognitive appraisal model sees emotions as being functional: our appraisal of the situation leads to a particular emotion, which in turn motivates us to respond to the situation appropriately. For example, if a stranger approaches you on a deserted street and you decide that you should feel afraid, you are likely to flee or seek help.

One of the issues facing cognitive appraisal theory is the role of arousal in emotional experience. In their original study, Schachter and Singer argued that emotions resulted from the way we interpret our physical arousal – that is, cognitive interpretations are the link between arousal and emotions. By contrast, Lazarus argues that cognitions are the primary determinant of emotions, independent of arousal. While this may apply to some situations, it does not seem to fit all the available data. For example, research on victims of spinal-cord injuries indicates that because the loss of sensation below the site of injury reduces awareness of many aspects of bodily arousal, it also results in feeling less emotional (Hohmann 1966). At present, there is no clear agreement on precisely how cognitions and arousal are linked, with several researchers proposing there are actually multiple mechanisms underlying emotions (Cacioppo and Gardner 1999; LeDoux 1995). For example, LeDoux has proposed that we actually have *two* systems for emotion – one which is cognitive (involving the hippocampus and cortex), and a more primitive, arousal-based mechanism (based in the amygdala). Support for this view comes from research using fMRI to identify the areas of the brain that are activated when we remember or learn about emotional events (Kensinger and Schacter 2007; LaBar and Cabreza 2006). Whatever the precise nature of the relationship turns out to be, the existing research clearly suggests that cognitions as well as arousal play a role in emotions.

Interestingly, the links between cognition and emotion seem to be bi-directional. That is, our emotions can affect our cognitive processes, just as our cognitive processes can affect our emotions. For example, emotions can affect the retrieval of information from long-term memory (Aupée 2007; Bower 1981; McFarland and Buehler 1997; Payne and Corrigan 2007). Even more striking is a case study reported by neurologist Antonio Damasio (Damasio 1994). Following removal of a tumour in the prefrontal cortex, the patient, a man named Elliot, reported an absence of emotions. When shown pictures that might reasonably elicit an emotional response (such as a gruesome accident), Elliot could recognize why they might be regarded as emotional, but he now felt 'nothing'. Equally striking was the effect on Elliot's ability to make decisions. While he could identify various factors which would be relevant to a given decision, he was unable to actually make a choice, even for something as trivial as picking a dessert! How can we make sense of this? It seems that without emotions, Elliot could no longer evaluate alternatives to make a 'rational' choice. To Damasio, the case demonstrates that emotions are inextricably linked with our cognitive capacities.

One of the puzzles that remains to be solved concerns cross-cultural differences. Since both cognitions and arousal seem to play a role in emotions, it is not immediately clear whether any differences in emotions that one observes across cultures are due to differences in cognitive appraisal, differences in arousal, or both (Lazarus 1995). In terms of the process of appraisal, comparisons of individuals in the USA, Japan and China found a high degree of consistency with regard to the factors that affect the appraisal of emotional situations, such as pleasantness/unpleasantness (Mauro *et al.* 1992). Based on studies of northern and southern Europeans, the same consistency may not apply in terms of physiological patterns of arousal (Rime and Giovannini 1986). For example, southern Europeans show greater blood pressure changes while experiencing joy, sadness and anger, while northern Europeans have more stomach sensations for joy and fear, and more muscle tension for anger. Why would these differences occur? Though not directly addressed in the study, it is likely that the differences are based on cultural learning rather than any sort of innate mechanism, given there is evidence for learning of autonomic functions (see Chapter 3). There are similarities in our facial expressions of emotions (see Figure 4.7), although there are differences in how people choose to express emotions (Stephan *et al.* 1996). For example, comparisons of American and Costa Rican college students found that Americans, seen as members of an individualistic culture, were less comfortable expressing emotions to strangers than to family members. By contrast, Costa Ricans, viewed as members of a collectivist culture, tended to put on a more positive front in public than did Americans (see also Box 4.6). Supporting the existence of differences between individualistic and collectivistic nations, when five nations in sub-Saharan Africa were studied, nations which were more collectivistic regarded guilt as a more desirable emotion, while less collectivistic nations regarded pride as less desirable (Kim-Prieto and Eid 2004).

Figure 4.7 Emotions and Facial Expressions One basic aspect of emotions is the facial expressions we use to indicate what we are feeling. As seen in the photos, men and women, and even individuals in different cultures, show great similarities in the way they express emotions. (See examples of happiness and disgust in North America and New Guinea.) Darwin believed facial expressions reflected the evolutionary origin of emotions.

Box 4.6 Events and Emotions

Our emotions evolved as an adaptive response to our environment, and external stimuli are still important.

In thinking about emotions, it should be remembered that emotions rarely occur in a vacuum – that is, there is always some event or stimulus to which we are reacting. While the chapter emphasizes the role of cognitive appraisal, it is also worth looking at the events themselves. (In fact, a behaviourist, Michael Weiner (1972), has argued one doesn't need to talk about cognition at all to explain results like Schachter and Singer's landmark study!) Sometimes, past experience determines our response to a situation, as when someone who has been previously bitten feels afraid when encountering a strange dog. Given the obvious potential for learned variability in our emotional reactions, it is interesting that when one looks at different cultures, so many basic emotional states are triggered by the same or similar events (Mauro *et al.* 1992).

We must also recognize that differences in eliciting events can be found across cultures. For example, in Russia, an even number of flowers in a vase is a sign of death that would be found at a funeral. Consequently, presenting a Russian with a lovely vase of a dozen beautiful red roses is more likely to elicit dread than pleasure! Another example is the fear of the number 13, experienced by many westerners in Europe and both North and South America. In fact, the 13th floor is labelled '14' in many high-rise buildings, because of the widespread superstition that 13 is an unlucky number. Kuwaiti Arabs, however, would experience no such fear: for them, 13 is just another number, like any other (Shiraev and Levy 2001). By contrast, many Chinese dislike the number 4, because in Cantonese the word sounds much like the word for 'to die'. Hence, even numbers can elicit emotional responses – and often people within a culture will share the same reactions.

Emotions likely originated through evolution as an adaptive mechanism, enabling quick assessments of situations – in essence, asking 'is it a threat or is it food?', not 'what is it?' (Cacioppo and Gardner 1999). However, emotions now play a much more nuanced role in our lives, thanks largely to the influence of cognitive processes. By means of perceptual interpretation and memory of past experiences, we appraise situations to feel not just fear or pleasure, but also love and sadness, pride and shame. As with many phenomena, the final understanding of emotion may involve a complex interaction of different factors – and cognitive processes will certainly be one factor.

Try it Yourself

Consider the following hypothetical scenarios:

1 Jurgen and Raj entered the classroom on what seemed like a normal day, only to hear their instructor announce a 'surprise quiz'. Jurgen immediately felt anxious, while Raj said cheerily, 'No sweat!'

2 Lisette and Jackie were invited to a party. Lisette looked forward to it while Jackie dreaded having to attend.

How would you explain the differences in the reactions of these characters to the same situations? Can you think of a case where you and another person (perhaps a friend) reacted with different emotions to the same situation? How would you account for this?

CONCLUSION

No other approach in psychology considers thinking processes in quite the same way as the cognitive approach. Some psychologists, like the behaviourists, ignore thinking processes, while others accept the existence of thought without examining its nature. One example is psychoanalysis: Freud's theory, despite emphasizing basic drives, would be empty were it not for the emphasis he gave to verbal behaviour (for example, Freudian slips) and to the symbolic meanings of actions. Yet, while he acknowledged the existence of thinking and symbols, he never focused on the processes involved in our *capacity* to use such symbols.

Despite its distinctive stance, and the successes of the cognitive approach thus far, significant challenges remain. One concern is that there is still a great deal of integration to do before the approach can lay claim to being an inclusive perspective on behaviour. While it is clear that problem solving, cognitive dissonance and emotion all involve mediational processes, the descriptions used tend to vary in each area. They are all 'cognitive theories', but as yet there is no *single* cognitive theory which links all of these areas in a coherent manner. A behaviourist can talk about operant conditioning, and use the same terms for any type of behaviour one considers, but no similar consistency exists currently within the cognitive approach. While this may be partly due to the lack of a single central theorist, whatever the cause, it remains a limitation.

A second problem concerns the use of the information processing model. This metaphor is borrowed from computer science, as reflected in terms like *input*, *storage* and *retrieval* of information. With respect to these terms, computers are infallible: errors are always the result of either human programming errors or equipment malfunctions. People, on the other hand, are clearly fallible. People forget; computers don't. People sometimes ignore available information; computers cannot ignore information provided to them. Given that such differences exist, one must remember that the information processing model is a metaphor, and however useful it is in some ways, like any metaphor it also has limitations. (Interestingly, attempts to link cognition to our understanding of the brain are leading to new analogies in terms of neural mechanisms, such as parallel processing in memory.)

In addition, while we are beginning to recognize connections between cognition and emotion, we still lack an emotional approach to cognition. That is, the *motivation* for actions has been largely ignored. Although Kohler recognized that perception and learning can be influenced by a motivational state (for instance, being highly motivated can increase functional fixedness), this aspect was never well developed in Gestalt theory, and has often been ignored in the cognitive approach. Tolman, in fact, was accused of 'leaving the organism lost in thought' – that is, in

The world today: Sports Psychology

Sports psychology examines the factors that affect athletic performance and how participation in sports and exercise affects the individual. A sports psychologist endeavours to improve the athlete's performance by psychological means (Tiger Woods has used the services of a sports psychologist with great success!). Research has demonstrated that the way athletes view their own performance and how they account for their successes and failures will impact on their subsequent performance. For example, Le Foll *et al.* (2008) gave 30 French students who had never played golf the chance to try their hands at putting. The researchers made sure that the distance from the novice golfer and the hole was far enough so that none of the students would experience very much success. After experiencing failure at their first attempt at golf, one group of the students was told that it seemed that they didn't have much ability for golf, a situation that is uncontrollable and unchangeable. A second group was told that while their performance was not very good, they could improve, that the situation was within their control and changeable. A third group was given no information directed toward understanding their lack of success (a control group). Subsequently, the researchers found that when the novice golfers were told that they controlled what happened and they could change their performance, they persisted in trying harder and felt more satisfied in attempting golf, as compared to the other novice golfers. The conclusion we can reach from this research is that by changing the way people interpret their failures, we can help their subsequent behaviour and feelings become more positive. This, of course, is more likely to lead them to ultimate success. This basic idea can be applied to areas beyond sports. Can you apply this to a common student situation, such as not doing as well on a test or essay as you had hoped?

distinguishing learning from performance, he failed to explain *why* behaviour occurs. This is not to say that cognitive research *never* considers motivation – for example, recent applications of the cognitive approach have examined the interaction of mediational processes and motivation (see *The World Today: Sports Psychology*). The concern is that, fundamentally, the cognitive approach has never explained what motivation really is, or its role in behaviour.

Several factors may account for cognitive theorists' tendency to overlook motivation. It has been suggested that the split of cognition and motivation goes back to psychology's philosophical roots, in that philosophers viewed cognition as distinct from emotion and motivation (see Eysenck 1993). The over-dependence on the information-processing metaphor may also be a factor, as 'motivation' is irrelevant in discussing a computer! Regardless of the reason, this oversight by cognitive researchers has not been shared by all approaches: although Freud tended to minimize the details of cognitive processes, he *was* vividly aware of the importance of motivational processes.

It remains for the future to solve some of these issues, particularly in terms of creating a general theory of behaviour. In this sense, the cognitive approach is no more perfect as a means of understanding human behaviour than is any other approach. With the trend towards 'cognitive science', we are seeing an increasing interchange among disciplines, including psychology, physiology, computer science and linguistics, and it is possible that further evolution lies ahead. There has already been tremendous change, from Tolman's cognitive maps, to today's information processing models. Yet even as the metaphors change, the questions remain largely the same. It is characteristic of human behaviour that we seek to understand the world, including our own actions. And it is characteristic of the cognitive approach that we will continue to ask how it is that we understand.

Putting It All Together – Cognitive Approach

One of Sam's major concerns is coping with his studies. He has found school difficult in the past, and he feels a great deal of anxiety when writing tests. As noted in Chapter 3, this anxiety may have arisen due to classical conditioning; however, from a cognitive perspective, it causes him to do poorly on tests, because it produces state-dependent forgetting. Thus, both his stress level (biological) and his performance (cognitive) are being affected by this learned anxiety (behaviourist) – an example of how different approaches can provide insight into the same situation.

The problems Sam has with schoolwork are probably also due to weaknesses in his study strategies. First, he is labelling his workload as an overwhelming mountain of tasks. By defining the situation vaguely ('I have tons of stuff to do!'), Sam has created stress for himself instead of a manageable challenge. Sam needs to use better problem solving techniques, such as defining the problem clearly; this requires being specific about both what needs to be done, and when things are due. Once he is clear about the situation, he would likely find it useful to break the 'mountain' into a series of 'molehills' (i.e., he would create sub-goals). He could then create step-by-step strategies for dealing with each task (and reaching each sub-goal). This would not only enable him to focus on small, manageable units, but would also provide satisfaction when he completes a sub-goal.

While the case doesn't specify, it is likely that Sam could make improvements in the way he goes about learning and remembering. While his anxiety is a problem, his performance will also suffer if he tends to simply repeat material when studying (maintenance rehearsal). If instead he focused on organizing the material, the organizational structure would provide retrieval cues that would be less vulnerable to forgetting, even if he is anxious. Mnemonic techniques could also be used to enhance the way he studies.

As noted in Chapter 2, while the body's response to a stressful situation is physiologically programmed, what defines a stressor is heavily influenced by the individual's perceptions. Thus, Sam needs to evaluate how he views his life situation. Are all of these demands really threats? Or should Sam view some of them (for example, going back to school to enhance his job skills) as an opportunity? Sam's perceptions of the situation, and also his depression, may be related to his attributional style. He is questioning his own ability to succeed, saying to himself, 'I'm not good enough'. Whenever something goes wrong, he blames himself, without considering the situation. Thus, his attributions about himself reveal a pattern of making a global negative assessment of his self-worth, and attributing all difficulties to internal causes. This pattern has been shown to be associated with high risk of depression (Seligman 1975). (As will be seen in Chapter 9, cognitive treatments for depression often focus on unrealistic beliefs and attitudes.)

Sam is also using some negative self-statements in his relationship with Vanessa. Clearly he is saying to himself, 'If I ask her out, she'll say no and this would be a disaster.' He is concluding that she will reject him on little or no evidence and is awfulizing (see Chapter 9) the result of such a rejection. A more positive style of thinking would both make him feel better and perhaps allow him to ask Vanessa for a date: 'If I ask her out, she might say yes.' 'If she says no, it's not the end of the world. She'll still be my friend.'

Overall, making changes in his thought patterns, and improving his study skills, would likely help Sam perform better, experience less stress and anxiety and feel better about himself.

CHAPTER SUMMARY

- The cognitive approach emphasizes the role of *mediating processes* in human behaviour. The central assumption is that behaviour can best be understood by looking at the processes which come between an environmental stimulus and the behavioural response.

- Models based on the role of mediating processes, such as the *information processing* model, have increased our understanding of phenomena like *memory* and *problem solving*, and also offered practical insights on enhancing their effectiveness.

- Memory is regarded as having three separate stages – *sensory memory*, *short-term memory* (STM) and *long-term memory* (LTM). Each stage has distinctive characteristics, with transfer between stages dependent on *attention*, *rehearsal* and *coding*.

- Forgetting from LTM can be interpreted in terms of either *interference* or *context-dependence*; each interpretation has been productive, though in recent years the concept of context-dependent forgetting seems to have attracted more attention.

- Problem solving involves a series of distinct *stages*. Problems can be described as either *convergent* or *divergent*, depending on the number of possible solutions and the process for reaching a solution.

- While Gestalt psychologists emphasized the importance of an appropriate *mental set* and *insight*, more recent research suggests that problem solving skills involve *learning to learn*.

- In terms of information processing theory, solving a problem requires defining the *initial state*, *goal state* and *operators*. With distinct stages generating solutions can involve the use of either *algorithms* or *heuristics*.

- *Language* is an open-ended system of symbolic communication, whose basis may be partially dependent on innate physiological capacities, and partly learned.

- Controversy exists concerning studies of language capacities in other species, particularly primates who have learned sign languages.

- There is an interactive relationship between thinking and language, with the language we use at least partially influencing the way we think.

- The cognitive approach has also been applied to issues of *social cognition* such as *cognitive dissonance* and *attribution theory*. *Cognitive appraisal theory* has been used to understand *emotions*.

🔓 Key terms and concepts

learning
information processing
cognitive map
mental set
memory
recall
recognition
priming
sensory memory
short-term memory
long-term memory
maintenance rehearsal
elaborative rehearsal
retroactive interference
proactive interference
availability
accessibility
context-dependent forgetting
cognitive appraisal theory

reconstruction
mnemonics
problem solving
initial state
goal state
operator
convergent problem
divergent problem
recentring
insight
algorithm
heuristic
creativity
language
language acquisition device
cognitive dissonance
fundamental attribution error
self-serving bias

Online
Learning Centre

When you have read this chapter, log onto the Online Learning Centre website at
www.openup.co.uk/glassman where you will find answers to these Test Yourself questions and
suggested answers to the Try it Yourself activities, plus many more learning resources to help
you study psychology.

Test yourself questions

1 What is the relationship between perception and cognition?
2 How much material can STM store? For how long?
3 How does forgetting occur in LTM?
4 How are algorithms and heuristics used in problem solving? Give an example of each.

Suggestions for Further Reading

■ For readers interested in an overview of the cognitive approach, there are two highly readable
accounts: **Howard Gardner's** *The Mind's New Science: A History of the Cognitive Revolution* (1985)
provides an entertaining overview, while **Bernard Baars's** *The Cognitive Revolution in Psychology*
(1986) allows many of those involved to speak for themselves, via interviews he conducted.

■ For an overview of memory, **Daniel Schacter's** *The Seven Sins of Memory* (2001) provides a
highly readable, non-technical account by a major researcher. For an emphasis on techniques for
improving memory, try **Kenneth Higbee's** *Your Memory: How It Works and How to Improve It*
(2001).

■ **Edward deBono's** books on problem solving are both interesting and entertaining; *Practical
Thinking* (1976) is perhaps more focused than some of his more recent books.

■ For a readable survey of all aspects of language, from development to animal studies, try **Joel
Davis's** *Mother Tongue* (1994). For more detail on language development, *Language Development:
An Introduction* (2007), by **Robert Owens**, is a popular source.

■ As noted in Chapter 2, **Damasio's** *The Feeling of What Happens* (1999) provides an interesting
view of cognition and emotions. A more comprehensive overview is offered by **Keith Oatley** *et al.*
in *Understanding Emotions* (2006).

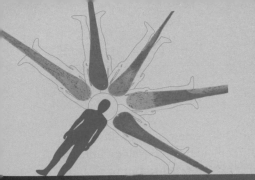

Chapter 5

The Psychodynamic Approach

Chapter contents

LEARNING OBJECTIVES

In this chapter, the objectives are to learn:

☑ the origins and nature of the psychodynamic approach

☑ the basic theories of Sigmund Freud, including
  • basic assumptions
  • theory of consciousness
  • dreams as an expression of the unconscious
  • Freud's model of personality
  • psychosexual stages of development
  • the nature of defence mechanisms and anxiety
  • examples of unconscious behaviour
  • an assessment of Freud's work and ideas

☑ neo-Freudian and non-Freudian alternatives within the psychodynamic approach, including the theories of
  • Carl Jung
  • Alfred Adler
  • Karen Horney
  • Erik Erikson

MOTIVATION AND THE MIND

Several years ago, while attending a conference, I (WEG) attended a preview of a new film about the work of Sigmund Freud. At one point, the film discussed Freud's ideas on development, and referred to the concept of identification, which involves a child copying the behaviour of a parent. To illustrate the concept, the film showed a father and his 5-year-old son doing chores in the yard. Suddenly, the audience (all psychologists) burst into gales of laughter. The film's producer, himself a psychologist, stopped the film to ask what was funny – clearly, he didn't expect it to be humorous. A member of the audience pointed out that the father was showing the boy how to cut a limb from a dead tree using a saw; to the speaker (and also the rest of the audience, including myself), this seemed much too blatant a reference to Freud's concept of castration fear. The film producer, showing a mixture of shock and embarrassment, could only mumble, 'You know, I never thought of it that way – we just thought it was an example of an ordinary activity ...'

Even if you know nothing of identification and castration fear, the basic point is clear: the film's content conveyed an obvious meaning of which the film's producer was unaware. One of the central assumptions of Freud's theory is that we often are unaware of the true reasons for our actions. In this incident, the film producer seemed to prove Freud right – ironically, while presenting Freud's ideas!

INTRODUCTION

If you were to do a survey in any western country, asking people who had never taken psychology to name a psychologist, you would likely get more people responding 'Freud' than any other figure, past or present. The image of Freud, stroking his beard and pondering the meaning of his patient's words and actions, has become almost a caricature of psychotherapy. As the founder of psychoanalysis, he has had a profound impact on the study of behaviour. Yet the approach which he pioneered has also spawned a number of variants; these theories share many of the same assumptions, but differ in their details. Hence it is appropriate to discuss the larger context of psychodynamic theories, as well as Freud's theory.

As discussed in Chapter 4, the cognitive approach deals extensively with mental processes within the person. In this sense, it is similar to the psychodynamic approach. However, one of the major limitations of the cognitive approach is its failure to address questions of intentionality – that is, it does not explain what *motivates* behaviour. By contrast, issues of motivation are central to the psychodynamic approach. As Robinson (1979) has pointed out, concerns about motivation are inevitably linked to the psychology of personality, since intentions must be held by *someone* – i.e., a person. Consistent with this view, psychoanalysis is both a theory of motivation and a theory of personality.

Psychoanalysis was the first psychodynamic theory, but over time a number of other theories have been developed, all of which share certain basic assumptions:

- *motivation*: psychodynamic theories assume that behaviour is motivated (caused) by mental processes, some of which operate outside the individual's awareness;
- *personality*: they see behaviour as part of a coherent whole (personality), which reflects both current motivation and past experience.

Thus, the *psychodynamic approach* focuses on the role of internal processes (for example, motivation) in shaping personality, and thereby behaviour.

In taking personality and motivation as its central focus, the psychodynamic approach is distinct from any of the approaches we have discussed. To the extent that behaviourism deals with motivation at all, it does so descriptively, in terms of an 'empty organism'. By contrast, inner processes, including notions of self and awareness, are central to the psychodynamic approach. By viewing behaviour within the context of personality, psychodynamic theories focus on the whole person, rather than the discrete mental processes characteristic of the cognitive approach. And while Freud himself was trained in neurology, in practical terms, psychodynamic theories operate at a very different level of description from physiological theories. Thus, the psychodynamic approach differs in important ways from the behaviourist, cognitive and biological approaches. Since Freud is certainly the pioneer of this approach, let us begin with him.

FREUD AND PSYCHOANALYSIS

Freud is probably one of the most complex, and most gifted, figures in the history of psychology. A contemporary of both James and Pavlov, he has become better known than either. By his own reckoning, expressed on several occasions, he was one of the three most important figures in the history of western science (Copernicus and Darwin being the other two). While this can be considered a form of exaggeration, there is no question that many Freudian concepts have become household words, including *ego*, *unconscious* and *Freudian slip*. More than most theories in psychology (or other fields), the man and his ideas are intertwined. In part, but only part, this is because his analysis of his own life significantly influenced his theorizing. So, let us begin by briefly setting the context of his life.

Sigmund Freud was born in Moravia (now part of the Czech Republic) in 1856, the eldest child in a closely-knit, middle-class family (since his father remarried, Freud actually had two elder half-brothers; as a result, he had a nephew who was slightly older than he!). He was educated in Vienna, and spent most of his life there. Entering medical school at the University of Vienna, he studied physiology with Ernst Brücke, whom he later described as the most influential person in his life (Fancher 1979). Brücke favoured a mechanistic view of both physiology and behaviour, which likely influenced Freud's own later thinking. Freud seemed to relish doing research in Brücke's lab, but practical considerations (including marriage) led him to focus instead on his medical studies, which offered greater economic rewards and recognition. He finished his degree in 1881, and in 1885 won a six-month fellowship to study with Jean Charcot, a leading French doctor who was interested in *hysteria* (neurological symptoms with no neurological basis) and hypnosis – both of which were to play a role in Freud's later career.

On returning to Vienna to practise, he specialized in neurological disorders, and became a leading figure in the area – a focus which eventually led to his search for new treatments and explanations. In 1919, well after he had become known for his writings on psychoanalysis, he was granted the title of professor at the University of Vienna (note, he was first nominated by the Medical Faculty in 1897, but the appointment was turned down by the government – a decision which greatly upset him). Freud became increasingly famous, and lectured internationally even as he continued treating individuals and writing books. In 1923, he was diagnosed with cancer of the jaw – the disease which ultimately killed him. Then, in 1938, the rise of anti-Semitism forced Freud (who, although not religious, was raised as a Jew) to move to London when Austria was annexed by Nazi Germany. He died there a year later at the age of 83, having outlived both James and Pavlov. (Given the connections between Freud's life and work, we will return to some details of his life in the course of discussing his theory.)

Key Thinker: **Sigmund Freud**

Sigmund Freud (1856–1939) was born in Moravia (now part of the Czech Republic) in 1856, the eldest of eight children in a closely-knit, middle-class family. He was educated in Vienna, and spent most of his life there. Entering medical school at the University of Vienna, he studied physiology with Ernst Brücke, whom he later described as the most influential person in his life; Brücke's mechanistic views seemed to influence Freud's own later thinking. While Freud seemed drawn to research, his marriage and other practical considerations led him to become a doctor, which offered greater economic rewards and recognition. In 1885 he received a post-degree fellowship to study with Jean Charcot, a leading French doctor. Through Charcot, Freud learned about hysteria disorders and techniques of hypnosis – both of which were to play a role in his later career.

On returning to Vienna to practise, he specialized in neurological disorders (including hysteria), and became a leading figure in the area – a focus which eventually led to his search for new treatments and explanations. In 1919, well after he had become known for his writings on psychoanalysis, he was granted the title of professor at the University of Vienna. In 1923, he underwent the first of a long series of operations for cancer of the jaw. As the cancer ate into his body, he also suffered social torments. Raised as a Jew, he became concerned about the anti-Semitism of the growing Nazi Party in Germany – his books were burned in a Berlin bonfire in 1933, where he was declared an enemy of the state. When Germany annexed Austria in 1938, Freud was reluctantly persuaded by family and friends to move to London. These personal and political concerns seem to be reflected in the dark tone of *Civilization and its Discontents*, his last major work. He died in London in 1939 at the age of 83.

Freud's Assumptions about Behaviour

As with other approaches, it is helpful to note some of the assumptions that Freud made in developing his theory.

■ *Psychic determinism.* As noted, Freud's early training in physiology under Brücke had a significant influence on his thinking, and one of Freud's most fundamental assumptions, psychic determinism, was partially derived from Brücke's ideas. **Psychic determinism** states

> **psychic determinism** the assumption made by Freud which states that all behaviour has a cause, and that the cause is to be found in the mind.

that all behaviour has a cause (i.e., is determined), and that the cause is to be found in the mind (*psyche* in Greek). As a doctor and scientist, Freud seemed to believe that ultimately his ideas could be reduced to physiological principles. However, he recognized that such a goal was not yet attainable, so instead he focused on mental constructs (*id, ego,* etc.). His work in physiology also converged with another influence – Darwin's work on evolution, which had been recently published (*The Descent of Man* 1871). The notion of biological continuity across species convinced Freud that human motivation is based on biologically-based, innate drives. (Note that, writing in German, Freud used the word *Trieb*, which in his usage is best translated as 'drive'; however, early translations into English used the word 'instinct'.)

■ *Importance of unconscious processes.* The second assumption, and perhaps the best known, was Freud's belief that much of behaviour is governed by processes that lie outside the individual's awareness – that is, that many crucial mental influences are *unconscious* (this will be elaborated in the next section).

- *Continuity of normal and abnormal behaviour.* Another important assumption for Freud was the *continuity of normal and abnormal behaviour*. In this regard, Freud was influenced by the enlightened view of mental illness pioneered by Phillipe Pinel roughly 100 years earlier. Pinel, while the head of the French asylum at Bicêtre, argued that mental disorders represented an illness, rather than spirit possession or degeneracy, as was then commonly believed. By taking this viewpoint, Freud was not only taking a humane attitude towards his patients; he was also justifying the use of clinical data in supporting a theory of normal personality. Since he believed normal and abnormal behaviour differed only in degree, not in kind, he felt justified in combining the two types of observations in developing his theory.

- *Value of clinical data.* The last point to consider is that although Freud was trained as an experimentalist (in Brücke's lab), most of his career was spent as a clinician, and he used *clinical observations* as his primary data. While he was as gifted an observer as he was a writer, clinical observations (that is, *case studies*) are inevitably limited in drawing conclusions. (As noted in Chapter 1, small samples, problems of representativeness and no control of causation all pose problems in interpreting case studies.) Since case studies represent a significant source of evidence for Freud's theory, we will have to return to this issue after discussing the theory itself.

Taken together, these four assumptions are the foundation on which Freud erected his ideas. (Note that these assumptions are consistent with the general emphasis on motivation and past experience found in all psychodynamic theories, but are more specific.) Having noted these points, we should explore the substance of Freud's work.

Try it Yourself

The notion that normal and abnormal behaviour are basically similar (differing only in degree) is central to Freud's theory. Do you accept this idea? Freud's view was based on beliefs about the underlying processes that govern behaviour, not on social judgements of normality, but our own perspective is likely influenced by social attitudes. Consider the following examples.

- Do you ever talk to yourself? 'Oh, Marilyn, be more careful!' mutters MH as she finds herself making typographical errors in preparing this text. Compare this to someone walking down the street while speaking loudly to themselves about their distaste for the government's latest policy. Is one instance normal and the other abnormal? Where is the cutoff point?

- Marjorie and Simone both keep an immaculate home. Marjorie enjoys having her grandchildren visit, but when they leave, she spends a great deal of time cleaning up after them. Simone, on the other hand, cleans every inch of her home with disinfectant before her grandchildren visit so they won't 'pick up germs'. When the grandchildren leave, Simone repeats this procedure, and sterilizes the glasses and dishes the children have used to remove any germs they may have deposited. Which woman would society consider a good housekeeper and which would be suspected of having an unhealthy preoccupation with cleanliness?

If we cannot readily draw a line between what is normal and what is abnormal, does that make Freud's assumption more plausible?

Exploring the Workings of the Mind

At the outset of his career, Freud attempted to specialize in cases of organic brain damage, and his work on cerebral palsy in children and on aphasia (a neurologically-based language disorder) was met with approval by the medical community. However, treatable cases of neurological disorders were relatively rare, and so he began treating patients with **hysteria** – disorders in which there are physical symptoms for which there is no apparent physical cause. (The term was used long before Freud; its origin, from the Greek for 'uterus', reflected a common belief that only women could show the symptoms – an idea Freud himself rejected in 1886.) Although neurology had advanced to the point that doctors could rule out physical causes, they were nonetheless confounded by the paradoxical nature of these disorders, and their inability to relieve the evident suffering of their mostly female patients. For example, in the phenomenon of *glove anaesthesia*, the patient complains of loss of feeling in the hand, as if it were covered by a glove. Neurologically, this poses a problem, since the pattern of nerves extends along the top of the forearm and back of the hand, and along the underside of the forearm and palm of the hand; consequently, it is nearly impossible to have neurological damage which affects the *entire* hand, and *no* part of the forearm.

hysteria a disorder characterized by physical symptoms for which there is no apparent physical cause; the term was used by Freud but actually predates him.

Like most doctors, Freud tried a number of techniques to treat hysteria, not always successfully. Two events were to point him in a new direction, which eventually led to the development of psychoanalysis. First, he had studied with Charcot, who used hypnosis in treating hysteria. Second, a Viennese colleague, Joseph Breuer, had reported successfully treating a case of hysteria by using hypnosis to prompt the recall of experiences associated with the onset of symptoms. Breuer found that re-experiencing the situation, which was usually emotional or even traumatic, produced relief from the associated symptom. In one case, a patient had developed a squint while trying to hold back tears at the bedside of her dying father. When she later was able to re-experience the situation, and express the grief she had hidden at the time, her symptom disappeared. While Breuer himself did not routinely deal with hysterias, his report intrigued Freud, who began his own explorations of the method. He quickly concluded that hypnosis was merely a tool; rather, the process of recalling emotionally charged experiences was the key factor. Freud concluded that recalling the traumatic event produced a release of emotional tension called **catharsis**. The striking thing about this discovery, easily overlooked from today's perspective, was that Freud was proposing that the *body* could be affected by processes within the *mind*. How was this possible? Freud began an exploration of the relations between mind and body which was to continue for more than 50 years, until the end of his life.

catharsis the release of drive energy in indirect form, either through the process of recalling emotionally charged experiences or involvement in symbolic activity.

Abandoning hypnosis, he developed the technique of **free association**, in which the patient says aloud whatever thoughts come into mind. Such thoughts were often jumbled and fragmentary, with no apparent patterns; however, listening to these thoughts, and occasionally asking questions, Freud would gradually see a pattern emerge, which typically climaxed in a highly emotional recall of forgotten events. The memory of these events had been *repressed* – blocked from conscious awareness. In turn, these repressed events were expressed through physical symptoms that were either directly or *symbolically* connected with the blocked memories (since Freud believed behaviour always had a cause, a lack of *direct* connection would not be taken as implying that no

free association a technique originated by Freud for studying the mind, based on asking a person to simply say whatever words floated into the mind, and then looking for patterns.

connection existed). Frequently, recall of a traumatic memory would produce relief, though in some cases, symptoms were *overdetermined* – that is, there were multiple events contributing to the symptom, each of which had to be uncovered and re-experienced. While the idea of associations in behaviour was not originated by Freud, his use of free association represented a new technique for studying behaviour – and one which is still controversial, as we will discuss later in the chapter.

Freud's Theory of Consciousness

The discovery of a connection between repressed memories and behaviour led Freud to propose a novel concept: that awareness is divided into different levels of consciousness. Those thoughts and feelings which we are aware of at a given moment are part of the **conscious** mind. Much like William James's 'stream of consciousness' (a phrase coined at about the same point in time), Freud saw the conscious mind as filled with a passing parade of ideas and emotions. Yet there is much more to the mind than this window of awareness; much of the contents of the mind are **subconscious** – that is, below the level of conscious awareness. The subconscious is divided into two levels – the preconscious and the unconscious. The **preconscious** contains all those thoughts, memories and emotions of which we are not presently aware, but which can be brought into the conscious mind by deliberate choice (for example, recalling something you did yesterday). By contrast, the **unconscious**, which may be much larger, contains all those ideas, experiences and feelings which are blocked from conscious awareness by the power of *repression*. The unconscious cannot be directly accessed by the conscious mind, but its contents 'leak out' in fragmentary intrusions into conscious awareness, either directly or in symbolic form (seemingly random thoughts, and images in dreams, could represent unconscious material). And, of course, the contents of the unconscious can cause pathology, as Freud found in treating hysteria.

conscious in Freud's theory, that aspect of the mind which contains those thoughts and feelings of which we are immediately aware at a given moment.
subconscious in Freud's theory, the portions of the mind which are below the level of conscious awareness.
preconscious in Freud's theory, that part of the subconscious mind which can be accessed by deliberate choice.
unconscious in Freud's theory, that portion of the subconscious which cannot be directly accessed by the conscious mind; nonetheless, impulses and thoughts from the unconscious can 'leak out' in fragmentary intrusions into conscious awareness, either directly or in symbolic form.

Today, the average person readily accepts the concept that consciousness is divided. Indeed, Freud's idea that mental events can occur outside of our awareness has become so widely known that it has become part of everyday language, as when someone says, 'I did it unconsciously.' However, its popularity does not automatically prove its validity, and the reality is that any *direct* proof is essentially unobtainable. (It is also worth noting that there are cultures, notably in Asia, where the notion of the unconscious does not traditionally exist.) Nonetheless, over time, a range of evidence has been collected supporting the idea that unconscious events can influence our behaviour (Davou 2002; Greenwald 1992; Kihlstrom *et al.* 1992; Westen 1999b). One example is the influence of subliminal verbal stimuli (too brief to be consciously recognized) on behaviour. The basic concept is that phrases which have emotional significance will influence the unconscious, even if the individual is not consciously aware of the message. In one such study, male college students presented with the phrase 'beating Dad is OK' before playing darts scored higher than those seeing the phrase 'beating him is wrong', who in turn did better than students presented with 'beating Dad is wrong' (Palumbo and Gillman 1984). Reviewing 56 studies using variations of this situation, Hardaway (1990) concluded that the effect, although small, is real. Another example is the role of unconscious processes in decision making, where research suggests consumers make better choices for complex issues (such as buying a house) when they rely on unconscious judgements (Dijksterhuis *et al.* 2006). Interestingly, even memory researcher Elizabeth Loftus, who is critical of many aspects of Freud's theory, has concluded that unconscious processes exist (Kantor *et al.* 2004; Loftus and Klinger 1992).

For Freud, the unconscious was a powerful concept, and a powerful force in behaviour: thoughts and feelings which a patient didn't even realize existed could manifest themselves in physical symptoms. While Freud found gaining access to the unconscious helped his patients, he was still faced with a problem: how can thoughts have such power to distort behaviour? To understand how Freud solved this question, we need to return to the cases he dealt with.

Initially, almost all his patients were middle-class women, living in the rather repressive culture of the Victorian age, in which women had rigidly prescribed roles as wives and mothers. Freud found that much of what they reported seemed sexual in nature, often implying assaults by family members or friends. This led him to propose that hysterias were the result of traumas which were sexual in origin. Breuer could not accept this, and Freud reported later that most of his colleagues greeted the concept with shock and rejection. (As will be discussed later, it is difficult in this context to separate the realities of what happened from Freud's perception. In point of fact, the idea of pathology having a sexual origin was not new with Freud, having already been proposed in the work of Kraft-Ebbing and Havelock Ellis – see Robinson 1979.) Whatever the reaction of his peers, Freud himself found it difficult to accept that sexual abuse could occur as frequently as his observations of his patients suggested. His own doubts, combined with the lack of support from his colleagues, gradually led him to the conclusion that the sexual traumas recalled were not true memories at all (interestingly, recent trends in research on sexual abuse would make it seem more likely that the assaults may have been real – for example, Faller 1988). But this posed a further dilemma – if they were not true, where did they come from? And how could false memories have such a powerful effect on the body?

Dreams and Symbolic Expression

Freud found answers to his questions about the role of false memories in his research on dreams. He was already aware of his patients' dreams, and had been interested in his own dreams from an early age – in *The Interpretation of Dreams*, he reported a dream which first occurred when he was about 10, portions of which later appeared in his adult dreams (Freud 1900). As he analysed these dreams, he came to the conclusion that dreams operate on two levels – the manifest content and the latent content. The **manifest content** is what the conscious mind is aware of, both during sleep and on waking. For example, one of Freud's female patients dreamt that she was holding a banquet, but had to cancel it because she had no food. However, this manifest content is merely a distorted or *symbolic* expression of the true meaning, which Freud called the **latent content**. In the above case (reported in *The Interpretation of Dreams*), the patient was recently married, and very jealous of other women. One woman in particular was of concern to the patient, but her husband had reassured her that the rival was too thin to be attractive. By dreaming of a banquet with no food, Freud explained, she was actually expressing the desire that the other woman remain thin, and therefore non-threatening.

manifest content in Freud's theory, the symbolic content of a dream (disguised by the dream censor) which the conscious mind is aware of, both during sleep and on waking.
latent content in Freud's theory, the true meaning of a dream, which is transformed by the dream censor into symbolic form as the manifest content.
wish fulfilment in Freud's theory, the symbolic expression of drives in fantasy form, as in dreams.

This dream expresses two characteristics of Freud's theory of dreams. First, he believed that dreams were basically motivated by **wish fulfilment** – expressing fantasies that were not acceptable or even possible in real life. Second, it shows how the actual nature of the dream (the latent content) is transformed into something less threatening to the conscious mind (the manifest content). The mechanism of this process was what Freud called the **dream censor**, whose function is to ensure that sleep is not disturbed by the unconsciously expressed desires that are the basis of dreams. To accomplish this, the dream censor converts the content of the dream into *symbolic* form (the *manifest content*). Thus, in order to understand the meaning of a dream (the *latent content*), one must interpret the symbolism expressed in what the person recalls. In therapy, this was rendered easier by the other knowledge Freud had of the patient, from direct report, from free association and other observations. In addition, Freud came to believe that some forms of symbols are nearly universal (for example, swords as phallic symbols, money as faeces). Recognizing common symbols was helpful to Freud when colleagues (or even strangers on the street) challenged him to interpret dreams. (In at least one case, Freud interpreted a dream described in a letter – see Benjamin and Dixon 1996.) Still, Freud felt that the majority of symbols were personal, and he regarded dream interpretation as a serious technique for gaining insight into the unconscious mind, not as a parlour game. (The issue of symbolism will be discussed further later in this chapter.)

Having decided that dreams were based on wish fulfilment, Freud returned to the subject of hysteria, and decided that, in a similar way, his patients' vivid descriptions were fantasies, not real events. This had at least two advantages: first, it produced a theoretical symmetry, in that both phenomena (hysteria and dreams) were now based on the same process (wish fulfilment). Second, it tended to placate his critics, who objected to his suggestion that sexual abuse was the source of all hysterias. Coupled with successes in treating a number of patients, this new interpretation led Freud to feel that he was indeed on the right track in understanding the mind. (The role of abuse in hysteria, and the reasons for Freud changing his interpretation, have generated considerable controversy, as we will discuss later in this chapter.) His biggest question still remained, however: what was the force that *motivated* these processes?

Try it Yourself

We all dream perhaps five or six times each night, yet we rarely remember all of these dreams. You may have had the experience of waking up after a dream and thinking 'Wow! I'll never forget that dream!' only to find, in the morning, that your memory of the contents of the dream is gone. By keeping a pad of paper and a pencil by your bed for a week, and trying to write down dream images as soon as you awaken, you will probably increase your memory of your dreams. After a week of doing this, look at what sorts of dreams you have had. Do any common themes emerge? Can you relate these themes to something that is happening in your life? For example, one of MH's students reported a series of dreams in which she was searching for something: for her hotel room in an unknown city, for her handbag at home, for someone to give her directions to a concert hall, etc. She immediately related this to her difficulty in choosing a programme of study at university, and was a little surprised. 'I didn't realize it was bothering me so much,' she said. 'But if I keep dreaming about this, maybe it is and I should make a choice.'

In exploring your dreams, it's useful to keep in mind two points: first, most dreams mean nothing (the 'daily residue', as Freud called them), and one isolated dream probably has little meaning. Second, even if dreams have deeper meanings, Freud (and most therapists) would say that self-analysis is generally neither productive nor advisable.

Drives and the Psychodynamics of Behaviour

As noted previously, Freud's own training in physiology, coupled with the ideas of Darwin, led him to believe that there was a biological continuity between humans and other species. This meant that the basic forces driving human behaviour were not greatly different from those driving animal behaviour. Survival needs, including the need for food, water and shelter, were obviously basic. In addition, the pressure for species survival made procreation (and therefore sexuality) a powerful force. As he worked with his patients and strove to understand both their behaviour and his own, Freud wrestled with the question of how to describe these biological forces. At first,

pleasure principle an early description by Freud of the basis of human motivation, which stated that we are driven to maximize pleasure (*Lust* in German), and to avoid that which is unpleasant (*Unlust*).

he thought that motivation could be described in terms of the desire to maximize pleasure (*Lust* in German), and to avoid that which was unpleasant (*Unlust*). This concept, which he dubbed the **pleasure principle**, was similar to the well-known philosophical concept of *hedonism* (a term coined by Jeremy Bentham in 1789). (One might compare the pleasure principle to Thorndike's *law of effect*, proposed at about the same time, and likewise influenced by Bentham.)

Of all the basic biological forces, Freud felt that sexuality was the most powerful, and for many years he conceived of it as the central force in behaviour. (It is worth noting, however, that Freud conceived of sexual energy in broader terms than simply adult sexual behaviour; all forms of physical, sensuous pleasure were based on the sexual drive.) This view gradually led him to develop a second model of motivation, building on the importance of sexuality. Freud first proposed this idea in a set of essays in 1905, but continued to reassess his thinking as time went on. By 1920, he had come to the conclusion that pleasure (sexuality) alone could not account for the behaviours and phenomena he observed (including sadism and masochism). This led him to argue for two basic drives, commonly referred to as *sexuality* and *aggression*; the change was described in *Beyond the Pleasure Principle* (Freud 1920).

By this time Freud had gone through many experiences, both professionally and personally. Between 1906 and 1920, not only had he received greater recognition for his work, but he had gone from middle age to the gateway of old age. (He was 64 when *Beyond the Pleasure Principle* was published.) In addition, World War I had taken place, with horrors previously unimaginable. To the rationalist culture of the late nineteenth century, the war was a stunning shock. It was in this context that Freud introduced aggression as being equal to sexuality as a basic drive. For most Freudians, this stage of his thinking represents the main form of his theory.

However, Freud was to approach the issue of motivation yet again, ten years later. In *Civilization and its Discontents*, he offered a sombre analysis of the workings of human society, and the drives which direct all human activity (Freud 1930). The horrors of World War I, and the signs of growing Nazi sentiment in Germany, led him to be somewhat pessimistic about the future of mankind. (We will return to this issue later, in discussing defence mechanisms.) Hence, he again revised his description of the motivating forces, referring now to Eros (named after the Greek god of Love) and Thanatos (the Greek representation of Death). *Eros* was seen as a positive, life-affirming force, expressed in human creative activities, including procreation (hence the link to earlier notions of a sexual drive). *Thanatos*, as its name implies, was a destructive energy, expressed both in aggression towards others, and in self-destructive behaviour. (It is interesting that Freud came to this view after witnessing World War I, and discovering he had cancer of the jaw – a condition possibly linked to his passion for smoking cigars.) Like his earlier concepts of motivation, Eros and Thanatos were seen as seeking continual expression and satisfaction. However, for the first time, he saw the two drives as also conflicting with each other. In fact, Freud ends *Civilization and its Discontents* by describing Eros as caught in a struggle to assert himself against his adversary Thanatos – and wondering what the outcome will be. Such comments suggest not simply a shift in theoretical viewpoint, but also a profound sadness, and possibly despair. Whether that means the theoretical shift is simply due to personal bias, is hard to say. Otto Zangwill, a psychologist but not a psychoanalyst, and an admirer of Freud the man, has simply said, 'though some of his [later] ideas are of great interest, their empirical foundation [is] decidedly weaker' (Zangwill 1987, p. 269).

As psychoanalyst Charles Brenner and many other writers have noted, Freud's writings sometimes pose a problem for those who wish to describe Freud's theory (Brenner 1957). In grappling with the puzzles of motivation, he was forced to *infer* the nature of the underlying drives from the observed effects on behaviour. Given the complexity of human behaviour, this is a difficult and uncertain process. Not surprisingly, therefore, Freud himself sometimes had doubts about his descriptions, and would revise his thinking. In terms of discussing his work, the difficulty comes from the fact that he was a prolific writer (his collected works fill 24 volumes), and in writing, he did not always make explicit when he was repudiating his earlier work. In addition, not all Freudian psychoanalysts necessarily agree with his later work, making it harder still to determine what is the 'true' version of Freud's thinking. In the end, it seems better to acknowledge the variations than to offer simplistic conclusions.

Clearly, there are difficulties in discussing Freud's conception of motivation, but the difficulties are also inherent in the underlying problem: we can *observe* behaviour, but must *infer* the reasons for it. (Even the behaviourists, in opting for a descriptive model based on stimuli and responses, are making inferences about the causal nature of the connections between the two.) Without getting into issues of Freud's intent, we will adhere to the generally accepted form, using the terms *sexuality* and *aggression* when discussing how the expression of drives fits into Freud's theory.

Thus far, we have seen how Freud dealt with two fundamental issues: the structure of consciousness, and the nature of the drives that motivate behaviour. This still leaves the large question of how these forces are expressed in behaviour. What determines, for example, whether something becomes repressed? And how do the small number of basic drives result in the wondrous variety of human behaviour? For Freud, these questions were answered by developing a model of *personality* based on his psychodynamic concepts.

Try it Yourself

As noted in the text, Freud developed three different models of motivation (pleasure vs. unpleasure, sexuality and aggression, or Eros vs. Thanatos). In the following examples, which model seems to explain each one best?

- Luke is upset about breaking up with his girlfriend. He starts drinking heavily, and then, while driving home, is nearly killed in an accident.
- Angela has an essay to write, but finds writing essays boring; so she decides to go shopping instead, hoping she will become 'inspired'.
- Damien has a crush on a girl in his chemistry class. However, whenever he attempts to talk to her, he ends up acting obnoxious in his attempts to impress her.

Can you think of an example of behaviour (your own, or that of someone you know) that seems to support each model? Overall, which model makes the most sense to you?

Freud's Psychodynamic Model of Personality

Freud's early theorizing was closely linked to his clinical observations, dealing with hysteria and neuroses. (A **neurosis** is a disorder in which high levels of anxiety are a primary symptom.) As such, his initial model was a model of pathological behaviour, not a general model of personality. However, by the time of writing his *Three Essays on Sexuality* (1905), he was discussing general human behaviour, not just pathology. The fullest formulation of his model came with the publication of *The Ego and the Id* (1923).

neurosis Freud's term for disorders in which high levels of anxiety are a primary symptom.

Similar to his analysis of the structure of consciousness, Freud conceived of personality in terms of a three-part structure – the id, ego and superego. The **id** (Latin for 'it') was the source of all basic drives; from the moment of birth, we are driven to try to obtain gratification of our needs. Motivation was based on *tension-reduction*: when a drive is active, we experience it as a form of tension, which we seek to reduce by obtaining the appropriate form of gratification. In Freud's view, a young infant is concerned only with obtaining what it needs – for example, if it is hungry or wet, it cries until its demands are met. To the infant, there is no right or wrong, no past or future, simply the pressing immediacy of its desire for gratification. The id lacks any sort of conception of reality, and consequently cannot distinguish between reality and fantasy; in this form of thinking, called **primary process thinking**, a wish and its fulfilment are equivalent, with no reference to reality. Thus, a hungry infant may conjure up an image of its mother's breast as a way of reducing the tension associated with hunger. Of course, since the image cannot provide food, such primary process thinking provides only a limited form of tension reduction.

id (Latin for 'it') in Freud's theory, the element of the psyche which is the source of all basic drives.

primary process thinking in Freud's theory, a form of thinking characteristic of the id in which no distinction is made between a wish and its fulfilment.

In an adult, the demands of id normally operate outside conscious awareness – we may experience the tension, but not be able to identify the source. In other cases, the focus of gratification may shift. For example, hunger may be satisfied by fixing a sandwich, going to a restaurant for a steak, or a range of other behaviours. The specific food, and the process for obtaining it, can vary; what remains constant is the tension induced by hunger. Some years ago, a popular song had the line, 'If you can't be with the one you love, then love the one you're with.' Such expressions (like many song lyrics) can be seen as supporting Freud's view.

Opposing the demands of id is the **superego** ('over the ego'), which is governed by moral constraints. Roughly speaking, it is the 'conscience' of the person (not to be confused with 'conscious'). Superego represents the moral demands of family and society, and opposes the desire of id for immediate gratification. (Sometimes this is referred to as the 'morality principle', but Freud did not use the term.) Not surprisingly, Freud saw id and superego as being fundamentally in conflict, since they attempt to direct behaviour in very different ways.

superego in Freud's theory, that portion of the psyche which represents the moral demands of family and society, and is therefore governed by moral constraints.

Mediating between the id and superego is the **ego** (Latin for 'I'), which provides the integrating of personality, and also mediates the links with the outside world. Ego provides the sense of self which is central to personality, yet it must also cope with the demands of id, superego and the external world. Because it must contend with constraints imposed by the real world, ego is described as governed by the **reality principle**. Ego's task is not an easy one, since it must deal with three very different sorts of

ego (Latin for 'I') in psychoanalysis, the element of the psyche which provides the integrating of personality by mediating between the id and the superego, and also mediates the links with the outside world.

reality principle in Freud's theory, the constraints imposed on the ego by the recognition of the demands of the environment.

demands, two of which (id and superego) are fundamentally irreconcilable. This means that conflict is a fact of life within personality, and the varying demands of id, superego and external world require a continuing balancing act by ego. The ways in which it does so are what determine behaviour. For example, a teenage boy sees an exotic sports car sitting parked, with the keys visible within. Id will see an opportunity to race around in a fast and powerful vehicle. Superego will insist that such behaviour would be stealing, and is morally wrong. Ego may note that people are walking on the street, and therefore the chances of being caught are very high. Thus, in this case, the outcome would likely be *not* to steal the car.

There is no hard and fast rule determining how ego resolves the ongoing conflicts within personality. Freud suggested, for example, that sometimes individuals will respond to the moral demands of superego even when this conflicts with external reality – as when a person risks their life to help another person. In other cases, ego may allow id's demands for gratification, despite the opposing demands of superego – as when a child impulsively steals a candy bar from a supermarket.

secondary process thinking in Freud's theory, a form of thinking used by the ego to direct the gratification of drives; unlike primary process thinking, secondary process thinking is accessible to conscious awareness, and recognizes constraints imposed by the external world.

Ego is capable of rational thought, which Freud called **secondary process thinking**. (In many ways, the cognitive approach is concerned with what Freud would call secondary process thinking.) Unlike the *primary process thinking* of the id, in which a wish and its fulfilment are synonymous, the ego in using secondary process thinking assesses gratification in terms of the constraints of the external world. Secondary process thinking also differs from primary process thinking in that it is accessible to the conscious mind, whereas primary process thinking cannot be directly accessed in conscious awareness. Only in limited circumstances does our conscious awareness make contact with the primitive nature of primary process thinking – such as in dreams, the physical symptoms of hysteria and the symbolism of artistic expression.

As suggested by the preceding, the relationship between the three aspects of personality and consciousness is rather complex. Primary process thinking was seen as characteristic of the id, which is unconscious. According to the descriptions in *The Ego and the Id*, Freud believed that ego was largely conscious, and that much of the contents of superego were also available to the conscious mind.

The complex relationships in Freud's psychodynamic model have often led to attempts to represent the theory visually. For example, the observation that ego and superego are largely conscious, while id is not, has led to a frequently-used analogy, in which ego and superego are at the top of an iceberg, with id at the bottom (see Figure 5.1a). The part of the iceberg which is above water is the conscious mind; that which is *visible* under the surface of the water is the preconscious; while the very bottom of the iceberg, where id lurks, cannot be seen from the surface – this is the unconscious mind. Like any analogy, this image has its limitations – not the least of which is the tendency to see the mind as composed of discrete boxes, instead of dynamic processes. An alternative is to describe personality in terms of the forces which press on ego, as in Figure 5.1b. Here, one can see that ego is at the centre of the mind, with the forces of drives (id), morality (superego) and reality all converging – and conflicting. It is ego's responsibility to maintain the integrity of personality. This task is not easy, but as ego interacts with the world, it continues to develop. To understand this, we need to look at Freud's model of personality development.

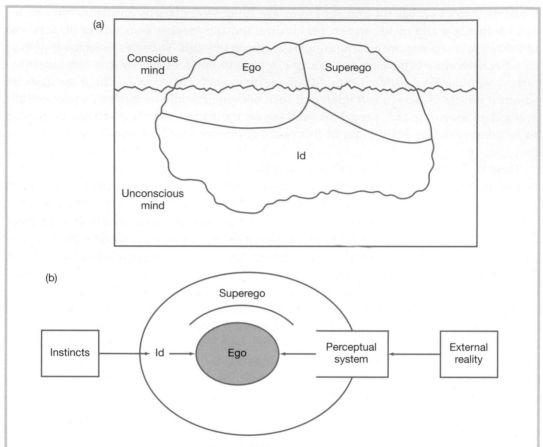

Figure 5.1 Visual Representations of Freud's Theory Many people have sought to present Freud's ideas in visual form. The iceberg model (a) emphasizes that the id is unconscious, while the ego and superego are mostly conscious. Freud himself proposed a vector model, emphasizing the various forces which bear on the ego. ((b) adapted from Fancher 1979)

Try it Yourself

Can you explain the following scenarios in terms of Freud's psychodynamic model?

- Tom is married, but finds himself attracted to Sarah, a co-worker. He decides that, if he is careful, his wife will never find out if he has an affair with Sarah.
- Margo cheated on her term test in psychology. She received a good mark, but she won't tell anyone what the mark is, and she finds her interest in psychology is diminishing.
- Helena knows she should eat a piece of fruit for dessert because she is dieting, but she craves chocolate. She goes to the store to buy some chocolate-covered raisins and happily eats them.

Can you think of any of your own behaviour that might be explained in terms of Freud's psychodynamic model as well?

Psychosexual Stages of Development

While the notion that our lives pass through stages was not invented by Freud (for example, Shakespeare referred to 'the stages of man'), Freud was the first to offer a detailed psychological model of human development based on stages. In one sense, stages are a counter-intuitive concept, since we experience our lives, day-to-day, as a more or less continual progression. Birthdays, graduations and other landmark events occur, but their timing is largely social, and bears no necessary relationship to underlying psychological processes. So what led Freud to conclude that there are discrete stages?

To understand Freud's model of development, one must bear in mind the importance he placed on biological drives. Throughout life, our behaviour is motivated by the need to satisfy our basic drives; however, Freud believed that the expression of these drives changes during the course of our lives. The objects which are the focus of gratification change, and so does the **mode of gratification** – that is, the area of the body which is the centre for gratification. To understand this, it is important to note that sexuality is not simply genital stimulation. It is also expressed through many parts of the body, called *erogenous zones*. Even as adults we can derive pleasure from our skin – a cool cloth applied to our neck on a hot day, a light touch on the arm to reassure us, and many other experiences. But at particular points during development, drive energy will be particularly focused on specific body regions (erogenous zones). Freud said that it is the shifts in mode of gratification, associated with different erogenous zones, that define the stages of development. Since these stages reflect differences in the expression of (sexual) drive energy, associated with changes in the functioning of the mind (psyche), they are called *psychosexual stages of development*. (Since aggression is also involved, the term 'psychosexual-aggressive' might be more accurate!) Altogether, Freud concluded that there are five stages, the first four of which occur in childhood. These stages play a central role in the development of personality (for a brief summary of the stages, see Box 5.1).

mode of gratification In Freud's theory of development, the way in which the individual satisfies basic drives – for example, in the *oral* stage, the mouth is the focus for obtaining pleasure (by sucking, eating, biting, etc.).

Box 5.1 Freud's Theory of Development

Freud saw development as a series of distinct stages, each defined in terms of the way drives are expressed and gratified.

Age	Stage and focus of gratification	Key issue
Birth – 1½ years	Oral – mouth	Beginnings of ego formation: weaning, learning to delay gratification, developing body image
1½ – 3 years	Anal – anus	Continuation of ego development: toilet training
3 – 5 years	Phallic – genitals and body awareness	Formation of superego: Oedipal conflict, parental identification
5 – puberty	Latency – drives repressed	Repression: childhood amnesia
Puberty – end of life	Genital – genitals	Symbolic gratification of drives: secondary process thinking

Oral Stage

oral stage in Freud's theory of development, the first stage, extending from birth to about 15 months, when the focus of gratification is on the mouth.

The first stage is the **oral stage**, when the focus of gratification is on the mouth. An infant is gratified by the pleasures of nursing; it cries to express its anger and frustration. In this context, nursing is not just a means of obtaining food – it is a primary source of pleasure, through oral stimulation. The new-born infant is governed by its drives – that is, only id is present at birth. It is a world dominated by immediate gratification and the magical powers of primary process thinking, where wish and fulfilment merge. Yet the child also has an interest in its surroundings, and its explorations are also linked to oral gratification – for example, if a 6-month-old baby girl is given a new object, the first thing she is likely to do is try to put it in her mouth. As infants develop teeth, biting becomes a way of expressing anger, but also is used to gain pleasure – for example, my (WEG) niece used to chew on the rails of her crib. From observations like these, Freud concluded that oral activity is so dominant because it provides the primary means of gratification – hence, the oral stage.

As the oral stage progresses, the beginnings of ego development occur. One aspect of this is the development of *body image* – the recognition that one's body is distinctly different from the rest of the environment. For instance, if an angry toddler hits the wall with a hand, their hand will feel the impact, but the child is not aware of how it affects the wall. By contrast, if the child hits their own face with their hand, both the hand and the face register the impact. Through such experiences, the child begins to recognize the boundaries of the body, and thereby develops a sense of self (ego). A second type of experience involves delays in receiving gratification. Id is responsive only to the inner drives, and when gratification is sought, the child wants it *now*! However, even the most attentive parent cannot respond so fully that the child never has to wait – so, inevitably, the child learns that gratification is not immediate. At first, the child will use primary process imagery to try to cope – for example, conjuring up the image of the mother's breast while waiting for mother to answer its cries. This is ultimately inadequate, but the child does gradually come to realize that it can initiate actions which lead to gratification. Infant specialists sometimes speak of babies 'settling', at around 2 months of age (Leach 1997). Before this time, their crying often seems purposeless – as if the infant itself doesn't know why it is crying. After this period, they begin to be calmer, and their crying seems more connected to specific wants. This change may well reflect the realization that crying can be used productively, to call attention to specific needs. (Parents often can distinguish between a 'hungry' cry and a 'wet' cry, for example.) Thus, delays in gratification ultimately lead to the realization that behaviour can be directed towards satisfying needs. Within the first year or so, these experiences have initiated the beginnings of ego.

One of the key experiences of the oral stage is *weaning*. While breast-feeding was the norm in Freud's day, even bottle feeding provides the infant with both food and intimate contact with the caregiver. Breast-feeding is particularly intimate, allowing the child to touch and smell the mother, hear her heartbeat, and so on. When weaning occurs, the child typically loses much of this regular intimate contact – eating in a high chair is not the same! Freud said that this is the first major experience of loss in the child's life, and that it affects both the immediacy of obtaining gratification and the child's awareness of self vs. external world. In fact, Freud saw weaning as the origin of the biblical story of being cast out of Eden, where food was plentiful and life was blissful.

Anal Stage

anal stage the second stage of psycho-sexual development (15 months to 3 years); during this stage the focus of drive energy shifts to the lower end of the digestive tract, and the major conflict is toilet training.

At around 18 months of age (the time boundaries of the stages are not precise), the focus of drive energy begins to shift. This shift of drive energy from the mouth and upper digestive tract to the lower end of the digestive tract characterizes the **anal stage**. Given the shift in focus of gratification, pleasure comes primarily from the process of elimination, and activities related to it (including handling of faeces). This stage also sees the further development of ego, based on the child's experiences with their surroundings.

As infants become toddlers, they gradually exert greater control over both their own body and their surroundings – crawling, walking, grasping objects of interest, and so on. By the age of 2, they have made dramatic advances, including the first beginnings of language. At this stage, they are likely to encounter another major challenge – toilet training. (Again, the timing is not exact; in the Victorian era when Freud made most of his observations, the tendency was probably to toilet train somewhat earlier than is the norm in our culture today.)

Compared to the need to delay gratification experienced in the oral stage, toilet training poses a greater conflict between the demands of id and the external world. For the child, bowel movements are intensely pleasurable. (Remember the focus on the anus as an erogenous zone at this stage.) As well, their own faeces are of significant interest – after all, they are produced by the child's body, so there is an intimate connection. Many a parent has witnessed a 2-year-old who wishes to play with their faeces, or who is dismayed at the prospect that their faeces will simply be flushed away. Parents, of course, take a very different view, seeing faeces as smelly, messy and germ-laden. To the extent that the parents impose demands about toilet training, the child is faced with a major conflict between the id and the most significant part of their external world: the choice is between heeding the demands of id and heeding the demands of the parents. Heeding the id means risking the negative reactions of the parents, who are the most important figures in the child's world; heeding the parents means denying the demands of id, which is the source of all motivation. The resolution of this conflict may be gradual and relatively untraumatic, or intense and stormy, depending on both the timing of the process and the parents' method of handling the situation. If the child tries to accommodate, and the parents are moderate, the child may gradually learn that self-control is useful, and that there can be value to order and cleanliness. If the parents place too much emphasis on this outcome, the child may become excessively concerned about cleanliness and discipline, laying the pattern for compulsive neatness and related behaviours in later life. On the other hand, if the child decides to heed the demands of id rather than the parents, the conflict is likely to be more intense. If the parents use harsh punishment, the child will eventually comply, but at the cost of a weakened sense of self (it is the parents, not ego, controlling the situation), and possibly a life-long resentment towards authority figures (for which the parents are the prototype). On the other hand, if parents give in when the child resists, the child may never fully learn to balance the demands of id against the realities of the external world. Not only could this lead to a sloppy, self-indulgent adult, but it may seriously hamper the development of ego.

These scenarios point out one of the significant features of Freud's model of development: while the order and approximate timing of the stages are fixed and universal, each individual will have different experiences, and will respond to them differently. To varying degrees, all childhood experiences affect personality in the adult; however, those most laden with emotion are likely to be the most influential, particularly if the conflicts involved are not adequately resolved. As the old saying has it, 'The child is the father to the man.' This aspect of development will be discussed further after we have considered the other stages.

phallic stage the third stage of psychosexual development, extending from about 3 to 5 years of age, during which gratification is focused on the genitals, although not in the form of adult sexuality.

Phallic Stage

As the ego grows stronger, through dealing with the conflict of toilet training and other experiences, the child begins to move into the third stage, which again is marked by a shift in the mode of gratification. In the **phallic stage** (from about 3 to 5 years of age), gratification is focused on the genitals. In Freud's day (and sometimes even today) the concept of childhood sexuality was seen as shocking, in part because it was interpreted in adult terms. Obviously, young children are still physically immature, and the expression of the drive is not the same as in an adult. However, they *do* seek gratification, and genital stimulation (to note one example) is experienced as pleasurable. Parents often find that children show an increased awareness of their body, including genitals, at this age, as well as a curiosity about other people's bodies. For example, 4-year-olds may take off their clothes to 'play doctor' with each other. A boy may ask his mother if she has a penis, or may want to see her body. Boys, like adult males, will sometimes have erections while sleeping. A girl may suddenly become jealous when her father is affectionate to her mother. All of these behaviours indicated to Freud that the genitals have become a focus of gratification – hence the *phallic* stage (after the Greek word for penis).

Oedipal conflict in Freud's theory of development, the major conflict associated with the phallic stage which challenges the developing ego; named after the Greek story of Oedipus, who unknowingly killed his father and married his mother.

As with the anal stage, the phallic stage is associated with a major conflict which challenges the developing ego. This conflict is called the **Oedipal conflict**, and is named after the Greek story of Oedipus, who unknowingly killed his father and married his mother. While the dynamics of the conflict are somewhat different for boys and for girls, Freud used the term Oedipal conflict to refer to both sexes. Early on, some analysts proposed calling the female variant the 'Electra conflict' (after another Greek myth), but Freud himself did not use the term (see Freud 1924). The central focus of the Oedipal conflict is the attachment to the parents, who as caregivers have become the focus of drive energy (and therefore attraction). Depending on family circumstances, the mother is typically the primary caregiver, and hence becomes a strong source of gratification for both boys and girls. However, as the child grows, the awareness of sexual differences increases, and with it, an increased sense of sexual identity. It is this difference which begins to alter the dynamics for boys and girls.

For the boy, the mother (who is already the primary source of gratification) becomes more intensely desired, in what is the prototype for all future love relationships. The father is a source of gratification, but now also becomes the focus of jealousy and rivalry; hence, the boy's feelings towards his father are *ambivalent*, a mix of affection and hostility. In primary process terms, the id wishes to unite with the mother, and eliminate the father as a rival. At the same time, ego is aware that the father is larger and more powerful, and may retaliate against the boy's feelings. This becomes expressed as a fear (called *castration fear*) that the father may take away the boy's source of gratification, through cutting off the genitals. (Of course, it is irrelevant to say such fears are not rational – the point is precisely that these feelings are at an unconscious, non-rational level.) Thus, there is an intense conflict created, which ego is poorly equipped to resolve. To deny the attraction to the mother is to prevent the experiencing of feelings that will later be crucial to forming love relationships. To attempt to act on the jealousy towards the father is to risk both an emotional and possibly a physical split. (This conflict is the basis for the impact of the message 'beating Dad is wrong' in Palumbo and Gillman's study of subliminal messages described earlier – see *Freud's Theory of Consciousness*.)

identification in Freud's theory, a defence mechanism which involves incorporating characteristics of a drive object into one's own ego.

The resolution of this conflict comes through adopting two *defence mechanisms* – techniques used by the ego to cope with anxiety. One is **identification**, which involves incorporating an object of conflict as part of one's own ego. This process is expressed in the old phrase, 'If you can't lick 'em, join 'em.' By adopting the values and behaviour patterns of the father, the boy seeks to reduce the threat associated with castration fear – in effect, 'If I'm like Dad, he won't want to hurt me.' The mother, too, is identified with, as the model for future attractions. As the old song says, 'I want a girl just like the girl that married dear old Dad!' Identification is important in reducing the conflict that the boy experiences, but also in triggering the development of superego; the earliest values of the superego are those derived from one's parents. (Later, other social values can also be incorporated.) The other mechanism used by the ego in dealing with the Oedipal conflict is **repression** – forcing the conflict into the unconscious, so that the conscious mind is unaware of the fears and attractions. (When adults would scorn his notions about the Oedipal conflict, saying they had never experienced such things as a child, Freud would argue that this was simply evidence of repression.)

repression in Freud's theory, a defence mechanism in which impulses, memories or ideas are actively blocked from the conscious mind.

For girls, the Oedipal conflict involves the same sense of attraction and rivalry, though the objects are reversed – now the mother is the rival, and the father is the object of attraction. Despite the basic similarity, the dynamics are rather different, for several reasons. First of all, the mother promotes greater ambivalence, since she is typically the first object (focus) of drive energy for the infant. Also, while the girl fears discovery of her jealous impulses towards the mother, the increased awareness of the body leads her to recognize that both she and the mother lack a penis. While a boy may fear the possibility of losing his penis (castration fear), the girl feels a sense of devastation at having *already* lost hers – leading to feelings of guilt and loss described as *penis envy*. The girl realizes that the mother, too, has been castrated, and this enhances the sense of identification with the mother. Faced with this attraction towards the father and ambivalence towards the mother, the girl's ego, like the boy's, seeks some way of resolving the conflict. As with the boy, this involves *identification* (the father as prototype for future lovers, the mother as role model) and *repression* (blocking conscious access to the underlying impulses). However, Freud believed the differences in the dynamics of the process make the Oedipal conflict more difficult for girls; he saw this as potentially creating greater submissiveness and lower self-esteem in adulthood.

In support of his conception of the Oedipal conflict, Freud used both evidence from clinical cases and also observations of normal behaviour. One observation he made in this regard continues to tantalize researchers: the phenomenon of *childhood amnesia*. Typically, individuals recall very little of their life before about age 5, other than a few fragmentary memories and stories that were likely heard from parents at a later age. Freud argued that childhood amnesia was due to the repression associated with coping with the Oedipal conflict. Interestingly, cross-cultural studies of North Americans and Asians indicate that the phenomenon is universal (Wang 2003). While other theories have been offered, ranging from changes in the myelination of brain neurons to changes in cognitive structure, no mechanism has been universally accepted; what is accepted is that Freud was the first to recognize the basic phenomenon. Freud also used the Oedipal conflict to explain the conflicts frequently seen among children in a family (called 'siblings'). He called these frictions *sibling rivalry*, and argued that they represented a redirection of the Oedipal conflict to a different object (i.e., from parent to sibling).

Freud's description of penis envy, and of the female Oedipal conflict more generally, has been heavily attacked in recent years, both for its negative view of women and for its narrow definition of family structure. This view was apparently based on Freud's observations of both his patients (who were primarily housewives) and his society (which emphasized the nuclear family, and generally kept women in a submissive role). However, modern evaluations have questioned his view that such patterns have biological, as opposed to social, causes – an issue which will warrant further discussion later on.

In both sexes, the Oedipal conflict is crucial both in the development of the superego, and in establishing the basis for sexual identity and formation of love relationships. Prior to this stage, the child is aware of moral principles, but such rules are regarded as part of the environment (Brenner 1955). For example, if a child wants a cookie, they may look to see if the mother is nearby. If she is, the child will refrain from taking the cookie; if she is not present, the child will proceed. That is, morality is evaluated in terms of getting caught, not right or wrong. As values become *internalized* through identification, they form the basis of superego. Now the child may take the cookie, but will feel guilty and could even confess the misdeed before being caught! Without identification, superego development will be weak or absent; Freud saw this as the origin of psychopathic behaviour (anti-social behaviour with no sense of guilt or wrong-doing). Identification is also necessary for developing a clear sense of sexual identity, and for the creation of a prototype love object as the basis for later relationships. Problems of identification can lead to an inability to form love relationships, or repeated difficulties with authority figures, who are seen as surrogate parents. If repression is emphasized over identification in trying to resolve the Oedipal conflict, the result in later life can be an individual whose life is dominated by excessive guilt and anxiety.

To Freud, the Oedipal conflict was the greatest challenge in the development of personality. Failing to resolve it can result in a distorted ego which sees all relationships in terms of the unresolved conflicts of the phallic stage. Freud saw the problems of many of his patients (sexual conflicts, guilt and anxiety) as stemming from this source. As a result, he came to the conclusion that most people fail to resolve the Oedipal conflict in a psychologically (as opposed to socially) satisfactory manner (Freud 1924).

Latency Stage

Whether the Oedipal conflict is successfully resolved or not, the imperatives of development push the child from the phallic stage to the stage of latency at around age 5. In the **latency stage**, which extends until puberty, the drives appear to be relatively inactive – hence they are seen as 'latent' or hidden. In part, the change is due to the use of repression in resolving the Oedipal conflict. Because this results in blocking conscious access to the id, gratification hereafter is related to *secondary process thinking*, and hence is never as direct or as immediate as the gratifications of early childhood. In latency, the repressed impulses are redirected into new activities, with new objects of gratification. Thus, sports, hobbies, school and friendships all provide opportunities for satisfaction of the drives. Problems during latency, such as excessive aggression, can be related to inadequate repression and/or the ego being unable to redirect drive energy into socially-approved outlets.

latency stage the stage of psychosexual development which begins at about age 5 and extends until puberty, during which the drives appear to be relatively inactive.

Genital Stage

At the onset of puberty, there is a resurfacing of drive energy, triggered in part by the physiological changes involved in sexual maturation. At this point, the individual enters the adult phase of development, called the **genital stage**. In this stage, drive energy is focused on the genitals, with adult expression of sexuality. The term 'genital' can be confusing, however, for the expression of drive energy is very different from the primary expression of id seen in the phallic stage. Ego's use of *secondary process thinking* has become

genital stage the final stage of psychosexual development (from puberty onward), when drive energy is focused on the genitals, with adult expression of sexuality.

well developed, allowing possibilities for *symbolic* gratification in a variety of ways. Symbolic expression is also encouraged by social influences, which direct the person towards new types of behaviours, including forming a love relationship, having children and assuming responsibilities in other socially-approved ways.

Curiously, given that the genital stage represents the major portion of life, Freud gave comparatively little attention to it. Primarily, he saw it as a period of trying to come to terms with the residues of childhood, such as an unresolved Oedipal conflict. The basic task for this stage was to separate oneself from one's parents. 'Only after this detachment is accomplished can he [the individual] cease to be a child, and so become a member of the social community' (Freud 1924, p. 346). Freud saw the genital stage as the final period of development, when the individual comes to maturity. While observing his patients provided many examples of the impact of problems in development, he said relatively little about what the outcome of successful development might be. This has been one aspect of psychodynamic theory that other theorists, such as Erik Erikson, have attempted to address, as we shall see.

Try it Yourself

In part, Freud defined his stages of development (especially the early stages) based on his behavioural observations. If you can, you might observe young children to see if their behaviour fits his descriptions. Also, if possible, ask your parents or other family members about your own behaviour as a child. Did you show any of the behaviours Freud described? For example, as a baby, did you ever play with your faeces? (As distasteful as this sounds, it's not uncommon!) Did you ever imitate your same sex parent? Did you have a 'crush' on someone when you entered puberty? Could Freud be right about what children do, without being correct about why they do it?

Fixation and Regression During Development

The failure to resolve the challenges of development results in **fixation** – the incomplete release of drive energy associated with a particular stage. This can occur if, during a stage, the child receives either too little or too much gratification. Under-gratification denies the individual the opportunity for drive satisfaction, leading to a desire for what was missed. For example, a new-born who is denied opportunities to suckle the breast will later be orally fixated. On the other hand, a child who is overindulged will not face the challenges associated with each stage, making them reluctant to move ahead in their development. For example, a 2-year-old who is still nursing, or a child who is given a bottle or pacifier at any indication of upset, will later be orally fixated. Fixation in turn is associated with **regression**, the tendency to revert to an earlier mode of gratification, usually under stress. Since direct access to the id has been cut off by repression in adults, regression is seen in *symbolic* forms of gratification. For example, a person who is orally fixated may binge on ice cream, or smoke, or chew their nails, or get drunk, or ... (the list of possibilities is obviously quite long). Fixation can also be expressed through *denial* of gratification, as when someone becomes a fanatical anti-smoker, or a teetotaller.

Each stage shows its own forms of fixation, representative of the focus of drive energy at that stage. For instance, at the anal stage, either overly rigid or overly permissive toilet training can

fixation the incomplete release of drive energy associated with a particular stage of psychosexual development, resulting in a preference for that mode of gratification.
regression in Freud's theory, a defence mechanism in which the individual reverts to behaviours characteristic of an earlier mode of gratification.

result in fixation. In later life, this will be seen in excessive sloppiness of either dress or living areas, a preference for activities that involve messes (for example, cooking or painting) or a preoccupation with money (seen by Freud as a symbol for faeces). Anal denial may be seen in compulsive neatness of clothes and surroundings, a preference for activities that involve order (such as cataloguing books), stinginess or an aversion to financial matters. Phallic fixations are associated with failures to resolve the Oedipal conflict, which later results in not psychologically separating from the parents. A man who continually fights with his boss, traffic officers and other authority figures, is showing a phallic fixation – trying to dominate the father figure. The man who is overly submissive is still complying with the father he dared not challenge. For a woman, phallic fixation may be expressed as seductiveness and a preference for older men (seeking to replace the mother), or as a desire to dominate men (symbolically castrating the father that rejected her). Freud would see such themes in a movie like *Fatal Attraction*. In latency, where direct expression of the drives is repressed, fixation results in behaviours which do not seem to involve drives – acts of altruism, for example.

One interesting aspect of the role of fixation is the way that Freud related it to career choices. Like many subsequent theorists, Freud believed that career decisions reflect personality at least as much as ability. Oral fixation, for example, would lead to careers that involve oral behaviour – a wine taster, a writer, a salesperson, even a university professor. Fixation at the anal stage, with its emphasis on cleanliness and bowel movements, leads to careers that involve messiness, order, and/or money. Thus, a banker, an accountant, a painter, a sanitation worker – all have careers reflective of an anal fixation. (Laboratory research in chemistry or biology, with its requirements for precision combined with messy procedures, seems to offer both indulgence and denial!) The phallic stage tends to lead to careers in which body image, sexuality and/or authority figures are involved. Thus, professional models (and the photographers who work with them) have made a choice based on phallic fixation, as have career soldiers, police officers and even prostitutes. In latency, the influence of repression means that drives must be expressed indirectly. Consequently, careers which seem unrelated to drive satisfaction, such as a clergyman, charity organizer or social worker, are likely choices for a person who is fixated at the latency stage.

One aspect of these descriptions that often bothers people is the non-obvious nature of many of the connections. This is inevitable, according to Freud, since the conscious mind of the adult is cut off (by repression) from direct access to the underlying drives. Consequently, the drives are always expressed in *symbolic* form, whether in the manifest content of dreams, or the choice of a career. In fact, from a Freudian viewpoint, adult actions and interests, being based on *secondary process thinking*, can *only* be regarded as symbolic. What differs is the degree to which the behaviour is adaptive or pathological. The man who collects swords (phallic symbols) may have an unresolved Oedipal conflict, but his method of dealing with it is more functional than the person who develops a psychogenic form of impotence.

There are other points that should be made concerning fixation and regression. First, in suggesting that these patterns exist, Freud was not making a value judgement. For example, he did *not* say that because a career reflects a particular form of fixation, it is therefore undesirable. His basic point was that behaviour is never random, and consequently behaviours like career choices simply reflect the developmental history of the individual (and, in instances of pathology, may give clues to the nature of the underlying conflict). Second, he saw such relationships as evidence that all behaviour is ultimately related to the basic drives – even those actions which seem remote from any connection with such motivating forces. Since expression in adults is symbolic, the fact that we have *no conscious awareness* of what motivates the behaviour in no way invalidates the connection. In fact, Freud argued that it is *necessary* that such connections be unconscious, in order to protect the ego from the threatening implications of recognizing what motivates us. To understand this, let us look at the concept of anxiety, and the methods the mind uses to cope with it.

Try it Yourself

Can you think of other behaviours or careers that seem to fit with Freud's ideas? Does being *consistent* with his theory prove that the theory is *correct*? Some Freudians have suggested that cultures, like individuals, can show fixations. If you were to apply Freud's model to our culture, at what stage would you say it is fixated? Does applying the theory in this way seem reasonable? Why or why not?

Anxiety and Defence Mechanisms

As we saw previously, adult personality is comprised of id, ego and superego. Ego, as the integrator, must contend with the divergent demands of id, superego and the external world. Meeting these demands is not simple at the best of times, and many circumstances (such as unresolved conflicts from earlier stages, or external threats) can make ego's task even more formidable. In such circumstances, the ego may experience anxiety. **Anxiety** arises when the ego is faced with a situation with which it cannot cope. This may be the result of an external danger, such as a civilian living in wartime conditions, or it may be due to an internal threat, related to the demands of id or superego. Since ego is unable to acknowledge the drives within the id, the breakthrough of unsatisfied id impulses into conscious awareness can trigger anxiety.

anxiety a negative emotional state associated with threat to the self; in Freud's theory, it arises when the ego is faced with an influx of stimuli with which it cannot cope, as a result of either external danger or the demands of id or superego.

Similarly, the moral demands of superego can be excessive, producing guilt and anxiety at the least suggestion of id gratification. Thus, the various forms of demands can threaten the integrity of the ego, which must protect itself.

Freud considered anxiety at several points in his writings, trying to find a way to understand this phenomenon. In *The Problem of Anxiety* (1926), he presented his mature views on the issue. Freud believed that anxiety was biologically based, and was intended as an adaptive mechanism – anxiety serving to warn the ego of a potentially overwhelming situation. However, ego has limited options: it cannot completely ignore id's desire for gratification, nor can it allow superego to make all decisions, without regard to either id or external reality (for example, it may be wrong to hurt others, but what if one's life is in danger?). Thus, ego must somehow cope with the conflicting demands, and also with the anxiety produced by awareness of them. Some forms of coping involve a reversion to *primary process thinking*, such as dreams, fantasy or the physical symptoms of hysteria. However, such methods were seen as signs of a weak ego, in that they involve ignoring external reality.

defence mechanism in Freud's theory, a technique used by the ego to protect itself from anxiety and the threats which give rise to it; many psychologists use the terms for specific defences as descriptions of behaviour patterns, without endorsing the Freudian interpretation of their origin.

More commonly, ego will invoke various defence mechanisms, a term actually coined by Freud's daughter, Anna, herself a distinguished psychoanalyst (A. Freud 1936). **Defence mechanisms** are techniques used by the ego to protect itself from anxiety and the threats which give rise to it. There are a number of such techniques,

Box 5.2 *Repression and Recovered Memories of Abuse*

A fundamental concept in Freud's theory is that our behaviour can be influenced by unconscious processes. When Freud first began treating patients suffering from hysteria, he discovered that most had been sexually abused as children, but had repressed the memories of the trauma. Though the conscious mind could not recall the events, at an unconscious level, the trauma was responsible for the patients' symptoms. Using first hypnosis, and later free association and other procedures, Freud tried to help his patients gain access to these repressed memories, and thereby begin to deal with the psychological impact of the abuse. Thus, regaining access to the memory of traumatic events, particularly sexual abuse, was a basic part of psychoanalytic therapy from the outset.

However, Freud later concluded that most of the events his patients related were actually fantasies, not real incidents of abuse. Both his original interpretation, and the subsequent change in his theory, remain the subject of controversy. The issue has become particularly significant in court cases of abuse, where sometimes the only evidence is the recovered memories of the accuser. Hence, a key question is, how accurate are memories of abuse recovered during therapy?

Evidence Favouring Repression

Apart from the general evidence concerning repression, there are a number of studies which have looked specifically at amnesia for sexual abuse. Typically, they find that gaps in childhood recall are quite common among abuse victims. (Briere and Conte 1993; Herman 1992). Even more striking evidence comes from a prospective study by Williams (1994a, b). Working from hospital records, Williams tracked down women who had been treated for sexual molestation 17 years earlier. Remarkably, 38 per cent were amnesic, even though many recalled other traumatic memories, including later incidents of abuse. Consequently, it seems reasonable to conclude that repression of sexual abuse may occur. But what about recall during therapy? Can such events be recalled accurately as a result of therapy?

Recovered Memories and Reconstruction

The basic premise of therapeutic recall is that the memories exist in their original form, if the repression can be overcome. However, memory is not simply a process of all-or-none retrieval; instead, we sometimes *reconstruct* events based on context and other factors (see Chapter 4). This may even extend to recalling events that never happened. For example, when given descriptions of real events (obtained from family members) along with false events (such as getting lost at a mall as a child), up to 25 per cent of college students recalled the false event as real (Loftus and Pickerel 1995; Loftus 1997)! In addition, recall of real events is rarely entirely accurate. Neisser and Harsh (1992) asked college students at the time of the *Challenger* shuttle disaster to describe how and where they heard of it. When contacted three years later, 50 per cent were incorrect on most details (like where they were or who they were with), and 25 per cent were completely wrong. Even when shown their own original notes, the students tended to react with disbelief! Consequently, critics argue that memories of abuse may be unreliable, possibly resulting from cueing in therapy. Unfortunately, it is not clear that the laboratory situations are equivalent to memory of real traumas, and sometimes the laboratory results are inconsistent, as when individuals with recovered memories are less prone to memory distortion than control groups (Clancy *et al.* 1999).

What Can We Conclude?

Sexual abuse, especially of children, is a serious issue. We know that abusers try to discredit their victims (Herman 1992), and we also know that abuse sometimes goes unreported until some time later (DelMonte 2000; Williams and Banyard 1999). Thus, it is important to treat reports seriously, even if they occur years later. At the same time, we know that memories are not always accurate, and therapists may sometimes cue false reports. Indeed, a survey of US and British therapists indicated that 94 per cent believe this can occur – though a strong majority reported that they believe *their* patients' memories were accurate (Poole *et al.* 1995)! In the end, in the absence of corroborating evidence, we cannot easily tell when recovered memories are true or false. Indeed, as Ost (2003) notes, there is still not even a 'middle ground' between the opposing groups examining the issue. As a result, both the issue and the dilemmas it creates are likely to remain unresolved for some time to come.

and frequently the ego will use a combination of them, rather than a single mechanism. There are several basic points to note about defence mechanisms:

- defence mechanisms operate unconsciously – otherwise, they would fail to protect the ego from awareness of the conflicts which are the source of anxiety;

- most defence mechanisms (with the significant exception of repression) operate by allowing gratification in some indirect way, typically involving either symbolic gratification or a substitute object; to the extent that this reduces id's demands, it can be a useful strategy;

- to be effective in protecting the ego, defence mechanisms must distort reality (since gratification is only indirect).

Before considering the implications of these factors, let us consider some of the specific defence mechanisms, several of which have already been mentioned in passing.

Repression, the blocking of id impulses at the unconscious level, is the most primitive of all defence mechanisms. Although Freud saw *repression* as universal (in the transition from phallic to latency stages), he also felt that it was extremely limited as a defence. The basic difficulty is that it fails to resolve the demands which led to its use, because no gratification occurs. Even worse, it can require significant amounts of mental energy to maintain the blockage against the increasing pressures for gratification. One can use an analogy to a boiling pot of water: as steam is generated, it starts to lift the lid off the pot. Putting a weight on the lid will help, but eventually the pressure will increase, until either a larger weight is needed, or the lid blows off. Similarly, maintaining repression, in the absence of any other response, will use up more and more of the mental energy that should properly go into other life activities. Since the ego is unaware of the underlying pressures, it experiences the fatigue without understanding its source. Thus, depression is seen by Freudians to be a result of excessive repression. Repression can also produce distortions of reality, as when memories are blocked which could trigger the leakage of underlying conflicts into conscious awareness. (The notion that traumatic memories can be repressed, and later recovered, has become a major source of controversy in recent years – see Box 5.2.)

Displacement, the redirection of drive energy towards a substitute object, is one of the most common defence mechanisms and is typically used whenever the direct expression of drives would be too threatening, due to either the disapproval of superego or a realistic threat associated with the original object; in such situations, we tend to seek a substitute object. For example, yelling at the boss when you

displacement in psychoanalysis, a defence mechanism which involves the redirection of drive energy from one object to a substitute object.

are asked to work overtime could result in being fired; instead, you complete the work, then cut someone off while driving home! Or, a teenage boy is attracted to Mary, but when she rejects him, he asks out Sally, in whom he initially had no interest. (In a classic cartoon, a man receives a speeding ticket while driving. Rather than yell at the officer, he goes home and yells at his wife; she in turn yells at their son; the boy then kicks the family dog, who goes out and bites a police officer!) In each case, there is displacement of drive energy onto a substitute object. The problem with displacement, of course, is that the substitutes are unrelated to the original object. Thus, while displacement allows release of drive energy, it clearly involves a distortion of reality in the process of doing so.

Identification involves incorporating characteristics of a drive object into one's ego. As discussed in relation to the Oedipal conflict, *identification* often occurs initially with one's parents; more generally, it occurs with individuals who are either admired or feared. For instance, hostages may come to adopt some of the values of their captors. More benignly, a young child may mimic a superhero seen on television. When we are unable to directly express sexual or aggressive impulses, we may adopt the guise of a figure in whom such impulses are acceptable. In movies, books or plays, identification with a character can provide a form of release called *catharsis* – the vicarious release of drive energy. While identification is necessary to resolving the Oedipal conflict, and may be a means of learning moral values, it still poses the risk of distorting reality, since the values incorporated are not freely generated by the ego. In extreme form, such as in delusional disorders, the identification may supplant the individual's own identity – for example, when someone believes they are Christ (see Rokeach 1981).

Regression, reverting to behaviour characteristic of an earlier stage under conditions of stress, is closely associated with fixation, as noted earlier. Like repression, regression is a fairly primitive defence mechanism. A 4-year-old child who has been toilet trained, for example, may begin wetting the bed after the birth of a sibling: faced with the stress of a rival for parental attention, the child regresses to an earlier stage. Working to meet a deadline, a smoker may begin smoking more heavily – a form of oral regression. (It is interesting to note that Freud himself was a heavy smoker of cigars. When once asked about the symbolic meaning of this, he apparently replied to the effect, 'Sometimes a cigar is a phallic symbol, and sometimes it is only a cigar. This is only a cigar!') Another person, faced with the same situation but being anally rather than orally fixated, may spend time rearranging everything on their desk as a means of getting some gratification. These behaviours allow for some gratification, but since the behaviours are to some extent inappropriate, they represent a distortion of reality. Freud argued that the seriousness of regression depends on both the stage of regression and the primitiveness of the response. For example, disaster victims will sometimes curl up in a ball, like an infant in the foetal position – a severe form of regression. Ultimately, regression is of limited value: since there is an inevitable shift of erogenous zones as one goes through stages, it is impossible to re-experience the satisfaction of an earlier stage in the original way.

rationalization in Freud's theory, a defence mechanism in which one explains behaviour by offering a reason acceptable to the ego in place of the true reason.

Rationalization is perhaps one of the most interesting defences; it involves offering an *acceptable* reason for behaviour in place of the true reason (acceptable to the ego, though the approval of other people may be a concern as well). When we engage in rationalization, we try to justify our actions. For instance, a person engaging in flirtatious behaviour may say, 'I was only being friendly.' Rationalization may be combined with other defences as well, to provide a justification for behaviour. For example, a person who wastes time organizing their desk may say, 'Oh, but I work better when everything is neat.' This may, in fact, be generally true – but the real reason for doing it *when facing the stress of a deadline* is in order to get some gratification through regression to the anal stage! 'White lies' offer an analogy to this form of defence: when a white lie is generated, both the liar and the person lied to may recognize that it is untrue, but may find it socially convenient to let the lie stand. Since rationalization prevents the person from recognizing the true motives for their actions, it represents a form of distortion of reality. It also suggests one should be wary of the 'rational' analyses people make of their own behaviour: while the ego is capable of rational thought, the potential for rationalization means that logic can serve reasons other than objectivity, and yet the ego will not recognize when that happens.

sublimation in Freud's theory, a defence mechanism in which drive energy is redirected towards a socially desirable creative activity.

Sublimation is one of the few defences which Freud saw as having a positive function beyond protecting the ego, and occurs when drive energy is redirected towards a socially desirable creative activity. While similar to displacement in the way it operates, it differs in terms of the restriction on outcomes. For example, an artist attracted to a married person may rechannel sexual energy into creating a beautiful statue of the person. A musician may create a patriotic anthem in a time of war, rechannelling aggressive energy. While sublimation is useful, because it results in a socially valued product, it is also limited: since gratification is very indirect, it cannot fully satisfy the demands of id. In addition, since it requires particular skills to be a painter, musician or other creator, it is not a workable mechanism for all individuals. Still, it is unique, in that Freud believed that the creative activity which sublimation supports makes it more than simply a response to neurotic anxiety.

There are a number of other defence mechanisms, but by now the basic point should be clear: defence mechanisms exist to protect the ego from anxiety, but they do so at the cost of distorting reality (see Box 5.3 for a summary). To the extent that defences work, they pose the risk of isolating the person from reality; in extreme form, Freud saw this as the basis of the major mental disorders, which he called **psychoses**. On the other hand, to the extent that the ego is *aware* of using a particular defence, distortion of reality is reduced, but anxiety will increase. Freud defined *neuroses* as disorders in which excessive anxiety is a primary symptom; in these circumstances defence mechanisms are not adequately protecting the ego. When we were in graduate school, the joke was, 'A neurotic worries about going crazy (distorting reality), but never will; a psychotic *is* crazy (distorts reality), but doesn't worry about it!' While obviously glib, it does capture the essence of the Freudian distinction between neuroses and psychoses.

psychosis a serious mental disorder characterized by severe disturbances of thought and behaviour (as in schizophrenia); according to Freud's theory, psychosis is the result of overuse of defence mechanisms.

In his later years, Freud was very interested in how the demands of society affect the growth of ego. In *Civilization and its Discontents*, he gave extensive attention to this issue (Freud 1930). One basic point was that living in society has a psychological price – we must cope with the arbitrary demands of society, as represented by the superego. Without a superego, a person would face fewer conflicts, since there would only be id and external reality to satisfy (note that asking 'what is possible?' is not the same as asking 'what is right?'). This point is illustrated by what Freud called psychopathic behaviour (today referred to as *anti-social personality disorder*). Such individuals, who are regarded by Freudians as lacking normal superego development, show no guilt (moral anxiety) for their anti-social behaviour. For the rest of us, being 'civilized' means we must deal with the demands of superego. This means that the opportunities for id gratification become largely symbolic and indirect. (Freud once commented to the effect that 'civilization began the first time an angry person cast a word instead of a rock'.) In addition to the demands of id, one must cope with the demands of superego itself, which may also conflict with reality. As a result, Freud believed that anxiety levels were increased by living in a civilized society.

At the same time, Freud was pessimistic about the possibilities of ego protecting itself from these threats to its integrity. He saw only two possible solutions that might satisfy society while permitting healthy development of the ego. One was sublimation, which, as we have discussed, is unlikely to be an adequate solution. The other (which is seldom mentioned in discussions of his theory) was love (Fancher 1979). *Love* is a defence mechanism, but it allows the drives to be gratified in the context of caring for another person, while meeting both moral and reality demands. Yet, while he believed love had the potential to benefit the ego, Freud also saw it as fraught with peril, since *losing* a loved one could leave the ego vulnerable to catastrophic pain.

Society, Freud concluded, creates a paradox for the individual: sublimation and love are only possible within the group structures which society provides, but it is also society that creates the constraints on id which make sublimation and love *necessary*! Unfortunately, in looking at the world as World War II was approaching, Freud felt that society was placing greater restrictions

Box 5.3 Defence Mechanisms and Behaviour

*Defence mechanisms like those in the chart exist to protect the ego from anxiety, but do so in ways that distort reality. (Note: those defences marked with * are not discussed in the body of the text.)*

Name	Definition	Example
Repression	Blocking thoughts, memories or impulses from the conscious mind	A troubled adult cannot remember having been abused as a young child
Identification	Incorporating characteristics of a drive object into one's own ego	A lonely teenager begins copying the clothes and actions of a popular peer
Regression	Reverting to behaviours typical of gratification in an earlier stage	Jim, an ex-smoker, starts smoking again after a romance ends
Displacement	Redirecting drive energy from one object to a substitute object	Marie is angry at her husband, but instead yells at her 5-year-old son
Sublimation	Redirecting drive energy into a socially acceptable activity	A sexually-frustrated woman becomes a writer of romantic novels
Rationalization	Explaining one's behaviour by offering an acceptable reason instead of the true reason	A student watches a football match instead of studying for a test, saying, 'I'm just taking a short break'
Denial*	Refusing to acknowledge anxiety-provoking thoughts or impulses	Sarah is an alcoholic but insists she is just a 'social drinker'
Projection*	Attributing one's unacceptable thoughts and impulses to others	A married man attracted to a colleague instead accuses her of being flirtatious
Reaction formation*	Reacting in a way which is opposite to one's actual impulses	John resents and dislikes his boss, but acts very friendly to him

on love, while at the same time directing aggressive energy into ever more dangerous forms. As quoted earlier, the conclusion to *Civilization and its Discontents* strikes an uncertain and pessimistic tone. To what extent this view was influenced by adverse circumstances (both personal and social), and to what extent it remains an accurate description of the ego's plight, is difficult to say.

Observing the Unconscious in Behaviour

One of the basic elements of Freud's theory is that id will always seek gratification, but that in adults, its expression is usually symbolic and indirect. This leads to the question of how one can provide supporting evidence. Since the id is by definition unconscious, one cannot simply analyse one's own actions to assess the validity of this conception. So how did Freud support his view? The key lies in one of his other basic assumptions – *psychic determinism*, which states that there is always a cause for behaviour, which can be found within the mind. This assumption meant that potentially *any* form of behaviour could provide evidence of the workings of the unconscious, especially the id. While we have already noted many examples of supporting evidence, it is worth reviewing some of the major types.

Freudian Slips

Perhaps the best known type of Freudian evidence are the everyday errors and slips of the tongue which he called **parapraxes**, but which have generally become known as *Freudian slips*.

---

paraprax an error or verbal slip due to an unconscious conflict; commonly called a 'Freudian slip'.

Since all behaviour has a cause, errors and slips are never accidental. While Freud conceded that fatigue and distraction could sometimes lead to errors and slips, he argued that the majority of cases reflected the workings of the unconscious. In arguing for this point of view, he made extensive use of examples from both his clinical cases and from everyday observation. In *Psychopathology in Everyday Life*, he offered detailed analyses of many such cases – for example, newspaper misprints involving, 'His Highness, the Clown Prince' (Freud 1904). In one case, a paper printed an apology for having said 'a battle-scared veteran' – but the apology appeared as 'a bottle-scarred veteran'! In such a case, Freud would argue that the errors reflected a latent hostility on the part of the writer. In general, Freudian slips can best be understood when they can be combined with other information about the individual, which can help in interpreting the underlying dynamics.

While everyday errors clearly occur, it is possible to interpret them in other ways. For example, cognitive psychologist Victoria Fromkin of UCLA has argued that verbal slips are linguistic in origin, not psychodynamic. Based on analysis of several thousand naturally-occurring verbal slips, she noted that slips are not random with regard to the linguistic units of words (Fromkin 1973). For example, phonemes may be transposed *within* a phrase (as in 'queer old dean' for 'dear old Queen'), but not *across* phrases (for example, 'the red ten on the pable' is not a likely result from 'the red pen on the table'). To explore this issue further, Michael Motley developed a procedure to study verbal slips in the laboratory (Motley 1985). In one study, subjects were asked to read aloud word pairs that were presented on a screen. In order to manipulate anxiety, subjects in one condition were told to expect a painful electric shock at some point during the experiment (aggression drive condition). In another condition, the experimenter was 'an attractive and provocatively dressed woman' (sexual drive condition). A control group was treated normally. Consistent with the Freudian view, each group made errors related to the type of drive stimulated – for example, 'varied colts' was frequently read as 'carried volts' in the aggression condition, and 'past fashion' became 'fast passion' in the sexuality condition (see Figure 5.2)! In addition, a pre-test of subjects in the sexual drive condition showed that those who scored highest on a test of sexual anxiety were the ones who made the greatest numbers of slips. While these results are consistent with Freud's theory of slips as anxiety-related, Motley, like Fromkin, notes that there are linguistic constraints on the types of errors that subjects make; he also argues that some errors, particularly in children, are not anxiety-related at all. For instance, my (WEG) 3-year-old son, returning from a historical site, called it 'pineapple village' rather than 'pioneer village'; the word 'pineapple' was already familiar to him, whereas the word 'pioneer' was new. However, as already noted, Freud himself suggested that not all slips have a psychodynamic cause. Thus, the evidence for linguistic constraints does not seem to contradict Freud's view, and overall the research seems to support his theory.

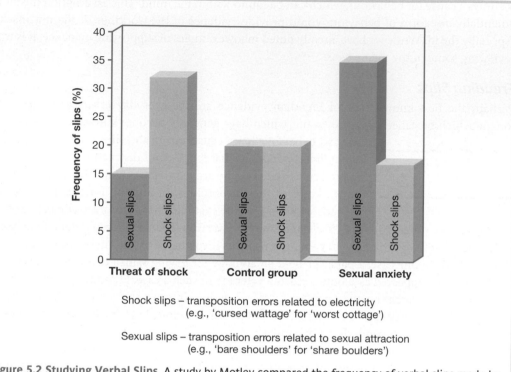

Figure 5.2 Studying Verbal Slips A study by Motley compared the frequency of verbal slips made by subjects who were either fearful of electric shocks or aroused by an attractive woman. Errors were typically Spoonerisms, in which syllables of two words are transposed, as indicated in the figure. (Data from Motley 1985)

Free Association

Asking patients to say whatever came to mind was used by Freud as a therapeutic technique very early, when he began to abandon hypnosis as a tool. Since he believed that thoughts, like behaviour, always have a pattern, listening to what his patients said could provide a means of accessing the unconscious mind. Freud's belief in the value of associations seems to have been influenced by the ideas of Theodore Meynert, his physiology teacher in medical school (Macmillan 2001). Meynert viewed associations as permanent physiological connections formed by experience; this view implied that free association could be used to access the original experience. As discussed in Chapter 4, the concept of associations is not new, and the organized nature of cognitive structure, including memory, is now well established. However, this does not mean that free association is necessarily a reliable technique. Since the particular pattern of associations is quite individual, even in the best of cases the use of free association in analysis is slow and painstaking, requiring considerable attentiveness by the therapist (sometimes, it also requires 'listening for what is not being said', which therapist Robert Fancher (1995) calls 'the greatest legacy of psychoanalysis'). In the worst case, the original associations may actually be modified by later experiences, which would imply that free association can never be certain to access the original event, such as a trauma. Indeed, evidence for reconstruction in memory suggests associations are likely to be impermanent (Spence 2001). Thus, while associative patterns clearly exist in the mind, it is not clear that free association can reliably access early memories.

projective test a type of personality test used by psychodynamics theorists in which an individual is asked to interpret an ambiguous stimulus; since the stimulus itself is ambiguous, the assumption is that whatever the person says reveals the workings of their own unconscious mind.

A related technique which Freud himself never used, but has subsequently become associated with psychoanalytic and psychodynamic approaches, is the use of a **projective test**. This presents the person with an ambiguous stimulus, which they are then asked to interpret. Since the stimulus itself is ambiguous, the assumption is that whatever the person says reveals the workings of their own unconscious mind (examples of projective test materials are given in Figure 5.3).

Like free association, the value of projective tests has been subject to dispute. Particularly controversial is the Rorschach inkblot test, whose ill-defined shapes are reminiscent of the game

Figure 5.3 Ambiguous Stimuli and Projective Tests Projective tests use the individual's interpretation of ambiguous stimuli to access the unconscious mind. Two popular tests are the Rorschach, which uses ink-blot stimuli similar to the top figure, and the Thematic Apperception Test, which asks individuals to tell a story about the people in a picture, similar to the lower figure.

'Blotto'. Some researchers have questioned whether it is of any value whatever (Lilienfeld *et al.* 2001), while others defend its scoring as highly reliable (Viglione and Taylor 2003). As Price and Crapo have noted, using tests like the Rorschach in other cultures is particularly problematical (Price and Crapo 2002). For example, the expected response to one card is that 'it looks like a bat' – but how could someone like an Inuit person respond, having never seen a bat? Whatever its real value, it appears that the test is still popular with clinicians, being used at least occasionally by more than 80 per cent (Mestel 2003).

Dreams

As previously discussed, dreams operate on two levels, the *manifest content* and the *latent content*. The manifest content is symbolic, having been created out of the original forms by the *dream censor*. Thus, a dream must be closely analysed to determine what the latent content actually is. While Freud believed that certain symbols were fairly universal (for example, guns and knives as phallic symbols, money as faeces, tunnels and flowers as vaginal symbols), he also recognized that some symbols have a meaning which is particular to the individual – a point sometimes overlooked in popular accounts and 'dream guides'. As with other techniques, proper analysis requires relating the dream to the person's overall behaviour. Though not directly addressing the symbolic meaning of dreams, recent research has suggested a possible neurological mechanism of dreaming which is consistent with Freud's model (Braun 1999; Solms 1995).

Cross-cultural Studies

In keeping with his belief that all behaviour is significant, Freud had a deep curiosity about similarities and differences across cultures. At the time of his death, he had amassed a considerable collection of primitive art (mostly carvings), which he valued both aesthetically and scientifically. One of his major attempts at cultural interpretation was *Totem and Taboo*, in which he noted the prevalence of incest taboos across many cultures, and explained such taboos in terms of the Oedipal conflict (Freud 1913).

Self-analysis

In keeping with his willingness to find evidence in any behaviour, Freud also used examples from his own self-analysis, which began after the death of his father in 1896. This event was terribly emotional for him; he later described the death of one's father as 'the most important event, the most poignant loss, in a man's life' (Fancher 1979, p. 227). Faced with this loss, he experienced anxiety and depression, and had trouble concentrating on work; this led him to begin an analysis of his own behaviour even while he was seeking a general framework for understanding the dynamics of behaviour. Self-analysis represents a potentially treacherous endeavour, both personally and as theoretical validation. The problem is that one can never be certain that what is discovered is genuine, rather than a distortion based on defence mechanisms. (Actually, at the time he began his self-analysis, Freud had not yet developed the concept of defence mechanisms.) In addition, self-analysis raises the danger of increasing anxiety, since it may impair the effectiveness of defence mechanisms before the underlying conflicts have been recognized and dealt with. Freud apparently found this was true, since he told friends and pupils that during this period he was sometimes afraid to cross the street, for fear of discovering some unexpected meaning in the act! Still, Freud had long been interested in his own dreams, and frequently used examples of his own dreams, as well as his other behaviours, in his writings.

Art

As discussed previously, Freud came to believe that art was the product of sublimation, and therefore was based on a healthy coping mechanism for the ego. At the same time, art is symbolic, and can be probed for unconscious meanings. While Freud was interested in art, particularly from other cultures, his discussions of art in his writings were restricted mostly to Greek dramas, like *Oedipus Rex*. Hence, the analysis of art is better regarded as an extension of his work, rather than a major part of Freud's own writings. One of the most interesting aspects of applying psychoanalysis to art is the ease with which it can be applied to pre-Freudian artistic creations. For example, the art of Hieronymous Bosch, a fifteenth-century Dutch painter, has frequently been cited for its Freudian imagery. Similarly, Herman Melville's *Moby Dick*, written about 50 years before Freud began developing his theory, has been extensively analysed; typically, the white whale is seen as a phallic symbol, representing Melville's latent homosexuality. It is more difficult to evaluate art created since Freud's time, since any symbolism could reflect either conscious or unconscious awareness of Freud's work. While psychoanalytic interpretations have become popular in relation to art, it poses problems similar to dream analysis – there is a danger that when too little context is available, the analysis may become a projective test, telling more about the analyst than the artist (for examples of visual symbols which have significance in Freudian theory, see Figure 5.4 later in this chapter).

Try it Yourself

Examples of Freudian symbols can easily be found in daily life. What do you think Freud would make of the following?

■ Ads which use attractive models to sell products.

■ Movie humour based on body functions like farting (for example, *Dumb and Dumber*).

■ The difference between a Ferrari and a Honda Civic.

What symbols do *you* see in everyday life that Freud might have an interpretation for? Does finding examples that fit with the theory prove that these interpretations are valid? Do you think other interpretations are possible?

Assessing Freud's Work

Attempting to evaluate Freud's work is a challenging endeavour, given both the range of his efforts and the impact which his work has had. As we will see in the next section, one way to evaluate his work is by examining what others have done subsequently. For the moment, though, let us deal with Freud in his own right.

Freud was a remarkable person: gifted intellectually, a keen observer, a fluent writer and, by some accounts, a very humane person (Zangwill 1987). While many of his basic assumptions were influenced by the work of others (such as Brücke, Darwin, Pinel), he was a tremendous synthesizer, and typically explored the implications of ideas more effectively than many of his predecessors (Robinson 1979). These are all admirable traits, but they do not really tell us much about the validity of his work. To determine that, we need to consider what makes a good theory.

falsifiability a criterion for evaluating a theory which states the theory should specify circumstances wherein it could be proven wrong.

One of the most basic criteria for a scientific theory is **falsifiability** – that is, one should be able to conceive of circumstances where a theory could be proven wrong. Typically, one of the most common criticisms of Freud's theory is that it is not falsifiable. There are several reasons for this criticism:

- Freud's assumptions dictate that many terms refer to variables that must be inferred rather than directly observed, which makes them hard to validate. For example, not remembering having an attraction to your opposite sex parent is explained by repression. 'I don't remember that.' 'That's because you've repressed it.' 'How do you know I've repressed something?' 'Because you don't remember it.'

- The large number of interrelated concepts, and the lack of precision associated with many of them, make it very difficult to set up critical tests. For instance, how do we measure fixation? Can one be a 'little bit' fixated? How much would a 'little bit' be?

- In many cases, the evidence used to *support* the theory is also *dependent* on the theory for its validity (for example, demonstrating the symbolic meaning of dreams is dependent on accepting the concept of latent content).

- The theory is primarily descriptive rather than predictive, which makes it more difficult to test its validity (see Chapter 1). For example, the theory does not predict which defence mechanisms a person will use in a particular situation, nor does it specify which experiences will be repressed.

- In some cases, there is also a problem of determining which theory to test, since Freud frequently revised his ideas without repudiating earlier work (see Brenner 1957).

All of these considerations make it difficult to directly test Freud's ideas. At the same time, his work has generated considerable attention, and there have been many attempts to test specific aspects of his work. Some examples have already been discussed, but it is worth considering the issue further. One of the most systematic attempts to explore Freud's ideas experimentally was the work of John Dollard and Neal Miller (Dollard and Miller 1950). Dollard, an anthropologist who became interested in psychotherapy, and Miller, an experimental psychologist (see *Autonomic Conditioning and Biofeedback* in Chapter 3), attempted to 'translate' Freudian concepts into behaviourally-based terms. Given that Freud's theory is expressed in terms of mental events, this is not an easy task. Some of their formulations were both creative and insightful – for example, they suggested that aggression could be described in terms of the circumstances that trigger it (see Chapter 7). In other cases, they found it difficult to provide behavioural definitions – for example, distinguishing fear from anxiety. (They *did* suggest, however, that the problems of anxiety seen in clinical practice involve more than the simple fear conditioning proposed by Watson and other behaviourists.) Their work caused a considerable stir at the time it was published, but has subsequently declined in influence. Whatever its limitations, one significant aspect of their work was that they considered Freud's ideas seriously, rather than dismissing his work as other behaviourists have done.

In keeping with the concern for falsifiability, more recent studies have focused on experimental testing of specific Freudian concepts – most notably repression, since it is so closely tied to the concept of the unconscious. As noted already, there is an active debate about repressed memories which surface in therapy (see Box 5.2). While this debate is unresolved, other researchers have looked at individual differences in the use of repression as a defence mechanism.

For example, Gary Schwartz and his colleagues have done a series of studies, based on first classifying individuals as likely to use repression or not. When exposed to sexual or aggressive written material, those classed as 'repressors' claimed not to feel anxious, but showed higher physiological arousal than non-repressors (Weinberger *et al.* 1979). In a related study, repressors spontaneously recalled fewer emotional experiences from childhood than non-repressors (Davis and Schwartz 1987). A more recent study similarly found that repressors were less likely to recall negative personal events than non-repressors (Boden and Baumeister 1997). While details of these studies vary significantly, the existence of individual differences in the use of repression seems well established, and is certainly consistent with Freud's theory. Thus, they provide some experimental support, but do not provide direct proof for Freud's interpretation of repression.

Obviously, these studies do not provide an adequate basis for judging the overall body of Freud's work, and it remains difficult to identify predictive tests. However, it is worth noting that there are some aspects which are well accepted at the *descriptive* level (that is, without reference to the specifics of Freud's *explanations*). For example, childhood amnesia is an accepted fact, even if its origin is still uncertain. Even more basically, most researchers accept the existence of the unconscious as reflecting processes which operate outside subjective awareness (Gedo 2002; Westen 1999b). Freud's view that many forms of abnormal behaviour have their origins in childhood experiences has also found support (Muris 2006). Similarly, therapists ranging in orientation from psychoanalytic to humanistic to even behaviouristic accept the utility of defence mechanisms as shorthand descriptions for particular behavioural patterns; where the approaches tend to differ is in the explanation offered for the existence of these patterns. These examples point out that Freud was a sensitive observer, who noted a number of behavioural phenomena that had previously been ignored. Similarly, his written descriptions of his case studies are vivid and detailed, often giving insights into his own thinking as well as the specifics of the cases. In this sense, they still make interesting reading. So, at the descriptive level, there is no doubt that Freud made major contributions to the observational base of psychology.

This raises a second criterion for judging theories: **generality**. This refers to the range of application of a theory; a good theory should apply to a wide range of situations. For example, a theory which only explains the behaviour of a particular species of rat in T-shaped mazes, and nothing else, is likely to be seen as trivial, no matter how accurate it might be. By contrast, Freud's work addresses almost the entire range of human behaviour. For example, he explicitly argued for the continuity of normal and abnormal behaviour. In addition, he discussed issues related to memory, art, cultural patterns, mythology and a wide range of other topics. Indeed, the assumption of psychic determinism meant that in principle the theory could be applied to understanding the motivational aspect of *any* behaviour. In this regard, Freud's theory still stands as probably the most comprehensive account of human behaviour produced by a single individual. (Skinner, who wrote on everything from superstitions to Utopian societies, may be a strong second.) The difficulty, of course, is that, without falsifiability, it is difficult to tell if it is *correct*. Just as a trivial but accurate theory is of little value, so too is a broad but false theory. But is Freud's theory necessarily false?

Without the objective standard of falsifiability, it becomes hard to evaluate Freud's theory (or *any* theory). While no theory can be *proven* true, a theory which cannot be tested also cannot be proven *false*. Instead, one tries to determine if it is self-consistent, by looking for evidence of distortions in the observations. A good theory should not be contradictory, and there should be no indication of *bias* or other distortions in interpretations of the data. Both of these points have

generality a criterion for evaluating a theory, which refers to the range of application of a theory; a good theory should apply to a wide range of situations.

been matters of controversy with regard to Freud's work. In terms of consistency, he frequently revised his thinking, as already noted, and did not always explicitly reject his earlier work. The changes were perhaps inevitable, given the difficulties of forming a theory based on inferred variables. However, the resulting contradictions remain, unless one decides to consider his latest work as reflecting what he ultimately thought.

In terms of distortion or bias, however, the situation is much more complex. Freud himself believed he had many opponents, as his letters and comments to friends indicate. Yet some authors have suggested that much of this opposition existed in his own mind (for example, Esterson 2002; Roazen 1975; Sulloway 1979). According to Sulloway, Freud seemed to thrive on challenge, and was at his best when defending his views from attack. But he also seems to have been very intolerant of real critics, which ultimately became a factor in his relationships with several colleagues and disciples. While his ventures into psychoanalysis began with his collaboration with Joseph Breuer, the two parted company when Freud developed his seduction theory of hysteria. Later, he had acrimonious splits with Alfred Adler, Carl Jung and Wilhelm Fliess – all one-time protégés.

More specifically, critics have charged that many elements of his theory reflect either personal or cultural bias. Two issues – the seduction theory and his views of women – have been at the centre of such criticisms. Early in his career, Freud proposed that hysteria arose from the trauma of sexual assault; this was the seduction theory of neurosis. Later, he decided that in fact the traumas were imagined assaults, not real attacks (see *Freud's Theory of Consciousness*). However, Masson (1984) has argued that Freud's shift was a mistake, and that Freud was unwilling to acknowledge the realities of sexual abuse of children. Masson based his argument in part on letters and documents accessed during his brief stint as project director of the Sigmund Freud Archives – a position which was abruptly terminated, and for which he later won a wrongful dismissal suit. By contrast, Esterson (2002) has argued that Freud's peers, and ultimately Freud himself, rejected the seduction theory because there seemed to be little supporting evidence. Without attempting to answer the question directly, Good has suggested that Freud's abandonment of the seduction theory had a chilling effect on psychoanalytic study of sexual trauma for more than 50 years (Good 1995). It is difficult to assess the issue fairly. Masson's point about the reality of child abuse seems consistent with modern research, but that does not prove that fantasy cannot cause trauma, as Freud came to believe. Interestingly, the disorder which Freud most closely associated with the seduction theory – hysteria – is today a rare phenomenon. (The term *hysteria* is not in common use today; the expression of psychological conflicts through physical symptoms is called *conversion disorder*. However, by whatever name, this type of problem is uncommon.) In the end, the key question about the seduction theory – whether sexual trauma is necessary for hysteria – remains unresolved.

Critics have also argued that Freud's ideas about women – especially the feelings of inferiority which he associated with penis envy – are wrong, and simply reflect the cultural attitudes of his time. In this regard, there is no doubt that attitudes in our culture have changed in the past 100 years, and it is possible that Freud, like any theorist, was influenced by the prevailing social norms. It is also possible that, because of the cultural restrictions women faced, the problems he saw in his patients were not representative of women in general. Later analysts (notably Karen Horney) have addressed the issue in different terms, suggesting that women's feelings of self-worth (inferior or otherwise) have nothing to do with biological mechanisms, but with the secondary position given to women in society (Horney 1950). Hence, at the very least, one can argue that alternative interpretations exist for explaining personality dynamics in women.

Some critics would go further, and argue that concepts like penis envy suggest that Freud was fundamentally anti-women. However, this seems hard to reconcile with other facts, such as his encouragement of women analysts, including his daughter Anna (Westen 1999a). Psychoanalyst Arlene Richards goes further, arguing that Freud in fact believed women were equal to men (Richards 1999). Whatever Freud may have personally believed, his theory's descriptions of women remain contentious.

At a broader level, cross-cultural researchers have questioned the basic tripartite model of the mind which is the foundation of Freud's work. As already noted, the concept of the unconscious is alien to traditional Asian societies. Clifford Geertz, a cultural anthropologist who has studied a variety of cultures, suggests that the idea of an individual awareness, as implied by the ego, is not only not universal, but is in fact relatively uncommon (Geertz 1984). This has significant implications if one considers how the same behaviour would be seen in other cultures. For example, if a man whose wife had just died appeared smiling in public, Freud would see this as indicative of repression; yet in Java, this would be seen as proper conduct, not concealment. As Geertz argues, to apply the Freudian standard would be to ignore the entire framework of the culture (Geertz

Box 5.4 *Culture and the Oedipal Conflict*

Freud's concept of the Oedipal conflict has long triggered controversy. At the everyday level, almost all adult men say that they cannot remember ever lusting after their mothers and wanting to take their fathers' place in their mothers' lives. Freud's answer to this was simply that men *repress* such threatening memories. But is this the case? Was Freud correct in believing that Oedipal conflict is universal? And even if behaviour which fits his theory (such as Oedipal symbolism in dreams) is observed, are alternate explanations possible?

If Freud is right, there should be signs of the Oedipal conflict in other societies. In the 1920s, anthropologist Bronislaw Malinowski lived with villagers in the Trobriand Islands of the remote South Pacific, and observed their lives closely (Price and Crapo 2002). In Trobriand society, boys were disciplined and taught by their mothers' brothers rather than by their biological fathers: this is called an *avuncular* society. Malinowski found that indeed the Trobriand boys did have dreams much like those that Freud observed in Vienna, but with their *uncles* as the target of underlying fears and even hatred, not their fathers! Given these observations, Malinowski argued that power, not sexual jealousy, is the basis of Oedipal tensions, since the uncles were not the lovers of the boys' mothers. Applying this interpretation, Segall *et al.* (1999) have pointed out that in Freud's time, fathers played two roles, that of the mother's lover and that of the children's disciplinarian. Hence, it is possible that Freud's theory was based on misinterpreting a *confound* of sexual jealousy and power relations. In this case, a son might resent the father, but for a different reason than Freud thought: 'I resent you because you boss me around and punish me' *not* 'I resent you because you sleep with Mom!'

Unfortunately, the issue is far from resolved. For example, Malinowski's original interpretation has been challenged, based on further research in the Trobriand Islands (Spiro 1982). Looking beyond Trobriand culture, a case study of a Nigerian man found evidence of problems consistent with an Oedipal explanation, but some dynamics seemed affected by cultural factors – for example, that the mother traditionally sleeps with the child, not the father, and that fathers could have multiple wives (Ilechukwu 1999). At present, it seems that evidence of the Oedipal conflict does exist in many other cultures, but is relatively rare in some (Bhugra and Bhui 2002). Further, Bhugra and Bhui suggest that more attention needs to be paid to specific factors, such as degree of jealousy between father and son. Of course, Freud himself would not be surprised that specific experiences affect development. However, the key question of what underlies apparent Oedipal behaviour remains unresolved.

1984, p. 128). Freud would likely respond that cultural beliefs may nonetheless mask hidden psychodynamics, but the issues of cultural bias are not likely to be resolved any time soon (see Box 5.4).

Many of these disputes seem inevitably to interweave the man and the theory. This is likely in part because he dominated the field for so long, and in part because of the difficulties of evaluating the theory in more conventional ways. However, claims of bias also raise an interesting conundrum: does bias prove that Freud was wrong, or that he was right? If Freud *was* biased, then it seems that he was *unaware* of the distortions to his thinking, since in most respects he adapted his thinking to fit new information. That means that he was *unconsciously* distorting his interpretations, which is precisely what his theory says: no person can ever fully understand their own behaviour, or be free of distortions induced by unconscious processes. So, if Freud's thinking (for example, about women) was biased despite his efforts to be objective, then that proves that his basic assumptions about the dynamics of the unconscious mind are correct! By the same reasoning, one would have to conclude that no one can offer a purely rational analysis of Freud's work – or of anything else in the world. (This point of view has in fact been suggested by some philosophers of science – see Kuhn 1970.)

It is precisely this 'Catch-22' nature of the theory that bothers some critics. If you accept the theory's basic assumptions, then it is nearly impossible to invalidate it. Consequently, some have argued that Freud's work is more of a story than a theory, weaving together the threads of human experience into a fictional tapestry (for example, Robinson 1979). More extreme critics see Freud's whole conception as simply wrong (Crews 1998; Shorter 1997). Others see that view as too negative – a case of seeing the faults, but not the contributions, of psychoanalysis (Gabbard 2005; Gay 1988; Wachtel 1977; Westen 1998). There is no doubt that Freud broke new ground in both his observations and his ideas. Given his pioneering role, it would seem unreasonable to expect him to have found the final answers to all questions – others could surely follow in his path. In this regard, a statement by psychoanalyst Charles Brenner, writing in a selected volume of Freud's writings, is apt:

> If the history of psychoanalysis is like the history of the other natural sciences, and we have no reason to doubt that it will be, the time will come when the theories Freud elaborated in the 1920s will be incorporated into and superseded by other more complete and more precise hypotheses which will be based on more extensive data and perhaps on different ways of viewing psychic phenomena. (Brenner 1957, p. 246)

That, indeed, is the way of science. Let us see just what Freud's successors have achieved.

NEO-FREUDIAN AND NON-FREUDIAN PSYCHODYNAMIC THEORIES

As his ideas became known, Freud attracted the attention of a number of doctors who were interested in his methods and theory. Several individuals became part of a closely-knit group of followers, who were to help Freud spread his ideas. Unfortunately, the relationships were not always amicable. Just as Freud was sensitive to opposition from the greater medical community, so too, he had limited tolerance for dissent within his group of followers. As a consequence, several early protégés either left or were cast out of the group. Wilhelm Fliess, who influenced Freud's thinking about the sexual origins of hysteria, was eventually relegated to the shadows (Masson 1984). More significant were the departures of Alfred Adler and Carl Jung, who split from Freud in the years just before World War I. Both men disagreed with various aspects of Freud's evolving theory, and ultimately became well known for their own theories. Interestingly, G. Stanley Hall, the American psychologist who sponsored Freud's first lectures in the USA, commented in 1924 that he hoped Freud would not make the mistake of making 'too abrupt a break with his more advanced pupils like Adler and the Zurich group' (Hall 1924, p. 7).

Even among those who stayed relatively close to Freud's basic views, a number of variants arose (see Padel 1987). The publication of The *Ego and the Id* (1923) led Freud's followers to go in two different directions, called the 'ego psychology' and 'object relations' schools. *Ego psychology*, promoted by Freud's daughter Anna, emphasized the mechanisms used by the ego to deal with the world (including defence mechanisms) (A. Freud 1936). Later, Erik Erikson, who worked with Anna, was to extend the conception of developmental stages over the entire lifespan, in the process placing greater emphasis on social influences. The *object-relations* school, which developed in England, focused on the relationships between the individual and those to whom there are significant emotional ties (particularly the mother, due to early rearing). According to object-relations theory, the infant's interactions lead to the creation of mental concepts, or 'objects'; distortions in these concepts (such as idealized or faulty expectations of the mother) create the foundation for later problems. Melanie Klein and Donald Winnicott were among the pioneers of this approach, which later influenced John Bowlby (Priel and Besser 2001). Bowlby, in turn, developed a highly influential model of the infant/mother relationship, which he called *attachment theory* (Bowlby 1969). Subsequent research has shown that early attachment patterns can often have a significant impact on later behaviour (Siegel 1999). For example, children with an *ambivalent* attachment often continue to have difficulty with relationships as adults, because they are preoccupied by their own emotional uncertainty.

Thus, Freud's work spawned a number of approaches, some closely related to his original ideas, some markedly different. Over time, the degree of divergence and variety of viewpoints has expanded. Thus, today one finds a number of viewpoints which are analytic, but clearly not Freudian, such as *transactional analysis* (Berne 1961). In addition, the humanistic approach, which differs in many ways from the psychodynamic perspective, was founded by individuals who were initially trained in analysis (see Chapter 6).

Given this diversity, and the considerable period that has elapsed since Freud's death, it is appropriate to reconsider Brenner's observation, quoted at the end of the last section: has the psychodynamic approach advanced, in the manner of the natural sciences, or are the ideas of Freud's successors simply variations on a theme? To get some sense of an answer to this question, let us briefly consider some major contributors.

Carl Jung and the Collective Unconscious

Carl Jung was born in Switzerland in 1875, the son of a Lutheran pastor. As a boy, he struggled to reconcile the religious differences between him and his father. In his autobiography, he contrasts his own ideas, based on the immediate experience of spirituality, with his father's, which were based on intellectual adherence to doctrine (Dourley 1992). These feelings, which sometimes led him to feel isolated in childhood, were later to influence his ideas about psychological growth. In university, he studied medicine, and in 1900 did a psychiatric internship at a major institute in Zurich. By 1905, he was lecturing in psychiatry at the University of Zurich, and conducting a psychiatric practice.

Key Thinker: Carl Jung

Carl Jung (1875 – 1961) was born in Kesswil, Switzerland, the son of a Lutheran pastor. Despite his vocation, Jung's father seemed more intellectual than spiritual, and his detached attitude led Jung, as a child, to feel isolated by his own spiritual interests. The feelings he experienced were later to influence his ideas about psychological growth. Jung was educated in Basel, and received his medical degree from the University of Basel in 1900; he then did a psychiatric internship at the Burgholzli in Zurich under Eugen Bleuler (who coined the term 'schizophrenia'). By 1905, he was lecturing in psychiatry at the University of Zurich and conducting a psychiatric practice. At this time, he contacted Freud to express interest in his work, and the two men developed a quick rapport; when they met in Vienna for the first time, they talked together for 13 hours! They had regular contacts after that, and Freud came to consider Jung as his protégé and successor (for example, when Freud was invited to speak in the USA in 1909, Jung was prominent among those who accompanied him). However, by 1912 they had clashed on a number of issues, and Jung left Freud's circle to develop his own theory and techniques. In later years, he continued to live in Zurich, where he conducted a private practice and wrote. Faced with heart problems that underlined to him the frailty of human life, he remained interested in the issues of individuation and growth until his death at the age of 86.

At this time, he contacted Freud to express interest in his work; thereafter, they were in regular contact, by mail and in person. As time went by, Freud came to consider Jung as his protégé and successor (Hall and Nordby 1973). Despite their personal rapport, the two men differed on matters of theory – Jung disagreed with Freud's emphasis on sexuality, and Freud questioned Jung's interest in spirituality, among other issues. (Jung saw psychic energy as being much more general than Freud's emphasis on sexuality.) As a result, they broke contact in 1912, and Jung continued to develop his own theory.

Apart from de-emphasizing sexuality, Jung's approach differed from Freud's primarily in two areas: the structure of personality (particularly the unconscious), and the process of development. It is not possible to provide a complete treatment here, but some general comments may help to suggest the nature of the differences. Jung's view of personality in some respects was more complex than Freud's. At the conscious level, Jung talked about the **ego**, which provides the conscious direction of our lives (much like Freud's conception), and the **persona**, which is the character or role we assume in presenting ourselves to the world. Both of these are distinct from the **self**, which comprises the totality of the person, both conscious and unconscious.

Jung's view of the unconscious differed significantly from Freud's, and was a source of friction between the two men. Jung acknowledged that part of the contents of the unconscious are related to the experiences of the individual; he called this portion (which paralleled Freud's conception of the unconscious) the **personal unconscious**. But in addition, there is a portion of the unconscious which reflects universal, not individual, themes and ideas; this portion, which he called the **collective unconscious**, was biologically based, not the

ego in Jung's theory, the element of the self which provides the conscious direction of one's life.

persona in Jung's theory, the conscious character or role we assume in presenting ourselves to the world.

self in Jung's theory, the totality of the person, both conscious and unconscious; the self is distinct from both the ego and the persona (conscious aspects of personality).

personal unconscious in Jung's theory, that part of the contents of the unconscious which relates to the experiences of the individual.

collective unconscious in Jung's theory, a biologically-based portion of the unconscious which reflects universal themes and ideas, not individual experience.

product of experience. While sometimes the collective unconscious is caricatured as a sort of 'race memory', Jung's actual intent was to suggest that just as the body has an evolutionary history, so does the mind (in biological terms, one might say the way the brain functions reflects its evolution).

One important element of the collective unconscious is the existence of organizing patterns called **archetypes**. Archetypes contain no content of their own, but instead serve to organize our experiences, almost like cognitive schemata (Knox 2001). The three most significant archetypes are the *animus*, the *anima* and the *shadow*. The anima represents the complementary qualities of the persona in a man – for example, if the persona is intellectual, the anima will be sentimental. In general, it represents the feminine side of the male. Similarly, the animus is the unconscious masculine complement to the woman's persona. The shadow represents the darker, primitive aspects of human nature – the negative counterpart to the ego. Ideas like 'being possessed by the devil' are expressions of the shadow. Jung saw archetypes as the basis of many fantasies, myths and symbols. For example, he

archetypes in Jung's theory, patterns or frameworks within the collective unconscious which serve to organize our experiences, providing the basis of many fantasies, myths and symbols.

Figure 5.4 Symbolism in Psychoanalytic Theories Both Freud and Jung believed symbols had meaning, although for Freud they represented the personal unconscious, as in the top figures; Jung saw symbols as expressions of the collective unconscious, as in the lower figures, which represent archetypes. (Try to figure out what each of the symbols represents.)

The world today: Harry Potter

Few books have been as popular with both children and adults as the J. K. Rowling *Harry Potter* series. The obvious reason is that they are exciting and transport us into a world in which magic reigns and good triumphs over evil, although only after much adversity. Carl Jung, however, would propose another reason: Harry Potter is a representation of one of the archetypes which we all possess, that of the Child-Redeemer. We have only discussed three archetypes in this book, but Jung proposed that there were, in fact, as many archetypes as there are common experiences for humankind (Jung 1967). The Child-Redeemer represents the journey that we all take through childhood and into adulthood, and the hope for the future that is inherent in children. Like Harry, we travel through a sometimes difficult childhood (the abusive Dursleys raise Harry, often keeping him in a room under the stairs and disparaging his character and his heritage) and we come to a greater understanding of ourselves and our uniqueness at puberty (Harry finds out about his true parentage and his magical abilities at the age of 11). Adolescence often finds us in confusion and torment, battling our conflicting emotions and physiological reactions, and the expectations placed upon us (Harry is expected to shine as a wizard, but is unsure of what his true abilities are and whether he will ever be able to fully use them effectively). As adolescents, we face the reality that the world is not always the way we think it should be and that our parents and adults in general cannot always help us, just as Harry is puzzled by adults' inability to see the evil threatened by Voldemort. With his friends, Hermione and Ron, he undertakes what Jung calls a hero's journey to rectify wrongs, often without the help of the adult characters. He undergoes the tests and trials, although in a form unlike that which typify our own adolescence. Just as we are marked by the experiences of our past, Harry is marked as well: in his case, the scar on his forehead is a visible reminder that his past has left a profound wound upon him. In general, all the ways in which Harry's experiences and feelings remind us of the tribulations of our own growing-up reflect the archetype of the Child-Redeemer. Why the Child-*Redeemer*? Because one of the reasons that the human race has valued children is because they represent our future, and we place in them the hope that they will make the future better than the present and will, perhaps, rectify our own mistakes and shortcomings.

Yeo (2004) points out that the archetype of the Child-Redeemer is present in much of the entertainment and literature of western society, from the Christian view of the Christ child to young Luke Skywalker in George Lucas's *Star Wars* trilogy. But what do you think? Is Harry Potter appealing because he represents an archetype? Or are J. K. Rowling's books just very good reading? Or does it matter?

explained the story of Oedipus as an expression of an underlying archetype, in contrast to Freud's view that it reflected a developmental conflict. At the same time, Jung agreed with Freud that the unconscious expresses itself in symbolic form, and he had a great interest in how certain symbols recur across different cultures (Jung and von Franz 1964) (see Figure 5.4). Like Freud, Jung also believed that analysing the meaning of symbols was helpful to understanding the dynamics of the mind. By exploring symbols, the individual can make contact with, and come to terms with, the unconscious portions of the self. See *The World Today: Harry Potter* for an interesting use of archetypes.

Jung's conception of growth and development, which he referred to as the process of **individuation**, was related to his conception of personality. The goal of human development, in Jung's view, was to expand conscious awareness by the ego making contact with the unconscious aspects of the self. For the *ego*, which reflects the conscious sense of identity, growth involves expansion of one's awareness of the world and of oneself. But for the *self*, which is the whole of one's being (including the unconscious), the goal is to

individuation Jung's conception of the goal of development, which he described as the expansion of conscious awareness by the ego making contact with the unconscious portions of the self.

transcend egotistical interests, achieving a union of the conscious with the unconscious. Jung perceived human growth and development as more open-ended than Freud's description of the genital stage, which was characterized primarily in negative terms. Instead, individuation was a life-long process of increasing awareness, whose ultimate end (the joining of the conscious and unconscious in the self) was unlikely to be fully achieved.

Taken as a whole, Jung's theory is rich in detail, and complex. The theory often deals with pairs of complementary opposites, such as conscious and unconscious, ego and shadow. (Another pair which has become well known is his description of personality in terms of *introversion* – being inwardly oriented – and *extraversion* – being focused on the outer world.) Like Freud, he was a prolific writer, and the large body of his writings makes it difficult to summarize all of his thinking. Like Freud, he often returned to the same themes and issues, seeking to clarify his earlier work. For example, late in his life, after a heart attack at 69, Jung returned to the issue of growth, relating it to his youthful concerns about the role of spirituality in human life. The increasing awareness associated with individuation, he concluded, was an affirmation of the meaning of human life. In his autobiography, he wrote, 'the sole purpose of human existence is to kindle a light in the darkness of mere being' (Jung 1963, p. 326).

Evaluating Jung's work is difficult. His theory has drawn many adherents, and provides a distinctive perspective on psychodynamic processes. His ideas about the collective unconscious raise interesting questions about the use of symbols in areas such as religion, mythology and children's art. In a classic study of myths across many cultures, Joseph Campbell found evidence for archetypes like the Hero and the Earth Mother in most cultures (Campbell 1968). Similarly, Jung argued that the colour black is a negative archetype, and studies indicate it is disliked or feared (even by pre-school children) in many cultures, including Japan, most of Europe and parts of Africa (Williams and Best 1990). Unfortunately, many of the observations offered as support for Jung's theory can also be interpreted in other ways. For example, children's art from around the world frequently shows mandalas and other archetypal symbols (Kellogg 1967). However, these shapes may simply reflect the development of perceptual and motor skills, or other non-Jungian mechanisms. Recently, it has been suggested that applying techniques used by cognitive researchers to study mental schemata might allow more precise testing of Jung's ideas about archetypes (Knox 2001). While an interesting idea, at present this is a proposal for research, rather than real evidence. In the end, the metaphorical nature of many of Jung's concepts has led critics to argue that his theory, while different than Freud's, comes no closer to being scientifically testable. As we shall see, this remains a concern when considering other psychodynamic theories.

Try it Yourself

Compare the symbols which Jung would call archetypes in Figure 5.4 with the Freudian symbols given. Which are easier to interpret for you? Is this a reasonable standard for determining their *validity*?
   What do you think Jung and Freud would say is the meaning of each of the following?

- Harry has a dream in which he is dressed like a ballerina.
- Sharon is seeking a 'guru' who can teach her to live a more fulfilled life.
- Twelve-year-old Jimmy wants to be Superman when he grows up.

Does being able to offer an interpretation prove that that theory is correct?

Alfred Adler and Individual Psychology

Born in Vienna in 1870, Alfred Adler had a difficult childhood, marked by the death of a younger brother when Adler was 3, and a near-fatal bout of pneumonia at the age of 5. These events seem to have influenced his later theorizing, with its emphasis on social factors and the importance of childhood experiences. When he survived the pneumonia, thanks to the interventions of a dedicated doctor, Adler decided to make medicine his career goal. While he initially specialized in ophthalmology, he gradually shifted to neurology and psychiatry. Although he had already begun his own theoretical work, he was drawn to Freud, who was becoming known in Vienna for his approach to hysteria. Like Jung, Adler was initially favoured by Freud, who nominated him as the first president of the Viennese Psychoanalytic Society in 1910.

As it turned out, Adler's favoured relationship with Freud did not last. Even when they first met, Adler had difficulty accepting Freud's views of the nature of drives, and the notion of the Oedipal conflict. As time went on, their disagreements became more evident, and more vehement. By 1911, Adler had split from Freud, and founded his own organization, called the Association for Individual Psychology. The group helped spread Adler's ideas in Europe; when he moved to the USA in the 1930s, interest also grew there. He continued to remain active, teaching and lecturing, until his death in 1937 (Fadiman and Frager 1976).

Adler's early views were shaped by his interest in organic dysfunctions and the implications of Darwinian theory. These influences led to the notion of *inferiority*, and subsequent attempts at *compensation*. While originally meant in a physical sense, these concepts gradually shifted towards the psychological, as Adler grew more interested in social relations. Gradually he evolved the notion that all children experience a sense of **inferiority** because of their size and dependence on others. In turn, inferiority can lead to attempts at overcoming the perceived

inferiority in Adler's theory, the notion that all children experience a sense of helplessness because of their size and dependence on others; this feeling can also be intensified by real or imagined physical defects, social rejection and other factors.

Key Thinker: **Alfred Adler**

Alfred Adler (1870–1937) was born in Vienna and had a difficult childhood. When he was 3 years old, his younger brother died in the bed they shared. In addition to this tragedy, he suffered from serious health problems, including a near-fatal bout of pneumonia at the age of 5. Adler struggled to overcome the impact of these early difficulties, and was popular among his peers. He received his medical degree from the University of Vienna in 1895. After practising initially as an ophthalmologist, he gradually shifted to neurology and psychiatry, and became one of the first members of Freud's inner circle in 1902, three years before Jung. Like Jung, Adler was an early heir-apparent, as shown by Freud nominating him as the first president of the Viennese Psychoanalytic Society in 1910. Unfortunately, Adler's favoured relationship with Freud was not to last, as they repeatedly clashed on theoretical issues. By 1911, the matters had come to a head, and Adler resigned as president of the society, just a year after taking the post. He went on to found his own organization, called the Association for Individual Psychology; some of the founding members were ex-members of the Viennese Psychoanalytic Society. The group flourished in Europe, helping to spread Adler's ideas. When Nazism began to threaten (like Freud, Adler came from a middle-class Jewish family), he moved to the USA, accepting a teaching post at Long Island Medical College. He died while on a lecture tour in Scotland in 1937, at the age of 67.

compensation in Adler's theory, a process of engaging in activities intended to produce a feeling of superiority over others, in order to overcome feelings of inferiority.

weakness (**compensation**); this process is motivated by the generalized drive which Adler called *striving for superiority*. In contrast to Freud's emphasis on sexuality and aggression, Adler saw motivation in terms of the desire for mastery over oneself and a striving for power (Ansbacher and Ansbacher 1956; Orgler 1976). Thus, striving for superiority was a lifelong process, guided by conscious goals and values rather than the forces of the unconscious.

For Adler, the experience of childhood inferiority is the most important influence on the development of personality. Some individuals are so overwhelmed by early feelings of helplessness that they develop a lifelong sense of inferiority, called an **inferiority complex**. Others attempt to mask their weakness by pretending to feel superior, when inwardly they lack self-esteem; this is

inferiority complex in Adler's theory, an intense feeling of insecurity based on failure to resolve the feelings evoked by childhood experiences of helplessness.

superiority complex in Adler's theory, a response to feelings of inferiority in which the individual attempts to mask their weakness by adopting an attitude of exaggerated self-importance.

style of life a term used by Adler to describe an individual's unique way of adapting to and interacting with the world, which is an expression of the person's life history and goals.

called a **superiority complex**. Early experiences like having a major illness, being overly pampered, or being neglected can have a major impact on how the child views their own capacities, and on the child's social interactions. (One can see in pampering and neglect a parallel to Freud's view of how over- or under-gratification create fixations.)

Adler argued that as an adult, a person is best understood as a whole, rather than in terms of individual behaviours; this emphasis on the whole person led to his theory being called *individual psychology* (Stone 2002). Each person has a unique **style of life**, a way of adapting and interacting, which is an expression of the person's life history and goals. For a healthy individual, unmarred by either inferiority or superiority complexes, the goals will include love, friendships and a commitment to society (which Adler called *social interest*).

Individuals who lack self-esteem will instead divert their energy into behaviours which are productive neither for the person nor society, such as blaming others for one's failings. Overall, Adler's model of personality places much more emphasis on social factors than does Freud's, and also offers a more positive conception of development as a growth process.

Adler's ideas have had a broad, but rather diffuse, impact. His emphasis on social interactions and self-esteem has influenced both other psychodynamic theorists like Karen Horney and Erich Fromm, and also the humanistic approach of theorists like Carl Rogers. In addition, his focus on childhood led him and his colleagues to pay considerable attention to educational processes, and 'Adlerian' schools still exist (Pryor and Tollerud 1999). While not proof that the theory is correct, the adoption of terms like 'inferiority complex' and 'style of life' in everyday language is an indication of how widely Adler's ideas have spread (for example, 'life style' as a concept in marketing research is really derived from Adler). In this sense, his influence has been significant.

In trying to assess Adler, it is not clear whether his theory should be considered a revision of psychoanalytic theory, or an alternative. The disagreements which led to the split between Freud and Adler (about the nature of basic drives and childhood complexes) clearly show the differences in the two theories. However, there is little evidence which addresses the issue of which view is more correct. Salvatore Maddi (1974) has argued that Freud's concepts can be applied to understand Freud's life; the same might be said of Adler and his theory. The difficulty with this sort of comparison, as Maddi notes, is that it is not a valid means of establishing scientific truth. While some evidence exists to support Adler's concepts of how self-esteem and social interest affect behaviour (Crandall 1984), many of his basic concepts remain difficult to assess. Lacking adequate evidence, it is difficult to draw clear conclusions about the validity of Adler's theory.

Other Psychodynamic Theorists

Jung and Adler are traditionally considered neo-Freudians, in part because of their early ties to Freud. However, there have been many other psychodynamic theories developed in the past 100 years, many of which view themselves as very different from Freud's theory. These non-Freudian theories nonetheless share some basic assumptions which make it appropriate to consider them psychodynamic. Among these assumptions are the importance of internal mental processes (especially motivation) in understanding behaviour, and the role of motivation and early experience in shaping personality. Despite this common foundation, psychodynamic theories nonetheless diverge – for example, in describing the nature of motivation. Hence, it is worth considering briefly some non-Freudian examples, in order to see some of the similarities and differences to Freud's theory.

Box 5.5 Anxiety, Insecurity and Culture

As noted in the chapter, Karen Horney found that her patients didn't seem to have the sorts of sexually-based problems that Freud had discussed. Rather, their problems seemed to revolve around anxieties and depressions that related to feelings of insecurity in the world (Horney 1950). Since Horney was practising during the Great Depression, a time of world-wide financial insecurity, it appeared to her that anxiety about whether one can feed oneself and one's family was pretty logical. When she moved to the USA in 1930, she found that the patients she dealt with exhibited symptoms predominantly related to this.

While the Depression could be considered simply as one type of economic circumstance, Horney's experiences led her to examine the role of culture in the formation of personality (Paris 1994). In particular, she emphasized what she referred to as the *hypercompetitiveness* of American culture. In Horney's view, American society had been founded on the strength of the individual pioneer, the individual entrepreneur. The conviction that capitalism and the competition bred by a free market were the basis of a strong democracy led to competition in other aspects of the culture. For example, possibly no other country in the world places such visible emphasis on competitive success, whether in sports events, beauty pageants, television game shows or climbing the corporate ladder. Coming to the USA from Europe, Horney marvelled at the American tendency to promote contests in sports even among very young children. For example, the 4-year-old boy who picks up a ball is quickly enrolled in a Little League of baseball, and the fun of just throwing a ball often becomes the serious business of winning. Given the emphasis on competitive success, Horney found it unsurprising that so many of her American patients showed insecurities at not 'measuring up'. Instead of being content with one's 'personal best' or recognizing the impossibility of some goals, Horney found that many of her American patients compared themselves to others so much that even their successes were not satisfying to them. Inevitably these people regarded themselves as being personally inadequate because they could not 'win the contest'.

Horney's basic concept – that cultural differences in competitiveness exist, and can influence the development of individuals – can be compared to work on *achievement motivation* by Harvard psychologist David McClelland (McClelland *et al.* 1953). McClelland found that achievement motivation is comprised of two primary components: the desire for success, and the fear of failure. (While the desire for success has greater influence on goal-setting, it is the fear of failure that is more readily related to Horney's concerns about anxiety.) Consistent with Horney's impressions, cross-cultural comparisons of five countries indicate that achievement motivation scores are highest in the USA, with its emphasis on individual success (Sagie *et al.* 1996). By contrast, collectivist countries like Japan and Hungary showed the lowest scores for achievement motivation. Obviously, culture is not the only source of anxiety, but as Horney noted, insecurity about achieving can be one more thing to worry about.

Karen Horney

Karen Horney (1885–1952) began as a psychoanalyst in Berlin; along with Anna Freud, she was one of the first female analysts. From the beginning, she was critical of what she saw as male-centred ideas in Freud's theory – particularly the concept of penis envy (in fact, Horney was the first to publicly challenge Freud on the issue, in 1926). Horney saw Freud's notion that women feel inferior as both biased and wrong. Instead, she argued that women are physiologically superior (partly because of their capacity to give birth), and that men seek to subordinate them out of fear (Horney 1967). Looking at different cultures, she noted that penis envy (which she called *privilege envy*, to emphasize the advantages men often receive) is not a universal.

Despite these differences, she agreed with Freud (and Adler) about the significance of early childhood in shaping personality. For Horney, the development of personality involved the fundamental *need for security*. This need is experienced from birth, as part of the **basic anxiety** experienced by a new-born child. Depending on the quality of early interactions between infant and caregiver, Horney said that individuals will develop a characteristic way of dealing with other people (see Box 5.5). She argued there are three primary patterns: a tendency to *move towards* other people (sociability), *move away* from others (isolation) or *move against* others (mistrust, aggression). In general, her theory, like Adler's, placed much greater emphasis on self-esteem than did Freud's work (Horney 1950). Her distinction between the *real self* (who we actually are) and the *ideal self* (an image of what we should be) also influenced the work of Carl Rogers (see Chapter 6). In addition, by examining how women's experiences, rather than their anatomy, shape their behaviour, she was a precursor of more recent feminist theories. While not well known by the general public, she influenced many of her peers and successors.

> **basic anxiety** in Horney's theory, an intense sense of isolation and helplessness which is the primary source of human motivation.

Erik Erikson

Erik Erikson (1902–94) originally studied under Anna Freud in Vienna, and later began to do research and child therapy in the USA. He evolved his own theory of development, which differed significantly from Freud's in both the nature of developmental stages, and also the drives which underlie them. First, he defined stages in *psychosocial* terms, not in terms of sexuality and aggression. To Erikson, the basic drives are social ones, which are biologically based. Development involves resolving a series of problems or conflicts which concern the individual's sense of self and relationships to other people. For example, infants must resolve their fears of helplessness by learning to trust their primary caregiver.

A second major distinction concerns the description of development. Whereas Freud's theory never elaborated on adult behaviour (the genital stage), Erikson's theory has eight stages, four of which focus on the years after puberty (see Box 5.6). In his view, personality continues to change in adulthood as we deal with issues like the search for intimacy, mid-life changes, and retirement and ageing. In this regard, his theory foreshadowed modern views on the study of human development (Erikson 1963).

Perhaps the best-known stage in Erikson's theory is that related to the period of adolescence (approximately ages 12–20). During this stage, an individual seeks to create a clear sense of 'who I am', or *identity*; failing to do so can create *role confusion*. Because of the distress, self-doubt and difficulties in relationships with others that can occur, role confusion can trigger an *identity crisis* – a term which is recognizable to many people who have never heard of Erikson. Interestingly,

Box 5.6 *Comparing Freud's and Erikson's Models of Development*

While the timing of early stages is nearly identical, Freud defined his stages in psychosexual terms (expression of drives), whereas Erikson defined his in psychosocial terms (social interactions).

Age	Freud	Erikson
0–1½	Oral stage – development of ego through body image, delaying gratification	Trust vs. mistrust – developing trust in others and self
1½–3	Anal stage – development of ego through toilet training	Autonomy vs. shame – learning self-control
3–5	Phallic stage – Oedipal conflict	Initiative vs. guilt – learning to plan and initiate new actions
5–12 (puberty)	Latency – drives repressed, little conscious conflict	Industry vs. inferiority – absorbed in activities like school; developing sense of competence
12–20 (adolescence)	Genital stage – development complete; gratification largely symbolic in form	Identity vs. role confusion – forming clear sense of self-identity
Young adult (20–25)		Intimacy vs. isolation – learning commitment and sharing in relations with others
Middle adult (25–65)		Generativity vs. stagnation – making contributions to family and society
Late adult (65+)		Integrity vs. despair – developing sense of completeness towards life, accepting past

Erikson was not the first to suggest that adolescence can be a difficult period; Anna Freud, for example, believed that such turmoil was normal (Freud 1958). Erikson himself saw adolescent storminess as a possibility, not an inevitability, but because of the popularity of the term 'identity crisis', his theory is often seen as supporting such views. In recent years, the notion that adolescent turmoil is universal has been challenged both across individuals and across cultures (Greenfield *et al.* 2003). For example, there are significant differences in experiences of loneliness for Canadian and Portuguese teenagers (Rokach and Neto 2001). While it is true that adolescents frequently have conflicts with their parents (Laursen *et al.* 1998), it seems that Erikson's view – difficulties are possible, not inevitable – is more accurate than Anna Freud's view that turmoil is normal.

While the evidence may favour Erikson's theory on this particular point, there has also been controversy on the broader issue of how universal the overall sequence and timing of stages are. Erikson himself did some work with adolescents from the Sioux and Yorok tribes, and later asserted that this experience was very influential on his thinking – implying that he saw no contradiction with the theory (Frager and Fadiman 1998). Other researchers, however, have raised doubts. For example, a study of South African men and women found indications that identity does not always precede intimacy (Ochse and Plug 1986). The same study suggested that factors like apartheid, poverty and fragmented living conditions could hamper the achievement of identity. However, until more cross-cultural data are available, it is not clear whether these results represent a fundamental challenge to Erikson's model, or simply reflect extremely adverse (and atypical) social conditions.

Erikson's interests were wide-ranging, and he did biographical analyses of historical figures like Martin Luther and Mahatma Gandhi (Erikson 1962). In doing so, Erikson pioneered the application of psychological analysis to the writing of biographies – an approach now sometimes called *psychohistory*. In some sense, his own life mirrored his view that development continues throughout life; he remained active well into his 80s, and was 91 when he died in 1994.

In the end, each of the above theories, both neo-Freudian and non-Freudian, seems to emphasize different concepts and structures. Yet it is not easy to determine if they are simply variations on a theme, as Robinson (1979) suggests, or whether one or more represent clear advances over Freud's pioneering theory. However they might disagree with Freud's concepts and theory, they clearly share the same difficulties of falsifiability.

Try it Yourself

Suppose that, for curiosity, you decided to see a psychodynamic therapist. Which theoretical orientation that we have discussed would you choose? Why? Is it because you think their theories are closest to the truth? Or because their general perspective is appealing? What do you think is important for an effective therapeutic relationship? (This question will be discussed further in Chapter 9.)

CONCLUSION

The psychodynamic approach attempts to understand behaviour by analysing how personality is shaped by past experience and the workings of the mind. In one sense, it is like the cognitive approach, in that both focus on processes which cannot be directly observed. At the same time, it is rather different from the cognitive approach, for it attempts to deal with the individual as a whole person, including what motivates behaviour. By contrast, the cognitive approach currently offers no integrated conception of the individual, and is essentially silent on the question of motivation. The biological approach also offers explanations of the mind, but its theories operate at a very different level of description from psychodynamic theories, and cannot be directly compared. (Ironically, Freud himself hoped that ultimately his theory could be supported by reference to physiological processes.)

Within the psychodynamic approach, there is no question that Sigmund Freud occupies the central place. His position as a pioneer has made his work the standard, rightly or wrongly, against which other psychodynamic models must be judged. Freud's theorizing, which is marked by numerous modifications over the course of his career, highlights the challenges posed in trying to infer the unobservable (the dynamics of the mind) from what can be seen.

At the same time, Freud's approach has inspired many others to develop psychodynamic models of behaviour, including some of his own close associates. Viewed together, it is possible to identify many kinds of similarities among these theories – but also many differences. One similarity is the emphasis placed on early childhood experiences in understanding adult personality. Unfortunately, the similar-yet-different nature of the various theories makes it hard to choose between them. To some extent, this seems unavoidable, given the goals and methods of the psychodynamic approach.

Ultimately, the goal of all psychological theories, psychodynamic or otherwise, is to account for actual behaviour; in that sense, it is inevitable that there should be agreement on some aspects. At the same time, psychodynamic theories are challenged by the necessity of inferring processes from observed behaviour. As discussed in Chapter 1, this process of inference makes it likely that different observers will create their own distinct organizing structures, which helps to explain the wide variety of conceptual structures found in psychodynamic theories. Seen this way, the theories represent different ways of viewing the same thing; as one analyst put it, 'Most conflicts in analysis are definitional' (Arlow, quoted in Karen 1992, p. 49). Thus, one is left with the sense that psychodynamic models are like cognitive schemata – each is shaped by the experiences and cultural background of the person who developed it.

While this might be reasonable in literature, science seeks to avoid such ambiguities by subjecting competing theories to experimental test. Unfortunately, the inference processes that lead to differing psychodynamic theories, and the emphasis on non-experimental forms of research, result in complex theories which are difficult to test. This difficulty is clear in Freud's theory, which can describe almost any aspect of human behaviour, but *predicts* very little. In general, there is no way to determine empirically which psychodynamic model is the most accurate, since they generally lack *falsifiability*.

Still, there are other ways to judge a theory. One way is in terms of *generality*: does a theory address the full range of human behaviour? Evaluating generality requires considering both what a theory covers *and* what it *doesn't* cover. One of the apparent omissions in Freud's work which has drawn criticism is the lack of a clear conception of the goal of development. Indeed, the genital stage, which represents the longest phase of life, is the stage which he elaborated the least. Interestingly, this omission helped to trigger the creation of the humanistic approach. Humanistic psychologists see development as a life-long process of growth, defined in terms of reaching one's maximum potential. In this regard, the humanistic approach is very different from the 'brutal pessimism' of Freud, and closer to the views of Adler and Horney.

Whether pessimistic or not, Freud's theory laid the foundation for the psychodynamic approach, and whatever their differences and limitations, all psychodynamic theories share certain basic assumptions. One of these is the belief that it is possible to understand an individual's personality objectively. Ironically, while often criticized today for lack of scientific rigour, Freud's work actually represented the first attempt to scientifically understand behaviour (Gedo 2002). Other approaches have subsequently been developed, with the behaviourists seeking even greater objectivity by discussing only observable events. By contrast, the humanistic approach argues that each individual is best equipped to know themself, and so humanistic theorists focus on the individual's own subjective perceptions. In this respect, we are reminded that each approach to psychology makes different assumptions, and therefore emphasizes different aspects of behaviour.

Putting It All Together – Psychodynamic Approach

Freud would say that many of Sam's difficulties likely relate to the *phallic stage*. The close relationship Sam has with his parents suggests he strongly *identified* with them (particularly his father) in seeking to resolve his *Oedipal conflict*. His *superego*, based on his father as a role model, demands that he work hard, get top grades and climb the ladder of success. Like his father, he wants to build a relationship with a woman much like his mother who is not particularly independent and works at a job that Sam associates with femininity (interior design). Hence Sam thinks that 'a real man', like his dad, should be able to get to the top of his field, support his family and excel at whatever he touches. But Sam's *id* sees his work/school/home responsibilities as being very onerous and unappealing, while his *ego* may well view them as realistically impossible to fulfil. This conflict creates *anxiety*, and to cope with this, Sam's ego uses *defence mechanisms*: rationalization (that he 'needs a break') and *repression* (resulting in his fatigue and depression). In addition, Freud might suggest that Sam unconsciously finds Vanessa's desire for a career as symbolically reflecting his potential inability to provide adequately for his family. While the case study says this relationship has not really begun as yet, it is likely that this simultaneous attraction to Vanessa and concern about her independence are adding to his *anxiety*.

To deal with his situation, Sam first needs to become aware of his internal conflict, so that he can find more effective ways to resolve it. This would require engaging in analysis with a therapist, so that he can develop *insight*. Typically, this could take an extended period of time – but Freud would argue that until he recognizes why he feels this way, he is unlikely to show any fundamental improvement.

Jung might say that Sam's *shadow* is manifesting itself by pulling Sam away from the difficult studying he must do and leading him to procrastinate instead. The anxiety Sam feels is a result of the conflict that is between Sam's *shadow* and his *persona*, which presents him as a competent, well-adjusted person who fulfils all his responsibilities. By failing to acknowledge the shadow, Sam is limiting his growth towards *individuation*, which requires becoming aware of his *collective unconscious*. Jung might also suggest that he is uncertain about entering a relationship with Vanessa because her independence does not fit with his *anima*, which represents, to Sam, a woman with a more traditional view of femininity.

Adler might say that Sam is feeling the pangs of an *inferiority complex*. In growing up, his parents' success may have seemed unattainable to him, and despite their encouragement he may have developed low *self-esteem*. Overall, he has been fairly successful in his *striving for superiority*, but as new, more rigorous demands are placed upon him and he becomes attracted to a bright independent woman, the old feelings of inferiority from his childhood return. It is also possible that his sense of inferiority is reflected in his *style of life*, whereby living on the brink of crisis has become part of how he sees himself. Until Sam can recognize the source of his feelings, it is unlikely that he can develop a more realistic pattern of behaviour, or better self-esteem.

As is evident from these assessments, while each theory uses a different set of concepts, they all agree that Sam's present emotional difficulties have their origin in unconscious processes. In addition, they would agree that his experiences in childhood have been a significant (but unrecognized) influence on who he is. Until he can develop more insight, he is likely to continue to struggle, and waste energy that could more productively be used to achieve his goals, and to enjoy his life.

CHAPTER SUMMARY

- The psychodynamic approach attempts to understand behaviour in terms of the workings of the mind, with an emphasis on motivation and the role of past experience. The approach was pioneered by *Sigmund Freud*, who developed *psychoanalytic theory*.

- Psychoanalytic theory emphasizes the importance of *psychic determinism* and *innate drives*, the role of the *unconscious mind*, and the *continuity* of normal and abnormal behaviour.

- In discussing the contents of the mind, Freud distinguished between the *conscious* mind and the *subconscious* (comprised of the *preconscious* and *unconscious*).

- Freud's theory of personality accounts for behaviour in terms of the dynamic relationships of the *id, ego* and *superego*.

- Freud described development in terms of five psychosexual stages distinguished by shifts in the underlying mode of gratification: *oral, anal, phallic, latency* and *genital*. Each stage is marked by particular challenges and conflicts; of these, the *Oedipal conflict* (in the phallic stage) is probably the most significant in terms of later development.

- Psychoanalysis, by making the assumption of psychic determinism, views all behaviour as having meaning; consequently, Freud looked at everything from dreams to *parapraxes* (Freudian slips) to art as expressions of the dynamics of the mind.

- Anxiety, which results from conflicts within the individual, is handled by the use of various *defence mechanisms*, such as *displacement* and *repression*, which reduce anxiety by distorting reality rather than resolving the conflict.

- While very comprehensive, Freud's theory has limitations (including problems of *falsifiability*), and even in his lifetime competing theories were developed, including several by his former students.

- The best-known of Freud's disciples are *Carl Jung* and *Alfred Adler*, who are considered *neo-Freudian theorists*; other psychodynamic theorists, such as *Karen Horney* and *Erik Erikson*, are generally regarded as *non-Freudian* psychodynamic theorists.

- Carl Jung's theory expanded on the nature of the unconscious, particularly by including a conception of a *collective unconscious* whose *archetypes* influence our interpretation of experiences. Jung rejected Freud's emphasis on sexual motivation, and instead emphasized the importance of *individuation*, the enhancing of awareness, as a motive for development.

- Alfred Adler was influential in the emphasis he gave to issues of *esteem*, and many of his terms, like *inferiority complex* and *style of life*, have become common usage.

- Psychodynamic theories provide a distinctive approach to the understanding of behaviour; the primary difficulty is finding an effective way to evaluate the various theories within the approach.

🔑 Key terms and concepts

psychic determinism
catharsis
conscious
subconscious
preconscious
unconscious
manifest content
latent content
dream censor
id
pleasure principle
ego
reality principle
superego
psychosexual stages of development
mode of gratification
Oedipal conflict
identification
repression
fixation

regression
anxiety
defence mechanism
displacement
rationalization
sublimation
parapraxes
projective tests
falsifiability
generality
persona
collective unconscious
archetypes
individuation
compensation
inferiority complex
style of life
basic anxiety
identity crisis

Online Learning Centre

When you have read this chapter, log onto the Online Learning Centre website at *www.openup.co.uk/glassman* where you will find answers to these Test Yourself questions and suggested answers to the Try it Yourself activities, plus many more learning resources to help you study psychology.

Test yourself questions

1 What are the basic assumptions that Freud makes about the human mind?
2 Describe three defence mechanisms.
3 What is the Oedipal conflict?
4 How did the neo-Freudians' theories differ from Freud's theory?

Suggestions for Further Reading

■ For the reader interested in more information on psychodynamic theories in general, **Bem Allen's** *Personality Theories: Development, Growth, and Diversity* (2005) provides a good general reference, organized by theorist.

■ The best way to get the flavour of **Freud's** work is by reading his own writings. *Psychopathology in Everyday Life* (1904), with its many examples of Freudian slips, provides an interesting starting point for the general reader. For those seeking a brief summary of Freud's theory, **Brenner's** *An Elementary Textbook of Psychoanalysis* (1955) is still a good brief guide, written by a Freudian analyst.

■ **Paul Roazen's** *Freud and His Followers* (1975) places Freud's work into historical context, and also explores his relations to Jung, Adler and others. *A History of Psychiatry*, by medical historian **Edward Shorter** (1997), provides a highly critical, but historically detailed, account of the development of psychoanalysis.

■ To explore **Jung's** ideas in more detail, *Man and His Symbols* (Jung and von Franz 1964), an edited collection of his writings, is a useful source.

■ To learn more about Adler, one of the best sources is **Ansbacher and Ansbacher's** *The Individual Psychology of Alfred Adler* (1956), an edited collection of his writings.

■ *Childhood and Society* (1963) offers an accessible introduction to **Erikson's** theory, and still makes interesting reading.

The Humanistic Approach

LEARNING OBJECTIVES

In this chapter, the objectives are to learn:

☑ the basic assumptions of the humanistic approach

☑ the theoretical framework of Carl Rogers, including
  - structure of personality
  - role of positive regard
  - conditions for growth

☑ Abraham Maslow's needs-based theory, including
  - the hierarchy of needs
  - the nature of self-actualization
  - Maslow's concept of healthy growth

☑ the extension of the humanistic approach to existential psychology, including
  - Frankl's logotherapy
  - the development of positive psychology
  - the modern application of the humanistic approach to coaching psychology

KEEPING THE PERSON IN 'PERSONALITY'

Freud's explorations of personality were initially driven by the suffering of his patients, and his desire to help them. In the same way, the origins of the humanistic approach can be traced to the desire to aid those in distress. To illustrate this, let us consider an experience that Carl Rogers, one of the founders of humanistic psychology, had as a counsellor. Rogers was working with a young man who suffered from schizophrenia, a serious form of mental disorder. The man was hospitalized in a state institution, and Rogers had been working with him for some time, with little evident progress. Then one day, something happened:

> [The man] made a few remarks about individuals who had recently left the hospital; then he remained silent for almost forty minutes. When he got up to go, he mumbled almost under his breath, 'If some of *them* can do it, maybe I can too.' That was all – not a dramatic statement, not uttered with force and vigour, yet a statement of choice by this young man to work toward his own improvement. (Rogers 1969, pp. 265–6)

Eight months later, the man was in fact discharged from the hospital. To Rogers, this represented, not a triumph for him as a therapist, but an 'experience of responsible choice' by the young man. In this event, as in all of life, 'It is the *meaning* of the *decision* which is essential to understanding the act' (Rogers 1969, p. 268).

This story is striking both for the improvement in the man's condition – which is remarkable in itself – but also for the way Rogers describes it. One can scarcely imagine Freud interpreting events in this way – a cure by *choice*? In what sense do choices determine our lives? And how can the meaning people give to their actions be incorporated into a psychological theory? In the humanistic approach, personal meanings are central to the understanding of behaviour – and behaviour is only one aspect of the whole person. To comprehend what this means, we must look at the origins of the approach.

INTRODUCTION

In the 1950s, the field of psychology, particularly in North America, was dominated by psychoanalysis and behaviourism. Clinically-oriented practitioners favoured psychoanalysis, while experimental researchers tended to follow the precepts of behaviourism. Supporters of each approach viewed it as a comprehensive system for understanding human behaviour. Not surprisingly, however, not every psychologist felt comfortable with the existing approaches. Some found behaviourism too limited, because it focused on specific responses, while ignoring the person as a whole. Others found psychoanalysis both too rigid and too pessimistic. (Some of the pioneers of the humanistic approach started their careers in the psychoanalytic tradition.) Many people who were not formally trained in psychology also felt vaguely uncomfortable with the conceptions of the human being that were being proposed by these psychological approaches. They felt, as you may also have felt up to this point, that they were more than a collection of biological and/or conditioned responses or feelings and actions dictated by processes of which they had no conscious knowledge. Intuitively, many people felt that they were more than this – that they were unique, thinking, feeling, hoping, dreaming, planning, growing beings that were special in their own unique ways. Out of these concerns emerged the humanistic approach.

The *humanistic approach* encompasses a variety of theorists, who have often applied other labels to their theoretical perspective, such as 'existential' or 'phenomenological' psychology.

Abraham Maslow, one of the pioneers of the approach, has referred to humanistic psychology as a 'Third Force', opposing the dominant perspectives of behaviourism and psychoanalysis (DeCarvalho 1990; Maslow 1968). While each label, and the associated theory, convey a slightly different meaning, collectively the various theories embody certain common elements which justify treating them together. These common elements are the assumptions which define the humanistic approach.

There are three assumptions which are basic to the humanistic approach: a phenomenological viewpoint, a belief in the capacity for choice, and an emphasis on meaning. Let us examine each, discovering why each assumption was considered radical and controversial to the study of psychology.

The Phenomenological Viewpoint

First and foremost, humanists believe that behaviour must be understood in terms of the subjective experience of the individual. If you wish to understand human behaviour, the humanists argue, you must understand the person producing the behaviour – *including* how the person sees the world (a **phenomenological** viewpoint). Only the individual can explain the meaning of a particular behaviour. To understand the challenge this poses, one must remember that psychologists have long been wary of dealing with subjective reports (as we have seen in earlier chapters), and consequently most approaches see little explanatory value in subjective experience. For example, the behaviourists have argued that what people think or say is irrelevant to the explanation of behaviour; instead, behaviourists focus on the role of the environment. Similarly, the psychodynamic approach also asserts that individuals cannot explain their own behaviour, because the causes are largely unconscious. Consequently, psychodynamic theorists argue that conscious explanations will be distorted by rationalization or other defences. The result is that both approaches devalue the significance of subjective experience. The explanation of behaviour ends up depending, not on the person who is behaving, but on the assessment of an observer (the researcher/theorist).

phenomenological pertaining to the way things appear or are experienced; in the humanistic approach, a reference to the emphasis on an individual's perceptions and feelings as defining the meaning of their behaviour.

The humanists reject these interpretations, and instead suggest that subjective experience is an important aspect of behaviour, *and* that it can be studied scientifically. Essentially, the argument is that *all data*, being gathered by human beings, are inherently *subjective*, and must be regarded as such (recall what has been said in previous chapters about the nature of perception). The traditional insistence on an objective observer is meaningless, since no one is objective. As a result, humanists argue that there is no reason to reject subjective experience in favour of third-party observations.

In favouring this view, Carl Rogers argued that, rather than making science impossible, the recognition of subjectivity establishes new criteria for legitimate scientific observations (Rogers 1964, 1985). Basically, any event or observation which can be agreed upon by two observers is a valid observation, even though each person is reacting out of their own subjectivity. This process of agreement, which Rogers called **intersubjective verification**, is seen ultimately as the basis of all science, as well as all human relationships. Since science depends on agreement among observers (for example, in using replicability as a test for the accuracy of experimental results), intersubjective verification is fundamentally no different from other methods. In this sense, rather than endorsing a dangerous

intersubjective verification a process for validating observations based on agreement by two observers; proposed by Rogers as a means of making subjective impressions useful as scientific data.

form of subjectivity, the humanists are simply making explicit how intersubjective verification is the basis of all observation, including traditional scientific methods.

The Capacity for Choice

The second major assumption is that behaviour is not constrained by either current circumstances or past experience. That is, the way we act is not simply a response to an immediate stimulus, nor determined solely by previous events. Instead, human beings *choose* and decide how to behave based on their subjective assessment of a situation; that is, we have free will. This assumption

determinism the assumption that all behaviour has specific causes.

contrasts with both behaviourism and psychoanalysis, which both assume some form of determinism. **Determinism** is the assumption that all behaviour has specific causes. For the behaviourist, behaviour is dictated by environmental factors, such as reinforcers. For the psychoanalyst, the individual is governed by innate drives whose influence is largely unconscious (psychic determinism). Ultimately, both see the individual as a kind of puppet, at the mercy of largely uncontrollable forces.

The justification for the humanist stance is complex, and has been a source of heated debate (see Rogers and Skinner 1956). In large part, the humanist position is connected to the view that the way we think affects our behaviour, independently of external factors. Note that the humanists are *not* saying that causes do not exist in the world; instead, they disagree with their opponents about what the primary causes of behaviour are. By focusing on the subjective perceptions rather than external stimuli or unconscious drives, the humanists argue that individuals make choices which cannot be controlled or predicted. Without trying to settle the dispute, let us point out that both determinism and choice represent *assumptions*, neither of which can be proved.

The Role of Meaning

A third characteristic of the humanistic approach, which emerges from the first two assumptions, is an emphasis on *meaning* – the purpose or value that a person attaches to their actions and experience. Traditionally, psychology has tended to avoid any discussion of meaning in relation to behaviour. At first glance, this seems strange, since questions of meaning lie at the heart of much of human experience – the myths we create, the stories we tell, the questions we ask ourselves about our lives, and so on. So why has psychology not tried to deal with the issue?

One reason psychology has ignored meaning has to do with the nature of modern science. Questions of meaning seem too closely tied to value judgements, and traditionally science has been regarded as 'value-free'. That is, science is neither intended nor equipped to talk about such questions. Today, of course, we recognize that *no* human activity, including science, is truly 'value-free'. What we choose to study, and the consequences of what we learn, have moral implications. Richard Feynman, one of the developers of the atomic bomb, admitted that he and other bomb researchers were slow to acknowledge the existence of this moral dimension in their work. Nonetheless, he concluded that it is an essential part of science (Feynman 1988). Hence, it is difficult to justify ignoring meaning as part of human experience by saying that science should not deal with values. Today, this is widely accepted, as most universities have centres for scientific ethics and conduct programmes in scientific ethics, and numerous international organizations of scientists promoting ethical considerations in science have been formed.

Like Feynman, many of the founders of the humanistic approach came to recognize the importance of meaning in behaviour because of personal experiences. World War II led to an exodus of thinkers and therapists from Europe to North America, and they brought with them both their ideas and their experiences. Many were psychoanalytically trained, and some, like Viktor Frankl, were survivors of the concentration camps. For these individuals, a value-free stance was inadequate to comprehend the atrocities of the war. Instead, questions of the meaning and value of human activity were central for these theorists, and their concern was a factor which helped shape the nature of the humanistic approach (for example, Viktor Frankl's best-known work is *Man's Search for Meaning* (1992)).

A second concern arises when talking about meaning in terms of the 'purpose' of behaviour. While purpose may imply a type of cause, one may be referring to factors which are remote from any immediately observable factor. This poses difficulties, since meaning in this sense cannot be directly observed, and often can be inferred only incompletely. To take a trivial example, if I go to the refrigerator, look in, and then close the door without removing anything, what can you infer? Was I looking for something, but discovered it was no longer there? Was I checking to see what I needed to buy at the store? Can you really determine just by observing? Given the difficulties of interpretation, many psychologists prefer to avoid discussion of meaning and purpose in favour of focusing on immediately observable causes. (See also the discussion of proximal vs. distal causes in Chapter 8.) Yet, if we accept that subjective experience is relevant to understanding behaviour, we cannot ignore the value that people place on their experiences. To do so is to once more exclude part of behaviour from study, the way Skinner tried to do with mental processes. As Gordon Allport, a personality psychologist, has said, psychology must deal with all aspects of the individual. 'If present-day psychology is not fully equal to the task, then we should improve the science until it is' (Allport 1955, p. 5). The humanists have responded to this challenge by accepting that questions of meaning – and the answers individuals identify – are central to understanding the way people behave. Of course, *acknowledging* meaning is not the same as *understanding* it, and ultimately the issue is whether the humanistic approach succeeds in constructing an effective framework for understanding. Only by looking closely at the theories will it be possible to evaluate them fairly in this regard.

To summarize, the humanistic approach evolved out of the psychodynamic approach, but was also a reaction to the deterministic viewpoint found in psychoanalysis and behaviourism. It is unique among the five approaches in emphasizing the importance of subjective experience in the understanding of an individual. Conscious awareness, the process of choosing and evaluating one's actions, and the meaning one gives to experience, are all part of this 'phenomenological' view.

Clearly, the underlying assumptions of the humanistic approach are very different from those of the other approaches. In some ways, the humanistic approach is the most accessible, because of its emphasis on personal experience. At the same time, it is perhaps the most difficult approach, for it does not permit one to take the relatively comfortable position of a third-party observer in understanding behaviour. To be valid within their own framework, the theories must be useful not only for understanding other people, but also for understanding one's *own* life. Hence, studying the humanistic approach should not be considered a spectator sport; as you read, you should think about how the concepts relate to your own experience.

CARL ROGERS'S THEORY

One of the most significant humanistic theorists, and one of the best-known psychologists of all orientations, was Carl Rogers. From a large, very strict, religious family, Rogers first studied for the ministry because of his interest in counselling. He realized, though, that counselling could take place outside the ministry, and combined with his own religious doubt, he committed himself to a career in psychology. After completing his PhD, Rogers began working in the area of therapy and counselling, dealing with both children and adults who suffered from a wide variety of problems. He found himself challenged both intellectually and emotionally by their suffering, and this drove him to seek better ways of understanding and helping. In this sense, his experiences were like those of Freud (and all those who seek to combine theory with treatment): the practical challenge of relieving suffering led to a journey of theoretical discovery. However, the path for Rogers was very different from that of Freud.

Try it Yourself

Skinner once said that freedom is an illusion, but a valuable one (Skinner 1971). Think about some decisions you have made in your life. Have you ever made a decision that was contrary to what other people expected of you? Why did you make that decision? Do you think this was a real choice, as Rogers would say, or could it be that you are simply unaware of the factors that determined your choice? If the latter, does that make freedom an illusion?

In humanistic terms, what we believe is as important as external reality. In Skinner's terms, what we believe about freedom changes our behaviour. Some direct support for this comes from a recent experimental study (Vohs and Schooler 2008). In this research, encouraging students to believe in determinism led to more cheating; not cheating was related to beliefs about free will!

For 12 years, Rogers worked at a child guidance centre, doing counselling and developing his own ideas about personality and therapy. Circumstances favoured this process, in that his superiors imposed few constraints in terms of treatment orientation. Along the way, he encountered Otto Rank (a student of Freud's who, like Jung and Adler, had parted ways with his mentor), and found that Rank's techniques (though not his theory) seemed similar to the direction that Rogers himself was moving in. His early thinking was summarized in *The Clinical Treatment of the Problem Child*, published while he was in Rochester, New York (Rogers 1939).

The book was well received, and led to Rogers being offered a full professorship at Ohio State University. In 1946, he was elected President of the American Psychological Association. In later years, Rogers observed that this chance to start at the top of the academic hierarchy freed him from the pressures and politics of academic life, and made it possible for him to move in new theoretical directions without fear of censure. In this sense, he encountered the conditions for growth which he eventually emphasized in his theorizing. To understand what this means, let us look at his theory.

Personality and the Self

As noted at the beginning of this chapter, humanistic theories emphasize understanding behaviour by understanding the way a person experiences the world. Rogers was a strong advocate of this view.

self theory a general term for theories of behaviour which focus on an individual's self-concept and subjective experience of the world.

As a consequence, his thinking is sometimes referred to as a **self theory**, since his ideas about personality focus on the notion of self (see Box 6.1). Rogers himself saw the theory as evolving out of his clinical work. Since the time of Freud, it had been assumed that it was the therapist's role to determine the direction and goals of therapy. This concept reflected the traditional view of medical practice, including the linguistic usage of calling a person seeking treatment a *patient*. By contrast, Rogers (consistent with his ideas about the

Key Thinker: **Carl Rogers**

Carl Rogers (1902 – 87) was born in Oak Park, Illinois, a suburb of Chicago. He came from a large, rather strict religious family. In his later writings, he has talked about his boyhood, and indicated that the rigid beliefs he grew up with contributed to feelings of loneliness and being an outsider (Rogers 1973). He sought refuge in his studies, and was an excellent student in high school. Only when he left home to attend the University of Wisconsin did he begin to develop wider horizons. In his second year, he began to study for the ministry, and the following year went to China in conjunction with a Christian student organization. The trip gave him new confidence, as well as an appreciation for other perspectives on life. He started graduate studies at Union Theological Seminary, but then decided to continue in psychology at Columbia University instead. The shift occurred partly from increasing doubts about his religious commitment, and partly through the realization that one could take a counselling role outside the Church. After obtaining his PhD in 1931, he began his career working in a child guidance centre in Rochester, New York, and also began developing his theoretical ideas. By 1945, he had become a professor at the University of Chicago, and was elected President of the American Psychological Association in 1946. Over a long and active career, he taught at several universities and lectured widely. His later years were spent at the Center for the Studies of the Person in La Jolla, California, which he had founded. He died in 1987 at the age of 85.

client-centred therapy an approach to therapy in which the person seeking treatment (termed a client), not the therapist, is seen as directing the process of therapy; later called person-centred therapy.

importance of self) came to believe that the person seeking treatment, not the therapist, should direct the process of therapy. To reflect this, the person seeking help was termed a *client* (implying a relationship of equals, not the subordination of the term *patient*); the process itself came to be called **client-centred therapy** (Rogers 1951). While Rogers, like Freud, developed his ideas largely out of a clinical context, his theory of personality, like Freud's, was intended as a general theory of behaviour.

The Organism and the Actualizing Tendency

Rogers's theory is grounded in experience, and this includes his ideas about the basic aspects of personality. One of the most fundamental aspects of human experience is the fact that we are living creatures – we are born, we grow and, eventually, we die. These basic realities are true for all

organism in Rogers's theory, the biological being which is the source of basic needs (such as food and water), and also the source of a growth motive termed the actualizing tendency.
actualizing tendency in Rogers's theory, an innate drive which reflects the desire to grow, to develop and to enhance one's capacities.

individuals, regardless of race, creed or social status. Our capacity for self-awareness tells us that however long we live, and however much we wish otherwise, we will in fact die. Cultures develop elaborate rituals to cope with death, but can do nothing to alter its finality. Yet what about what happens while we are alive? What needs must be fulfilled? What directs the path we walk through life? For Rogers, the answers to these questions stem from the biological reality of our existence: as living creatures, we need food, water, shelter, and so on. These needs arise out of our biological being, termed the **organism**.

At the same time, Rogers believed there is a broader motive that directs our lives. This motive, called the **actualizing tendency**, reflects the desire to grow, to develop and to enhance one's

Box 6.1 Theories of Self

As noted in the main text, Rogers's theory of personality is considered an example of a *self theory*. But what exactly do we mean by '*self*'? It's easy to recognize that it relates to being an individual, to our experience of who we are – but is it possible to define it any more clearly?

The notion of self has a long history within both psychology and philosophy, with various definitions being offered. William James in his *Psychology* (1890) considered the many possible meanings of 'self', and reduced the issue to its essential aspects. James identified what he called the *self as subject*, the awareness that we associate with 'I', and the *self as object*, the reflexive awareness that we associate with 'me'. While he did not pursue the issue further in any significant way, James set the context for much of the work which followed – as with many issues he examined!

In distinguishing self as subject vs. self as object, James was identifying what have become two different traditions for exploring the self. The self as subject primarily concerns the individual's conscious awareness, both of existing, and of their environment; this approach to self is associated with phenomenology in philosophy, and psychological theories of self such as the ideas of Horney and Rogers. While acknowledging that self is partially reflective, in emphasizing the importance of immediate awareness, it readily lends itself to a focus on subjective experience, as seen in Rogers's theory.

The other tradition, emphasizing self as object, was elaborated by George H. Mead (Mead 1934). Mead was a philosopher who studied at Harvard in the 1880s. (Interestingly, although he did take psychology, and served as a live-in tutor to James's children, he apparently never took a course with William James!) Despite being trained in philosophy, Mead was influential in shaping the early development of both sociology and social psychology. Though he accepted James's original distinction, Mead focused on the self as the object of thought and reflection – essentially, self-consciousness rather than simple consciousness. (To Mead, simple consciousness did not imply a sense of self; for example, an animal might have consciousness, but not a self.) More importantly, he argued that this 'self' develops out of our social interactions with others. In doing so, Mead placed a crucial component of self *outside* the individual, in terms of the attitudes of others. In effect, we know who we are by interpreting how others see us.

Mead's approach, blending cognitive processes and social interactions, was the precursor to the study of social cognition, which underlies much modern research in the area of social behaviour, including Kelly's personal construct theory, and attribution theory (see Chapters 4 and 8). Not surprisingly, this approach is associated with the idea that behaviour can be studied objectively – a scientific framework that fits better with experimental research than with the clinical emphasis of Horney or Rogers (see Ellemers *et al.* 2002). Unfortunately, this means psychology must still contend with multiple meanings of 'self'. Possibly, a new definition of self will emerge which can blend the two traditions, as Martin and Sugarman (2001) have tried to do by defining self as based on the process of *understanding*. (Note that other cultures have developed other ideas about what the 'self' is, as we will consider later in the chapter.)

capacities; Rogers saw this as an intrinsic property of life. It is the actualizing tendency that stimulates creativity, that leads us to seek new challenges and skills, and that motivates healthy growth in all the myriad aspects of our lives. The actualizing tendency motivates the baby to learn to walk. It nurtures our curiosity and our appreciation for beauty. It even underlies our desire for human contact, from sex to friendship to love. When a person is 'in touch' with the actualizing tendency, it becomes a powerful guide for directing behaviour into ways that foster positive growth and happiness. (As we shall see, individuals can also be influenced by other forces, often to the detriment of healthy growth.)

The Phenomenal Field and the Self

If awareness of being alive is the most basic of human experiences, shared by all, there are also many ways in which individual experience differs. Fundamentally, we each live in a world of our own creation, formed by our processes of perception. Rogers referred to an individual's unique perception of the world as their **phenomenal field**. As we saw in Chapter 1, perceptual processes structure our experience of the world according to our individual cognitive schemata; the way we perceive a situation is influenced by our past experiences, our needs and our expectations. In many respects, our perceptions match the external world, but as Rogers noted, 'We live by a perceptual "map" which is never reality itself' (Rogers 1951, p. 485). Some aspects of what we experience are internal, including thoughts and feelings. For each of us, the world we experience is personal and private. Hence, Rogers argued that external reality is not what shapes our lives – our *perceptions* of it, expressed through our phenomenal field, are what guide our behaviour.

phenomenal field for Rogers, an individual's unique perception of the world.

The way in which each of us sees the world affects the way we interact with each other. Very often, misunderstandings arise because two individuals perceive a situation differently, and are each unable to see the other's point of view. A teacher looks at the course material in terms of what 'should' be in the course; a student may look at the content in terms of whether it relates to their personal interests. A pregnant woman sees her body changing, and fears that her husband will no longer find her attractive; her husband may welcome the changes as positive signs of a much-desired child, and never imagine his wife needs reassurance. Such differences can lead to disagreements, but they can often be resolved when we attempt to see the other person's point of view. (Rogers believed this process of *empathy* plays an important role in healthy growth, as we shall see later.) In more extreme cases, distortions of reality expressed in our phenomenal field can lead to inappropriate behaviour: desire may lead to misinterpreting a friendly smile as a flirtatious invitation; a driver frustrated by pressures at work may see an unintentional error by another driver as a deliberate act of aggression. Whether it is consistent with the external world or not, the phenomenal field is the reality that we experience.

Overall, our phenomenal field reflects the way we see the world, and often how we act. Within this framework, the most significant element is our sense of self. While we all tend to perceive our self as a stable entity, in fact, it is a fluid, changing thing, a unity comprised of many elements. Rogers called the **self** 'an organized consistent gestalt, constantly in the process of forming and reforming' (Rogers 1959, p. 201). The self reflects our view of 'who we are' at a given moment, and is influenced by all those factors which shape perception in general, including past experiences, the present situation and our expectations for the future. If we are in touch with our own being, then the self will be guided by the actualizing tendency as it relates to the present situation. Whereas psychoanalytic theory sees personality as the product of past experience, Rogers argued that the past is only relevant to the extent that we *perceive* it to be relevant. If you believe that the way you act is based on your childhood, and you perceive certain childhood experiences (positive or negative) as highly significant, then your behaviour at this moment will be strongly influenced by those experiences. On the other hand, if you 'let go' of the past, and emphasize your current needs and aspirations, then the past will play a much less significant role. Rogers related how, in therapy, a young man came to focus on how his life had been 'distorted and spoiled' by his parents. Then, as he reflected on his own analysis, he said, 'Maybe now that I *see* that, it's up to *me*' (Rogers 1969, p. 266). The self may well reflect the past,

self for Rogers, a fluid perceptual structure based on our experience of our own being.

but it is not constrained by it; it is always possible for a new pattern to emerge, even based on a seemingly minor alteration of the phenomenal field (Rogers 1959).

The Ideal Self, Congruence and Incongruence

Apart from the self, there is another aspect of the phenomenal field which relates to our sense of our own being. The **ideal self** refers to our notions of who we would *like* to be, and the goals and aspirations we have for our lives. Depending on what these goals and aspirations are, the ideal self may either be quite similar to the real self, or radically different. However, like the self, the ideal self is not a stable entity, but a dynamically changing construct, reflecting both the actualizing tendency and external forces. When we talk of a dying person who is 'at peace with himself', we are implying that their ideal self is consistent with their self. By contrast, when we perceive our behaviour as falling short of our desired goals, we can experience it as powerfully negative. A vivid example of this occurred in a class I (WEG) taught a few years ago. While I was returning papers to a class of university students, a young woman burst into tears. Since I knew she had received an excellent grade (94 per cent), this seemed a very strange response. When I discussed it with her after class, she explained that she had seen the grade for the person seated next to her, which was 97 per cent. Since she had always tried to be the best, to discover that someone else had scored higher than she had was a source of considerable distress – *regardless* of the objective quality of her own work. While I tried to console her, and suggest that her standards were perhaps unrealistic, this aspect of her ideal self was not something she could easily relinquish.

ideal self in Rogers's theory, a dynamically changing construct which represents an individual's goals and aspirations.

Obviously, the relationship between the self and the ideal self is an important factor in how we view ourselves, and consequently it forms a central issue in Rogers's theory of personality. To the extent that the self and ideal self match, the individual experiences a sense of **congruence**. It is further expressed as consistency between what one experiences (phenomenal field) and what one expresses (communicates to others). Implicitly, one is saying 'I am what I want to be, and I feel free and secure to let others see what I am.' By contrast, if a person experiences contradictions in their sense of self and surroundings, then this will produce a feeling of incongruence. **Incongruence** represents a mismatch between self and ideal self, between what we experience and what we communicate. For example, imagine going to a party which you thought was casual, only to find everyone else dressed formally. The discomfort and embarrassment you would feel would reflect incongruence. Similarly, the student who was distressed that someone else had received a higher grade was experiencing incongruence. Underlying such experiences is a feeling that 'I am not what I want to be, and I don't feel my real self is good enough.'

congruence in Rogers's theory, a feeling of integration experienced when the self and ideal self match.
incongruence in Rogers's theory, a feeling of conflict or unease experienced when there is a mismatch between the self and ideal self.

Obviously, no one deliberately tries to feel out of place, and it seems equally obvious that incongruence is a very unpleasant experience. So why does it arise? Wouldn't it make sense to shape our perceptions so that such discrepancies don't arise? To some extent, we *do* in fact engage in such perceptual filtering. As we have seen, our perceptions can be influenced by our needs and expectations – a process Freud described in terms of the use of *defence mechanisms*. While Rogers disagreed profoundly with Freud's theory, he would acknowledge that perceptual distortions like those Freud described certainly can occur. However, he would disagree with Freud's explanation of their basis. In addition, Rogers would disagree with his more general assertion that conflict (or incongruence) within personality (the trigger for using defences, in Freud's view) is inevitable. Instead, the question becomes: how does incongruence arise?

Try it Yourself

Are there particular situations in which you experience incongruence? Why do you think this occurs? Does your feeling of incongruence help to motivate you to do more, or is the discomfort simply disruptive? (For example, some students procrastinate on starting an assignment because they worry the end result will not achieve their desired mark.) In order to experience congruence, we must define our ideal self in terms of goals which foster growth, but which are not based on standards which are impossible to achieve.

Sometimes, our culture creates expectations that can become part of our ideal self. An example of this is the concept of the 'Superwoman', which was popularly discussed a few years ago: the concept imagined a woman who could hold down a full-time job, raise several children with constant attention, be a loving and desirable partner to her spouse, cook gourmet meals each evening, have several creative hobbies, and so on. It's exhausting to even read this list, yet many women aspired to this ideal, and berated themselves when they found they could not attain it. They found their self-esteem sinking as they told themselves about all the things they 'should' be doing and couldn't seem to manage. Given how unrealistic this ideal is, why do you think some women took it seriously as part of their own ideal selves?

Personality Development and Conditions for Growth

Rogers regarded incongruence as a result of unhealthy growth – that is, it reflects a problem in development. Like Freud, he recognized that development can be distorted by negative experiences; however, his general model of development was very different from Freud's. For Rogers, development is influenced by the kind of social interactions an individual has, not the changing expression of sexual and aggressive drives.

Philosophers and social theorists have long noted that people like company – very few seem to welcome long periods of isolation. Rogers, too – perhaps influenced by his own experiences of loneliness as a boy – believed that social contact and positive relationships are essential to human growth. Contact with others can provide us with a feeling of belonging, of being valued and loved. Rogers referred to the need for such love and caring as the **need for positive regard**. Any form of attention and praise is positive regard. Little Johnny does a picture, and Mummy gives him verbal praise and a hug. Mary tells a funny story, and Daddy laughs and smiles. Such incidents provide positive regard, and play a crucial role in development.

need for positive regard a need for positive social contacts like love, which Rogers regarded as universal.

At first glance, positive regard may seem very reminiscent of the behaviourist concept of positive reinforcers. However, behaviourism emphasizes how reinforcers change *behaviour*, while Rogers emphasized the *feelings* that positive regard induces, and how these affect our sense of self. While it might be argued that some forms of regard (like praise or attention) are essentially conditioned reinforcers, Rogers cared little about such interpretations. He saw the need for positive regard as universal, and was not concerned about how it originates: 'Whether it is an inherent or learned need is irrelevant to the theory' (Rogers 1959, p. 223).

Conditions of Worth and the Would – Should Dilemma

Positive regard is so important, that finding ways to obtain it can lead to ignoring other aspects of self. For example, if Mary finds that telling funny stories makes people laugh, she may begin finding other ways to make people laugh, even if at heart she feels her actions are foolish and inappropriate. Earning positive regard becomes the measure of self-worth, and pleasing others

conditions of worth in Rogers's theory, restrictions imposed on self-expression in order to earn positive regard.

can become an end to itself. The restrictions imposed on self-expression in order to earn positive regard are called **conditions of worth**. Sometimes, these conditions are self-created, as in the example of Mary trying to be funny all the time. However, conditions of worth can also be created by others (such as parents or teachers). If Tommy hurts his knee and starts to cry, but is told that big boys don't cry, then crying may later be suppressed as a possible emotional expression. If Jane gets angry, but is told that ladies don't show a temper, then she may come to suppress all feelings of anger. Rogers encountered many individuals in counselling who seemed out of touch with their emotions; typically, this could be related to parental demands in early childhood. As we internalize conditions of worth into the ideal self, we lose touch with our actual perceptions and emotions – with who we really are.

In accepting various conditions of worth, we also incorporate the values implied by these conditions as part of our ideal self, a process Rogers described as **introjection of values**. (The

introjection of values for Rogers, the incorporation of values into the ideal self due to accepting conditions of worth imposed by others; the term was first used by Freud to refer to a defence mechanism.

term '*introjection*' was first used by Freud to refer to a defence mechanism – hence this is a case where Rogers has accepted the behavioural description, but not the underlying explanation.) As the ideal self comes to represent the values and standards of other people, it is likely to become more and more discrepant with one's real nature (the self). This in turn creates the basis for incongruence. When pleasing others becomes more important than satisfying one's own actualizing tendency, then healthy growth is threatened. Thus, conditions of worth, and the resulting introjection of values, result in the negative experiences of incongruence.

In one sense, conditions of worth are unavoidable: parents and society inevitably set standards for conduct, and at least some of these standards will be arbitrary, or at least conflict with personal needs. As teachers, we have sometimes encountered students who are pursuing a career goal which does not seem to suit them. When probed, they often say, 'Well, my mother's a nurse, so I feel I should be one, too,' or 'My parents want me to be an engineer,' or similar statements. In such cases, the individual often has other aspirations – art, or accounting, or whatever – which are being submerged in order to maintain parental approval. The result, of course, is incongruence, and feelings of being in conflict with oneself.

The conflict between one's own needs, expressed through the actualizing tendency, and the demands of others, expressed through the ideal self, is referred to as the **would–should dilemma**.

would–should dilemma in Rogers's theory, the conflict between one's own needs, expressed through the actualizing tendency, and the demands of others, expressed through the ideal self.

While the values represented by the ideal self may have *originated* with other people, once they are introjected as part of the ideal self, they are *experienced* as internal in nature. Hence, rather than seeming to be a conflict between oneself and another person (who might reasonably disagree), the conflict is experienced as internal, between two parts of one's own being. This type of internal conflict is much more threatening and anxiety-provoking than disagreements with another person. This conflict can take many forms: when a student *would like* to study art, but feels they *should* study nursing, this is experienced as a would–should dilemma. Two young teens *would like* to engage in sex, but feel they *should* wait until they are older. A parent *would like* to spend time playing with their children, but feels they *should* spend extra time at work.

In the would–should dilemma, there is a conflict between personal needs and goals, and perceptions of expected behaviour. Freud described this in terms of the conflicts between superego (parental values) and id (one's own needs), and believed that such conflicts were inevitable. By contrast, Rogers saw such conflicts, described as the result of incongruence between self and ideal self, as both undesirable and avoidable. Furthermore, he did not see them as reflecting a simple conflict between personal needs and society, because concern for others is an inherent part of the self. That is, a healthy person is naturally motivated to consider the impact of their actions on other people when choosing how to act. Still, if conflicts like the would–should dilemma are *not* inevitable, then how do they arise? To understand this, we must look at the distinction between conditional and unconditional positive regard.

Try it Yourself

Re-examine your conception of your ideal self. Do you see how it might have arisen? If your ideal self is one of unrealistic standards of performance, consider whether your parents or teachers might have suggested to you that you could only meet their conditions of worth if you achieved these unrealistic levels. Do you think they really meant to convey this message to you? Do you think the intentions of others determine the impact of conditions of worth, or how the individual experiences those conditions?

Now consider what conditions of worth you impose on others. For example, what do you expect of another person in order to classify that person as your friend? What condition of worth would they have to violate to lose your friendship? Seen in these terms, we can begin to see growth as interdependent, with each of us influencing, and being influenced by, other people.

Conditional and Unconditional Positive Regard

As noted earlier, the need for positive regard, in the form of approval and love, is seen by Rogers as universal. Ideally, we would all receive such regard on a free and open basis, both as children and adults. Such **unconditional positive regard** is acceptance and caring extended simply because the person is a human being. Religions have traditionally urged individuals to adopt this attitude, hence the injunction to 'hate the sin, but love the sinner'. But we all recognize how difficult it is to put into practice. For example, in their best moments, all parents value their children; unfortunately, it is harder to maintain a feeling of unconditional regard if Jimmy has just broken an heirloom vase while trying to get at the cookie jar. Instead, we tend to give love and praise based on the child doing things of which we approve. When regard is given only for meeting certain standards of behaviour, it is called **conditional positive regard**. If Sean clears up his toys, he gets praised; if he leaves them scattered about, he is likely to get scolded, or at least ignored. In later life, we find that regard is given for good performance at school or at work; we may even find friends welcome some actions, and heap scorn on others (peer pressure is an example of such forces in operation). In all these cases, positive regard is given for certain actions, but not for others. The problem with this is that conditional positive regard often leaves the person feeling that it is their *self*, not their *behaviour*, which is unacceptable: for example, Jimmy's father reacts to the broken vase by saying, 'Jimmy, you idiot! How could you break that vase? You know better than to take cookies without asking! Honestly, I don't think you ever listen to me!' While remarks like this may deter future incidents, they may also leave Jimmy feeling that making *any* error means he is bad and unacceptable.

Ideally, it should be possible to value a person as a human being without implying that one

> **unconditional positive regard** in Rogers's theory, acceptance and caring given to a person as a human being, without imposing conditions on how the person behaves.
> **conditional positive regard** in Rogers's theory, acceptance and caring given to a person only for meeting certain standards of behaviour.

accepts all of their actions – that is, regard for the *person* would be unconditional, but regard for their *actions* would be conditional. This would mean that one could withhold regard for particular actions – such as when a child has a tantrum – and yet still show regard for the person. In practice, however, both the person *giving* regard and the person *receiving* it often find the distinction between person and action hard to maintain. A scolded child tends to feel rejected, even if the mother says, 'I love you, but …'; the criticism of the child's behaviour tends to overshadow the expressed regard. When one's performance at work is criticized, it is hard not to take it as a criticism of one's general competence and worth. When too much conditional regard is given, it undercuts the person's sense of self, and contributes to the development of incongruence. To avoid this, one must focus on the conditions which instead foster congruence.

Congruence and Conditions for Growth

Rogers believed we are all born congruent, because the discrepancies which create incongruence arise through life experiences. Thus, his theory implies that it should be possible to develop in a way that *maintains* this sense of congruence. What fosters congruence, and how can one avoid incongruence? The answer to this question lies in recognizing the conditions under which healthy development of personality occurs – the **conditions for growth**: unconditional positive regard, openness and empathy. Let us consider each of them separately.

conditions for growth the conditions under which healthy development of personality occurs; defined by Rogers as unconditional positive regard, openness and empathy.

As discussed in the preceding section, *unconditional positive regard* is based on accepting that each person has value, without any reference to what they do or don't do. 'It is an acceptance of this other individual as a separate person, having worth in his own right. It is a basic trust – a belief that this other person is somehow fundamentally trustworthy. Whether we call it prizing, acceptance, trust, or by some other term, it shows up in a variety of observable ways' (Rogers 1969, p. 109).

By not imposing external conditions of worth, *unconditional positive regard* makes it possible for the individual to develop a sense of self based on their own actualizing tendency and their individual perceptions and experiences. Without the distortions introduced by external demands, the values which develop as part of the ideal self are likely to be self-consistent, and hence maintain congruence. Thus, receiving unconditional positive regard is the most basic requirement for healthy growth and congruence.

While truly unconditional regard is extremely rare, it can help if we distinguish between the person and the action, as seen in the following incident. Several years ago, I (WEG) was meeting some friends for dinner. The husband was on time at the restaurant, but his wife was nearly an hour late. Since this had happened on other occasions, the husband was furious when she finally arrived. Quickly recognizing this, she attempted to defuse his anger by saying, 'Oh, sweetie, don't you love me any more?' The message implied by this was, 'If you love me, you'll overlook my being late' – clearly setting up conditional regard. Instead, the husband replied, 'Of *course* I love you – *but that has nothing to do with it*: you shouldn't be late!' In effect, he distinguished between loving her, and yet not accepting her action.

Obviously, though, most of the time we encounter a mixture of conditional and unconditional positive regard. Yet Rogers believed that growth was possible even if not all the regard we receive is unconditional. (Otherwise, *no one* would be likely to grow!) Basically, it requires an opportunity to interact with at least one person who can provide mostly unconditional positive regard – whether a family member, a friend, a counsellor, a co-worker or whomever (in counselling,

Rogers called this *client-centred therapy* – see Chapter 9). For instance, in a healthy relationship, spouses accept each other even though each has faults. (Indeed, sometimes the 'flaws' become points of endearment rather than friction – much the way parents complain of noisy children for years, and then miss the noise when they leave home.) Unconditional positive regard allows the individual to take chances with their feelings and behaviour – and in the process to explore and develop their sense of self.

The second condition for growth is **openness**, which refers to a person freely expressing their own sense of self, rather than playing a role or hiding behind a façade. Like unconditional positive regard, openness can be found potentially in any situation. For example, consider a person who attends a dull party. When approached by the host, the person musters a forced smile, and insists the party is 'wonderful'. Politeness dictates the verbal response, which differs significantly from the person's actual feelings; this contradiction creates incongruence. However, this could change, depending on the host's response. Suppose the host were to respond by saying, 'It's nice of you to say so, but I really think I've been to livelier *funerals!*' By expressing his own feelings instead of relying on social conventions, the host is exhibiting openness. In doing so, the host may open the door to a more honest assessment by the guest, whereby both host and guest gain. It's not that the party is no longer a disaster, but at least the two individuals have been able to make real contact with each other, free of social constraints. (It is worth noting that Rogers did *not* advocate deliberate rudeness in the guise of honesty; the goal is to be open while also being respectful of the other person as a human being.)

openness behaviour characterized by a person freely expressing their own sense of self, rather than playing a role or hiding behind a façade; seen by Rogers as a condition for growth.

Rogers believed that this quality of openness (which he also called 'realness') creates greater self-awareness, and thereby the possibility of personal growth. By contrast, when we adopt a façade which is based on our social role or other external constraint, we inhibit any genuine expression of feelings – either for ourselves, or those we interact with. For example, Rogers noted 'the tendency of most teachers to show themselves to their pupils simply as roles', not as real persons with doubts, fears and other human limitations (Rogers 1969, p. 107).

The third condition which can foster growth is **empathy**, the ability to understand the other person's point of view. Ideally, this encompasses their perceptions, thoughts and feelings. This concept is expressed in a proverb popular in the prairie regions of Canada, which says, 'Never judge someone until you've walked ten miles in their boots.' If you meet someone who seems rude (for example, in a store), does this mean they are always rude? Are they having a bad day? Could they have a headache or other problem? While we are often quick to jump to the conclusion that the person is simply rude, the reality is that we cannot properly judge from a brief interaction like this. (As noted in Chapter 4, this tendency to explain others' behaviour in terms of personality when situational factors are more likely is called the *fundamental attribution error*.)

empathy the ability to understand another person's perceptions and feelings; seen by Rogers as a condition for growth.

Like unconditional positive regard and openness, empathy is a quality that is readily recognizable, but not so readily found. Teachers, for example, are supposed to empathize with their students, but differences in background, as well as situational factors, can make such understanding difficult to achieve. Faced with this difficulty, teachers will sometimes adopt a smiling, tolerant façade – not empathy, but a pretence of it. Rogers believed that this compounds the problem of not understanding with the problem of not being real. Faced with students one doesn't understand (and may even dislike), Rogers believed that 'it is almost certainly more constructive to be *real* than to be pseudo-empathic, or to put on a facade of caring' (Rogers 1969, p. 113). Note that being real may sometimes imply expressing negative feelings. For example, a teacher faced with a messy classroom might say, 'I can't function when things are a mess!' While clearly disapproving, the response reflects the teacher's feelings, not simply disapproval of the students. This is likely more honest – and also more productive – than saying, 'You kids don't know how to be tidy!'

In the end, the three conditions of growth tend to be interwoven – experiencing one factor involves the others as well. Rogers noted this when he commented, 'To be genuine, or honest, or congruent, or real, means to be this way about *oneself*. I cannot be real about another, because I do not *know* what is real for him. I can only tell – if I wish to be truly honest – what is going on in me' (Rogers 1969, p. 113). In effect, empathy results from openness and congruence, which are themselves closely connected.

The conditions for growth are meant to allow the individual to evaluate their experiences in terms of their own internal standards, based on the actualizing tendency. Like most things in the world, the conditions exist on a continuum, not as either/or alternatives. Consider, for example, empathy: at first glance, the statement by Rogers quoted in the previous paragraph seems to imply that empathy is impossible – we can never truly know what another person feels. In fact, the reality is more complex. First, when he speaks of empathy, he means the *attitude* of *trying* to empathize, even if the effort doesn't fully succeed. Second, since the same basic elements are common to all human existence – we are all 'siblings under the skin' – empathy may often result from being open to our own experience of the situation. The conditions which foster personal growth are also the conditions that will foster positive interactions with others. It is this fact – that what favours my growth will also favour yours – that makes Rogers optimistic about the possibilities for growth in everyday life.

Try it Yourself

Think about the people who are important to you. Do they provide you with unconditional positive regard, openness and empathy? Have you ever wished that you received more of any of these elements from some of these people? Does what you receive from others influence your choice of friends? Sometimes we are attracted to people because of their status or other factors, rather than what they provide to us; how could you explain this in terms of Rogers's theory?

Human Potential and the Fully Functioning Person

In describing personality, Rogers's theory repeatedly contrasts the factors which foster healthy growth, and those factors (such as conditional positive regard and conditions of worth) which obstruct growth. But what exactly is a healthy personality? One could say that a healthy person is one who lives up to their potential, but what would *indicate* that a person is fulfilling their potential?

The idea that there is some sort of optimal result for personality development is one of the unique features of the humanistic approach. In this respect, the approach is very different from psychoanalysis. Freud's theory was based largely on his clinical observations, dealing with people who often had severe problems, including physical symptoms. Perhaps as a consequence, his theory tended to emphasize the negative aspects of development. While Freud's ideas on pathology were very detailed, his conception of healthy development was never fully elaborated;

overall, he seemed pessimistic about the possibilities for growth unburdened by fixations and neurotic conflict. By contrast, Rogers argued that personality development naturally moves towards healthy growth, and it is only negative external factors which lead to distortions of personality.

Rogers described the ideal of growth as being a **fully functioning person**. The term itself suggests that anything less than optimal growth is a deviation from proper functioning – that is, healthy growth should be considered the *norm*, not some super form of development. In many respects, being fully functioning is equivalent to being congruent. Congruence produces self-confidence and high self-esteem, which in turn make possible the openness to feelings and experiences that Rogers saw as central to growth. The individual trusts their own ability to deal with the world, and consequently shows a high degree of spontaneity, compassion and self-direction. Instead of being preoccupied with conflicts, the person is able to engage in activities with energy and enthusiasm. You may have experienced a sense of this at moments when you are fully immersed in doing something you enjoy: time flies, and you feel energized by your involvement – a feeling that has been described by Mihaly Csikszentmihalyi (1990) as *flow*. (For more on this concept, see *Positive Psychology*, later in the chapter.)

fully functioning person described by Rogers as the ideal of growth, closely related to congruence; healthy growth is characterized by openness, a high degree of spontaneity, compassion and self-direction.

One characteristic which is *not* part of being fully functioning is aggression. Aggression for Rogers is a result of unhealthy growth, in contrast to Freud's view of aggression as an innate drive. Rogers saw aggression as one of the consequences of too much conditional positive regard. When a person is offered only conditional positive regard, they will often alter their behaviour to meet the imposed standards, since the need for positive regard is so powerful. However, this will often mean denying one's own preferences and feelings, which results in both incongruence *and* frustration. Aggression then arises as a natural response to the denial of one's own needs and feelings. If aggression seems widespread in the world, it is presumably because the use of conditional positive regard is so common. Unconditional positive regard contributes to healthy growth, and also reduces the likelihood of aggression.

If this seems abstract, consider the following example. Garry is an only child whose parents were very strict and demanding when he was a child. As a result, he incorporated their standards into his ideal self, and as a teenager has become a very rigid, argumentative person who criticizes and challenges all those whom he sees as making errors, whether peers or authority figures like teachers. At the same time, he is dissatisfied with his own behaviour, which cannot meet his own high standards. This combination of being highly critical and having low self-esteem leads Garry to get into many disagreements, resulting in his being rejected by others. His peers see Garry as a loner with a chip on his shoulder, and generally avoid him. Inside, Garry feels frustrated and lonely. Rogers would see this as a typical example of how excessive emphasis on conditional positive regard during Garry's childhood has led to incongruence and aggressive behaviour. Depending on the circumstances (for example, a social environment where drug trafficking is prevalent), Garry could end up expressing his frustrations in criminal form, while being scornful of the society that he sees as having failed him.

Healthy development thus depends on the conditions for growth. When these are fulfilled, the individual will move towards being a fully functioning person; in their absence, incongruence and aggression will arise. In one sense, this conception of human potential is very specific, in that it implies that a fully functioning person will show little anxiety, an ability to evaluate situations independently, an openness in dealing with other people, and so on. At the same time, it is very broad and vague, in that it implies very little about the specific behaviours, or even values, of a congruent person.

The issue of values is a significant one to humanists like Rogers. Whereas modern science has generally argued for a value-free approach to theorizing, humanistic psychologists believe one cannot understand human behaviour without understanding the values which often direct a person's choice of actions. Rogers addressed this issue in an essay in 1964, and then revised it five years later (Rogers 1969) (see Box 6.2). He noted that infants have clear preferences: they value food, security, human contact and new experiences, while clearly disliking aversive events like pain, bitter tastes and sudden loud sounds. He noted that as we grow, however, we begin to incorporate values dictated by society, such as 'disobedience is bad' and 'making money is the highest good'. These values may be reinforced by various sources, ranging from parents to advertising. Often these values seem directed towards social acceptance, and are rigidly held, without being open to question. Not surprisingly, the result is that the person is often out of touch with their own feelings and internal sources of satisfaction.

Box 6.2 *Values in the Mature Person*

Rogers believed that healthy individuals who had reached a mature stage of development would be likely to hold particular types of values. (Adapted from Rogers 1969)

Characteristics Which Are Negatively Valued

Valuing genuineness – pretence and defensiveness are negatively valued.
Moving away from 'ought' – acting because one values the action, not because one feels one 'ought to' do it.
Moving away from others' expectations – pleasing others as an end in itself is negatively valued.

Characteristics Which Are Positively Valued

Being real – being 'who one is' and expressing one's feelings honestly.
Self-direction – taking pride and confidence in making choices in one's life.
Valuing one's own being – viewing one's self and one's feelings positively.
Focusing on life as a process – instead of valuing the goal, one values the process of living, without concern for reaching a particular goal.
Valuing openness – being open to both one's inner and outer experiences, recognizing one's own feelings and those of other people. This is a particularly important value.
Valuing other people – accepting other people and appreciating them for what they are, just as one accepts oneself for what one is.
Deep relationships are valued – to be close to another person, able to fully communicate and share, is a very basic need.

By contrast, Rogers believed that a fully functioning person will be self-directing in forming values, and will tend to evaluate choices according to the immediately experienced situation. While this sounds like a form of situational ethics, Rogers also argued that the importance of the actualizing tendency will imply certain criteria for making moral choices. Life is seen as a process, not as a series of goals to be reached. Relationships, especially to family and close friends, become more important than material accomplishments. This attitude has been captured effectively in the quip, 'Nobody ever died wishing they'd spent more time at the office!'

While seemingly consistent with his overall conception of the actualizing tendency, Rogers's ideas about values in the fully functioning person are otherwise hard to evaluate. He seemed to believe that there is a biological basis for these characteristics, as when he said that mature persons share 'an organismic commonality of value directions' (Rogers 1969, p. 252). At the same time, he wanted to leave individuals free to make their own choices, unrestricted by him or anyone else: 'I do not expect that every [person] would agree with what I have to say here ...' (p. 239). In the absence of any hard evidence that these characteristics are innate, Rogers's position creates a dilemma, in that it seems to argue for a universal framework of values, while making the individual the ultimate arbiter of morality. If individuals are free to decide their values, how can he be sure that all individuals, even those who are fully functioning, will value the same things? While this clearly seems to be a contradiction, Rogers himself apparently never saw the contradiction, or at least never addressed it directly.

The problem of defining ideal development is a fundamental one, both for Rogers's theory, and more generally for any humanistic theory. To talk about the goal of development as being objectively definable suggests a universal standard. However, both the values proposed by Rogers (such as valuing immediate experience over long-term goals) and the underlying model of self seem inconsistent with cross-cultural studies of personality. For example, while Rogers felt that social relationships are important, his theory is clearly focused on the individual. This might seem both obvious and necessary but, in fact, reflects a view of our selves and the world that is by no means universal. Instead, many cultures foster a definition of identity which is based on our ties to others, especially family and friends – a framework often called *collectivism* (Triandis 1990). In such cultures, social relationships and obligations are more important than the individual. Researchers have suggested the description applies to a number of cultures, ranging from the Cheyenne of North America, to Japan, to various Latino societies (Levine and Padilla 1980; Markus and Kitayama 1991; Straus 1982). An example of how this can affect individuals' perceptions and experience is illustrated by a study which compared Americans and Japanese. When asked if their sense of self changes in different situations, only 5–10 per cent of the Americans said yes, but almost 100 per cent of the Japanese said yes (de Rivera 1989). While there may be many reasons for this result, such evidence suggests that notions of the self may well vary with culture.

If the way individuals experience their own identity (or *self*) can differ across cultures, what about values? How can one argue for universal values as part of a model of ideal development, especially within an approach that sees each individual as the ultimate arbiter of such matters? One possible explanation lies with the actualizing tendency as a universal, biologically-based motive. If it *does* in fact favour certain characteristics, then the answer may ultimately be that there is no contradiction in Rogers's interpretation. (Wilson's (1998) arguments for morality as having a biological basis would seem to favour this view.) Alternatively, the interpretation made

Try it Yourself

Consider the list of values in Box 6.2: do you agree with Rogers's choice of values? If not, what would you omit? Why? What values would you add to this list? Ask some of your friends and family members what they would omit or add. Do their answers indicate common values or are there points of disagreement?

by Rogers may represent a distortion of his own phenomenal field, whereby certain values of his own culture were interpreted as being universal.

At present, no one can really prove whether Rogers's theory fails on these points or not. He himself would likely argue that while some cultures may emphasize collectivism, culture is a human construct, and cultures may not always work to foster human potential (a viewpoint that seems supported by the existence of many totalitarian societies over the course of human history). Thus, the fact that collectivist cultures *exist* is not necessarily proof that they are *healthy*. At the same time, one must be wary of accepting arguments for universal values when there seems so little direct support. At present, no clear resolution is possible. What *can* be said with certainty is that his ideas have been influential both within the domain of humanistic psychology, and beyond it, in fields like education and social work.

ABRAHAM MASLOW'S THEORY

Rogers was not alone in pioneering the humanistic approach. Others, working independently but with similar assumptions, have also shaped the development of the approach. One of the main figures in this regard was Abraham Maslow. Like Rogers, he rejected the psychoanalytic and behaviourist approaches, which he saw as ignoring the positive aspects of human life, such as creativity and love. Instead, Maslow believed that there is an internal force which directs human development towards its highest potential. In describing this motivating force, called 'self-actualization', he focused on the potential for human growth, and the characteristics of healthy individuals. While this emphasis, too, seems reminiscent of Rogers's work, Maslow's perspective differs from that of Rogers in a number of ways, as we shall see.

Abraham Maslow was born in New York in 1908, the son of Jewish immigrants. His initial training in psychology belied his future interests, as he studied primate behaviour at the

Key Thinker: **Abraham Maslow**

Abraham Maslow (1908 – 70) was born in New York, the son of Jewish immigrants. He received both his undergraduate and graduate training at the University of Wisconsin, where he studied with, among others, Harry Harlow, an eminent expert on primate behaviour, and with Clark Hull, a behaviourist theorist. After receiving his doctorate in 1934, he went back to New York to teach psychology at Brooklyn College. While his graduate studies focused on primate behaviour, as time went on, Maslow became more interested in human concerns, in part because of events related to World War II. In the late 1930s, New York had become a gathering place for a number of European intellectuals, many of whom were fleeing the Nazi rise to power. At this time he met such distinguished psychoanalysts as Alfred Adler, Karen Horney and Erich Fromm. He also encountered scholars from a range of other perspectives, including Max Wertheimer, one of the pioneers of Gestalt psychology. World War II seemed to emphasize for him how little psychology had contributed to solving social problems, and he began to focus on social psychology and personality theory. His emphasis on real-world issues was also expressed in his interest in applying psychology to business – a domain often disdained by research-oriented psychologists. In 1951 Maslow moved to the newly-established Brandeis University near Boston; as first chairperson of the psychology department, he fostered the school's growth until 1968. In 1967 – 68, he also served as President of the American Psychological Association – an indication of the influence of his work. He died in 1970.

University of Wisconsin under Harry Harlow. After receiving his doctorate in 1934, he went back to New York to teach psychology at Brooklyn College. In the late 1930s, New York had become a gathering place for a number of European intellectuals, many of whom were fleeing the Nazi rise to power. While teaching, Maslow met a range of scholars who had emigrated from Europe, including distinguished psychoanalysts (Alfred Adler, Karen Horney and Erich Fromm) and Gestalt pioneer Max Wertheimer.

Maslow's ideas evolved significantly over the course of his career. His early training under Harlow taught him the importance of scientific methodology and observation, and exposed him to the work of social anthropologists. His contacts with Wertheimer and other Gestalt psychologists, however, led him to see the importance of viewing the whole person, not just single responses. World War II seemed to emphasize to him how little psychology had contributed to solving social problems and he began to focus on social psychology and personality theory, eventually even applying psychology to business. He was also influenced by psychoanalysis, both through his contacts with therapists like Fromm and Horney, and by his own experience of psychoanalysis. In fact, in the early 1950s, he saw psychoanalysis as the best therapeutic approach available. However, he gradually became disenchanted with the emphasis on innate influences and past experience in the Freudian approach. By the late 1960s, he had rejected the gloomy determinism of Freud in favour of what he called the 'Third Force' in psychology (psychoanalysis and behaviourism being the first two). In a well-known quote, he stated, 'To oversimplify the matter somewhat, it is as if Freud supplied to us the sick half of psychology, and we must now fill it out with the healthy half' (Maslow 1968, p. 5).

'The healthy half' in fact became the primary focus of Maslow's work, as he strove to describe and understand the limits of human potential. He referred to this potential in terms of *self-actualization*, the full utilization of a person's talents and capacities (self-actualization will be discussed in detail below). To Maslow, this focus on healthy people, in contrast to Freud's emphasis on pathology, was the proper subject matter for psychology. While he preferred to avoid doctrinaire disagreements between approaches, he commented in an interview not long before his death, 'We shouldn't have to say "humanistic psychology". The adjective should be unnecessary' (Hall 1968, p. 57). This was said, not as a rejection of other approaches, but with the conviction that psychology must ultimately concern itself with the betterment of human life – that is, 'humanistic' as a concern with humanity. In his writings, most notably *Toward a Psychology of Being* (1968) and *Motivation and Personality* (1970), Maslow developed a theory of personality based on his ideas and experiences.

Motivation and the Hierarchy of Needs

At the core of Maslow's theory is a description of basic human needs, which he saw as influencing every aspect of our behaviour. This emphasis on motivation seems to reflect the influence of psychodynamic models on Maslow's thinking. However, unlike the two basic drives which Freud described, Maslow saw a whole constellation of needs which could influence our behaviour. Before considering these needs in a formal way, let us consider an example.

In our society, work forms a central part of our lives. Every now and then, most of us entertain fantasies about receiving a monetary windfall, and quitting our job. Yet, studies show many lottery winners keep working. If people buy lottery tickets in hopes of quitting work, why don't they quit when they win? In order to understand, Maslow would suggest we look at the person's needs. The most basic need fulfilled by working is having the money to buy food, shelter, clothing and other necessities for survival. At the same time, working can fulfil other kinds of needs. Most people work in jobs that involve various kinds of human interaction; often, co-workers become friends. In this sense, working can satisfy social needs for contact with others; some lottery winners may continue working because they want to preserve these relationships. In addition, successful job performance (whether as a custodian or a neuro-surgeon) provides feelings of competence, which can foster both self-esteem and recognition from others. Lottery winners, like many retirees, often fear the loss of meaning in their lives if they no longer have a job to perform. In some cases, a person may even enjoy their job – it may provide opportunities for creative challenge and self-expression. (This can be as true of a salesperson or electrician as an artist or writer – it is only the *form* which creativity takes which differs.) If this is the case, a lottery winner may see no reason to stop an activity which gives them satisfaction. Thus, what seems to be a simple situation on the surface, may in fact be very complex. Ultimately, only the individual can determine what course of action will best fulfil their needs.

hierarchy of needs   Maslow's model of basic human needs, which he saw as organized in a hierarchical structure; needs range from physiological (most basic) to self-actualization (top of hierarchy).

Maslow recognized the complexity of motivation, and sought to describe it in terms of a **hierarchy of needs** – a hierarchical structure of different types of needs (see Figure 6.1).

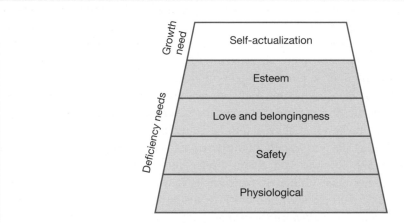

Figure 6.1 Maslow's Hierarchy of Needs Maslow's theory states that more basic needs must be fulfilled before higher needs become significant – hence the pyramid, with the most basic needs at the bottom. The higher up the pyramid one goes, the more advanced the needs, and the more variable their expression. Self-actualization, unlike the other needs, is not triggered by a deficit, but is growth-oriented instead.

- *Physiological needs.* The most basic needs are those which are linked to survival – the physio-logical needs for food, air, sleep and so forth. When these needs are unfulfilled, nothing else matters. As Maslow put it, 'It is quite true that man lives by bread alone – when there is no bread' (Maslow 1970, p. 38). Once these needs are fulfilled, other types of needs are experienced.

- *Safety needs.* The next level of needs are safety needs, which relate to both physical (freedom from danger) and psychological (stability, order) safety. Thus, earthquake victims will con-tinue to feel safety needs long after the quake itself is over, because of the disruption of their ordinary routine. Similarly, a worker who feels that their job is threatened by a corporate restructuring will experience a high safety need. However, when these needs are being met, we begin to focus on the next level of needs.

- *Love and belongingness needs.* The next level of needs are related to love and belongingness: giving and receiving acceptance and affection. (Sex would be a physiological need, but can play a role in the development of love.) These needs are normally met through our interactions with family and friends; however, it requires little insight to recognize that not all family relationships are fulfilling. So, too, there are many people, especially in large cities, who often feel lonely and isolated. Dating clubs, personal ads and similar phenomena are an expression of such needs.

- *Esteem needs.* Assuming the needs for love and belongingness are fulfilled, then the individual will experience esteem needs – a feeling of self-respect and the sense of being competent at what one does, as well as receiving regard from others. It is interesting to note that Maslow regarded love as more basic than self-esteem; perhaps this is why individuals sometimes are drawn into relationships which offer affection only at the cost of self-respect. In any event, esteem needs are secondary to love and belongingness, and consequently less likely to be satisfied.

deficiency motives in Maslow's theory, needs whose motivating power is triggered by the absence of the underlying requirements, such as the physiological or esteem needs.

metaneeds in Maslow's theory, need states which are based on a desire to grow rather than an underlying deficiency; expressed as the need for self-actualization.

self-actualization for Maslow, self-actualization is the most advanced human need, and is based on the desire to grow and use one's capacities to their fullest; as such, it is process-oriented, not based on an underlying deficiency

All of the above needs reflect **deficiency motives** – that is, we are driven to satisfy them by the *absence* of the underlying requirements. In this sense, they are similar to behaviourist notions of drive motivation, and also psychodynamic concepts of motivation, both of which assume that behaviour is triggered by an underlying deficiency. However, many human activities seem to involve no intrinsic need – hobbies, for example, may have no clearly defined function other than 'having fun'. Freud attempted to deal with this problem by suggesting that drives can be satisfied in *symbolic* ways – for example, collecting stamps may reflect an anal fixation. Maslow rejected both the convoluted nature of such explanations, and also the underlying assumption that all behaviour must be based on fulfilling a deficiency. Instead, he argued for **metaneeds**, based on a *growth motive*, which he called **self-actualization**.

- *Self-actualization.* As a metaneed, self-actualization is based on using one's capacities to their fullest. Much like Rogers's actualizing tendency, self-actualization is an expression of the potential for growth which is part of all life. Not being based on a deficiency, it can also never be fully satisfied; unlike other needs, the expression of self-actualization is a process, not a goal. It is expressed through the moment-to-moment experiences of living, of facing challenges to one's abilities, and of interacting with the world in all its diverse aspects.

As noted, the structure of needs was seen as a hierarchy, rather than as simply a collection of equally important motivational states. Maslow believed that the needs differed in several ways: The more basic the need (for example, physiological), the more powerfully it is experienced, and the more difficult it is to suppress or ignore. For this reason, the most basic needs, like hunger, are universally experienced, whereas the higher needs (esteem, and particularly self-actualization) are less commonly experienced (see Figure 6.1). To put it in simple terms, a person who is starving is not likely to worry about whether they are being creative. Hence, a person will only experience higher needs when the more basic ones have been satisfied.

Taken in the most literal form, the notion of a hierarchy of needs seems to contradict reality: for example, it cannot explain why a parent would sacrifice their own life to save the life of their child, since physiological survival should be more potent than love. Maslow attempted to deal with such contradictions by suggesting that the hierarchy is not completely rigid: different needs may vary in intensity across individuals, and more than one need can be experienced at a given time. Normally we do not experience higher needs until more basic ones have been fulfilled, but, once experienced, the higher needs may become salient for a particular person. This qualification would account for parental sacrifice, as well as an artist who would rather live in poverty than compromise their creative aspirations by producing 'popular' art. Even so, most people will rarely, if ever, experience a strong need for self-actualization, because the circumstances of life prevent the lower needs from ever being satisfied. Whether one considers poverty in underdeveloped countries, or loneliness in major cities, the complexity of our deficiency needs can be hard to satisfy. Even if the basic needs are satisfied, the comparative weakness of the need for self-actualization can make it easy to ignore.

Needs and Self-development

Maslow saw understanding the nature of our needs as an important part of self-development, since the various needs can affect all aspects of our lives. For instance, deciding to make a career change can involve physiological needs ('Will I have money to live on if I don't get a new job?'), safety needs ('Will I have to move?'), belongingness ('What about my friendships at my old job?'), esteem ('Will I be recognized for my abilities?') and self-actualization ('Will this alleviate the boredom I've been feeling at work?'). Given the wide-ranging impact of our needs, it should not be surprising that they influence all aspects of our lives, including our perceptions. Maslow suggested that when deficiency needs are dominant, we tend to see the world in terms of objects that can satisfy the dominant need. Hence, a hungry person will pause before a restaurant and see only the food; a person concerned with esteem will focus on the decor and perceived status of the restaurant. In each case, perception is distorted according to the dominant need. (Compare this notion to Freud's view of how distortions of reality arise.) By contrast, a person experiencing the need for self-actualization is likely to see the world more accurately, because objects are seen in relation to themselves, not as a means of fulfilling a deficiency. (For some further examples of how needs and behaviour interact, see Box 6.3.)

In the same way, the frustrations we experience depend on which needs are dominant. A person with unsatisfied safety needs may complain about unsafe working conditions and a lack of job security; a person who 'has everything' (in terms of deficiency needs) may nonetheless feel unfulfilled, and see life as devoid of meaning – an expression of the self-actualization need. In fact, Maslow saw such complaints as an indication of a basically healthy state, since they imply that the deficiency needs are more or less fulfilled. Like Rogers, Maslow did not view aggression as an innate drive, but rather as a possible response to frustration of one's needs; in a healthy person living in a benign environment, aggression should not occur.

The relationship between needs and the environment is an important factor in understanding the behaviour of an individual. For example, a person may be irritable and antagonistic at work, despite being well paid and secure in their position. How are we to make sense of this? Maslow would suggest that it is only possible to understand the dynamics of this behaviour by exploring the situation thoroughly. Is the job itself boring? Are there unfulfilled aspirations at play? How do co-workers react to the person? If it turns out that significant needs are not being met in the work situation, then one could argue that the environment is at fault. However, this does not mean that the individual should accept the situation passively.

Box 6.3 Interactions of Needs and Behaviour

Depending on what need is dominant, we engage in different behaviours to satisfy the need. Being unable to satisfy a need leads to deficiencies; sometimes people will show maladaptive ways of responding to needs, resulting in pathology. (*Note that, as a meta-need, self-actualization is open-ended.)

Need	Means of satisfying	Effect of deprivation	Pathology associated with need
Physiological	Hunger – eat a meal	Malnutrition, illness	Over-eating; anorexia
Safety	Get a good job	Anxiety, insecurity	Phobias
Love and belonging	Fall in love, Join a club	Loneliness	Anti-social personality
Esteem	Receive praise or an award	Feeling inferior or worthless	Depression
Self-actualization	Create a sculpture, help others*	Boredom, life seeming meaningless	Cynicism, alienation

Although the environment may be the source of the problem, Maslow did not see individuals as simply victims of circumstances. Whereas the deterministic notions of the behaviourists might lead to saying 'it's not my fault' and giving up, Maslow believed an individual has a responsibility to strive for growth and self-actualization, regardless of circumstances. Self-actualization is not simply a natural unfolding, but an active process that often involves making choices and overcoming obstacles. In this sense, his views echo Carl Rogers's ideas about individual autonomy. In the case above, the individual must carefully assess the situation, to determine an appropriate course of action: can the job conditions be changed? Is it worth changing jobs? Only by identifying what needs are not being met, can the person hope to find a workable solution.

One of the things which can interfere with recognizing, and therefore satisfying, one's needs is *cultural conditioning*. In modern western society, we are taught to focus on material sources of satisfaction, which are associated primarily with physiological and safety needs. By comparison, love and esteem are seen as secondary, and personal growth has been almost completely ignored (to the extent that esteem is acknowledged, it also tends to be addressed in material terms – i.e., 'status symbols'). As a consequence, we have been conditioned to interpret the behaviour of others through a schema which emphasizes the lower needs. For example, employee relations are often seen by managers in very limited ways. Consider the case of an airline which several years ago was going through financial difficulties, and was seeking cooperation from the employee unions for various cutbacks. At the same time that the management was seeking employee support, they informed employees of lay-offs by posting names on company bulletin boards! Not surprisingly, the efforts to win union support for cutbacks failed, sending the airline into bankruptcy. The company president spoke of the 'greed' of the employees, assuming they were concerned with physiological and safety needs, while completely ignoring the issues of higher esteem needs raised by the insensitive way the lay-offs were handled.

The tendency to view satisfaction of needs in material ways can be seen in other behaviours. Thus, someone who has been rejected by a lover may go shopping to try to ease the pain. Similarly, we tend to view a person who is well-off financially as 'having everything', but in Maslow's view, this could still mean that many needs are unmet. For example, the person may be going through a marital crisis, or suffer from low self-esteem. Even if the individual's love and esteem needs are met, self-actualization may be completely lacking.

In broader terms, a focus on consumerism may actually interfere with recognizing and fulfilling our real needs (McCarthy 2004). Having been raised to focus on material sources of satisfaction, which originally were associated only with the lower needs, we tend to evaluate needs in these terms, both for ourselves and in perceiving others. Unfortunately, while money can buy food and shelter, it cannot buy love or respect, and so these needs can continue to go unsatisfied. Ironically, in emphasizing material forms of satisfaction, and successfully finding ways to fulfil them, western society has actually made it more likely that people will satisfy material goals – only to end up asking themselves, 'Is that all there is to life?'

Try it Yourself

What needs are important to you at this point your life? Where in the hierarchy do they fit? Do you perceive needs which don't fit within Maslow's hierarchy? One issue to consider is that people sometimes mislabel their needs. For example, Pierre claims that he 'needs' a new car, even though his old car still runs perfectly well. He contends that a new car would satisfy his safety needs. But is that the real reason? Is it possible that, deep down, he wants to buy a new automobile to fulfil his esteem needs? (One indicator would be whether Pierre would be satisfied buying a basic, low-cost vehicle, or insists on getting a fancy car that he can't really afford.) Examine your own needs in this light – only you can determine where, on Maslow's hierarchy, they really fit.

Self-actualization and Peak Experiences

Self-actualization is a complex need, whose nature sometimes seems hard to grasp. Kurt Goldstein, from whom Maslow borrowed the term, saw it as a drive to actualize one's capacities, which is found in every organism (Goldstein 1939). Unlike basic drives such as hunger, which seem focused on reducing tension, Goldstein noted that self-actualization often involves *increasing* tension, as when we seek out new situations to master. Rather than representing a tranquil state of rest, self-actualization can be a painful process of struggle in order to grow. Despite this, we are driven to stretch ourselves, to reach new limits, whether they be physical (like an athlete) or mental (like a novelist). For example, many of us would not willingly choose a job which was repetitive and boring, even if the pay were high; a job that was challenging and interesting would be preferable, even if lower-paying. As Maslow said, in words that echo Goldstein, 'capacities clamor to be used' (Maslow 1968, p. 152).

While struggle seems to be a common circumstance in life, self-actualization is not. Indeed, Maslow estimated that only 1 per cent of people ever really experience the need. Yet, for those who do, it can alter profoundly the individual's perceptions of the world, and the way they relate to others. How can the rest of us understand this type of experience? One way that Maslow used was to discuss peak experiences.

peak experience for Maslow, a transient experience of deep intensity which involves enhanced awareness, often accompanied by feelings of being 'fully alive'.

Peak experiences represent moments of deep intensity in which we feel ourselves most fully alive. Such moments may occur when a parent first sees their new-born child, while viewing a great work of art, enjoying the beauty of nature, or in any of a myriad of other ways (Maslow 1964). Maslow believed that such experiences provide a glimpse of what it really means to be self-actualized. In contrast to the sense of routine and drabness that sometimes seems to pervade everyday life, peak experiences represent moments of intense joy and excitement, coupled with a sense of fully living, of being truly *part* of the world. Lovers in the first glow of romance often have this feeling, as do religious mystics; Maslow saw both as examples of peak experiences. Curiously, such moments can even come in the face of adversity, as in the aftermath of a natural disaster, or following the death of a close friend. Whatever the circumstances, peak experiences are perceived as moments of insight into the potential of life.

Peak experiences by nature are both unexpected and relatively short-lived; they seem to come and go unexpectedly, regardless of the individual's desires. While they last, they are typically very intense and clearly distinct from ordinary living. Yet these characteristics also set these experiences apart from self-actualization, which is a less intense, ongoing process. Instead, peak experiences are more like a mystical rapture, reminiscent of the Zen experience of *satori*, or enlightenment. Zen practitioners may discipline themselves for years, seeking the moment of enlightenment, without any assurance about when, or even if, it will come. When it does, it is often experienced as an intense rapture, a feeling of suddenly being fully awake for the first time. Yet, like peak experiences, this feeling often fades somewhat after the initial rapture.

plateau experience for Maslow, an experience which produces an intensified awareness of the world, and a heightened appreciation for life; a more enduring but less intense state of enhanced awareness than a peak experience.

A longer-lasting form of heightened awareness occurs in what Maslow called plateau experiences. A **plateau experience** is a more enduring but less intense state of awareness than a peak experience (see Figure 6.2). One of the primary characteristics of a plateau experience is a change in one's perceptions of the world. The experience produces an intensified awareness of one's surroundings, and a heightened appreciation for life (Maslow, in Krippner 1972). Maslow came to this point of view as a way of accounting for more enduring changes than those of peak experiences, but also because of his own experience. After suffering a heart attack late in life, he found himself more deeply aware of the transience of human life, and this led to a profound change in his own view of the world. Commenting on this, he once remarked, 'If I could teach a person only one thing, it would be to live each day as if it were the last day of their life.' The point, of course, is not that if we're dying, nothing matters; rather, it is that if we are about to die, how we spend our last moments matters very much.

The transcendence of ordinary perceptions which occurs in peak and plateau experiences is not always part of self-actualization. All three concepts emphasize the sense of living to the fullest, but some people seem to live productive, self-actualized lives without ever experiencing the shift of awareness characteristic of peak and plateau experiences. Conversely, some people seem to have peak experiences, without ever being able to integrate this insight into a process of self-actualizing. In essence, self-actualization requires an overall balance and satisfaction of lower needs, not just a sudden insight (this view obviously contradicts the idea, expressed in some books and workshops, that brief experiences can radically change one's life). Hence, the transcendent awareness of peak and plateau experiences is neither a requirement nor a defining characteristic for self-actualization. Even so, Maslow believed that those self-actualizers who *did* have such experiences were more likely to be creative, and to see life as magical or miraculous. It is also worth noting that the transcendence associated with peak and plateau experiences does not preclude involvement in everyday affairs: 'You can run a grocery store and pay the bills, but still carry on this sense (of the mystical) ...' (Maslow, in Krippner 1972, p. 115).

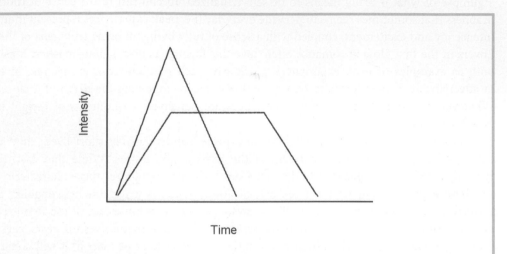

Figure 6.2 Peak vs. Plateau Experiences In Maslow's view, peak experiences are intense but relatively brief: by contrast, plateau experiences are not as intense, but the positive effects tend to persist significantly longer.

Try it Yourself

Have you ever had an experience that you would describe as a peak experience? If you have, did it seem to arise because of a particular situation, or did it arise without a clear cause? If it was triggered by a particular situation, was it a positive moment, or not? As Maslow recognized, sometimes even negative situations provoke peak experiences. For example, adults whose parents die often report that although they grieve greatly, the bereavement has made them more loving and appreciative of their remaining families and friends, and more determined to fulfil their own potential (Marshall 2004; Petersen and Rafuls 1998; Pope 2005). Peak experiences seem to lead individuals to be more intensely aware of life, and even loss can lead someone to transcend purely personal concerns and relate more openly and appreciatively to life and to the people around them.

Maslow's Concept of Healthy Growth

Self-actualization refers to making full use of one's talents and capacities (Maslow 1970). Yet, in order for such a description to be meaningful, one must have some idea of what constitutes 'full use' – that is, one must have a conception of the *goal* of growth and development. Maslow recognized this, and tried to describe this goal by studying the lives of individuals whom he regarded as highly self-actualized. He began with the examples of two of his own teachers, Ruth Benedict and Max Wertheimer, both of whom seemed to show high levels of fulfilment in both their professional and personal lives. Over time, he expanded the study, eventually basing his description on 18 people – 9 of whom were contemporaries and 9 of whom were historical figures. Among the latter were Jane Adams, Albert Einstein, Abraham Lincoln and Eleanor

Roosevelt. (It should be noted that one does not have to be famous to be self-actualized; Maslow chose historical examples in part because they would be familiar to most readers.)

Maslow's rationale for this methodology was that he was interested in the psychology of healthy people, and that outstanding individuals would provide the best possible indicator of what it means to fulfil one's potential. (This is in marked contrast to Freud, who dealt primarily with pathology, and never developed a clear model of the ideal of adult development.) Based on seeking common characteristics in the lives of the 18 individuals, Maslow proposed a list of characteristics of self-actualized people (see Box 6.4). The list is rather daunting, and is apt to make one question whether *any* person could meet such standards. However, in proposing this description, Maslow was offering an ideal, which no individual would fully achieve – each would show some characteristics more strongly than others. Indeed, in describing these characteristics, Maslow commented, 'There are no perfect human beings! Persons can be found who are good, very good indeed, in fact, great ... And yet these very same people can at times be boring, irritating, petulant, selfish, angry, or depressed.' For example, Oskar Schindler, the subject of a popular book and movie, sacrificed his considerable wealth to save the lives of over a thousand Jews during World War II – yet he was also a womanizer and con-artist (Keneally 1982).

While suggesting that the characteristics he identified represent a sort of ideal for human growth, Maslow also noted that an ideal is a static concept, and self-actualization is itself not a static thing. Rather than being an *end*, a fixed goal which one can reach, Maslow emphasized that in fact self-actualization is a *process*, for which there is never an end. Like a journey, our lives can encompass detours and even backwards movement; what matters is what we do along the way, not the destination. Seen in this way, it is understandable that no one person will show all of these characteristics all of the time.

Nonetheless, the attempt to define self-actualization in terms of an ideal of human development has drawn a number of criticisms. One concern is that Maslow's only basis of judgement was from what could be publicly observed of individuals. In some sense, this contradicts the most

Box 6.4 *Characteristics of Self-actualized Individuals*

Like Rogers, Maslow believed that healthy individuals would come to show certain characteristics. This list is based on his study of a group of famous individuals (see text for details). Compare this list to Box 6.2. (Adapted from Maslow 1970)

1 More efficient perception of reality
2 Acceptance (of self, others and world)
3 Spontaneity and naturalness
4 Problem-centred rather than ego-centred
5 Need for privacy and being detached from situations
6 Independence from both cultural and environmental influences
7 Freshness of appreciation of all experience
8 Having mystical or peak experiences
9 Feelings of kinship to others
10 Deep relationships with others
11 Democratic attitudes
12 Distinguishing between means and ends, good and evil
13 Philosophical, not hostile, sense of humour
14 Self-actualizing forms of creativity
15 Forming attitudes and values independently of culture

fundamental assumption of the humanistic approach, which is that behaviour is only meaningful from the individual's own perspective. Would the people on Maslow's list have considered themselves to be self-actualized? If Maslow could have 'walked in their boots', would he still have considered them to be self-actualized? Since Maslow could not see inside their minds, he contented himself with dealing with the public perception of their lives, knowing that his goal in compiling his list was to illustrate what self-actualization was, not to glorify individuals.

Another obvious concern is that in selecting individuals for his sample, Maslow was selecting those who exhibited the traits he hoped to find, and that therefore the process was both biased and circular. That is, these individuals met the criteria for self-actualization that Maslow set. Maslow himself claimed to be surprised at the similarities he found, but one cannot rule out unconscious bias. Even without assuming such bias, there are concerns. Maslow wished to believe that the named characteristics, and the values associated with them, somehow stem from the very essence of human nature: 'Some values are common to all (healthy) mankind' (Maslow 1970, p. 150). Culture, he thought, could 'warp or suppress or build upon' the individual's potential, but does not change the fundamental nature of human beings (Hoffman 1989). Clearly, Maslow believed that his criteria for self-actualization were valid. Yet, he also recognized that individuals differ in many ways, which could affect their actions and values: 'To the extent that capacities differ, so will values also differ' (Maslow 1970, p. 152). Hence, he was caught in the conundrum of arguing for a universal ideal, while simultaneously acknowledging that great variability exists among individuals. In essence, he seemed to say that his criteria for self-actualization were valid for everyone while not valid for some!

As we have already discussed with Rogers's theory, the attempt to identify universal values is a complex issue. Maslow seemed to argue that the nature of self-actualization is independent of culture. For example, he proposes that *resistance to cultural influences* is one of the characteristics of self-actualized people. Thus, Oskar Schindler, by not accepting the Nazi view of Jews, was showing a form of self-actualization. But does this make every societal rebel self-actualized? And if the overall culture does accept the values of the individual, does this mean that the individual is not self-actualized? Clearly the answer to both questions is no. If societal acceptance or non-acceptance (including Maslow's acceptance or non-acceptance) is not a criterion for self-actualization, couldn't it be argued that self-actualization is whatever each person thinks it is? And if so, is Maslow's definition anything more than a reflection of his own values? As one critic put it, 'The question of just what is "natural" to man is, of course, the most vexed in the history of thought, and cannot be settled even by something as lofty as "the universal experience of clinicians" (Robinson 1979, p. 257). Obviously, this line of reasoning poses a problem for Maslow's view, and he tries to avoid this conclusion by pointing to cross-cultural commonalities for certain characteristics and values. For example, studies he did with the Blackfoot tribe in Canada in 1938 convinced him that human nature transcends culture. Although Rogers and others have argued for similar values and characteristics as Maslow (compare Boxes 6.2 and 6.4), it is unclear whether this is truly an expression of 'human nature', or simply a consensus of like-minded people.

Reviewing the available cross-cultural research indicates that Maslow may be at least partly correct (see, for example, Baumeister and Leary 1995; Inglehart 1990; Sheldon and Kasser 2001), although the evidence is not entirely consistent. For example, a study of Maslow's needs done in China argued that belongingness was seen as more basic than physiological needs, and that self-actualization was perceived in terms of contributions to the group, not individual development (Nevis 1983). By contrast, studies of subjective feelings of well-being have indicated that, for the most part, the same kinds of factors (such as satisfaction with friends and family) affect the ratings people make, independent of culture (Diener *et al.* 2003). This implies that sources of satisfaction may in fact be fairly universal. Hence, at present one cannot draw a final conclusion about the universality of Maslow's framework (for a further discussion of the role of culture, see Box 6.5).

In the end, Maslow's ideas have proved influential more because of their capacity to inspire than for their empirical foundation. If one compares his work to that of Carl Rogers, one finds that Rogers has made a more concerted effort to validate his ideas through research. This is

---

Box 6.5 *Culture and Concepts of Self*

Does culture affect an individual's experiences and values? And if so, does this affect the person's sense of self? While many researchers have asked questions like these, answering them is not easy. First, one has to clarify what 'self' refers to. As noted in Box 6.1, psychologists have tended to use the term in two ways, with humanists emphasizing the subjective, experiencing self (what William James called the self as 'I'). However, research typically has focused on 'self-concept', which is closer to the objective, reflexive self which James called the self as 'me'.

Because the objective self can be influenced by others' attitudes and expectations, researchers have looked for differences in self-concept in terms of *individualism* vs. *collectivism*. To say that a culture is individualistic means that it emphasizes personal rights and freedoms; by contrast, a collectivist culture is one that emphasizes a person's connections and obligations to the social group (family, society, etc.). A number of studies have suggested that many western societies (particularly the USA) are primarily individualistic, whereas many Eastern societies (particularly China) are collectivist (Markus and Kitayama 1991; Price and Crapo 2002). Consistent with this, many studies have found that Europeans and Americans tend to focus on personal identity in defining their self-concept, while Koreans, Japanese and Chinese tend to define self-concept more in terms of social relationships. However, a recent review by Daphna Oyserman and her colleagues presents a more complex picture (Oyserman *et al.* 2002). Because various studies measure individualism vs. collectivism and self-concept in different ways, Oyserman argues that it is not clear that cultural difference is the appropriate explanation of observed differences in self-concept. In addition, since 'self-concept' is closer to the interpretive, objective self than the experiential, subjective self, this research cannot directly answer whether culture affects the 'self' in the sense that humanists use the term.

While the objective/subjective split in discussing the self has persisted for more than 100 years in psychology (see Westen 1992, and Singer's 1992 reply), there are other ways of thinking of the self. For example, consider the self as seen in Mahayana Buddhism, which has a long history in Tibet, China, Japan and Korea, and is the basis of Zen Buddhism (Page and Berkow 1991). According to Mahayana Buddhism, one can distinguish between the lesser self and the greater self. The lesser self is the ego that we are aware of, our day-to-day consciousness which includes our feelings, our attitudes and our behaviours. This self is also the source of feelings of separateness from the world, and the goal of life is to transcend this lesser self, and to identify ourselves with the greater self, or the Cosmic Whole. To fully develop, then, we must abandon the notion that we are an individual self. Hence, both the self as 'me' and the self as 'I' are seen as distortions to be transcended. While Maslow saw transcendence as a possible aspect of self-actualization, he did not see it as central in the way that Mahayana Buddhism does. However, it is worth noting that similar themes arise in Islamic Sufism (Shah 1981) and even Judaism (Buber 1958). Given that millions of people across the globe are following these traditions, one cannot lightly dismiss the relevance of such concepts as an influence on behaviour. While the objective self favoured by social psychologists may have the advantage of being easier to measure, clearly 'self' can mean different things to different people, and in different places.

somewhat ironic, since Maslow began as an experimental psychologist, while Rogers began as a divinity student. Maslow also poses a contradiction when compared to psychodynamic theorists. While he rejected the pessimism and determinism of Freud, his own theory, like Freud's, rests on a foundation of analysing fundamental human needs. In one sense, he incorporated elements from various psychodynamic theorists – Freud for physiological needs, Horney for safety and love, and Adler for esteem. To this structure, Maslow then added self-actualization. In doing so, he clearly made a shift from pathology to growth, as he intended. However, to reach the level of self-actualization, one must satisfy the lower needs, and clearly there are echoes of the psychodynamic approach in the lower needs of his hierarchy.

In one sense, the similarities between Maslow's theory and the psychodynamic approach should not really surprise us: while each approach to psychology has its own perspective, the subject matter – human behaviour – is common to all. Consequently, some convergence of descriptions would seem inevitable. At the same time, the distinctive elements of Maslow's work – the capacity to adapt in meeting our needs, the emphasis on self-actualization – make it clearly humanistic, not psychodynamic. In domains as disparate as personality theory and diplomacy, Maslow's ideas live on.

Try it Yourself

When I (MH) was 12 years old, I told my great-grandmother that I was 'mature'. My great-grandmother responded, 'Really? I'm 86 years old and I'm not. But I'm working on it.' If someone said to you, 'I'm self-actualized,' would you believe them? Why or why not? Given that self-actualization is a process, not an end, do you think a self-actualized person would make such a statement?

Do you know anyone personally whom you would consider highly self-actualized? What leads you to think so? Do their values seem consistent with Maslow's description? If you can, talk to them – do they consider themselves to be self-actualized?

EXTENDING THE HUMANISTIC APPROACH

As noted at the beginning of this chapter, the humanistic approach has no single theoretical founder. Instead, it encompasses a number of theorists, of whom Rogers and Maslow are simply the best known. Within the approach, each theorist uses a somewhat different vocabulary, and tends to emphasize slightly different concepts and issues. What lends coherence to the approach is a set of shared *assumptions* – a belief that behaviour can only be understood through an individual's subjective experience, and a belief in choice rather than determinism. In order to better understand this unity within diversity, we will briefly consider another viewpoint which shares many of the characteristics of the humanistic approach: existential psychology, particularly as seen in *Frankl's logotherapy*. In addition, we will look at a framework which originates from outside the humanistic tradition, but which nonetheless shares a concern with fostering human potential: *positive psychology*.

Existential Psychology

The origins of existential psychology lie in early twentieth-century philosophy. In the wake of World War I, with its horrors for both soldiers and civilians, European philosophers began to question whether life had any objectively definable purpose or meaning. Thinkers like Jean-Paul

Sartre (1948) argued that life has no purpose, except what an individual gives it through their actions. Sartre felt that individuals are capable of making choices about how they live, and that those choices are what create meaning.

existentialism a twentieth-century philosophical movement concerned with the meaning of individual existence in a universe which lacks objective meaning or purpose.

The work of Sartre and similar philosophers, known as **existentialism**, influenced a number of psychologists, particularly therapists, in the period after World War II. As they shared ideas and insights, existential psychology developed, based on the same general premises as existentialist philosophy (May 1961). If you recall the introduction to this chapter, Sartre's view may seem familiar, since the humanistic psychologists also believe that individuals are capable of making choices, and that the meaning of behaviour is subjective. In this sense, there is clearly an overlap between existentialist and humanistic viewpoints. (In fact, Rollo May's early book, *Existential Psychology* (1961), included contributions by Rogers and Maslow!) The primary difference is the emphasis which the existentialists place on the issue of meaning. The human capacity for awareness means that we are capable of reflecting on both our own lives and the world around us. Out of this comes two major realizations: first, that both we and those we love will inevitably die; and second, that suffering is an unavoidable part of life. What, then, makes life worth living?

Addressing this question is the central focus for existential psychologists. Not surprisingly, they do not see simple answers. Instead, they see many problems that individuals have as being the result of failing to resolve the issue of meaning. Irvin Yalom, an existential therapist, says that anxiety is a result of trying to cope with the painful realities of suffering and death, not repressed desires or childhood traumas (Yalom 1980). Ernest Becker, another existential theorist, argues that acknowledging the reality of death is so threatening that cultures foster beliefs and values which symbolically deny the reality of death (Becker 1973). Some existential theorists see Becker's view affirmed in the way other approaches in psychology ignore the issues of suffering and death. For example, it seems unsurprising that some elderly people feel concerns about coming to terms with their approaching death. Yet, instead of dealing with this, developmental researchers tend to focus on issues like how cognitive abilities change with ageing (Vandenberg 1993).

Like Sartre, existential psychologists believe there is no universal answer to the questions of suffering and death, and no universal meaning to life. Instead, it is up to each individual to find their own meaning. This may seem like a very grim conception of life, far from the optimism of Rogers or Maslow. Yet in the end, the existential viewpoint shares more than simply the basic assumptions of the humanists. As we will see with Frankl, existential psychology asserts that finding meaning is the path to healthy development.

Frankl's Logotherapy

In some ways, Viktor Frankl's life parallels that of Sigmund Freud. Both were Jewish and both went to the University of Vienna to study medicine, with an initial interest in neurology. However, there are also many differences, beginning with the fact that Frankl was born when Freud was already in middle age (Frankl was born in 1905, when Freud was 56). In addition, while Frankl was interested in neurology, he soon changed his focus to the treatment of mental illness; he also earned a doctorate in philosophy along with his medical degree. While exposed to Freud's ideas during his early training, he gradually evolved his own framework, which rejected many of the assumptions of Freudian analysis. Rather than the drives of sexuality and aggression, Frankl felt the most important motive for human behaviour was the desire to find a meaning for life.

This belief was greatly strengthened by Frankl's incarceration in Nazi concentration camps. While there, he saw some inmates survive seemingly insurmountable horrors while others appeared to give up and died in a short period of time. He concluded that the difference between these people was in the way that some found a meaning and purpose to go on living while others didn't.

logotherapy Viktor Frankl's theory of development and therapy, which is based on the argument that finding a meaning for life is central to individual growth and happiness.

Frankl is probably best known for his book *Man's Search for Meaning* (Frankl 1992). Originally, he intended to publish it as an anonymous memoir of his experiences in the concentration camps, but ultimately decided that it required a personal framework to be meaningful. Even so, it was not initially meant as a full exposition of his theoretical ideas. (Its original English title was *From Death-camp to Existentialism*.) However, the book proved remarkably popular, and over four editions, the theoretical background, which he refered to as **logotherapy**, was gradually expanded.

To understand Frankl's theory, and how it fits into the humanistic approach, let us consider his view of some of the basic assumptions. Like Rogers, Frankl argued against the determinism found in both behaviourism and psychoanalysis: 'Man is *not* fully conditioned and determined but rather determines himself' (Frankl 1992, p. 133). While he grants that there are conditions which limit this freedom, the real issue 'is not freedom from conditions, but it is freedom to take a stand toward these conditions' (p. 132). Even in the concentration camps, individuals could 'choose one's attitude in a given set of circumstances' (p. 9). In this sense, Frankl's views are similar to other humanistic theorists.

A second assumption concerns the value of a *phenomenological framework* in understanding behaviour. At the very outset, he distinguishes between 'facts' and 'experiences'. Facts are objective observations, devoid of subjective context and meaning, while experiences are descriptions which are anchored in an individual's perspective – that is, subjective meaning. While he acknowledged that psychology as a science has traditionally emphasized detached objectivity, he suggested that in trying to understand experiences like those of concentration camp survivors, a

Key Thinker: **Viktor Frankl**

Viktor Frankl (1905–97) was born in Vienna, the son of Orthodox Jewish parents. He was educated at the University of Vienna, where he distinguished himself by earning doctorates in both philosophy and medicine. In medical school, he initially trained in neurology, but found himself drawn to concerns about mental illness. In this sense, his training mirrored an earlier Viennese physician – Sigmund Freud. Like Freud, he faced a threat from the rise to power of the Nazis, and in fact was granted a visa to go to the USA shortly before they entered World War II. However, because his parents were still living in Vienna, and unable to emigrate with him, he chose to stay. Consequently, he was imprisoned after the Nazi takeover of Austria, and spent three years struggling to survive in various concentration camps (primarily the notorious camps at Auschwitz and Dachau) until the end of the war. Only one person in 28 survived in the camps, and the experience was to play a significant role in Frankl's later theorizing. After the war, he became a professor of neurology and psychiatry at the University of Vienna, where he spent the remainder of his career. Frankl died in 1997, having lived through almost the entire twentieth century.

detached observer 'is too far removed to make any statements of real value' (Frankl 1992, p. 20). That is, the meaning of human experience can only be determined by the individual having the experience. Like Rogers, Frankl saw the understanding of meaning as central to understanding behaviour. Thus, his framework is essentially phenomenological.

As the early title of his book (*From Death-camp to Existentialism*) suggests, Frankl's views are also heavily existential. Like Jean-Paul Sartre and other existentialists, he saw the basic issue of life as the challenge of finding meaning in a world which often seems meaningless. For Frankl, however, meaning is not an abstract philosophical issue, nor is it based on some universal principle. Rather, meaning is viewed as a personal outcome which is related both to the immediate context of one's experiences, and to the attitudes one takes towards those experiences. That is, rather than there being a general meaning to life, there is only 'the specific meaning of a person's life at a given moment' (Frankl 1992, p. 113). In this sense, Frankl emphasized the need to focus on the here-and-now of experience (in contrast to psychoanalysis, which tends to emphasize the person's past). While meaning may refer to future possibilities, it can only be derived from the present moment. Like life itself, meaning is changing and transient; rather than existing 'out there', it is created by the individual (such a view, as has been noted, is a familiar feature of humanistic theories).

Like other humanistic theories, logotherapy has its own specific structure and concepts. Not surprisingly, Frankl placed issues of meaning at the centre of his theory. Whereas Freud saw concerns about meaning as being a rationalization of instinctual drives, Frankl argued that 'striving to find a meaning in one's life is the primary motivational force in man' (Frankl 1992, p. 104). In emphasizing the motivational role of meaning, Frankl rejected drive-reduction as being the goal of motivation (as Freud believed). In fact, he suggested that 'mental health is based on a certain degree of tension … between what one is and what one should become' (p. 110). This view also places him in seeming contradiction to Rogers, who suggested that optimal functioning occurs when there is congruence (that is, no conflict) between the self and the ideal self. The open-ended nature of the search for meaning is more like Maslow's conception of self-actualization (which, like Frankl's view of motivation, is not based on tension reduction). However, he saw self-actualization as a 'side-effect' of seeking meaning, 'not an attainable end' in itself (p. 115).

noögenic neuroses in Frankl's theory, conflicts within an individual which are based on existential frustrations, rather than the conflicts of id, ego and superego which Freud saw as the source of anxiety.

Meaning or its absence has profound effects on a person's life, in Frankl's view. In fact, issues of meaning produce what he calls **noögenic neuroses** – conflicts based on existential frustrations (rather than the issues of anxiety which underlie traditional neuroses). Frankl believed that such problems are more common than anxiety neuroses, and criticized psychodynamic theories for ignoring issues of meaning. In one case, he encountered a diplomat who had been through an extended period of therapy, and had been told that his concern about his work reflected unresolved feelings about his father. After only a few sessions with Frankl, the man recognized that his problem was really a dislike for his current career. As a result, he decided to change careers, and five years later, had shown no recurrence of his former problems (Frankl 1992, p. 107)!

While existential concerns are not themselves pathological, they can result in pathology, and Frankl cited examples ranging from aggression to alcoholism. The interaction is seen most clearly in cases of depression (Frankl 1992). At one point, Frankl was working with unemployed individuals (in the economic downturn of the 1930s) who suffered from depression. While he could do nothing to change the economic conditions, Frankl found that those patients who began doing voluntary work for community groups also showed mood improvement. Unemployed individuals, he suggests, may be given social assistance to acquire food and shelter, but this is not the real issue: 'people have enough to live by but nothing to live for' (Frankl 1992, p. 142). (Unfortunately, like most clinical studies, this result is correlational, and consequently one cannot be certain that the voluntary work was the cause of improvement; it may be that only the healthier patients were willing to volunteer, or the result could be coincidental.)

Frankl's view of the interactions between an individual and their surroundings is also different from other humanistic theorists. Ultimately, life has meaning only in terms of the way we relate to our surroundings: 'being human always points, and is directed, to something, or someone, other than oneself.... The more one forgets himself ... the more human he is and the more he actualizes himself' (Frankl 1992, p. 115). Yet, while our relationships to people and things around us can be the source of meaning, they can also be the source of problems. This is clearly evident in the case of those who struggled to survive in the Nazi concentration camps, but can also be true in less extreme circumstances. For example, Frankl suggested that cultural beliefs can negatively influence the search for meaning in ways that may not be obvious. In this regard, he was very critical of modern western culture, suggesting that its belief in determinism (both in science and therapy) has encouraged a feeling that life has no meaning: 'Existential vacuum is the collective neurosis of the present time' (Frankl 1992, p. 131). In this sense, he went beyond Rogers's view (which emphasizes how conditional regard given by others affects growth), suggesting that the factors which distort development can be *cultural* rather than individual.

One of the most interesting aspects of Frankl's theory is his position on the nature of human values. As has been discussed, both Rogers and Maslow argued that certain types of values are intrinsic to any healthy human being. By contrast, Frankl resisted any such notion. Instead of advocating particular values, he argued that it is up to the individual to find meaning by making choices about what matters in life:

> Logotherapy tries to make the patient fully aware of his own responsibleness; therefore, it must leave to him the option for what, to what, or to whom he understands himself to be responsible. That is why a logotherapist is the least tempted of all psychotherapists to impose value judgements on his patients. (Frankl 1992, p. 114)

Rather than imposing values or other beliefs, the therapist's role is to help the individual discover their own values. In a sense, the *process* (though clearly not the concepts used) seems very much like Rogers's notion of providing the appropriate conditions for growth. The person must discover the truth for themselves, but the therapist can help, much the way an ophthalmologist 'tries to enable us to see the world as it really is ... so that the whole spectrum of potential meaning becomes conscious and visible ...' (Frankl 1992, pp. 114–15).

It is possible that Frankl's unwillingness to assert particular values was a reaction to his experiences in the concentration camps – after all, could anyone who lived through such horrors really believe that all people are fundamentally good? Even to survive required suspending conventional notions of morality: when selections were made of those who were to be killed next, 'All that mattered was that one's own name and that of one's friend were crossed off the list of victims, though everyone knew that for each man saved another victim had to be found' (Frankl 1992, p. 18). In such circumstances, it seems hard to claim the high ground of moral superiority; indeed, many survivors were haunted by the implications of having survived. Frankl alluded to this when he said, 'We who have come back ... we know: the best of us did not return' (Frankl 1992, p. 19). Whatever its basis, Frankl's view that values are personal rather than universal means that, in contrast to Rogers and Maslow, he had no fixed value system to defend.

Although Frankl did not argue for a particular meaning to life or a particular set of values, he *did* suggest three ways in which meaning can be *created* in life:

1 *Achievement.* Meaning can be created by doing something, achieving something. For Frankl himself, his focus on his desire to complete a book about his ideas provided the will to live when he was in the concentration camps. Note that, in humanistic fashion, what defines an important achievement is subjective, and hence might differ for different individuals. For example, when first reading Frankl, I (WEG) realized that providing for my family was more important to me than writing a book (including this book)! One person might find meaning in accumulating a million dollars; another might find meaning in raising a million dollars for charity.

2 *Transcendent experience.* In many ways, this is similar to Maslow's concept of peak experiences. Frankl believed that being in love, having an appreciation of the beauty of nature, or other 'transcendent' experiences, could provide a sense that simply being alive has meaning.

3 *Attitude toward unavoidable suffering.* This may seem rather strange, at least in a western context. (By contrast, the 'Four Noble Truths' of Buddhism state that existence is suffering, which is caused by our failure to deal with our desires.) As Frankl noted, our culture seems to emphasize pleasure-seeking and the avoidance of suffering. While this fits well with drive-reduction notions of motivation, it has the consequence of encouraging denial of unpleasant realities, and even makes the experience of suffering degrading. However, there are clearly individuals who face death – such as terminal cancer or AIDS – with grace and calm. For Frankl, their attitude bears witness to 'the uniquely human potential ... when we are no longer able to change a situation ... to change ourselves' (Frankl 1992, p. 116). In his view, 'life has a meaning up to the last moment' (p. 118). Indeed, he would likely be alarmed at the growing interest in euthanasia and assisted suicide, since seeking to terminate life in this manner seems based on the assumption that suffering is not only meaningless, but something to be actively avoided.

Like other existential thinkers, Frankl's ideas are grounded in some of the harshest realities of human experience – suffering, death and the apparent pointlessness of some events (Becker 1973; Yalom 1980). In this sense, his theory strikes a very different emotional tone from the sometimes Pollyanna-like optimism of Rogers and Maslow, who talk of 'unconditional regard' and 'peak experiences'. Consequently, it is all the more interesting that his thinking leads to a similar result – that life is worth living, and we have both the freedom and the responsibility to determine our own actions and their meaning. Of course, this similarity does not provide unequivocal evidence that Frankl's theory is correct; indeed, it suffers from many of the same difficulties of evaluation as the theories of Rogers and Maslow. Nonetheless, logotherapy clearly fits comfortably within the humanistic framework, and Frankl himself provided an inspiring example of finding meaning in life. Despite his harrowing time in the camps, Frankl was optimistic – and if *he* can be, should we not be, too?

Try it Yourself

Have you ever been through a difficult experience which nonetheless had a positive influence on your life? Why was it ultimately positive?

Consider this example: I (MH) once had a student who was denied admission to law school. Bitterly disappointed, he entered a graduate programme in education instead. Years later, he contacted me to say how much he enjoyed teaching in developing countries, and how fulfilling his career was. 'Thank heaven I wasn't accepted to law,' he said. 'That would have been a disaster for me!'

In suggesting that suffering could be a possible source of meaning, Frankl was not saying that we should welcome hurt and pain, but rather that meaning truly lies in how we interpret experience. Frankl found personal meaning even while confronted with the horrors of the concentration camps; can we find meaning in the challenges that *we* face?

Positive Psychology

As we have discussed, humanistic psychologists have long emphasized the importance of developing human potential ('a psychology of health', as Maslow expressed it) – a view which has typically not been shared by other approaches. Recently, however, American psychologist Martin Seligman has expressed a similar concern, and has advocated a focus on what he calls *positive psychology*. This term was first used by Maslow to characterize his approach in his book *Motivation and Personality*, originally published in 1954. To understand what positive psychology is, and how Seligman came to this interest, it is necessary to go back to the early stages of his career in the 1970s. Seligman, an experimental psychologist (see discussion of *preparedness* in Chapter 3), was looking at how dogs reacted when they repeatedly experienced unavoidable aversive

learned helplessness a condition found in animals exposed for prolonged periods to unavoidable aversive stimuli, resulting in passive, 'helpless' behaviour.

stimuli (electric shocks). He found that, while initially they would try to escape, eventually they sank into passivity. Seligman called this phenomenon **learned helplessness**, and it led him to explore how learning might play a role in depression (Seligman 1975). This in turn led him to develop an interest in clinical psychology more generally; over the past 30 years, he has had a distinguished career as a researcher, teacher and clinician. In 1998, he became President of the American Psychological Association (a position based on a vote by association members) and was elected with the largest plurality in any election to date.

Over time, Seligman found his interests moving from a focus on negative aspects of behaviour (learned helplessness and depression) to positive aspects, particularly the role of optimism in psychological health. When he became president of the APA, he used this as an opportunity to create interest in a new psychological focus on the understanding and fostering of healthy development, which he named 'positive psychology'. Garnering support from colleagues, the theme became a focus for several special issues of journals – most notably in the issue of *American Psychologist*, January 2000.

As described in the lead article by Seligman and Mihaly Csikszentmihalyi (2000), positive psychology arose out of a concern with perceived deficiencies in contemporary psychology – particularly the emphasis on mental disorders and human suffering, which they called 'negative psychology'. They argued that this negative focus affected not only clinical attitudes, but also theoretical views and directions for research. As Seligman put it, 'making the lives of all people better, and nurturing genius, were all but forgotten'. Psychology, they argued, should have

Key Thinker: **Martin E. P. Seligman**

Martin E. P. Seligman (1942–) was born in Albany, New York, on 12 August 1942. As an undergraduate, he majored in philosophy at Princeton University, graduating *summa cum laude*. He went to the University of Pennsylvania, receiving his PhD in psychology in only three years. After teaching at Cornell University for three years, he returned to the University of Pennsylvania, first in the department of psychiatry, and then in the department of psychology, where he has remained. A man of broad interests in psychology, he has made contributions in animal learning, the study of depression and optimism, has served as director of the Clinical Training Program in psychology, and served as the primary consultant for a major study on the effectiveness of long-term psychotherapy for consumer reports. A prolific writer and recipient of numerous awards, he served as President of the American Psychological Association in 1998, which led to his current focus on positive psychology. Married, and the father of six children, Seligman continues to be active as Fox Leadership Professor of Psychology at the University of Pennsylvania.

something to contribute to society in terms of the positive: optimism, interpersonal skills, faith and so forth.

In several ways, positive psychology has strong similarities with humanistic psychology. In particular, Seligman and Csikszentmihalyi are concerned with fostering human growth; moreover, they are interested in understanding the subjective experiences which people find positive, such as contentment, hope and satisfaction. They also believe that individuals are not simply pawns of their genes and environment, but can make choices which influence both their surroundings and their experiences. Further, they argue that a science of human beings should not be defined simply by methodology, but should seek to understand both what behaviour is and what it *could be*.

In all these respects, positive psychology shares much with the humanistic theories we have discussed. Indeed, Seligman and Csikszentmihalyi acknowledge the influence of Rogers, Maslow and other humanists. In addition, their sense of dismay that contemporary psychology seems more concerned with pathology than health echoes the reaction of the humanists to the perceived negativity and limitations of the psychodynamic approach and behaviourism in the 1950s and 1960s. However, despite the similarities in concerns and interests, there are also significant distinctions which make the relationship of positive psychology to humanistic theories less clear.

First of all, while acknowledging that subjective experience is relevant to understanding behaviour, positive psychology argues that it is insufficient by itself to develop a scientific understanding of behaviour. Not only does an exclusive focus on subjective experience lead to difficulties in evaluating theories (as we have discussed), but at its worst it opens the door to almost anything dealing with human experience claiming to be part of 'psychology' (crystals, aromatherapy and so forth). In this respect, humanistic psychology is criticized for failing to generate a significant empirical base to underlie its theories, although Carl Rogers maintained a commitment to scientific inquiry. Hence, positive psychologists see a role for subjective reports of experiences, but also argue for quantitative studies (surveys, experiments, etc.) of topics like happiness (see Myers 2000).

Apart from this possible methodological difference, positive psychology also encompasses two areas of interest which the humanists have traditionally ignored. One is the notion of personality *traits* – enduring characteristics of an individual which influence behaviour across a variety of situations (see Vaillant 2000). The other is a concern with the *social context* of behaviour – understanding how communities, institutions and cultures affect experience and growth, and *also* how individuals selectively interact with their social environment to foster well-being (see Massimini and Delle Fave 2000).

Both of these areas have traditionally been largely ignored by humanistic psychologists, for reasons related to basic humanistic assumptions. While the study of personality traits has a long history (see Chapter 7), humanists have rejected such measures because they categorize and objectify the individual's experience. As a result, humanists are traditionally not interested in using traits as an explanatory mechanism in understanding behaviour. In terms of the relevance of social context, although Maslow acknowledged that specific environments can affect our ability to meet our needs, the social group was not the focus of concern. Moreover, in the long run, the humanists see culture as irrelevant to defining (and possibly understanding) healthy growth. (As discussed, the assumption of universality has been criticized, but the issue remains unresolved.)

Hence, in terms of the range of interests and methods, positive psychology overlaps with humanistic psychology, but also shows some distinct differences. Seligman's advocacy has led to a flurry of material being published, including special issues of *American Psychologist* (January 2000; March 2001), the *Journal of Humanistic Psychology* (winter 2001) and the *Journal of Social and Clinical Psychology* (January 2001), as well as several books (for example, Peterson 2006; Seligman 2002; Snyder and Lopez 2002, 2006).

It is not possible to summarize all of the studies here, but a couple of examples of research themes will perhaps help to illustrate the framework. One focus is the nature of happiness, a topic explored by social psychologist David Myers in an article which appeared in the first special issue of *American Psychologist* (Myers 2000). He looked at the nature of happiness and how three factors relate to it (interpersonal relationships, faith and wealth), using a mixture of primarily survey data, interspersed with anecdotal accounts by individuals. The data reveal that, in the long run, wealth does not affect happiness, either for individuals (for example, the 100 wealthiest Americans) or nations (based on both international comparisons and longitudinal studies of single countries). By contrast, faith and relationships seem to have a significant influence on how happy people say they are. (The value of relationships is an important theme within positive psychology; in this case, Myers attributes it in part to a 'need to belong', thereby echoing Maslow.) Subsequent research has provided further support for Myers's conclusions (Kesebir and Diener 2008). In addition, Kesebir and Diener's review provides evidence that personality traits like being extraverted are significant contributors to happiness, and that being happy contributes to both good health and career success. In the same vein, a cross-cultural study of the USA and Switzerland found that in both countries, traits like hope and a zest for living were strongly related to both life satisfaction and a sense of meaning (Peterson *et al.* 2007).

A second example concerns the research of Mihaly Csikszentmihalyi, Seligman's co-author in the inaugural article on positive psychology. Csikszentmihalyi was already well known for

flow a positive state of subjective experience associated with engaging in tasks which are involving and challenging.

his research on what he calls **flow** (Csikszentmihalyi 1990), which is a positive subjective state that arises when one feels very involved in a task, even though that task may be difficult or even risky. For example, musicians, chess players, surgeons and even rock climbers have reported experiencing this state. Interestingly, while a variety of studies have confirmed the existence of flow states, and have identified variables which can influence them (such as paying attention and setting clear goals), the concept is essentially defined experientially, not objectively. In a recent study, Csikszentmihalyi has looked at flow (and its opposite, boredom) in adolescents (Hunter and Csikszentmihalyi 2003). As Hunter and Csikszentmihalyi note, increased affluence in western countries has enabled most people to readily obtain the basics of life, leaving the door open to focus on higher needs (see Maslow's hierarchy). Unfortunately, instead of finding positive experiences of flow, many adolescents experience boredom, especially in school. To explore this, the researchers used a technique called the 'experience sampling method', which requires individuals to self-assess their mood state at random intervals over several days. The results showed that adolescents experiencing relatively high levels of flow also tend to show higher self-esteem, and are more optimistic about the future. Unfortunately, because of the correlational nature of the study, one cannot be certain about the cause of the results. (As noted above, one of the goals of positive psychology is to develop methodologies which can address causation, to avoid the limitations which most humanistic research has posed.) Interestingly, the subjective nature of measures of flow would not be out of place in a humanistic context – though humanistic researchers would avoid averaging data across individuals, as Hunter and Csikszentmihalyi do.

Not surprisingly, humanistic psychologists have taken a keen interest in positive psychology, and not all of the reactions have been positive. After the initial *American Psychologist* issue appeared, several psychologists responded that positive psychology gave too little credit to the influence and accomplishments of humanistic psychology (Bohart and Greening 2001; McLafferty and Kirylo 2001) and cited the humanistic tradition as a large part of the founding basis for positive psychology (Resnick *et al.* 2001; Strümpfer 2005). In addition, articles appeared arguing that, contrary to the assertions of Seligman and Csikszentmihalyi, humanistic psychology can and does generate empirical, quantitative research (Deci and Ryan 2000; Sheldon and Kasser 2001; Taylor 2001). Ultimately, though, the issue will not be decided by the volume of research each side produces. Clearly, there is overlap between positive psychology and humanistic psychology. In this respect, positive psychology has the potential to trigger a humanistic renaissance by increasing awareness among psychologists of the importance of fostering human growth. Although positive psychology is still in its infancy, it appears at present to be thriving. For example, in the year 2000 in the USA, there were no under-graduate courses offered in the area. By the year 2003, there were over 100 (Murray 2003). The British Psychological Society's publication, *The Psychologist*, devoted a special issue to positive psychology in March 2003, reflecting the continuing interest in the area. Today, the APA has a positive psychology section in its Division 17 (Society of Counseling Psychology), and the area has developed its own journal, *The Journal of Positive Psychology*, which began publishing in 2006.

Coaching as an Application of Humanistic and Positive Psychology

'I don't need therapy! I just need to know how to communicate my ideas to others in a way that they can understand!', 'I just can't seem to decide what kind of career I want.' These are two examples of the many problems that people may face in their lives – problems that may impact both their personal and professional lives, yet which do not fit within the traditional domain of 'abnormal behaviour'. If not therapy, then where can one go for help in areas such as these? Often,

The world today: **Coaching of Project Management**

In the working world, project managers have two major tasks: first, they must manage the technical parts of a project, such as budgets, schedules, monitoring results, etc., and second, they must manage the workers involved in the project to motivate them to a successful completion (Neuhauser 2007). This is clearly demanding, and many people feel that they do not have the expertise to be effective in managing all these diverse areas. Most particularly, many people with strong technical skills find the second task, managing people, to be a source for concern. Coaching psychology has been used very effectively in helping these people develop the skills they need. Berg and Karlsen (2007), of the Norwegian School of Management, have developed a generic model of stages that successful coaching should go through, while noting that these stages are flexible and specific techniques should be adapted to the needs and desires of the person being coached.

The first stage is that of developing trust between the coach (let us call her Dr C.) and the person being coached (Martha, the 'coachee'). This involves the coach listening to the coachee, with respect and openness. Dr C. and Martha need to talk honestly about what success in the project will mean, what potential pitfalls exist and in what areas Martha is feeling unsure of herself.

The second stage is that of 'diagnosis'; that is, clarifying the situation facing the coachee, and determining the strengths and weaknesses of the coachee in this situation. For example, Dr C. needs to continue talking to Martha to find out how she thinks and acts. This allows Dr C. to form a picture of Martha's customary functioning, and allows Martha to gain more insight into herself.

In the third stage, defining goals, the coach and the coachee examine what results the coachee wishes to obtain. Dr C. and Martha will discuss two major areas: first, what changes Martha wishes to make in herself, such as becoming better at delegating responsibilities to others or becoming more effective at resolving conflicts; and second, what final results Martha wants to see from the project, such as greater profit margins or customer satisfaction. Change is difficult, and a great deal of change may be unrealistic. Part of Dr C.'s job is to make sure that the goals that Martha wants to achieve are realistic and achievable.

The fourth stage is the hardest and yet most flexible part of the model: it involves planning and implementing the changes that the coachee wants to make. Dr C. and Martha will discuss how she can go about making the changes in herself, such as delegating responsibilities more effectively. Dr C will then monitor Martha's actions, challenging her to implement her changes and overcome obstacles, while encouraging her realistically with the belief that the process will be successful.

The final stage is that of follow-up and feedback. The coach should continue to monitor the coachee, examining how successful the coachee has been in making personal changes and how successful the project has been. Dr C. may not only talk to Martha, but also to the members of the project team to determine the success of the coaching. Dr C. will give Martha feedback on the changes she has made and point out areas that may need more work in the future. It will be up to Martha, however, to decide whether she wants to make further changes.

If coaching has been successful, the coachee feels less stress from their work, more confidence in their ability to handle future projects, and an overall sense of empowerment. The stages outlined by Berg and Karlsen may look simple, but it should be noted that generally successful coaches are professionals who are well trained by an accredited institution. The job entailed in being a coach is highly rewarding, but not easy, and should not be attempted by those without adequate training.

people have turned to 'coaches', a term originally associated with athletics, but more recently applied to many other domains. Unfortunately, professional standards for coaches have often been vague (Seligman 2007), a problem that coaching psychologists have been addressing in the last few years and trying to remedy with regulation and accreditation of training institutions (Grant 2006; Olson 2007; Whybrow and Palmer 2006). The advent of positive psychology, with its focus on enhancing quality of life, has provided a natural link to coaching psychology. As a consequence, both the British Psychological Society and the Australian Psychological Society have formed sub-groups devoted to applying psychological principles to coaching (Australian Psychological Society 2008; British Psychological Society 2008). The links between this area and positive psychology are based on their joint emphasis on human beings' desire and ability to become better functioning and more satisfied with their lives (Linley 2006).

Although the techniques used by coaches come from a variety of sources, depending on the goals and needs of the individual, coaching psychology specifically credits the humanistic approach for its orientation and many of its theoretical underpinnings (Linder-Pelz and Hall 2007; Stelter 2007). Philosophically, coaching involves a person-centred approach in which the assumption is made that '... people are intrinsically motivated toward creative, fulfilling, and optimal ways of living ...' (Joseph 2005, p. 3). This is a statement of the actualizing tendency that Carl Rogers discussed (Joseph 2006). The individual, whose rights of self-determination are respected, sets specific goals and together with the coach formulates explicit plans that the individual can implement to reach these goals. The coach strives to comprehend the individual's framework of understanding the situation (the *phenomenological framework*) and to help the individual clarify what needs to be done for them to achieve the desired end. Basic humanistic assumptions in coaching are that the individual is capable of growing and developing, and that the role of the coach is not one of advising or interpreting, but of helping the individual find clarity and answers themselves. (See *The World Today: Coaching of Project Management* for an example of how coaching is done.) Joseph (2006) contends that much of the therapy that Carl Rogers engaged in was, in fact, coaching! In keeping with the scientific emphasis of positive psychology, the focus is often on behavioural and cognitive techniques, but with an underlying humanistic philosophy intact.

At present, coaching psychology is in its very early days, and how research in positive psychology will benefit coaching psychology, and vice versa, remains to be seen. But it is fair to say that coaching psychology's emphasis on 'the systematic application of behavioural science, which is focused on the enhancement of life experience, work performance and wellbeing' (British Psychological Society 2008) is a natural fit with positive psychology and the humanistic tradition. Given this, it is likely that the founders of the humanistic approach would be gratified to find their views so influential in the twenty-first century.

Try it Yourself

What makes you happy? Have you ever looked forward to buying/doing something, only to find that when you finally did, you weren't happier as a result? One way to explore what makes you happy is to keep a record for a week of your mood state, especially times when you feel happy. What do you think you'll find? For example, do you think that playing with your children or pets will result in happiness? Or that finally finishing a term paper will make you happy? After a week, see if your predictions match the situations in which you felt happiness. In thinking about what makes you happy, can you relate your experience to the positive psychology research on happiness?

CONCLUSION

The humanistic approach encompasses a number of theorists and theories, all of which (as the name implies) seek to understand behaviour in human terms – that is, as it is experienced by the individual. Behaviour itself is only one aspect of human experience, and the humanists believe one can only understand human experience in terms of the meaning an individual gives to it. This emphasis on subjective experience, often referred to as a phenomenological viewpoint, distinguishes the humanistic approach from all the other approaches to psychology, which seek to eliminate subjectivity by emphasizing objective observation. However, humanists like Carl Rogers suggest that the distinction is more apparent than real, and question whether it is possible for *any* observations by humans to be free of subjectivity.

Evaluating the humanistic approach by traditional scientific criteria is difficult, because of its phenomenological emphasis. The sources of evidence used to support the theories are almost entirely *correlational* (case histories and interviews), which (unlike experiments) do not produce *falsifiable* predictions. While humanistic theorists would argue that prediction is ultimately irrelevant to understanding behaviour, without it, evaluation of a theory becomes very difficult. For most psychologists, the basic issue is *accuracy* (how well does the model fit reality?) – yet when assessments are dependent on subjective judgements, this is hard to determine. Only when individual preferences are reflected in a common consensus do scientists trust personal judgements. On this basis, there is some ground for supporting humanistic theories – for example, one can see many points of agreement between Rogers and Maslow. However, when differences exist between theories, it becomes hard to determine which theory (if any) is actually correct. (As we have seen, this lack of testability is also a concern with psychodynamic theories, and has resulted in a similar debate about the value of the individual theories.)

Within the humanistic approach, there are several areas that require further consideration. One is the question of cross-cultural validity, which arises in regard to the definition of self and also when discussing values in human development. As noted, some cultures foster a collective sense of identity, rather than the individualistic version emphasized in humanistic theories. Does this mean that the humanistic concept is biased, or could it be that collectivist cultures artificially constrain the individual? And is there a universal set of optimal values? Both Rogers and Maslow suggested there is a common set of values for healthy individuals, yet Frankl rejected this view. Even if one supports the notion of innate values, as E. O. Wilson (1998) does, identifying what they are is not easy (Robinson 1979).

Culture may also be relevant to how we define the nature of healthy development. Viktor Frankl has commented that 'every age has its own collective neurosis, and every age needs its own psychotherapy to cope with it' (Frankl 1992, p. 131). Further, he suggested that the increase in secularism in our society has changed the accepted source of help: 'Some of the people who nowadays call on a psychiatrist would have seen a pastor, priest or rabbi in former days' (p. 119). The notion that attitudes and expectations have changed was echoed by Perry London, a clinical psychologist (London 1974). London has remarked that to Freud, a patient was someone who felt bad (i.e., suffered from an obvious problem), while for the humanists, it is sufficient that a person doesn't feel good (i.e., is not reaching their full potential). Whether this reflects refinements in our understanding, or simply a cultural shift, is not clear. Ironically, while promoting positive psychology as an alternative to the humanistic approach, Martin Seligman has also detailed how non-humanistic psychology has again begun to focus on pathology instead of health (Seligman and Csikszentmihalyi 2000). (While it is impossible to discuss fully the relationship of theory to culture at this point, the issue will recur in Chapter 10.)

Both by its assumptions and the content of its theories, the humanistic approach has enlarged psychology's domain and provided a basis for new areas of interest and research. By emphasizing the importance of meaning in the lives of individuals, it has challenged other approaches to provide their own answers to such questions. Our capacity to be self-aware, to reflect on our own existence, and even to imagine its ending, is as much a part of human life as our capacity to learn or to feel emotion. The answers given by current humanistic theories may be incomplete or even inaccurate, but until the role of meaning in human experience is understood, psychology must not shrink from exploring the issue.

Putting It All Together – Humanistic Approach

Rogers would say that Sam's anxiety and negative feelings about himself suggest that he is experiencing *incongruence* – a gap between his *self* and his *ideal self*. While his parents are loving and supportive, as Sam grew up, their high expectations for him created *conditions of worth* which he has integrated into his ideal self. Now, as he faces increased demands at school and home, his immediate experience of struggling clashes with his idealized concept of being competent and successful. The result is a lowered sense of self-worth, and a fear that others may withhold *positive regard* if he does not succeed. By procrastinating, Sam may be trying to reduce his incongruence, because it would be easier to accept a failure due to circumstances ('lack of time') than to find he is not capable of meeting the expectations of his ideal self. Unfortunately, his incongruence drains his energy and enthusiasm, leaving him feeling tired and depressed. In a similar vein, he avoids pursuing his friend Vanessa even though he is attracted to her because her potential rejection of him would contradict his idealized concept of being attractive and desirable. A rejection from her would again lower his sense of self-worth. By avoiding asking her for a date, Sam can use the excuse 'I never tried' which is less incongruent than facing a blow to his ideal self.

Despite his problems and low self-worth, Sam's situation is not hopeless. His *actualizing tendency* will encourage him to work through his difficulties, and his family is a likely source of *empathy* and *unconditional positive regard*. If he can gain some *insight* into his own expectations, it is likely that he will find it easier to set realistic goals and meaningful priorities. Rogers would say that not everyone should aspire to get straight As (or feel bad if they don't get them), and not every romantic overture will meet with success, but everyone can make choices that will foster a sense of congruence. Since personal expectations play a role in our perception of stress, with greater insight Sam will likely experience less stress, and more satisfaction, regardless of the challenges he faces.

In terms of Maslow's hierarchy of needs, Sam's *physiological* and *safety* needs seem to be mostly satisfied, though the pressure to get a degree may be related to concerns about whether he will eventually get a secure job. Having supportive parents and good friends help to satisfy his need for *love and belongingness*, although he wants more love from a relationship with Vanessa. The major deficit for Sam right now seems to be his need for *esteem*. Giving his upbringing, Sam also feels that esteem comes from being 'the best', as his parents told him; it is also possible that he feels achievement is linked to getting love. Now, the increased load he is facing has aroused concerns that he is in danger of not being able to fulfil these expectations. As a result, he seeks simpler ways of satisfying his needs: increasing his feeling of safety by doing household chores, and his feeling of love and belongingness by remaining friends with Vanessa while fantasizing about her. Unfortunately, given that esteem is already a need he has experienced, diverting his time and energy in this way is not going to satisfy the deficit. If Sam can complete his courses successfully, he may find his esteem needs being more fulfilled. If not, he may have to seek other routes (and goals) to satisfy this need. As Maslow noted, a culture which creates high standards for achievement can make it difficult to meet the need for esteem. In fact, he said most people are never fortunate enough to fulfil all the deficit needs, thereby experiencing the need for self-actualization.

In considering the above analysis, it is important to remember that humanistic theories do not suggest any single answer to Sam's problems. Rather, they would argue that there are many possible paths through life – and ultimately, only Sam can determine what are the best choices for him.

CHAPTER SUMMARY

- The *humanistic approach* is characterized by two basic assumptions which distinguish both its methodology and its theories from other approaches: the focus on subjective experience (*phenomenological* viewpoint), and a rejection of *determinism* in favour of individual choice. Among the humanistic theorists, the ideas of *Carl Rogers* and *Abraham Maslow* are certainly the best known.

- Rogers developed a model which focuses on the relationship between what we feel we are (the *self*) and what we feel we should be (the *ideal self*). When the two are experienced as being similar, the individual is *congruent* or *fully functioning* – the goal of development. When a gap exists between the self and the ideal self, the person will experience this as *incongruence*.

- Being congruent depends on encountering people who provide the *conditions for growth*: *empathy, openness* and *unconditional positive regard*. Incongruence results from other people setting up *conditions for worth*, expressed through *conditional positive regard*.

- Like other humanistic theorists, Rogers was optimistic about human growth. In describing the potential of human development, he described the characteristics of *fully functioning individuals*, including the *values* which he felt such individuals were likely to hold. His ideas have been very influential in counselling and therapy, where his theory forms the basis of *client-centred therapy*.

- Abraham Maslow attempted to understand behaviour in terms of the needs which motivate an individual. The recognition that not all needs are alike led him to formulate his *hierarchy of needs*, which ranged from basic safety needs to the creative desires represented in *self-actualization*.

- Unlike other needs, self-actualization is based on the desire to grow, not on some form of deficit. Maslow believed that individuals can experience self-actualization during *peak experiences*. Like Rogers, Maslow tried to describe the nature of optimal human growth; to do so, he used historical examples of *self-actualized individuals* (both men and women).

- While Rogers and Maslow are the best-known humanists, the approach can also include *existential theories* like that of *Viktor Frankl*. Frankl argues that issues of *meaning* are central to all human experience. Unlike Rogers and Maslow, he rejects the view that particular values are necessary to human growth.

- Recently, Martin Seligman and others have advocated the creation of *positive psychology*. While sharing the humanistic concern for fostering human growth, it differs in its use of objective as well as subjective methodologies and concepts, and its concern for the role of social context in understanding behaviour. At the same time, concepts like *flow* clearly overlap with humanistic concepts of optimal functioning.

- Among the approaches, the humanistic approach is unique in emphasizing questions like the role of meaning and spirituality in human life. It remains a challenge to find ways to effectively evaluate the differences among theories, and the approach itself.

🔑 Key terms and concepts

phenomenological	conditions for growth
intersubjective verification	fully functioning person
client-centred therapy	hierarchy of needs
actualizing tendency	deficiency motives
self	self-actualization
ideal self	peak experience
congruence	existentialism
incongruence	logotherapy
conditions of worth	noögenic neuroses
would–should dilemma	learned helplessness
unconditional positive regard	flow
positive psychology	coaching psychology
conditional positive regard	

Test yourself questions

1 What does Carl Rogers consider to be the conditions for growth in human beings?
2 What is self-actualization?
3 What do existential psychologists such as Viktor Frankl believe is the most important part of human experience?
4 Why is positive psychology included in a chapter on the humanistic approach?

When you have read this chapter, log onto the Online Learning Centre website at
www.openup.co.uk/glassman where you will find answers to these Test Yourself questions and
suggested answers to the Try it Yourself activities, plus many more learning resources to help
you study psychology.

Suggestions for Further Reading

- **Rogers** wrote a number of books on different aspects of his work, but perhaps the best for a reader seeking a general overview is *Freedom to Learn* (1969), which discusses his ideas of personal growth in the context of education.
- **Maslow's** best-known book, *Toward a Psychology of Being* (1968), is also one of his best in terms of conveying an overall view of his ideas.
- For the reader interested in **Viktor Frankl's** ideas, *Man's Search for Meaning* (1992) is the primary source.
- One source for learning more about positive psychology is **Martin Seligman's** own book, *Authentic Happiness* (2002). Another good and highly readable source is **Christopher Peterson's** *A Primer in Positive Psychology* (2006).

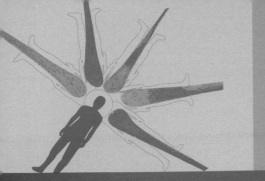

Chapter 7

Perspectives on Development

Chapter contents

LEARNING OBJECTIVES

In this chapter, the objectives are to learn:

☑ the methods employed in studying development, including
- longitudinal, cross-sectional and sequential designs

☑ issues that are central to the study of development, including
- continuity vs. discontinuity of developmental processes
- generality vs. specificity in models of development
- the role of heredity and environment

☑ basic concepts of personality

☑ how personality development is regarded by
- the biological approach
- the behaviourist approach
- the cognitive approach
- the psychodynamic approach
- the humanistic approach

☑ how the development of gender roles is viewed by each of the five approaches

OBSERVING THE JOURNEY OF LIFE

Writing a book is sometimes compared to having a child, with a long gestation period followed by release into the world. For a textbook like this, each edition shares similarities, yet is unique – much like siblings. Despite the parallels between writing and parenting, as someone who is both a writer and a parent, I (WEG) feel strongly that parenthood is far more significant. My ties to my two sons extend well beyond biology; each day's interactions are a process of discovery that is always unpredictable, and often joyful. To see a child grow seems an affirmation of life and its potential; it simultaneously leads us into thoughts of the future, and into recollections of the past. Sometimes I watch my younger son, and am reminded of similar moments when his older brother was that age. Like any parent, I also see glimmers of my own life journey in the lives of my children. And, like any parent, I am also a child – and watching my own parents as they aged, and died, has carried portents of the road that lies ahead. At whatever point on the journey we may be, life is a process that moves ever forward.

The start of a new life is a remarkable process: we are conceived as a joining of sperm and ovum, each of which bears only a half set of DNA, but which together provide the genetic pattern for a new being. Nine months later, we emerge from the womb as an infant – small, frail, dependent on others for survival, but still recognizably human. This, of course, is only the beginning of an ongoing process of growth and development – from infant, to toddler, to child, to adolescent, and onwards through adulthood and ageing. The process by which we reach our full potential is a slow one: altogether, it takes nearly two decades for physical and intellectual capacities to mature. Thus, given a lifespan of approximately 75 years, we spend about *one quarter of our life* simply reaching our full size and skills!

This prolonged developmental period is remarkable – few animals spend such a large portion of their life reaching their full capacities. In fact, it has been suggested that in many ways our nature is best seen as based on a kind of delaying of the developmental timetable. For example, compared to the most genetically-similar species, chimpanzees, we are more like a foetal chimp than an adult chimp – like human adults, foetal chimps show a relative absence of body hair, no brow ridges, and a spine–brain connection which makes an upright posture possible (Campbell 1982). By contrast, the appearance of mature (adult-like) capacities in a new-born is generally found only in lower species. It almost seems as if slow development is necessary to form the capacities we have (Bjorklund 1997).

Comparing human development to other species can pose many difficulties, but the desire to compare is driven by a basic question: why do we develop the way we do? The question quickly leads to a host of other questions: what guides our development? What kinds of factors can influence it? Such questions – and there are many others that are closely related – are basic to the study of developmental psychology.

INTRODUCTION

In its most general form, **developmental psychology** is concerned with the processes that produce changes in behaviour over time. These changes are most dramatic in the first two decades of life, so it is not surprising that early researchers tended to focus on this period of human life. Hence, for many years, 'developmental psychology' really meant 'child development'. More recently, the field has broadened to consider events during the ensuing years as

developmental psychology the study of the processes which underlie growth and change in behaviour over time.

well. While the changes that occur in adulthood are generally less obvious, it is clear that we do not simply remain static after childhood and adolescence. Indeed, the long period of preparation would seem to be pointless if nothing important followed! So, today, researchers are interested in questions of growth and change as related to the whole span of life, from birth to death.

The study of developmental psychology represents a different sort of division within psychology than do the approaches we have considered thus far. What unites the area is the emphasis on the processes of growth and change, not a particular theoretical perspective. In fact, the questions of development can be looked at from each of the approaches, as we will see. At the same time, developmental researchers (of every perspective) are concerned with asking certain types of questions about behaviour, and it is the focus on these questions that gives the area a thematic coherence.

The most basic question in development has already been raised: what makes us the way we are? While simple to ask, it is exceedingly difficult to answer. For one thing, one could ask it about one individual (for example, what makes Sabrina different from Jill), about particular groups (for example, based on gender or nationality), or about humans as a species (as in the earlier comparison to chimpanzees). Long before psychology emerged as a distinct discipline, philosophers asked similar questions – and often disagreed about the answers. As far back as ancient Greece, Plato argued that all human knowledge and virtue was innate – that is, we are what we are born to be. By contrast, John Locke, a seventeenth-century English philosopher, suggested that a new-born child is like a blank slate, on which experience writes its messages; in essence, we are what we experience. In modern psychological terms, these polarities would be represented by the factors of heredity and environment, and debates about the importance of each are a long-standing issue. But trying to answer this age-old question requires first answering some more basic questions.

Methods of Studying Development

The first step required for understanding is to be able to describe what development actually involves. That is, what are the changes that go on during a person's life? The physical changes of childhood may seem very obvious, but as with many phenomena, the interesting parts lie in the details. Consider a simple question (one which concerns nearly all parents): at what age does (should) a child begin talking? To answer this question, we might study language acquisition in a representative sample of children; this provides us with a description in terms of what is typical – that is, a *norm*. In all likelihood, there will be some noticeable variability across the group; this, in turn, may spawn a whole new series of questions, aimed at understanding why such variability occurs. (To answer the 'simple' question, children typically say their first words before their first birthday, but even this generalization ignores many details – for example, not all speech sounds (called *phonemes*) are acquired at the same age, as Prather *et al.* (1975) noted.)

Determining norms for basic aspects of development is an important element in describing the process of development as a whole (for an overview, see Box 7.1). However, even this task becomes complicated when one wishes to find relationships between events – for example, do children who are slow to begin talking also lag behind in other respects, such as learning to walk? Or are the behaviours independent of each other? And do children who begin talking early continue to show superiority in language skills later on? While in principle one could establish norms for any single behaviour by selecting a representative sample, it becomes more complicated when one wants to make comparisons at different ages (for example, as in looking

longitudinal study a research design in which a group of individuals are studied over a period of time.

at the pace of language acquisition). One way to answer the question is to select a group of individuals who are all the same age, and then continue to study them during the period of interest (for example, from 6 months to 6 years). This approach is called a **longitudinal study**, since it represents a long-term study of a given group.

Box 7.1 A Basic Framework for Looking at Development

This chart describes the major dimensions of development, and highlights some of the landmarks in each area. The cognitive landmarks are partly based on Piaget's theory (see Box 7.2), while the socio-emotional landmarks reflect Erikson's (see Chapter 5) and Kohlberg's (1969) theories.

Dimensions of Development			
Age	*Physical*	*Cognitive*	*Socio-emotional*
Birth to 5 years	Crawling, walking	Talking, pre-operational thinking	Attachment, start of gender roles pre-conventional morality
5 – 12 years	Growth in size, strength, skills	Concrete operational thinking	Developing sense of competence, conventional morality
12 – 20 years	Puberty – development of secondary sex characteristics	Formal operational thinking	Identity formation, adolescent egocentrism
20 – 60 years	Physical peak years (20 – 40) Loss of resilience, posture/weight changes (40 – 60)	Peak speed of processing (20s)	Intimacy commitments, contributing to family and society Post-conventional morality
60 years to death	Increased risk of stroke, bone fractures, illness	Cognitive slowing, risk of dementia due to stroke, Alzheimer's, etc.	Dealing with loss Resolving life issues

---

While highly informative, longitudinal studies are also difficult to do. The most obvious problem is the time required – the study takes at least as long as the time period of interest. While the duration will vary depending on the question being researched, in some cases (such as the language issue described above) it may take years. This requires a tremendous commitment on the part of the researcher (whose own life is passing along with those of the subjects), as well as the cooperation of the subjects. (In the case of children, obviously this means their parents must *also* be supportive.) Even so, participants sometimes move away, die or drop out for other reasons. If too many of the initial group fail to complete the study, the representativeness of the results can be jeopardized, eroding the value of the work. Despite these obstacles, there are instances in which subjects have been studied for decades or longer, providing a remarkable extended portrait of lives unfolding. One example is a study of patterns of adult personality which continued for over two decades (see White 1975).

Longitudinal studies, though very useful, represent only a small percentage of all developmental studies. In many cases, neither researchers nor subjects are willing or able to make the commitment required. In addition, depending on the question being asked, a longitudinal design may not be necessary. For example, if a researcher simply wants to determine the age range at which a particular behaviour occurs (such as producing two-word sentences), a longitudinal design is not required to get an answer. As a result, many developmental studies are based on selecting representative groups of each age and comparing them, thereby getting a sort of snapshot of behaviour at each age. This approach, which draws comparisons across time by looking at different age groups, is called a **cross-sectional study**. For example, the study of speech acquisition referred to earlier (Prather *et al.* 1975) used a cross-sectional design. Cross-sectional studies have the obvious advantage of minimizing the time required for the study.

cross-sectional study a research design based on selecting representative groups who vary on a particular characteristic; when the characteristic is age, this design provides a means of making developmental comparisons.

For example, one could simultaneously study changes across adulthood by selecting groups of individuals who are aged 20, 30, 40, 50, etc. This advantage is one reason for the popularity of cross-sectional studies.

Unfortunately, this advantage can often be offset by the disadvantages of the design, particularly when studying individuals across wide age ranges. As a type of *quasi-experiment*, a cross-sectional design limits our ability to interpret causation (see Chapter 1). The primary problem is that such studies cannot control for any factors that change along with age – for example, the fact that the subjects of different ages were born at different points in time. Such differences can be very important in terms of the role of cultural and historical influences – for example, comparing the attitudes of teenagers today and their parents (who were most likely teenagers in the 1990s) would have to contend with differences in areas such as school curricula, social attitudes and the spread of technology like computers, cell phones, and MP3s. When such outside influences (called **confounding variables**) are present, they can sometimes dramatically alter the interpretation of development. By their nature, confounding variables represent something which has been overlooked in planning the research, and it is often only after the fact that they can be identified. For example, cross-sectional studies have suggested that intelligence test scores begin declining by age 50; however, when a longitudinal design is used, it becomes clear that scores typically remain constant up to age 70 or later (Labouvie-Vief 1985)! In this particular case, the contradiction may be related to differences in the groups selected for the cross-sectional studies. Since the older subjects were born decades earlier than the younger subjects, there would be differences in educational level, age of first exposure to television, etc. (for example, likelihood of attending university increased over the twentieth century). These differences among the groups, which might affect performance on the intelligence tests, would thus represent a confound with age. The possibility of such confounds, which are often difficult to anticipate, means that cross-sectional studies require careful assessment, particularly when attempting to compare behaviour over wide age ranges. In this sense, cross-sectional studies can be useful for identifying the age at which a behaviour occurs, but are sometimes not as helpful as longitudinal studies in clarifying the processes which underlie development.

confounding variable a factor in research which varies jointly with a variable of interest, making it impossible to properly identify the role each variable has in affecting behaviour; typically, a confounding variable represents something which has been overlooked in planning the research, and is only identified after the data have been collected.

One way of compensating for the risks of cross-sectional studies is to use a hybrid design which has features of *both* longitudinal and cross-sectional studies. This approach, called a **sequential design**, uses groups of different ages, which are then observed for some period of time, such that the groups eventually overlap. Comparing behaviour of individuals from different groups at the same age then allows an evaluation for possible confounds or other problems which

sequential design a research design which combines features of both longitudinal and cross-sectional studies by selecting groups of different ages (like a cross-sectional design), and then following them over a period of time (like a longitudinal study) sufficient to create overlap in the ages represented by different groups.

sometimes arise in simple cross-sectional studies. For example, a study of adolescents might select four groups, aged 12, 14, 16 and 18. All subjects would then be followed for two years. At this point, those who were originally 12 would now be 14 – and their behaviour could be compared to that previously recorded for the group who were *initially* 14. If no differences exist based on this comparison (and similar comparisons for the other groups), the researchers would be more secure in suggesting that no confounds are present. (The problem would come, of course, if the results based on the age-matching were not similar – one is then left to ponder whether the difference represents a confound, or simply sampling variability.) Thus, the sequential design would allow the study of behaviour over a ten-year span, but would only require two years to complete – in some sense, the best of both worlds (see Figure 7.1 for a comparison of the three research designs).

Try it Yourself

The term 'generation gap' was coined to describe differences in values and preferences between generations which were considered to provide an insurmountable obstacle to mutual understanding. While it is highly debatable whether any such obstacles are truly insurmountable, differences between people of varying generations *do* exist. Explore these yourself by asking a parent, grandparent or some other older adult about their experiences at your age – what were they doing, what they were interested in, and so on. Then ask them about their current preferences in music, books, etc. Assuming their current preferences are different from your own, can you decide whether this is due to the age difference, the difference in prior experience, or some other factor? What does this tell you about the difficulties of interpreting developmental research?

Issues in Interpreting Development

Obviously, one cannot understand development without knowing something about what actually occurs. However, gathering accurate information about behaviour at different ages is only part of the puzzle. As discussed in Chapter 1, description is only the starting point in understanding behaviour. Understanding also requires explaining *why* things happen as they do, and this requires *interpreting* what we know, in terms of a theory. In the case of development, the goal is to understand the changes in behaviour that occur over time. However, we recognize that time itself is not the active force – it is processes going on *within* time that account for the changes. Hence, the task becomes one of identifying and describing these underlying processes. As we have seen in considering the various approaches, the same behaviour may be interpreted differently by different theories. When it comes to development, there are three major issues that arise in interpreting developmental changes:

1 Is development a continuous unfolding, or discontinuous stages?
2 Can a single model describe all aspects of development, or do different aspects require fundamentally different models?
3 What is the relative importance of heredity and environment in determining the course of development?

Because they apply to all the approaches, we will consider each of these questions in more detail.

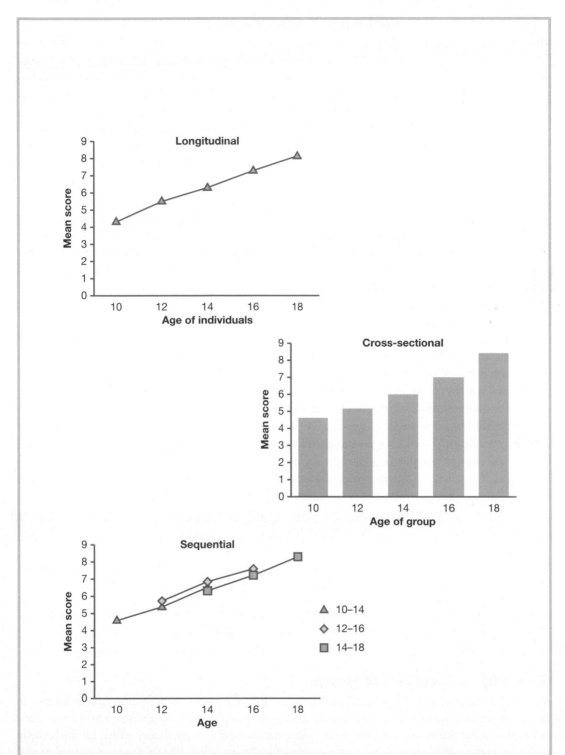

Figure 7.1 Research Designs In Developmental Research As the graphs indicate, longitudinal, cross-sectional and sequential designs can all be used to explore developmental change. (These graphs represent a hypothetical study of changes in logical reasoning from age 10 to age 18.)

continuity the view that changes in development occur through a continuous, gradual process, rather than as a series of discrete stages; continuity is an assertion about the processes which underlie development, as well as the changes observed in behaviour.

stages the belief that development is based on distinct periods with clear boundaries, with behaviour at each stage governed by different underlying processes; Freud's theory of psychosexual stages is one such theory.

Continuity vs. Discontinuity

The most basic issue is concerned with the **continuity** of development. One of the most obvious aspects of development is the fact that many changes occur during the course of life. For example, the reasoning skills of a 3-year-old are dramatically different from those of a 20-year-old. At what point are these differences so great that they represent a new skill (a *qualitative* change), rather than simply more of the same (a *quantitative* change)? To put it another way, are there distinct **stages** in development, with clear boundaries, or is development a more or less continuous process? (Sometimes this issue is described as one of *continuity vs. discontinuity*, and sometimes as *gradualism vs. stages*.) For example, a 10-year-old can use language in much more complex ways than a 4-year-old. Does this mean the 10-year-old processes language differently (is in a different stage), or does it simply reflect the effects of six years of practice (continuity)?

While strikingly different in their implications, the concepts of continuity and discontinuity are nonetheless hard to evaluate in practice. In one sense, it is obvious that development is continuous – physical growth is a gradual process, and many skills, like walking or talking, are acquired only gradually.

At the same time, it is tempting to categorize behaviour into stages, just as we form other sorts of categories. The physical changes which occur at puberty, while gradual, nonetheless seem to herald a new stage of life. Similarly, we talk about adolescence vs. adulthood, implying that the two periods are distinct. Are these stages really distinct in the way that pre- and post-puberty are? Asserting that stages exist implies several things about the underlying processes – most importantly, that each stage is characterized by *distinct underlying mechanisms*. In addition, discontinuity frequently implies that there is a specific *order* to the stages, and possibly even specific *timing* of the occurrence of each stage. (Freud's theory of personality development, for example, involves all three aspects – changing mechanisms underlying stages, a specific order of stages, and specific timing of stages.) As we consider some of the specifics of development, the issue of continuity vs. discontinuity will arise repeatedly.

Try it Yourself

A few years ago, a well-known television talk show host was trying to alert the public to the dangers of physical punishment administered to children. Attempting to arouse empathy, she asked adults to imagine how they would feel if they were beaten for mistakes. She then went on to state that this is how children feel, that they are little adults who simply haven't learned as much as adults have. Do you think she was correct in her interpretation of childhood? If not, why not?

Generality vs. Specificity of Models

A second issue concerns the *generality* of theories of development. A basic principle in science is the notion of *parsimony* – that is, a simpler theory is preferable to a complex one, assuming both can explain a particular set of results. In the same way, having a single theory which can be broadly applied is preferable to using several narrow ones. Ideally, we would like to have one general model to describe all aspects of development. At present, this seems out of reach, but we can still ask whether specific aspects of development (for example, cognitive development or social development) can be explained in terms of a single set of principles. A broad theory, because it attempts to encompass many areas or 'domains' of cognitive functioning, is

domain-general model a theory which attempts to account for many aspects of behaviour in terms of a single set of principles.

domain-specific model a theory which focuses on only a single aspect of behaviour in the belief that different aspects of behaviour involve different processes, and therefore require different theoretical explanations.

equilibration Piaget's term for the process of maintaining balance between our environment and the mental structures which we use to represent that environment.
assimilation Piaget's term for a process of integrating new knowledge or experience into our existing cognitive schemata.
accommodation Piaget's term for a process of modifying our cognitive schemata in response to new knowledge or experience.

sometimes called a **domain-general model** (Rosser 1994). In contrast, some researchers believe that different cognitive functions require different theoretical explanations; that is, for example, how problem solving skills develop and how social understanding develops might require different theoretical orientations to explain them. A theory which focuses on only one function or domain is called a **domain-specific model**.

The Swiss theorist Jean Piaget, one of the great pioneers in the study of cognitive development, believed that a single set of principles could account for the development of all sorts of cognitive skills, from understanding numbers to spatial reasoning (Piaget 1954). His work has been highly influential, and his theory represents an example of a domain-general model. In his theory, he emphasized certain general principles which he believed were applicable to all aspects of cognitive development. The most fundamental of these principles was **equilibration** – the desire to maintain a balance between our surroundings and the mental structures we use to represent those surroundings. Often this means that we integrate new information or experiences into our existing cognitive structure (a process Piaget called **assimilation**). In other circumstances, new experiences require us to change our existing representations; Piaget called this process **accommodation**. To Piaget, this search for balance (equilibration) was the process underlying all cognitive activity. Despite seeing equilibration as fundamental to all cognitive processes, Piaget nonetheless saw cognitive development as a series of discrete stages, as can be seen in Box 7.2.

Piaget's work has been very influential, and has generated a great deal of research. Not surprisingly, some studies have been critical, suggesting that the broad picture of cognitive processes which his theory paints seems wrong in some of its details (Baillargeon 2002; Bremner *et al.* 2006.; Krøjgaard 2005; Lacerda *et al.* 2001; Pramling 2006). Of particular concern is its applicability to other cultures – for example, most Australian Aborigines never reach the stage of formal operations, at least using Piaget's standard tasks (Dasen 1975; Flavell 1992). Trying to

Key Thinker: **Jean Piaget**

Jean Piaget (1896–1980) was born in Neuchatel, Switzerland on 9 August 1896, the son of a professor of medieval literature. A precocious student, Piaget began working in the local natural history museum at the age of 10, getting paid in specimens! While in high school he published his first scientific paper, on the sighting of an albino sparrow. After high school, he studied natural sciences at the University of Neuchatel, where he obtained a PhD in zoology at the age of 21. After a semester at the University of Zurich studying psycho-analysis, he went to France, working with a colleague of Alfred Binet (the developer of the first standardized intelligence test). There, he did his first experimental studies of cognitive development. In 1923, he married Valentine Châtenay; the couple had three children, who became part of many of Piaget's pioneering studies of intellectual development.

Over the next 30 years, he held a number of different positions in psychology, sociology and history of science, sometimes being cross-appointed at various institutions. In 1955, he created and directed until his death the International Center for Genetic Epistemology. Throughout his career, he was concerned with epistemology (the study of the origins of knowledge), both experimentally and as a philosophical issue. During a long and prolific career, he published more than 60 books and several hundred articles, receiving numerous awards and honorary degrees. He died in Geneva on 16 September 1980.

Box 7.2 Piaget's Theory of Cognitive Development

Piaget viewed cognitive development as consisting of four distinct stages, which were characterized by qualitatively different thinking processes; these stages were seen as age-related, and as always occurring in the same order.

Age	Stage	Major characteristics
Birth to 2 years	Sensorimotor	Egocentric thinking – inability to conceive of the world as existing apart from one's own experience of it
		Development of object permanence – understanding that objects exist independent of one's sensory experience
	Preoperational	Development of language skills
2 – 4 years	Preconceptual (sub-stage)	Use of symbols – using words as category labels
4 – 7 years	Intuitive (sub-stage)	Using concepts – sorting objects by size, shape or colour
7 – 11 years	Concrete operations	Mastery of principles of conservation – understanding that mass, volume and number remain constant despite perceptual changes in grouping or form
11 years to adult	Formal operations	Mastery of abstract thinking – ability to use inductive and deductive reasoning, using symbolic representations to analyse problems and formulate ideas

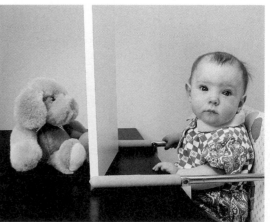

Figure 7.2 Cognition in Infancy Piaget argued that very young children lack object permanence – the capacity to understand that objects continue to exist when they are no longer visible. As seen in these pictures, this 5-month-old boy does not search for the toy when it is blocked from view.

evaluate the issue is complex, especially given the influence of factors like differences in tasks and test conditions (Keen 2003). Nonetheless, it does illustrate that getting the details right often represents the biggest difficulty in trying to develop a comprehensive (domain-general) model. Partly in response to these concerns, other researchers have put forward theories which deal with only limited aspects of cognitive development. For example, Lawrence Kohlberg developed a theory of moral development (how we make judgements of right and wrong) (Kohlberg 1966). His work grew out of Piaget's, but its narrower focus on moral thinking makes it an example of a domain-specific model.

animism Piaget's term for the small child's tendency to ascribe human-like qualities to inanimate objects.
egocentrism Piaget's term for the small child's tendency to assume that their perspective of the world is the only one possible.

The differences between the theories of Piaget and Kohlberg illustrate the dilemma which developmental theorists face. Basically, the problem is a conflict between the principles of parsimony (a general model would be simpler than invoking several different models) and accuracy (a general model may fail to do justice to the complexities of development). In practice, the issue is often not as clear-cut as it is expressed here, but we nonetheless have to recognize that there are often competing demands involved in deciding what is a good theory.

Try it Yourself

When MH was 4 years old (so the family story goes), she watched eagerly as her father made her a slice of toast and put butter and then jam on it for her. But to her dismay, Daddy didn't put enough jam on the toast. She complained, 'The butter's looking through at me!' This illustrates two biases in the thinking of a small child: first, the butter is assumed to have humanlike qualities as it looks at her (Piaget termed this **animism**); second, she saw the world in terms of how it related to her, with the butter specifically looking at *her* – what Piaget called **egocentrism**.

Ask your parents or other family members if they can recall 'funny' things you said when you were small. Do these 'funny' statements reveal the particular way a small child thinks?

To see differences in the way children think for yourself, talk to children of different ages and ask them questions, such as why the sun seems to set in the west each evening, or why it sometimes rains. Do you find that at different ages children have widely disparate explanations for such phenomena? Are animism and egocentrism revealed by the children you speak to?

Heredity and Environment

The broadest issue in forming a theory of development, and in some ways the most contentious, concerns the *origins* of the changes which occur over the span of life. In some ways, development represents a paradox: there is the obvious sense of change, while at the same time there seems to be a central thread of constancy. For example, parents of grown children often recall ways in which the infant or child foreshadowed the adult. Is this constancy real or imagined? And if real, what is it based on?

The traditional answer to the question of constancy has been to assert that the basic characteristics of a person are innate – that is, the constancy is due to the influence of *heredity*. In essence, this is the modern version of Plato's nativist theory. The role of heredity is evident in the development of a foetus, whereby cells differentiate to form the various parts of the body. Even after birth, the regularity of growth strongly suggests the influence of genetic timetables (see Purnell 2003). The alternative to explanations based on heredity is to look for *environmental influences*. At first glance, it may seem hard for environmental models to explain either constancy over time in an individual's behaviour or the developmental similarities found across individuals. Yet, as Skinner (see Chapter 3) and others have noted, it is possible to talk about environmental constancies and similarities as sources of behavioural consistency.

Thus, traditionally, the issue has been seen as polarized between those who see development as based on heredity (the *nativist* view), and those who credit the environment (the *empiricist* view). (Note that the terms *nature vs. nurture* and *innate vs. learned*, are generally synonymous with 'heredity vs. environment'.) In recent years, developmental researchers have come to recognize that either/or statements about heredity and environment are both pointless and misleading. For example, as we gain a greater understanding of the underlying mechanisms of heredity, we have come to recognize that genetic mechanisms do not operate in a vacuum. Instead, they must be expressed in the context of the individual's environment – and while one can speak of an impoverished environment, there is always *some* environment. Thus, the proper question is not whether development is based on heredity or environment, but rather how, and to what degree, the two *interact*. Donald Hebb, a noted Canadian psychologist, once suggested that the interaction is akin to the way the area of a field is determined by its length and width: one can have fields of different shapes, but every field has *some* length and width (Hebb 1953)!

reaction range in genetics, the limits on the variability of a phenotype (observed characteristic) determined by the genotype; in essence, the limits set by the genes on how environmental influences (whether deprivation or enrichment) can affect the trait.

There are a number of ways that heredity and environment can interact. At the simplest level, the **reaction range** of the genotype may set the limits on how environmental influences (whether deprivation or enrichment) can affect the trait (Hirsch 1963). For example, white American males are, on average, taller than Japanese males; this difference appears to be based on genetic factors. At the same time, however, there is overlap between the two groups, and within each group variations are associated with differences in nutrition – an environmental factor. Hence, heredity determines a range for the person's height, with actual height determined by the nutritional environment.

epigenetic effects a term to describe processes whereby stable changes in the expression of genes occur during development; such changes can be transmitted during cell division, but do not involve mutations of DNA itself.

A second process, which is just beginning to be understood, is the role of the environment in turning genes on and off. Such influences, which can result in local genetic changes during development which are passed on during cell division, are called **epigenetic effects**. These effects have been implicated in the expression of parental behaviour, aggression and risk-taking behaviour in some non-human species, and the development of some psychiatric disorders in humans (see Cushing and Kramer 2005 for a review of the literature).

Identifying the boundaries for the influence of heredity and environment can be very difficult. For example, most people probably think of environmental influences as beginning at birth, when the infant emerges from the womb into what William James called a 'booming, buzzing confusion of sights and sounds'. In reality, environmental influences exist *within* the womb as well. One reflection of this is that maternal behaviour and health have measurable effects on the unborn child. For example, smoking and drinking by the mother have both been shown to adversely affect the developing foetus. In the case of alcohol, the amount of impact on the child may possibly vary with genetic make-up (Gemma *et al.* 2007). Exposure to certain drugs in the womb can even affect the development of sex characteristics (Money and Tucker 1975). Thus, interactions of heredity and environment must be assumed to occur right from the time of conception.

Prenatal influences are also a concern when looking at twins. Studies of identical twins in particular are popular because one can be certain of the genetic relationship between the twins, and similarities are often cited as examples of genetic influence (see Box 7.3). Unfortunately, such studies often overlook the role of prenatal influences, despite evidence that the prenatal environment may contribute to any observed similarities. For example, fraternal twins (conceived from separate zygotes) often seem more similar than other siblings in part because they share a common prenatal environment. Thus, simply knowing the genetic relationship between two individuals is insufficient to determine the relative role of heredity and environment. In addition, it is easier to specify genetic similarity (at least in the case of identical twins) than it is to precisely measure environmental similarities and differences (Dick and Rose 2002; see Chapter 2 for a related discussion).

Box 7.3 Heredity and Environment in Studies of Twins

Studies of identical (MZ) and fraternal (DZ) twins reared together and apart can suggest the influence of both heredity and environment: greater similarities for MZ twins than DZ twins suggest heredity; greater similarities for twins reared together than apart suggest environment. Note that the data for stress reactions do not fit the expected pattern, since twins reared apart are more similar than twins reared together. (Data from Tellegen et al. 1988)

Trait	Reared together		Reared separately		
	MZ	DZ	MZ	DZ	
Well-being	.58	.23	.48	.18	Results fit genetic model: MZ > DZ, reared together > reared separately
Achievement	.51	.13	.36	.07	
Positive emotionality	.63	.18	.34	−.07	
Stress reaction	.52	.24	.61	.27	Results don't fit genetic model: reared separately > reared together

More recently, researchers have begun to look at more complex ways in which heredity and environment interact (Bronfenbrenner and Ceci 1994). In part, the goal is to recognize the complex nature of interactions between the individual and their environment. Thus, parents may seek to treat siblings equally, but the temperament of one child may lead to differing parental reactions. The child's temperament may reflect heredity, but the family environment is altered by the way that the child's behaviour affects other family members. Similarly, Sandra Scarr has argued that individuals tend to create their own environment (by their activities, interests, etc.), and that these *active choices* are influenced by heredity. That is, individuals with different genotypes are likely to choose different environments. Evidence which is consistent with this view comes from studies of intelligence test scores, in which as children get older, typically their score becomes less like that of their parents and siblings; in effect, older children exert more control over their environment than do younger children (Scarr and McCartney 1983). Further support for this idea comes from a study in which family environment was found to be more similar for identical twins than fraternal twins – presumably because they elicit more similar responses from family members (Plomin and Bergemen 1991). Such interactions imply that the genotype will influence the environment, as well as the environment affecting the expression of the genotype.

In some circumstances, it can seem that there is very little interaction between heredity and environment. For example, some aspects of development seem to occur independent of variations in specific environmental conditions, a process known as **maturation**. One example of this is walking, where there is relatively little variability across different cultures: in North America, a child typically begins to walk at about 12 months; in France, at 15 months and in Uganda at 10 months (Gardiner and Kosmitzki 2002). (The advantage for Ugandan children appears to be related to a cultural emphasis on walking, with children being given exercises and encouragement; despite this, the age for walking is very similar.)

maturation a term referring to processes in development which seem to be relatively independent of environmental influences, such as depth perception and walking; implied in the term is the assumption that the characteristics are governed by heredity.

Even when dealing with seemingly straightforward situations of maturation, one must be careful about the assumptions one makes. For example, consider the development of depth perception. Most mammals (including human infants) are able to perceive depth by the time they are able to move about in the world (Richards and Rader 1983). Obviously, this has adaptive value in terms of avoiding falls, and seems to arise as a result of normal visual experience. With infants, the study of depth perception usually involves using the 'visual cliff', a well-known test in which the toddler is confronted with a glass-covered surface, beneath which there is an obvious drop. Typically, infants old enough to crawl will not venture over the apparent 'edge', despite the support of the glass. This is interpreted as evidence of depth perception, whereby vision (the perceived drop) overrides touch (the support of the glass surface). However, psychologist Neil Carlson notes that when his 6-month-old daughter was tested, she went unhesitatingly across! Since it seemed impossible that the toddler could not perceive depth, the perplexed researcher, a colleague of Carlson, could not understand this result – until it was explained that the family had a glass-covered coffee table, and the child had often crawled on it. Thus, rather than indicating a failure of depth perception, the results reflected the difference in her prior environment (Carlson 1990).

Closely related to maturation is the existence of *critical* or 'sensitive' *periods*. Essentially, the concept is that there is an optimal time during development for particular experiences to occur. For example, while the language one speaks depends on early experience – that is, the environment – it appears that the *timing* of language learning is governed partly by genetic programming, with an optimal interval during early childhood (Chomsky 1988; Morgan and Kegl 2006). Deprivation at this time – for example, because of an undiagnosed hearing impairment in a 3-year-old – may have long-term repercussions for language learning. (See Chapter 4 for a related discussion.)

Given the complexities already discussed, most discussions about development today tend to assume an interactionist view of heredity and environment. However, this does not preclude emphasizing one aspect or the other, as we will see when we consider how each of the approaches views development. In addition, it is worth noting that developmental researchers are increasingly interested in the role of culture in development. While technically it might be considered simply an aspect of the overall environment, explicitly including culture in analyses can often shed additional light on the nature of development (van de Vijver and Poortinga 2002).

To recap our discussion, there are three major issues that underlie the study of development, which are reflected in the interpretations made by each approach. These issues are:

1 Is development a continuous process of gradual changes, or a series of distinct stages?

2 Can one theory describe the processes which underlie all development (domain-general theory), or are specific models needed to account for different aspects of development (domain-specific theories)?

3 What is the relative importance of heredity (genetic make-up) as compared to the environment (especially learned experiences) in explaining the outcome of development?

As we consider selected aspects of development, you may want to think about the possible answers to these questions.

In the end, these questions can only be answered by considering what we actually know about growth and change over the course of life. After all, the issues, as well as the theories which attempt to answer them, have meaning only with regard to the actual events of development. It is beyond the scope of this chapter to provide a full review of what is currently known about development across the lifespan. Instead, we will focus on one aspect of development: the patterns of behaviour which we see as characteristic of an individual. Some of these patterns seem distinctive to the individual, and represent what we call the person's 'personality'. Another type of pattern, which is both part of personality, and separate from it, is the tendency to show gender-related behaviours (called gender roles). In the remainder of this chapter, we will look at these issues from the point of view of each of the five approaches.

Try it Yourself

It's not uncommon to see the children of people with great talent in some area to show such talent as well. In the world of music, for example, the children of talented people such as Frank Sinatra, John Lennon, Woody Guthrie and Nat King Cole also show musical talent. Can you think of examples of children 'taking after' their parents in other fields, such as sports? Do you think this reflects genetics, or environmental influences, or a combination of both?

Assume that there is a gene which affects athletic ability. What sort of environmental factors do you think might interact with it to affect athletic performance? What would enhance it? What might impair it?

PERSONALITY AND GENDER ROLE DEVELOPMENT

Personality and its Origins

Several years ago, I (WEG) had the chance to get together with college classmates at a reunion. Some individuals I hadn't seen since our graduation, 25 years before. Not surprisingly, it was a bittersweet occasion, with many shared laughs about long-ago incidents, but also more muted reflections on the passage of time, and of those friends whose lives had already ended. But what struck me most of all was the sense that most people seemed to be 'still the same' – that apart from bodily changes (greying/thinning hair, weight gained or lost), much was unchanged. Tom was still shy, Laurie was still extraverted – in other words, there seemed to be a strong sense of consistency in their behaviour, even after 25 years. As a psychologist, how can I account for this?

personality patterns of behaviour which are characteristic of an individual and which tend to be consistent across situations and over time.

Traditionally, we talk about such consistency in terms of the individual's personality. **Personality** refers to those behaviour patterns which are characteristic of an individual and which tend to be consistent across situations and over time. The concept of personality provides a simple way to talk about consistency *within* the behaviour of an individual, but we sometimes also make comparisons *between* individuals. In this case, we typically refer to specific characteristics, called personality **traits**. We say 'he's shy', or 'she's outgoing', and people nod knowingly, accepting the terms both as a way of describing the individuals, and as a means of predicting how they might act in a particular situation, such as at a party.

trait a behaviour pattern which occurs consistently across a range of situations; a specific personality characteristic.

To the average person, the study of personality may be the most interesting issue in psychology. Indeed, it has been suggested that we are all 'personality theorists', since in our interactions with others, we make interpretations based on our cognitive schemata about what people are like. These schemata, called **implicit personality theories**, have been shown to influence our social relationships. For example, a study of dating couples found that when individuals believed that people don't easily change, this also affected their view of their partner and of the quality of the relationship (Ruvolo and Rotondo 1998). In this sense, ideas about personality may stem from our own perceptions, rather than external reality (see also Chapters 1 and 4).

implicit personality theory a general cognitive schema about human behaviour which is used in making interpretations of the behaviour of other people.

At the same time, most people, and even most psychologists, would argue that at least *some* of the perceived consistencies are real, just as some of the perceived differences between individuals are real. For example, two longitudinal studies done at the Institute of Human Development at Berkeley followed randomly selected children from early childhood until mid-life, and found signicant correlations over time on several personality measures (Block 1971). Given that each individual is a unique combination of genes and experiences, what shapes the *person* in the 'personality'? To try to understand this, let us look at how each of the five approaches views the origins of personality.

Try it Yourself

Have you had an experience of reuniting with someone you haven't seen for many years? Did they seem the same to you as they were years ago, or did they seem to have changed? How do you think they perceived *you*: as the same or changed?

In what ways do you think you are consistent? Try to identify four or five of your traits; then ask a friend to list what they perceive as your major traits. How do the lists compare? What does this tell you about implicit personality theories? Do you and your friend put the same emphasis on particular traits, or do you emphasize some traits in yourself which your friend finds less noteworthy? Does your friend's list of your traits give you more insight into yourself, or into your friend's view of personality traits?

Perspectives on Personality

Earlier in this chapter, we noted that there are three major issues which arise when considering theories of development:

1 the role of heredity vs. environment;

2 whether development is continuous or based on discrete stages; and

3 whether development involves a single process that can be understood in terms of a single

model (domain-general), or involves different processes that require separate models (domain-specific).

Not surprisingly, each of the five approaches tends to have its own view of these issues, and therefore offers different insights when it comes to considering the origins of personality.

The Biological Approach

The biological approach, as the name implies, places heavy emphasis on the role of heredity and physiological structure in shaping behaviour. In looking at personality, the approach has tended to focus on those aspects of personality associated with temperament. **Temperament** refers to basic behavioural tendencies, such as emotionality, sociability and fearfulness, which are believed to be determined by heredity (Rothbart 1981). Two types of evidence support the view that temperament is largely innate: studies of twins and longitudinal studies.

temperament behavioural tendencies which are believed to be determined by heredity; examples include emotionality, sociability and fearfulness.

Twins have long been favoured in studies of nature vs. nurture, because of the ability to look at degree of genetic relationship (see Chapter 2). Comparisons of fraternal and identical twins indicate that identical twins are more alike in activity level, irritability and sociability than are fraternal twins (Plomin *et al.* 1988). A long-running study of twins separated early in life, the Minnesota Twin Study, has reported similar findings about heredity influencing temperament (Bouchard *et al.* 1990). The researchers have also reported finding evidence of significant hereditary influence on such higher-level aspects of personality as recreational and vocational interests (Lykken *et al.* 1993). Other twin studies indicate that there appears to be a genetic component to what has been called the *alpha* (*α*) factor which is defined by agreeableness, conscientiousness and emotional stability, and the *beta* (*β*) factor which is defined as incorporating extraversion and intellect. Moreover, these results appear to hold in Canada, Germany and Japan (Jang *et al.* 2006).

As already discussed, twin studies can be difficult to evaluate. Both body structure (itself genetically influenced) and the reactions of other people to physical attributes like attractiveness may influence some aspects of behaviour that we associate with 'temperament'. Such influences would represent an interaction with environment, not a pure genetic factor. Support for this interactionist view of temperament comes from a longitudinal study which followed a group of children from the age of 3 months until adulthood (Chess and Thomas 1987; Thomas and Chess 1977). The researchers found that there are interactions between the temperament of a child and the caregiver, which over time can affect behaviour. For example, mothers may tend to respond more favourably to babies who are not irritable. This type of temperament–environment interaction may even extend across generations: the way parents interact with their babies may be influenced by the parent's own genetically-influenced temperament, which subsequently affects the baby's behaviour, which then further affects the parent's responses to the baby (Caspi *et al.* 2005)!

The second type of evidence used to suggest a biological basis for personality comes from longitudinal studies. In many ways, such studies seem better suited than twin studies to determining the stability of traits, hereditary or otherwise. Developmental psychologist Jerome Kagan has used this approach to look at a trait he calls *behavioural inhibition* – the tendency to withdraw from unfamiliar people or situations. Inhibited children tend to be shy, and experience anxiety when faced with novelty. Those children who were either inhibited or uninhibited at 21 months of age tended to remain so both at age 7 and at adolescence (Kagan 1989). A subsequent study

Key Thinker: **Jerome Kagan**

Jerome Kagan (c. 1929 –) started his career studying psychology and biology at Rutgers University in New Jersey, and then received his PhD in psychology from Yale University in 1954. After a two-year stint in the US Army during the Korean War, he joined the Fels Research Institute, where he was involved in a longitudinal study which first drew his attention to differences in temperament in children. Given his early interest in biology as well as psychology, the study of the role of temperament in behaviour was a natural direction to pursue; it has been a major focus of his developmental research for more than 35 years, resulting in many articles and books, including *Birth to Maturity* (1962), *The Second Year* (1981) and *Three Seductive Ideas* (1996). Since 1964, he has been a professor at Harvard University, and in 1997 he became a co-director of Harvard's Mind – Brain – Behavior initiative, a cross-disciplinary exploration of human nature involving neuroscientists, social scientists and humanists. Kagan has received numerous honours for his work, including the Distinguished Scientist award from the American Psychological Association. He continues to live and work in Cambridge, Massachusetts.

by Kagan and his colleagues has found the patterns extend into adulthood as well (Schwartz *et al.* 2003). Thus, studies of temperament support the biological perspective in suggesting that important components of personality are due to heredity. Taken as a whole, there is considerable evidence for a strong genetic influence in personality traits (Caspi *et al.* 2005).

With regard to the other two issues, the biological approach is less consistent. *Maturation*, the genetically-programmed development of characteristics over time, often involves the idea of *critical periods* for development, as noted earlier. Essentially, a critical period represents a discontinuity in development – the individual will react differently depending on the timing of experience. While difficult to prove in humans, many researchers believe that there are critical periods for both social attachment and language learning during the first few years of childhood (Bornstein 1989). According to this view, a child who does not form close emotional ties, or receive exposure to language, at this time will show a permanent deficit in these behaviours (Bowlby 1988; Lenneberg 1967). While the notion of a critical period suggests that discontinuities or stages exist in development, in other areas, such as temperament, the biological approach emphasizes the continuities of development. Hence, one cannot make a simple generalization about how the biological approach views the issue of continuity vs. discontinuity.

In terms of the third issue, the validity of domain-general vs. domain-specific models, the biological approach seems to favour domain-specific models. As suggested in the previous paragraph, various aspects of development are seen as having different characteristics, and this implies different underlying sub-processes. At the practical level, no one within the biological approach has suggested a comprehensive, domain-general model of development, though Zuckerman has proposed a model for personality (Zuckerman 1991). Thus, it seems reasonable to describe the biological approach as advocating domain-specific models of development.

The Behaviourist Approach

Compared to the biological approach, the behaviourist approach takes a polar-opposite view of the importance of heredity vs. experience. In fact, Skinner has suggested that physiological processes within the organism are of no concern, provided one can find meaningful links between stimulus conditions and behavioural responses (Skinner 1974). All behaviour is seen as determined by experience, based on the principles of *classical* and *operant conditioning*. Rather than being based on discrete stages, the approach views behavioural change (development) as a continuous process. Since the principles of conditioning are seen as applicable to all behaviour, the behaviourist approach represents a domain-general model.

The main problem this approach faces, in terms of explaining personality, is how to account for the apparent consistency of behaviour. After all, the principles of learning would seem to imply that change is as probable as consistency, since there is no explicit factor pushing for constancy. Skinner and other behaviourists have responded to this problem by suggesting that 'personality' is simply a perceived pattern, with no basis within the individual. Instead, they suggest two factors which could produce the consistencies which are ascribed to personality. One factor is the cumulative effect of reinforcement (Salzinger 1996). Each time we are reinforced, the influence of that reinforcer is *in addition to* all prior reinforcement in the same or similar situations. Rarely is one experience so significant as to override our entire past **history of reinforcement**. (This is one reason that attempts at changing behavioural patterns like bad habits overnight rarely succeed.) Hence, the consistency of behaviour, particularly in adults, is largely a product of prior patterns of reinforcement.

history of reinforcement in operant conditioning, the sum of all prior reinforcement for a particular behaviour; behaviourists assert that the cumulative history of reinforcement is more important than any single reinforcement in determining behaviour.

The other factor which behaviourists point to in explaining behavioural consistency is the role of *environmental consistency*. Skinner has argued that in trying to explain behaviour, we tend to give credit to the individual, not the environment, especially when we are unaware of the contingencies which govern the behaviour (Skinner 1971). In the case of the consistencies which we attribute to personality, we tend to overlook the degree to which the typical person's environment is consistent. For example, most of us have daily routines which are quite regular, we associate primarily with the same group of friends and acquaintances, we tend to live in the same place for relatively extended periods, and so on. These patterns of activities contribute to making our environment relatively consistent, thereby increasing the consistency of our behaviour (Caspi and Roberts 2001). At least partial support for this comes from further analyses of the Berkeley longitudinal study (mentioned previously), which found that married couples who were rated as more similar in personality tended to engage in more similar activities (Caspi *et al.* 1990).

Given these processes, it would be surprising if our behaviour were *not* fairly consistent. Beyond that, behaviourists are not obliged to suggest a mechanism for *perfect* consistency, since nearly every study of personality shows that consistency is generally far from absolute (Caspi *et al.* 2005; Lewis 2001). Thus, behaviourists would argue that the behavioural patterns which we call 'personality' are simply the result of the cumulative effects of reinforcement, together with overlooked sources of environmental consistency.

The Cognitive Approach

The cognitive approach is interested in how cognitive processes influence behaviour. In this sense, cognitive psychologists are as interested in why we *believe* in the concept of personality as in the factors that promote actual behavioural consistency. Let us consider first our tendency to believe that behaviour is consistent.

Over 30 years ago, Walter Mischel challenged the trait view of personality by arguing that while consistencies in behaviour may exist, they are much more situation-specific than most people realize (Mischel 1968). In this sense, perceived consistencies may reflect a form of mental bias rather than true characteristics. Explaining the origins of such biases is part of the

social perception the study of the social aspects of perception – how we see other people, and ourselves in relation to others.

study of social perception. **Social perception** is concerned with the social dimension of perception – how we see others, and ourselves in relation to others. As noted earlier, cognitive theory argues that we actively interpret our experiences, forming mental schemata about both people and situations. One example of this is the study of *attribution theory*, which deals with the kinds of inferences we make about the causes of behaviour – both our own, and that of other people (see Chapter 4). For example, the *fundamental attribution error* states that we place too much emphasis on internal characteristics (personality), and too little on environmental influences (the situation) when interpreting other people's behaviour (Ross 1977). Such bias would lead to overestimating the actual consistency of behaviour, and thus our willingness to believe that personality traits exist.

If personality does not represent inherent traits, then how do the consistencies arise? The answer proposed by Mischel and others is based on **cognitive social learning theory**, which

cognitive social learning theory (sometimes simply 'social learning theory') a theory derived from the cognitive approach which asserts that behaviour can be learned from observing other people, and that behaviour is mediated by cognitive schemata.

looks at behaviour from a cognitive and social perspective (Bandura 1986, 1991; Berkowitz 1984). Cognitive social learning theory is based on two premises: first, it argues that much of our behaviour is learned from interactions with others, especially through imitation (hence the 'social learning' component). *Imitation* (also called 'observational learning' or 'modelling') is concerned with learning based on observing others, as opposed to direct experience. Second, it asserts that the mental constructs that we form (values, expectations and other schemata) mediate our behaviour in ways that produce our personality (hence the 'cognitive' component). Since constructs are generally closely tied to specific situations, the theory argues for the kind of limited behavioural consistency cited by Mischel. (More recently, Mischel has modified his position, suggesting that personal schemata interact with the specific situation – see Mischel 2004; Mischel and Shoda 1995). One area where social learning and social cognition (including social perception) seem to play a significant role is the effect of parenting styles and parental expectations on children's behaviour (Baumrind 1991; MacKinnon-Lewis *et al.* 1997). (For a further discussion of parenting, see Box 7.4).

Box 7.4 *Personality, Parents and Culture*

How much influence do parents have on the personality of their children? And what role does culture play in parenting practices? Obviously parents matter, in that they determine both the genetic make-up and the domestic environment of their children. In terms of psychological theories, the idea that parents' behaviour shapes children's personalities can be traced back to Freud. His developmental theory argued that the importance of events in the first five years was crucial to later development. In particular, the child's superego is formed by identification with their parents. Later researchers, while often rejecting Freud's model of development, have focused on the role of parents as a source of reinforcement (behaviourist) as well as imitation and mental schemata (cognitive). Over time, a large body of research has supported the idea that factors like parenting styles, for example, have a significant impact on children's personality and behaviour (see text).

While parents clearly matter, one way to understand variations in parenting is by looking at other cultures. In every culture, there is a belief system about the role of parents, what goals they should have in raising their children, and the best way to go about this. The parental belief system in any society is influenced by the overall beliefs of the culture, and is entwined with many other aspects of life in that society. In turn, the belief systems of the parents influence their treatment of their children, and also the values they transmit to their children. For example, a Malaysian manual for Islamic parents notes that rewarding children for proper behaviour is very important under Islamic law, but that Malaysian culture and language do not encourage praising children (al' Mahdi 2002). In general, current cross-cultural research shows clearly the influence of culture on parenting practices, but is less clear in linking variations in parenting to outcomes for children.

In one study, Richman *et al.* (1988) found that, compared to middle-class mothers in the USA, Gusii mothers of Kenya look at and talk less to their 9- to 10-month-old babies. However, the Gusii mothers hold and physically soothe their babies more. This appears rather paradoxical until one examines the Gusii culture and beliefs. The Gussii believe that children under the age of 2 years do not understand language, and that eye contact is to be avoided in all cases. Holding and physically soothing, however, are seen (appropriately) as aiding in the child's survival. By contrast, American parents often believe that stimulation in infancy (and even prenatally) is important to maximize development. In fact, a few years ago, the state of Georgia distributed CDs of Mozart's music to new mothers, in hopes of providing enrichment (Kagan 1998)!

Another example concerns the Efe, a Pygmy group who live in the Congo (Gardiner and Kosmitzki 2002). The Efe live in extended family groups of about 20 to 30 people, because in their jungle environment survival depends on group cooperation and sharing in all matters, from food gathering to child rearing. The Efe strongly believe that a new mother should not be the first to hold her new-born child. This assures that other family members, including the father, will be present at the birth, thereby increasing the physical aid for the mother and child, and enhancing the extended family's feeling of responsibility for the child. This practice also ensures that the child will quickly become accustomed to multiple caregivers – a pattern reinforced by the constant presence of others, and the common practice of a woman other than the mother breast-feeding the child. Through this form of multiple caregiving, the children are prepared for a life of interdependency and social interaction that will enhance their chances for survival in a dangerous environment. In the end, parenting is a universal source of influence in development, but the practices of parenting can vary significantly with culture.

Not surprisingly, the cognitive approach is strongly environmentalist, and largely ignores the role of heredity in behaviour. This is evident in the rejection of trait concepts of personality, which typically assert that traits are based on innate factors. In terms of the issue of continuity vs. discontinuity, the theory largely favours continuity. For example, when children are allowed to observe adults doing Piagetian tasks before being tested themselves, their performance is not always consistent with Piaget's model of cognitive stages (Rosser 1994). With respect to the issue of domain-specificity, the cognitive approach appears to be domain-general, in that it views many aspects of development as open to explanation, from cognitive development to personality and moral development. However, this conclusion is largely tied to the two previous points: if development is seen as a continuous process of learning, it is open to a domain-general model. As yet, however, no one has attempted to use cognitive social learning theory as a general developmental framework.

The Psychodynamic Approach

While the psychodynamic approach encompasses a number of theorists, Freud is still the dominant figure. The psychoanalytic theory which he developed provides a framework for interpreting nearly every aspect of behaviour, including the origin and nature of personality. In Freud's view, all behaviour is motivated by innate drives, whose mode of expression changes over the course of development. These changes in expression of the drives define the *stages of development* which shape the formation of adult personality: the oral, anal, phallic, latent and genital stages. Personality is based on the three components of *id*, *ego* and *superego*, which dynamically interact to direct behaviour. Id, the source of the drives, is present from birth. By contrast, ego and superego are formed over time, with the first five years of life being of central importance.

While the drives determine the sequence and timing of the stages of development, Freud believed that *experience* was an important factor in the shaping of personality. In particular, the way the individual learned to handle the expression and gratification of the basic drives would determine the conflicts and coping strategies which defined much of adult personality. Unfortunately, by emphasizing early development as the source of personality formation, Freud had little to say about possible changes during adult life. Neo-Freudian theorist Erik Erikson has addressed this issue by creating a model of personality development with stages across the entire lifespan (see Chapter 5).

Freud's theory is fairly explicit in terms of the basic issues of development. His emphasis on innate drives clearly argues for the role of heredity – indeed, his view of aggression as innate has been a frequent focus of criticism. At the same time, he clearly recognized the importance of nurture, particularly in terms of the effects of early experiences. Consequently, it is appropriate to classify Freud as an interactionist in relation to heredity vs. environment – he saw both factors as important to development. With respect to the issue of continuity, it is apparent that Freud saw development as discontinuous. His stages were biologically defined by the expression of the innate drives, and hence fixed both in sequence and timing. In terms of domain specificity, Freud's theory is clearly domain-general. Freud did not invoke different processes to distinguish the development of cognitive capacities (largely connected to ego) from the development of personality. In his view, all of behaviour could be understood in terms of the same basic processes. Indeed, while the specifics of his theory have been frequently challenged, his work still stands as one of the most remarkable attempts at creation of a comprehensive theory of behaviour.

The Humanistic Approach

The humanistic approach includes a large number of specific theories, which share certain basic assumptions, but differ in many details. One respect in which they differ is the degree of attention paid to questions of development, with some theorists, like Viktor Frankl, scarcely using the word 'personality'. Hence, in order to provide a useful basis for comparison in this context, we will focus on the work of Carl Rogers (Rogers 1969).

Rogers sees all of growth and development as motivated by the *actualizing tendency*, a biologically-based drive to reach one's full potential. However, the primary factors which influence the process of growth are cognitive and experiential, not biological. Like other humanists, Rogers emphasizes the way individuals see themselves in relation to their surroundings. This *phenomenological* approach means that behaviour can only be understood in terms of the meaning the individual gives to it.

In Rogers's theory of personality, over time each person comes to define their *self* and their *ideal self*. The self stems largely from the actualizing tendency, and reflects innate tendencies; however, the ideal self is strongly influenced by experience, particularly interactions with other people. This influence is expressed largely through the type of *positive regard* we receive. Rogers sees the outcome of healthy development as a *fully functioning person*, which is defined in terms of an ongoing process rather than a static end state. Thus, Rogers sees development as a lifelong, continuous process rather than a series of specific stages.

In terms of the nature–nurture issue, Rogers supports aspects of each view. For example, he acknowledges the importance of the innate actualizing tendency, and has gone so far as to suggest that particular values are embedded in the actualizing tendency (Rogers 1969). He also sees our need for positive regard as having an innate basis. Thus, the forces which motivate growth are largely reflective of heredity – but the same is not true of the factors that shape personality. The most significant aspect of personality functioning for Rogers is the relationship between the self and the ideal self, which is largely influenced by our interactions with others. The *conditions for growth* which Rogers has specified (openness, empathy and unconditional positive regard) are all provided by other people; hence, in this respect, his theory emphasizes the importance of experience. Overall, his theory can be seen as reflecting an interactionist view of heredity and environment.

The remaining question is whether he views development as domain-specific or not. Overall, he seems to present a domain-general model, since he does not explicitly divide development into different aspects or processes. However, one must also note that he says very little about some aspects of development, such as physical and cognitive development. Given these omissions, one can only really evaluate his theory in terms of what it *does* consider, personality development. Within this domain, it does seem to present a general model, but as a theory of development, it is clearly not as comprehensive as the theories of Freud and Skinner.

Summary

The five approaches view personality very differently, ranging from the biological view that personality is innate, to the behaviourist/cognitive assertion that personality does not exist. While the differences are significant, one should consider the approaches as providing insight on different aspects of the issue, not as simply being right or wrong. The reality is that the behaviour patterns we call 'personality' are complex, and as Jerome Kagan has noted, there is a temptation to oversimplify, especially when using words like 'temperament' (Kagan 1998). Hence, it may be the case that no single approach is sufficient to explain the development of personality. To explore this in a more specific way, let us look at the issue of gender role development.

Try it Yourself

Are you similar or dissimilar to your parents? For example, do you have 'your father's temper' or 'your mother's stubbornness'? What do you think accounts for this? Does your explanation fit with one of the approaches discussed? How would each of the five approaches account for the similarities and dissimilarities between you and your parents? Overall, which approach's explanation of personality do you find most compelling?

The Development of Gender Roles

'Boys will be boys,' states an old saying. Unfortunately, this simple statement belies the complexity of the questions which underlie it. What *are* boys like? Do they really act differently from girls? And if so, *why*? We know there are differences associated with sex – for instance, males are typically larger and stronger than females – but do these differences account for why, for example, boys play with trucks and girls play with dolls?

gender roles patterns of behaviour which a culture defines as being appropriate for each gender.

The existence of two physical sexes is one of the most obvious characteristics of human beings. This biological fact is often regarded as equivalent to a psychological imperative – that is, that behaviours *associated with* sex (gender roles) are directly *determined by* gender. However, the realities are not as simple as this view implies. For one thing, **gender roles** refer to the behaviours which a culture considers appropriate for each gender, and differences exist across cultures (Ford and Beach 1951; Mead 1935; Price and Crapo 2002). Therefore, there is no universal definition of 'male' and 'female' gender roles; instead, the definition depends on the culture one lives in. In talking about gender roles, we encounter the same kinds of questions of individuality and causation that are part of the larger domain of personality in general. To try to understand such behaviour, let us consider how each theory interprets the development of gender roles.

The Biological Approach

The physical differences in body structure which are associated with gender are obviously rooted in heredity. Chromosomally, males have an XY pattern, while females have an XX pattern. In turn, the expression of this genetic pattern is dependent on the actions of hormones, which affect the development of physical sex characteristics. In particular, the presence or absence of **androgens**, the male hormones, determines prenatal physical development: if androgen is present, the foetus develops male characteristics; if it is not, the foetus develops female characteristics. Normally, the amount of androgens present is determined by the genes associated with the sex chromosomes. However, there are cases where the process

androgens hormones whose functions are related to masculine characteristics; the most important is testosterone.

goes awry, either because of genetic defects or environmental factors (such as the presence of drugs which affect androgen levels). In such cases, the development of physical characteristics, including genitalia, can be affected. Thus, at the level of the physical characteristics associated with gender, the nativist position of the biological approach is well supported.

The crucial question, though, is whether *behaviour* is determined in the same way. The biological approach would say it is, and therefore that gender role differences are the result of biological/evolutionary processes. For example, Buss has drawn on evolutionary theory to suggest that the different reproductive challenges faced by men and women have led to them having different gender roles (Buss 1995). Certainly, the existence of cultural stereotypes of males and females is consistent with this view. For example, males are typically seen as more aggressive than females in nearly all cultures (Williams and Best 1982). While such observations support the biological view, we need to ask if there is any direct evidence for innate behavioural differences based on gender, since stereotypes may influence behaviour in ways unrelated to heredity.

One area where there seem to be innate differences is in physical activity. A number of studies have found that boys are typically more physically active than girls, even in early infancy (Eaton and Enns 1986). The early appearance of this difference suggests an innate factor, which might be mediated by hormonal influences. That is, hormones seem to affect development of the brain as well as the body, and this results in gender-related differences in behaviour (Kimura 1999). Evidence for hormonal influence comes from cases of androgenized females (genetic females exposed to high levels of androgens prenatally). In these cases, physical development is affected, but also behaviour – the girls are typically more physically active and tomboyish than their peers (Berenbaum and Hines 1992; Money and Tucker 1975). In addition, a study of British fraternal twins found that girls with twin brothers were more active and adventurous than those with a twin sister (Resnick *et al.* 1993). Why would this be? The researchers attributed the results to the influence of prenatal exposure to androgens from the sibling. (Socialization seemed an unlikely explanation, since boys with twin sisters were not less active than boys with twin brothers.) Hence, physical activity level may be a gender difference which has a hereditary origin.

Hormonal effects on brain development have been directly demonstrated in other mammals, and apparent differences in the brains of men and women have been interpreted in the same way (Kimura 1999). In terms of how this might affect behaviour, Kimura cites the tendency for men to outperform women on certain spatial tasks, while women outperform men in fine motor coordination. While not directly proving that performance differences are hormonal, research has linked testosterone levels in men, and hormonal menstrual variations in women, to differences in spatial performance (Choi and Silverman 2002; Silverman and Phillips 1997). This difference, however, seems to be affected by the content of the measures used (Alexander and Evardone 2008; Alexander and Son 2007), so the issue is not completely settled. Hormonal levels have also been linked to other behavioural measures, including speed of speech (Wadnerkar *et al.* 2006) and aspects of sexuality (see *The World Today: Hormones and Sexuality*).

The world today: **Hormones and Sexuality**

Many women believe that their sexuality is dictated by their learning and their choice, and this is undoubtedly true to a great extent. But there is noteworthy evidence to suggest that women are also affected by the cyclical nature of their hormones when it comes to their preferences in men. For example, Little *et al.* (2007) report on studies which demonstrate that during the fertile phase of a woman's menstrual cycle, she may prefer men with:

- more masculine facial features;
- a more masculine voice;
- greater height;
- more dominant behaviour.

In addition, their research demonstrates that at this time, women also prefer more masculine body shapes in men. Little and his colleagues found, however, that this effect was found mainly when women were contemplating short-term, not long-term relationships, and not in women using hormonal contraceptives. They speculate that women may be evolutionarily prepared to value masculine physical and behavioural characteristics denoting strength and survival significance in men when the chance of their becoming pregnant and passing on these genes to their children is greatest. But for long-term relationships, looks and 'macho' behaviour may not be so valued!

One fact which tends to work against the biological view, at least in the simple form that sex determines gender roles, is the tremendous variation in behaviour *within* each sex, which results in overlap *between* the sexes. Compared to this, the overall differences which can be associated to sex are fairly small: Deaux (1985) has estimated that only 5 per cent of individual differences among children can be attributed to sex. This leaves the question of how such small differences can produce stable and well-differentiated gender roles. In essence, if boys and girls are so similar, how can their gender roles be so different? In this regard, John Money has argued that socialization, not hormones, determines an individual's sense of **gender identity**, and hence gender role (Money and Tucker 1975) (see Box 7.5 for more on gender identity).

gender identity an individual's belief about whether they are male or female.

Similarly, while arguing that gender differences have an evolutionary origin, Kenrick and Luce (2000) acknowledge that both culture and cognitive processes influence the observed behaviours. Hence, gender roles seem to involve more than simply biological sex; to understand this, we must see what other approaches have to say about the development of gender roles.

Box 7.5 Nature, Nurture and Gender Identity

While the origin of gender roles may be complex, at first glance gender identity seems very straight-forward – after all, it's pretty obvious who is a boy and who is a girl. Or is it? While human beings consist of two biological sexes, the experience of gender identity is not so simple. Some individuals grow up feeling they were 'born with the wrong parts', and feel their body is inconsistent with their gender identity. Such transsexuals may even seek surgery to make their body's appearance consistent with their sense of gender identity. Other individuals, of either sex, may exhibit appearance and behaviour which seems to be a blend of male and female – an androgynous gender identity. Hence, sex does not automatically determine gender identity.

The complexities of gender identity are vividly illustrated by a disorder called TFS. A genetic disorder, TFS causes biological males to be insensitive to the prenatal effects of male hormones. Consequently, they are born with ambiguous genitals and are typically raised as females. However, more male hormones are produced at puberty, and those with TFS suddenly develop secondary sex characteristics such as beards and a generally masculinized appearance. While rare overall, TFS is common among particular groups who share the genetic defect, including a particular group in the Dominican Republic, and the Sambia of New Guinea.

Given the ambiguity of gender at birth, and subsequent changes at puberty, it is interesting to consider how TFS affects gender identity. Imperato-McGinley *et al.* (1979) studied 18 of these individuals and found that 16 of them made what seemed to be an easy transition to being male after spending their childhoods as females. Of the remaining two, one chose to retain a female identity, and the other chose a male identity but continued to dress as a female. What can we make of this? One obvious possibility is that the children's early socialization as females was much less important than the effect of the male hormones that surged through the children's bodies at puberty. Hence, nature seems to win in determining gender identity. However, Ehrhardt (1985) has suggested an alternative. It is possible that the parents of these children, knowing of the prevalence of TFS in their group and seeing the ambiguity of their children's genitals, treated them differently. That is, these children may not have had a typically 'feminine' socialization. Also, since children in this society would often bathe together in the river, they undoubtedly had the opportunity to see for themselves that they were not similar to other girls. Consequently, this may have caused them to be less committed to the feminine role. Hence these differences in experience could potentially account for the relatively easy and swift transition these children made to the male sex. Another possibility is suggested by an investigation of TFS in the Sambia of New Guinea (Herdt and Davidson 1988). For these children, a switch to a male role seemed to be based more on social factors, specifically the argument that they could not bear children as females, but could father children as males. Then again, the possibility that male hormones at puberty play the largest role in the changing gender identity cannot be ruled out. Gender identity, like gender roles, can be complex.

The Behaviourist Approach

Behaviourists like Skinner argue that all behaviour is shaped by reinforcement, so if variations exist across individuals, this implies differences in reinforcement history. In terms of gender roles, this view is supported by research showing that right from birth, boys and girls are treated differently (Maccoby and Jacklin 1974; Pomerlau *et al.* 1990). This pattern occurs in childcare settings as well as at home, and possibly increases in later childhood (Chick *et al.* 2002; Huston *et al.* 1986; Sanford 2006). Thus, the behaviourist approach would argue that the behaviours associated with gender roles, like other cultural patterns, are shaped by reinforcement, and hence are learned, not innate (see Guerin 1992).

This approach is consistent with the observation that gender roles differ across cultures, for both men and women (Gibbons 2000; Whiting and Edwards 1988). Cultural variations, of course, are generally easier to explain in terms of learning than in terms of heredity. The behaviourist approach also makes it easy to explain individual differences, since experiences can differ for each individual.

One disadvantage of the behaviourist view, however (a problem shared by all environmentalist theories) is the difficulty of explaining the *origin* of gender roles. If the patterns are entirely learned, then where did they come from in the first place? *Why* should males and females be treated differently? The behaviourist approach gives no specific answer to this question, but would suggest two possibilities:

1 small biological differences are selectively amplified over time by differential reinforcement; or

2 the pattern is random, somewhat the way different pigeons respond differently to the same schedule of non-contingent reinforcement (see Chapter 3).

If the first explanation is true, then in fact there is a biological component to gender roles; as already noted, this seems consistent with data on male–female differences in aggressiveness. The second interpretation seems less plausible, since it is not clear how random reinforcement would result in differences based on sex, as opposed to simply random variation across individuals. Like evolutionary theories of gender roles, directly testing these two proposals would seem to require going back in time, which is clearly not a viable option. However, based on the available evidence, it seems likely that biological differences became elaborated by reinforcement. If so, it strengthens the view that development depends on an interaction between nature and nurture. As we will see, the cognitive approach agrees that reinforcement is one factor which contributes to gender roles, but sees it as only one part of the process.

The Cognitive Approach

The existence of gender roles, from the cognitive viewpoint, implies that individuals have a mental schema which tells them what is appropriate behaviour for their sex. This is supported by the evidence that sexual stereotypes exist. For example, university students in the USA identify certain attributes as masculine or feminine (see Box 7.6). The formation of such **gender schemata** seems to begin very early: 2-year-olds can already identify the gender of individuals based on clothing or style of hair (Thompson 1975), show preferences for toys which they perceive as congruent with their

gender schema (pl., schemata) a cognitive representation which organizes an individual's knowledge of cultural norms for male or female behaviour.

gender (Campbell *et al.* 2002) and can identify gender stereotypes of household tasks (Serbin *et al.* 2002). By the time children are 5 or 6, their memory for events differs based on whether what they are asked to recall is gender-consistent or not (Martin and Halverson 1983). At the same time, the development of such schemata is gradual, and often children as old as 5 have not yet grasped that gender is a permanent attribute, and full gender constancy may not be achieved until the ages of 6 or 7 (Carver *et al.* 2003). For example, they may believe that someone can change gender by wearing clothes usually worn by the opposite sex (Marcus and Overton 1978)!

How do children form such concepts, either about others or about themselves? Cognitive theory argues that the behaviour of others, particularly adults, provides an example which is *imitated*, through the process of social learning (Perry and Bussey 1979). Any parent can readily cite examples of children attempting to copy adult actions, ranging from Daddy using a

Box 7.6 Gender Roles and Stereotypes

One way that gender roles are expressed is through stereotypes of men and women – for example, that men are 'forceful' and women are 'tender'. Not surprisingly, individuals within a culture will often show high consistency in evaluating what sort of traits are considered masculine or feminine. A recent study looked at ratings by students in an American college, and compared them with results on the same scale, collected almost 30 years ago, with a similar sampling of university students (Auster and Ohm 2000). The lists below give some of the main results:

Masculine attributes	Feminine attributes
Acts as a leader	Compassionate
Aggressive	Gentle
Ambitious	Loves children
Dominant	Sensitive to needs of others
Forceful	Tender
Independent	Understanding

On all of the attributes listed, there was a significant agreement by both men and women – and this had not changed in the period between the two surveys (completed in 1972 and 1999). Yet, as Auster and Ohm note, during this period there were significant changes in American culture, particularly in terms of the work environment. For example, the proportion of married women working went from 40 per cent to 70 per cent, the percentage of female law graduates went from 5 per cent to almost 50 per cent, and men were more likely to be involved in childcare and enter 'female' occupations like physiotherapy. So does this mean that work behaviour had changed, but attitudes had not? Actually, the study also indicates several attributes for which ratings had changed. For example, where men were originally seen as more 'analytical' and women as more 'yielding', both men and women agreed that there was now no significant difference on these attributes. Interestingly, the study indicates that most changes in ratings reflect changes by men – for example, men no longer saw any difference between the genders for 'individualistic', 'self-reliant' or 'willing to take a stand' – but women continued to see these traits as masculine. Ironically, it appears there had been change in both the workplace and men's attitudes, but the women students in the study had yet to integrate these changes into their own ideas about gender roles.

screwdriver to Mummy cooking. Once children enter school, peers are also significant as models to be imitated; older siblings are also a model for social learning of gender roles (McHale *et al.* 2001). Albert Bandura has suggested that such observational learning is a major factor in gender role development (Bandura 1977). However, other researchers have indicated that children are more concerned with gender-consistency of behaviour than with the sex of the model, until at least about age 6 (Masters *et al.* 1979). For example, boys will still play with a truck, which they regard as a boy's toy, after watching a girl play with it. It is not until the concept of gender as a permanent attribute of a person is established (around age 7) that the sex of models seems to influence children's behaviours. Although it does not rule out other forms of learning (such as direct reinforcement) as a factor in gender role development, this finding does suggest that imitation is not a sufficient explanation by itself.

As children learn about gender schemata, they also learn about what the *norms* for their society are, and how a violation of a gender role norm is viewed. Does it surprise you to learn that boys with feminine hairstyles and clothing are viewed more negatively than are girls with masculine hairstyles and clothing? A study by Blakemore (2003) found that children as young as 3 were likely to react negatively to clothing and behaviour that violated gender role norms. Hence, children learning about gender roles are forming concepts of appropriate behaviour and also social expectations.

Overall, the cognitive approach emphasizes how mental schemata interact with the effects of social experience (reinforcement and imitation) in directing gender role behaviour. For example, in general, the cognitive approach offers a more specific model for the role of experience in gender role development than does behaviourism. Indeed, since many of the reinforcers that children receive are social (such as praise from a parent or teacher), the approach in some ways incorporates the behaviourist notion of operant learning. Despite this, there are still many details unresolved, and competing models exist within the cognitive approach (for example, Eagly 2001; Martin *et al.* 2002).

One aspect that remains unclear is the role of biological factors. Since gender schemata obviously include the recognition of sex, the influence of sex distinctions cannot be ignored in formation of gender roles. Similarly, the fact that certain attributes seem to be associated with gender roles in nearly every culture remains to be explained (Williams and Best 1982). While social learning addresses the process of forming gender roles *within* a culture, why should cultures across the globe share particular attributes (such as males being more aggressive) in their gender roles? (Of course, as already noted, considerable variation exists for other attributes.) The willingness to address such issues in understanding gender roles has waned and waxed in the past 30 years, sometimes reflecting political attitudes which are themselves probably socially learned (see Eagly 1995; Eagly and Diekman 2006). Although no final answer can as yet be given, it may well be that future cognitive models will require integration with some biologically-based factors.

The Psychodynamic Approach

As noted earlier, Freud's theory of development acknowledges both biological and experiential factors. Biological influences are reflected in the innateness of the sexual drive which is seen as motivating much of our behaviour, and in the biologically-determined *stages of psychosexual development*. The existence of the sexual drive cannot itself explain gender roles, however, since Freud did not see the drive as gender-oriented. Instead, he saw the development of gender roles as a product of the child's attempt to resolve the *Oedipal conflict* during the *phallic stage* of development (Wittkower and Robertson 1979). For a boy, the mother is the prototype for future relationships, while the father is a rival for the mother's attention. In order to cope with the anxiety created by the Oedipal conflict (including fears that the father will retaliate by castrating him), the boy uses the defence mechanism of *identification*, thereby modelling his behaviour on that of his father. This process of identification establishes the boy's gender role. Although the dynamics are somewhat different for girls, ultimately identification still provides the basis for the formation of gender roles in both sexes. Freud believed that the absence of a parent, particularly the same-sex parent, could distort the normal process of development, with consequent effects on gender role development. For example, a boy without a father, lacking both a model and the need to identify, might fail to develop male gender role behaviour.

In limited ways, Freud's theory is consistent with the available evidence. For example, he correctly identified the period around ages 3 to 5 as being significant in the formation of gender

The world today: **Parents' Reactions to Gender Nonconformity**

It seems clear that all the approaches discussed in this book admit that parents encourage, reinforce and model their children's chromosomal gender identity. Yet it is equally clear from cross-cultural research that what constitutes a society's conception of 'male' and 'female' may differ from culture to culture. In western society, it seems intuitively obvious that this society's conception of what constitutes 'male' and 'female' has changed over time as well. The Women's Liberation Movement, started in the early years of the twentieth century and coming into great prominence in the 1960s and 1970s, heralded changes in laws governing equality of rights, opportunities and pay scales for men and women. Didn't parents start to raise their children differently, then? Didn't they become less rigid in their ideas about what behaviours, clothing and toys were suitable for their sons and their daughters? Yes and no, replies Emily Kane (2006). She interviewed a diverse group of parents in the northeastern part of the USA and found some mixed results. First, these parents appeared to endorse a greater range of behaviours for their children than indicated by a traditional conception of gender roles. Thus, they (mothers in particular) thought it was acceptable for their children to have interests typically associated with the opposite sex: both boys and girls were encouraged to learn domestic skills such as cooking that have been traditionally thought of as being in the feminine domain, and athletic skills that have been traditionally thought of as being in the masculine domain. The parents wanted both their sons and their daughters to be nurturant and empathic, traits traditionally associated with females. But they indicated more constraint with their sons than their daughters; that is, they seemed more comfortable with their daughters following a masculine gender role than with their sons following a feminine gender role. While there was little worry about a 'tomboyish' daughter, there was far more worry about a 'girlish' son, especially from fathers. In fact, Kane entitled her article 'No way my boys are going to be like that!' The parents might give their sons dolls and cooking sets as gifts, but they became upset if their sons tried using nail polish or expressed interest in dance (especially ballet). Parents were particularly upset if their sons expressed an interest in Barbie dolls. One mother compromised with her son who asked for a Barbie doll by getting him a NASCAR Barbie, and one father expressed great relief that his son seemed more interested in a Ken doll than in Barbie! Parents were also concerned if their sons cried openly or showed passivity, but they were far more tolerant of this in their daughters. Kane found that the parents' concern about traditionally feminine behaviours in their sons revolved around the possibility that their sons might be or might be perceived as being homosexual. Her conclusion is that while it is clear that there have been changes in adherence to traditional gender role rearing in western society, there is still a clear devaluation of what has been considered feminine.

identity (Fagot 1985). In addition, there is some evidence that when boys have no father figure to identify with, their gender role behaviour is often less masculine (Stevenson and Black 1988).

Beyond these points, Freud's theory doesn't fare very well. Since identification, like social learning theory, predicts that children will imitate parents, one might expect that any studies favouring imitative behaviour would therefore support Freud's theory. However, identification is seen as based on anxiety and fear, not positive feelings. Instead, the evidence suggests that nurturance produces more imitative behaviour than does parental dominance (Hetherington and Frankie 1967). Overall, the evidence, while not extensive, is not very supportive of Freud's theory as applied to gender roles.

The Humanistic Approach

The humanistic approach is perhaps the most difficult to evaluate in the present context, since little is said about specific elements of development. Even Rogers's theory is problematical, since he did not directly address the issue of gender roles. As an aspect of the *ideal self*, gender roles would be influenced by the *conditional positive regard* that a child receives. That is, parents and others would set expectations related to gender roles by establishing *conditions of worth*. In order to receive positive regard, the individual would then *introject* these expectations into the ideal self as definitions of appropriate behaviour. For example, a 5-year-old girl who shows an interest in playing with a toy truck may be told, 'Oh, trucks are for boys. You should play with your doll instead!' Similarly, a boy may be told that 'cooking is for girls'. Such messages can easily be incorporated in the ideal self, effectively instilling cultural norms for gender roles (see *The World Today: Parents' Reactions to Gender Nonconformity*).

Beyond such general points, Rogers's theory offers few insights into the process of gender role development. Since he never specifically addressed the topic of gender roles, there has been no research to explore the issue from within the Rogerian framework. However, in some respects, Rogers's theory is consistent with interpretations offered by other approaches. Since positive regard in Rogers's theory functions in ways that are similar to positive reinforcement in behaviourist theory, it reflects a similar emphasis on learning and experience. One can also draw a parallel between the Rogerian view of *self* as based on the individual's perceptions and experiences, and the cognitive concept of a *mental schema*. Since both the processes and predicted outcomes are very similar, it will require further research to distinguish whether there are fundamental differences, or simply different conceptual labels for the same underlying process.

Summary

Overall, the two most plausible approaches for understanding gender roles and sexual identity are the biological and the cognitive. While very different in their interpretations, each is well developed theoretically, and supported by a wide range of relevant research. The behaviourist model, emphasizing the role of reinforcement, is clearly relevant, but seems like a limited version of cognitive social learning theory, with no specific advantages of its own in explaining gender role behaviour. The theories of Freud and Rogers, as representative of the psychodynamic and humanistic approaches, are largely inadequate, albeit for rather different reasons: Freud's theory does not seem consistent with the available evidence, and Rogers's theory is not sufficiently specific to be seriously evaluated. However, there are still many aspects of this topic, like development as a whole, which are not resolved. At present, the evidence suggests that what is needed is a model which incorporates elements of both the biological and cognitive approaches – interactionist, and able to integrate heredity, learning and culture.

Try it Yourself

Does your name immediately reveal your gender to others? Have you noticed anyone who knows your name being surprised at seeing you for the first time? Many parents today are giving their children names that do not directly reflect the gender of the child in western society (for example, Jordan, Mackenzie, Casey). Why do you think parents are choosing these names? Suppose that parents of a new child, in order to avoid gender-bias, took this further and decided to raise their new baby as an 'it' rather than as a boy or girl. What would be the advantages of this? What problems might arise? What would each theory predict in terms of the effects this would have on the development of a gender role?

CONCLUSION

Developmental psychology is concerned with the changes that occur during human life. This interest in understanding the course of life is not unique to psychology; for example, biographers also try to capture the span of life. What distinguishes the study of development in psychology are the questions asked and the methods used. A biographer seeks to understand a single person's life, and in doing so, tends to emphasize the events which are unique to that person – for instance, how their place of birth, family or particular experiences shaped their development. By contrast, developmental psychologists are interested in the principles which are common to all lives – the processes which describe development in general. The challenge is to identify and understand these common principles.

As we have seen, there are several basic issues which arise in the study of development. For example, is development a continual unfolding, or a series of discrete stages? Asking about *continuity* vs. *discontinuity* is not just a matter of how we *describe* development, but also of identifying the *processes* which direct it.

An equally major concern is the role of *heredity* and *environment*. Although often oversimplified, the issue is not whether development is controlled by one factor or the other, but rather *how* does each one influence a given behaviour, and how do they *interact*? Phrased in this way, the study of heredity and environment becomes the foundation for all developmental research.

The challenges of developmental research are clearly seen in the way each of the five approaches views the process of development, and the fact that, at present, no approach seems capable of offering a comprehensive (*domain-general*) model. This may partly reflect the limitations of each framework, but also suggests that development is not a single process, but many.

This complexity is seen even when one looks at specific aspects of development, such as gender roles. While the explanations proposed by the various approaches are relatively clear, the evidence is very difficult to interpret. It is easy to recognize that human beings are divided into two sexes, but the relationship of behaviour to gender is less clear-cut. Models which emphasize only one type of factor, such as the role of heredity, seem inconsistent with the available data. In the end, it seems that what is needed is a multi-process model which can *combine* the effects of heredity and learning (and also culture). At present, there are still significant gaps in our understanding.

Overall, the study of development can be one of the most challenging, but also frustrating, areas in psychology. In writing this chapter we were struck, not for the first time, by the seeming lack of coherence in the area. The number of questions to contend with (and the diversity of answers offered) seem to defy attempts at theoretical integration. Given the desire for a full understanding, this fragmentation appears to be an obvious failing. Yet, one should not be too hasty in blaming developmental theorists for failing to provide a cohesive framework. In some sense, the study of development is a microcosm for all of psychology, since in various ways it touches on nearly every aspect of behaviour and experience. As there is no comprehensive theory of psychology at present, it should not be surprising that there is no comprehensive theory of development. Yet, by pointing out what is needed for a successful theory, the study of development may in fact help to clarify issues for the field as a whole. In that sense, the lack of integration currently found in developmental psychology may ultimately prove to be a benefit. In the meantime, it provides us glimpses of insight into the remarkable journey which we are all taking: the journey of life.

CHAPTER SUMMARY

- *Developmental psychology* is concerned with understanding the changes that occur over the course of human life, and the processes which govern the changes.

- In order to study changes over time, researchers tend to use *longitudinal studies* or *cross-sectional studies* involving groups of different ages; in some cases, researchers will use a *sequential design*, which combines elements of both of the other two.

- Three general issues pervade the study of development: *continuity* vs. *discontinuity* in the developmental process, the relative importance of *heredity* and *environment*, and the value of *domain-general* vs. *domain-specific models*. Piaget's theory of cognitive development is a limited form of a domain-general model.

- The origin of *personality* patterns and traits provides a useful focus for comparison of how the five approaches view development.

- The *biological approach* emphasizes the *role of temperament* in personality development, as being based on heredity.

- The *behaviourist approach* emphasizes the importance of environmental influences, particularly the role of *environmental consistency* and the person's *history of reinforcement* in accounting for the consistencies which are attributed to 'personality'.

- The *cognitive approach* interprets development in terms of cognitive social learning theory, which emphasizes the role of imitation in learning and the importance of *cognitive schemata* in structuring behaviour.

- The *psychodynamic approach*, as represented by Freud's psychoanalytic theory, favours an interactionist interpretation of development. His theory explains personality in terms of physiologically-based *psychosexual stages of development* and the role of early experience.

- The *humanistic approach* offers the least detailed analysis of development. Partly this is because it emphasizes individual experience and subjective perceptions, while developmental researchers favour the search for common principles based on objective observation. To the extent that it can be evaluated, Rogers's theory seems to favour an interactionist interpretation of development.

- The study of *gender role development* presents a clear example of the challenges of developmental research. At present, no one approach seems to offer a fully satisfactory model of the origin of gender roles or *gender identity*, though a model combining the biological and cognitive approaches might have significant value.

- Overall, developmental psychology represents the field of psychology in microcosm, since development involves virtually all aspects of behaviour. To the extent that no single model currently seems adequate, it reflects the realities of the current limits of our broader understanding of behaviour.

❶ Key terms and concepts

longitudinal study	maturation
cross-sectional study	critical period
sequential design	personality
continuity	trait
stages	implicit personality theory
domain-general models	temperament
domain-specific models	history of reinforcement
assimilation	gender roles
animism	gender identity
egocentrism	gender schema
reaction range	

Test yourself questions

1 What are the differences between a longitudinal and a cross-sectional design? What are the advantages and disadvantages of each?
2 Explain the issue of continuity vs. discontinuity in the study of development.
3 How does the behaviourist approach explain personality development?
4 How does the cognitive approach explain gender role development?

Online Learning Centre

When you have read this chapter, log onto the Online Learning Centre website at **www.openup.co.uk/glassman** where you will find answers to these Test Yourself questions and suggested answers to the Try it Yourself activities, plus many more learning resources to help you study psychology.

Suggestions for Further Reading

- For a current overview, *Human Development*, by **Diane Papalia** *et al.* (2007), provides a reasonable choice. Jerome Kagan's short book, *Three Seductive Ideas* (1998), provides an interesting discussion of selected issues in development, and *Human Development: Traditional and Contemporary Theories* (2007) by **Doris Bergen** takes another look at theoretical approaches to understanding.

- For two different views of the role of heredity and environment, consider **David Moore's** *The Dependent Gene* (2003), which offers a conventional interactionist view, and **Matt Ridley's** *Nature Via Nurture* (2003), which emphasizes how the environment affects the actions of genes.

- For an example of the potential of longitudinal studies, **White's** *Lives in Progress* (1975) is a fascinating demonstration of what can be learned by a researcher who has both patience and sensitivity.

- Development as seen cross-culturally is highlighted in **Gardiner and Kosmitzki's** (2007) book entitled *Lives Across Cultures: Cross-cultural Human Development*.

- For a readable overview of gender role development, particularly in terms of differences across cultures, **Williams and Best's** *Sex and Psyche* (1990) is a good choice. More current, but also more technical, sources are *The Developmental Social Psychology of Gender* (2000), edited by **Eckes and Trautner**, and *Gender and Development* (2003) by **Janet Momsen**.

- In various ways, all of the approaches touch upon development; readers interested in a particular approach should refer back to the suggested readings in the appropriate chapter.

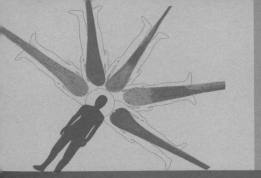

Chapter 8

Perspectives on Social Behaviour

LEARNING OBJECTIVES

In this chapter, the objectives are to learn:

- methods employed in studying social behaviour, including experiments vs. correlational methods

- the challenges of reactivity and experimental realism

- important issues in the study of social behaviour, including
  - role of person vs. situation
  - proximal vs. distal causes

- the nature of aggression, and how it is explained by
  - the biological approach
  - the behaviourist approach
  - the cognitive approach
  - the psychodynamic approach
  - the humanistic approach

- the debate about how media violence affects aggression

- the nature of prosocial behaviour and how it is explained by each of the five approaches

- the relationship between altruism and bystander behaviour

THE INDIVIDUAL AND SOCIETY

At the time of the Cold War, amid fears of nuclear war, there was a science-fiction drama on television in which a man was the only survivor of a cataclysmic disaster. In his case, he relished being alone, because it freed him from the incessant chatter of other people. He looked forward to the quiet, to being able to sit and read as he pleased, without being disturbed. His joy lasted until he broke his only pair of glasses, and realized there was no one to provide a new pair! The story, of course, was meant to be ironic, but it also raised an interesting question: what would it be like to be the only person in the world? How do you think you would react? Unlike the man in the story, most people would likely see it as a calamity, not a blessing; part of being human is being involved with other people.

It is an oft-repeated truism that human beings are social creatures. Four hundred years ago, the English poet John Donne observed that 'no man is an island, entire of itself'; instead, he said, we are all bound together, each of us 'a piece of the continent, a part of the main'. At birth, we are linked to others by our dependence on them for survival. Later, when we have become physically independent, we still seek others for companionship, affection and mutual support. Indeed, even when we are alone, we are influenced by others – in the memories we carry, in the way we think, and in our perceptions of both ourselves and our surroundings.

Thus far, we have been focusing primarily on the understanding of individual behaviour. That, after all, is what psychology is all about; other fields, like sociology and anthropology, look at the behaviour of groups and cultures. Yet, we also recognize that one cannot study individuals without acknowledging that they interact with, and are influenced by, other people. We have seen examples of this in examining the various approaches – for example, we are reinforced by the praise we receive from others (behaviourist), we learn from observing others (cognitive) and so on. In the end, no study of psychology can be complete without considering the social dimensions of individual behaviour.

INTRODUCTION

The study of the social aspects of behaviour is the focus of **social psychology**. While it is evident that as individuals we do not (normally) live in isolation, understanding *how* our interactions with others affect our behaviour is not so obvious. Even deciding how to study the interactions is difficult, as is indicated by the way the boundaries between social psychology and sociology (and even anthropology) sometimes blur. In fact, one of the first books to be entitled 'Social Psychology' was actually written by a sociologist (Ross 1908)! As we will see, however, social psychology focuses primarily on the individual, with other people representing the *context* for the individual's behaviour. Before looking at specific aspects of social behaviour, let us look at some of the underlying issues in social psychology.

social psychology the study of how interactions with other people affect an individual's thinking and behaviour.

As discussed in Chapter 1, one of the things that makes the study of psychology challenging is the complexity of behaviour. As the different approaches reveal, there are many aspects and dimensions of human behaviour, and a potentially limitless range of variables which can affect it. Even when we focus on a single individual, the task of gathering data is complicated by the person's awareness and potential for *reactivity*. Therefore, it should not be surprising that trying to understand *interactions* between an individual and other people can be even more daunting. To deal with this, social psychologists have had to develop ways of defining the issues, and also methods of studying social behaviour.

social behaviour any behaviour which involves others or is implicitly oriented towards others (for example, both conformity and social expectations that become part of our mental schemata).

One basic question is what do we mean by social behaviour? While any situation where two or more people interact would obviously qualify, many psychologists would say that behaviour can have social dimensions even when a person is alone. For example, when shopping for clothes, a person may think about how other people would react to a particular style or colour. Hence, social behaviour could be interpreted broadly as any behaviour which is basically social in orientation – even if only implicitly.

One way of organizing this rather large domain is in terms of social cognition and social interaction. As noted in Chapter 4, *social cognition* refers to the mental processes involved in understanding ourselves and other people. For example, the way we form *stereotypes*, and the factors that influence our *attitudes*, are both aspects of social cognition. As its name implies, the study of social cognition arose largely as an outgrowth of the cognitive approach. Hence, just as the cognitive approach began to overtake the behaviourist approach in the 1960s, social cognition began to overtake a more behaviourist-influenced focus on social situations within social psychology. As interest grew, some researchers began to argue that social cognition was central to *all* of social psychology. This assertion was not entirely unreasonable, since humans are capable of thought, and there is no clear boundary between situations that involve thinking and those that don't; in fact, some texts *do* claim that social cognition is part of all social psychology (see Smith and Mackie 1995). However, most social psychologists – even those involved in the study of social cognition – would not make this claim (see Fiske 2003). In fact, assuming that social psychology is only 'cognitive' is both historically inaccurate, and leads to ignoring questions that may not fit easily within the cognitive approach (Berkowitz and Devine 1995). According to Haslam and McGarty (2001), the proportion of social psychology research which includes interaction by participants declined from about 40 per cent in the 1960s to about 10–15 per cent in the 1990s!

While it might be tempting to view social cognition as simply a sub-area within the cognitive approach, in fact many cognitive phenomena can also be addressed by other approaches (for example, within the biological approach, evolutionary psychology discusses prejudice in terms of kinship relations). Nonetheless, the cognitive approach does play a dominant role in the study of social cognition. Indeed, various aspects have already been introduced in previous discussions, including *attribution theory*, *cognitive dissonance* and various aspects of *social perception* (including *stereotypes* and *gender schemata*) – see Chapters 1, 4 and 7. Because of this, and because the focus of this chapter is to explore how *all* approaches contribute to understanding social behaviour, we will not pursue the above topics further in this chapter.

The other sub-domain within social psychology is the study of *social interactions* – that is, situations that directly involve other people. One important aspect of this is the study of **social influence**, which is concerned with the ways that an individual's behaviour is affected by others. Not surprisingly, the term covers a wide range of situations, from group decision making to *obedience to authority* (see Chapter 1). One common form of social influence is *conformity*, when social pressures lead us to go along with group norms; for example, a person may dress in a particular way in order to fit in with their peers. In this chapter we will be exploring social influence in more detail, including conformity and the role of social influence on *prosocial behaviour*.

social influence a general term for the various ways in which an individual's behaviour is affected by others, such as conformity pressures and group dynamics.

There are also types of social situations where the focus is not purely on how others affect an individual's behaviour, but instead are concerned with social relationships. For example, romantic *attraction* between individuals is typically reciprocal (see Box 8.1). Similarly, *altruism* (helping others) has no meaning except in a social context. In other cases, such as *aggression*, the concern is to understand what motivates such behaviour against others. In this chapter, we will touch on a number of aspects of social interaction, including all the issues mentioned above. In particular, we will explore how each of the approaches contributes to our understanding of aggression and prosocial behaviour.

Box 8.1 Friends and Lovers

'You've gotta have friends' and 'love makes the world go round' are familiar sayings – but what qualities are important in friendships and love? The question is easy to ask, but harder to answer.

One characteristic which seems important in any close relationship is familiarity. In general, we are drawn to people that we know well; typically friends and lovers are people who may have grown up together, gone to school together, work together or take part in the same activities (such as sports) (Brehm 2002). In one early study of friendship patterns in university, the best predictor of friendship formation was how close together the individuals' rooms were – in other words, you tend to become friends with people you see frequently.

Another significant factor in relationships is similarity. A variety of research indicates that we tend to prefer to associate with people whom we perceive as similar (Berscheid 2000). But what *kind* of similarity? Attitudes? Interests? Appearance? Research indicates that the types of similarity that we perceive as important or relevant depend on both the situation and the person, and can also be influenced by culture (Hamm 2000; Michinov and Monteil 2002; Mills *et al*. 2002).

Physical attractiveness is another variable that can influence relationships. While we may tend to think of it in terms of romantic attractions, it can also play a role in friendships and even career advancement (Berscheid 1988; Collins and Zebrowitz 1995). While the standards for physical attractiveness can vary across cultures and even in one culture over time (Buss *et al*. 2001; Lamb *et al*. 1993), symmetrical features are often evaluated as attractive – in part, evolutionary psychologists say, because they are an indicator of genetic fitness (Grammer and Thornhill 1994).

Not surprisingly, culture also plays a role in relationships, particularly love. The emotional intensity which people associate with love ('it was love at first sight') is what psychologists call romantic love. Interestingly, this idea was largely non-existent as a cultural phenomenon until the Middle Ages, when it was associated with chivalry. Today, romantic love is a familiar idea, especially in western societies. Perhaps because of this, romantic love is rated as more important for choosing a partner in individualistic cultures (like the USA, Canada and the UK) than in collectivist cultures (Dion and Dion 1993). Dion and Dion also found that psychological closeness (intimacy) is valued more for love relationships in individualistic cultures; in part, because collectivist cultures tend to view intimacy in terms of one's entire social network, not just one's partner. However, there are indications that these patterns are changing in collectivist cultures like Japan and China.

In the end, who we're attracted to as friends and lovers, and why, is a complex phenomenon. Would you really want it to be simple?

Together, social cognition and social interaction touch on virtually every aspect of the relationship between an individual and society, and thus help to outline the subject matter of social psychology (for an overview, see Box 8.2). At the same time, social psychology is a broad field, whose boundaries are not easy to define. As one moves from the individual to the group, it begins to move towards sociology. As one looks at social behaviour across cultures, it begins to verge into anthropology. What distinguishes social psychology is that the focus of study is the *individual*, rather than the group (sociology) or the culture (anthropology). The diffuseness of social psychology is also evident in the role of theories within the field. Like development, social psychology is defined by its subject matter, not a theoretical framework. That is, its unity stems from its emphasis on behaviour in a social context, just as the study of development is unified by the emphasis on changes over time. Thus, the defining element of social psychology is still the focus on the social dimensions of individual behaviour.

Box 8.2 Topic Areas in Social Psychology

Social behaviour has many aspects; some of the major areas are identified in this chart

Social cognition	Social interaction
Impression formation	Obedience to authority
Stereotyping	Conformity
Prejudice	Group dynamics
Attitudes	Attraction and love
Cognitive dissonance	Aggression
Attribution theory	Prosocial behaviour

Methods of Studying Social Behaviour

In developmental research, the focus on changes in behaviour over time makes longitudinal studies and other time-based designs the primary methods of investigation. In social psychology, the desire to identify the causes of behaviour has led to an emphasis on doing experiments. Other methods, including case studies, participant observation and quasi-experiments, are sometimes used, but are less attractive because of the lack of clear causal patterns. In the past few years, structured equation modelling, which uses mathematical models to make predictions involving multiple variables, has been gaining in popularity as an alternative to gathering experimental data. For example, Agnew *et al.* (2000) used this technique to study the origins of prejudice, and Ferguson *et al.* (2008) have used it to explore the relationship between playing violent video games and aggression. However, experimental research is still the primary method used in studying social behaviour.

At first glance, this emphasis on doing experiments may seem puzzling. After all, many of the interesting questions about social behaviour arise out of everyday events. For example, in Chapter 1 we discussed the death of Kitty Genovese, an incident in which 38 people observed the fatal attack on a young woman, but did not intervene. Why didn't they help? One can speculate about the reasons, and her death did in fact generate considerable conjecture at the time, but ultimately no amount of speculation can ever provide the evidence necessary for sound explanations. Instead, social psychologists prefer to do experiments, which provide the kind of controlled conditions necessary for making clear interpretations of causation. (It should be noted that this emphasis has been stronger in North American psychology than in European psychology, and is not without its critics, as will be discussed in Chapter 10.)

Conducting experiments on social behaviour can pose a number of challenges, all related either directly or indirectly to the conditions required for performing sound experiments. As

Try it Yourself

Have you ever asked any of the following questions?

- Do you find the tests in this course hard?
- What should I wear to the party?
- What do you think I should do?
- Which CD would you recommend?
- Do you think that is a good restaurant?

In all of these cases, you are looking for social input to help you make decisions. Whether you follow the advice given by anyone is, of course, up to you, but social influence is a part of the decision making process for most of us. Are you more likely to be influenced by some people than others? For example, consider how you dress: Are you a 'preppy'? A 'goth'? Is there another term that fits? What does this tell you about social influence? Do you consider being approved of by others either bad or good? Why?

discussed in Chapter 1, one of the advantages of the experimental method is that it allows the researcher to control the situation – manipulating the desired variable(s) and keeping other factors constant. Such control is important to interpreting the causes of behaviour. However, experimental requirements can sometimes interfere with the very behaviour one is interested in studying, particularly with social behaviour. One difficulty is that when people know they are being observed, they may react differently than they would otherwise – a phenomenon called *reactivity*. Concerns about reactivity are not unique to social psychology; the problem can occur in many kinds of psychological research. Consequently a number of techniques have been devised to deal with it, including deliberately withholding information from participants, or using deception (see Chapter 1 for a further discussion of reactivity). However, a second difficulty, related specifically to social behaviour, is the fact that the behaviour of other people is often a key element of the research design. Not surprisingly, it is harder to maintain control and consistency when dealing with such variables than, for example, controlling the frequency of a food reinforcer to an animal. The use of confederates and taped materials can often help address these concerns, but the reality is that doing well-controlled social research is challenging.

A second major issue which can affect social research is the need to create a convincing situation. In everyday life, social interactions elicit emotional as well as cognitive responses, and these emotions can sometimes be intense. For example, a person may feel stage fright about speaking before a group; two drivers involved in an auto accident may get into an angry confrontation; a person may become embarrassed by a social slip. In order to provide meaningful results, an experimental situation must be sufficiently involving that participants will react genuinely. If the person thinks, 'Oh, well, this is just an experiment', then that perception will likely lead to behaviour which is very different from 'real' situations. The social psychologist Elliot Aronson has referred to the importance of natural reactions as the need for **experimental realism** (Aronson 1976). This is not quite the same as saying that the situation must be life-like in the sense that it is familiar in daily life. Stanley Milgram's study of obedience, in which a 'researcher' encouraged participants to give apparently dangerous electric shocks to another person, was not a situation

experimental realism a quality of involvement whereby research participants respond without regard for the laboratory context, as they would in an ordinary situation.

which most people encounter in daily life; in this sense, it was not 'realistic' (see Chapter 1 for a description of Milgram's study). However, the subjects found the situation highly involving (not to say emotionally distressing), and there is little reason to doubt that their responses were genuine. In this sense, Milgram's research satisfied the need for experimental realism. Essentially, a realistic experiment shows us 'the way people would react if a similar set of events *did* occur in the real world' (Aronson 1976, p. 292).

Creating a convincing situation often requires considerable ingenuity. In essence, the experiment must be sufficiently complex to be involving, yet sufficiently simple to allow proper experimental control. In addition, because people would likely not behave naturally if they knew the true purpose of the study, it typically requires *deception*. An example of this is a classic study on **conformity** by Solomon Asch (1951).

conformity the tendency to adjust one's opinions and behaviour to comply with group norms in response to explicit or implicit social presssure.

Earlier research on group behaviour had demonstrated that people are influenced by the judgements of others when evaluating an ambiguous stimulus – that is, a group norm emerges to which people conform (Sherif 1936). Asch believed that the results were due to the ambiguity of the situation, which provided little guidance for individual judgement. Instead, he asked people to make comparative judgements of line length – a presumably straightforward situation (see Figure 8.1). The situation called for individuals to give their judgements publicly, in a group of eight people; of the eight, only one was a real participant, with the others being confederates of the researcher, who had been instructed on their answers. For the first few trials, everything went normally, with everyone making correct judgements. Then came a trial on which seven people (the confederates) gave the same wrong answer – and then the real participant had to respond. Faced with this situation, people blinked, hesitated – and then, on one-third of the trials, gave the same wrong answer as the group! As Asch noted in his analysis, on average, individuals still went against the group two-thirds of the time – but individually, responses varied tremendously. One-quarter of all participants remained independent for all 12 test trials (out of 18 trials in total, of which 6 were not rigged). However, almost one-third of individuals conformed at least half the time, and one individual conformed with the group's wrong answers on 11 out of 12 test trials! Given the obvious nature of the stimuli (deviations ranged from 20 per cent to almost 50 per cent of the standard), it seems hard to believe that anyone could err. So what was happening? According to Asch's description, individuals who conformed gave visible signs of social stress: grinning embarrassedly, appearing nervous and confused. Yet, despite the contrary evidence of their senses, they felt pressure to go along with the group. (In subsequent experiments, Asch found that conformity pressures are considerably reduced in smaller groups, or with non-unanimous majorities.)

Conformity has been extensively studied, and the basic phenomenon as a form of social influence is well established. In addition, it is now known that many other factors, including status of both the group and the individual, affect conformity (Campbell *et al.* 1986). A cross-cultural review has also confirmed Asch's general findings, but two points are worth noting: overall, conformity in tasks like Asch's appears more likely in cultures with a collectivist orientation, like China, but within the USA seems to be declining since Asch's time (Bond and Smith 1996; Hornsey and Jetten 2005).

The Asch study, and the research on conformity which it spawned, are classics within social psychology. However, it is relevant to this discussion of research methods because the group pressure depended on two key elements of *deception*: the confederates were presented as being genuine participants, and the answers they gave on test trials were lies. Thus, it highlights the fact that many studies of social behaviour (especially social influence) require the use of deception. While ethical standards of the time did not require it, Asch did *debrief* his participants – although it appears this was partly intended simply to gather subjective reports about their experience. Today, the significance of Asch's research is clear – but it is equally clear that it would have been impossible to do without deception.

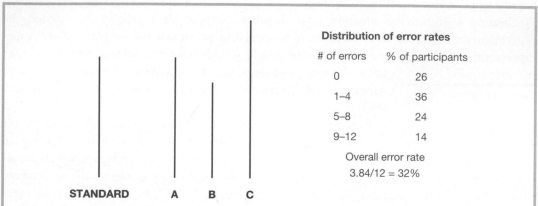

Distribution of error rates

# of errors	% of participants
0	26
1–4	36
5–8	24
9–12	14

Overall error rate
3.84/12 = 32%

STANDARD A B C

Figure 8.1 Line Length and Conformity In the classic experiment by Solomon Asch, participants compared stimuli like those shown here, and had to decide which line most closely matched the standard (in this case, the confederates chose 'C'). As shown by the summary of results, individuals agreed with faulty judgements by the group on one-third of all trials – in other words, they conformed to the group's erroneous choices. (Data adapted from Asch 1951)

This poses a continual ethical dilemma for researchers – can the knowledge gained justify the process? Most researchers in social psychology believe that deception is a necessary procedure, despite its disagreeable implications. (Presumably, if they did not feel this way, they would not do any research involving deception!) At the same time, serious researchers agree that one should try to minimize the manipulative aspects of research, and any possible negative consequences of experimental procedures. One way of mitigating harm is to always discuss the true nature and goals of the research with participants when the experiment ends – that is, to *debrief* participants. Alternatively, a researcher may use observational techniques (such as non-obtrusive measures or surveys) which do not require the use of deception. Unfortunately, this option *also* precludes the possibility of identifying causal relationships. Thus, the potential conflict between methodological requirements and ethical concerns remains. Ethical issues, obviously, can arise in most psychological research, but they are particularly vivid in social psychology precisely because social interactions are so central to human experience. (The ethical dimensions of social research become particularly significant in cross-cultural studies, where the need for experimental realism may conflict with varied social norms.) In the end, researchers must grapple with both the complexities of the research situation, and the need to be considerate of their participants – a balance which is not always easy to achieve (see Chapter 1 for discussion of ethical standards and issues).

Issues in the Study of Social Behaviour

Developing effective and appropriate methods to study social behaviour is important, since we cannot hope to understand social behaviour without reliable data. However, gathering accurate information is only the starting point, since the goal of research is to understand *why* behaviour occurs, rather than just *describing* it. This is true whether we are talking about development, or abnormal behaviour – or social behaviour. In each area, there are basic issues that must be addressed by any theory in order to interpret and explain the observations.

In the case of social behaviour, the most challenging issues relate to interpreting the causes of behaviour. As noted earlier in the chapter, doing experimental research on social behaviour is complicated by the fact that individuals are aware, and also that social variables (involving the actions of other people) can be more difficult to control than many other types of variables. The resulting complexity and interactions can make doing research very challenging – and also affect the ability to interpret the results. Consider a simple situation: Mike is walking down the street, and a poorly dressed man lying on the ground asks Mike for help. What will determine whether Mike helps or not? Many people would want to know more about Mike – for example, whether he has helped people in the past. Others would want to know more about the situation – for example, whether Mike is in a hurry or not, or whether other people are nearby who might help. Obviously, there are many factors that might potentially influence Mike's behaviour, so how can we make sense of it? What really matters?

The above scenario outlines one of the basic issues in social psychology: what is the relative importance of the individual's characteristics vs. the situation? This issue, often called the **person–situation debate**, has a long history within social psychology. The earliest studies of social behaviour were mostly influenced by the behaviourist approach, and hence emphasized the importance of stimulus variables (the situation). In the 1930s, Gordon Allport and others began arguing that individuals show tendencies to act in particular ways across many situations – that is, that behaviour is influenced more by personal characteristics than by the situation (Allport 1937). Thus was born the person–situation debate.

person–situation debate an ongoing issue concerned with the relative importance of personal characteristics vs. situational variables as influences on behaviour.

To illustrate this debate in a research context, think back to Asch's studies on conformity, discussed earlier (Asch 1951). The fact that some individuals showed significant conforming, while others did not conform at all, suggests the role of personal influences. By contrast, the fact that large groups which agree unanimously on a wrong answer produce more conformity than small, non-unanimous groups suggests the role of situational influences. Over time, one side or the other has marshalled evidence that seems to advance its case. Some have even gone so far as to suggest that personal variables are illusory. For example, in the 1960s, cognitive psychologist Walter Mischel asserted that interpreting consistencies in behaviour in terms of personal characteristics is an error based on ignoring situational influences (Mischel 1968). (Note that in everyday contexts this is equivalent to the *fundamental attribution error*.) Mischel himself subsequently modified his position to acknowledge that individual differences in behavioural tendencies exist which are relevant to understanding social behaviour (Mischel 2004; Wright and Mischel 1987). However, the debate continued. A book written by Lee Ross and Richard Nisbett, called *The Person and the Situation* (1991) represented a major attempt at resolution, and essentially argues for an interactionist view that acknowledges both the role of experience in shaping cognitive schemata, and also the ways in which people select and modify the situations in which they function. As reasonable as this seems, the debate has not ended (see Bem 1992; Roberts and Caspi 2001; Ross 2001; Sternberg and Vroom 2002; Trope 2004). At the heart of the issue lies the difficulty of accurately separating personal influences from situational ones – a problem which Ross and Nisbett (1991) saw as unsolvable in any absolute sense. Nonetheless, all five of the approaches involve interpretations about person vs. situation, as we will see.

The person–situation debate is not the only difficulty which arises when trying to interpret the causes of social behaviour. A further problem relates to the fact that 'cause' can have different

proximal cause a factor which is a direct influence on behaviour, such as one's attitude or an aspect of the immediate situation.

distal cause a factor which has an indirect effect on behaviour, such as previous experiences in similar situations.

meanings – for example, one can talk about immediate causes as compared to those which only indirectly affect behaviour. For example, in the scenario discussing whether Mike will help a stranger, an immediate influence would be whether he is late for work. A less direct cause might be the values he was taught as a child, which would affect his current attitude towards helping others. The two types are sometimes distinguished as **proximal** (immediate) vs. **distal** (indirect) **causes**. Proximal causes are often relatively easy to identify, as in the above example – that is, one can easily verify if Mike is late. Distal causes, by their nature, are more difficult to identify and measure (such as Mike's early childhood experiences, which he may not even consciously recall).

From a theoretical point of view, both proximal and distal causes may be relevant to behaviour, but from a research perspective they are not equally accessible to study. As a consequence, research on social behaviour often tends to emphasize proximal causes, which can be readily linked to experimental variables. When attempts are made to analyse both types of causes, it often involves non-experimental methods like structured equation modelling. For example, Agnew *et al.* (2000) used structured equation modelling in a study of the origins of prejudice. In this study, they were able to determine that the influence of distal variables like family structure and the context of exposure affected proximal variables like beliefs in determining prejudicial attitudes. As with the person–situation debate, one must distinguish between what individuals believe about causation (attributions) vs. determining the actual role of proximal vs. distal causes. For example, a study by Gillen and Muncer (1995) compared men's and women's beliefs about the causes of date rape. While gender differences about proximal (for example, male dominance) and distal (for example, social norms) causes were found, unfortunately the data do not tell us about the *actual* causes of date rape. Despite such difficulties, it is important to remember that both types of causes exist, and each approach tends to make assumptions about the relative importance of each type of cause.

Social behaviour is both diverse and complex, and challenging to understand. Yet this complexity underscores the richness of our interactions with others, which are central to what it means to be human. To their credit, researchers have not shrunk from the challenges involved in trying to understand social behaviour. To see this more clearly, let us look at how each of the approaches has dealt with two key aspects of social interactions: why we hurt each other, and why we help others.

PERSPECTIVES ON AGGRESSION

There is little question that aggression represents one of the darker aspects of human behaviour. We seem to be both able and willing to hurt each other, despite our social orientation. Aristotle once described humans as 'the social animal'; given the history of aggression, some would suggest the emphasis should be on 'animal' rather than 'social'. Today, it often seems that the news media provide daily reminders of the human capacity for violence. Several years ago, all of England, and indeed the world, was horrified by the story of two boys, not yet in their teens, who kidnapped and tortured a 2-year-old boy, and then left him to die on the railway tracks. Not long ago, a local newspaper reported the story of a man who pushed a woman into the path of an underground train, killing her; she was a stranger to him, her death a seemingly random act of violence. In several places in the world, civilian populations are under attack by military forces. Both individually and in groups, we seem only too capable of causing harm to each other.

Such incidents cast a bleak picture, and the past includes many comparable examples. The long history of such violence has led many to assume that such actions represent an intrinsic part of human character. However, we must not be too quick to label 'aggression' as an innate drive – in part because doing so presumes that we already have the answer before we have really posed the question. The question, of course, is 'what is the origin of aggressive behaviour?'. Unfortunately, before we can answer, we must be clear about what we mean by 'aggressive behaviour'.

Defining Aggression

Most people would say that if someone deliberately harms another person, this is undesirable behaviour. But is it therefore *aggressive* behaviour? And what if someone *intends* to harm another person, but does not succeed? Is aggression the same as violence? Can there be aggression if there is no actual violence? Although we use (and seem to understand) the terms 'aggression' and 'violence' in everyday language, like many words, their meaning can be somewhat ambiguous, shifting according to the context. In order to be useful in the context of scientific explanation, we need to define the terms unambiguously.

The basic problem in defining aggression is whether the focus should be on the behaviour, the intention or both. *Violent* behaviour is that which causes harm to other people, regardless of intent. (Some researchers, like Moyer (1983), would also include property damage.) However, violence is not necessarily the same as aggression, in that violence may occur accidentally. For example, a golfer's errant ball may hit someone in the head, causing serious injury; given that there was no *intent* to cause harm, most people would not view it as an aggressive act.

In our culture, we are accustomed to considering a person's intentions, as well as the outcome, in evaluating behaviour. For instance, judgements of guilt in our legal system emphasize the consideration of a person's motives. In the same way, researchers have often sought to consider the motivational component of behaviour in defining aggression. Thus, Elliot Aronson has defined aggression as 'behavior aimed at causing harm or pain' (Aronson 1976, p. 143). By focusing on the *intention* of the behaviour, Aronson is able to make some seemingly useful distinctions. For example, a football player who inadvertently injures another player is not being aggressive, although it results in harm (and is therefore violent behaviour). By contrast, a football player who deliberately sets out to injure an opponent is being aggressive – even if he fails to actually cause harm.

The trouble with focusing on intentions in defining aggression is that, like any form of motivation, aggressive intent is difficult to measure. Among other things, one has to consider whether intentions can be expressed symbolically. Freud was willing to talk about symbolic forms of aggression which seem unconnected to violent acts, but this is because he assumed aggressive intent is always present (after all, he believed aggression was an innate drive). Hence, a hotel maid punching the pillows as she makes a bed could actually be expressing aggression. If one doesn't make this assumption, then it must be acknowledged that measuring aggressive intentions is a difficult task. For example, if a writer satirizes a real person in a story, is that aggression? How do we judge the intent?

It seems that defining aggression is very much tied up with our assumptions about its origins. Those who believe aggression is a learned behaviour (like Aronson) typically emphasize behaviour in defining aggression (in other words, it must result in harm, and hence is equivalent to violence). By contrast, those who believe aggression is an innate drive (like Freud) prefer to emphasize intentions (which may be expressed symbolically). There is no simple resolution to this dilemma, because the word 'aggression' has many connotations. (If we were to examine other

aggression behaviour which causes intentional harm to another person.

cultures, there would be even greater variability.) In this chapter, we will generally try to adhere to a compromise definition which includes both components – that is, **aggression** is behaviour which causes intentional harm to another person (Anderson and Bushman 2002; Berkowitz 1975). This definition likely excludes some forms of aggression, but at least has the virtue that nearly every theorist would agree that such behaviours are aggressive.

The very fact that it has taken more than a page simply to try to define aggression – and then, only with partial success – gives an indication of how complicated it is to explore this topic with some semblance of objectivity. For many people, ideas about aggression are closely linked to beliefs about human nature. Similarly, the way each approach views aggression reflects the interpretations it makes about social behaviour in general, as we will see.

Try it Yourself

'You would be so pretty if you lost some weight.'
'Hey, that's a pretty smart idea coming from somebody like you!'
'Now that your head is shaved, I can see that you really do have a funny-shaped head.'

Are these statements of aggression? Does deliberately embarrassing someone constitute aggression? If you *imagine* embarrassing someone, but don't actually do so, are you being aggressive? Freud would likely call verbal taunts *symbolic aggression*. Do you agree that such behaviour is aggressive? Would you be willing to make similar interpretations about other forms of behaviour, such as love? Why or why not?

Methods of Studying Aggression

Before considering the interpretations offered by the approaches, it is useful to return to the question of research methods: how can one study aggressive behaviour scientifically? As already noted, social psychologists typically prefer experimental research, because experiments allow one to make interpretations about the causes of behaviour. Yet experimental studies of aggression face several stumbling blocks. One concern is that individuals may act differently in a laboratory than in everyday life; if they do, this would create distortion and bias in the results. A second concern is the need for *experimental realism*. While this is an issue in all social psychology experiments, it is particularly significant when dealing with aggression, because researchers cannot ethically explore the full range of aggressive behaviour in the laboratory (no one wants to incite individuals to lose all self-control, and no one would do an experiment leading to actual physical harm). Yet restrictions on the intensity and types of aggression examined may limit the *external validity* of a study – that is, the extent to which one can generalize to other situations involving other forms of aggression. For example, does punching an inflatable doll really tell us whether someone would punch another person (see Bandura *et al.* 1961)? This is not to say that laboratory studies are irrelevant to the study of aggression, but they are difficult to design well, and there may be limits to their generality. Interestingly, the consistency one finds between real situations and the predictions from laboratory studies indicates that the external validity of aggression research may actually be reasonably good (Anderson and Bushman 1997).

In order to avoid these problems, researchers sometimes prefer to avoid laboratory research when studying aggression; instead, they may perform field experiments or use correlational designs based on real-world observations. A *field experiment* involves conducting an experiment in a real-world setting, such that the subjects are not aware they are participating in a research study. As discussed in Chapter 1, field experiments pose the two-fold problem of trying to maintain proper controls in a natural setting, along with concerns about the ethics of doing research without the informed consent of participants. This is particularly troublesome when dealing with aggressive behaviour and, consequently, relatively few field experiments have been done, compared to either lab experiments or correlational studies. *Correlational studies* involve some form of observation of variables in a natural setting (for example, naturalistic observation, longitudinal studies) in which one tries to find patterns between particular variables – for example, viewing violence on television and aggressive behaviour. Because the aggression observed is 'the real thing', not a laboratory analogue, correlational studies often seem more convincing than laboratory experiments. Unfortunately, this advantage is offset by the fact that these studies, like all correlational studies, do not allow one to draw clear conclusions about cause and effect.

In the end, there is no single research design which can optimally address the issue of aggression. Ideally, one would like to employ all three types of studies, because finding similar patterns of results in a variety of contexts enhances one's confidence that the underlying theory may be valid. As you consider the explanations of aggression offered by the five approaches, ask yourself what sort of evidence each offers, and what limitations it may have.

Theories of Aggression

The most basic issue in the study of aggression is explaining its origin. As with many aspects of behaviour, the various theories tend to split into two groups: those that see aggression as innate, and those that see aggressive behaviour as learned. This split is relevant to both the *nature–nurture* controversy (see Chapters 2 and 7) and the *person–situation* debate, since theories which emphasize innate characteristics are also suggesting that characteristics of the person are the primary influence on social behaviour. Conversely, to suggest that aggression is learned is to emphasize the power of the situation (although past learning may also have influenced the person). The position taken on these issues has particular significance for aggression, because explanations of its origin *also* imply specific ways of trying to *limit* it. Since society has an interest in limiting at least some forms of aggressive behaviour, understanding its causes is a matter of practical as well as theoretical interest. Hence, in looking at the theories proposed by the various approaches, one should consider both how they explain the causes of aggression, and also how they suggest society could or should deal with it.

The Biological Approach

Not surprisingly, the biological approach looks at social behaviour in terms of the role of heredity. In fact, one of the first social psychology texts was written with the view that all social behaviour stems from innate tendencies or drives (McDougall 1908). This means that the biological approach emphasizes characteristics of the person, not the situation, in explaining social behaviour. Given this emphasis, it should not seem surprising that aggression is viewed as an innate characteristic of human beings. At present, no one has directly demonstrated a genetic mechanism for aggression, though accumulating evidence suggests that genetics plays at least a part (Buckholtz and Meyer-Lindenberg 2008; DiLalla 2002). Beyond a direct genetic factor, biological theories put forward various forms of evidence to argue for aggression as innate, as we shall see.

As discussed in Chapter 2, one of the great success stories of physiological research has been the mapping of the human brain to identify the areas responsible for specific aspects of behaviour. Based on this idea of *localization of function*, researchers have sought to identify areas of the brain which control aggressive behaviour. Generally, the focus has been on the hypothalamus and the amygdala, in the evolutionarily older regions of the limbic system (Delgado 1969; MacLean 1990). As with the ethological argument, it turns out on close examination that much of the argument depends on analogy to animal studies, and consequently the theories seem to go further than the evidence warrants. Despite this, some supporters of this view have gone so far as to suggest that certain violent criminals might be better handled by brain surgery than by imprisonment (Mark and Ervin 1970).

A more limited physiological approach has been to look at the connection between pain and aggression. As Moyer has noted, there is a large body of research suggesting that stimuli which cause pain will often trigger aggressive behaviour (Moyer 1976). There is likely a strong defensive component to such behaviour – that is, it seeks to stop the painful stimulation. However, this appears to be only part of the picture, since many factors affect the likelihood of pain-mediated aggression, not all of which have a biological foundation. Since much of the work in this area has involved animals, it is useful to look at the issue in a human context. In this regard various studies have found evidence suggesting that aversive (painful or unpleasant) stimuli can also trigger aggression in people (Anderson *et al.* 1998; Berkowitz 1983, 1993a; Kristin *et al.* 2007). Leonard Berkowitz, however, is qualified in his support, suggesting that there is strong evidence that aggressive responses to such stimuli are cognitively mediated, not simply a reflexive response. In other words, as a form of arousal, pain is an indirect (distal) cause of aggression, while cognitive processes are the direct (proximal) cause. This view has also been put forward by Anderson and Bushman (2002), and will be discussed further in relation to the cognitive approach.

Studies of gender differences in aggression have also been suggestive of a biological mechanism. Many researchers have asserted that men are generally more aggressive than women (Harris and Knight-Bohnhoff 1996; Knight *et al.* 1996). One mechanism which could explain such differences is gender-related physiological differences, such as the role of hormones. For example, a longitudinal study of adolescent males found a relationship between testosterone levels (measured in saliva) and some forms of aggressive behaviour (von Bokhoven *et al.*, 2006). Various studies have also found links between androgen levels and various measures of aggression in women (Cashdan 2003; Hermans *et al.* 2008; Pajer *et al.* 2006). Unfortunately, these results are typically correlational, and studies using other methodologies have provided only mixed support for a biological basis for gender differences in aggression (White 2001). This pattern may occur for several reasons: First, it may be that hormones actually have only a limited influence on gender differences in aggression. Second, it may be that hormonal effects are mediated by some other process, such as cognitions (Klinesmith *et al.* 2006), or that gender differences are a result of both genetics and shared environment (Vierikko *et al.* 2003). Thus, current data on gender differences provide only limited evidence that aggression is primarily biological.

If aggression does have an innate foundation, it is likely that it is the product of evolution; as a consequence, theories have been put forward based on presumed analogies between human and animal behaviour. Among these, one of the best known is the work of Konrad Lorenz. Lorenz was one of the founders of ethology, an approach to the study of animal behaviour which originated as an offshoot of zoology, not psychology. Ethologists study behaviour primarily in natural settings, not in the laboratory; this difference in methodology, along with theoretical differences, led to early disputes with behaviourist psychologists. Influenced by Darwin's work on evolution, Lorenz believed that many human characteristics were based on inherited mechan-isms. Aggression to Lorenz served an evolutionary function, promoting selective survival of the strongest individuals; in other words, it evolved as a biologically useful characteristic (Lorenz 1967).

Key Thinker: **Konrad Zacharias Lorenz**

Konrad Zacharias Lorenz (1903–89) was one of the founders of ethology, an approach to the study of animal behaviour which originated as an offshoot of zoology, not psychology. Lorenz was born and educated in Vienna; he attended the University of Vienna, receiving both a medical degree and a PhD in zoology. The study of animal behaviour attracted him more than did the practice of medicine, and he began to focus on the role of genetic factors in animal behaviour. Together with Nikolaas Tinbergen and Karl von Frisch, he developed a new approach to the study of such behaviour, largely in natural settings. The approach became known as *ethology*, and culminated in the three sharing the 1973 Nobel Prize in Physiology or Medicine. Lorenz's focus on natural settings rather than the laboratory was one of the factors which distinguished ethology from behaviourism as a method of studying behaviour. Lorenz was also influenced by Darwin's work on evolution, and it led him to focus on inherited mechanisms in explaining behaviour. Aggression to Lorenz served an evolutionary function, promoting selective survival of the strongest individuals; in other words, it evolved as a biologically useful characteristic. His best-known book, *On Aggression*, drew a large popular audience for his ideas about both animal and human aggression, though it also attracted many critics. Lorenz died in Vienna at the age of 86.

Lorenz viewed aggression as a biologically-based drive which must be periodically satisfied through behavioural expression. This concept, sometimes referred to as a 'reservoir' model, states that the drive level builds up over time, like a reservoir filling with water; the expression of associated behaviours reduces the drive level, much like draining water from the reservoir. Normally, the expression of aggressive behaviour is controlled by environmental cues called **sign stimuli**, which regulate the initiation and inhibition of aggression. In many species, such as cichlid fish, the intrusion of one individual into the territory of another is a sign stimulus for attack; by contrast, a wolf that is losing a fight will roll over on its back, averting its eyes and exposing its jugular to the other wolf's teeth – a sign stimulus which inhibits further aggression by the victor. Lorenz viewed the existence of sign stimuli as a crucial factor in understanding aggression. By regulating the nature of aggressive encounters, sign stimuli allow the expression of aggression, while minimizing fatal violence and enabling members of a species to establish stable social hierarchies. (In essence, the existence of an aggressive drive is a distal cause of aggression, but sign stimuli would be the proximal cause regulating behaviour.)

sign stimuli in ethology, environmental cues which regulate the expression of behaviours related to innate drives.

Lorenz's theory has several implications for human aggression. First of all, it implies that since aggression is innate, it is also unavoidable. If society attempts to suppress all forms of aggression, then the reservoir will simply 'overflow', resulting in random acts of violence referred to as **vacuum activities**. Lorenz was also concerned that human technology had outstripped biology, in that the sign stimuli that inhibit most fatal aggression require close

vacuum activities in ethology, behaviours which arise in the absence of appropriate environmental stimuli when drive levels are very high.

contact between aggressors (for example, averting the eyes). Methods of killing at a distance, such as bombs dropped from planes and even guns, render such inhibitory stimuli inoperative. Hence, he believed that activities like war, while channelling aggression into socially-sanctioned forms, bypass the controls that evolved to limit excessive violence.

Given the potential for either random violence or mass destruction, what is society to do? Lorenz argued that society should encourage specific forms of substitute activity, such as sports. Such activities allow expression of aggression in limited ways, and thereby reduce drive levels. This process, often referred to as *catharsis*, is a solution frequently proposed by advocates of nativist theories of aggression (both biological and psychodynamic). Presumably, Lorenz would be neither surprised nor alarmed at the violence expressed by soccer fans or hockey players; instead, he would most likely argue that such limited expressions of aggression are preferable to more extreme forms. Ultimately, since aggression will always exist, all society can do is try to channel it into minimally damaging forms.

The work of Lorenz and other ethologists has been important to our understanding of animal behaviour, but his ideas on human aggression are seriously weakened by the absence of supporting human evidence. In essence, the basic assumption – that aggression is innate – is also the point which must be proved. Generally speaking, finding analogous behaviours in different species does not prove that they have the same cause. For example, showing that aggression is innate in wolves does not prove that it is also innate in humans. Similarly, no one has identified specific sign stimuli which categorically inhibit aggression in humans, casting doubt on the relevance of his theory to humans. Despite the lack of direct evidence, Lorenz's view has an understandable appeal. There is no doubt that humans *do* have an evolutionary heritage, and seeing aggression as innate fits well with many cultural beliefs – what Klama (1988) has called 'the myth of the beast within'. Nonetheless, there are still many gaps in Lorenz's argument, and given its implications (that we can only redirect aggression, not eliminate it), we must be wary of accepting his view without further evidence.

Try it Yourself

Many cultures have blatant expectations that one gender (generally boys) will behave in aggressive ways, and even have sayings such as 'boys will be boys'. Indeed, in some cases, boys who do *not* behave aggressively in some situations are looked upon with doubt. Do you think that one gender is more predisposed than the other to be aggressive? Does your answer depend on your definition of aggression? Do you think boys and girls can be aggressive in different ways? If you do see differences between the genders, do you think a non-biological explanation is possible?

Many of the arguments offered by Lorenz and other biological researchers are based on analogies to animal behaviour. In what ways do you think such analogies are or are not appropriate in trying to explain aggression?

The idea that aggression is innate has also been advanced by evolutionary psychologists (de Waal 1989; Konner 1982). Unlike Lorenz, however, they do not necessarily argue for a reservoir concept of drive energy. Instead, they see aggression as involving a series of physiological mechanisms that evolved in response to threats to survival, reproduction or similar situations. Unfortunately, like the ethological arguments, most of the evidence offered is based on comparative studies of other species (Lore and Schultz 1993). While there are studies with humans where the results are explained in terms of evolutionary psychology (for example, Archer and Latham 2004), the studies cannot provide direct evolutionary evidence, and other explanations are clearly possible.

Overall, the evidence for a biological basis for aggression seems more suggestive than conclusive. Minimally, it supports the position that *some* forms of aggressive behaviour (but by no means all) have a physiological foundation which is largely independent of learning (Filley *et al.* 2001). While some researchers advocate the stronger view that *all* aggression is rooted in the structure of the brain, at present, some form of interaction between nature and nurture seems more probable.

The Behaviourist Approach

Unlike biological researchers, the behaviourists view social behaviour, including aggression, as learned (for example, social reinforcers like praise and attention are based on learning). 'Aggression' refers not to an internal drive, but to a particular class of voluntary responses, which are acquired and modified by means of *reinforcement*. This viewpoint emphasizes the role of the situation rather than the person, since the availability of reinforcers is situational (Salzinger 1995). (At the same time, the concept of *reinforcement history* can be used to account for differences between individuals in aggressive behaviour.) While this general interpretation can be applied to any example of aggression, there are really two aspects of aggressive behaviour which have been emphasized by behaviourist theorists: instrumental aggression and the role of frustration in aggression.

instrumental aggression aggressive behaviour which is maintained because it is positively reinforced.

Instrumental aggression is aggressive behaviour which is maintained because it is positively reinforced. For example, suppose Mary sees that her younger brother Tommy has a candy, and takes it away from him so as to eat it herself. In this case, her aggressive behaviour (taking someone else's possession) is reinforced by the outcome (having the candy to eat). Although later Mary may be scolded or otherwise punished for her misdeed, the most immediate consequence is positive reinforcement. In effect, Mary will learn that some desired outcomes can be achieved by the use of aggression. Behaviourists describe this as instrumental aggression because the aggressive behaviour results in acquiring the desired reinforcer; the only difference between this situation and any other case of positive reinforcement is that we label the particular response as 'aggressive'. In the same way, behaviourists would argue that many forms of anti-social behaviour represent instrumental aggression. For example, although we may be dismayed to read that a well-dressed person has been attacked and robbed, we are not likely to be surprised by the event – the money simply represents a tempting reinforcer to a thief.

Examples of instrumental aggression like those above are all too familiar in life. Whatever our *moral* perspective, in *practical* terms, force sometimes works. Consequently, the behaviourist perspective would suggest that such aggression will be common enough to be mistaken for 'innate'. To prevent instrumental aggression, one must alter the environmental conditions so that such behaviour no longer pays off. For example, a child who hits other children in order to get something will alter this behaviour if adults intervene, ensuring that hitting not only does not lead to the desired outcome, but is punished instead. On the broader level of society, preventing all instrumental aggression would require similar interventions – a requirement which is not easy to fulfil (for example, if conviction rates for bank robberies are low, robbing banks can be reinforcing).

Despite the pervasive nature of instrumental aggression, we must also recognize that some instances of aggressive behaviour do *not* appear to be instrumental. Consider an athlete who yells at a referee after an unfavourable call, or a homeowner who kicks a lawnmower that won't start, or a child who misbehaves at home after having problems at school. In each of these cases, the behaviour seems unlikely to lead to a positive reinforcer (i.e., a favourable ruling by the referee, a working lawnmower, expressions of approval). In fact, in most cases, we would expect the behaviour to *worsen* the situation. So, if such aggressive acts cannot reasonably be viewed as instrumental aggression, how can we explain them? The answer given by the behaviourists is to examine the role of frustration in aggressive behaviour, in terms of what is called the frustration–aggression hypothesis.

The frustration–aggression hypothesis traces its origins to work by John Dollard and his colleagues at Yale in the 1930s (Dollard *et al.* 1939). (One colleague was Neal Miller – see Chapter 3.) Consistent with the behaviourist ideas of Watson, they sought to operationalize, and thereby render precise, the everyday concepts of frustration and aggression. In part, they were reacting to Freud's theory, which argued that aggression was innate; later, the original work was extended by Dollard and Miller as an attempt to translate Freudian concepts into behaviourist terms (Dollard and Miller 1950). The **frustration–aggression hypothesis** stated that *frustration* (defined as blocking a goal-oriented response) was the sole cause of aggression. If circumstances create frustration, then this will arouse a drive which motivates aggressive behaviour. The intensity of the aggressive response is determined by the intensity of the frustration, and also by prior punishment of aggressive behaviour (the stronger the punishment, the weaker the aggressive response in the future). For example, if a football player is blocked from scoring a goal, this may result in aggression against another player. If, however, this results in a heavy penalty for the offending player, such behaviour is likely to be inhibited in the future. Instead, the aggressive tendencies aroused by frustration may be channelled into expending more effort in legitimate ways. An example of this occurred in North American hockey, which in the 1980s experienced a trend towards bench-clearing brawls. When a rule change led to stiff penalties being imposed on the third person to enter a fight, the number of brawls decreased dramatically. These examples illustrate the basic elements of the frustration–aggression hypothesis: frustration leads to increasing the potential for aggression, but punishment does seem to decrease its expression.

frustration – aggression hypothesis a theory of aggression developed by Dollard and Miller which states that frustration (defined as blocking a goal-oriented response) is the sole cause of aggression.

The notion that frustration can elicit aggression has an intuitive appeal – after all, we have all felt frustrations that have led to some form of 'letting loose', whether verbally or physically. An interesting example of this in a real-world setting was a study by Stanley Milgram and his colleagues, which found that someone cutting into a line at a ticket booth could trigger aggressive responses (Milgram *et al.* 1986). Starting with the Dollard *et al.* book, and including work by Neal Miller (1941), the frustration–aggression hypothesis was the dominant framework for research on aggressive behaviour for about 25 years. While the basic idea that frustration could lead to aggression received some support, over time the evidence also indicated weaknesses in the original hypothesis. In its strongest form, the hypothesis states that frustration *always* results in aggression, and aggression *only* occurs as a result of frustration. Both of these principles have been challenged. For example, aggressive behaviour can be produced by reinforcement, even in the absence of frustration (Berkowitz 1978). Even when frustration *does* seem to elicit aggression, the relationship has been interpreted as due to the instrumental value of the aggression (Buss 1963).

The issue is further complicated by the fact that a particular frustrating situation may elicit different types of aggressive response in different people. For example, if a soft drink machine accepts money without giving the selected beverage, one person may kick the machine, another may write an angry letter to the company, and a third may walk away depressed, wondering, 'Why does it always happen to *me*?' Thus, aggression may be directly expressed towards the immediate source of frustration, or *displaced* towards another object. Displacement extends the frustration–aggression hypothesis to situations where there is no *immediate* source of frustration, and may also account for some instances of aggression that instrumental aggression cannot explain. However, because it is hard to predict the exact form of displacement, it also makes the theory less precise and testable. A further modification to the theory has been put forward by Berkowitz, who has proposed that frustration will only lead to aggression if failing to reach a goal is accompanied by a negative emotional state (Berkowitz 1989). In the end, the various extensions do not fully resolve the weaknesses of the frustration–aggression hypothesis. Instead, it seems reasonable to conclude that frustration is *one* possible cause of aggression, but not the *only* cause. (See Fortman 2005 for a recent examination of the relationship between frustration and aggression.)

Taken together, instrumental aggression and the frustration–aggression hypothesis can account for many cases of aggressive behaviour. While each has weaknesses and limitations, they are at least partially complementary, as suggested above. Most importantly, both suggest ways in which aggressive behaviour can be *learned*, and hence pose an alternative to nativist views (such as the biological approach or Freud). If aggression really is learned, then no amount of catharsis is going to solve the problem, despite Lorenz's assertions. Hence, the behaviourist perspective suggests that we need to focus on identifying those elements of the social environment that encourage aggressive responses, and alter them so as to produce more socially-desirable behaviour.

Try it Yourself

Have there been any times in your life when you have been reinforced for acting aggressively? What was the reinforcer? Have you observed other people being reinforced for aggressive behaviour? Can you identify the reinforcers they received? Would you ever reinforce someone for being aggressive? If so, under what conditions? Under what conditions would you punish aggressive behaviour? If aggression *is* sometimes instrumental, do you think that aggressive behaviour can ever be eliminated?

The Cognitive Approach

Like the behaviourists, cognitive theorists see social behaviour as learned, not innate. They also accept that reinforcement can influence learning, and hence that some aggression is instrumentally-based. However, the cognitive perspective sees the behaviourist viewpoint as too limited, because it ignores the role of mental processes in learning. Interestingly, because the cognitive approach emphasizes how people perceive a situation (which in turn is affected by one's expectations and other cognitive schemata), the models give significant weight to person variables, even while acknowledging the role of learning and the situation (Berkowitz 1998). Thus, cognitive theorists would say one cannot understand aggression without considering mental processes.

Cognitive theorists point to two ways in which mental processes seem to affect behaviour: first, we are capable of learning by observing what others do (imitation); and second, our thoughts and perceptions may directly influence behaviour, as opposed to behaviour depending on external stimuli. Let us consider how each of these factors is applied to the understanding of aggression.

imitation the learning of behaviour by observing the behaviour of others; sometimes called 'modelling' or 'observational learning'.

The role of **imitation** (or modelling) in learning is the focus of *cognitive social learning theory*. According to the theory, much of what we learn is based on observing the behaviour of others, rather than direct experience and reinforcement. For example, if you see someone who has just jumped into a swimming pool suddenly show a stunned expression and howl, 'Yikes! It's freezing!' you do not have to touch the water to know it is cold. In the same way, we can learn aggressive behaviour from observing others.

Albert Bandura is one of the theorists who has argued for a social learning interpretation of aggression (Bandura 1973). In a well-known series of studies, Bandura and his colleagues examined the effects on children of observing aggressive behaviour by an adult. In one typical study, children individually observed an adult who either acted aggressively (for example, hitting and kicking an inflatable doll) or non-aggressively (playing quietly with toys). Later, the experimenter frustrated the children by taking away a toy they were playing with, saying a child in another room needed it. Aggression was measured by observing the child's behaviour after the experimenter left the room. (Note that this procedure implies acceptance of the frustration–aggression hypothesis!) The results indicated that exposure to an aggressive model significantly increased imitative aggressive responses, and somewhat increased non-imitative aggressive behaviour (such as verbal remarks or hitting other toys). Interestingly, the effects tended to be stronger for both boys and girls when the adult model was the same sex as the child (Bandura *et al.* 1961). Although there are flaws in this experiment (including the use of frustration, and the obvious differences between punching an inflatable doll and hitting a person), the study illustrates the basic premise of social learning theory in this context: aggressive behaviour can be learned from observing aggressive acts by others. Later studies both by Bandura and others have extended the original study to a variety of contexts (for a review, see Bandura 1973).

Key Thinker: **Albert Bandura**

Albert Bandura (1925–) was born in the small town of Mundare in Alberta, Canada. After receiving his bachelor's degree from the University of British Columbia, he emigrated to the USA, receiving his PhD in psychology from the University of Iowa in 1952. The next year, he received a position at Stanford University, where he is currently the David Starr Jordan professor in social sciences. Bandura's interests in social psychology and development led him to the study of learning in children, which led to several ground-breaking studies on the role of imitation in human learning. Together with Leonard Berkowitz, he has been one of the pioneers of the social learning approach, which emphasizes the importance of imitation and cognitive mediation in learning. His influence has been recognized on many occasions, including a Distinguished Scientist award from the American Psychological Association and a Guggenheim Fellowship. He lives with his family in Stanford, California, where he continues to teach and write.

The implications of the theory are both broad-ranging and serious: exposure to aggressive behaviour, in whatever form, is likely to increase the potential for aggression in observers. For example, parents who use physical punishment to discipline their children are likely to make the children more aggressive, since it teaches them that physical force is an appropriate means to control others. This interpretation is supported by a variety of studies which find a correlation between the use of physical discipline by parents and levels of aggression in children (Lefkowitz *et al.* 1978; Maccoby 1992; McCord *et al.* 1961). Other studies have demonstrated that negative or hostile parental behaviour, which includes criticism and derogatory comments (indirect aggression) to the child, is correlated with the child's subsequent use of criticism or derogatory comments to others (Barnow *et al.* 2005; Vaillancourt *et al.* 2007). Conversely, exposure to models who remain calm in provocative situations may foster non-aggressive behaviour (Baron 1983).

While there have been a tremendous number of studies exploring cognitive social learning theory, support for the theory does have certain limitations. Most significantly, the crucial links to serious human aggression typically are either correlational (as in the case of punishment), or else arguments by analogy (if children imitate one form of aggression, they will imitate others). In neither situation can one draw direct conclusions about the causes of serious forms of aggression. This is not a trivial concern, and we will return to it in relation to the debate about violence in the media, later in this chapter. Nonetheless, cognitive social learning theory clearly represents a possible explanation of the origins of many forms of aggressive behaviour.

Apart from social learning, the cognitive approach would argue that the *cognitive schemata* which guide individuals' behaviour can generally also affect the possibilities of aggressive behaviour. As was discussed in Chapter 1, we each develop a variety of schemata which influence both the way we perceive the world and the way we act. For example, we develop schemata that tell us how to act in a restaurant – waiting to be seated, selecting from a menu and so on (Schank 1984). These schemata are in turn influenced by the experiences we have. For example, people who watch large amounts of violent programming on television are more likely to perceive their surroundings as dangerous than those who don't watch such programmes. But can such schemata account for aggressive behaviour?

One example of a cognitive schema which relates to aggressive behaviour is what sociologist Elijah Anderson has called 'the code of the streets' (Anderson 1994). This code is a set of norms which govern interpersonal relations in the inner cities of the USA, particularly for African-American teenagers. Like other cognitive schemata, the code provides an internalized guide for behaviour. The most basic premise is that self-esteem is dependent on receiving 'respect' (defined as deferential behaviour) from others. 'Dissing' (expressions of disrespect) must be dealt with in kind, to prevent erosion of self-esteem. Since self-esteem is vulnerable to perceived insults, the code results in aggressive posturing and quick, violent responses to even imaginary wrongs. Unfortunately, since both parties operate on the same tit-for-tat premise, the violence can quickly escalate, even to fatal levels. Thus, Anderson argues that the assumptions of the code are a contributory factor to inner city violence. He notes, however, that the code is not universal: 'decent' kids (those trained in mainstream values) use the code only when necessary to minimize confrontational situations; by contrast, 'street' kids, imbued with the code, have no alternative schema. In this sense, what is most striking about Anderson's observations is the implication that different cognitive schemata can have a very real effect on the likelihood of aggressive behaviour.

priming a phenomenon whereby a thought or memory increases the activation of associated thoughts or memories (the term is analogous to 'priming a pump' by using a small quantity of water to enhance the flow of water).

cognitive neo-association theory Berkowitz's theory that thoughts, memories and behaviour may be triggered by affective states and/or priming.

Apart from such specific schemata, it is possible that violent thoughts may elicit violence through a kind of **priming** effect – the notion that any thought or memory is capable of increasing the activation of associated thoughts or memories. Leonard Berkowitz, one of the early supporters of cognitive social learning theory, has endorsed this idea to account for non-imitative forms of aggression. Berkowitz refers to the underlying model as **cognitive neo-association theory** (Berkowitz 1990). Whereas social learning theory requires that a particular aggressive behaviour must be observed in order to be learned, neo-association theory suggests that violent cognitions can increase the potential for *any* related behaviours. For example, Berkowitz notes that suicide rates go up after highly publicized aeroplane crashes; while both represent violent events, it is clearly not a case of imitation. In one experiment, Berkowitz looked at the effects of violence-related stimuli on subsequent aggression by angry individuals. Individuals who were shown pictures of guns were more willing to punish another person (with electric shocks) than those shown pictures of neutral objects, such as a badminton racquet (Berkowitz 1984). The tendency for guns to evoke hostile thoughts has been confirmed in a variety of studies (for example, Anderson *et al.* 1996; Klinesmith *et al.* 2006). In one interesting study, experimenters found that hunters displayed higher levels of aggression when primed with pictures of assault rifles (vs. hunting rifles), whereas non-hunters showed higher aggression when primed with pictures of hunting rifles rather than assault rifles (Bartholow *et al.* 2005)!

As with social learning theory, much of the evidence for neo-association theory depends on broad extrapolations of experiments, with only correlational data for real-world aggressive behaviour. While field experiments would provide more convincing evidence, the lack of such studies must be understood in the context of the ethical constraints on research involving aggression. Nevertheless, the available data suggest that the way we think can influence the way we act.

general aggression model (GAM) a theory of aggression developed by Anderson and Bushman which attempts to integrate cognitive social learning theory, cognitive neo-association theory and biological data on arousal.

Recently, Anderson and Bushman have attempted to combine social learning theory and neo-association theory, along with the biological data on arousal. The result is what they call the **general aggression model**, or **GAM** (Anderson and Bushman 2002). Acknowledging the role of both personal and situational variables, GAM provides a useful integration of much of the existing cognitive and physiological evidence, and also suggests some future directions for research. For example, imagine a person who is bumped in a crowded room. Depending on their current cognitive state, they may interpret this as accidental or (if angry already) as hostile – a process called 'immediate appraisal'. However, GAM states that whether this will lead to an immediate (aggressive) response or a further review of the situation (reappraisal) will depend on both the person's personality and situational constraints (like having time to reassess before reacting). By combining both cognitive and biological evidence, and suggesting that aggression is the result of an interaction of the person and the situation, GAM seems to offer a larger view of aggression. Support for the model has been demonstrated in subsequent research which looked at the interaction of priming and exposure to externally-administered testosterone (Klinesmith *et al.* 2006). This view is also endorsed by Cohen and his colleagues, who urge that this examination of aggression be expanded even further by looking at the entirety of the situation, including the victims of the aggression, the group with whom the aggressor is currently interacting, and the form the aggression takes (Cohen *et al.* 2006).

In summary, the cognitive approach suggests that aggressive behaviour is learned, and can be influenced both by what we observe (imitation) and by the way we think (the role of schemata). These assertions have been the subject of extensive research, most of which is consistent with the underlying hypotheses, although critics have tended to focus on the technical limitations of the research. In general, by asserting that aggressive behaviour is learned, the cognitive approach suggests that such behaviour is not inevitable. In fact, it implies that the same principles can be applied to foster prosocial behaviour. In essence, it argues that humans are neither inherently evil nor inherently good: how we act depends on what we have learned.

Try it Yourself

Newscasts and newspapers often pay detailed attention to fighting in professional sports, such as replays of fights in a sports broadcast. What effect do you think this might have on young and amateur athletes? Will they be more likely to get into fights? If so, how would you explain this in cognitive terms? How would the cognitive approach suggest that fighting in professional sports be handled by the media? What could parents do so that their children who view these incidents don't become violent themselves?

The Psychodynamic Approach

The psychodynamic approach traces its roots to Freud, and psychoanalysis is still probably the best-known theory within the approach. While the cognitive and behaviourist approaches see aggressive behaviour as learned, and therefore avoidable, Freud viewed aggression as an innate drive, and therefore an unavoidable reality of human life. Hence, Freud saw aggression as related to the person, not the situation. While certain situations might be more likely to trigger aggression, the nature of the response was seen as a function of the individual's psychic processes.

The aggressive drive was seen as part of the *id*, the aspect of the mind and personality which motivates our behaviour, while *ego* and *superego* often oppose the aggressive impulses of the id, creating conflict within the psyche. To cope with this conflict – and the aggressive tendencies – we use *defence mechanisms* which block conscious awareness of the underlying conflicts, and attempt to ameliorate the tensions in various ways – for example, by *displacing* the aggression onto a substitute object. For example, a man who plays a hard game of squash after having a disagreement with a colleague at work could be viewed as engaging in displacement as he bashes the ball.

In Freud's view, we can never eliminate aggression, we can only seek to control it by channelling it in particular ways which involve *symbolic* gratification. The most desirable form of release is through *sublimation* – the creation of socially-approved products like art or music. Since most of us are not proficient at such activities, a more common form of coping is the use of displacement, as noted above. Fantasy, seen in both dreams and other activities, is another possible outlet for aggressive energy. For example, imagining that the driver who just cut you off gets stopped by the police is an expression of aggression through fantasy. Underlying these and other defence mechanisms is the principle of *catharsis* – the release of drive energy through indirect gratification. For example, catharsis implies that if one watches violence (for example, a war movie), then one will symbolically release aggression through one's involvement with the characters. (Note that Lorenz also advocated catharsis, although the details of his theory are somewhat different.)

Unfortunately, the evidence regarding the value of catharsis is rather mixed, with more studies challenging the idea than supporting it. In one of the few experimental studies to provide support, Seymour Feshbach aroused aggressive tendencies by insulting the participants, and then provided one group with the opportunity to engage in fantasy activities (Feshbach 1955). When compared to a control group, this group showed a significant reduction in aggressive impulses, as measured by projective tests (a measure of symbolic aggression).

However, when looking at more direct forms of aggression, most studies have found that opportunities for catharsis *increase*, rather than decrease, aggressive behaviour. For example, in one study, participants were first given electric shocks during a learning task (arousing aggressive tendencies), and then half the subjects were allowed to retaliate against their tormentors, which presumably would reduce aggressive tendencies (Geen *et al.* 1975). Instead, in a follow-up to this situation, those subjects who had retaliated subsequently gave *more* intense shocks than those in the group which had no chance to retaliate previously. Hence, rather than reducing aggression, the initial opportunity to retaliate increased subsequent aggression – a result more consistent with social learning than catharsis. Similarly, a study by Bushman found that even when people are *told* that catharsis will reduce aggressive tendencies, the result is an increase in aggressive behaviour (Bushman *et al.* 1999). In the end, it seems necessary to conclude that there is little evidence in favour of catharsis. While this does not directly prove that aggression is not an innate drive, it does lead one to question the validity of Freud's views on regulating aggression.

Like the biological perspective, psychoanalysis asserts that aggression is innate. For the most part, Freud used case studies and anecdotal observations to support his theory; in addition, by emphasizing the symbolic nature of behaviour, he was able to ascribe even non-violent actions to aggressive motives. However, the dependence on case studies and symbolic interpretation must be considered weak evidence for the innateness of aggression. Furthermore, experimental research has largely contradicted his ideas of catharsis as a control mechanism for aggression. At the theoretical level, it is worth noting that some of Freud's early associates, including Adler and Jung, disagreed with his interpretation that aggression was innate. As Freud clearly recognized, aggressive behaviour is a common human phenomenon – but explaining *why* is the issue, and its pervasiveness does *not* constitute direct proof that it is innate. Given these realities, we can only conclude that the case for Freud's view is open to serious doubt.

Try it Yourself

Think about exciting action movies or television programmes you have seen. How did you feel afterwards? Did you feel calm and content? Did you feel excited and aroused? Pay attention to how you feel the next time you see an action movie. Do your impressions support the concept of catharsis? Do you think that the idea of catharsis might be applicable to any other situations? For example, do you think that watching a sad movie would help you cope with a sad situation in your own life? Or would it make you feel sadder?

The Humanistic Approach

In general, humanistic theory emphasizes the role of the person, not the situation, in behaviour, including social behaviour. Since individuals are seen as able to make choices, the humanists reject the determinism implied by situationism. In terms of aggression, humanistic theorists explicitly reject the idea that aggression is innate or in any way inevitable. Since aggressive behaviour clearly exists, how can humanistic theories account for it? To understand, let us look at the theories of Maslow and Rogers.

Maslow's hierarchy points out that a number of different needs exist, and that for any individual, particular needs will be more pressing at various times. Conspicuously absent from his hierarchy is any mention of aggression. Instead of being an innate drive which must be satisfied, aggression arises in response to circumstances where fulfilment of one of the basic needs is obstructed. In this sense, Maslow's view of aggressive behaviour is somewhat akin to the frustration–aggression hypothesis: aggressive behaviour is a possible response to particular circumstances. However, Maslow does not endorse the strong form of the frustration–aggression hypothesis, which states that frustration (blocking satisfaction of a need, in Maslow's terms) *always* results in aggression. Instead, he sees aggressive behaviour (particularly instrumental aggression) as only one possible response among many.

To understand this concept of aggression as only one possible response, let us consider an example. What would you do if an intruder broke into your house? Interestingly, a friend once faced this situation in real life. As the intruder entered the bedroom, Tony was awakened by his wife – just in time to see the stranger lunging at him with a knife. Fortunately, Tony (who was trained in the martial arts) disarmed the intruder, *without retaliating,* and held him until the police arrived. While they waited for the police, Tony talked with the teenage intruder, whose actions had been prompted by economic desperation. Despite nearly being killed (the knife tip came close enough to scratch Tony's chest), Tony felt sorry for the teen, and almost regretted having phoned the police! As this example shows, even threats to physical safety do not inevitably result in aggressive behaviour as a response. Hence, aggressive behaviour may arise in reaction to deprivation of needs (as the teen demonstrated), but is only one possible response. In the absence of any deprivation, Maslow would see aggressive behaviour as highly unlikely. Therefore, in his portrayal of self-actualized individuals, aggressive behaviour is largely absent; since self-actualization is not a deprivation need, it does not provide even this minimal reason for aggression.

Carl Rogers's theory uses a different set of concepts from Maslow's, but leads to a similar conclusion concerning aggression. Rogers sees human development as based on the *actualizing tendency,* which is a positive force for growth. Aggression, therefore, is not an innate drive. Instead, aggressive behaviour is one of the possible consequences of a state of incongruence. *Incongruence* occurs when individuals experience a conflict between their sense of self and their ideal self. Typically, this arises when other people impose *conditions of worth* as a requirement for giving positive regard. For example, teenagers frequently resent the rules of conduct which their parents attempt to impose, resulting in various forms of resistance, including acts of aggression. In Rogers's terms, there is a conflict between the teenager's own values (part of the self) and the parental values on which they were raised (part of the ideal self). As awareness of their own values grows, it results in resentment towards the parents, who use *conditional regard* to try to maintain the prior values. Aggressive behaviour is one possible response to this situation.

Another possible way in which aggressive behaviour might arise is if a person adopts aggressive norms due to the need for positive regard. For example, an adolescent exposed to the type of street code which Anderson (1994) has described may be reluctantly drawn into aggressive behaviour in order to get peer approval. Note that in both of the preceding examples, Rogers would not see aggression as inevitable, or even as the most appropriate response; it is simply a *possible* response.

Given that conditions of worth are frequently encountered in everyday life, we should not be surprised that aggressive behaviour is relatively common. However, Rogers believes that when individuals are in touch with the actualizing tendency, they will recognize aggressive responses as inappropriate. This is reflected in his description of the values which are associated with healthy growth, which make no mention of aggression, but include 'sensitivity to others and acceptance of others' (Rogers 1964, p. 166). Rogers notes that under the conditions which foster growth, 'I do not find, in such a climate of freedom, that one person comes to value fraud and murder and thievery, while another values a life of self-sacrifice ...' (Rogers 1964, p. 167). In other words, given the conditions for healthy growth and the development of congruence, Rogers believes that aggressive behaviour will not occur.

While the interpretations of aggression offered by Maslow and Rogers are consistent with their overall theories of behaviour, neither theorist provides much in terms of direct empirical support for their views. In part, this is due to the humanists' methodology, which emphasizes the subjective nature of experience rather than traditional experimentation. As a consequence, much of the evidence involves case studies and anecdotal observations drawn from their experiences with individuals in therapy. Unfortunately, as noted with the psychodynamic approach, such data are very limited as a means of proving causation.

Box 8.3 A Cross-cultural Look at Aggression

There is no doubt that different cultures may show different levels of aggression. Among the Semai of Western Malaysia, aggression is discouraged, and physical violence is extremely rare (Price and Crapo 2002). To the Semai, to be angry and show it in any way indicates a person's immaturity and lack of worth. While Semai behaviour would not surprise humanistic psychologists, not every culture is alike. By contrast, to the Dobu of the Trobriand Islands, aggression is central to most interactions: the Dobu believe a reasonable person is one who keeps neighbours in check through intimidation and threats. Even within a culture, the levels of aggression that are viewed as appropriate differ widely among sub-cultures: thus, to North American street gangs, aggression may be a sign of worth and manhood (Anderson 1994), while to American Quakers or the Amish, aggression is seen as completely unacceptable.

Whether approved of or not, aggression in some form occurs in all cultures. One of the most pervasive cross-cultural findings is that males (particularly adolescents) commit more aggressive acts than do females (Berry et al. 2002). As noted in the chapter, the biological approach would suggest this aggression is caused by high levels of the male hormone testosterone. While there is some evidence that high levels of testosterone are linked to aggressive behaviour, the data are mostly correlational (for example, Dabbs and Morris 1990), so inferring that testosterone causes aggressive behaviour is unjustified. More importantly, the variations in levels seen in aggression across both individuals and cultures strongly suggest that learning, including learning from one's culture, is a significant determinant of how aggressive one will be.

One way to account for the pervasive gender differences is based on the behaviourist approach. Essentially, the argument is that societies in some way accept, and even encourage (by reinforcement), aggressiveness in boys, but actively discourage it in girls. This idea was explored by Barry et al. (1976) in an examination of nearly 150 societies. These researchers found that in only 20 per cent of the societies studied was there a difference in teaching boys and girls about the acceptability of aggression.

Besides testosterone and differential teaching of boys and girls, other factors also seem to be implicated in the development of aggression. One factor suggested by Segall et al. (1999) is the 'gender-making' function that aggression may serve. In almost all cultures, rearing of the young child is done predominantly by females, with limited male presence. This may lead to an over-identification of the young boy with a female identity. Such a 'mistake' is corrected later, either by deliberate and often severe adolescent initiation rites, or by the individual effort of the boy to assert his masculinity, often in aggressive ways. Segall et al. (1999) call this behaviour, which typically appears at adolescence, 'compensatory machoism'. This concept can readily be linked to cognitive concepts like the formation of gender-role schemata; of course, the concept of identification can also be related to Freudian psycho-dynamic theory.

Thus, contemporary cross-cultural research suggested that aggressive behaviour involves multiple factors. In terms and explanations, the five approaches are all relevant in various ways, but none seems sufficient on its own.

By suggesting that life circumstances (such as deprivation of needs and conditions of worth) can affect behaviour, the humanists are proposing a person–situation interactionist model, despite their apparent emphasis on the individual. In essence, their assertion that aggression is not innate rests on two claims: first, that aggressive behaviour is based on thwarted development (situational); second, that some individuals function largely without resorting to aggressive behaviour (personal). The first point, as already noted, is problematical at best, since no direct proof is given. The second point is interesting, but also ambiguous. Since no one is *fully* self-actualized or *fully* congruent, and definitions of aggression differ, how one assesses an individual's non-aggressiveness is likely to be influenced by one's assumptions. (Culture also plays a role, as noted in Box 8.3.) For example, instances of aggressive behaviour in a supposedly self-actualized individual might be seen as refuting the humanistic view, or simply as an indication that the person is less than perfect. Even if someone showed no real sign of overt aggression, such as Mahatma Gandhi (the father of passive resistance as a form of political protest), some critics might say his behaviour reflected indirect or symbolic aggression. In the end, judging the appropriateness of the humanistic view of aggression seems (like other aspects of experience) dependent on one's own perceptions.

Try it Yourself

Imagine that you are raising a child. Based on the humanistic view, what would you do to ensure the child did not grow up to be aggressive? What does the humanistic view suggest to you about reducing violence within society? Is it about changing the person or changing society?

The view of aggression as one response among many possibilities is also supported by existentialist psychologist Rollo May, who asserts that aggression may be one response to an individual's perceived feeling of powerlessness in the world. Thus, if a person interprets their position as one which they can do nothing to affect, they may decide that their only recourse is to be aggressive in asserting their rights. In May's view, this can account for not only individual acts of aggression, but also violent incidents of civil unrest in countries where personal freedoms are withheld from individuals (May 1972).

Summary

The five approaches vary considerably in their perspective on social behaviour, and aggression in particular. (See Box 8.4 for a summary of the approaches' interpretations.) Of the five, the humanistic appears the weakest in terms of providing either evidence or a testable model. Of the other four, those theories which propose an *innate drive* – the biological and psychodynamic – have little direct supporting evidence. The argument that aggression is common, and therefore must be innate, is really only circular reasoning. Furthermore, the mechanism which Lorenz and Freud proposed for reducing aggression – *catharsis* – has yielded more negative than positive experimental results.

Research on the physiological aspects of aggression suggests that there is a relationship between pain and aggression, and possibly emotion and arousal more generally. That is, painful or unpleasant stimuli often elicit aggressive behaviour. As evolutionary theories have argued, it is likely that we have developed behavioural mechanisms for dealing with threats, and one interpretation of the pain–aggression relationship is that the behaviour is a defensive response, intended to eliminate the aversive stimulus. However, not all situations involving pain lead to aggression, so there seem to be mediating mechanisms involved.

The alternative to assuming aggression is innate is to explain it in terms of learning, and several theories have done so. The behaviourist concept of *instrumental aggression*, which says that aggression is reinforced by experiences in which it is effective in accomplishing a goal, is plausible, and has received some experimental support. It can also be related to other theories, such as aggression as a defensive reaction to pain: such reactions can be seen as a form of instrumental aggression if the person succeeds in eliminating the painful stimulus. Hence, instrumental aggression is one likely cause of aggressive behaviour. By contrast, the *frustration–aggression hypothesis* has weaker support. There seems no question that frustration can elicit aggression, but there are many qualifiers on the relationship, including the perceived likelihood of retaliation. Indeed, it may well be that frustrating circumstances simply represent a particular category

Box 8.4 *Perspectives on Aggression*

This chart provides a comparison of the five approaches in terms of how they view the origin of aggression, and the means by which it can be controlled.

Approach	Explanation of cause	Method of reducing
Biological	Ethology – innate drive Physiology – response to aversive stimuli	Catharsis (e.g., via sports) Minimize aversive stimuli
Behaviourist	Instrumental aggression – using aggression to reach a goal is reinforcing	Change contingencies so aggressive responses not reinforced
	Frustration–aggression hypothesis – frustration leads to aggression	Minimize sources of frustration, punish aggression
Cognitive	Social learning theory – aggressive behaviour is imitated	Reduce opportunities for observing aggression
	Neo-association theory – aggressive events trigger related thoughts and actions	Reduce exposure to aggressive stimuli
Psychodynamic (Freud)	Aggression innate drive (in id)	Catharsis (especially sublimation)
Humanistic (Rogers)	Aggression is one response to distortions of growth due to conditions of worth	Provide more unconditional positive regard

of aversive stimuli, in which case the hypothesis really reduces to a special case of the pain–aggression relationship.

At present, the most promising approach is the cognitive approach. While accepting the principle of instrumental aggression, the approach adds two further mechanisms to account for aggressive behaviour: *social learning* and the role of cognitive schemata (*neo-association theory*). More recently the *general aggression model* has proposed an integration of these mechanisms (and implicitly, instrumental aggression) along with biological arousal. Research thus far seems mostly supportive, and it has great potential to provide a more coherent theory of aggressive behaviour. (See *The World Today: Serial Killers* for a glimpse of how the five approaches might address this extreme form of aggression.)

The world today: **Serial Killers**

The newspapers, the movies and television programmes talk about them frequently. Serial killers, it appears, walk among us all too commonly (although not as frequently as the entertainment media portray, but exact numbers are unknown). They kill many people, (at least three people in a period of over 30 days), for no reason apparent to anyone except perhaps them. Often there seems to be some sort of sexual motive included in the killings, as many serial killers combine their murders with rape or sexual degradation.

The biological approach focuses on brain pathology as a causal agent in extreme aggressiveness, citing, for example, instances of violent behaviour in some people with epilepsy (Ito *et al.* 2007). From the behaviourist viewpoint, serial killers kill because of the reinforcing value of killing, and many do, in fact, express pleasure at seeing the suffering of their victims. Again there is a question, however: what makes the sight of suffering and death reinforcing to some people? The cognitive viewpoint points to the fact that many serial killers come from violent homes in which they witnessed brutality and physical aggression. They then model (to the extreme) in adulthood what they have seen in childhood (Knight 2007). Freud explained killing of others as manifestations of *Thanatos*, the innate drive to destroy, to be aggressive, to deny the life-affirming drive of *Eros*. Serial killers, then, may be conceptualized as people who have not been able to integrate the morals of society into their psyches, and so have no control over their destructiveness: they have a compulsion to kill to release the tension of Thanatos within them. Contemporary psychoanalysts have a somewhat different view of this. For example, object relations theorists believe that serial killers have had early experiences which have led them to believe that the world is bad, hateful and threatening to them, physically or psychologically. Their killings are in response to the perceived threat that constantly confronts them (Knight 2006). The question of why everyone who has had a terrible childhood does not become a serial killer is left open.

Humanists, such as Rollo May, contend that the perception of powerlessness leads to violence. Serial killers kill to gain the power they have been deprived of in their individual lives and, sometimes, in the society in which they live. The extreme violence seen in civil disturbances in some countries in which groups of people have felt oppressed and denied civil rights may stand as an example of this (May 1972). For both the cognitive and the humanistic approaches, however, questions still remain. Why doesn't everyone who has lived under such conditions become a serial killer? Why are some serial killers from backgrounds which do not include such hostile elements?

The foregoing are admittedly very abbreviated explanations given by the various approaches, but none seem to adequately explain serial killing on their own. There is consensus among researchers from all viewpoints that there are many factors which go into the making of a serial killer; these include neurological, social, psychological and environmental factors (Knight 2007). But the exact aetiology of serial killing is unclear.

Aggression and the Media

For many years now, there has been a debate about the relationship between observing violence portrayed in the media and aggressive behaviour. Whether one considers the news media or the entertainment media, there is no question that images of violence are readily encountered. However, the issue is not whether such portrayals occur, but whether media violence increases aggressive behaviour or not.

The debate is largely between the cognitive approach and those theories which see aggression as innate (the biological approach and psychoanalysis). The cognitive approach argues that observing violence may increase the potential for aggression, through both imitation and priming. The nativist theories, drawing on the concept of drive-reduction, suggest that observing violence can lessen aggressive energy through catharsis. It is also possible that, in the real world, no consistent relationship exists between observing violence and aggressive behaviour. This could happen if both theories are wrong, or if the effects of watching are mediated by other variables (making it only a distal cause), or even if the two kinds of processes somehow offset each other, producing no net change in the potential for aggressive behaviour.

At an intuitive level, many people favour the cognitive view. For example, after seeing an action film in which the hero triumphs by killing the bad guys, most people feel some degree of arousal, not relaxation. Does this mean that they will then scour the streets looking for criminals? Probably not. Behaviour is influenced by many factors, so the real issue is simply whether observing violence has a significant effect on aggressive behaviour or not.

As noted previously, there is little evidence to support catharsis; consequently, most of the research has focused on the hypothesis that observing violence *increases* aggressive behaviour, as the cognitive approach suggests. Over the past three decades, there have been hundreds of laboratory experiments on social learning of aggressive behaviour, and several reviews of the published literature. While details of the studies vary, they have looked at modelling of aggression by both sexes over a wide age range, and using a number of measures of aggressive behaviour (including willingness to give electric shocks to other people). Within the laboratory context, it appears quite clear that observing violence will increase the likelihood of aggressive behaviour. (For reviews, see Bandura 1973; Freidrich-Cofer and Huston 1986; Wood *et al.* 1991.) The difficulty with these studies is that laboratory findings may not generalize very well, for reasons discussed earlier in this chapter.

Because of the limitations of laboratory experiments, researchers have also tried to look at the effects of observing television violence in natural settings. One way that this can be done is through the use of correlational studies, which involve making observations without the controls required for experiments. Indeed, one of the earliest studies reporting a link between observing television violence and aggressive behaviour in children was based on an incidental finding from a broader study of child-rearing practices (Eron 1963). Subsequently, a positive correlation between observing violence on television and aggressive behaviour has been confirmed in a large number of studies, involving a variety of groups in several different countries (Belson 1978; Bushman and Huesmann 2001; Huesmann *et al.* 1984; Singer and Singer 1981).

While these studies have shown a link, the results are nonetheless limited, in that no correlational study can identify the cause of an observed pattern. That is, on the basis of the correlational data alone, one could argue that aggressive children choose to watch more violent television (reversing the direction of causation), or that an unidentified third variable accounts for the link (possibly family influences), or that the pattern is simply coincidental (unlikely, given how common the pattern is). Ideally, one would like to gather experimental evidence in a natural setting – in other words, do a field experiment.

One interesting study, conducted by a group of Canadian researchers, was described as 'a natural experiment' (technically, a quasi-experiment done in a field setting) (Joy *et al.* 1986). The research examined the impact of the introduction of television in a small isolated Canadian town, referred to in the study as Notel (for 'no television'). The investigators examined behaviour both before the advent of television, and for two years after its introduction (in 1974). As a control comparison, they also examined behaviour in two other Canadian towns which, while similar in size and demographic profile, already had access to television. Aggressive behaviour was measured in two ways: by direct observation of children's verbal and physical aggression during play periods at school, and by student and teacher ratings of aggressiveness. As shown in Figure 8.2, aggressive behaviour rose in Notel, while there was no significant increase in such behaviour for children in the other two towns. What is particularly striking is that the increases occurred for a wide range of children – both sexes, those who were initially high or low in aggressiveness, and those who watched large or small amounts of television. Hence, the study suggests a strong link between exposure to television and aggressive behaviour. One difficulty with the study is that the experimenters did not have direct control over the *content* of what children watched, so the effects cannot be specifically linked to observing violence. However, it seems reasonable to assume that some portion of the viewing (and the results) involved violent programming. Still, it illustrates the difficulty of doing field experiments (and natural-setting research in general) – one cannot control all elements of the situation.

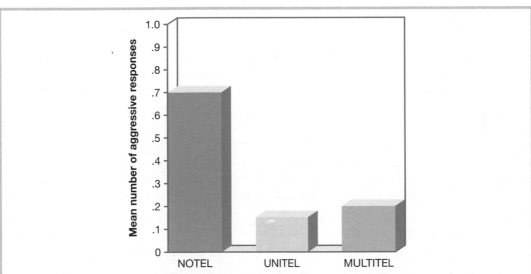

Figure 8.2 Effects of the Introduction of Television The graph shows the results of a field experiment in which physical aggression by children was compared as a function of the introduction of television to the Notel community. Unlike in the two communities which already had televisions at the time of the study, the children in Notel showed a significant increase in physical aggression. (Adapted from Joy *et al.* 1986)

Another field experiment focused on altering the *attitudes* towards violent content, without trying to control what viewers watched (Eron 1982). In this experiment, 169 boys who had already been identified as viewing high levels of violence were randomly divided into two groups. One group was given training intended to reduce aggression by altering attitudes toward television violence, the other group was a control group. Based on peer ratings of aggression collected four months after the end of the training, the experimental group showed significant reductions in aggressive behaviour, while the control group showed no change. The general pattern of results suggests that it is not simply the viewing of violence which increases aggressive behaviour; instead, it depends on how the viewer interprets the meaning of what they watch. That is, cognitive processes mediate the effects of observing violence. Support for this conclusion comes from other studies which suggest that parental guidance can alter both children's perceptions of violence *and* subsequent aggressive behaviour (Mattern and Lindholm 1985; Kirsh 2006). Thus, the connection between media violence and aggressive behaviour seems to involve an interaction between the person and the situation. The role of the person has been further reinforced by research indicating that gender differences and motivation (the reason why people watch violent programming) can mediate the general connection between media violence and aggressive behaviour (Haridakis 2006). The relationship is indeed complicated.

Taken as a whole, all three types of research point to a connection between observing television violence and aggressive behaviour. However, none of the studies we have mentioned is without flaws, and critics continue to challenge the conclusion that a relationship exists (Freedman 1984, 1986). Freedman acknowledges that the correlation between viewing television violence and aggressive behaviour is most likely genuine. However, he also concludes that the effect is small (a correlation coefficient of 0.10 to 0.20), and that weaknesses in the experimental research suggest that the evidence for a causal connection is minimal. (For replies to Freedman, see Freidrich-Cofer and Huston 1986; and Liebert and Sprafkin 1988.) In part, Freedman is justified in being sceptical, since each of the studies we have discussed *does* have flaws. However, it should be noted that they are not the *same* flaws in each case, and that the general nature of the results remains the same in all cases.

The questions raised by Freedman's analysis go to the heart of our understanding of social behaviour. Psychology has traditionally (but not exclusively) modelled its methods on those of the physical sciences, a domain where many of the phenomena are relatively simple compared to human behaviour. Within psychology, social behaviour may well be the most complex area, since it involves *interactions* between individuals. Beyond this, social psychologists are often limited in their research methods by ethical considerations. All of these factors create constraints on the effectiveness of research. Consequently, it seems unlikely that one could conceive of *any* one study in social psychology which would adequately satisfy the conflicting needs for experimental control, experimental realism, external validity and ethical responsibility. Thus, one must proceed hesitantly by exploring the problem from as many angles as possible. Looked at in this way, Freedman's analysis seems overly critical, and possibly disingenuous, in that it seems unlikely that *any* generally-accepted finding in social psychology would meet his standard of proof.

Overall, it seems reasonable to believe that *some* relationship does exist between observing violence and aggressive behaviour, even if it involves an interaction between the person and the situation in which viewing occurs. (It is worth noting that video games yield similar – and similarly complex – data to the results found for television violence: see Ferguson *et al.* 2008; Giumetti and Markey 2007; Konjin *et al.* 2007.) At the same time, it is important to note that no serious researcher believes that observing violence on television is the *only* factor in aggression. For example, instrumental aggression (including real violence in the home) and other forms of social learning (for example, attitudes of parents and interpersonal skills) also play a role in aggressive behaviour. As Anderson and Bushman's general aggression model makes clear, aggression is multi-factorial – but observing violence can interact with many of the other elements (Anderson and Bushman 2002; Cohen *et al.* 2006; Klinesmith *et al.* 2006).

More than any other area of psychology, social psychology seems to invite extrapolation to everyday life. Thus, if one *does* accept that there is a causal connection between observing violence and aggressive behaviour, then shouldn't society do something about it? And if so, what? Ban all violence in television and movies? Prohibit all violence in sports? Such prospects can evoke strong feelings among both advocates and detractors. The problem is, psychological research may help us *understand* behaviour, but it cannot directly address the moral questions of what behaviour *should* be. In this sense, psychological research cannot be the sole criterion for framing social policy.

At the same time, to ignore what psychology has learned when we consider social issues (either individually or collectively) seems equally undesirable. To do so implies that the search for psychological understanding has no bearing on our lives. As a parent, for example, I (WEG) am concerned with the upbringing of my children, and with the kind of society in which they live; in both respects, I feel it is important that, as a society, we try to understand the factors that affect aggression.

Try it Yourself

What conclusion do you draw about the relationship between observing violence and aggressive behaviour? Have you played computer/video games which feature graphic violence? How do you feel about the relationship between such games and aggression? Do you think that the age of the viewer or game-player makes a difference? What guidelines would you draw up for parents who are concerned about the effects of viewing violence on their children?

PERSPECTIVES ON PROSOCIAL BEHAVIOUR

Thus far, our examination of social behaviour has focused on one of the most negative forms of behaviour, aggression. While not demonstrating that *all* aggressive behaviour is learned, the research on observing violence certainly suggests that the potential for such behaviour can be increased through learning. What about behaviour that is socially desirable? How does it arise? And are there ways to encourage such behaviour? For example, does reading stories about people who help others (such as the Good Samaritan) have any impact on actual helping by children?

Defining Prosocial Behaviour

Prosocial behaviour can be defined as socially desirable behaviour which in some way benefits another person, or society as a whole. While **altruism** is the most frequently studied category of prosocial behaviour, it also includes a number of other kinds of behaviour (see Box 8.5). In day-to-day life, we all engage in prosocial behaviour – for example, when we play a team sport, when we offer sympathy to a friend who is upset, or when we refrain from dropping litter. Hence, the working of society is largely dependent on the occurrence of prosocial behaviour. In this section, we will focus on altruism, and how each of the approaches explains it.

prosocial behaviour socially desirable behaviour that is beneficial to another person, or to society as a whole.

altruism any behaviour intended to help others.

Altruism may bring to mind images of someone heroically intervening in an emergency, such as rescuing a drowning stranger. In that sense, it might seem that altruism is quite rare, for few of us would claim to be heroic. Yet, we all engage in small acts of helping, whether contributing

> ## Box 8.5 *Categories of Prosocial Behaviour*
>
> *Just as various forms of aggression exist, there are also various forms of prosocial behaviour. Here are some categories suggested by Rubenstein* et al. *1974. (Adapted from original)*
>
> Altruism – sharing, helping and cooperation with people or animals
> Control of aggression – behaviours intended to prevent or eliminate aggression by self or others
> Explaining feelings – communicating with another person about thoughts, feelings or actions with intent of increasing understanding and fostering positive outcomes
> Reparation for wrongdoing – behaviour which is clearly intended to make amends for previous wrongful actions
> Resistance to temptation – resisting temptation to engage in socially-prohibited behaviours
> Sympathy – expressing concern for others and their problems
> Task persistence/delay of gratification – actions intended to fulfil commitments by persisting at a task or delaying gratification

to a charity or holding the door for a stranger. Thus, although altruism refers to helping others, the term can cover a wide range of behaviours. In order to study altruistic behaviour, we need to have some way to define it which is specific enough to be testable, and which does not assume a particular theoretical basis. One of the most common ways that researchers have tried to do this is by looking at whether people will assist someone in distress, called 'bystander intervention'.

The converse of bystander intervention is *bystander apathy*, the failure to intervene in an emergency. Historically, bystander apathy was the starting point for modern research into the conditions which foster or inhibit altruistic behaviour. As noted in Chapter 1, this concern was stimulated in part by the unfortunate death of Kitty Genovese in New York in 1964. Here was a young woman being repeatedly attacked on the street, and screaming for help, to no avail. As it turned out, none of the 38 individuals later identified as having observed the attack had even telephoned the police. The event shocked many people, and was seen by many as a sign of the callousness of modern urban life. After all, in doing nothing to help, the bystanders had indirectly contributed to her death. Conversely, if any one person had acted, Kitty Genovese might still be alive. (Note: the original incident, and the behaviour of the bystanders, have recently been revisited by Manning *et al.* (2007). While in no way challenging the basic research on bystander apathy, it offers a new interpretation of the original event.) Before examining more closely the research on bystander intervention and bystander apathy, let us consider how each approach views altruistic behaviour.

Theories of Altruism

As with aggression, each of the five approaches has an interpretation of how socially desirable behaviour arises. In general, both the person and the situation seem to influence altruism. In

ethical hedonism (also called 'egoism') the principle that individuals engage in moral behaviour, such as altruism, because it provides some personal benefit.
genuine altruism the principle that individuals will assist others without deriving any personal benefit.

terms of the situation, theories tend to suggest either that altruistic behaviour benefits the helper in some way (**ethical hedonism**), or that it occurs without regard to personal benefit (**genuine altruism**). Partly because of the difficulty of identifying all possible benefits, some researchers argue that genuine altruism cannot be demonstrated (Cialdini 1991; Krebs 1991). As we will see, most of the approaches invoke some form of ethical hedonism to explain helping behaviour, though the mechanisms proposed differ significantly.

The Biological Approach

For the biological approach, altruistic behaviour has its roots in our evolutionary history. In general, evolutionary theorists argue that displaying altruism confers an advantage in terms of natural selection. For example, Melvin Konner (1982) has suggested that prosocial behaviours like altruism occur only to enhance reproductive success and foster the transmission of one's genes (called **kin altruism**). Thus, a parent might sacrifice their own life to save their child, because the child carries half of their genes and can in turn preserve them by procreating. For similar reasons, one would be less likely to help a more distant relative like a cousin, and very unlikely to help a total stranger, whose genetic similarity is unknown. Support for this idea comes from studies of people faced with hypothetical life-or-death decisions (Burnstein *et al.* 1994). In general, individuals favoured those who would be most likely to contribute to preserving their genes, such as close kin over distant relatives, and the young (who are likely to reproduce) over the old.

kin altruism the concept that individuals help those who are close relatives, because it fosters the transmission of their genes.

One difficulty with explaining altruism in terms of reproductive success is that it cannot account for helping those who are not genetically related. For example, why help a total stranger who is in distress? In order to deal with such situations, evolutionary psychologists have developed the concept of **reciprocal altruism**. Essentially, reciprocal altruism says we will help others in the expectation that they will help us when we are in need, as long as the expected long-term benefit exceeds the immediate cost (Trivers 1971). Thus, a group of people on a subway platform may respond to an attack on a stranger, because the risk to each person is quite small, but the future benefit of other people helping if one of them were to be attacked would be large. Alternatively, in a variant of kin altruism, Elliott Sober (2002) has suggested that helping strangers is based on compassion. Under this model, being compassionate to one's relatives has survival advantages, and this is correlated with extending compassion to others; that is, the more one feels compassion to kin, the more likely it is one will be sensitive to the suffering of strangers (and therefore respond by helping). Yet another model, suggested by Tom Walker (2008) notes that *sexual selection* may be at the root of altruistic behaviour: if a male helps others, even those who are not genetically related, it suggests that he has resources and is biologically fit, thereby making him more desirable as a mate. But incompatible with this is the research finding that men often report refraining from intervening in a violent situation because of their fear that they might appear weak and feminine if they showed any objections to aggressive behaviour (Carlson 2008).

reciprocal altruism the concept that individuals help strangers if the expected benefit of future help from the strangers exceeds the short-term cost of helping.

Other evolutionary models have been put forward, including *competitive altruism* (McAndrew 2002). While differing in various specifics, they all pose similar challenges in terms of evaluation. For instance, sexual selection altruism, kin altruism and reciprocal altruism all reflect forms of ethical hedonism, with the assumed benefit being defined in terms of reproductive success and survival advantage. Of these concepts, kin altruism is perhaps the most interesting, both because its predictions about choices seem difficult to explain without referring to genetic relatedness, and because of the empirical support which exists for these predictions. On the other hand, reciprocal altruism can be interpreted as simply a restatement of the principle of reciprocity, which has a social history going back at least as far as the biblical 'golden rule'. Since it is almost impossible to identify, let alone measure, the implied costs and benefits, reciprocal altruism seems very hard to test. Sexual selection altruism (seeking to be a more desirable mate) seems like a *post hoc* explanation: for example, one might argue that non-altruistic behaviour might be regarded more favourably by a potential mate since it might indicate that resources would not be spent indiscriminately. Indeed, several different models have been put forward, but at present none can claim much experimental support (Caporael and Baron 1997; Simon 1990). One indirect piece of evidence comes from work showing that older adults who provide social support to others live longer than those whom they help – that is, reciprocal altruism may confer a health benefit (Brown *et al.* 2003). Other studies have found similar health benefits (for example, Li 2007), but the correlational nature of the data makes it difficult to rule out other explanations, such as lowered stress. At present the explanations offered by evolutionary psychology must be considered tentative, but they do warrant further exploration.

The Behaviourist Approach

To the behaviourists, prosocial behaviours, like aggressive behaviours, are acquired through reinforcement. For example, if parents and others reinforce a child for sharing or helping others, then the child will learn such behaviours. Like the biological approach, the behaviourist view of altruism is based on an assumption of ethical hedonism. However, the underlying benefit is seen in terms of reinforcers, not survival advantage. In this context, the publicity and other rewards which society bestows for major acts of altruism (such as rescuing a drowning person) can be seen as social reinforcers. (It can also be argued that they serve as discriminative stimuli to encourage other people to act similarly.) In essence, altruism is seen as instrumental, just as aggression can be; an individual does the action because of a perceived reinforcer.

While it is likely that children are reinforced for various forms of prosocial behaviour, it must be acknowledged that there is little supporting evidence (Maccoby 1992). Interestingly, the anthropological evidence cited by McAndrew to support *competitive altruism* could also support the behaviourist model of instrumental altruism (McAndrew 2002). That is, when someone makes public sacrifices based on a perceived long-term benefit, it is hard to distinguish competitive from instrumental reasons. Hence, like the evolutionary models, the concept of instrumental altruism seems rather vague. For example, there are circumstances where individuals may actually risk their lives in order to help another. In such circumstances, what is the reinforcer that could be worth losing one's life? Or must we assume that the person is unaware of the risk in order to make sense of such behaviour? It may well be that heroic acts are extraordinary, and not easily explained. But at present, the behaviourist view of altruism seems too unsupported to consider seriously.

The Cognitive Approach

Like the behaviourists, the cognitive approach views prosocial behaviours as learned by the same processes as those involved in learning anti-social behaviours like aggression. That is, both types of behaviour are learned by *imitation*, and are influenced by the schemata we form concerning social interactions. Hence, altruistic behaviour can be influenced by what we observe others do, and by the ideas which we are exposed to in everyday life (via *priming* effects).

Some cognitive researchers have tested these ideas by doing experiments to try to enhance altruistic behaviour. Sprafkin and her colleagues looked at the effect of positive media examples by exposing first grade children to one of three television shows: one conveyed a message to help others even at personal cost, while the other two represented control conditions with no such message (Sprafkin *et al.* 1975). Subsequently, over 90 per cent of children exposed to the helping message chose helping a puppy over a chance for personal gain; in neither control group did more than 50 per cent similarly intervene. One way to explain this result is in terms of imitation, since the helping message also involved rescuing an animal. However, Berkowitz has suggested that these and similar studies involving media exposure can better be explained in terms of *priming* – that is, exposure to concepts of helping serves to activate related schemata in the individual (Berkowitz 1984). The activation of these prosocial schemata then makes it more likely that the person will intervene if an emergency – even one dissimilar to the original example – arises. For example, if you hear on the radio that a young child has given their allowance to a charity, you may be more likely to help a stranded motorist while you are driving to work. Priming may also contribute to a phenomenon in which having helped someone leads to further helping behaviour: when individuals believed they had been helpful (termed 'gratitude'), they were subsequently more likely to render aid when requested by a stranger (Bartlett and DeSteno 2006).

Thus, both priming and social learning are consistent with the conclusion that it is possible to enhance prosocial behaviour by exposing individuals to examples of prosocial concepts. However, they do differ in significant ways. One difference is that priming is generally seen as relatively transient, lasting hours or days (Berkowitz 1984). By contrast, social learning effects can often be detected months or years later (for example, Eron 1982). While hardly conclusive, these experiments at least demonstrate that it is possible to enhance altruistic behaviour by applying cognitive principles.

However they are formed, the development of prosocial cognitive schemata seem to produce stable effects on behaviour. For example, a longitudinal study of schoolchildren found that ratings of prosocial behaviour in grade 3 were a strong predictor of prosocial behaviour five years later (Caprara *et al.* 2000). Possibly, these effects are related to schemata for making moral judgements, as engaging in altruistic behaviour has been shown to be associated with higher levels of moral reasoning in both adolescents and adults (Comunian and Gielen 1995).

One fundamental limitation of the cognitive view of prosocial behaviour is that neither the research nor the theory really explains *why* people help. That is, do people help because they receive a benefit from helping (ethical hedonism), or simply out of a desire to do good (genuine altruism)? Because the theory does not address the issue of motivation, it seems impossible to decide which assumption should apply. In a sense, we are left with a model which seems to work (at least for many cases), but we don't know why! Hopefully, future work may clarify this aspect of the cognitive approach.

The Psychodynamic Approach

In contrast to the cognitive approach, Freud saw prosocial behaviour as closely linked to motivational processes. Essentially, altruism results from a defence mechanism, whereby one engages in good deeds in order to block awareness of one's own aggressive nature. In developmental terms, individuals who consistently engage in altruistic acts are fixated at the latent stage, where overt expression of the drives is repressed. For example, a doctor who treats the poor without charging a fee may do considerable good in helping others, but Freud would say the underlying motivation is based on redirecting the drive energy of the id. In his view, such behaviours have social value, but their occurrence is dependent on the dynamics of the psyche, particularly in terms of how ego handles the competing demands of id and superego. In this sense, his theory is clearly based on ethical hedonism, with benefits being defined in terms of the ego's ability to minimize anxiety and cope with external reality.

Like many aspects of Freud's theory, his explanations of altruistic behaviour are not easily testable. A modern psychoanalyst, Daniel Kriegman, has examined Freud's ideas, and has suggested that altruism is better accounted for by other psychoanalytic models than by Freud's original theory (Kriegman 1990). Unfortunately, Kriegman provides little direct evidence to support his argument, instead drawing analogies to work in evolutionary psychology. Interestingly, Shapiro and Gabbard have challenged the Freudian idea that altruism results from a defence mechanism – and have used evolutionary theory to support their argument (Shapiro and Gabbard 1994). Hence, there seems to be no convincing support of Freud's view of altruism.

It is worth noting that Freud's theory says little about how society might foster altruistic behaviour, other than by ensuring a well-developed superego. This is somewhat surprising, given that the theory puts forward a clear mechanism (catharsis) as a means of reducing aggression. The absence of a specific mechanism may reflect the fact that altruism, unlike aggression, is not seen as an innate drive. Consequently, the methods for fostering altruistic behaviour (like the use of defence mechanisms) cannot be directly promoted. Hence, in terms of understanding and fostering altruistic behaviour, his theory seems too vague either to test or to utilize.

The Humanistic Approach

As discussed previously, the humanists take a positive view of human behaviour, including prosocial behaviour. For Rogers, the motivation for altruistic behaviour comes from the actualizing tendency, and hence is a basic human capacity. In part, helping others can be seen as a form of reciprocity which is fostered by *empathy*; we can recognize others' suffering, just as we recognize their need for positive regard. Thus, Rogers would say we help someone who is in distress because we recognize their distress, not because helping is of direct benefit to us. As such, altruistic behaviour can be seen as genuine altruism, rather than ethical hedonism.

The idea that empathy fosters altruistic behaviour has been explored in several experiments by Daniel Batson (Batson 1991, 1998). Batson has found that under conditions which foster empathy, individuals will choose to help someone who is suffering even if it implies that they themselves might suffer. For example, in a variant of Milgram's obedience situation (see Chapter 1), subjects watched another person receive electric shocks; when given the option, individuals often agreed to take the person's place. In some studies, individuals chose to help even if walking away led to a cash incentive! Thus, Batson's work seems to confirm that empathy can be a source of altruistic behaviour. Furthermore, contrary to the claims of critics (see earlier discussion), Batson has asserted that it is possible to distinguish between *genuine altruism* (based on empathy) and *ethical hedonism* (based on self-interest) (Batson *et al.* 1999). In an experiment testing both types of altruism (in different conditions), he found that while both principles can motivate private actions, ethical hedonism is reduced when actions are public, but empathy is not. Hence, while not absolutely conclusive, it suggests that empathy can motivate altruism, and is different from ethical hedonism as an influence on behaviour. (See also Eisenberg 2005 for a review of the relationship between empathy and prosocial behaviour.)

Maslow looked at the motivation for behaviour in terms of his *hierarchy of needs*. At the top of the hierarchy is self-actualization, which is a growth need, rather than deficiency-based. Thus, he would likely say that altruistic behaviour is based on genuine altruism, rather than ethical hedonism. Indeed, he noted that people are capable of responding based on a higher need, even if it implies ignoring a more basic need. For example, someone could risk their life (threatening safety needs) in order to help a friend or loved one (love and belonging needs), or even a stranger (self-actualization). In the case of a stranger in distress, self-actualization would imply helping simply because (as a human being) it is the appropriate thing to do. Similarly, Maslow's theory would suggest that self-actualized individuals are the most likely to engage in consistent acts of altruism (for example, Mother Teresa). Interestingly, later in his life, Maslow suggested that there may be a level beyond that of self-actualization in which the dichotomy between 'me' and 'them' is transcended. The person at this level would engage in prosocial or selfless behaviour simply because they identify more with the whole of society than with themselves and their own self-actualization (Greene and Burke 2007; Maslow 1971).

In terms of evidence to support Maslow's description of altruism motivated by the need for self-actualization, there are many anecdotal examples, as well as correlational studies, that show a relationship between self-transcendent values and prosocial behaviour (for example, Caprara and Steca 2007). However, there is little experimental evidence to support this interpretation of altruistic behaviour. In part, this reflects the emphasis that the humanists place on subjective experience rather than experimental control. However, as Batson's work shows, it is not impossible to develop experiments that can be related to the theories.

In terms of promoting altruistic behaviour, Rogers and Maslow seem to offer similar views. By providing the conditions for healthy growth (Rogers) and satisfaction of deficiency needs (Maslow), society can foster the development of individuals who will reach their potential in all respects – including their capacity to respond to individuals in distress. In short, if we wish to create a society of individuals who help others, we need to create a society which helps everyone. Clearly, this concept is not likely to be tested in the near future (though we might wish it could be).

Summary

As we have seen, each of the five approaches offers a distinctive interpretation of altruism. In this regard, the biological and psychodynamic approaches seem similar in their views of the origin of aggression (as innate), and also agree in terms of the basis of altruism (that is, as ethical hedonism). However, currently evolutionary models of altruism are attracting a great deal of interest, while psychodynamic theory seems of little practical relevance. The behaviourists explain prosocial behaviour primarily in terms of instrumental benefits, which also seems consistent with cognitive models. In general, cognitive models seem to have the best empirical support, but there are still large gaps – including explaining what motivates altruistic behaviour. The humanistic approach is the only one which seems to be clearly based on genuine altruism – a concept which is still controversial. As research on altruism continues, it will be interesting to see how this issue is resolved, and whether empathy can be applied to provide the motivational foundation of a cognitive model.

At present there are many unresolved questions about the origins of prosocial behaviour. Given this, it is not surprising that we know relatively little about ways to foster it, despite the potential social value. To understand the difficulties, let us return to the issue of bystander intervention as a form of altruism.

Altruism and Bystander Behaviour

While there are many ways that we can help others, responding to an emergency is perhaps the most significant. Thus, **bystander intervention** is clearly a form of altruistic behaviour. Similarly, it seems surprising to find situations where someone is in distress, yet onlookers don't respond – the phenomenon of *bystander apathy*. Thus, examining the reactions of bystanders to emergencies provides a practical example of the factors which affect altruism.

bystander intervention the act of assisting strangers in an emergency.

One element to consider is the type of circumstances under which people do or do not intervene. As Latané and Darley (1969) noted, most emergencies represent a complex situation, and several steps are required for intervention to occur (see Figure 8.3). First, one must recognize that there is an emergency, and some situations can be ambiguous. For example, a diabetic suffering from insulin shock may appear drunk, including sweetish breath. Given that perception is an active construction (see Chapter 1), it is possible for people to misinterpret the situation, or simply fail to notice that there is an emergency. Second, one must evaluate what response is appropriate. Given that emergencies are both unpredictable and rare, many people are unsure what to do when faced with a situation in which someone needs help. Consequently, they will often consider the behaviour of others in order to determine how to respond. Hence, this is the stage where social dynamics are typically significant. Third, the person must decide whether they have the appropriate skills to intervene. For example, if the emergency is a heart attack, the person may consider whether they are capable of performing CPR (cardiopulmonary resuscitation). The possible reasons for failing to act are many, and include fear for one's own safety, lack of specific skills and even legal barriers. For example, in some jurisdictions, bystanders are not legally compelled to intervene in an emergency, but may be held liable for consequences if they do intervene. In such cases, this legal stance can serve as a deterrent to becoming involved. (Some places have passed so-called 'good Samaritan' laws protecting those who try to help from liability, in order to encourage intervention.) Thus, the decision to intervene requires a series of assessments, in a situation which often requires an almost immediate response.

Given this complexity, the failure to intervene may reflect processes that have little to do with lack of caring. (Because of this, some prefer the term 'bystander non-intervention' to bystander apathy.) In their research, Latané and Darley focused on the second stage of the process: how people decide what to do. Typically, individuals look to others for clues as to how to act – a form of *social influence*. Thus, if others are present and do nothing, one might conclude that there is no reason to intervene. (Latané and Darley found that when a confederate of the experimenter deliberately remained passive, few people responded to the emergency.) Even if no one else is present, social influence may play a role, in terms of calling upon previously learned social schemata. For example, a teenager might think, 'What would my Dad do in this situation?' Consequently, social influence is a major factor in determining altruism or its converse, bystander apathy. As Mark Levine (1999) has noted, the assumptions individuals make about the situation are an important determinant of helping – for example, when individuals see a man assaulting a woman, they are much less likely to intervene if they think the man and woman know each other (see also Carlson 2008).

Try it Yourself

Most of the interpretations of empathic behaviour suggest that we help others because 'there's something in it for us'. It may be because we anticipate rewards of some kind, such as praise from others, an increase in our own sense of esteem, or a reduction in our (empathic) suffering. Or, it may be because we are genetically programmed to engage in behaviour that will ultimately benefit our own survival or the propagation of our genes. Thus, most explanations suggest that we intervene for our own benefit, not out of genuine altruism. Consider some possible situations. Some wealthy individuals donate large amounts of money to charities, while making sure that their donations are highly publicized (possibly even expecting a building to be named after them) – but sometimes donations are anonymous. Or, consider that individuals sometimes risk their lives in emergencies, such as running into a burning building to rescue strangers, and report afterwards that they even didn't think about the risk to themselves. Do you think genuine altruism is possible? Explain why or why not.

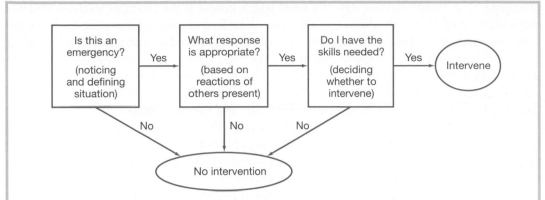

Figure 8.3 Determining Response to an Emergency As discussed in the text, responding to an emergency requires a series of decisions, and a negative response to any step will preclude taking action.

diffusion of responsibility a lessening of an individual's feeling of responsibility in a situation which involves other people.

Latané and Darley also identified a second factor which could influence responding, **diffusion of responsibility**. In any situation where others are present (not just emergencies), individuals often feel less personal responsibility for what happens. In an emergency, this can result in a perceived lessening of the onus to act. For example, when Kitty Genovese was killed, interviews indicated that people assumed that *someone else* had already called the police – and so no one did!

While both factors seem relevant to the likelihood of bystander intervention (Christy and Voigt 1994), much of the early work on bystander apathy focused on diffusion of responsibility by looking at group size effects (Latané and Nida 1981). One reason for this may be the fact that it is easier to control group size when doing experiments than it is to control the cognitive schemata that underlie social influence. Ironically, if one is seeking to enhance the likelihood of bystander intervention in the real world, social influence may be more relevant than diffusion of responsibility, since group sizes at real emergencies are unpredictable. In any case, to avoid confounding these two possible factors, much of the research on enhancing altruism has utilized situations involving single individuals.

Consistent with these considerations, most researchers have attempted to increase intervention by manipulating social influence. In one study, a variant of Latané and Darley's 'lady in distress' scenario was used; the difference was that, in this version, the confederate reacted to the sound of someone falling in the next room (Staub, reported in Goleman 1993). In one case, the confederate said, 'That probably has nothing to do with us.' In this condition, fewer than 25 per cent of subjects intervened to offer help. In the other condition, the confederate said, 'That sounds pretty bad – I'll go get the experimenter and maybe you should go check what's happening next door,' and proceeded to leave the room. In this case, 100 per cent of subjects moved to render aid. In effect, the comments of the confederate served to define what was appropriate behaviour in the situation. In another study, people who interpreted another person's facial expression as indicating fear were more likely to render aid (Marsh and Ambady 2007). Hence, one way to enhance altruism is by creating situational interpretations which encourage intervention.

Other research suggests additional factors that may foster intervention. As discussed earlier, both exposure to positive models and priming with prosocial ideas can increase the likelihood of helping. Consistent with this view is a study which looked at the effects of teaching students about research on bystander apathy and altruism. Compared to students that were not given the same information in class, they were more likely to help when they encountered an apparent emergency two weeks later (Beaman *et al.* 1978). The notion that people can be primed to engage in prosocial behaviour is also central to the notion of 'behavioural nudging' – for example, simply making people aware of how their energy consumption compares to the norm in their community leads people to reduce their usage (Thaler and Sunstein 2008).

Intervention is also more likely when the person in distress seems similar to the bystander (Graf and Riddle 1972). In a recent study, researchers made British students very aware of their European (rather than British) identity, and found that they were then more likely to help in a fictitious disaster that was said to occur in mainland Europe than one in South America (Levine and Thompson 2004). The precise mechanism for this similarity effect is uncertain; it could reflect a form of kinship altruism, or it may indicate that perceived similarity increases feelings of empathy. A third possibility is that similarity effects are cultural, since a study of Chinese individuals found no difference in prosocial behaviour towards in-group vs. out-group members (Leung and Bond 1984).

Overall, this research is consistent with the cognitive approach, which suggests that the likelihood of bystander intervention depends on the way we perceive and evaluate the situation. Furthermore, the indications are that prosocial behaviour can be modified by processes like priming and social learning. Of course, the existing research does not prove that all prosocial behaviour is learned, nor does it imply that no limits exist to modifiability. Hopefully, over time we will develop further insights into prosocial behaviour, and will be able to apply that understanding in our communities.

One aspect that has not been addressed in our discussion of altruism is the role of culture. While it is clear that social behaviour varies across cultures, identifying the causal factors is not easy. One factor that has been studied extensively is the difference between *individualist* and *collectivist* cultures. Describing cultures in this way has limitations, since it reduces complex differences to a single factor. In addition, finding differences across cultures does not directly tell us which elements affect the likelihood of helping. Despite these limitations, some interesting differences emerge (see Box 8.6).

One element of social experience which does seem influential is the urban environment. Some years ago, Stanley Milgram looked at large cities vs. small towns, and proposed that higher population densities and less social cohesion lead to greater diffusion of responsibility, and consequently, less helping (Milgram 1970). This finding was confirmed in a subsequent study by Robert Levine which looked at 36 American cities of varying sizes (Levine *et al.* 1994). Overall, the best predictor of helping was population density; however, other factors also seemed to play a role, including economic conditions. Consequently, Levine and his students went on to look at helping in cities in 23 different countries (Levine 2003). Interestingly, when comparing a range of cultures and city sizes, the best overall predictor was economic status, not population size or density – people in poor places were more likely to help than those in wealthy cities. Unfortunately, the correlational nature of the data makes it impossible to determine causation in these studies. However, the results do pose fascinating questions about the role of culture in prosocial behaviour. For example, the second most important factor, an attitude called *sympatico*, was associated with Spanish and Portuguese cities. Despite variations in things like crime rate, people in Latin America and Spain were the most likely to help strangers. Hopefully, future research will be able to clarify the underlying influences.

Box 8.6 *Culture and Expectations of Prosocial Behaviour*

Most cultures view helpful behaviour in a very positive manner, although some, such as the Dobu of the Trobriand Islands, qualify this. To them, non-family members are potential threats and should be either avoided or treated as enemies (Fortune 1963). In many cultures, however, empathy, cooperation and helpfulness are not just seen as desirable – they are regarded as obligatory. As discussed earlier in the book, collectivist societies such as China or India have a value or orientation that emphasizes the welfare of the group one belongs to. By contrast, individualist societies, such as the UK, the USA or Canada, value the individual's welfare more highly than the group's. For example, in an individualist society, visiting or caring for elderly relatives is often seen as an act of kindness 'above and beyond the call of duty'. In collectivist societies, however, caring for an elderly relative is a duty; hence, it is a responsibility of one group member to another, not an unusual act deserving praise (Brislin 2000). Similarly, in a collectivist society, grandparents or other extended family members would not be seen as doing a kindness by babysitting children; rather, they would be *expected* to take on part of the responsibility for raising children.

In an individualistic society, the phenomenon of social loafing is common. Social loafing refers to people making fewer contributions while working with others than while working alone. Part of the reason for this is related to diffusion of responsibility: when working in a group, one's individual effort is less likely to be seen and potentially rewarded – a large consideration to people raised in an individualist culture. But in a collectivist society, one's co-workers are considered to be members of one's group, to whom one owes assistance. Not surprisingly, social loafing is rarely found in these cultures. Gabrenya *et al.* (1985) found that in a strong collectivist society such as Taiwan, not only did social loafing not occur, but the opposite, social *striving*, was found. The Taiwanese were more productive when working with others than when working alone, indicating the strong emphasis placed on the value of the group.

There are other sorts of social expectations in the workplace, too. A worker in an individualist society might feel that an employer or supervisor who asks personal questions and gives advice about the worker's family and home life is being inappropriate, intrusive and possibly even violating the worker's civil rights. However, in the collectivist societies of Asia, such personal involvement in workers' lives may be expected and seen as part of a good employer's responsibility towards their employees (Brislin 2000).

These examples point out some of the difficulties in studying prosocial behaviour cross-culturally. What is seen as altruistic in one culture may be seen as a responsibility in another. They also support the idea that prosocial behaviour may be increased by the activation of prosocial schemata. That is, an individual may respond in a more socially helpful and cooperative manner if they are in some way reminded of the desirability of doing so. Collectivist societies seem consistently to promote cooperative and prosocial schemata, while in individualist cultures, their activation is not as frequent. This raises the question: do different cultures create these different schemata, or is it the existence of the schemata that leads us to describe cultures as individualistic or collectivist? Is it an interaction, or which comes first?

While social learning processes are doubtless one of the elements involved in cross-cultural differences, the issues are extremely complex. Without looking at how different societies define concepts like altruism, we risk misinterpreting the meaning of behaviour; that is, we may be able to identify a response (such as helping a blind person cross a street), but not how it is perceived or why it occurs. In the end, such questions seem to lead from social psychology to related disciplines, such as anthropology – and hence back to where we started in our exploration of social behaviour.

Try it Yourself

One of the challenges of researching bystander intervention is a lack of *external validity* – simply put, most of the experimental research involves situations that are not very dangerous or violent, whereas real-world emergencies may well be. So what of situations in which the bystander can readily ascertain that intervention is necessary, but which also pose significant risks? Fischer and his colleagues (2006) performed a study in which low-danger situations were compared to high-danger situations. When the danger seemed low, the usual effect was found: a bystander was more likely to help when alone than when other bystanders were present. Interestingly, when the danger was perceived to be high, the effect disappeared – it didn't matter whether the bystander was alone or with another person. Unfortunately, in the situations considered, no more than 50 per cent of the participants tried to help someone in trouble, no matter what the circumstances. So what can we conclude about real-world helping?

Have you ever encountered an emergency? Did you intervene? Can you relate your behaviour to the principles discussed above? Does knowing these principles seem likely to affect how you will react to future emergencies (priming suggests that it should)? If you've never been involved in an emergency, under what conditions do you think you would intervene?

CONCLUSION

Social psychology is concerned with the social dimensions of individual behaviour. As such, it deals with both how we think about ourselves and others (*social cognition*), and also how we relate to other people (*social interaction*). Interest in social behaviour is, of course, not restricted to psychology – indeed, it has been studied within the disciplines of biology, sociology and anthropology. What distinguishes social psychology from these other fields is largely its focus on the individual, and its emphasis on experimentation as a methodology.

In some ways, social psychology is the most appealing area within psychology. In a very fundamental way, it touches on the social concerns that are basic to our lives. By exploring questions of how we respond to, and are influenced by, other people, it seems to be both 'real' and 'relevant'. This is evident, for example, in the debates about aggression. Yet, one cannot consider social psychology closely without also recognizing the limitations of the area in terms of what we know, and how we know it.

One of the basic difficulties is the complex nature of social research, and the limits it places on finding definite answers. Experimental *control*, *reactivity*, the need for *experimental realism*, *external validity*, *ethics* – all of these factors (and others unmentioned) place constraints on how one does social research, and on the quality of the answers one obtains. Consider the problem of observing violence: after almost 30 years and hundreds of studies, there is still controversy about drawing conclusions. At some stage, this inexactitude can frustrate even the most dedicated researcher. Leon Festinger, at one time one of the most noted social psychologists in the world, suddenly stopped doing social research, and shifted his attention to the study of colour vision. Perhaps (and this must be considered speculation) he concluded that it was better to pursue an area where definite answers are more attainable. If this *was* his reason, it is easy to feel empathy for him.

In the end, the problem may be too much emphasis on scientific rigour, rather than too little. As British psychologist Colin Fraser has suggested, the desire for rigorous methods has led to defining social behaviour in terms that can be addressed experimentally (Fraser 1987). This can result in limiting attention to those questions that can be answered (for example, 'will children imitate an adult who hits an inflatable doll?'), while being unable to answer broader questions which may be of greater importance (for example, 'what role does culture play in aggressive behaviour?'). In effect, anything that doesn't fit the mould gets ignored (such as the effects of social structures on individuals), or else subject to the endless doubts of empirically-minded critics (as with the issue of observing violence). It remains a concern that social psychology has not yet found satisfactory ways to answer the questions that people find most interesting. Without that ability, its contributions to our understanding of behaviour are likely to remain far less than its potential.

CHAPTER SUMMARY

- *Social psychology* is concerned with the social dimensions of individual behaviour. As such, it deals with both the way we think about ourselves and others (*social cognition*) and also the way we relate to, and are influenced by, other people (*social interactions*).

- Research on social behaviour faces many challenges, including the need for *experimental realism* and *external validity*. While researchers prefer the controlled conditions of laboratory experiments, it can be difficult to meet these requirements convincingly in a laboratory, due to participants' awareness of being in a study. Consequently, researchers also use *field experiments* and *correlational research* (such as *naturalistic observation*). In the end, the three methods each have advantages and limitations.

- Given the complexity of social behaviour, determining causation is a significant challenge. In general, the approaches differ in their emphasis on *personal* vs. *situational* factors. In addition, there is a tendency to focus on *proximal* rather than *distal* causes.

- Perhaps the most intensively studied aspect of social behaviour is *aggression*. As with other issues, each approach has its own interpretation of the origins of aggressive behaviour.

- The biological approach sees aggression as physiologically-based, in the form of an innate drive (ethology) or as a response to aversive stimuli.

- The behaviourist approach views aggression as learned behaviour. In particular, it is seen as behaviour which is sometimes reinforced as a means to a desired goal (*instrumental aggression*), or as the response to *frustration* (*frustration–aggression hypothesis*).

- The cognitive approach also sees aggression as learned, but emphasizes the role of *imitation* (*social learning theory*) and *priming* (*neo-association theory*). Recently, the *general aggression model* has attempted to combine the various cognitive mechanisms, along with the role of biological (physiological) factors.

- The psychodynamic approach, as expressed in Freud's theory, views aggression as an innate drive, which can be redirected by *catharsis* and *defence mechanisms*, but cannot be eliminated. Unfortunately, the available evidence seems to challenge the validity of catharsis.

- The humanistic approach sees aggressive behaviour as a response to circumstances which threaten the individual's ability to satisfy needs (Maslow) or as a reaction to arbitrary conditions of worth (Rogers). However, the humanists argue that even in adverse circumstances, aggressive behaviour is only one possible response, and is not inevitable.

- *Prosocial behaviour* (such as *altruism*) has also interested social psychologists, though it has been less intensively studied than aggression. The approaches differ in their views of whether altruism is innate or learned, and whether it benefits the person helping (*ethical hedonism*) or occurs without regard to benefit (*genuine altruism*).

- The study of bystander behaviour in emergencies (*intervention* and *apathy*) provides a practical focus for the study of altruism. Available research suggests that *social influence*, and *diffusion of responsibility* can affect the likelihood of intervention, as can *priming* and *social learning*.

- Social psychology is an appealing area, but the difficulties of doing research on complex social issues means that at present it is very hard to draw clear conclusions about the causes of social behaviour, as is seen in studies of the role of *culture*.

🔒 Key terms and concepts

social cognition	instrumental aggression
social interaction	frustration–aggression hypothesis
social influence	imitation
experimental realism	priming
conformity	prosocial behaviour
person-situation debate	altruism
proximal vs. distal causes	ethical hedonism
aggression	kin altruism
sign stimuli	reciprocal altruism
vacuum activities	empathy
catharsis	diffusion of responsibility

Test yourself questions

1 What are the major issues in the study of social behaviour?

2 How do proximal and distal causes differ?

3 What can you conclude from the evidence about how media violence affects aggression?

4 How does the humanistic approach explain prosocial behaviour?

When you have read this chapter, log onto the Online Learning Centre website at **www.openup.co.uk/glassman** where you will find answers to these Test Yourself questions and suggested answers to the Try it Yourself activities, plus many more learning resources to help you study psychology.

Suggestions for Further Reading

- For more detail on many of the aspects of social psychology mentioned in this chapter, the *Handbook of Social Psychology*, edited by **Gilbert** *et al.* (1998), is an excellent source. For a less technical source, there are a number of general texts on social psychology; *Social Psychology* by **Aronson** *et al.* (2006) is a reasonable and readable choice.

- For a book about attraction and relationships, **Brehm's** *Intimate Relationships* (2002) is an excellent choice.

- There have been many books about aggression, expressing various points of view. One of the most interesting is an overview by **John Klama**, *Aggression: Conflict in Animals and Humans Reconsidered* (1988). The authors ('John Klama' is a pseudonym for John Durant, Peter Klopfer and Susan Oyama) provide a history of the concept of aggression as an innate drive, as well as a critique of theories. Alternatively, **Berkowitz's** *Aggression: Its Causes, Consequences, and Control* (1993b) provides a thorough review by one of the major researchers on the topic. The more recent book by **Ervin Staub** *The Psychology of Good and Evil: Why Children, Adults, and Groups Help and Harm Others* (2003) provides another very thought-provoking look at the areas of both aggression and altruism.

- The relationship between observing television violence and aggressive behaviour has been extensively studied. *The Handbook of Children and the Media* (2001), a collection edited by **Singer and Singer**, provides information on many of the aspects of this issue.

- For a review of altruistic behaviour, see **Batson's** chapter in the *Handbook of Social Psychology* (1998).

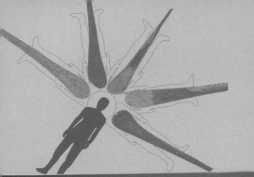

Chapter 9

Perspectives on Abnormal Behaviour

Chapter contents

LEARNING OBJECTIVES

In this chapter, the objectives are to learn:

☑ how abnormal behaviour is classified

☑ the aetiology and treatment of abnormal behaviour according to
  • the biological approach
  • the behaviourist approach
  • the cognitive approach
  • the psychodynamic approach
  • the humanistic approach

☑ the aetiology of schizophrenia according to
  • the biological approach
  • the behaviourist approach
  • the cognitive approach
  • the psychodynamic approach
  • the humanistic approach

WHO AND WHAT IS NORMAL?

When I (WEG) was a graduate student in psychology, I had an experience which affected me so deeply that even now, many years later, it still seems fresh and vivid. On a summer evening, I was standing on a quiet residential street, talking to a friend. As we talked, we noticed a young man, perhaps 24 years old, wandering down the street in our direction. He halted periodically, peering intently, and would then continue. His movements seemed erratic, weaving left and right as he went. It was difficult not to notice him on the quiet street, and at first I thought he was inebriated, or possibly on drugs. I commented to my friend that he seemed to be acting strangely, and she agreed. Then, as he neared us, she spoke to him. The conversation went something like this:

'Can we help you?'

'No,' he said, then added, 'Yes. Umm ...', looking around, 'can you tell me where the garbage is?'

'You need a garbage can?', I asked.

'No, no, it's ...' he said. 'Where does the garbage go?' As I pondered this, he abruptly changed the subject, turning to my friend and asking, 'What's your name?'

'Hope,' she said. (It really was her name!)

'That's what I need,' he replied, still looking around.

I was beginning to suspect that he was neither drunk nor on drugs, but rather suffering from a mental disorder. As the conversation continued, this impression become stronger; finally, with his consent, we led him to my car, and drove him to a local psychiatric hospital. On the way, Hope was able to elicit his name, and confirm that he lived in our city. At the hospital, we explained the situation, and the staff checked their records, which confirmed that he had been a patient there on several occasions. The diagnosis: schizophrenia. They agreed to admit him, and we left.

I think of this experience whenever I consider abnormal psychology. It represents one of my few encounters in everyday life with an individual classed as 'abnormal'. Taking him to the hospital made me feel I was doing him a kindness – but it also served to alleviate my own distress at dealing with someone who acted very differently from most people.

Consider another episode: in my second year of high school, a new student arrived. By the standards of his peers, he was rather strange: he was a vegetarian, and also refused to wear animal products – meaning he wore plastic belts and plastic shoes, even in midwinter. He had wavy blond hair that by the standards of the day was very girlish. He had no interest in sports, instead preferring to study foreign languages. On many occasions, he would go through the school singing operatic arias, while most students' taste ran to The Beatles and similar groups. Needless to say, he was not very popular. The question is, was he abnormal?

Both of the individuals described above behaved unusually, and in that sense might be called abnormal. But is that the same as saying someone has a mental disorder? What defines a mental disorder? And what can be done to help someone suffering from such a disorder?

INTRODUCTION

Abnormal psychology is concerned with the understanding and treatment of mental disorders. However, defining the boundaries of the field can be difficult: many of those who treat such disorders are doctors, not psychologists; in other cases, help is provided by social workers, clerics or other types of counsellors. Even the term 'mental disorder' is not universally accepted – other terms include *mental illness*, *psychopathology* and *abnormal behaviour*. For our purposes, we

abnormal behaviour behaviour which is regarded by society as deviant or maladaptive; according to DSM-IV, an individual must be suffering or show maladaptive functioning in order for behaviour to be described as abnormal.

will use the terms mental disorder and **abnormal behaviour** as interchangeable, and largely avoid the other terms.

Defining abnormal behaviour is a complex issue. Literally, the word 'abnormal' means 'away from the norm', and traditionally, the term has been used to describe behaviour which departs from an accepted norm. However, norms can be defined in two ways – *statistical abnormality* refers to behaviour which is rare, while *unconventionality* refers to behaviour which departs from social standards. The boy who sang operas in high school would likely be considered abnormal in the sense that he was unconventional. Historically, the standard of conventionality was often a significant element in judgements of abnormality – not conforming was viewed with suspicion, or worse. Today, however, standards of conformity are somewhat looser, and someone who does not 'fit in' is not automatically viewed as having a mental disorder. Behaviour which is unconventional is also often statistically rare, in that most people behave according to the social standards of the culture they live in. However, statistical rarity, like unconventionality, poses difficulties as a criterion for mental disorders. It is true that many mental disorders are relatively rare, as the statistical criterion would imply. Yet some are fairly common (such as phobias and depression), and there are many rare forms of behaviour which we would not consider indicative of mental disorder – for example, musical genius. Hence, *neither* of these standards is commonly used today by psychologists as part of the definition of abnormal behaviour. The difficulties these definitions pose are partly due to the complexity of abnormal behaviour, but also reflect how easily value judgements can creep into the process of evaluation. To see this more clearly, let us consider briefly the history of concepts of abnormality.

Abnormality in Historical Context

Throughout history, there have been reports of individuals who acted in aberrant ways. In early pantheistic cultures, whose members believed spirits permeate the world, abnormal behaviour was often explained as possession by evil spirits. More than 4000 years ago, holes were made in people's heads with the apparent intent of allowing spirits to escape (Porter 2002). The notion of mental disorders as demonic possession has also been common in our own culture. In 1692, in Salem, Massachusetts, 20 young women were executed for being 'bewitched by the Devil' because they exhibited visions, sensory distortions and other odd behaviours. Today, scholars believe they were actually suffering from poisoning from ergot, a fungus which sometimes grows on rye, and is related to LSD (Caporael 1976). Spirit possession is also central to the origin of the term *hysteria* (used by Freud and others to describe physical symptoms of paralysis and pain of unknown origin). The disorder, whose name comes from the Greek word for 'uterus', was attributed in the Middle Ages to the Devil controlling a woman's uterus.

Even when abnormal behaviour was not attributed to spirits, the sense of moral condemnation was often strong. For example, in the pre-Civil War USA, a doctor asserted that slaves who attempted to run away were suffering from a disorder dubbed 'drapetomania' (Eakin 2000). Those with mental disorders were commonly seen as degenerates, less than human. Consequently, common forms of treatment included beatings and imprisonment. This attitude slowly began to change as doctors began to conceive of the behaviour as having physical causes. One of the early pioneers in this regard was Phillipe Pinel, a French doctor who ran the Bicêtre asylum in Paris at the end of the eighteenth century (just after the French Revolution). Contrary to the notions of demonism and degeneracy, Pinel saw his patients as *ill*, suffering from physical disorders. As a result, he argued for treating them like other patients, rather than chaining them in dark cells. By suggesting that abnormal behaviour was like other forms of illness, Pinel's work marked a shift towards more humane and rational treatment.

At the same time, by suggesting that mental disorders have physical causes, Pinel helped introduce what has become known as the **medical model** of abnormal behaviour. (Today, this approach is closely linked to the biological approach, as we shall discuss further.) The medicalizing of abnormal behaviour led to doctors becoming the *de facto* authorities on the treatment of such disorders. This trend lasted well into the middle of the twentieth century, and in some ways the medical viewpoint is still dominant.

medical model a theory of abnormal behaviour which assumes that all such disorders have physiological causes.

One consequence of the medical model was a move towards rational systems of diagnosis. Doctors, like scientists, had learned the value of classification systems as a means of understanding the world. Diagnosis of physical illness was based on matching symptoms to known diseases; now, the same approach began to be applied to the understanding of mental disorders, with behaviour representing the symptoms. This process accelerated after World War II, spurred on by the American Psychiatric Association in the USA, and the World Health Organization internationally. (**Psychiatrists** are medical doctors who specialize in treating mental disorders.) The systems developed by the two groups are known respectively as the Diagnostic and Statistical Manual of Mental Disorders (DSM), and the International Classification of Diseases (ICD). Though differences still exist, increasingly the two systems are similar, and the groups hope to resolve remaining disparities in future versions. (The current major version of the DSM system is DSM-IV, published by the American Psychiatric Association in 1994; a minor update, DSM-IV-TR, was released in 2000.) To understand how classification works, and its value and limitations, let us look more closely at the nature and use of the DSM system.

psychiatrists medical doctors who specialize in treating mental disorders; by comparison, clinical psychologists typically have a PhD rather than an MD degree.

Try it Yourself

It's common for us to say 'I must be crazy' or 'You would have to be nuts to do that!' What do we really mean when we say such things? Are we really referring to behaviour that might be classified as mentally disordered? Do you think that the use of such expressions adds to our confusion and sometimes discomfort about mental disorders?

Have you ever encountered a stranger whose behaviour you considered abnormal? What was unusual? How did it make you feel? Do you think other people react in the same way? Ask your friends what comes to their minds when they hear that someone has a mental disorder.

Classifying Abnormal Behaviour

The most fundamental issue of diagnosis is to define what we mean by abnormal behaviour. This is not always easy, especially since many theorists (including Freud) believe there is a continuum between normal and abnormal, with no absolute dividing line. As discussed earlier, defining abnormality in terms of social norms or frequency of occurrence seems questionable. Instead, DSM-IV-TR uses two primary criteria to determine whether a person's behaviour warrants being described as a mental disorder: suffering and maladaptiveness.

agoraphobia anxiety disorder in which a person feels anxiety about experiencing panic attacks in public, and therefore avoids public situations.

anti-social personality disorder a behaviour pattern in which an individual shows a history of disregard and violence towards others, unaccompanied by guilt; although these individuals may not report either suffering or unsatisfactory functioning (the generally accepted standard for abnormality), their behaviour is still deemed abnormal because it violates society's norms in such significant ways.

Suffering implies that the behaviour causes the individual distress or anxiety; *maladaptiveness* implies that the person's functioning in daily life is significantly impaired. For example, a person who experiences intense anxiety at the prospect of venturing out of their home would be viewed as suffering; this type of anxiety reflects a disorder called **agoraphobia**. Maladaptiveness could take many forms, affecting work, school or social relationships: drinking which interferes with work performance, disordered thinking which prevents communicating with others, uncontrollable outbursts of rage, and so on. Most psychologists and other mental health professionals agree that behaviour must fit one or both of these criteria in order to be considered abnormal. However, exceptions exist even to these criteria. For example, an individual with **anti-social personality disorder** may show a history of acts of violence towards others, unaccompanied by guilt. These individuals may not report either suffering or unsatisfactory functioning, yet their behaviour is still deemed abnormal.

The intention of using suffering and maladaptiveness as criteria is to free the definition of abnormality from arbitrary social judgements (such as unconventionality). However, even these criteria can be open to interpretation. For example, if a person prefers beachcombing to banking, does this suggest maladaptation? The possibility of social bias in diagnosis is a particular concern when factors like culture and ethnicity are involved (Fabrega 1994). For example, belief in communication with the dead is common in Cuban culture, but could lead to a diagnosis of psychosis for a Cuban-American being assessed by a non-Cuban (Alonso and Jeffery 1988). Such problems tend to occur when there is a mismatch of ethnicity and/or language for therapist and patient. For example, a study in the UK found that English doctors were less likely to recognize depression in Punjabi patients, and Asian doctors were less likely to recognize depression in English women than men (Bhui *et al.* 2001). Similar effects were found in the USA for various aspects of treatment for Asians, blacks and Native Americans (Sue *et al.* 1991).

In general, there has been a significant increase in awareness of the ways that culture interacts with diagnosis, with consequent attempts to improve practitioner knowledge (American Psychological Association 2002b; US Department of Health and Human Services 2001). Hence, one major goal of DSM-IV was to provide guidance to clinicians with respect to the influence of culture, ethnicity, age and gender on diagnosis and treatment (see Box 9.1). Still, the interaction between culture and diagnosis remains a problem (Escobar and Vega 2006). While the risk of misdiagnosis due to such factors is a genuine concern, it must be acknowledged that in many circumstances the standards are quite obvious – for example, someone who complains of intense anxiety is obviously suffering.

Assuming that a person's behaviour is regarded as abnormal, DSM-IV-TR tries to identify the particular form of disorder, using five major dimensions (axes) for assessment (see Box 9.2). Axes I–III represent the basic types of disorders (for example, mood disorders, anxiety disorders, psychotic disorders like schizophrenia, substance-abuse disorders, etc.) and ongoing psychological or physical conditions that could affect adjustment. Axis IV looks at the stressors in the person's life which may contribute to a problem (such as the recent death of a family member). Axis V looks at the person's general adaptation in three areas of daily life (social relations, work and leisure); this helps in determining the severity of the current problem, as well as influencing the prognosis for recovery. For example, someone diagnosed as depressed will have a

Box 9.1 Culture-bound Psychological Disorders

Some psychological disorders, such as schizophrenia and depression, are seen in all cultures, with only a few dissimilarities. But many cultures have disorders that are unique to them: they exist in that culture and nowhere else. In order to assist with diagnosis, DSM-IV-TR lists several of these:

- **Koro** Koro is an anxiety disorder found mainly among young men in southern China. In this syndrome, the man worries about his sexuality and virility, leading him to suffer from the delusion that his penis is shrinking and retracting into his abdomen. He has the panic-stricken belief that he will die when the retraction is complete (Yap 1965).
- **Kayak angst** This is an extreme form of anxiety found among Eskimos of western Greenland. It occurs after or during periods of sensory deprivation, such as kayaking alone on a slightly wavy sea on a sunny day. This condition resembles a panic disorder, with the individual experiencing cognitive and perceptual distortions, and a terror that the individual will die if he moves.
- **Amok** Amok is a dissociative disorder (see *depersonalization*) found in Malaysia. First the individual experiences a period of brooding, then there is an extremely violent, even homicidal, outburst directed at other people or objects.
- **Zar** In Northern African and Middle Eastern societies, the term *zar* refers to the possession of an individual by a ghost. People with zar may show a variety of symptoms: in some, there is withdrawal, apathy and loss of appetite. In others, there may be crying, shouting, laughing, singing or self-injurious behaviours.
- **Shinbyung** This is a syndrome found in Korea during the course of a prolonged psychosomatic illness. In this disorder, the individual believes that he or she has been possessed by the spirit of a dead ancestor. The cure comes through a dream or hallucination in which the individual is persuaded to become a shaman (Simons and Hughes 1985).
- **Eating disorders** While not restricted to a specific culture, eating disorders seem to be particular to cultures and parts of cultures where food is plentiful and thinness is seen as desirable (not surprisingly, North America and Europe have the highest incidence of these disorders). Because of distorted concerns about body image and weight, in *anorexia nervosa*, the individual exercises and starves himself or herself to the point of emaciation; in *bulimia nervosa*, an individual induces vomiting and/or diarrhoea to reduce weight (Dragnus 2001).

In general, it seems that culture-specific disorders are related to particular concerns within the culture. An example can be seen within western culture in terms of historical changes in the content of common paranoid delusions: in the early part of the sixteenth century, common delusions might have centred on witchcraft and Satan, but in the twentieth century, the main themes ranged from 'the Communist menace' in the 1950s, to today's preoccupation with secret governmental plots involving aliens.

Thus, culture can play a significant role in the nature and expression of abnormal behaviour, which becomes important both in diagnosis and in treatment.

better prognosis if their general life history suggests a high level of functioning than if they have a history of mood problems, poor social relationships and an erratic employment record. By making such assessments part of the overall diagnosis, DSM-IV-TR tries to provide a more detailed, individualized description.

How common are mental disorders? A general answer has been given by the National Institute of Mental Health, which estimates that 26.2 per cent of Americans over the age of 18 years suffer from a diagnosable mental illness in a given year (National Institute of Mental Health 2008). To try to answer the question more specifically, a number of studies have attempted to measure incidence rates for various disorders (Lewinsohn *et al.* 1997; Newmann and Bland 1998; V. Bijl *et al.* 2002). While research designs and diagnostic criteria have tended to vary somewhat, studies done in the USA, Canada and the Netherlands have shown broad agreement overall (see Figure 9.1). One of the most comprehensive studies, in terms of range of disorders, was done in five cities in the USA (Regier *et al.* 1988). Researchers attempted to identify the incidence rates (percentage of population) for various disorders measured over a one-month interval; lifetime risks are typically regarded as about twice as high. There are a couple of points about these results that are worth noting. First, there are significant differences in the frequency of occurrence of different disorders, and in most cases, the rates for men and women also differ. (This has sometimes led to charges of sex bias in diagnosis – hence the concern to address the issue in DSM-IV-TR.) Second, one should note that many of these disorders are not very rare: if one extrapolates to lifetime rates, then about 22 per cent of the population will suffer from a serious phobia at some time in their lives, and about 17 per cent will experience depression severe enough to merit treatment. By comparison, Swindle *et al.* (2000), using a non-technical criterion of disorders, found that one-third of Americans surveyed felt that at some point in their life they had had 'a mental health problem'.

Classifying mental disorders, as with other forms of medical diagnosis, is intended to help identify the cause of a problem and to guide treatment. While the value of diagnosis has been

Box 9.2 *Classifying Mental Disorders*

As noted in the text, DSM-IV classifies behaviour using five dimensions or 'axes'. (Categories copyrighted by American Psychiatric Association 1994)

Classifying Abnormal Behaviour Using DSM-IV		
Axis I	Clinical syndromes	Primary classification of disorders, based on behavioural symptoms: e.g., phobias, depression, drug abuse, obsessive-compulsive disorder; also includes developmental disorders like attention-deficit/hyperactivity disorder
Axis II	Personality disorders and mental retardation	Personality disorders – long-standing patterns of maladaptive behaviour: e.g., narcissistic and antisocial personality disorders
		Mental retardation – disorders causing significant intellectual impairment – e.g., Down's syndrome, PKU
Axis III	General medical conditions	Any physical problems which may be relevant to the person's condition
Axis IV	Psychosocial and environmental factors	An assessment of the severity of factors stressors which contribute to the person's condition.
Axis V	Global assessment of functioning	A general evaluation of functioning during the past year in terms of work, leisure and social relationships

well established in general medicine, its use is more problematical for mental disorders than for other forms of illness, because we do not yet know the causes (**aetiology**) of most mental disorders. (As we will see in the next section, this is a major source of disagreement among the five approaches.) In fact, some critics have focused on this lack of knowledge as part of a challenge to the entire concept of classification. For example, the absence of a theoretical model of aetiology within DSM-IV has led to the criticism that the system is untestable (Follette and Houts 1996). Even those who support use of the DSM have noted that ultimately there is room for improvement, including the need for a more explanatory system (Beutler and Malik 2002; Frances and Egger 1999).

aetiology the study of the causes of a disease or mental disorder.

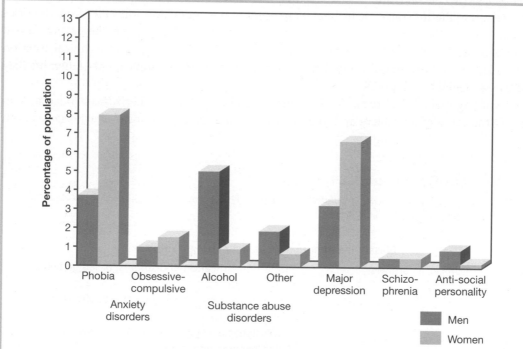

Figure 9.1 Incidence Rates for Mental Disorders This chart shows the frequency of occurrence for some of the most common disorders. The percentages are for incidence rates over a one month period in the USA; lifetime risks are roughly twice as high (except depression, where lifetime rate is 17 per cent). (Most data from Regier *et al.* 1988; data on phobias and depression based on Blazer *et al.* 1994)

A more extreme view is that we cannot identify the causes because there is no such thing as a mental disorder. Thomas Szasz, himself a psychiatrist, has argued that mental disorders are a 'myth' (Szasz 1974). To Szasz, identifying behaviour as abnormal is simply a way for society and clinicians to justify interfering in an individual's life. One example is the use of *community treatment orders*, which can force an individual diagnosed with a mental disorder to comply with treatment recommendations, including possibly medication, while otherwise freely living in the community. Similarly, Stanley and Raskin (2002) argue that abnormality is simply a social construction, not a real condition within the individual. Sarbin and Mancuso (1980) have charged that schizophrenia is just a label applied to those who live outside society's norms; in essence, they believe that our society still defines abnormality in moral terms.

Most clinicians reject such claims, and emphasize the practical value of diagnostic classification in their work. At the same time, in recent years because use of the DSM system is based on categorization, there is the risk that one focuses on the diagnosis rather than the person (Tucker 1998). Within our culture, the term 'mental disorder' has a negative connotation; as a consequence, diagnosis assigns a label to someone which identifies them as being different, or *deviant*. Such labels serve as a form of **stigma**, a marking which is used by society to treat someone as an outsider (Goffman 1963). In the case of mental disorders, this results in problems of social rejection which often make recovery more difficult (Canadian Mental Health Association 2000; Clausen 1981; Corrigan 2007; Lysaker *et al.* 2007). To some extent, this problem has been recognized in DSM-IV-TR, which recommends referring to an individual *having* a disorder, in contrast to the earlier common practice of equating the disorder with the person. For example, one should refer to 'a person with schizophrenia', not 'a schizophrenic'.

stigma a mark or label which identifies an individual as deviant, resulting in social rejection.

The stigmatizing effects of diagnostic labels illustrate the ultimate dilemma involved in defining abnormality: balancing the benefits and detriments of the classification of behaviour. Advocates of diagnostic systems tend to believe that mental disorders are purely objective phenomena, like a tumour or tuberculosis, while critics of such systems argue that abnormality is simply a reflection of arbitrary social norms. The truth is likely somewhere in between. On the one hand, stigmatizing and misdiagnosis for cultural or other reasons are possible, as critics have charged. However, diagnostic categories seem useful in understanding an individual's behaviour, and may aid in treatment. The basic standard of abnormality employed in DSM-IV-TR – that the individual shows significant distress and/or maladaptive functioning – is one that most people would likely find reasonable. Indeed, the autobiographies of those who have suffered from disorders like depression and schizophrenia suggest that they view their disorders as real, not as an arbitrary social conceit (Endler 1982; Jamison 1995; Vonnegut 1975).

At present, there are no final answers to this debate. In part, disagreements over the issue of classification reflect differences in assumptions about the underlying causes of abnormal behaviour. Because it is descriptive in nature, DSM-IV-TR does not address causes, and so cannot resolve such debates. If we could be certain of the origin of particular disorders, many of the questions of bias, misdiagnosis and arbitrariness of standards would be resolved. For now, most clinicians, faced with what they see as real suffering, simply do their best to help.

Try it Yourself

As Figure 9.1 indicates, various forms of abnormal behaviour are more common than many people think. In addition, there are cases where it can seem difficult for us to draw a line between what constitutes a mental disorder and what is simply a personal idiosyncrasy. Consider, for example, a 'neat freak' who cannot abide even a little bit of dust or clutter. Do you think that this might qualify as a diagnosable disorder? What if the person refused to have company because they might make a mess, or would not go outdoors because of the dust in the air? Would that change your opinion? What if the person claimed to be quite happy, and thought that *you* had a problem because of your attitude?

Do you know anyone who suffers from a serious phobia, or has had a mood disorder such as depression? Would you react differently to the person in the two cases? What does this tell you about your own attitudes towards abnormal behaviour?

PERSPECTIVES ON AETIOLOGY AND TREATMENT

To a large extent, treatment methods tend to be linked to ideas about the causes of abnormal behaviour. Consequently, one cannot discuss theories of treatment without also discussing theories of *aetiology* (the study of the causes of a disorder). What makes this difficult is that many types of factors can contribute to a particular behaviour. When one speaks of 'cause', one may actually be referring to *predisposing factors* (genetic inheritance, prior experiences and beliefs), *precipitating factors* (immediate stressors like loss of a family member), or *sustaining factors* (consequences of a disorder that help to perpetuate it, such as reactions of family or society). In addition, in any particular case there may be more than one causal factor of a given type. For example, children of individuals with schizophrenia may be at risk because of genetic factors and also because of growing up with parents who provided a faulty model for behaviour. (Both of these would be predisposing factors.) It is also possible that different forms of abnormal behaviour have different aetiologies; for example, schizophrenia may have a very different origin from depression. For all of these reasons, the search for a single cause, and a single form of treatment, may be fruitless. Nonetheless, each of the five approaches tends to emphasize particular types of causal factors, and given the current state of evidence, each feels justified in utilizing the particular treatment techniques which it does. To see how they differ, let us consider how each approach views aetiology and treatment.

The Biological Approach

As noted earlier, the biological approach to abnormal behaviour is based on the *medical model*, which assumes that disorders are based on physical causes. Given the role of the brain in the control of behaviour, the causes are usually attributed to abnormalities in either the structure or functioning of the brain.

The strongest justification for this approach has come from advances in *psychopharmacology* (the study of drugs which affect mental processes and/or behaviour). Although the use of drugs to alter behaviour has a long history (alcohol, for example, has been used in some form in nearly every culture), the greatest advances have come in the last few decades (National Institute of Mental Health 2002). Today, a large and growing range of drugs exists to deal with many forms of disorders. For example, tranquillizers are used to relieve anxiety, antidepressants help relieve depression, and anti-psychotics relieve hallucinations and mental confusion (Davis *et al.* 2002). In addition, sedatives often take the place of physical restraints, such as straitjackets. Not only do drugs frequently seem to alleviate symptoms, but drug therapy also seems relatively efficient: compared to alternative treatments like psychoanalysis or behaviour modification, it is relatively low cost, fast-acting, and requires comparatively little of the doctor's time. For all of these reasons, the use of psychoactive drugs has become extremely common both in the formal treatment of mental disorders and as part of the practice of many family doctors.

depression a mood disorder characterized by sleep disturbances, fatigue and low self-esteem; in major depressive disorder, the symptoms are severe enough to seriously hamper normal functioning, and can be accompanied by thoughts of suicide.

To understand the role of drugs, let us consider the case of **depression**. Clinically, depression is a mood disorder which can affect sleep, thoughts, energy level and a range of other aspects of functioning. Under the DSM, depression is only diagnosed when several symptoms have been present continuously for at least two weeks. In practice, many doctors regard less severe but ongoing symptoms (technically called 'dysthymia') as depression; overall, the reported incidence rates for depression have been growing in North America, and probably Europe, for more than two decades (Costello *et al.* 2002). Cross-cultural studies of depression in Iran, Japan, Switzerland, Colombia, Canada and the USA have found a common core of depressive symptoms (sad affect, loss of enjoyment, anxiety, lowered concentration and low energy levels), supporting the idea that depression has a biological basis (Brislin 2000). The precise cause of depression is uncertain, though there is accumulating evidence that it affects functioning of both the prefrontal cortex and limbic structures, notably the hippocampus and the amygdala (Belmaker and Agam 2008; Davidson *et al.* 2002). At the neurotransmitter level, attention has focused on the role of serotonin, and to a lesser extent, norepinephrine. Today, depression is frequently treated by giving drugs which selectively enhance the availability of serotonin (see Figure 9.2 and Chapter 2). Thus, depression provides an example of how both aetiology and treatment are addressed by the medical model of the biological approach.

At the same time, the use of drugs is not without problems. First, treatment using drugs is still largely based on symptom relief, and does not directly address the issue of causation. While our understanding of how drugs work is becoming much more precise, this is not necessarily the same thing as identifying the cause of the disorder. Indeed, many aspects of the available data suggest that drugs may not be addressing the root causes of disorders (Luyten *et al.* 2006). For example, one of the unsolved problems of antidepressant use is why, since the drug reaches the brain in a matter of hours, there is often a considerable time lag between the onset of usage and improvement of mood (intervals of two weeks are typical). In addition, individuals who show comparable symptoms often do not respond equally to a particular drug. (In the case of anti-depressants, about one-third of individuals with depression don't respond to any available drug. For more on the role of drugs in depression, see Box 9.3.)

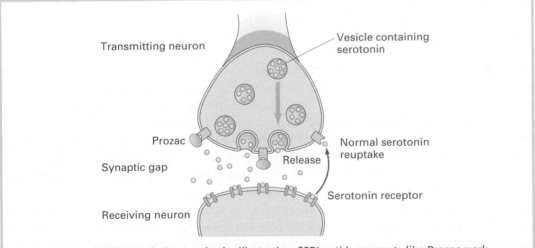

Figure 9.2 How SSRIs Work As seen in the illustration, SSRI antidepressants like Prozac work by selectively blocking the reuptake of seratonin into the synaptic vesicles, thereby enhancing seratonin's availability to stimulate the receiving neuron. (See also discussion in Chapter 2.)

Apart from questions about the effectiveness and mechanism of action of drug treatments, there is also the possibility that many problems for which drugs are prescribed may be self-limiting. For example, according to its manufacturer, Xanax (alprazolam) is a drug which is designed to alleviate panic disorder (frequent attacks of intense anxiety and panic). The clinical trials which led to its approval showed that after four weeks, 50 per cent of patients taking Xanax were completely free of symptoms, compared to 28 per cent of those taking a placebo. Interestingly, however, after eight weeks, there was no significant difference between the two groups (Editors 1993). More broadly, psychiatrist Peter Kramer contends that the use of medication as treatment for behaviours like depression has the capacity to alter the individual's sense of self, an attribute which involves cultural conceptions as much as physiological reactions (Kramer 1993).

At present, there are still many questions associated with using drugs to treat abnormal behaviour. At a practical level, drugs often do seem to be useful in alleviating symptoms, but that does not prove they are actually addressing the causes of disorders. Nonetheless, drug therapy is consistent with the medical model, and as we shall see in examining schizophrenia, may very well hold important clues to the understanding of abnormal behaviour.

Another application of the biological approach to the study of mental disorders is genetic research. For example, researchers have used concordance studies to examine the role of genetics in disorders like schizophrenia and bipolar mood disorder (formerly called 'manic-depression'). The results of such studies are often very variable, and open to conflicting interpretations. For example, reports of a genetic link for bipolar disorder, announced in the late 1980s, were later found to be flawed (Kelsoe *et al.* 1989). Robert Plomin, a long-time believer in genetic factors in pathology, has argued that early studies attempted to find a single genetic factor, when the reality is more likely that there are multiple genetic factors, each having only a small effect, and interacting with environmental influences (Plomin and McGuffin 2003). At present, the available evidence does not show conclusively that any major form of abnormal behaviour is *solely* genetic. Instead, as Plomin has suggested, it is likely that genetic factors, if any exist, interact with environmental factors. Consistent with this, recent studies have reported direct evidence of a genetic factor that significantly increases the risk of depression – but *only* if the person has experienced repeated major stresses (Caspi *et al.* 2003; Holden, 2003b; Kim-Cohen *et al.* 2006). In individuals with the defective gene who had not experienced high stress, there was no increase in the rate of depression compared to people with the normal gene. Hence, while genetic contributions to mental disorders may be confirmed in future research, the likelihood is that the picture will be one of interactive effects, not simple genetic causation (Rutter *et al.* 2006). In any case, it must be noted that genetic analysis at present can only indicate an individual's risk – there are no current treatments designed to address mental disorders at the genetic level.

In summary, the biological approach sees abnormal behaviour as having a physiological cause, an assumption known as the *medical model*. Within this framework, its greatest success has been drug therapy, which has produced significant benefits in the past few decades. However, until we understand more about the causes of abnormal behaviour, it is not clear if it addresses the root of such disorders, or simply masks the symptoms. Genetic research may eventually prove useful, *provided* the primary causes of disorders are in fact genetic in origin. For the biological approach, as for all the approaches, the only criterion for testing a theory at present is to try to evaluate its success in alleviating the suffering associated with mental disorders.

The Behaviourist Approach

As one might expect, the behaviourist approach interprets abnormal behaviour in terms of faulty learning. Like all behaviours, abnormal behaviour is acquired through a process of conditioning and learning. In the absence of known organic problems, this explanation does not assume there is any underlying causal factor, as the medical model does; instead, the behaviourists say the behaviour is the problem. Consequently, behaviourists have relatively little interest in classification, since learned behaviour is too variable to make categories very meaningful. To the extent

Box 9.3 Do Antidepressant Drugs Actually Work?

The use of drugs to treat depression is common, but not without controversy. At heart, the controversy involves two aspects – the role of the placebo effect, and the limitations of our understanding of how antidepressant drugs work.

As noted in Chapter 2, an inert substance which is represented as a drug (a placebo) will often have a measurable effect. Such placebos are often used as a control condition in medical research, to reduce subject bias (see the Appendix). However, re-analyses of the clinical trials done in order to gain government approval of drugs in the USA have led to surprising effects in the case of antidepressants (Kirsch *et al.* 2002). When compared to placebos, antidepressant drugs typically show very modest benefits – approximately 80 per cent of the improvement noted with the drugs was duplicated in the placebo groups. As Kirsch (2002) notes, what is surprising is not that there is a placebo effect, but that the effect of the drug is so small (since whatever underlies a placebo effect is presumably present in the drug group, too).

Not surprisingly, other researchers have challenged this pessimistic assessment. For example, both Brown (2002) and Rush and Ryan (2002) have noted that drug companies usually seek to ensure that government drug trials involve relatively mild cases of depression, uncomplicated by other disorders – a situation unlike the real world, where individuals may suffer from severe depression and coexisting problems. Hence, Brown argues that only mild benefits should be expected, since the individuals have only a mild disorder. However, other studies, presumably involving a broader range of depression, consistently show that placebos produce better than 50 per cent of the efficacy of antidepressant drugs (Hollon *et al.* 2002). In addition, cognitive and interpersonal therapy appear to be at least as effective as drugs in the short term, and possibly better than drugs in preventing relapses. If psychotherapy is better at preventing relapses, it raises questions as to what it is that drugs are actually doing.

Unfortunately, answering the question of how drugs treat depression is also complex. As Rush and Ryan (2002) note, we still lack a proper understanding of the neurobiological mechanism for antidepressant drugs. This is highlighted by the fact that different individuals and types of depression will respond better to one drug than another, but we don't know why (nor can anyone reliably predict which drug will work best in a given case). The problems are even further underlined by the fact that no drug typically produces a measurable benefit for more than 60 per cent of patients (Hollon *et al.* 2002).

So does this mean that antidepressants don't actually work? Despite the title of this box, it is likely that they do have benefit, even if their effects are less than optimal. While a variety of evidence suggests this conclusion, one example will help illustrate. When PET scans are taken before and after treatment, measurable changes in brain activity can be identified – and the degree of change correlates with the degree of improvement in symptoms (Drevets *et al.* 2002). At the same time, the limitations of current drugs, along with the significant placebo effects observed, suggest two conclusions: first, that depression may have multiple mechanisms, and second, that the potential role of experience in both causation and treatment cannot be ignored.

that classification is seen as at all useful, it is typically as a shorthand description – for example, phobias represent learned fears.

The emphasis on learning leads the behaviourists to reject the medical model. Similarly, their focus on behaviour rather than mental processes places them in opposition to the other three approaches, all of which suggest that cognitive processes of various sorts mediate the behaviour. In addition, the behaviourist approach to treatment is largely ahistorical, since what matters is not the circumstances under which abnormal behaviour was acquired in the past, but the need to identify ways to modify it in the present. Because of the emphasis on changing the undesired behaviour, therapy based on the behaviourist approach is generally referred to as behaviour modification. (Often, practitioners abbreviate this to 'behaviour mod'.)

systematic desensitization a technique based on classical conditioning which is designed to treat phobias (unrealistic fears) and related anxiety disorders by gradually diminishing the undesired response.
phobia an irrational fear of a specific object or situation which is severe enough to interfere with an individual's functioning in daily life.

Several forms of behaviour modification exist, based either on classical or on operant conditioning. One of the earliest techniques, derived from classical conditioning, is **systematic desensitization**, which is designed to treat **phobias** (unrealistic fears) and related anxiety disorders. As noted in Chapter 3, Watson had demonstrated with little Albert that it was possible to develop a fear by classical conditioning. Although he was subsequently unsuccessful in eliminating Albert's conditioned fear, the notion that phobias could be explained in terms of classical conditioning was established.

Eventually, Joseph Wolpe developed systematic desensitization, which seeks to eliminate the fear response by replacing it with a competing response of relaxation (Wolpe 1973).

In conception, systematic desensitization is very simple, being based on two fundamental principles of conditioning: first, an individual cannot produce two competing reflex responses at the same time (such as fear and relaxation). Second, classical conditioning often involves *stimulus generalization*. In practice, the desensitization procedure requires elements of timing and judgement which make it more than a mechanical process. Typically, the clinician works with the individual to identify the type of stimuli which trigger the phobia – that is, the *conditioned stimulus* (CS). For example, someone afraid of bees might panic if a bee buzzed near their head.

hierarchy of fears in systematic desensitization, a list of fear-evoking stimuli, ranging from very mild to very intense,

Next, the individual is taught techniques for inducing relaxation, often associated to a cue (which becomes a CS for relaxing). Then, the clinician and individual develop a list of fear-evoking stimuli, ranging from very mild to very intense. This list is called a **hierarchy of fears**, since stimuli are listed in order of the intensity of fear which they elicit. Then, working gradually, the therapist attempts to recondition the person so that the stimuli in the hierarchy become associated with relaxing rather than fear. For example, the

---

Box 9.4 *The Basic Procedure for Systematic Desensitization*

Applying Systematic Desensitization

1 Identify fear-arousing stimulus (CS) – for example, person is afraid of snakes.
2 Person practises relaxation techniques (relaxation is an unconditioned response which is incompatible with fear).
3 Develop hierarchy of fears – list of stimuli which arouse fear, arranged from least fearful to most fearful.

Examples	seeing a picture of a snake in a book	(least fearful)
	seeing a snake on television	
	going to a zoo and seeing a snake in a cage	
	walking in the woods and seeing a snake	
	approaching a snake	
	holding a (harmless) snake	(most fearful)

4 Gradually proceed through hierarchy – at each step, person must imagine the fearful stimulus (from hierarchy), and deliberately relax; once person can imagine the weakest stimulus and remain relaxed, proceed to next stimulus, etc.

Original situation: CS (snake) elicits CR (fear)

After desensitization: CS (snake) elicits new CR (relaxation)

person might think of driving by a beehive in a closed car; once they can imagine this without fear, they would proceed to the next stimulus – seeing a bee outside the window, and so on. Once the person can confront the stimulus which originally evoked the greatest fear (imagining a bee buzzing near their head) and yet remain relaxed, then the phobia has been eliminated (see Box 9.4).

Systematic desensitization has been successfully employed for a wide variety of fears, ranging from the fear of snakes or heights to more unusual fears like the fear of music (Goldfried and Davison 1994; Wolpe 1973). Airlines have even sponsored desensitization sessions for individuals who are afraid of flying, based on the very reasonable premise that such individuals otherwise will not be potential customers! While systematic desensitization is often effective, rarely does the success rate for treatment go higher than about 70 per cent, and improvements may not be maintained over the longer term (Choy *et al.* 2007). This has prompted concerns about how to improve the effectiveness of systematic desensitization. For example, there have been recent attempts to enhance desensitization by using computer-generated 'virtual reality' stimuli (Choy *et al.* 2007; Maltby *et al.* 2002; Weiderhold *et al.* 2001). We will return to this issue in discussing the cognitive approach, but one should not overlook the fact that systematic desensitization is relatively time- and cost-efficient, as well as frequently successful.

The underlying principle of systematic desensitization – substituting a competing response for the undesired response – is sometimes referred to as *counter-conditioning*. Just as it can be used to eliminate a fear, it has also been employed to *induce* an aversive response to stimuli which are associated with existing undesirable behaviours. This procedure, called **aversive conditioning**, has been applied in dealing with a range of disorders, from sexual fetishes to alcoholism (see Figure 9.3). For example, an alcoholic might be given a drug called antabuse, which when present in the body reacts with alcohol to cause extreme nausea and vomiting. Then, if the person drinks, they will get sick, thus establishing an association that alcohol leads to sickness rather than pleasure. In practice, this procedure is only moderately effective – in part because drinkers quickly realize that by not taking the antabuse, they can drink with impunity (Forrest 1985). Hence, to be successful requires consistent long-term supervised administration of the drug, which suggests it is the physiological effect of antabuse, not aversive conditioning, that is the primary factor at work (Krampe *et al.* 2006*)*. More than other forms of behaviour modification, aversive conditioning is controversial, since it involves deliberately causing pain or discomfort. Consequently objections have been raised, even by psychologists who support non-aversive forms of behaviour therapy (McConnell 1974).

aversive conditioning a form of behaviour modification which is designed to induce an aversive response to stimuli which are associated with existing undesirable behaviours.

Operant conditioning has also been used in therapy, albeit with more limited success. Therapeutic attempts to alter operant behaviour through conditioning are dependent on controlling the relevant reinforcers (Hayes *et al.* 1995). Since people can potentially respond to a wide range of reinforcers, this can be a difficult task. Indeed, one writer has suggested that failures of conditioning derive from the individual getting more reinforcement from making the therapist look foolish than from the *intended* reinforcers (Carlson 1990)! Thus, the use of shaping and operant reinforcement has generally been most effective in situations which are highly structured.

token economy a form of behaviour modification based on operant conditioning; most commonly used in institutional settings, it involves giving conditioned reinforcers (tokens) for doing specific behaviours.

One such operant application has been the establishment of institutional programmes where conditioned reinforcers are given for specific behaviours. Such programmes, called **token economies**, allow individuals to earn tokens (conditioned reinforcers) for doing

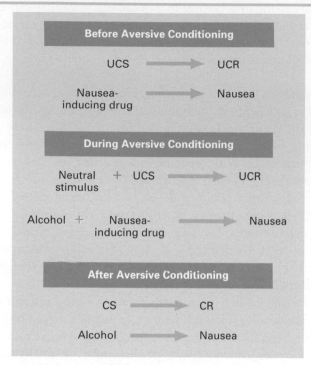

Figure 9.3 Aversive Conditioning as a Form of Classical Conditioning As illustrated, the drug antabuse causes nausea when combined with alcohol; consequently, alcohol becomes associated with the aversive experience of getting nauseated, which should deter drinking in the future (avoidance of the CS of alcohol).

things like making their bed, arriving at meals on time, or similar simple tasks. In turn, the tokens can be exchanged for desired items like candy or cigarettes, or used to buy privileges like television viewing or day passes. In effect, the tokens become a form of money (which is itself a conditioned reinforcer), for which individuals will perform work. Since access to such reinforcers can be readily controlled in an institutional environment, and the desired behaviours easily monitored, token economies can be very effective in establishing behavioural goals (Ayllon and Azrin 1968; Chen and Ma 2007; Dickerson *et al.* 2005; Fox 1998). Their primary disadvantages are the careful planning required, the need for a structured environment – and, like other forms of behaviour modification, the ethical problems which some perceive. With regard to the latter point, Skinner has noted the irony in popular attitudes: if we directly (and efficiently) seek to modify behaviour, people get concerned, but if we seek to do it indirectly (and thereby less efficiently), then that is considered acceptable (Skinner 1971)! While token economies do seem to work, their practical limitations are such that today they are relatively uncommon in the treatment of mental disorders.

Behaviour therapy today takes many forms, and has been applied to many sorts of problems (Hayes *et al.* 1995). In general, the techniques reflect the assumption that the goal of treatment is to change the undesired behaviour. As indicated, these techniques often show relatively high success rates, and the course of treatment is often very brief. Despite these advantages, behaviour modification has been criticized by other approaches on both ethical and theoretical grounds. Certainly, the focused nature of behaviour therapy makes informed consent very important – but the same thing could be said of any form of therapy. However, other approaches have also challenged the assumption that abnormal behaviour has no underlying causes – this issue has already been discussed in relation to the biological approach. Let us see how the other approaches explain the origins of abnormal behaviour.

The Cognitive Approach

cognitive behaviour modification an extension of behaviour modification which uses cognitive mediation (such as observing a model) in addition to basic conditioning techniques.

cognitive therapy a form of therapy which focuses on the role of faulty beliefs and thought patterns in abnormal behaviour; because it also encourages testing beliefs via behavioural strategies, it is sometimes called 'cognitive behavioural therapy'.

Cognitive theorists reject the behaviourist assumption that abnormal behaviour has no underlying cause. Instead, they view it in terms of underlying mediational processes – either symbolic mediation of conditioning, or the influence of faulty cognitions. **Cognitive behaviour modification** focuses on the role of symbolic mediation in treating abnormal behaviour, and is really an extension of behaviour therapy. By contrast, **cognitive therapy**, such as Albert Ellis's *rational emotive therapy*, emphasizes *faulty cognitions*; this focus links it more directly to the cognitive tradition. Theorists like Ellis (Aaron Beck is another example) focus on how behaviour is affected by distortions in *how* we think and *what* we think – such as false assumptions about ourselves and the world, inappropriate schemata and unrealistic expectations of life.

Cognitive behaviour modification can be traced back to the work of Albert Bandura, one of the pioneers of cognitive social learning theory. Bandura's experimental research on imitation had already led him to recognize that imitation can often be more effective than reinforcement for learning. He began applying this concept to the use of behaviour modification for treating phobias.

As noted earlier, systematic desensitization rarely has a 100 per cent success rate; one factor which may account for this is the dependence on *imagining* fear-evoking stimuli, rather than dealing with actual stimuli (imitation, of course, would involve actual stimuli). One way to separate out this component is to compare the effects of observing a model (an individual who acts out the desired behaviour) with actually imitating the behaviour of the model. This can be seen in a study in which Bandura compared the effects of three conditions: systematic desensitization, observing a model and *participant modelling* (where the individual actually does what the model does) in the treatment of a snake phobia (Bandura 1970). Individuals using systematic desensitization and those using simple modelling showed similar improvement compared to a control group; thus, simply using real stimuli did not enhance treatment. However, those who used participant modelling did significantly better than either of the other treatments, with 11 out of 12 individuals showing complete elimination of the phobia in follow-up tests. Thus, active imitation of the desired behaviour seemed more effective than either observing a model or conventional behaviour modification.

Subsequently, Donald Meichenbaum extended this approach to the imitation of thought processes (Meichenbaum 1977). The individual and therapist work together to identify problem areas, and then develop new self-statements that will be more effective. For instance, a person who has given a speech thinks, 'I was really boring; nobody will want to invite me again.' This negative assessment is self-defeating, in that it does not focus on any ways to improve behaviour in the future. Instead, the therapist might encourage the person to frame the assessment in more productive ways, such as thinking, 'That talk was pretty dry; I'll plan a better opening next time, and vary the pacing more.' By observing and imitating alternative ways of thinking, the individual can develop different strategies that lead to more effective behaviour (Freeman and Reinecke 1995).

The emphasis which Meichenbaum places on thought patterns is very similar to the work of Albert Ellis, although Ellis works within a different theoretical framework. Ellis focuses on the relationship between thoughts and emotions, using what he calls 'rational-emotive therapy' (Ellis 1993). **Rational-emotive therapy** argues that negative emotions arise from people's faulty interpretations of experiences, not from the experiences themselves. Using what he calls the *ABC principle*, Ellis says an activating event (A) triggers a faulty belief (B), which in turn triggers an emotional consequence (C). While we tend to assume that A causes C, it is really the belief (B) that is responsible for our emotional reactions. For example, Bob meets someone for the first time at a business conference, and comes away feeling that the person did not like him (the activating event). He then feels unhappy (the emotional consequence). Ellis would point out that this emotion was triggered by the irrational expectation (belief) that everyone Bob meets should like him. Realistically, there are always people who don't like us; while this is unfortunate, a realistic attitude is to accept this, rather than feeling devastated. Similarly, people who focus excessively on negative events are engaging in what Ellis humorously calls *awfulizing*.

rational-emotive therapy a form of therapy developed by Albert Ellis which focuses on the relationship between thoughts and emotions, particularly negative emotions which arise from an individual's faulty interpretations of experiences.

Faulty beliefs represent distortions in schemata pertaining to oneself, the world and the future. Thus, Ellis works in very directive ways to modify the beliefs which lead to negative emotions. This process, called **cognitive restructuring**, is designed to develop realistic beliefs and self-acceptance (Ellis 1993; McGinn 1997). (Box 9.5 gives some examples of how a person might react positively and negatively to difficult situations.) At first glance, Ellis's emphasis on self-worth and developing beliefs which foster growth seems similar to the humanistic approach. However, his technique is much more directive, and he believes that the therapist should focus on the individual's cognitive patterns and behaviour, rather than being concerned about empathy.

cognitive restructuring in Ellis's rational-emotive therapy, a process for modifying faulty beliefs and the negative emotions they produce, in order to develop realistic beliefs and self-acceptance.

Ellis originally developed rational-emotive therapy as a means of treating depression, but it has been subsequently applied to a range of other problems, including personality disorders, panic disorder and other forms of anxiety, and eating disorders (Beck 1993; Freeman and Reinecke 1995). Studies of its effectiveness as a treatment for depression suggest it is at least as effective as other forms of therapy (Dobson 1989), and may be better than older forms of *antidepressants* (so-called tricyclic drugs, as compared to newer drugs like Prozac) in preventing relapses (Antonuccio *et al.* 1999; Hollon *et al.* 1992). In fact, today rational-emotive therapy and its relatives, known as cognitive behaviour therapy, are considered to be a mainstay approach to depression (Kuyken *et al.* 2007). As a treatment for panic disorder, it seems to work as well as behaviourist relaxation therapy, and better than brief non-directive psychotherapy (Beck *et al.* 1992, 1994). More broadly, rational-emotive therapy has been significant in making clinicians aware of the role cognitions play in abnormal behaviour, and has contributed to the development of cognitive therapy more generally (Wirga and De Bernardi 2002).

Despite these apparent successes, we still know very little about what the significant elements of the therapeutic process are (Haaga and Davison 1993). (Compared to cognitive behaviour modification, for example, rational-emotive therapy is both more complex and less specific.) Perhaps the most interesting question is *why* focusing on cognitions sometimes seems more effective than focusing on the behaviour itself. This question is particularly interesting given the bi-directional links between cognition and behaviour. While cognitive theorists emphasize how thoughts mediate behaviour, from a practical standpoint, we recognize that changing behaviour can also affect cognitions, making the direction of causation less than clear. Cognitive therapists frequently suggest that emphasizing the cognitive mediators produces broader-scale changes (that is, more generalization) than does modifying specific responses. While this may in fact be true, at present our understanding of this question is still quite limited. The relationship between thoughts and behaviour remains an important issue when we look at psychodynamic and humanistic techniques, both of which emphasize the importance of cognitive insight in changing abnormal behaviour.

Box 9.5 Negative and Positive Self-statements

Many situations can be interpreted in different ways. As the text discusses, depression is often associated with making negative assessments of oneself.

Situation	Negative self-statements	Positive self-statements
Losing a job	'I'll never be able to find another job.'	'I'll have to look hard so I can get a job quickly.'
Having a relationship break up	'I have nothing to live for now.'	'It seemed good, but maybe the next relationship will be even better.'
Not getting accepted to the school one prefers	'I must be too dumb to qualify.'	'I have other choices, and I could always apply for a transfer later.'
Facing a difficult task	'I can't do this, it's too hard for me.'	'I'm going to have to work hard, but I can do it.'

Try it Yourself

Can you think of a situation when you found yourself being self-critical? Do you think your criticisms were realistic or unrealistic? If they were unrealistic, did you recognize it at the time? Ellis (1994) suggests that we can use his technique on our own to avoid unrealistic criticisms of ourselves. He adds a 'D' to his ABC model to help us:

A *Identify the antecedent event(s).* For example, if you are feeling down because you have just been turned down for a date, the antecedent event is the other person's refusal.

B *Identify the belief.* What are you thinking about this? For example, you may be thinking, 'Nobody wants to date me' or 'I must be a real loser if he/she doesn't want to go out with me.'

C *Identify the consequence.* The result of your negative thoughts is to make you feel rejected and to lower your self-esteem.

D *Dispute the unreasonable thoughts* you have and *develop more reasonable alternatives* to them. So, you might think, 'Just because one person said no doesn't mean everyone will' or 'He/she may have other reasons why they don't want to go out with me that I don't know about.' These are more realistic statements than the ones you previously said to yourself, and they will make you feel better.

To stop the irrational thoughts going through your head, you need to say or think 'Stop!' to yourself, or even snap a rubber band on your wrist. (Yes, it's supposed to hurt a little! That's what will stop you!) (Hadad and Reed 2007).

The Psychodynamic Approach

The various theories which make up the psychodynamic approach all assume that abnormal behaviour is the product of some form of inner conflict. For Freud, this was seen in the dynamics of id, ego and superego. For other theorists, the conflicting elements vary (for example, Jung emphasized the relations between the ego and the collective unconscious). However they view the source of conflict, all psychodynamic theorists agree on two points: first, that abnormal behaviour is only the *symptom*, not the *cause* of the problem; and second, that treatment requires gaining awareness and understanding of the underlying conflicts which represent the true cause of disorders (Jones and Pulos 1993).

In asserting that behaviour is a symptom, not the problem itself, psychodynamic theorists have been critical of behaviour therapy. Since the behaviour is only an expression of the problem, they assert that trying to change the behaviour without addressing the underlying cause will prove ineffective. Instead, it will simply lead to **symptom substitution**, the expression of the problem in a new way. For example, if a person complains of a fear of snakes, and this reflects denial of sexual impulses, then eliminating the fear of snakes without addressing the sexual conflict will only lead to some other problem – possibly a different phobia, possibly a very different manifestation. However, this concept has found little experimental support. For example, bedwetting might be interpreted by a Freudian as reflecting Oedipal conflicts, yet behaviour therapy can successfully eliminate it while simultaneously increasing self-esteem (Baker 1969). Overall, the evidence suggests that symptom substitution does not occur in behaviour therapy (Kazdin and Wilson 1980).

> **symptom substitution** in psychodynamic theory, the assumption that changing overt behaviour without addressing the underlying dynamics will lead to the expression of the problem in a new way.

The second point, that successful treatment requires awareness of the underlying conflicts, is basic to the therapeutic techniques used by psychodynamic theorists. The development of **insight** into the causes of behaviour represents the basic goal of treatment. Using a variety of techniques, the therapist analyses the underlying conflicts, and helps the individual to understand how they are related to outward behaviour. Once the individual understands the causes of their difficulties, then change in the behaviour should follow. (In practice, the process of change is often gradual, rather than occurring immediately as insight is gained.)

> **insight** in psychotherapy, awareness of the underlying conflicts which are regarded as the causes of behaviour.

At first glance, the psychodynamic approach's emphasis on insight seems similar to both the cognitive and humanistic approaches to treatment. However, there are differences among the three in both the process and the types of cognitions emphasized. As noted earlier, the cognitive approach is largely present-oriented, whereas psychodynamic theories tend to focus on how present behaviour is related to past experience. In addition, cognitive theories like Ellis's view faulty beliefs as being the direct cause of disorders, while psychodynamic theories see the unconscious conflicts as the actual cause. While both psychodynamic and humanistic therapy emphasize insight, the types of conflict involved are different, as is the role of the therapist. In psychodynamic therapy, it is typically (though not always) the therapist's responsibility to analyse the behaviour and identify the underlying causes; in humanistic therapy, as we shall see shortly, the individual, not the therapist, is the final judge of what is significant. Hence, while all three approaches utilize insight, there are differences as well as similarities in how they do so.

The prototype for all psychodynamic therapies, and still probably the best known, is Freudian psychoanalysis. Since the development of his theory of personality was largely related to his clinical practice, Freud began with a desire to treat abnormal behaviour. His experiences with patients shaped not only his ideas about how the mind works, but also his views on treatment techniques. One of his basic assumptions was the value of *catharsis* – the release of emotions associated with the underlying conflict, often through remembering traumatic experiences. This emotional release, in turn, could help to foster insight.

Freud used a number of techniques to identify the underlying causes of conflict, all based on analysing various aspects of the individual's behaviour. Among the most important were free association, transference and resistance. (Note that *projective tests* like the Rorschach ink blot test came later, and generally have been shown to be poor assessment tools (Blatt 1975).) *Free association* involves having the person relax, and say whatever comes into awareness – thoughts, feelings, even bodily sensations. Freud would then seek to interpret the contents of such reports by looking for patterns and symbolic meanings. Freud also believed that the relationship between the individual and the therapist could come to represent other past relationships, often between the individual and a parent. The analysis of the emotions involved in this **transference** could then provide an important tool for understanding the development of current conflicts. In the same way, if a patient rejects the analyst's interpretations of the meaning of behaviour, this **resistance** can represent a defence against acknowledging the identified conflict. Thus, in various ways, all aspects of the therapeutic situation become relevant to analysing the underlying dynamics which produce the disorder.

transference in psychoanalysis, the displacement of drive energy from past relationships, often between the individual and a parent, to the relationship between the individual and the therapist.
resistance in psychoanalysis, the rejection by an individual of the analyst's interpretations of the meaning of behaviour; regarded as a defence mechanism.

Critics have often pointed out that Freud's approach to therapy places the therapist in a position of great power. Only the analyst can determine what is significant and what is not; in fact, if a patient objects to a particular interpretation, that is simply taken as evidence of resistance! Another limitation is that traditional psychoanalysis is a very open-ended process, potentially lasting several years. (Partly in response to this limitation, more recent theorists have worked on developing forms of brief psychodynamic therapy.) In fairness, one must evaluate these criticisms in the context of the overall effectiveness of Freud's therapeutic techniques.

One concern in evaluating Freudian therapy is finding appropriate measures of efficacy, since psychoanalysts seek not simply symptom relief, but also broader changes in the awareness and functioning of the individual. (Other psychodynamic therapies would generally make the same claim.) Consequently, comparing psychodynamic techniques to alternatives which emphasize narrower goals, such as behaviour therapy, can pose difficulties. In addition, since real-world evaluations involve individuals who are suffering, there are also ethical limits on the comparisons possible in research (for example, one cannot deliberately deny people access to treatment in order to create control groups, or deliberately offer inferior forms of treatment).

These limitations can make it difficult to draw clear conclusions, but have not prevented researchers from attempting to address the issue. A recent review provides a pessimistic picture for the effectiveness of psychoanalysis, but notes that there are serious methodological problems in evaluating the research (Fonagy *et al.* 2005). Nonetheless, some researchers claim that meaningful research can be done on the effectiveness of psychoanalysis (Sandell 2001). One well-controlled study, done at a clinic in Philadelphia, USA, randomly assigned individuals suffering from anxiety disorders to either behaviour therapy or psychoanalytic therapy (Sloane *et al.* 1975). A control group consisted of those on a waiting list for treatment. After four months, all three groups had shown some improvement, although the results were much better for those in treatment than for the control group (see Figure 9.4). Interestingly, in this study, there was no significant difference between psychoanalysis and behaviour therapy. Obviously, this represents only one study, and it involves a type of disorder for which psychoanalysis may be fairly well suited. A review of four major outcome studies concluded that 60–90 per cent of 'suitable' patients derived 'substantial therapeutic benefit' from psychoanalytic therapy (Bachrach *et al*. 1991). However, the word 'suitable' is an important qualifier, and the authors concluded that effectiveness is not easily predicted from initial patient assessments. Interestingly, a separate analysis of one of the studies reviewed, done by the Menninger Foundation, suggests that much of the benefit may come from the empathy and concern which the therapist shows, rather than from the specific insights (Wallerstein 1989). Since this is potentially a factor in *all* forms of therapy, we will return to it when discussing the general issue of evaluating the treatment of abnormal behaviour.

While the relatively vague treatment goals of traditional psychoanalytic therapy have tended to limit assessments of efficacy, other variants of psychodynamic therapy have been developed which are more focused. One increasingly popular variant is interpersonal psychotherapy, which is an outgrowth of object relations theory (see Chapter 5). **Interpersonal psychotherapy** (often called **IPT**) is a short-term therapy which focuses on the individual's current interpersonal problems, rather than early childhood experiences (Book 1998). The structure of therapy is based on identifying a few key problems, developing strategies for dealing with them, and then building confidence to be able to function beyond therapy (Weissman *et al*. 2000). IPT has been frequently applied as a treatment for depression, with efficacy approximately equal to cognitive therapy and drug therapy, and better than psychoanalytic therapy (Hollon *et al*. 2002; Kelly *et al*. 2007).

interpersonal therapy (IPT) a short-term, focused psychodynamic therapy which emphasizes current interpersonal problems and the development of strategies for dealing with them.

Overall, the available studies suggest that psychodynamic therapy, including psychoanalysis, produces some benefits for at least some types of patients and disorders, though the results

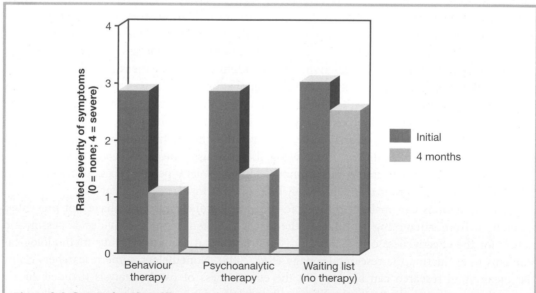

Figure 9.4 Comparing the Efficacy of Behaviour Modification and Psychoanalysis In a carefully controlled experiment, individuals sought treatment at a psychiatric outpatient clinic in Philadelphia; most suffered from anxiety disorders. Since the clinic had a waiting list, this group was used for a control comparison for initial condition and a follow-up after four months. (Data from Sloane *et al*. 1975)

are not without ambiguities, as noted. Two key questions, which will be explored further in discussing the evaluation of therapy in general, are worth keeping in mind. Is insight crucial to improvement of behaviour? And can improvement occur for reasons which are not specific to the form of therapy?

The Humanistic Approach

The humanistic approach argues that the meaning of behaviour can only be understood in terms of an individual's own perceptions and experience. This *phenomenological* emphasis, as it is referred to, is central to all of the various humanistic theories, and has particular significance when considering abnormal behaviour. Since judgements of what is appropriate or 'normal' depend on an individual's own perceptions, objective definitions of 'abnormal' are meaningless. As such, humanistic therapists have little use for classification systems like the DSM (Bugental and Sterling 1995). Instead, the humanists emphasize the potential for human growth, and focus on helping the individual grow. In effect, it is a psychology of health, not a therapy for abnormal behaviour.

Although the emphasis is rather different from the other approaches, humanistic therapy is still dealing with the same human beings as other therapists, no matter how the process is described. That means that the humanistic therapist must still deal with the reality that individuals seek help because they are suffering in some way. This suffering is interpreted as due to distortions of growth, usually caused by the demands of other people. The desire to meet these demands can result in frustration and despair, as well as loss of awareness of one's own feelings and preferences. Consequently, humanistic therapy tends to focus on creating conditions under which the individual can increase self-awareness and begin to make choices that will enhance the process of growth.

Although each humanistic theorist uses slightly different concepts and techniques, in practice the different therapies tend to be similar in several respects: the emphasis on the individual's own perceptions and feelings, the importance of self-awareness or *insight* as a tool for growth, and the responsibility of the therapist to respect the individual's autonomy. Among the various therapies, however, the work of Carl Rogers has become perhaps the best known.

As noted in Chapter 6, Carl Rogers developed his approach to therapy partly as a reaction against the pessimistic image of human growth which psychoanalysis offered. Over time, he developed a technique which was initially called 'client-centred therapy', and later, **person-centred therapy** (Bohart 1995; Raskin and Rogers 1989; Rogers 1951). (The early emphasis on the term 'client' was meant to contrast with the traditional usage, by both psycho-analysts and other therapists, of the term 'patient'.) In Rogers's view, the therapeutic relationship was between equals; the therapist's role was to provide a sounding board, not to make judgements as an authority figure. Hence, 'client' seemed preferable to 'patient'; the later shift to 'person-centred' was simply a further step towards acknowledging that the therapeutic relationship is essentially an interaction between two human beings.

person-centred therapy (also called 'client-centred therapy') a form of therapy developed by Carl Rogers which empha-sizes the responsibility of the individual to determine the direction of change within therapy.

Rogerian therapy is based on the therapist trying to provide the *conditions for growth*: empathy, openness and unconditional positive regard. The therapist must act in an *open* and genuine way, not hiding behind a professional façade. By trying to understand the individual's perceptions and feelings, the therapist provides *empathy*. *Unconditional positive regard* comes through demon-strating caring and acceptance of the individual and their concerns. By showing these qualities, the therapist can help the person to become more self-aware and more self-confident.

Despite the seemingly subjective nature of person-centred therapy, Rogers was very concerned with the importance of demonstrating that therapy actually helps people. Consequently, very early on he began keeping detailed transcripts of therapy sessions, and used them as a tool for evaluating therapeutic change (Rogers and Dymond 1954). Typically, as therapy progressed, an individual would make more statements relating to feelings, wishes, and having a sense of control over life. For example, a person might go from saying, 'I'm a failure; I always disappoint my parents' to saying, 'I realize how important my parents are to me; but I also realize I have to make my own career decisions.' Changes like this are consistent with what the theory would predict, and suggest Rogerian therapy is effective. Unfortunately, we recognize that what people *say* is not always what they *do*, and the data provide no direct evidence of behavioural change. Indeed, a study by a psychologist who was allowed to observe Rogers conducting therapy found that *only* statements indicating progress regularly led to positive comments by Rogers (Truax 1966). In effect, Rogers's comments provided a form of social reinforcement for the individual to make appropriate statements. Based partly on this finding, Rogers abandoned the term 'non-directive therapy' as a description of his therapeutic technique; while the therapist may try to be neutral, the reality is that *any* human interaction is influenced by the attitudes and preferences of each person. Nonetheless, Rogers continued to assert that the process of therapy must emphasize the individual's own potential for growth, not the judgements of the therapist. In this respect, the dynamics of Rogerian therapy seem very different from psychoanalysis.

This issue of implicit control is one basis on which person-centred therapy has been criticized. Another criticism is that, as an insight-oriented therapy, it requires a high level of verbal interaction. As such, critics suggest, it works best for problems of living – anxiety, depression and, particularly, self-esteem. There is some evidence to support this view, although Rogers himself also worked with individuals with more serious disorders, including schizophrenia (Rogers *et al.* 1967).

As with other forms of talking cures, which seek large-scale changes in the individual, Rogerian therapy is very difficult to evaluate. Nonetheless, research exists for anxiety disorders and depression, among other conditions. For example, it is as effective as cognitive therapy in dealing with anxiety disorders when each is used in combination with relaxation training (Borkovec and Matthews 1988), but slightly less effective than either cognitive therapy or relaxation when each is used independently (Borkovec and Costello 1993). For depression, studies indicate that it is comparable to cognitive therapy in effectiveness (Elliott *et al.* 1990). While offering some indication that person-centred therapy may be useful, these studies provide neither an absolute standard for comparison (for example, therapy vs. no treatment), nor any specific indication of what the key therapeutic factors are. Even if its primary effects are due to social reinforcement and the empathic support which the therapist provides, one thing is clear: Rogers has been highly influential on other clinicians. When a survey in the 1980s asked American therapists who had had the greatest influence on their work, Rogers was cited more frequently than anyone else (Smith 1982). More recently, a similar study of Canadian therapists (completed four years after Rogers's death) found him still in second place (Warner 1991). Overall, evaluated in terms of the amount of literature that has been published in the area of person-centred therapy and the number of journals, institutes and professional organizations dedicated to this approach, we can conclude that Rogers's influence is still strong, and the person-centred approach is still popular in the twenty-first century (Kirschenbaum and Jourdan 2005). As a model of a caring and compassionate therapist, Rogers seemed to fit his own theory very well indeed.

Try it Yourself

A Rogerian therapist strives to be genuine, empathic and accepting. He or she tries to provide an atmosphere of unconditional positive regard. To some, this sounds like a wonderful friend or even parent; but that doesn't guarantee the relationship is positive – even friends and parents can exert a powerful influence, and someone seeking help from a therapist (no matter how kindly) is potentially vulnerable. What do you think? Is client-centred therapy a kind of manipulation? Or is it a normal, day-to-day use of social influence in a caring relationship? How do you think it compares to behaviour modification, where the therapist can use reinforcement to change the individual's behaviour? What makes therapy 'manipulative' or not? And which type would *you* choose?

Evaluating Therapeutic Techniques

Clearly, there are differences in how each of the approaches views the origins and treatment of abnormal behaviour (for a summary, see Box 9.6). In discussing the approaches, we have often made reference to the apparent effectiveness, or **efficacy**, of the treatment techniques. The issue of efficacy is important, because obviously a treatment which doesn't help is worthless. To the average person, though, the question would probably be expressed in terms of 'which one is best?' As simple as it seems, this is a very difficult question to answer.

efficacy the measured effectiveness of a treatment technique in medicine or psychotherapy.

Box 9.6 Aetiology and Treatment: Comparing the Approaches

As summarized in the chart, the various approaches show both similarities and differences in their views of abnormal behaviour.

Approach	View of aetiology	View of treatment	Example of treatment
Biological	Physiological and/or genetic defects	Use of drugs	SSRIs for treatment of depression
Behaviourist	Reinforcement of maladaptive behaviour	Behaviour modification by conditioning and/or reinforcement	Systematic desensitization for treating phobias
Cognitive	Distorted and/or inappropriate thought patterns	Change thought patterns as mediators of behaviour	Rational-emotive therapy for depression
Psychodynamic	Unresolved conflicts related to early development	Develop insight into nature and origins of conflicts	Interpersonal therapy for depression
Humanistic	Incongruence due to conditions of worth imposed by others	Providing conditions of growth	Person-centred therapy for low self-esteem

Diversity is part of the problem: not only are there five broadly recognized approaches, but within each, many possible variants of treatment exist. This diversity of choices can create confusion – what behaviour therapist Joseph Wolpe has called 'the babble of conflicting voices' (Leo 1985, p. 39). Not surprisingly, one result has been an increased interest in comparative evaluations of the various types of therapy.

Unfortunately, it is not easy to design comparative studies. Therapeutic approaches often have different goals (for example, modifying personality vs. eliminating a specific behaviour), which can make it difficult to define a common standard of evaluation. Indeed, some suggest that standardized procedures to measure outcomes are inappropriate, since they ignore the differences in both processes and goals (Goldfried and Wolfe 1998; Persons 1991).

The question of the proper way to do assessments was raised by a major study completed by *Consumer Reports* in the USA. The study looked at the experiences of 2900 patients who were treated with some form of psychotherapy, with or without drugs as an adjunct. (**Psychotherapy** is a general term used to describe treatment which is basically verbal in nature.) The results indicated that all therapies were equally useful, regardless of type of disorder, and that generally longer periods of treatment were better than shorter. The study caused considerable controversy, because there was no standardization of treatment methods and duration, severity of symptoms, etc. – in short, all the factors which conventional research tries to control. Despite this, Martin Seligman (himself a cognitive-behaviourist researcher) argued that the study was useful, precisely because it allowed therapists and patients to make the decisions about duration and type of treatment (Seligman 1995). Nonetheless, the fact that the study found no appreciable differences in effectiveness among the therapies seems both odd and unhelpful.

> **psychotherapy** any variety of treatment for abnormal behaviour which is primarily verbal in nature, rather than based on the use of drugs.

This phenomenon of 'no difference' has been the typical outcome in studies comparing various types of therapies in their overall long-term efficacy for a wide variety of disorders. This has been termed the 'dodo bird verdict', referring to the judgement of the dodo in *Alice in Wonderland,* that everyone had won the race, and so should have a prize (Luborsky *et al.* 2002). On the other hand, there have been several criticisms of the studies showing the 'dodo bird verdict' for their methodological problems (for example, Beutler 2002; Chambless 2002). One major concern is the use of variable (and hence vague) standards for assessing outcomes; in order to draw reasonable conclusions, most researchers and clinicians feel that there must be at least some minimal common standard for assessment.

A further problem in trying to assess the effectiveness of therapy is the possibility that an individual may show improvement even *without* treatment – what is referred to as spontaneous remission. Obviously, if **spontaneous remission** is not considered, then some apparent improvements will be credited to treatment, instead of coincidence! Yet, there is an obvious ethical problem in deliberately denying treatment simply to create a control group.

> **spontaneous remission** in medicine or therapy, improvement in an individual's condition in the absence of treatment.

As a result, control groups are usually either based on soliciting informed consent to delay treatment, or else created by selecting individuals from waiting lists for treatment. (Unfortunately, many treatment centres are unable to meet immediate demands.)

Another issue which can complicate assessments is the role of culture. As noted earlier in discussing the DSM, cultural differences between therapist and patient can affect the accuracy of diagnosis. It can also affect communication within therapy, assumptions about the nature of the disorder, and identification of the appropriate goal for therapy. For example, a Sri Lankan Buddhist who talks about life as suffering may be reflecting religious beliefs, not depression (Bhui *et al.* 2001). While the importance of empathy is often emphasized, there can be a temptation to seek to get beyond the cultural barrier, when in fact culture may well provide the context for therapy (Ruskin and Beiser 1998). Hence, both the therapeutic process and assessment of outcomes are made more difficult whenever cultural variations exist.

Having noted these difficulties, let us consider some of the findings of evaluation studies. One of the best-controlled comparative studies was conducted by the National Institutes of Mental Health, a

US government agency (Elkin *et al.* 1989). In this study, 28 clinicians of various orientations worked with 240 individuals diagnosed as having major depression. Individuals were randomly assigned to treatment using either an antidepressant drug (imipramine), psychodynamic therapy (not psycho-analysis) or cognitive therapy. In addition, a control group was given a placebo pill, along with brief weekly meetings with a psychiatrist. The placebo/drug groups were conducted as a *double blind* design, so that neither the doctor nor the individual knew which was which. All individuals were assessed at the start, after 16 weeks of treatment, and again 18 months later. The results of the study are complex, and do not point to the type of clear-cut result one might hope for. For example, all three types of treatment produced greater improvement than did the placebo. Drug therapy produced faster improvements than did the insight therapies – but was also associated with higher rates of relapse of symptoms. Even in the placebo group, some of the individuals with only moderate depression showed improvement. (This improvement is not evident in the final results, because these individuals tended to drop out before the study was completed.) Subsequent studies comparing cognitive, interpersonal and drug therapy have tended to show similar results (Hollon *et al.* 2002; Scott 2000). Of course, these studies only looked at efficacy in treating *depression*; while relatively common, depression is obviously only one form of disorder.

A different approach to comparing treatment techniques was used by Mary Lee Smith and her colleagues (Smith *et al.* 1980). Drawing on the hundreds of previously published evaluations of various forms of therapy, Smith did a meta-analysis of 475 studies, statistically analysing the combined results according to various factors, such as theoretical orientation and type of disorder treated (a partial summary of results is shown in Figure 9.5). The major finding was that *all* of the various approaches seemed to produce significant improvement, and that there was little difference in ratings of overall effectiveness. However, when the analysis was broken down in terms of *types of disorders*, there *were* significant differences between approaches. For example, humanistic therapy seemed the *least* effective approach to treating anxiety, but was the *most* effective approach for problems of self-esteem.

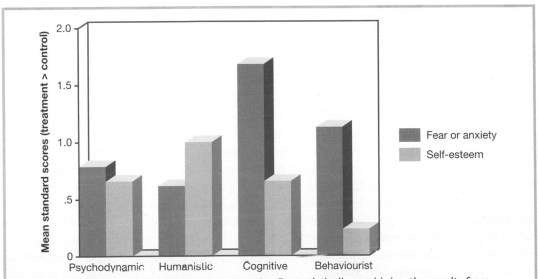

Figure 9.5 A Meta-analysis of Treatment Results By statistically combining the results from 475 different studies, researchers were able to do a comparative study of four approaches to the treatment of anxiety and self-esteem. The scores are 'standard scores'. which are expressed in units of the standard deviation. A score of 1.0 would mean approximately 84 per cent of those in the treatment group improved more than those in the control group; any positive score indicates greater improvement in treatment than in control groups. (Data adapted from Smith *et al.* 1980)

The type of analysis used by Smith and her colleagues, while interesting, poses many difficulties. For example, studies used different assessment criteria and durations of treatment, and possibly varied in accuracy of diagnoses and assessments of severity, among other factors. In addition, Smith *et al.* did not include treatment based on the medical model (drugs), which limits the possibility of complete comparisons. Overall, the finding that *all* methods show *some* efficacy (also noted in the *Consumer Reports* study and other general studies, as discussed above) suggests that there may be factors which are common to all types of treatment.

The idea that there are *non-specific factors* associated with treatment has been recognized for many years. As noted earlier, this was raised in a study of the effectiveness of psychoanalysis (Wallerstein 1989), and the idea has also found support in research on the relationship between therapist and patient in the treatment of eating disorders (Constantino *et al.* 2005). In a classic book called *Persuasion and Healing*, psychiatrist Jerome Frank suggested that the common factors in all forms of treatment are the clinician's commitment to helping, and the belief in improvement which this instils in the individual (Frank 1963). More recently, this has been echoed by other researchers; one study suggested that the primary non-specific factors are *support* and *hope* (Stiles *et al.* 1986). The importance of support has been affirmed by psychodynamic therapist Hans Strupp, who states that creating an atmosphere of acceptance and empathy is itself of great therapeutic value (Strupp 1989). Hope, which may be created by the therapist's attitude or even a placebo, also seems to be a general feature of effective therapy (Babits 2001; Bergin and Walsh 2005).

While it is easy to dismiss such factors as relevant only in the context of humanistic therapy, that does not appear to be the case. A study of rational-emotive therapy for treating depression makes this point clearly (Castonguay *et al.* 1996). According to Ellis's theory, the therapy works by challenging false beliefs, and research indicates that such therapy is as effective as medication in alleviating depression, and probably better at preventing relapses (see earlier discussion). However, an analysis of the factors that contribute to successful treatment showed that the commitment of therapist and patient, and the emotional involvement of the patient, were the significant elements. Surprisingly, the degree of emphasis that therapists put on distorted cognitions did *not* predict treatment success, contrary to the assumptions of rational-emotive therapy. The commitment of therapist and patient to the therapeutic process (sometimes called the *therapeutic alliance*) is now widely recognized as an important element of therapy (Langhoff *et al.* 2008), even by behaviour therapists (Hayes *et al.* 1995).

Given that the various studies have not led to the assessment that one method is consistently superior, should one conclude that all therapies are the same? Probably not. As noted in Smith's review, some approaches work better than others for certain problems. In part, this may reflect the reality that abnormal behaviour does not have a single cause. Instead, genetic predisposition, prior experiences and current circumstances all likely play a role – and therefore are also factors in treatment. In addition, the relative importance of each factor is likely to vary across disorders and even across individuals. Consequently, the finding that each approach has some benefit may reflect the realities of complex causation, as well as the non-specific treatment factors discussed above. So, it should not be surprising that drug therapy combined with experientially-based therapy is often more effective that either alone.

Given that no type of therapy is consistently superior, it is interesting that a significant number of practitioners describe their approach to treatment as *eclectic* – that is, they draw upon a range of techniques on a case-by-case basis, rather than adhering to a single theoretical model. In a study of therapeutic orientations, anywhere from 30–40 per cent of Canadian and American psychologists described themselves as eclectic in orientation – more than any single approach (Warner 1991). While this seems a reasonable attitude, it may or may not work in practice: without clear knowledge of which technique works best in a given circumstance, eclectic approaches could conceivably result in the *worst* of all methods, rather than the *best*. In the end, we still know too little about causes, and clearly, we need to know more about what works, and *why*.

Try it Yourself

The risks of eclectic styles of therapy are illustrated by an old puzzle: which is more accurate, a watch which doesn't work, or one which loses five minutes per day? (The answer: the broken watch, because at least it will be right twice a day, while the one which loses time may *never* be correct!) Suppose that you had a problem such as severe depression. What type of therapist would you go to? Why? What questions would you want to ask them before beginning therapy? Would you go to the same therapist if your problem were low self-esteem? Why or why not? Do you think that finding the right therapist for you depends on the approach the therapist uses or the personal characteristics of the therapist? Ask a friend what he or she would look for in an ideal therapist. Do you and your friend agree or disagree?

UNDERSTANDING SCHIZOPHRENIA

At the beginning of this chapter, we described the case of a young man who had been diagnosed as having schizophrenia. The symptoms he manifested – confusion, incoherent speech, possible delusions – are common in schizophrenia. As a disorder, schizophrenia is relatively rare, affecting about 1 per cent of the population (compared to a lifetime risk of serious depression of about 15 per cent). However, schizophrenia and its stereotypes are closely associated with the popular conception of abnormal behaviour as 'madness'. Of all the forms of mental disorders, it is perhaps the most frightening to the average person, and the most difficult to understand.

What we now call schizophrenia has been recognized in various forms for centuries. Even in ancient Greece, Hippocrates described its basic symptoms. The term 'schizophrenia' was first used by a Swiss psychiatrist named Eugen Bleuler. Drawing on the Greek words for 'split mind', Bleuler coined the term to refer to disorders in which there seemed to be a separation of cognitive and emotional functions, resulting in mental confusion and either inappropriate emotions or the absence of emotional expression. (It should be noted that schizophrenia, despite the connotation of 'split personality', is *not* the same as **multiple-personality disorder**, a severe form of dissociative reaction which can result in several independent personalities being manifested.)

multiple-personality disorder a severe form of dissociative reaction which can result in several independent personalities being manifested.

Schizophrenia represents a severe form of disorder in which there can be distortions of perception, thought, language and emotions. While no two cases are likely to be identical, DSM-IV-TR requires that there be cognitive or perceptual distortions which impair the person's contact with reality, and also significant deterioration in general functioning (as in working and caring for oneself). In addition, there are several types of symptoms which may occur. Some are called **positive symptoms**, because they represent

schizophrenia a severe form of mental disorder in which there can be distortions of perception, thought, language and emotions.
positive symptoms behaviours associated with a mental disorder which would not occur in a healthy person; for example, hallucinations in schizophrenia or sleep disturbances in depression.

delusions false beliefs which are maintained in the absence of clear evidence to the contrary.
hallucinations false perceptions in the absence of relevant sensory stimuli, such as hearing voices or seeing objects which are not present.
thought disturbances distortions of thinking processes such as violations of logic, incoherent speech and inappropriate shifts in word usage.
negative symptoms the absence of expected behaviours; negative symptoms of schizophrenia include bodily immobility, limited speech, flattened affect (absence of emotional expression) and social withdrawal.

behaviours that are commonly associated with schizophrenia: delusions, hallucinations and thought disturbances. **Delusions** are false beliefs which are maintained in the absence of clear evidence to the contrary. For example, psychologist Milton Rokeach once encountered three individuals with schizophrenia, each of whom believed himself to be Jesus Christ (Rokeach 1981). **Hallucinations** are false perceptions – most commonly, hearing voices. When asked to describe the source of such voices, individuals typically say they come from within their own head. Interestingly, one study suggests the perceived voices originate by the same process as ordinary silent verbalizations ('talking to oneself' without speaking aloud), but are instead perceived as actual voices (Bick and Kinsbourne 1987). **Thought disturbances** can take many forms – apparent violations of logic (called *paralogic*), incoherent speech and shifts in word usage (as when the young man in the Introduction responded to the name Hope as 'that's what I need'). In addition, schizophrenia can be indicated by **negative symptoms**, which involve the absence of expected behaviours. Negative symptoms can include bodily immobility, limited speech, flattened affect (absence of emotional expression) and social withdrawal, among other forms.

Although not all of these types of symptoms occur in every patient, the predominance of one type is often used to diagnose a particular sub-type of schizophrenia: *paranoid schizophrenia* involves delusions of grandeur (as in the three Christs) and persecution; *catatonic schizophrenia* is characterized primarily by negative symptoms, particularly non-responsiveness to environmental stimuli; the *disorganized schizophrenia* type shows disturbances of thought and flattened or absent emotional expression. A fourth category, *undifferentiated schizophrenia*, is used for those cases that meet the primary criteria (cognitive or perceptual distortions, and generally poor functioning) but do not fit one of the three specific sub-types. In addition to these four types, DSM-IV-TR provides a fifth category, *residual schizophrenia*, for circumstances in which there has been partial recovery after an acute episode of schizophrenia, but lingering problems of adaptation which are associated with the disorder (see Box 9.7).

The definition of schizophrenia, and the description of sub-types, are still a matter of some controversy. In part, this reflects the complex mix of possible symptoms, and the necessity of defining the condition (at least at present) purely symptomatically. This is a serious issue, because if the categories are invalid, then classification may actually impede our understanding of aetiology. To give an example: excessive use of amphetamines can result in **amphetamine delusional disorder**, which presents symptoms nearly identical to paranoid schizophrenia. While the ambiguity in this case can be readily resolved by a period of observation in hospital (which removes access to amphetamines), it illustrates that symptoms are not always a direct indicator of cause. (We will return to this concern in discussing how the approaches deal with schizophrenia.)

amphetamine delusional disorder a form of mental disorder resulting from the excessive use of amphetamines; its primary symptom, extreme paranoid delusions, can make it appear symptomatically identical to paranoid schizophrenia.

Despite these difficulties, there is little question that there are individuals with these general symptoms who experience significant distress, and who seem unable or unwilling to function effectively. In recent years, the estimates of the frequency of schizophrenia have tended to centre on 0.5–1 per cent of the population (lifetime risk), with men and women equally likely to be

Box 9.7 *Major Sub-types of Schizophrenia*

Diagnosis of schizophrenia under DSM-IV can fall into one of five categories, depending on the symptoms and history. (Adapted from DSM-IV, American Psychiatric Association 1994)

Type of schizophrenia	Major symptoms
Paranoid	Hallucinations (e.g., hearing voices) and delusions (e.g., of being persecuted, or of exaggerated self-importance)
Catatonic	Excessive motor behaviour, or unresponsive, inactive stupor; sometimes alternating between the two extremes
Disorganized	Incoherent speech and thought, inappropriate emotional expression, bizarre behaviour
Undifferentiated	Mixture of symptoms, not fitting one of the above types
Residual	Moderate symptoms (often flat affect and limited speech) occurring after an acute episode of schizophrenia

affected, but with men often showing an earlier age of onset (late teens to early twenties, vs. late twenties or later for women) (Jablensky 2000; Narrow *et al.* 2002; Regier *et al.* 1988). Since most clinicians *do* accept that the behaviours associated with schizophrenia exist, it is worth considering what we know about its origins and possible treatment.

Try it Yourself

Elijah is a 48-year-old man who wears a straw hat, a bulky sweater, plaid shorts and army boots every day, rain or shine, as he stands on a busy street corner. Sometimes he seems to be having arguments with people who are not there; sometimes he laughs uproariously for no apparent reason; sometimes he is completely unresponsive when people attempt to speak to him. If someone tries to take him to a homeless shelter, he angrily rejects their overtures, insisting that they should mind their own business.

Elijah has many of the symptoms associated with schizophrenia. Can you identify them? Is the presence of these symptoms enough to make you conclude that he has this disorder? Is there other information you might want before you made this judgement? Are there circumstances where these behaviours might *not* reflect schizophrenia?

The Biological Approach, the Medical Model and Schizophrenia

Of the many theories of the causes of schizophrenia, perhaps the best known is the idea that it is biologically based. This view, consistent with the biological approach's general interpretation of abnormal behaviour, reflects the *medical model*. Suggesting that there is some sort of fundamental physical defect seems consistent with the apparent severity and generally poor prognosis for permanent recovery found in schizophrenia. In addition, such a view may also be socially attractive. That is, by suggesting there is a fundamental physiological difference between those with schizophrenia and those who don't have it, it may be reassuring to people who want to believe that 'it can't happen to me'. As we explore what is known about schizophrenia, we will return to the question of social dynamics.

One of the first significant clues suggesting a biological origin was the development of chlorpromazine, the first of the modern antipsychotic drugs. Heinz Lehmann, a Canadian doctor who is usually credited with introducing chlorpromazine in North America, said that after giving chlorpromazine to patients for a few days or weeks, most of the positive symptoms disappeared. 'In 1953, there just wasn't anything that ever produced something like this' (Shorter 1997, p. 252). For doctors like Lehmann, accustomed to being able to do little for individuals suffering from schizophrenia, this was a startling breakthrough.

The success of chlorpromazine and similar drugs has led to the development of theories which say that schizophrenia is related to abnormalities in neurotransmitter function. The first of these was the **dopamine hypothesis**, which asserts that schizophrenia is related to overactivity in neural pathways which depend on dopamine as a neurotransmitter. The primary evidence in favour of this hypothesis comes from clinical experience with drugs which affect dopamine activity. For example, *neuroleptics* like chlorpromazine reduce positive symptoms of schizophrenia, and are known to reduce the activity of dopamine in the brain (Wender and Klein 1981). Conversely, drugs like amphetamines, which stimulate dopamine levels, are known to induce psychosis with excessive use (Angrist *et al.* 1980). Similarly, the drug commonly used to treat Parkinson's disease (a muscle-control disorder whose treatment involves enhancing dopamine levels) can worsen the symptoms of schizophrenia (Kendell 1987). (Interestingly, a side effect of neuroleptic drugs can be muscle tremors reminiscent of Parkinsonism.) Hence, in various ways, the clinical evidence has pointed to a link between dopamine and schizophrenia. Over time, the dopamine hypothesis has been refined to focus on one of several types of dopamine receptors, the D2 receptor (Hirvonen *et al.* 2005). At present, available drugs cannot target just one type of dopamine receptor, but even without this concern, there are a number of difficulties with the dopamine hypothesis.

dopamine hypothesis a theory which argues that schizophrenia is based on over-activity in neural pathways which depend on dopamine as a neurotransmitter.

The most basic problem is that not all patients respond to neuroleptics (Garver *et al.* 1997). Moreover, there is currently no clear sense of how dopamine is responsible, and physiological studies have been inconsistent (Heinrichs 2001). For example, many of the studies which have found abnormalities in dopamine receptors in individuals with schizophrenia have depended on post-mortem analyses. Since most individuals with a lengthy history of schizophrenia also have a long history of taking neuroleptics, one cannot rule out drug-induced changes in the neural pathways. A further problem is that the drugs usually reach the brain very shortly after ingestion, yet there is typically a lag of days or weeks before clinical improvement occurs. If excess dopamine is the problem, why doesn't behaviour change as soon as dopamine levels drop? Today, it is recognized that the original dopamine hypothesis was too simplistic, and that a more reasonable dopamine hypothesis is that some people suffering from schizophrenia have abnormalities in a specific dopamine receptor, the D2 receptor.

The picture is also muddied by clinical studies with newer drugs, such as clozapine. These drugs, called 'atypical antipsychotics', seem to be even more effective clinically than the earlier neuroleptics (notably chlorpromazine), yet produce fewer side effects (such as muscle tremors). However, they do so by affecting different neural pathways (Meltzer 2002; Tandon and Kane 1993). Over time, this has led to studying the role of other neurotransmitters, including glutamate and serotonin (Dubertret *et al.* 2004; Meador-Woodruff and Kleinman 2002; Meltzer 2002). Interestingly, the finding that low levels of glutamate are related to schizophrenia (Goff and Coyle 2001) lends support to the idea that dopamine has a role in the neurochemistry of schizophrenia, since dopamine receptors inhibit the release of glutamate. Unfortunately, these alternative hypotheses have also produced inconsistent physiological evidence (Heinrichs 2001). As intriguing as the neurotransmitter hypotheses are, they do not directly explain the *cause* of schizophrenia; that is, why should some people's brains show a problem with regulation of neurotransmitters? This question has led researchers to look for a more fundamental explanation.

Over the years, various studies have suggested a number of physiological differences between individuals with schizophrenia and the rest of the population. One theory is that the cognitive deficits found in schizophrenia are due to frontal lobe pathology. For example, scans of the brain using positron emission tomography (PET scans) have shown that there is less frontal lobe activity during attention tests in individuals with schizophrenia (Gershon and Rieder 1992). Heinrichs has noted that a substantial number (although a minority) of individuals with schizophrenia show about the same performance deficit as patients with frontal lobe damage – but in both cases, there is considerable variability, and overlap with control groups of healthy individuals (Heinrichs 2001).

Thus, while such studies are promising, they still do not offer a clear explanation of the basis of schizophrenia. One mechanism that seemingly *could* account for such physical differences is heredity. In the case of schizophrenia, there have been hundreds of studies, and a general pattern has emerged. Studies of concordance rates for family members suggest that there is a genetic predisposition for schizophrenia (Gershon and Rieder 1992; Nicol and Gottesman 1983). These findings indicate that for relatives of individuals with schizophrenia, the closer the genetic relationship, the greater the risk. Moreover, results from cases in which family members were separated early in life suggest that the observed pattern is *not* due to the effects of growing up in a home where someone has schizophrenia (Kety *et al.* 1994).

Still, there are limits on what these findings tell us. First of all, they do *not* mean that schizophrenia is purely genetic – even identical twins reared together show no more than a 50 per cent concordance rate. As Nicol and Gottesman (1983) note, there are very few cases involving separated identical twins with schizophrenia, and those cases may not be representative of the general population. Most importantly, while a genetic factor does seem implied, no one knows exactly what it is, despite years of searching (for example, Brzustowicz *et al.* 2000; Klar 1999; Macgregor *et al.* 2002). Today, researchers are looking for specific genes that may account for some of the symptoms of schizophrenia (Harrison and Owen 2003), but so far there are no definitive results. Consequently, researchers have begun to look at alternative mechanisms to account for the occurrence of schizophrenia.

Some researchers have begun to speculate that schizophrenia is actually several different disorders which have different causes – and the variants do not necessarily match the DSM-IV-TR categories (Andreasen 1999; Garver 1997; Heinrichs 1993). If this is the case, then any attempt to identify a single factor – whether neurotransmitter, gene or structural defect – is hopeless. As Weinberger (2002) notes, this is not to say that physiological defects do not exist; instead, it suggests that the origin of schizophrenia involves *multiple* factors.

Given this possibility, the 'two hit' model, developed by Mednick and his colleagues, is gaining increasing attention (Mednick *et al.* 1998). According to this model, schizophrenia requires two types of adverse events, or 'hits'. Since many of the identified brain anomalies seem likely to arise early in development of the brain, the model proposes that the first hit occurs during the second trimester of pregnancy. A genetic defect could be one cause, but others are possible. For example, several studies have pointed to the possibility that the damage is due to the mother contracting influenza (flu) during this portion of the pregnancy (Byrne *et al.* 2007; Mortenson *et al.* 1999; Venables 1996). One of the interesting implications of this is that a viral mechanism would show up in twin studies as genetic, since twins share the same prenatal environment. This might explain why concordance rates for both identical and fraternal twins are greater than zero, but not high enough to suggest a purely genetic factor. It might also explain why schizophrenia has persisted as a human trait, since normally natural selection would lead to disappearance of traits that affect adaptation in such negative ways (Hooper 1999). (Other factors besides influenza have also been suggested as posing risks during the second trimester, including cold temperatures and malnutrition.)

The second hit would be a subsequent environmental stress, including possibly trauma during birth or negative rearing conditions. This factor may also be relevant to reinterpreting the studies of adopted twins, since the conditions which led to being separated may also be the factors triggering the onset of schizophrenia (including poverty or marital breakdown). Even when looking at onset in adults, one cannot rule out the role of environmental factors in producing some of the changes, since we know that experience modifies brain structure (see Chapter 7). Environmental influences could include deprivation during early rearing, malnutrition, social isolation and treatment-related factors like drug effects and institutionalization. In support of the idea of environmental influences, a large cross-cultural study sponsored by the World Health Organization found a pattern of stressful events preceding acute onset of schizophrenia (Day *et al.* 1987). More recently, the stress of social disadvantage that may come with immigration and social dislocation has been implicated in incidence rates for schizophrenia across a range of European countries (Cantor-Graae 2007; Hutchinson and Haasen 2004).

The new model which is emerging is reminiscent of what has been called the **diathesis-stress model** of abnormal behaviour. According to this theory, abnormal behaviour arises as a result of the combination of a predisposition (usually genetic) and a stressful environment. In the absence of a stressor, the predisposition will not be manifested. (Thus, a genetic defect or influenza during the second trimester could be the diathesis, and childhood poverty could be the stress.) According to one version of this model, in individuals with a predisposition, stress raises dopamine levels, and thereby increases

diathesis-stress model a theory which views abnormal behaviour as being due to a combination of a physiological predisposition (diathesis) and a stressful environment.

symptoms (Walker and Diforio 1997). One implication of this model is that it may be possible to reduce the environmental stressors which result in schizophrenia in those who are vulnerable, or teach them skills to cope with stress more effectively (Zubin and Spring 1977). The ideas about schizophrenia which are currently being developed are exciting, and seem to make sense of a complex and confusing disorder. However, history suggests that we should be cautious, since there have previously been claims to having found 'the cause of schizophrenia'. (Both Whitaker (2002) and Brown and Herrnstein (1975) have provided scathing reviews of the history, almost 30 years apart!) Even if the two-hit (diathesis-stress) model is correct, the biological approach is less suited to considering environmental factors than are the other approaches. Consequently, let us look at how each of them deals with schizophrenia.

Alternatives to the Medical Model of Schizophrenia

The biological approach uses the medical model to explain schizophrenia in terms of genetic and physiological processes. In contrast, the other four approaches all emphasize environmental influences. While the specific factors emphasized differ, each approach offers theories to explain the aetiology of the behaviour, and also treatment techniques derived from the theory. In comparing these various theories, we face a basic problem of evaluation. While we can attempt

Try it Yourself

Do you find the medical model interpretation of schizophrenia convincing? Why or why not? If you were in charge of administering funding for research into the causes of schizophrenia, how would you allocate the money? (Surprisingly, although schizophrenia affects about one in a hundred people worldwide, it receives relatively little research funding.) Suppose one of your parents or grandparents had schizophrenia; would this affect your desire to have children?

to measure the effectiveness of the treatments, this does *not* directly prove that the associated theory is correct in explaining the cause of schizophrenia. The problem, for both the environmental theories and the medical model, is that nearly all of the evidence is *retrospective*. That is, we are unable to do controlled experiments to test the theories; instead, researchers have to work backwards, after the disorder has already been diagnosed. At best, one can try to identify individuals who are defined as being at risk, and observe whether they in fact develop schizophrenia – but even in this case, the results are technically correlational, and prone to errors such as sampling bias. The problems of evaluation are further complicated by the disputes about the validity of current diagnostic categories, since recent evidence (see previous section) may either mean that multiple factors contribute to the occurrence of schizophrenia, or that we are currently lumping together disorders with very different origins. With these difficulties in mind, let us consider what each of the other approaches can contribute to our understanding of schizophrenia and its treatment.

The Behaviourist Approach

As previously discussed, the behaviourist approach interprets abnormal behaviour as simply maladaptive learning. In this respect, schizophrenia is not regarded any differently from other forms of abnormal behaviour. Indeed, behaviourists would view the term 'schizophrenia' as having no aetiological value. Even viewed descriptively, the term would be seen as useful only to the extent that it reliably describes particular patterns of behaviour.

As an explanation of the origin of schizophrenia, the behaviourist view has several weaknesses. First, although learning by reinforcement is a well-demonstrated general principle, there is no direct evidence for the acquisition of *schizophrenic* behaviour. There are also several ways in which the model seems inconsistent with the available evidence. For example, while it is possible to use learning to suggest why children of individuals with schizophrenia are at greater risk, it is hard to see how this applies in cases where children are reared *apart* from the parent with schizophrenia. Also, although one can conceive of a particular symptom being learned, it is not clear why particular combinations of symptoms should occur so regularly (for instance, delusions coupled with hallucinations). It has been argued that by regarding all behaviour as alike, behaviourists give little attention to the kinds of problems people tend to develop (Wachtel 1977).

One exception is 'immediacy theory', which argues that hallucinations and delusions are the result of focusing on immediate rather than more distant stimuli (Salzinger 1998). For example, a delusion could result from interpreting being bumped as an attack, rather than related to being on a moving train. While this bears some resemblance to the cognitive model of *defective attention*, Salzinger's model deals primarily with treatment, not aetiology. Overall, the behaviourist approach does not seem to contribute greatly to our understanding of the causes of schizophrenia.

In terms of treatment, a number of studies have shown that reinforcement can be effective in modifying the behaviour of individuals with schizophrenia. For example, in one case, a 40-year-old man had been hospitalized for 19 years, and had not spoken to anyone in all that time. The researchers discovered that he loved chewing gum, and used it as a reinforcer to successfully reintroduce speech, by a process of shaping (Isaacs *et al.* 1960). In an experimental study of individuals with auditory hallucinations and delusions, behaviour modification was compared to generic supportive therapy (Leibman and Salzinger 1998). Over a six-week period, target behaviours declined by 66 per cent with behaviour modification, while most measures actually *increased* in the control group.

Other studies have focused on shaping the behaviour of entire wards, by establishing a *token economy* (Atthowe and Krasner 1968; Schaefer and Martin 1966). These studies have typically reported success in improving specific behaviours (such as dressing and going to meals), and also improvements in overall functioning. What is most striking is that these studies involved individuals who had already been institutionalized for long periods – in the Atthowe and Krasner study, the median age was 57, and the median duration of hospitalization was *22 years*. Despite the negative prognosis this would imply, 90 per cent of the 87 men on the ward participated actively in the programme, and showed improvements over a two-year period.

Token economy programmes represent one of the most frequent applications of the behaviourist approach within mental institutions (Ayllon and Azrin 1968). One obvious reason for this is that the institutional environment makes it possible to control reinforcers sufficiently to make tokens meaningful. However, these programmes also raise questions about the effects of an institutionalized environment on behaviour. Schaefer and Martin note the passivity of the patients, a characteristic noted by many observers (Rosenhan 1973; Schaefer and Martin 1966). Indeed, concern about the negative effects of institutionalization partially explains the shift from hospitalization to out-patient treatment after the discovery of drugs like chlorpromazine. This shift led to dramatic drops in hospitalization rates: from a peak in the early 1950s, hospitalization rates in the USA for mental disorders (of which schizophrenia represented a large proportion) dropped almost fourfold over the following 20 years (Bassuk and Gerson 1978). To some critics, the shift to minimal hospitalization (supplemented by out-patient services) has not been entirely positive. As negative as most hospital environments were, the failure to create appropriate community-based supports for individuals with schizophrenia and other disorders has often led to even greater neglect (Albee 2002; Shorter 1997; Thomas 1981).

The reason for engaging in this digression is twofold. First, it indicates that many of the behaviours modified in the above studies may have been related to *institutionalization*, not schizophrenia. Consequently, these studies may tell us little about the validity of the behaviourist model in terms of schizophrenia proper. Second, the emptying of institutions described above (a pattern repeated in most western countries) has meant that there are fewer opportunities to apply the behaviourist approach – particularly token economies. This, at least in part, accounts for the paucity of studies since the late 1960s. However, many of the principles of behaviour modification, if not the name, have been integrated into the repertoire of 'eclectic' therapists (see Krasner 1976).

Overall, the evidence suggests that certain forms of maladaptive behaviour can be modified by reinforcement, and this may have some benefit for overall functioning of individuals with schizophrenia. Beyond that, there seems little basis to suggest that maladaptive learning based on reinforcement is the sole, or even primary, *cause* of schizophrenia.

The Cognitive Approach

In dealing with schizophrenia, the cognitive approach has tended to focus on analysing the various types of symptoms, and suggesting explanations based on *faulty cognitive processing*. While these models do not represent a coherent whole, they nonetheless suggest interesting insights into the nature of schizophrenic behaviour. There are three aspects that we will focus on: delusions, language and thought disturbances.

At first glance, *delusions* are easy to define – they represent beliefs which seem to contradict reality. The difficulty with this, as Roger Brown has pointed out, is defining what constitutes reality (Brown 1972). When Milton Rokeach encountered three individuals who each believed himself to be Jesus Christ, he thought that confronting them with each other would be an effective therapeutic tool (Rokeach 1981). In fact, each remained steadfast in his belief, convinced the *others* were deluded. Ultimately, Rokeach came to regret his own actions, which did little to help the three men, citing his own 'Godlike delusion that I could change them by omnipotently and omnisciently arranging and rearranging their daily lives'.

While the three Christs fit the stereotype of delusions, in practice most individuals show much more limited delusional beliefs; for example, out of 25,000 patients in Michigan, USA, Rokeach found only a handful who had delusional identities. Moreover, delusional individuals typically recognize as false the delusions of *other* patients (Brown 1972). Hence, there is not a complete loss of commonly-defined reality, but only in specific content areas. For the moment, let us leave aside the question of *why* this might occur.

At one time, the *language* of individuals with schizophrenia was regarded as an incoherent babble, a 'word salad' or regression to infantile speech. However, in recent years, a number of analyses have suggested that this picture, like the stereotype of delusions, is inaccurate. Roger Brown, who is a specialist in the development of language, has declared that he has never encountered evidence of childlike utterances in individuals with schizophrenia (Brown 1972). Instead, words are simply used in ways that other individuals find strange. Often, it seems that particular words will have private significance to the individual, which can only be interpreted by a patient observer (Forest 1976; Maher 1972). Sometimes the difficulty seems to be a looseness of *connotation* – the associations which a word suggests, rather than its specific meaning (*denotation*). For example, the word 'life' might conjure up human birth (a new life), a magazine (*Life*), a party ('the life of …') and so on, leading to 'the baby came in the magazine and the noise was too much'. Unfortunately, developing a consistent model to explain such utterances on a case-by-case basis is a nearly impossible task (Rochester 1977). What is needed is an understanding of *why* individuals with schizophrenia sometimes use language in such idiosyncratic ways. Recent research has suggested that people with schizophrenia may have a particular difficulty in monitoring language, including their own speech, for errors (Stephane *et al.* 2006), but why this impairment should exist is unknown.

Similarly, *thought disturbances* can seem very puzzling. Two aspects that have garnered attention are faulty reference and logical errors. **Faulty reference** (sometimes considered a form of delusion) involves misinterpreting the significance of stimuli and events. For example, if a person on the street is observed frowning, the individual assumes that it is directed at them. A branch knocks against a window, and it is taken as a sign from God. In such cases, the person attributes a meaning to the event which most people would not. Logical errors, apparent lapses in reasoning, are a matter of some

faulty reference an error involving misinterpreting the significance of stimuli and events; while sometimes considered a form of delusion, it can also arise through faulty perceptual processing.

contention. Some theorists, like Silvano Arieti, believe such errors are based on the individual using a different form of reasoning (Arieti 1974). For example, the person may say, 'The Virgin Mary is a virgin. I am a virgin. Therefore I am the Virgin Mary.' In this case, the person is creating an identity based on the predicates of the first two statements being alike; in conventional logic, this is considered improper. However, if the person reasons this way consistently, then it could still be considered 'logical', albeit using unconventional rules. On the other hand, other theorists reject the idea that individuals with schizophrenia reason better, worse or differently, compared to normal individuals (Brown and Herrnstein 1975). For instance, there is a fairly consistent finding that people with delusions of persecution show biases in their reasoning, such as misattributions of the actions of others – but no more so than is found in the general population (Freeman 2007).

Considered together, these various phenomena can seem very puzzling, and somewhat bizarre. Yet one must remember that not all individuals with schizophrenia show all of these behaviours; in fact, even those that do manifest these symptoms tend to do so in limited ways. This leaves the question, how can these behaviours be explained? From a cognitive standpoint, one explanation suggested is that individuals with schizophrenia have a problem of **defective attention** – a difficulty in selecting and attending to the relevant stimuli in a situation (Braff 1993). Even Bleuler, in first defining schizophrenia, noted that individuals with schizophrenia seemed unable to keep their thoughts focused. Many individuals who have developed schizophrenia have described their early symptoms in terms of behaviours like memorizing trivial details, being easily distracted, or misinterpreting instructions (Chapman 1966). What is particularly striking is that they describe these behaviours not as personal preferences, but as something which they are *unable to control*.

defective attention a theory which argues that schizophrenia is due to difficulties in selecting and attending to the relevant stimuli in a situation.

Looked at in this context, many of the above symptoms seem understandable. Typically, we assume two people focus on the same 'evidence' when evaluating beliefs; if a person holds an anomalous belief, it is clearly a 'delusion'. Instead, delusions and faulty reference may arise from idiosyncratic selection and/or interpretation of information. Similarly, word salads and other language problems could arise because of an inability to ignore the connotations of words. The cumulative effect of such attention deficits could be to develop atypical beliefs (delusions), and to have difficulty with language and thought in ways that would hamper social interactions. In turn, the negative responses of other people would aggravate the social impact of the initial problem of defective attention. This pattern has been supported by studies indicating that attentional difficulties are one of the risk factors for developing schizophrenia (Alvarez-Moya *et al.* 2007; Cornblatt and Keilp 1994). Further support comes from prospective studies of children with a family history of schizophrenia, which indicate that attentional problems are relevant in identifying which children are at risk (Erlenmeyer-Kimling *et al.* 1993; Green 1993).

To understand *why* attention is defective, it is useful to think about the physiological basis of cognitive processes. As discussed in relation to the biological approach, a number of studies have identified various physiological defects, particularly in the frontal lobes, which are involved in many aspects of cognition. As a result, researchers are increasingly trying to find the basis for the cognitive impairments (Barch 2003; Holden 2003a). For example, Robert McCarley and his colleagues have collected EEG data indicating deficits in areas of the left hemisphere associated with language and attention (Craven 2002; McCarley *et al.* 2002; Potts *et al.* 2002). Studies utilizing tests which specifically reflect hemispheric competencies indicate that *left* hemispheric impairment is related to *negative* symptoms of schizophrenia, while *right* hemispheric impairment is related to *positive* symptoms (Caligiuri *et al.* 2005). Hence, the cognitive and biological approaches seem to be converging in their attempts to understand schizophrenia.

While no specific treatment technique has emerged from the defective attention theory, it does pose some interesting implications. One obvious attraction is that it suggests a common mechanism underlying many seemingly disparate symptoms, as discussed above. Also, it provides an explanation for why individuals with schizophrenia can function normally in some respects, while other behaviours seem very bizarre. Given the convergence with biological research noted above, knowledge about the cognitive aspects of schizophrenia may be increasingly useful in aspects like the evaluation and development of better drugs. Certainly, the future appears promising for more interaction between the approaches.

The Psychodynamic Approach

The psychodynamic approach views schizophrenia as a severe distortion of psychological functioning; that is, ego functioning is impaired, resulting in the loss of reality testing. To Freud, for example, schizophrenia reflected a regression to the oral or anal stages, during which the ego first develops. Because the child fails to develop a clear sense of the boundaries between the self and the outside world, the ego is later unable to effectively maintain reality testing, or cope with the demands of id. Freud saw this as resulting in the variety of symptomatic behaviours which we associate with schizophrenia. For example, the self-neglect and behavioural passivity found in schizophrenia, particularly the catatonic form, can be attributed to the distorted body image of a damaged ego. Similarly, the incomprehensible language is interpreted as infantile regression.

Objectively, there is little evidence to support the Freudian interpretation. As noted above, Roger Brown has challenged the notion that the language behaviour found in schizophrenia bears any resemblance to children's speech (Brown 1972). In terms of treatment, Freud himself did little with patients suffering from psychoses (severe distortions of reality), including schizophrenia. Since therapy involved developing insight into unconscious processes, there was a strong verbal component to treatment which often made it unsuited to such disorders (Luborsky and Spence 1978).

Other psychodynamic theorists have also offered interpretations of the origins of schizophrenia, and have attempted to provide treatment. In particular, analysts of the *object relations school* developed models based on the effects of early relationships (see Chapter 5). For example, Margaret Mahler, a neo-Freudian theorist who focused on personality development in infancy, suggested schizophrenia develops from the child's inability to separate from the mother. Mahler viewed this separation process as difficult for all individuals: 'not even the most normally endowed child, with the most optimally available mother, is able to weather the separation … process without crisis …' (Mahler *et al.* 1975, p. 229). In the case of schizophrenia, the mother and child form an intense interdependency, called a *symbiotic attachment*, which prevents the child from developing a healthy, distinct ego. This focus on mother–child relationships was most evident in Bateson's **double-bind hypothesis** (Bateson *et al.* 1956). Bateson suggested that the mother gives contradictory messages, like urging the child to 'come closer', but then shrinks from physical contact, which creates confusion and ambivalence for the child. However, this model has been attacked for depending largely on retrospective analysis of communication patterns within families of individuals with schizophrenia. This makes it impossible to know if

double-bind hypothesis a theory of schizophrenia developed by anthropologist Gregory Bateson and his colleagues, which argues that faulty communication patterns within the family are the cause of schizophrenia.

the way family members communicate is the cause of schizophrenia, or a *result* of trying to cope with the behaviours associated with schizophrenia.

At this point, the double-bind hypothesis has been largely discredited (Neill 1990). However, the idea that family relationships play a factor in the development of schizophrenia has led to interest in **expressed emotion**. Expressed emotion refers to communication patterns which are marked by high levels of criticism, hostility and emotional intensity (Butzlaff and Hooley 1998; Jenkins and Karno 1992). Unlike the double-bind hypothesis, the theory does not focus on expressed emotion as a *cause* of schizophrenia; instead, it focuses on *relapse rates*. Essentially, the theory argues that relapse rates are much higher when individuals with schizophrenia reside in families with high levels of expressed emotion (for example, see McNab *et al.* 2007). In effect, criticizing and blaming the individual for their disorder seems to create a stressor of the type described by the diathesis-stress model. In the past decade, studies have indicated that expressed emotion is a factor in relapse rates in many countries, despite cultural differences in average levels of expressed emotion. For example, a study done in Iran found that high family levels of expressed emotion were related to relapse rates, especially for males with schizophrenia (Mottaghipour *et al.* 2001). (We will return to this point at the end of the chapter.) In one sense, expressed emotion theory is an offspring of the double-bind hypothesis, which first focused attention on communication patterns within the family. However, expressed emotion theory has a much narrower focus, emphasizing recovery rather than causation. While this may be realistic, it means the theory does not help to clarify the origins of schizophrenia.

> **expressed emotion** a pattern of communication within families which is characterized by high levels of criticism, hostility and emotional intensity.

In terms of treatment, we must conclude that psychodynamic approaches do not seem well suited to treatment of schizophrenia (as Freud first noted), though individual analysts have claimed some success (Kohut 1977). While research on expressed emotion seems promising, the psychodynamic approach generally does not fare very well in dealing with the complexities of schizophrenia.

The Humanistic Approach

Like the psychodynamic approach, the humanistic approach emphasizes distortions of development. However, it interprets the origins of the distortions very differently from Freud or other psychodynamic theorists. The behaviours which are labelled as 'schizophrenia' represent the individual's response to the world, however distorted it may seem to other people. For the therapist, the essential concern is to try to understand what the person is experiencing. As Rollo May has said, focusing on the *how* and *why* of the individual's condition will result in understanding 'everything except the most important thing of all, the existing person' (May 1961, p. 25). Not surprisingly, humanistic therapists tend to de-emphasize diagnostic schemes like the DSM, which are intended to categorize people in restrictive ways.

What is it that the person is experiencing in schizophrenia? In some sense, it seems that the person sees the demands of the environment as conflicting intensely with the needs of the self. R. D. Laing, a psychoanalytically-trained British psychiatrist who came to adopt a humanistic view, talked about it as 'the divided self' – a split created by the need for 'compliance with the other person's intentions or expectations for one's self' (Laing 1965, p. 98). In Rogerian terms, externally imposed *conditions of worth* lead to an extreme lack of congruence. For some individuals, the incongruence created by the demands of others can result in a virtual dissolution of the individual's sense of self (for example, Vonnegut 1975). If the external demands are sufficiently threatening, then withdrawal from social interaction can seem a reasonable option in order

depersonalization a type of dissociative reaction in which the individual psychologically withdraws from a situation, often accompanied by feeling that their body is not real or belongs to someone else.

to preserve some part of the self. This withdrawal, accompanied by a 'splitting off' of the self, is sometimes called **depersonalization** by clinicians; it is worth noting that such reactions are at least occasionally experienced by most people under stressful circumstances. As Brown and Herrnstein have noted, it is a sense of looking at the situation from outside, accompanied by the feeling that 'this isn't really happening to *me*' (Brown and Herrnstein 1975).

However the process is described, humanistic theories argue that the threats to the self produce a profound sense of distress and loss of self-awareness, which result in the characteristic behaviours seen in schizophrenia. Since withdrawal from social interaction is often part of the response, it seems hard to fathom how humanistic therapy could proceed. However, Rogers and other clinicians have successfully used *person-centred therapy* in working with individuals with schizophrenia (Rogers *et al.* 1967; Teusch 1990). Basically, the process depends on the therapist first convincing the individual that the therapist is concerned, and is not a threat. Often, this may require long periods, sitting quietly with the person, waiting for a sign of possible interaction. In one case, Rogers worked with a 28-year-old man named Jim who had been hospitalized for two and a half years. After months of weekly meetings which passed mostly in silence, Jim finally began to speak. After several more sessions, he began to reveal feelings of bitterness, mistrust and worthlessness. Near the end of one session, Jim, expressing his frustration, said, 'I want to go, 'cause I don't care what happens.' Rogers responded to this by saying, 'I'd just like to say – I care about you. And I care what happens' (Rogers *et al.* 1967). The conversation in which this exchange occurred marked a turning point in the therapeutic process; several months later, Jim was discharged from the hospital and began a job. Eight years later, he spontaneously wrote to Rogers to say that he was still employed, had friends and felt content with his life (Meador and Rogers 1979).

While this example typifies the Rogerian approach, and suggests that it may be useful with schizophrenia, there are a number of unresolved issues. Given the poor reliability of diagnostic standards in the early 1960s, it is conceivable that Jim would not be diagnosed as schizophrenic under current criteria. More generally, there is a concern that, like other insight therapies, person-centred therapy is not likely to have a very high overall success rate, because of the need for verbal interaction. Prouty (1990) has claimed that person-centred therapy is possible with a variety of 'non-verbal' individuals, including those with mental retardation as well as schizophrenia. However, the number of cases may be too small to be very representative.

In summary, the humanistic approach suggests that schizophrenia is an expression of the vulnerability of the self, and an attempt to adapt to a threatening social environment. Although this notion of social stress seems consistent with the *diathesis-stress* model of schizophrenia, humanists have been largely silent on the question of *diathesis*. That is, is there a physiological defect which predisposes someone to develop schizophrenia, as the biological approach asserts? Or is it simply a psychosocial phenomenon? Humanists don't address this, because their concern is with the person's experience and suffering, not potential physiological defects (whether as causes or consequences of the disorder). In the long run, it remains to be seen if this is sufficient for understanding schizophrenia. In the meantime, it is clear that Rogerian therapy emphasizes the caring which has been identified as a beneficial factor in all therapies (Frank 1963; Stiles *et al.* 1986). If expressions of hostility and criticism hamper recovery (as research on *expressed emotion* indicates), then caring and acceptance by others may in fact open the door to growth, and rediscovery of the self.

Try it Yourself

Given the discussion of how the various approaches view schizophrenia, do you believe that psychotherapy should be seen as an alternative to the use of drugs, or simply an adjunct? And which approach do you see as most suitable to this role? Do you think that one form of therapy might be better than others for individual symptoms of schizophrenia? For example, which therapy would you recommend if the primary symptoms were delusions? What if the primary symptoms were negative symptoms?

Evaluating Our Understanding of Schizophrenia

As we have seen, each of the approaches has something to say about the nature of schizophrenia, and how to help those who suffer from it. The explanations offered differ significantly, however, and so do the attitudes which are implied. In this sense, schizophrenia provides perhaps the clearest example of how the approaches differ in their views of abnormal behaviour.

Resolving these differences requires a better understanding of what schizophrenia is. Is it a physiological disorder? A form of learned dysfunction? An arbitrary social construct? All of these? One way of gaining some perspective on the issue is by looking at how other cultures view it. A major study by the World Health Organization in the 1970s looked at schizophrenia in ten countries, reflecting both industrialized and developing societies (Jablensky *et al.* 1992). Using agreed-upon diagnostic criteria, the researchers in each country identified new cases of schizophrenia, and followed the course of treatment for two years; altogether, they considered almost 1400 cases. In terms of overall incidence rates, types of symptoms, and even average age of onset, there was remarkable similarity across cultures. This tends to suggest that there is some common cause which is unrelated to culture – in other words, a physiological factor (for more details, see Box 9.8).

While there was broad consistency in incidence rates and diagnosis, the results of treatment were startling: over two years, the rate of recovery in industrialized countries was only 37 per cent, whereas in developing countries it was 63 per cent – nearly double! This result is surprising, since we tend to view medical care as superior in industrialized countries. (In fact, individuals in the developing countries were more likely to seek folk remedies, and less likely to receive drugs.) Unless one is prepared to argue that drugs actually hamper recovery (an unlikely possibility), how can one account for the pattern of results? A number of possible factors may contribute, including social structures. For example, individuals in developing countries may find it easier to remain part of society by finding useful work, because jobs tend to be less specialized. In addition, extended families living together are more common in developing countries, which places less of a burden for support on just one or two caregivers.

While these things may play a role, a more significant factor seems to be differences in attitudes (Lin and Kleinman 1988). People in developing countries typically have less rigid conceptions of abnormality, and are less likely to view the behaviour as permanent, thus reducing *stigmatizing*. In general, families in developing countries are more supportive towards a member who has schizophrenia than is true in industrialized nations (Jenkins and Karno 1992). The reasons for this may have to do with *expressed emotion*, and also *attributions*. While families high in expressed emotion can be found in all cultures, they appear to be more common in industrialized nations. This may reflect the fact that the industrialized (western) nations tend to favour

Box 9.8 A Cross-cultural Look at Schizophrenia

In 1973, the World Health Organization began conducting cross-cultural studies on schizophrenia. Over time, these studies have expanded to include more than 20 countries. The results, and those of other researchers, indicate that the occurrence rate of schizophrenia is roughly the same across cultures. In addition, the same core symptoms seem to be universal: restricted affect, lack of insight, poor social rapport, widespread bizarre delusions, incoherent speech and thinking aloud. As noted in the chapter, the commonality of symptoms across cultures is most readily explained in terms of an underlying physiological mechanism – thus supporting the biological approach to the understanding of schizophrenia.

However, research has also indicated that there can be culturally-specific variations in symptoms. For example, in Columbia, India and Nigeria, waking early, depressed facial features, and expressions of extreme elation appear commonly as symptoms. Also, in India, schizophrenic symptoms tend to cluster around self-isolation, in contrast to the traditional emphasis on interdependence in Indian culture. In Nigeria, individuals with schizophrenia tend to show more suspicious orientation toward others with bizarre fears and thoughts, in common with the traditional Nigerian view of illness being caused by evil forces. For example, in Nigeria, one man's schizophrenia was preceded by his mother's confession that she practised witchcraft (Brislin 2000).

While cultural differences point to the influence of learning rather than physiology in the expression of schizophrenia, specifying the relevant element is difficult. For example, several studies have found differences in symptoms for members of the same ethnic group living in different places. Thus, African-Caribbeans living in London were more likely to exhibit delusions and paranoia than African-Caribbeans living in Trinidad (Bhugra *et al.* 2000). Similarly, Pakistanis living in London showed more similarity in the content of delusions and hallucinations to native Britons in London than to Pakistanis living in Pakistan (Suhail and Cochrane 2002). Thus, while cultural background may be relevant to the type of symptoms expressed in schizophrenia, the local environment also seems to matter. For clinicians trying to diagnose and offer treatment, the complexities can be daunting.

As noted in the chapter, the World Health Organization's studies have indicated that the prognosis for recovery is better for poorer patients living in developing countries such as India and Nigeria than for those living in Europe and North America. While the reasons for this are still not entirely clear, Draguns (2001) attributes it to the fact that less industrialized, more collectivist societies tend to provide more social and practical support for the schizophrenic individual, thereby aiding recovery. Whatever the explanation is, the cross-cultural data strongly suggest that recovery is *not* simply a matter of taking the right drug. As in discussions of aetiology, treatment of schizophrenia seems to involve an interaction of physiological and environmental factors.

individualist rather than collectivist notions of the self, and to emphasize personal responsibility. Given these attributional biases, families within this cultural context tend to blame the mentally ill for their actions, and believe they can control their symptoms 'if they just try' (Hooley and Campbell 2002). These effects suggest that cultural factors must be integrated as a basic element of our understanding of schizophrenia and other forms of abnormal behaviour (Fabrega 1995).

Certainly, the differences in recovery rates cannot easily be explained if one assumes that schizophrenia is purely physiological. Instead, it seems that environmental factors, including culture, play a role as well. This conclusion, which seems to support the diathesis-stress model, may help explain why each of the approaches has *some* benefit as therapy. At the same time, it leaves us to ponder how our *own* culture views schizophrenia and abnormal behaviour in general.

CONCLUSION

Abnormal psychology is concerned with the understanding of *abnormal behaviour*. The question of what constitutes abnormal behaviour is a difficult one. While it always implies some form of *deviance* from expected norms of behaviour, deviance is not in itself a reasonable basis for defining mental disorders, since it is too dependent on cultural values. Instead, the generally accepted definition today is that abnormal behaviour involves significant *suffering* and/or *maladaptive functioning*. Although these criteria seem intuitively reasonable, they still pose problems of *who decides* what is maladaptive and what represents significant suffering.

Viewed conceptually, abnormal psychology involves three aspects: diagnosis of the problem, understanding the cause of the problem, and therapy to treat the problem. In practice, the three elements are closely intertwined, making it hard to assess one element independently of the others. Hence, while each of the five approaches has its own interpretation of the origins of abnormal behaviour, at present the primary means of assessing the various theories is by examining their *efficacy* as therapies.

To the extent that it is possible to determine, the evidence suggests that *all* the approaches have some value, but that *no* approach is superior for *all* forms of disorders. One explanation for this outcome may be that there are *non-specific effects* of therapy in general, such as emotional support provided by the therapist, and the individual's belief that therapy can help. Another possible reason for the partial effectiveness of most therapies is that many patterns of abnormal behaviour may have multiple causes. For example, a particular disorder may be triggered by a physiological imbalance, which can be treated with drug therapy. However, in trying to adapt to that imbalance, the individual may have developed other maladaptive behaviours which drugs will not change. Because mental states can affect the functioning of the body, it is also possible that observed physiological factors represent a consequence, rather than the cause, of abnormal behaviour (for example, experiencing serious depression seems to produce brain changes that leave the individual more vulnerable to depression in the future). Whether as cause or consequence, to deal with behavioural aspects, some form of psychotherapy may be appropriate – though at present we have too little information to determine which approach is best in a particular circumstance, or why.

The limitations of our current knowledge are particularly evident when considering *schizophrenia*. While neuroleptic drugs have proven effective in alleviating delusions, hallucinations and other positive symptoms of the disorder, the *medical model* on which drug therapy is based has not yet produced a clear explanation of the mechanism of action. Similarly, the *diathesis-stress* model, which suggests that schizophrenia results from a combination of a physiological disposition and the effects of environmental stressors, seems promising, but is as yet unproven.

At this point, we must admit that we still have no clear understanding of the causes of schizophrenia, or how to treat it. Interestingly, some cultures seem to deal with it better than we do – a reminder that there is a social dimension to abnormal behaviour. While most clinicians believe that normality and abnormality are part of a continuum, too many people in our society still view mental disorders as something strange and frightening – and 'different'. Not only does this limit the understanding of abnormal behaviour, it also hampers treatment by *stigmatizing* individuals with mental disorders. Consider this example: suppose that schizophrenia really is based on *defective attention*, which leads people to behave in idiosyncratic ways. In itself, this defect may hamper the individual in some ways, but if the quirkiness of their behaviour (or society's perception of it) leads to the person being stigmatized and rejected, then the effects of social isolation will create further problems. (On the other hand, psychopathology has often been linked to creativity. To evaluate this, see *The World Today: Creativity and Psychopathology*.) The challenge is to understand the core problem, but respond to the *person*, not simply the problem.

The world today: **Creativity and Psychopathology**

It's not surprising that many people have likened psychopathology to creativity. Some of the delusions that people with schizophrenia reveal may seem like the product of a highly creative mind, as may the original use of language in the word salad that may be heard. But are there really linkages between psychopathology and creativity? Research indicates that the answer depends on what kind of psychopathology and what type of creativity are being examined. A review of studies examining the relationship between mental disorders and creativity found that some sort of relationship does exist, but it is far from clear-cut (Lauronen *et al.* 2004). In the case of schizophrenia, the reviewers concluded that the evidence suggests that while some creative people can develop schizophrenia, in general most people with schizophrenia are less creative than usual. Interestingly, though, there may be an exceptional number of creative people among the relatives of those who have schizophrenia. This suggests that some of the symptoms shown in schizophrenia may also be present in a less extreme form in relatives (who share some genes), and that these qualities may be related to creativity. Supporting this is evidence from studying schizotypal personality disorder. This disorder shows some of the positive symptoms characteristic of schizophrenia, such as magical thinking and unusual perceptual experiences. People with schizotypal personality disorder have a greater vulnerability to developing schizophrenia than people without the disorder, but most do not. These people also show better performance on measures of divergent thinking and creativity, as well as more activity in the prefrontal right cortex (Fisher *et al.* 2004). Nettle (2006) studied this further, paying particular attention to different areas of creativity. He found that poetry and art are more closely associated with divergent thinking, schizophrenia and mood disorders, while mathematical creativity is more closely associated with convergent thinking and autism. Mood disorders, especially those with manic components (bipolar disorder, hypomania or cyclothymia) show a stronger relationship to creativity than any other mental disorder (Lauronen *et al.* 2004).

That there is a relationship of some sort between some forms of mental disorders and some forms of creativity seems clear, but again we must stress the limitations of the research. All studies examining this are, of course, correlational. Recall that this means that we cannot conclude that mental disorders *cause* a person to be more creative, or that creativity *causes* a vulnerability to mental disorders, or whether some other factor or factors may be instrumental in the occurrence of both creativity and mental disorders. It is interesting to speculate, however, that perhaps some traits in some people lead to creativity, while more extreme expression of these traits leads to psychopathology. Much more research will need to be conducted, however, before we can speculate further on this.

In the end, behaviour, whether normal or abnormal, is still *human* behaviour. As travellers on the human journey, we are all alike, and ignoring this reality ultimately diminishes our capacity to understand *any* aspect of human experience. As R. D. Laing said in *The Divided Self*, there is still too much talk of Them, and not enough of Us (Laing 1965).

One may argue that this is a social issue, not a scientific one. Yet the whole premise of this book is that psychology is the product of human beings, and is therefore influenced by the processes which affect all human behaviour. Each of us brings to the study of behaviour our own perceptions and cognitive schemata, based on our past experience. Part of that past experience, of course, is the culture we live in. If our culture encourages us to view abnormal behaviour as Us vs. Them, then that perception will influence our theories as well. This is not to suggest that everything is a construction of our minds – the behaviour we seek to explain is real. Instead, it is simply meant to point out that we each tend to see only part of the overall picture, and this partial vision tends to be reflected in our theories. In this sense, the struggle to understand abnormal behaviour, and the perplexities that surround it, reflects the larger challenges which face psychology as a whole.

CHAPTER SUMMARY

■ *Abnormal psychology* is concerned with the understanding of *abnormal behaviour*. While definitions have varied historically, it has typically been defined in terms of *deviance* from society's norms. Today, *DSM-IV-TR* identifies significant *suffering* and/or *maladaptive functioning* as the primary criteria.

■ Critics have questioned the value of classification systems like DSM-IV-TR, citing problems of misdiagnosis and the *stigmatizing* effects of labels, but most psychiatrists and other clinicians find classification useful.

■ Each of the five approaches has its own interpretation of the origins of abnormal behaviour, such as *depression*; evaluation of these theories is closely tied to the assessment of the efficacy of therapies based on the theories.

■ The *biological approach* emphasizes physiological and genetic factors, in terms of the *medical model*. The effectiveness of drug therapy has made great progress as our knowledge of psychopharmacology has grown in recent years. As evidence for prenatal trauma as well as environmental influences grows, the *diathesis-stress* model is drawing more attention.

■ The *behaviourist approach* sees abnormal behaviour as based on learning of inappropriate responses. Techniques of *behaviour modification*, such as *systematic desensitization*, have been used to treat a variety of problems; *token economies* have been used in institutional settings like hospitals.

■ The *cognitive approach*, consistent with its general view, emphasizes the role of cognitive mediators in abnormal behaviour. Social learning theory has been applied to the use of behaviour modification, resulting in *cognitive behaviour modification*. Other *cognitive therapies*, such as Ellis's *rational-emotive therapy*, have focused on the faulty beliefs which accompany maladaptive behaviour. Like psychodynamic and humanistic therapies, cognitive therapy places an emphasis on *insight* into one's behaviour.

■ Within the *psychodynamic approach*, Freud saw abnormal behaviour as the result of unconscious conflicts within the psyche; therapy was based on helping the individual gain awareness of the underlying dynamics. Psychodynamic therapy can be difficult to evaluate, since its goals are often fairly global, involving modifying the whole structure of personality. However, *interpersonal therapy* seems to be effective in treating depression. With regard to schizophrenia, while the *double-bind hypothesis* has been largely refuted, it has led to interest in *expressed emotions* in families as a factor in relapses.

■ The *humanistic approach* rejects classification in favour of trying to understand how the individual experiences the world. Abnormal behaviour is regarded as a distortion of growth, with the maladaptive behaviours representing an attempt to cope with threats to the *self*.

Rogers's *person-centred therapy* often results in changes in how individuals express their feelings and goals, but it is harder to assess whether it leads to behavioural change.

- *Schizophrenia* is one of the most challenging forms of mental disorder, and has been the focus of considerable research. Though the term itself is less than a hundred years old, the primary symptoms of *delusions, hallucinations, thought disturbances* and *distortions of emotional expression* have been recorded since ancient times.

- The effectiveness of neuroleptic drugs in treating the primary symptoms has led to theories of schizophrenia based on neurotransmitter imbalances. These theories, such as the *dopamine hypothesis*, have drawn considerable attention, but difficulties still exist with both the theories and the use of drugs in treatment.

- Studies of *heredity* and physiological factors have failed to identify a single factor present in all cases, even for specific sub-types of schizophrenia. This has led to development of the *diathesis-stress model*, which suggests that schizophrenia results from a combination of a physiological predisposition and the effects of environmental stressors. This 'two-hit' model has the advantage of not specifying a single genetic or physiological cause, and seems consistent with the available evidence on both predisposing factors and the impact of environmental stressors.

- The other approaches interpret schizophrenia in terms of *maladaptive learning* of various types. Of these, the *defective-attention theory* of the cognitive approach seems to offer the greatest potential to enhance our understanding, possibly in conjunction with the medical model. However, it has not yet resulted in any specific therapy.

- In the end, the study of abnormal behaviour, including schizophrenia, challenges our perceptions of ourselves and our relationship to other people. In this sense, progress in understanding abnormal behaviour is likely to depend on our progress in psychology as a whole.

Key terms and concepts

abnormal behaviour
medical model
stigma
depression
phobia
behaviour modification
systematic desensitization
aversive conditioning
token economy
cognitive behaviour modification
rational-emotive therapy
cognitive restructuring
insight
symptom substitution
transference

resistance
interpersonal therapy
person-centred therapy
efficacy
psychotherapy
spontaneous remission
schizophrenia
positive symptoms
negative symptoms
dopamine hypothesis
diathesis-stress model
defective-attention theory
expressed emotion
depersonalization

Online Learning Centre

When you have read this chapter, log onto the Online Learning Centre website at **www.openup.co.uk/glassman** where you will find answers to these Test Yourself questions and suggested answers to the Try it Yourself activities, plus many more learning resources to help you study psychology.

Test yourself questions

1 Describe the axes of the DSM classification system.

2 What role does the biological approach believe that genetics plays in the aetiology of mental disorders?

3 What are positive symptoms of schizophrenia? What are negative symptoms of schizophrenia?

4 What is expressed emotion? What role does it play in schizophrenia?

Suggestions for Further Reading

■ For readers wondering what it is like to have a mental disorder, **Dale Peterson's** *A Mad People's History of Madness* (1982) provides a remarkable collection of autobiographical accounts. For an individual account of schizophrenia, read **Mark Vonnegut's** *The Eden Express* (1975).

■ For a layman's guide to understanding depression and other mood disorders, try *Depression and Bipolar Disorders* by **Virginia Edwards** (2002). For a candid account of a mood disorder by a psychologist who suffers from one, read **Kay Redfield Jamison's** *An Unquiet Mind* (1995).

■ For a fascinating exploration of society's attitudes towards abnormal behaviour in the recent past, *Back to the Asylum*, by **LaFond and Durham** (1992), covers legal and social as well as scientific aspects.

■ While no longer completely current, **Samuel Baronides's** *Molecules and Mental Illness* (1993) effectively conveys the biological approach to mental disorders in a brief, readable book. For approaches other than the biological, two sources are recommended: *The Evolution of Psychotherapy*, edited by **Jeffrey Zeig** (1987), provides the views of 26 well-known therapists, based on an extraordinary conference which brought them together to discuss their ideas. For a more technical overview, **Gurman and Messer's** *Essential Psychotherapies: Theory and Practice* (1995) provides reviews of 12 major forms of therapy (including all of those discussed in this chapter).

■ For an overview of research on various aspects of schizophrenia, **Walter Heinrichs's** *In Search of Madness* (2001) provides a broad-ranging, albeit somewhat technical, source. *Reconceiving Schizophrenia*, a book of readings edited by **Chung et al.** (2007), is also worth exploring. **Robert Whitaker's** *Mad in America* (2002) provides both a history of schizophrenia and a withering critique.

■ You may also want to consider **Sylvia Nasar's** *A Beautiful Mind* (1998), or the movie of the same name adapted from it. While the movie is somewhat dramatized, both chronicle the life of John Nash, a brilliant Nobel Prize-winning mathematician who suffered from paranoid schizophrenia, but with a supportive wife and community, has recovered to be a professor at Princeton University.

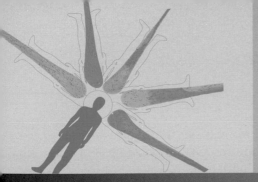

Chapter 10

Psychology in Perspective

LEARNING OBJECTIVES

In this chapter, the objectives are to learn:

- ☑ the way perception affects theory formation
- ☑ the role of paradigms within psychology
- ☑ the limitations of the scientific method
- ☑ new methodologies, as exemplified by chaos theory and systems theory
- ☑ the role of culture in studying psychology
- ☑ the possibilities of convergence or pluralism in the future of psychology

SEARCHING FOR ANSWERS

There is an old story about a man who had accomplished many things in his life – inventing new products, acquiring a great fortune and becoming famous. Yet still, he felt a sense of incompleteness, as though somehow the real meaning of life had eluded him.

One day, he heard of a hermit who lived on a far-off mountain. Despite the remoteness of the location, many people journeyed to visit the hermit, because he was reputed to know the secret of life. Like these travellers, the dissatisfied man decided to seek out the hermit.

After a long and difficult journey, the man finally located him. He lived in a simple shack, with no running water or electricity – yet his eyes glowed with what seemed great joy. Sensing that the rumours might be true, the man pressed the hermit for the secret of life. The hermit looked at him, with his fine clothes and belongings, and said, 'If you wish to know the secret, you must first give away all your money and possessions.'

At this, the man hesitated. He thought about it for some time, and finally agreed, having realized that his possessions had not made him happy anyway.

Finally, the hermit spoke. 'The secret of life is –' He paused, drawing out the suspense, and then whispered, 'there *is* no secret!'

INTRODUCTION

Like the man in the story, you have been on a journey. Rather than crossing unfamiliar terrain, you have been venturing into a domain of new ideas. In some ways, such journeys are more difficult than physical journeys, because they challenge us to think in new ways. Having gone through the previous chapters, you should have a better understanding of what psychology is, and what research has been able to tell us about human behaviour. Hopefully, you have found the experience both interesting and challenging. Interesting, in that psychology is concerned with who and what we are, and most of us would like to understand more about both ourselves and other people. Challenging, because psychology is full of unanswered questions and controversies, and this book has tried to explore those controversies, rather than hide them behind a mass of facts. Exploring ideas is a kind of adventure, and psychology is fertile territory for such adventures. In much the way that a hired guide helps explorers, this book has tried to guide your experience, to help you past the worst difficulties and confusions. While it is hoped that you will venture further in the future, it seems an opportune moment to look back over the ground we have covered, and try to get some sense of what may lie ahead.

RECONSIDERING THE ORIGINS OF THE APPROACHES

In the preceding chapters, we have explored five major approaches to the study of human behaviour. Each approach seems to offer its own interpretation, and on many issues, there seems to be significant disagreement – for example, in explaining the origins of aggression. Consequently, it is understandable if at this point, like the man in the story, you are tempted to ask for a simple answer to a basic question: 'Which one is right?' Like the man in the story, you may be disappointed at the response.

The answer, of course, is all of them, and none of them. All of them, in that each approach has had significant impact on our view of ourselves. None of them, in that no one approach has been able to successfully explain the full range of human behaviour and experience. As we have discussed, each approach still leaves gaps, and major questions unanswered. While often the approaches are complementary rather than conflicting, there are still significant issues on which they continue to disagree.

The diversity of approaches poses a contradiction: while the approaches differ in assumptions, methods and explanations, each claims to be offering the appropriate basis for psychology. Normally, a discipline is defined by its assumptions and methods, as well as its subject matter. How can one speak of psychology as a single discipline, when there is no single framework which underlies it? One answer, suggested by cognitive psychologist George Miller, is to assert that what unites psychology is the faith that eventually a common framework will be found (Miller 1985). This framework will provide 'a science of immediate experience' – Miller's description of psychology's central focus. But why isn't there such a framework already? And if no such framework exists after more than 100 years, is it reasonable to hope for one in the future? In order to answer these questions, we need to return to the subject of how different approaches originate.

Perception and Theory Formation

In Chapter 1, we looked at some of the basic principles of perception, and noted that the way we see the world depends both on what is 'out there' to be experienced, and on the mental processes 'inside' the person. That is, perception is based on the interaction of external stimuli and our cognitive processes (selection, organization and interpretation). Because of those internal processes, what we experience in any situation is influenced by what we expect to experience. In extreme cases, our perceptions may depend more on our interpretation than on the actual stimulus, as illustrated by the following incident. A few years ago, a Japanese exchange student in Louisiana, USA, was seeking directions to a party. Lost, he approached a house to get information; the owner, perceiving him as a threat, shot and killed the student before he even spoke. We can call it a tragedy, which it certainly is, but we must also acknowledge the power of the processes that led to that tragedy (for example, what experiences and attitudes led the homeowner to fear the approach of a stranger?). Given the vast range of stimuli we encounter, we select certain elements, and then interpret them using our current cognitive schemata. In this sense, the reality we experience is individually constructed.

As human beings, psychologists are also dependent on the processes of perceptual selection and interpretation. This is reflected in the different assumptions and methods which are central to the various approaches. As Sigmund Koch, a psychologist noted for his interest in such issues, has commented, 'Different theorists will – relative to their different analytical purposes, predictive or practical aims, perceptual sensitivities, metaphor-forming capacities and pre-existing discrimination repertoires – make asystematically different perceptual cuts upon the same domain' (Koch 1985, p. 93). In effect, all theorists, having differing interests and expectations, will perceive the world in their own way, and will develop their theories accordingly. Philosopher Bertrand Russell had this in mind when he commented that animals in psychological research seem to match the theories of their experimenters: American (behaviourist) animals use trial and error, while German (cognitive) animals are reflective (cited by Skinner 1974, p. 18)!

cognitive pathology a phenomenon whereby researchers selectively ignore simplifying assumptions and other limitations which are part of the foundations of their theories and methods.

Hence, the origin of any approach is dependent on processes which are partly subjective. Failing to recognize this can lead to becoming blind to the limitations of one's own approach – what Koch has called **cognitive pathology**. Cognitive pathology is reflected in practices like making simplifying assumptions that lead to restrictions in what one observes, and then developing 'total amnesia' for those assumptions and restrictions. This could happen, for instance, if a researcher operationally defines aggression as punching an inflatable doll in a laboratory, and then assumes *without further evidence* that the results of a study based on this definition can be applied to homicide. Similarly, when researchers assume a behaviour is 'universal' without examining other cultures, this would be a form of cognitive pathology. Indeed, it can be argued that without recognizing the role of underlying assumptions and methods, it is impossible to properly evaluate any conclusion. In this regard, the tendency for many authors to present psychology as a collection of facts has questionable value, and may even be hostile to the possibility of real understanding.

Because our assumptions affect our judgement about what is relevant in interpreting a situation, different approaches may view the same event differently. For example, suppose two researchers examine the same experiment, dealing with the effects of television viewing on aggression in children. One asserts that the results can be generalized to everyday life, while the other insists that the laboratory study lacks realism, and cannot be applied to the real world. If the argument actually reflects differing assumptions about the causes of aggression, but this is not acknowledged, then no real dialogue is possible. It is not simply the validity of generalizing, but the entire meaning of the evidence, that is at issue.

The idea that our assumptions affect the way we reason was supported in a study conducted by Eric Amsel (Amsel *et al.* 1991). In conjunction with a lawyer and another psychologist, Amsel studied the way that lawyers and psychologists evaluate the causes of events. They found that lawyers are trained to reason mechanistically, using counterfactual arguments, whereas psychologists are trained to reason statistically, using covariance arguments. As a result, the two groups tend to explain behaviour differently. For example, consider this situation: David was watching TV, and the picture was poor. He kicked the set, and the picture improved. Given this scenario, a lawyer might justify David's behaviour by suggesting that if he had not kicked it, the picture would not have improved (a counterfactual argument). By contrast, a psychologist might explain it by noting that on several past occasions, kicking the set led to the picture improving (a covariance argument). The point here is not that one argument is necessarily better than the other, but that they depend on different assumptions about what makes an argument convincing. In the same way, advocates of different approaches make different assumptions about behaviour. Understanding those assumptions can help to clarify the ways in which the approaches disagree – hence the emphasis throughout this book on the assumptions that the different approaches make.

While perceptual processes help us to understand how different approaches can arise, they do not answer the question of whether one approach is better than another. After all, the fact that advocates of various approaches perceive the world differently does not automatically mean that all see it *equally accurately*. Instead, it is *logically* possible that one theory is superior at explaining the world. Does it therefore follow that one approach actually is better? And how do we decide?

Try it Yourself

Did you find yourself drawn to any of the five approaches? Which of the five do you prefer? Why? Did you find that any of the approaches didn't appeal to you? Why not? Try to poll some of your classmates, to see their preferences. What do you conclude from these results?

Objective Evidence vs. Shifting Paradigms

Traditionally, psychology has been founded on the premise of **logical empiricism**, a principle shared with the sciences in general. Logical empiricism says that it is possible to evaluate theories in terms of how well they account for the evidence (Savage 1990). This principle is an extension of the basic belief in *empiricism*, which states that observing the world is the way to gain knowledge. However, accepting that observation is *necessary* in science does not necessarily imply that observational evidence is a *sufficient* basis for evaluating a theory. Consequently, logical empiricism is a possible, but not inevitable, result of accepting the importance of observations.

logical empiricism in philosophy of science, the assumption that it is possible to compare and evaluate theories in terms of how well they account for the evidence.

Logical empiricism says that theories are evaluated, and either accepted or discarded, on the weight of the evidence. As the history of the natural sciences over the past 200 years has demonstrated, it can be a very productive framework for enhancing knowledge, especially when dealing with the inanimate world of atoms and molecules. However, it does have limitations. For one thing, evidence is more useful for discarding an incorrect theory than for determining what is a correct theory. Indeed, statistical theory tells us that observations cannot directly prove a theory to be true (see the Appendix for further discussion of this point). In addition, it has been argued that demonstrating a 'good fit' between the evidence and a theory is too limiting as a means of evaluation (Roberts and Pashler 2000).

Given these limitations of logical empiricism, it is important to remember that it is not the only possible framework – and in recent years, it has been challenged. The primary alternative interpretation for why theories get accepted is **social constructionism**, which looks at science in terms of the role of social processes. One of the earliest, and best-known, expressions of this view was a book called *The Structure of Scientific Revolutions*, by philosopher of science Thomas Kuhn (Kuhn 1970). Kuhn asserts that science operates in terms of **paradigms** – frameworks which are endorsed by a group of adherents. Rather than being simply a theory, a paradigm represents an entire way of seeing the world. As Kuhn states, in a new paradigm, 'old terms, concepts, and experiments fall into new relationships with each other' (Kuhn 1970, p. 148).

social constructionism in philosophy of science, the idea that the formation and assessment of theories are primarily influenced by social processes rather than empirical evidence.

paradigm in Kuhn's analysis of science, a super-ordinate framework or world view accepted by a group of researchers, which shapes both theories and evidence; since the paradigm influences the observations one makes, no observations can ever be used to evaluate the paradigm.

As a basic framework for our concepts, a paradigm is more basic than a theory; indeed, different theories can exist within the same paradigm (for example, Pavlov and Skinner both developed theories within behaviourism as a paradigm, each dealing with different types of responses). Since theories exist within a particular paradigm, sometimes a new theory actually represents a change in paradigm as well. For example, Einstein's theory of relativity required physicists to move from a Newtonian paradigm to a relativistic one as a way of seeing the structure of the universe. Instead of space and time being independent, as in Newton's framework, space and time became inseparably linked in the new paradigm represented by Einstein's theory.

The crucial element of Kuhn's view is his conception of how one framework replaces another. Paradigms change not because a new one proves better at explaining the evidence than the old paradigm, but because the new one becomes more *popular*. Citing the shift from a Newtonian to an Einsteinian universe, Kuhn argues that the change came because the newer paradigm came to be preferred to the older one. Indeed, he cites a famous remark by physicist Max Planck (who helped shape the 'Einsteinian revolution'), that '... a new scientific theory does not triumph by convincing its opponents and making them see the light, but rather because its opponents eventually die, and a new generation grows up that is familiar with it' (Kuhn 1970, p. 150).

In Kuhn's view, because a paradigm is an entire way of seeing the world, observations cannot be made independently of the paradigm. Any piece of evidence only makes sense in terms of the underlying framework which generated it. As a result, observations cannot be used as the basis of choosing between paradigms. This conclusion, which is in direct contradiction to logical empiricism, means that the reasons for preferring one paradigm to another are not simply the result of a better fit to the data. While one may refer to the simplicity or elegance of a model, Kuhn argues that ultimately the choice is more social than rational.

To anyone accustomed to thinking of science as rational and objective, this is a rather startling notion, and Kuhn's argument has not gone uncriticized. Indeed, the very term 'paradigm' is a slippery one, and Kuhn has been attacked for not defining it precisely. However, as Baars points out, Kuhn was writing in reaction to the notions of logical empiricism, and in that sense, most readers have little trouble grasping his intended meaning (Baars 1986). Still, Kuhn's view is disturbing, because it suggests that a paradigm is essentially an arbitrary framework for describing the world. This limits the value of evidence in science, because observations will have very different meanings depending on the paradigm. For example, consider how a behaviourist and a humanist would interpret someone saying, 'I feel depressed.' For the behaviourist, the statement is simply a verbal response which has been previously reinforced; for the humanist, it is a valid description of an internal emotional state.

While Kuhn's analysis has been both controversial and influential, it has not led to the complete abandonment of empiricism. Most philosophers of science still seem to believe rational choices can be made between theories, and assume that observations can be made independently of a theoretical framework. In this view, theories may be subjective structurings of the world, but observations are still useful in evaluating theories (Savage 1990).

Paradigms in Psychology

Whether Kuhn's notion of paradigms is correct or not, it has been frequently applied to psychology (for example, Baars, 1986; Berlyne 1975). However, unlike physics, psychology has never had a single paradigm – there have been several, denoted by the different approaches we have discussed in this book. Hence, we cannot talk of 'paradigm shifts' in the sense of a complete reorientation of the discipline. Instead, psychology has several competing paradigms, none of which enjoys complete dominance. Over time, though, the approaches have varied in their level of acceptance, and it is interesting to look at the changes in their *relative* popularity as paradigms.

With the exception of the humanistic, all of the approaches can trace their origins back to at least the early decades of the twentieth century. Within that time frame, there have certainly been indications of shifts in popularity. From the 1930s until the early 1960s, the dominant paradigms were the psychodynamic (mainly psychoanalytic) and behaviourist approaches. The former was favoured by clinicians, and the latter by experimentalists. As has already been discussed earlier in the book, these two approaches differ in many of their assumptions and methods, and have frequently been highly critical of each other. However, over time, both have lost influence, and today the most active approaches appear to be the cognitive and biological.

Many authors have talked about the striking shift from behaviourism to cognitivism (for example, Baars 1986; Berlyne 1975), whereby mental processes have gone from being essentially irrelevant to being the central concern. The shift from behaviourism can be seen, for example, in changes in citation patterns in major psychology journals (Robins *et al.* 1999). One element in this shift was almost certainly the development of new experimental techniques and results (see Chapter 4). While in some cases the cognitive approach might be seen as an extension of behaviourism (for example, cognitive behaviour modification; the role of imitation in learning), in other cases it has led to the study of different phenomena (for example, organization in memory; attribution theory). Hence, the shift may reflect the rise of a 'better' paradigm, or it may be that, in Kuhn's terms, the primary factor was the shift in interests of a new generation of researchers.

The decline of the psychodynamic approach, and the rise of the biological, are not as simple to describe. In a clinical context, the development of new drugs, beginning with neuroleptics for treating schizophrenia, has certainly altered treatment options for many disorders (Shorter 1997). As a result, the shift among clinicians from the psychodynamic approach to the biological may well represent a paradigm shift. However, the biological approach is also increasingly popular among researchers, and this seems unrelated to any decline of the psychodynamic approach, which has traditionally never been a major influence among experimental researchers (recall the discussion of testability in Chapter 5). Instead, researchers seem to be attracted by the possibility of using new techniques to improve our understanding of behaviour. For example, tools like fMRI scans have enabled researchers to study brain activity during cognitive tasks (see Chapter 2). Thus, by using fMRI, Servos and his colleagues were able to identify an error in Penfield's mapping of the cortex (Servos *et al.* 1999). In fact, increasingly one sees studies which involve cognitive variables being linked to biological measures – a phenomenon which will be discussed later in the chapter.

Whether Kuhn's argument about the role of social processes in paradigm change is correct or not, it is clear that psychology is very different from most disciplines. Whereas physics involved a shift from one broadly accepted paradigm to another, to this point there has never been a single dominant paradigm within psychology.

Psychology has been defined in various ways, but the most widely accepted view, reflected in this book, is that psychology must deal with *both* behaviour *and* experience. It is not, as the behaviourists suggest, purely the study of overt responses, nor is it solely concerned with inner experience (thoughts, feelings, and so on). This duality has always been a source of difficulty. Wundt's attempts to analyse experience in terms of sensory inputs ultimately came to little, and the awkward position of the humanists in contemporary psychology shows that dealing with subjective experience is still problematical. As Daniel Robinson has suggested, it seems we are forced to choose between a psychology which is not scientific, and a science which is not psychology (Robinson 1985)! That is, Robinson believes that although questions of inner experience are central to psychology, they cannot be addressed scientifically.

To understand this comment, one need only consider some of the ways in which researchers have tried to handle inner experience and the questions of thought, feeling and desire that it raises. The introspectionists tried to reduce conscious experience to objective sensory properties, to little avail. Radical behaviourists like Watson and Skinner have sought to side-step the problem by insisting that inner experience is irrelevant. The humanists, aware of the failures of others, have tried to suggest changes in how we conceive of science. However, the methods they advocate have not been widely accepted.

All of these responses acknowledge that 'inner experience' and 'science' seem hard to combine, and this dilemma has certainly contributed to the disagreements between approaches. Conceivably it may be possible to adapt the methods of natural science to address at least some aspects of the mind, as Martin Seligman (2002) is seeking to do with positive psychology (see Chapter 6). By trying to blend subjective experience and experimental rigour, Seligman is also implicitly acknowledging that some of the polarities within psychology have arisen because of disagreements about research methods, not just theories. To understand this, let us reconsider some issues related to the role of research methods.

Try it Yourself

Assuming Robinson is right, would you rather see a scientific psychology which ignored inner experience, or a non-scientific psychology which included the study of inner experience? Why? Do you think the two can be meaningfully combined? Do you think any of the five approaches discussed in this book try to do that?

PSYCHOLOGY AND SCIENCE

Depending on how one chooses to look at it, the source of the continuing fragmentation lies either with the limitations of science, or with our expectations of psychology. Let us consider the second point first. Our experience as human beings leads us to ask about the causes of behaviour. In everyday life, we generate such explanations constantly, invoking our individual and collective notions of personality, motivation, and so on. Science, including psychology, often charges that these notions are not really explanations at all, but simply muddled generalities. However, saying that people's everyday explanations are worthless does not itself enhance understanding – and understanding human experience is precisely what people are seeking. Thus, unless science is itself willing to tackle the task of explaining experience, its criticisms lack credibility (Robinson 1985). In this sense, asserting that psychology should not address these issues (as Watson and other radical behaviourists have said) seems to miss the point.

Limitations of the Scientific Method for Psychology

Instead of rejecting people's interest in the mind and subjective experience, one can argue that the problem lies with the scientific method. That is, the inability of science to provide insights which are both rigorous and relevant is largely due to the way science operates. Critics have suggested that science has two limitations when it comes to addressing inner experience.

One limitation involves science's search for causal explanations. While this has proved highly successful in dealing with many phenomena in the natural sciences, it encounters difficulties when applied to psychology. Ross and Nisbett (1991), looking at social behaviour, have questioned whether we will ever be able to make predictions – and the challenges are even greater when considering mental states. The crucial difficulty is that mental states are not directly observable, and neither they, nor the behaviours which are used to indicate them, can be uniquely associated to particular causes (Robinson 1985). Instead, the result is often a kind of circularity, like trying to pull yourself up by tugging on your shoes: inner experience is used to explain the behaviour which is meant to indicate inner experience. For example, Johan says he is unhappy. We then examine Johan's facial expression, tone of voice and other behaviours as a means of validating this statement. In turn, we then 'explain' the behaviour by referring to the fact that he is unhappy! While this is a simplified example, it illustrates how difficult it is to explain inner experience independently of behaviour. In this regard, the traditional model of causation which is used in science seems ineffective when dealing with thoughts, feelings, motives and other aspects of inner experience. In some cases, we can use different forms of behaviour to converge on a mental process (as when we compare thinking aloud protocols and patterns of errors in problem solving); but fundamentally, what we can observe of other people is inevitably different from what they experience within themselves. In that sense, subjective experience can never be directly translated into objective behaviour. Thus, trying to generate a causal explanation becomes difficult, because one is moving between two different domains. (Making linkages between 'mind' and 'body' in literal terms poses similar problems.)

The second limitation concerns the use of the experimental method. The logic of experiments, with their need for strict control and assumptions of objectivity, falters when applied to complex behaviour (as opposed to simple behaviours, like isolated muscular responses). The central difficulty is that human beings are *aware* of being studied, which makes it difficult to obtain an objective assessment of behaviour – particularly when awareness is part of what researchers hope to explain. Thus, as medical ethicist Richard Zaner has commented, an experiment is really an interaction: even as one tries to study the behaviour of individuals, the individuals will be studying the experimental situation (Zaner 1985).

This tendency for behaviour to be altered by the experimental context is emphasized by the concept of **demand characteristics** in research settings. Martin Orne coined the term to describe

demand characteristics the overt and covert cues present in an experimental situation which can influence how participants behave.

how participants in experiments respond to both the overt and covert cues of the situation (Orne 1962). Orne suggested that participants will attempt to figure out what is expected, and will use this information in guiding their behaviour. Consequently, he suggested, the only reliable experiment is one that produces a different outcome from what people expect. Otherwise, one cannot be sure whether the results obtained are a result of natural behaviour, or simply a self-fulfilling prophecy by the participants. For example, Orne did an experiment in which individuals in one group were hypnotized, while individuals in the control group were asked to *pretend* they were hypnotized. In effect, the control subjects were acting the way they *thought* a hypnotized person would act. In this case, they acted differently from the genuinely hypnotized participants, suggesting that the behaviour of hypnotized individuals could not be explained by demand characteristics. (If hypnosis was simply play-acting, they should have reacted like the control group.)

Orne's work challenged the notion that psychological research could be as objective as physics, in the way that the radical behaviourists like Watson asserted (Rosnow 2002). Instead, over time, Orne's work has been reinforced by related research, such as Robert Rosenthal's (1966) studies of *experimenter bias* (see the Appendix). As a result, researchers today recognize that individuals participating in psychological research are capable of dynamically interpreting the situation – *reactivity*, not objectivity, is the reality. Nonetheless, researchers differ in their assessments of how damaging such influences are to the validity of laboratory research; judging by the number of studies that omit quasi controls and *double-blind* procedures, most researchers are unconcerned. However, at the very least, researchers must acknowledge that individuals in laboratory experiments are aware of being in an experiment, and this can obviously affect their behaviour. Reflecting this, Daniel Berlyne suggested that researchers should 'form the habit of asking what a subject would do without a psychologist at his elbow' (Berlyne 1975, p. 77)!

As discussed in Chapter 8, concerns about how individuals react to being studied are particularly strong in dealing with social behaviour. British psychologist Colin Fraser has expressed concern that the emphasis on experimental methods ends up distorting the kinds of questions that are asked, and thereby our understanding of social behaviour (Fraser 1987).

Indeed, American social psychologist William McGuire suggests that 'our social psychological knowledge is a delusional system which represents reality only poorly, the representation being distorted by our limited intellectual apparatus and distorted by our cognitive systems and our wishes, values, and expectations' (McGuire 1985, p. 585). In one sense, he is offering an indictment of the traditional experimental method; but at the same time, he is not advocating the wholesale abandonment of observation and enquiry. Rather, he argues for recognizing the limitations of scientific knowledge, and working to minimize distortion and oversimplification. At heart, the problem may be that researchers are driven to use experiments because of the desire to answer questions about causation. Paul Meehl, a former president of the American Psychological Association, has argued that psychology places too much emphasis on experimental methods and the search for causes (Meehl 1971). He notes that other methods may not give direct information about causation, but they are nonetheless empirical, and therefore scientifically useful.

In summary, there are two key concerns, both related to the nature of 'objectivity' in psychological research. First, subjective experience cannot be properly captured, or explained, by objective measures of behaviour. Second, the dynamic qualities of how participants respond to experimental situations, and possibly to any overt observation, seriously weaken attempts to view behaviour in purely objective terms. Granted, it is possible to at least partially compensate for these limitations (for example, linking self-reports to other measures of behaviour, using double-blind procedures). Nonetheless, it seems likely that psychology will never be successful by trying to model its methods on those traditionally used in physics. Of course, this leaves a large question: if not the methods of the physical sciences, then what?

The Search for a New Methodology

The difficulty of applying the scientific method to inner experience has been a problem throughout psychology's history. Traditionally, science has evaluated theories by generating a hypothesis, which is then tested by doing an experiment; essentially, the hypothesis is a prediction about what will occur. Making predictions is then seen as a basic part of doing research and evaluating theories. In particular, experiments have been valued because, in the deterministic world of Newtonian physics, they provide insights into cause and effect. For a variety of reasons, psychology in its early years adopted this model as well.

Unfortunately, this has led to a variety of difficulties. As already noted, observing behaviour is more complicated than observing inanimate objects, and this poses significant challenges. In addition, the emphasis on experiments as the preferred research design has also influenced both the data we gather, and possibly the kinds of theories we generate. Typically, it has resulted in the study of situations which are simple enough to control, thus allowing the assessment of theoretical predictions, and then generalizing the conclusions to the larger world (Hunt 1991). Unfortunately, experiments have limitations, as discussed above – and these limitations are particularly significant when studying social behaviour (McGuire 1973). However, doing research this way is not the only possibility, and questioning it does not mean abandoning empiricism as such. (Indeed, observing behaviour, in a variety of ways, has been very productive within psychology.) Rather, the problem seems related to the emphasis on generating causal predictions, and therefore using methods (experiments) that make testing such predictions possible.

Ironically, the emphasis placed on experimental methods may be not only inappropriate, but unnecessary. After all, it is possible to generate theories which do not generate causal predictions, or which cannot be directly evaluated through experiments (Freud's theory is an example of the first case; evolutionary theory is an example of the second). Nonetheless, moving away from models of simple causation would have significant implications for psychology. Before considering this issue more closely, let us consider some examples which suggest how such theories might be developed, and why they might be appropriate.

One relatively recent development in basic science which challenges the appropriateness of prediction is the study of non-linear dynamics associated with **chaos theory** (Hilborn 1994). Chaos theory tells us that many physical systems are *non-linear*; that is, they are not predictable, because very small changes in initial conditions can result in radical differences in outcomes. This phenomenon is sometimes called 'the butterfly effect', after meteorologist Edward Lorenz's comment that the flap of a butterfly's wing in Brazil could ultimately trigger a tornado in Texas (Lorenz 1993). Similarly, a small measurement error could radically alter the expected outcome of an experiment. Hence, while still subject to the laws of causation, chaotic systems defy any serious attempts at predictability. A second characteristic of chaotic systems is *complexity*. Complex phenomena are those that involve a large number of variables; for example, neural activity in the brain is complex. Not all complex phenomena are chaotic – otherwise, science would not have advanced this far with predictive models! However, in general, the more complex the situation, the more likely it is to be chaotic. For example, simple reflexes are basically linear and non-chaotic, but the brain's functioning as a whole is complex, and likely chaotic.

In some ways, chaos theory represents a framework for analysis rather than a specific theory – in Kuhn's terms, it is a paradigm. Hence, it has the potential to lead to a new approach to understanding human behaviour, although at present its impact has been much more limited. For example, neuroscientist Walter Freeman has proposed a chaos-based model of how signals from sensory neurons get translated into perceptions by the brain (Freeman 2000). Similarly, Davison and Neale (1997) have been influenced by chaos theory in considering the process of therapy. Given the limitations on predictability which chaos theory implies, they have argued that therapists should be cautious in assuming they can anticipate, let alone influence, all the factors that affect the behaviour of their patients. As researchers and psychological theorists become more familiar with chaos theory, it will be interesting to see what emerges.

Another alternative to traditional linear, deterministic models is **systems theory**. First developed by Norbert Weiner to deal with the complexities of aiming anti-aircraft guns (where the movement of the shell, the plane and wind all affect the accuracy of the outcome), systems theory is increasingly being applied in the human domain. According to Robert Jervis, a system exists whenever there are multiple elements which interact, and where the properties of the system are different from those of the parts (Jervis 1998). In this sense, an individual could be considered a system (with the functioning of the various parts of the nervous system being elements, for example). Similarly, social groups could be considered a system, with the individuals as elements (for example, social psychologists have long noted situations where choices by a group are different from the sum of the individual members' choices). The functioning of a system is governed by two basic processes, negative feedback and positive feedback. **Negative feedback** serves to maintain stability in the system, while **positive feedback** amplifies disturbances,

chaos theory a branch of mathematics dealing with non-linear functions which has been applied to the modelling of situations such as the weather and stock markets; non-linear systems are not predictable, because very small changes in initial conditions can result in radical differences at a later point.

systems theory a theoretical framework designed for understanding phenomena which involve multiple interrelated elements, where the properties of the whole are different from the properties of the parts; systems are viewed as governed by processes of negative feedback (which promotes stability) and positive feedback (which promotes instability).

negative feedback a process within a system which serves to dampen disturbances, promoting stable functioning.

positive feedback a process within a system which reacts to disturbances by amplifying the effects, triggering a major change in functioning.

thereby promoting a change in the response of the system. For example, a person driving a car continually makes adjustments to maintain their direction. As long as the car is going in the intended direction, the adjustments are small (negative feedback). However, if the car loses traction and starts to skid, they will react by quickly turning the wheel the other way (positive feedback). Unfortunately, because they may overreact, it is possible that the car will begin skidding the other way, rather than simply returning to its original direction. This instability is inherent to positive feedback, and can result in non-linear effects. (In the example, the difference between the amount of steering required to compensate for a skid, and the amount that will make the car skid the other way, is quite small.)

As the preceding example suggests, systems theory, like chaos theory, suggests that complex behaviour may be difficult to predict. By their nature, models based on systems theory are relational rather than linear (unlike, for example, the stimulus-response framework of behaviourism). Causality is often indeterminate, both because of the way elements interact, and because feedback processes affect the system as a whole, rather than just one element. For example, in a confrontation, threats may sometimes serve to cause escalation of aggression, or may lead to both sides backing off (Jervis 1998). Without knowing all of the elements of the system (which becomes difficult in complex systems), predicting the outcome may be impossible. Thus, applying systems theory within psychology may require new methods of testing theories. Nonetheless, both Hunt (1991) and McGuire (1985) see systems theory as a potentially productive approach to psychological issues.

One well-known application of systems theory is the pioneering work of developmental psychologist Urie Bronfenbrenner (Bronfenbrenner and Ceci 1994), who argues that development is best understood by recognizing that individuals do not develop in isolation, but are always part of larger systems – the family, the community (peers, school, etc.), the society (culture), etc. Looked at in this way, nature and nurture are not a dichotomy, but elements which interact as part of a larger system. (As noted in Chapter 7, heredity and environment are increasingly being viewed as interacting rather than distinct.) Partly because of Bronfenbrenner's influence, systems theory has become popular in the study of behaviour within families. For example, Mohammad Besharat has argued for a systems-based model for looking at the behaviour of couples in therapy (Besharat 2003). Compared to a behaviour-focused approach, he argues that a systems approach influences both the way behaviour is seen (embedded in the family and community, not individual), and also the goals of therapy (modifying the family system, not reducing symptoms). Moreover, more established family therapy techniques are now being reconceptualized in terms of systems theory with the aim of making the therapies more understandable and effective (Gardner et al. 2006). Assessing the value of this model is difficult, as for many kinds of therapy (see Chapter 9). However, systems theory has also been applied to other issues in psychology, including creativity (Csikszentmihalyi 1999), emotions (Eynde and Turner 2006; Sander et al. 2005), psychopathology (Tschacher and Kupper 2007), addictions (Chambers et al. 2007), psychotherapy (Hayes et al. 2007), self-concept (Schleicher and McConnell 2005) and adolescent behaviour (Granic et al. 2003). Systems theory has even been used as a method of understanding psychoanalysis (Seligman 2005).

Thus, chaos theory and systems theory challenge the deterministic model of the world which psychology has often used. If non-linear systems are characteristic of behaviour, then deterministic models, and the predictions they generate, are inappropriate. However, abandoning prediction (or at least de-emphasizing it) would not be a death blow to psychology. Indeed, there are already precedents within many of the approaches. Freud's theory is essentially non-predictive, as is the phenomenological framework of the humanistic approach. Even in the biological approach, non-predictive models have sometimes been met with acceptance. Evolutionary theory is one example; pain theory provides another. Pain is a complex phenomenon, influenced by a variety of interrelated processes – just the sort of situation suited to systems theory. While not called a systems theory (it's called the neuromatrix theory), the best current model of pain phenomena, developed by psychologist Ronald Melzack and physiologist Patrick Wall, is essentially a systems model, including forms of positive and negative feedback (Melzack 2005; Melzack and Wall 1982).

Of course, without prediction, the danger is that it is harder to reject a faulty theory – particularly one which is vague enough to describe almost any observed outcome. (Freud's theory has frequently been criticized in this regard; even Melzack and Wall's pain theory is difficult to test in many respects.) In simple systems, it may still be possible to talk about descriptive accuracy, but as noted earlier in the chapter, simply fitting the data is often not a sufficient criterion for testing a theory. At present, it is not clear what criterion could be used to evaluate chaotic theories of human behaviour, or complex system models. Still, it would be unwise to suggest that no resolution of this issue is possible; rather, we must recognize that it is possible for new answers to emerge for old questions.

Psychology and Culture

Another issue which needs to be considered is the role of culture. As we have noted throughout this book, psychology is a human endeavour, influenced by the processes of human perception and thinking. This has at least two obvious implications for the research process. First, it means that observations may be open to perceptual distortion or bias. Second, it means that theories tend to reflect the mental schemata of the theorist. Both of these points challenge the idea that research can be wholly objective, as discussed earlier in the chapter. At the same time, it is important to note that this does not mean that psychology is wholly subjective, nor that we must abandon any hope of agreement about understanding behaviour. As even Rogers asserts, agreement about what is observed, and what it means, is central to attempts at understanding. Rather, it means that we need to remember that decisions regarding both *what* to observe and *how* to observe it are rooted in the very kinds of processes we are trying to understand (the workings of mind and behaviour).

At an individual level, it is clear that perception is influenced by both the immediate situation and also our past experience, which is reflected in our schemata about the world. Thus, the ideas and interests that any one psychologist develops (like any individual) will reflect their own perceptual processes. For example, Freud became convinced that sexuality was a basic human motive because of the observations he made of his patients. At the same time, science is a social process, meaningful only through the *sharing* of ideas and observations (this is true even if Kuhn's ideas about the social aspects of paradigm change are wrong). Thus, we should also consider what types of perceptions might be common to a group of individuals – that is, we need to consider the role of culture.

culture a relatively organized set of meanings, shared by members of a group, which affect how people, objects and events are interpreted.

Culture can be defined in many ways, but one aspect which is part of most definitions is a set of shared meanings within a group (Smith and Bond 1999). These shared meanings are largely based on our common attitudes and experiences. As individuals, part of how we each perceive the world is a reflection of the culture we live in. In terms of psychology, this becomes important, because cultural ideas can play a role in how researchers think about behaviour. For example, it is generally accepted that Victorian ideas about sexuality influenced Freud's thinking. Similarly, it is likely that behaviourism became more popular in the USA than in Europe because it was a better fit with the democratic culture of the USA, as compared to the history of monarchs-by-birth in Europe. (When Bertrand Russell spoke of the behaviour of 'German rats' vs. 'American rats', he was of course referring to the differences in the researchers who studied them, not the rats themselves!) One reason to be interested in culture, then, is that culture may influence the mental schemata of researchers, and therefore affect the kinds of theories which they develop.

Culture is also significant because of its effects on the observations we make, and how we interpret them. As noted at a number of points in this book, people from different cultures do not always react the same way to similar situations. If one only makes observations in a single culture, it is possible to unintentionally over-generalize about the results. As noted in Chapter 4, the *fundamental attribution error* is actually not fundamental to all cultures, but is most common among North Americans. However, since most of the initial research was done in North America, and consistently produced the effect, it is understandable that researchers concluded it was a universal human trait. A similar example has been documented for group decision making (Smith and Bond 1999). Based on studies of American students, it was originally concluded that groups tend to make riskier decisions than the individuals who comprise the group. Only when research was done in a variety of other countries did it become evident that the real effect is one of *group polarization*. That is, the dynamics of groups often leads to decisions which depart from the average of the members – but whether group decisions are riskier or more conservative depends on culture, as well as other factors. Cultural differences can also affect the interpretations psychologists make about individuals. For example, cultural differences between therapist and patient can affect diagnosis and treament of abnormal behaviour (see Chapter 9). Thus, awareness of the influence of culture on behaviour is important because it can bias the way observations are interpreted. While we may not completely avoid such misinterpretations, being sensitive to the role that culture plays is still desirable.

A third reason for studying cultural differences is because culture clearly affects the way individuals behave, and no understanding of individual behaviour can be complete without recognizing that. In this regard, it is encouraging that cross-cultural research is a growing area within psychology (see Gardiner and Kosmitzki 2008; Laungani 2007; Price and Crapo 2002; Shiraev and Levy 2001). For example, there are studies of language and thinking processes, social interactions, gender roles and concepts of self, among other topics. Recognizing cultural differences is also increasingly important in terms of professional ethics, although implementing this is sometimes harder in practice than in theory (Gil and Bob 1999; Rice and O'Donohue 2002).

Unfortunately, simply acknowledging that culture can affect behaviour does not guarantee a proper understanding of the role of culture. As Pittu Laungani (2002) has noted, applying traditional methodology risks oversimplifying the nature of culture: instead of seeing culture as the ecological context of behaviour, it reduces it to just one more variable affecting behaviour. The result can be research which is shaped by methodology, rather than by the desire to develop a framework for proper understanding. A similar argument has been made by Shinobu Kitayama (2002), who has asserted that many analyses of individualism vs. collectivism (such as Oyserman *et al.* 2002) are based on a faulty concept of what cultures are (see Chapter 6 for a description of Oyserman's study). These criticisms are not trivial, as they suggest that analysing behaviour in terms of cultural differences may well distort the underlying processes. For example, consider the various boxes in this book which discuss the role of culture: while intended to offer a more nuanced understanding of behaviour, it must be acknowledged that, if taken out of context, they pose the same risk of oversimplifying behaviour. Ultimately, this issue is not about respect or sensitivity; rather, it is about how to conceptualize the role of culture in behaviour.

This concern is not easily resolved, as it is not 'simply' a matter of dealing with the potential for bias in research. Rather, it is a question of what sort of paradigm is appropriate for understanding culture. In that sense, it raises the same concerns that were discussed in relation to methodology: can psychology really develop a unified understanding of behaviour (including the role of culture) without modifying the methods it uses?

To summarize our discussion of psychology and science, we can point to three themes: the limitations on observing behaviour, the concern to develop new models or even paradigms, and the importance of recognizing how social factors, particularly culture, affect the nature of psychology (and conversely, how the nature of psychology affects our understanding of culture). Clearly, psychology faces many challenges, both theoretical and practical, as it seeks to move forwards. Over time, it is likely that both the methods we use and the theories we embrace will evolve, for that is the way knowledge and understanding develop. In this regard, it is likely that the issues and ideas discussed above will be among the factors which influence the future direction of the field. Whatever the challenges, we must seek ways to resolve the problems; doing otherwise would mean abandoning attempts at improving our understanding.

Try it Yourself

What is your cultural background? Do you think that this affects the way you view the world and the people in it? Does it affect the way you view yourself? Ask your friends with different cultural backgrounds how they think this affects their perceptions of the world, other people and themselves. What differences and similarities among people of different cultural backgrounds emerge from your questions? What differences and similarities do you see in the way the five approaches look at culture? Do you think that culture should be considered as simply a variable, or as one of several systems of which individuals are elements?

THE MANY AND THE ONE

Having come this far, you may still be hoping for an answer to the question, 'which one is right?', or at least 'which one *will* be right in the future?' As noted at various points in this book, casting the question in such terms tends to oversimplify the issue. For the most part, it may be more productive to consider how each approach contributes to our understanding of behaviour.

At the same time, there are issues that remain unresolved. Clearly, there are points of disagreement among the approaches which cannot be ignored. In addition, as noted in this chapter, psychology as a discipline still faces many basic challenges which need to be resolved. Without a crystal ball or similar device, no definite answer to these concerns is possible. However, it does not seem likely that some new framework will suddenly arise which will resolve all the shortcomings of the current approaches. Instead, it is likely that the future will to some degree be an extension of the present. In that sense, it is possible to look at developments in the past several years, and note the conflicting tensions between pluralism (the many) and convergence (the one).

Seeking Convergence

Given the history of distinct approaches, it may seem odd to imagine that psychology could move towards a unified approach. However, in the larger context of the history of science, the search for theoretical unity is well established. In physics, for example, there has been a trend to develop theories which link together combinations of the four fundamental forces of nature (gravity, electromagnetism and the strong and weak atomic forces). Thus far, physicists have not been successful in developing a 'grand unified theory' which would integrate all four, but efforts continue, and some physicists are optimistic about reaching that goal.

In psychology, as in physics, the desire for convergence in theorizing stems in part from the value placed on *parsimony*. That is, needing fewer theories to account for a range of phenomena simplifies both research and our understanding of the world. In addition, some scientists assume that there is an underlying unity to the universe, such that complex phenomena can ultimately be explained in terms of simpler processes at a more fundamental level of analysis. For example, one might argue that all of genetics is ultimately reducible to chemistry. This assumption, called **reductionism**, has a long history, and is still popular. For example, biologist E. O. Wilson has argued for a unification of all knowledge, under a framework he calls 'consilience' (Wilson 1998). When closely examined, consilience embodies most of the elements of reductionism. (Much of psychology, in his view, would be merged into existing fields like biology and physiology, for example.)

> **reductionism** the assumption that phenomena at one level of description can be understood in terms of principles at a more basic level of analysis; for example, that biology is 'reducible' to chemistry.

Reductionism has a controversial history, and has never been fully achieved. However, its appeal is certainly comprehensible. When understanding is fragmented, theoretical disagreements are almost inevitable, as we have seen in comparing the approaches. Even if the differences represent conflicts between paradigms, not contradictions about the underlying reality, they are nonetheless problematical. Since differences between theories in a very limited domain are often resolved by combining elements of the two into a new theory, convergence between approaches seems at least worth attempting, even if we are unsure of the outcome.

As discussed throughout this book, there are many areas in which one can find agreement between different approaches. However, to talk about convergence is to suggest that somehow two (or more) approaches might be merged into a single unified framework. In the past decade, there have been a number of attempts at convergence between various approaches. For example, Paul Wachtel has tried to reconcile psychoanalysis and behaviourism as forms of therapy (Wachtel 1977, 1997). By contrast, John Kihlstrom has tried to reconcile psychoanalysis with 'scientific psychology', which he construes as essentially the methods of the cognitive approach (Kihlstrom 1994). Physiological researcher Roger Sperry, noted for his work on the split brain, has called for a new framework that allows for both physiological processes and subjective mental states (Sperry 1993, 1995). While Sperry justifies his proposal in part by referring to the successes of the cognitive approach, essentially he is trying to deal with subjective experience, and thereby points towards a relationship between the biological and humanistic approaches. Not surprisingly, his ideas have not met with universal acceptance (Morf 1994).

> **cognitive neuroscience** a hybrid discipline aimed at identifying the biological bases of cognitive processes by combining techniques for the study of cognitive processes with measures of physiological processes.

Of all the possible mergers, the one which is most advanced, and seems most likely to succeed, is the linking of the biological and cognitive approaches. While individually they represent the two most popular approaches in psychology today, the combination (often called **cognitive neuroscience**) has the potential to draw upon the best of both domains. In the process, it can address new questions that do not fit either approach, and thereby provide new insights into behaviour. Many researchers, like physiological researcher Michael Gazzaniga (whose mentor was Roger Sperry), welcome the convergence as an opportunity for cross-disciplinary synthesis (Gazzaniga *et al.* 1998).

Does the emergence of cognitive neuroscience indicate that a new paradigm is emerging which can unify psychology? At this stage it is premature to judge, but it is worth noting that at present the merger is still too limited in its frame of reference to encompass all aspects of psychology. For example, Gazzaniga seems less interested in including subjective mental states than is his mentor Sperry. It is also not entirely clear whether cognitive neuroscience represents a new approach to psychology, or simply a sub-area of the hybrid field called cognitive science. Cognitive science is seen by some as a new discipline, which draws upon cognitive and biological psychology, but also philosophy and computer science (Osherson and Smith 1990). Possibly this convergence will produce the kind of sharing of knowledge which E. O. Wilson (1998) seeks. However, it is also possible that cognitive neuroscience will simply define some questions (like subjective experience) out of existence, the way the behaviourists did.

The advance of cognitive neuroscience could also affect other approaches, and therefore psychology as a whole. For example, if the cognitive and biological approaches merge, but ignore subjective experience, then psychology as a whole may become more fragmented even as some parts converge. At the same time, some researchers fear that cognitive neuroscience will lead to a 'hollowing out' of psychology. This possibility is reinforced by a study which attempted to gauge the influence of four of the approaches (humanistic was not included) by looking at publication citations (Robins *et al.* 1999). The authors looked at the frequency with which major journals in each of the four approaches were cited between 1967 and 1994. Over this period, behaviourism showed a major decline, and the cognitive approach showed a dramatic increase, becoming the dominant area. (Psychoanalysis was low throughout the period examined, but the focus on 'psychoanalysis' as a citation term underestimates the influence of psychodynamic theories more generally.) However, what was most striking was that the biological approach showed very little increase. When the researchers looked more closely, they found that neuroscience journals are among the most widely cited in science – but not in psychology. If this trend continues, then cognitive neuroscience may ultimately split from psychology, rather than providing an integrative framework for the discipline.

Another option for convergence also exists, which cuts across several approaches: positive psychology. As discussed in Chapter 6, **positive psychology** seeks to integrate subjective experience and objective research with the goal of advancing our understanding of how to foster human growth. While still in its infancy, research to date has combined humanistic themes with cognitive, biological and even behaviouristic research methods (see Seligman 2002). In some ways, what is most interesting is what is left out: there is little attention given to pathology, and no real role for traditional psychodynamic models. In addition, as noted in Chapter 6, some humanists have objected to what they see as appropriation of humanistic concerns, but a rejection of humanistic theories. At this stage, it is too early to say whether positive psychology will flourish, and if so how it will evolve as it develops. Nonetheless, it represents perhaps the first real attempt at a new paradigm in more than 40 years. On that basis alone, it will be fascinating to see how it unfolds.

positive psychology an initiative to combine objective research and subjective experience, with the aim of improving our understanding of how to foster human growth and happiness.

To summarize, there have always been ways in which particular approaches have overlapped, but no way to reconcile the differences in assumptions and methods. As a result, psychology has always consisted of several paradigms. Recent initiatives related to cognitive neuroscience and positive psychology have the potential to evolve into new paradigms which may provide greater convergence, but at present, it is premature to predict.

Embracing Pluralism

A second way of resolving the contradictions within psychology is to endorse the notion of pluralism. Koch has argued that psychology can never be a coherent field, and that we should welcome the diversity of approaches (Koch 1985). In some sense, this brings us back to a metaphor which was mentioned in Chapter 1: the story of the blind men and the elephant. Just as each of the blind men comprehends only part of the whole elephant, so, too, each approach has limitations. Rather than engaging in a divisive – *and* fruitless – attempt to seek the triumph of one approach, Koch suggests that psychology acknowledge the value of multiple approaches.

One virtue of multiple approaches, each with its own constraints, is that the domain of phenomena to be explained by any one approach is limited, and therefore should become more manageable. That is, one can explicitly decide to focus on only limited aspects of the world. The radical behaviourists like Watson and Skinner have in fact done this – although they then proceed to declare that the rest of the world is irrelevant, anyway! What Koch advocates instead is a decision to set limits, but *without* suggesting that what lies outside those limits is without value or relevance to a broader understanding.

Although this idea of setting limits on the field of study (the *domain*) contradicts the goal of developing a comprehensive theory, it may be a more realistic way to proceed. Somehow, we expect a psychological theory to answer everything, yet we don't expect the same of other sciences. For example, Berlyne has pointed out that botany largely ignores the existence of animals, the geology of soils and the astrophysics of the sun (Berlyne 1975). Instead, botany deals with a world of plants – even though we *know* that animals, soils and the sun exist, and in various ways affect the way plants function (for example, insects, birds and other animals can be crucial to the distribution of seeds). No theory is likely to explain everything, particularly if the domain is a large one. Even physics, with a much longer history than psychology, has yet to achieve a grand unified theory of forces. Indeed, as noted, in Chapter 1, physicists invoke the concept of *complementarity* to deal with the existence of two models which are both useful, but not directly reconcilable. If psychology were to be seen as a set of complementary domains, each with its own value, then possibly there would be less concern over differences and disagreements. In this regard, Robert Sternberg (a former president of the APA) has decried the splits within psychology, and has asserted that psychology will only be unified by accepting the value of different approaches (Sternberg and Grigorenko 2001). As Cambridge University psychologist Paul Whittle notes, by acknowledging their different roles and styles, even psychoanalysis and the cognitive approach could learn from each other (Whittle 1999).

Constraining the domain may be useful, *provided* that researchers do not set such narrow limits as to make the enterprise worthless (recall Koch's comments on cognitive pathology earlier in this chapter). Most psychologists see this as a mistake of the radical behaviourists (like Skinner), though not necessarily of behaviourism more generally. For example, Tolman, who is often seen as one of the pioneers of the cognitive approach, considered himself a behaviourist. Similarly, observational learning (imitation), which laid the foundation for *cognitive social learning theory*, originated within behaviourism.

The problem of where to set the limits is essentially one of context: creating an artificially simple situation often leads to overlooking elements of the situation which are crucial to understanding. This is particularly tricky in psychology, given the complexity of behaviour. An example of the pitfalls of oversimplification concerns the type of materials used in the study of memory. Hermann Ebbinghaus (1885) pioneered the experimental study of memory over 100 years ago; in doing so, he chose to use nonsense syllables (meaningless combinations of letters) as a way of stripping memory processes to the essentials. Since there was little opportunity to utilize meaning, subjects performed in ways that seemed to reflect rote associations. The result was that early memory researchers ended up developing theories (like interference theory) that were associationistic. It was not until the 1960s, when researchers finally began to study more realistic tasks, that our understanding changed. By using meaningful material, researchers like Endel Tulving realized that memory is organized, not based on random associations, and that remembering is *context-dependent*. The possibility of recognizing this had been impeded by using nonsense materials (Tulving and Madigan 1970). Unintentionally, the constraints placed on the study of memory hampered our attempts at understanding.

It may well be that simultaneous exploration of different approaches is the best way to ensure that limits are not set too narrowly. For example, the cognitive approach became dominant over behaviourism not simply as a change of taste, as Kuhn might suggest. Instead, it occurred because people who insisted on pushing the limits of the framework (like Tolman, Krechevsky and Levine) demonstrated that there were phenomena that behaviourism could not explain.

Koch's call for pluralism seems reasonable, at least given current realities. In some ways, acceptance of the validity of multiple approaches is already the case: for example, most counsellors view themselves as eclectic, using techniques drawn from several approaches, rather than being bound to a single approach (Warner 1991). Indeed, contrary to Koch's criticism that many researchers show cognitive pathology, most psychologists seem aware that there are limits to their particular approach. Along with this awareness of limitations goes a (sometimes grudging) acceptance of other approaches. For example, even John B. Watson, the founder of behaviourism, seemed to harbour the tiniest of doubts in his attacks on psychoanalysis. Near the end of *Behaviourism*, he commented that if he ever developed a symptom like paralysis for which no physical cause could be found, 'I should hasten to my psychoanalytic friends and say, "Please, in spite of all the mean things I've said about you, help me out of this mess"' (Watson 1930, p. 301).

CONCLUSION

Amid these criticisms of the past and worries about the future, one should not lose sight of psychology's accomplishments. Even if one restricts the assessment to simply observing behaviour and cataloguing the results, there have been impressive accumulations of information. In some areas, the results have added greatly to our understanding – for instance, the functions of the brain, and the workings of memory. There have been important insights into social behaviour, despite its complexity. For example, consider a problem we discussed in Chapter 1 – social intervention in emergencies. The work of Latané and Darley, and others, has put the lie to the common-sense notion that people don't help because they simply don't care. Instead, the factors that govern intervention are often related to social influence – and knowing that fact may help us find ways to increase intervention in emergencies. Hence, even when our understanding is incomplete, it can be argued that psychology has increased our awareness of possibilities.

Whether the future is one of pluralism, convergence or new paradigms, it is sure to be both interesting and challenging. As Stephen Chorover has suggested, the ferment in psychology is interconnected to the ferment in society (Chorover 1985). We are living in a world with complex problems, including population growth, environmental degradation and conflicts between nations and cultures. At the same time, our intellectual traditions are also being questioned. While science has long been based on the premise that knowledge can aspire to objective absolutes, this view has been challenged by notions of knowledge as a social construction. (Kuhn, of course, has contributed to this, but deconstructionists like Michel Foucault (1965) have been more extreme.) The study of the human dimensions of science has been useful, for it has helped us recognize points of weakness in the scientific process. However, like many ideas, the notion of knowledge as a social construct can be dangerous if carried too far. When taken to the extreme, it leads to the conclusion that no absolutes exist in the world. The framework for psychology then becomes just one more arbitrary choice in a world of arbitrary choices – and therefore meaningless. This view, which is associated with deconstructionism in the arts, seems far too pessimistic as an assessment of science, as Wilson (1998) has noted. Furthermore, to say that nothing is understandable through science ignores what we have learned about behaviour.

In this book, pains have been taken to acknowledge the limitations of current knowledge, and where possible, to suggest what the difficulties are. Yet, however limited psychology's understanding of behaviour, it should be clear that this book does not accept the view that the search for understanding is either completely arbitrary, or meaningless. While our understanding of reality can be affected by our personal beliefs and biases (that is, our cognitive schemata), there is something 'out there' to be explained. The existence of human behaviour is not simply a construct of the mind, nor is its nature purely imaginary. Indeed, our desire to understand ourselves is an affirmation of our existence and our capacity for awareness. Consequently, far from being arbitrary or meaningless, the search for understanding is central to our being.

Psychology, like the behaviour it studies, is rich and diverse, and full of unanswered questions. If we can proceed with an appreciation of the wondrous complexity we are seeking to explain, and a suitable humility before that complexity, then psychology should bring us closer to a proper understanding of what we are, and why.

Try it Yourself

This book, as an introduction to psychology, is of course limited in many ways. There are probably many questions about behaviour you would like answered which this book has not discussed. What are they? Make a list. Ask classmates what questions their lists would contain. Try looking for an answer, through the references given, a library, etc.

CHAPTER SUMMARY

- One of the most basic issues in psychology is how to deal with the existence of different approaches.
- The formation of a theory, and the gathering of evidence, cannot be fully understood without considering the *processes of perception*.
- Whereas *logical empiricism* asserts that theories can be judged by seeing how well they fit the available evidence, Kuhn's theory of *paradigms* suggests that both theories and observations are influenced by the broader frameworks (paradigms) which we use to view the world.

- The various approaches within psychology can be seen as examples of paradigms, but this does not resolve the disagreements among them about the nature of behaviour.
- Using the methods of the physical sciences in psychology has two limitations:
  1 Subjective experience (including mental events) cannot readily be defined by objective measures,
  2 Participants' awareness of their surroundings makes it difficult to maintain control and objectivity in experiments.
- In exploring these difficulties, some argue that we should focus on theories and paradigms which do not require causal predictions, such as *chaos theory* or *systems theory*.
- Psychologists now recognize that *culture* influences both the theories we generate, and the way that observations are interpreted; consequently, cross-cultural studies are increasingly important. At the same time, there is debate as to whether culture represents simply another variable, or a context in which behaviour is embedded.
- It is unclear whether psychology in the future will move towards *convergence* of approaches, as in *cognitive neuroscience* and *positive psychology*, or towards *pluralism*, and acceptance of the existence of different approaches/paradigms as a form of *complementarity*.

🔑 Key terms and concepts

cognitive pathology

logical empiricism

paradigm

demand characteristics

chaos theory

systems theory

negative feedback

positive feedback

culture

reductionism

cognitive neuroscience

positive psychology

complementarity

Test yourself questions

1 How might a scientist's perception affect the type of theory he or she formulates?

2 Why is it said that the scientific method is limited?

3 How does systems theory relate to psychology?

4 Why is it important to study the role of culture in psychology?

Online Learning Centre

When you have read this chapter, log onto the Online Learning Centre website at **www.openup.co.uk/glassman** where you will find answers to these Test Yourself questions and suggested answers to the Try it Yourself activities, plus many more learning resources to help you study psychology.

Suggestions for Further Reading

- For a better understanding of the concept of paradigms in science, **Thomas Kuhn's pioneering** book, *The Structure of Scientific Revolutions* (1970) provides an authoritative view. While it is not light reading, Kuhn proposes some provocative ideas. For a lucid exploration of the philosophy of science, an excellent choice is *What Is This Thing Called Science?* by **Alan Chalmers** (1999).

- For an introduction to chaos theory, **James Gleick's** *Chaos: Making a New Science* (1997) is still one of the more readable choices. For an introduction to system theory, try *System Effects*, by **Robert Jervis** (1998).

- For a better understanding of the role of culture, **Price and Crapo's** *Cross-cultural Perspectives in Introductory Psychology* (2002) and **Gardiner and Kosmitzki's** *Lives Across Cultures* (2008) provide good current overviews. For a less experimentally-oriented view, **David Matsumoto's** *Culture and Modern Life* (1997) is a good brief source.

- One of the most interesting sources for assessments of all aspects of psychology is **Koch and Leary's** edited collection, *A Century of Psychology as a Science* (1985). Written to commemorate the centenary of Wundt's first laboratory, it contains chapters written by a variety of eminent modern psychologists. While it is not the type of book one sits down to read from cover to cover, it makes fascinating browsing. A more recent collection, albeit one that ignores the humanistic approach, is *Psychology: Theoretical-Historical Perspectives*, edited by **Robert Rieber and Kurt Salzinger** (1998). *The Philosophy of Social Science* (2008) by **Alexander Rosenberg** addresses the assumptions and biases inherent in several approaches to studying the social sciences, asking some very provocative questions.

Appendix: Research Methods and Statistics

MAKING SENSE OF THE EVIDENCE

Most people initially think that the study of research methods and statistics is both dull and meaningless – something that only professional researchers should be concerned with. In fact, however, we all encounter situations in which we must make sense out of information which we encounter. Sometimes this is presented as research results (for example, in a newspaper report), and sometimes it may appear unrelated to research issues. Consider the following situations:

■ A politician running for re-election claims that the average family income has risen by $3,000 in the past two years. Does this really mean that most people are better off than they were?

■ A friend goes on a business trip to France. Before leaving, she expresses concern that the French are not friendly to foreigners. On her return, she reports several instances of situations where people were rude and hostile to her. Does this mean that her preconception was correct?

■ Your doctor proposes to do a diagnostic test to find out why you don't feel well. When it comes back positive, he says you should go for exploratory surgery. What do you need to know about the test before agreeing to surgery?

In none of these situations have we used the words 'research methods' or 'statistics', but all of them are in fact examples of basic issues in the design and analysis of research. As we explore these issues, think back to the situations mentioned here, and see how you can apply the principles you encounter. Far from being dull and irrelevant, the material in this Appendix can lead you into a number of challenging insights.

INTRODUCTION

Throughout this book, we have emphasized that psychology is an *empirical* pursuit – that is, the knowledge gained is based on observation of behaviour. The process of gathering observations is commonly referred to as 'doing research'. Research provides the basic information that is used to formulate and test theories. Although the various approaches differ in the kinds of research methods used, all agree on the importance of observation.

In Chapter 1, we discussed the basic methods, both correlational and experimental, which are most commonly used in psychological research. At various points, we have focused on particular aspects of research methods – for example, the use of time-based studies in developmental psychology, and the difficulties of doing experiments on social behaviour. Regardless of the problem studied or the method used, there are some basic considerations that apply to all psychological research. In this section, we will look briefly at some of these points.

THE LOGIC OF RESEARCH

Making Observations: Measurement and Sampling

One basic concern in research is how to describe what we observe. It takes very little insight to recognize that people vary in many ways. For example, people differ in size, age, education, and so on. Obviously, they also differ in the way they behave. Any characteristic which shows variation can be called a *variable*, and so in essence the information we collect is based on observing different variables. The choice of variables is one of the things which distinguishes the approaches – for example, the behaviourist's use of reflex responses, or the humanist's use of subjective reports of feelings.

Unfortunately, not all variables are alike. For example, variables may be simple descriptive labels, as when we refer to eye colour as green, blue, brown, and so on. Such labels are very limited when it comes to making comparisons between individuals. We can put people in groups (for example, all those with blue eyes), but we cannot really say how *much* they differ. For example, is the difference between blue and green greater than the difference between blue and brown? Whatever our intent might be in asking the question, there is no meaningful way to answer it from the information provided by the labels.

ratio variable a characteristic whose measurements are based on a continuous scale, with an obvious zero point.

In order to make relative comparisons, we must use variables which provide more information. The most detailed information is provided by **ratio variables**, which use measurements based on a continuous scale, with an obvious zero point. For example, we can measure age in years, weight in kilograms (or pounds), and so on. Ratio variables are highly useful, because they allow a wide variety of comparisons. For example, one can say John and Bob together weigh as much as Jim, or Mary is three times as old as her daughter Jane, and so on. As implied in the examples, ratio variables are fairly common when measuring physical characteristics. They are less common in dealing with psychological variables, many of which do not have a clear zero point. For example, what would it mean to say someone has 'zero intelligence'? Without a clear zero point, we cannot say that someone who has an IQ of 140 is 'twice as intelligent' as someone with an IQ of 70. Thus, one concern in making observations is deciding what kinds of comparisons are appropriate for particular variables.

Another way in which variables can differ is how easy they are to measure. Variables which refer to physical characteristics are relatively simple to measure (although errors can still occur), but measuring psychological variables, like 'intelligence' or 'aggressiveness', is more difficult, since they cannot be directly observed. Hence, in gathering data, we have to be concerned about the measurement process. Basically, we want our measurements of any variable to be both reliable and valid. **Reliability** means that the measuring process gives consistent results; **validity** means that the variable measures what it claims to, as opposed to some other characteristic. That is, the measurement process should be both consistent (reliable) and accurate (valid). There are several effective ways to measure reliability, all of which basically compare the consistency of repeated measurements of particular cases. Validity is more difficult to assess, because one must have an independent means of measuring the same property (called the validity criterion); this means you cannot measure the validity of any characteristic for which you don't already have an accurate validity criterion. To take a simple example, you can't determine whether a ruler is accurate unless you already have an accurate ruler (or other measuring device) with which to compare it! Having measurements which are reliable and valid is important to effective research; without dependable observations, the whole enterprise is threatened.

reliability a criterion for evaluating a measurement process, which assesses the consistency of measurements; often measured by comparing the correlation between repeated observations.
validity a criterion for evaluating a measurement process, which assesses whether the variable measures the intended property, as opposed to some other characteristic.

Assuming one has confidence in the measurement process, there is still the question of *who* to observe and measure. In practical terms, a researcher can only observe a limited number of individuals, yet would like to draw conclusions about all human beings. That is, we make observations of a limited group (the *sample*), but we wish to generalize about the larger group from which the sample is selected (the *population*). This leads to concerns about sampling – the process by which one selects observations. In sampling, the goal is to select a *representative sample*, one which can be assumed to fairly reflect the population.

sampling the process by which one selects observations for research (the sample).

There are normally two ways to obtain a representative sample: random sampling and cross-sectional sampling. A **random sample** is one in which everyone in the population has an equal chance of being selected. In the case of the election poll, suppose the researcher went to a large shopping centre in Toronto at lunch time, and stopped every third person that went by: would that be a proper random sample? No – since not every Canadian voter is likely to be found at that site, it would not be a random sample. Similarly, if survey forms were mailed out based on voter registration lists, the researcher would have to be concerned about how many were actually returned. Although the initial mailing might be random, if only a small percentage actually responded,

random sample a sample obtained through a selection procedure in which everyone in the population has an equal chance of being selected.

self-selected sample a sampling procedure which allows members of the population to decide whether to be included or not, as when a survey has a low rate of response.

the results would no longer be random, due to possible differences between those who answered and those who didn't. With a low response rate, the sample becomes **self-selected** rather than random. This point – the need to ensure a high response rate in the target sample – is sometimes overlooked. For example, consider a book based on a survey of women's attitudes towards men (Hite 1987). The author made much of the fact that almost 5000 women had responded; unfortunately, since over *100,000* survey forms had been distributed, the response rate was so low as to make the results of questionable value. Similarly, a recent article noted that typically only 5 per cent of Americans contacted by telephone to participate in political surveys agree to take part (Klein 2003). In such a circumstance, one must wonder about the reasons why the other 95 per cent don't answer – and whether the resulting polls should be taken seriously.

Another possible difficulty arises when practical constraints result in the pool of potential participants differing from the actual population (this is more likely to occur in laboratory research than in surveys). The result can be a quasi-random sample called a **convenience sample**. For example, in the past few decades, the most common participants in North American laboratory studies have been university students. When using a restricted sample pool, researchers typically do so on the assumption that there are no crucial differences between the group they have sampled and the actual population. Unfortunately, while university students are readily accessible to researchers (for example, participating as part of their enrolment in a psychology course), it turns out they are not representative of the broader population in age, education and other variables. As David Sears (1986) has noted, the distortions this creates in results can be particularly significant when looking at social behaviour – but distortions can also occur with other aspects of behaviour. For example, performance in *short-term memory* actually differs in university students compared to middle-aged, non-university educated individuals, very young children, the elderly, etc. While this result may not seem surprising, sometimes it is difficult to predict if a restriction on sampling is significant. For example, is a sample drawn from only one country unrepresentative? Early research on the *fundamental attribution error* (which happened to be done in North America) assumed it was a universal phenomenon; only when studies were done in more collectivist cultures did differences appear (see Chapter 4). Yet, in other situations, the influence of differences like age and culture may not matter. In the end, determining when limitations on sampling make it non-representative is difficult. If particular characteristics *are* important, random sampling is not always the most effective method of obtaining a representative group.

convenience sample a quasi-random sampling procedure in which the potential sample pool actually differs from the population – for example, selecting university students instead of people in general; the impact on representativeness (if any) often depends on what behaviour is being studied.

cross-sectional sample a sample which is deliberately selected in such a way that the sample matches the population for particular characteristics, such as age and income.

The primary alternative to random sampling is a cross-sectional sample. As the name implies, a **cross-sectional sample** is deliberately selected so that the sample matches the population for characteristics which are particularly relevant. For example, in a election survey, one would want the sample to reflect the age, income, sex and geographic origin of the population, among other things (for example, if 20 per cent of the population live in Ontario, one would want 20 per cent of the sample to come from Ontario). For a voter survey, such data could be obtained from census figures; for other types of survey, depending on the focus, other sources might be used to determine population data.

The primary limitation of using cross-sectional sampling is the problem of determining the population characteristics to be matched. Sometimes, a factor that is important may be overlooked – for example, the above example neglects native language, which would be a relevant factor in surveying Canadian voters, since differences likely exist between English- and French-speaking voters. At the same time, it is obviously impossible to match a population for every known characteristic. Even more importantly, it is impossible to create a proper cross-sectional sample if the population characteristics are *unknown*.

In doing research, the goal of sampling procedures is to avoid serious *bias*, or systematic error. For example, if I am interested in how children react to watching violence on television, it might make a difference if I study children in a university day-care centre, or children in a home for delinquents. In this case, either sample would be biased; that is, neither sample is likely to be typical of the larger population (all children in the world). In terms of the logic of research, there is one thing to keep in mind: even when using generally accepted procedures for sampling, it is still possible to get a set of observations which are not actually representative of the population. This potential for **sampling error** is one of the main reasons we use statistical analysis in interpreting the results of research.

sampling error an error caused by having a non-representative sample, due either to using a biased sampling procedure, or the inherent variability associated with the sampling process.

Try it Yourself

If a researcher were to do a survey of people's favourite television programme by randomly dialling listings from the telephone book, would this be a representative sample of the population of television viewers? Why or why not?

Designing Research

The concerns about types of variables, measurement procedures and sampling apply to all psychological research. In this sense, they are independent of both the question being asked, and the research method used. Nonetheless, doing research always involves a number of choices, which begin with the question one seeks to answer, and end, hopefully, with the results providing the answer. In between, one must consider how the question is to be stated, in terms of the *hypothesis* to be tested, what *research method* is to be used to collect the observations, and how the *variables* are to be measured. All of these choices are part of the general domain of *research design*.

The decisions involved in designing a study are not cut and dried. In practice, one could give the same question to several researchers, asking each to design a relevant study, and find that each one produces a different design for addressing the question. (Consider, for example, the many studies which have looked at the relationship between observing television violence and aggressive behaviour, as discussed in Chapter 8.) In each case, the reasons given for the resulting design could be very sensible, despite the differences.

Research design is a creative activity, and like other forms of creation, can be both challenging and gratifying. We cannot deal with all of the complexities here, but it is important to realize that designing and doing research is not a dry and mundane task; it is an inventive process for exploring the unknown. There are rules, to be sure, but within those rules, there is tremendous opportunity for the mind to imagine new possibilities.

Pitfalls in Experimental Research

In general, using experiments to gather information can be more complicated than using non-experimental observational procedures. In order to draw clear conclusions, one must maintain consistent conditions in the experimental situation, and ensure that no unwanted factors distort the results. The issues of proper design and execution of an experiment are part of the issue of **internal validity**. (You may recall that concerns about the ability to generalize from the results, particularly with laboratory experiments, are related to *external validity*.)

internal validity the assessment of the degree to which the design and execution of an experiment are free from bias, confounds and other sources of error.

Confounds

Broadly speaking, there are two kinds of factors that can detract from internal validity: confounds and bias. A **confound** represents a situation where two variables change simultaneously, making it impossible to determine their relative influence (that is, there is a *confounding variable*). For example, suppose that in Latané and Darley's field experiment (see Chapter 1), it turned out that all the subjects in one group were male, and in another group were female. In this situation, one could not tell whether differences in helping behaviour were due to the independent variable, or the sex of the subjects. Similarly, if an experiment designed to compare two teaching methods used two classes which met at different times of day (one early morning, one mid-afternoon), then differences in results (for example, student grades) might be due to the teaching methods, or the time of day, or a combination of both factors. Such situations are undesirable, because they represent a confound of two variables.

confound in experimental research, a situation where two variables change simultaneously, making it impossible to determine their relative influence.

Basically there are two ways to avoid confounds. The most common approach is to hold constant factors which are not of direct interest; this is a key feature of experimental design. For example, in the experiment on teaching methods, one would plan it so that the groups met at the equivalent times (for example, morning or afternoon on alternate days). The other approach to avoiding confounds, used when the variables involved are of direct interest, is to use multiple independent variables. In the Latané and Darley field experiment, the number of customers and the number of robbers were both intended to be independent variables; by using four groups (which reflected all possible combinations of the independent variables), they were able to avoid the difficulties of confounding. Generally, careful planning of the experiment should be able to prevent most confounds, although in research as in everyday life, the unexpected can still create surprises. In this regard, the greatest risk is that an unrecognized variable will turn out to be confounded with a planned independent variable, resulting in the kind of ambiguities we have noted.

random error non-systematic error produced by the variability in sampling or other natural processes.

While confounds can make it difficult to interpret the results, various forms of *error* can directly affect the results obtained. So-called **random error**, produced by natural variability in sampling or other processes, is an inevitable part of research. (For example, in doing a survey, no two samples of a population will be identical; the differences represent a form of random error.) Generally speaking, random error can be dealt with in the analysis of results, and does not threaten the basic legitimacy of the research. By contrast, systematic forms of error, called bias, are a more serious concern.

Bias

Systematic error, as its name implies, means that some factor is at work which consistently influences the results in a particular way; since this influence is not a planned part of the research design, its intrusion is undesirable. Systematic error (bias) can arise in many ways: Suppose that Latané and Darley had told their subjects the purpose of the research; do you think that people would react differently if they knew the researchers were interested in helping behaviour? One possibility is that more people would intervene, in order to create a better impression of themselves. If this were true, the results would be biased, since the information led people to intervene more than would otherwise be the case.

To consider a different example, suppose an experiment was designed to test a new drug; the independent variable will be the presence or absence of the drug. In its simplest form, this would mean that some subjects would receive medication, and others would receive nothing. Unfortunately, this would mean that subjects in the control group would know they were not getting treatment, since they were not given anything. As in the Latané and Darley example, this could distort the results by creating a confound (see Figure A.1a). In both of these examples, bias is created because of what the subjects know; consequently, this form of bias is commonly called **subject bias**. In order to prevent subject bias, experimenters usually try to set up an experiment in such a way that participants do not know anything which might lead to bias. An experiment planned in this manner is commonly called a **single-blind design**, since subjects are kept uninformed or 'blind' to the purpose. Sometimes this is done by withholding information or by active deception, as in the Latané and Darley experiments. In drug studies, those not given a real drug are usually given a placebo – an inert substance which they believe is a drug (see Figure A.1b). (In some cases, both those receiving the drug and those receiving the placebo are kept in doubt; in this case, the expectation in both groups is one of uncertainty.) Since bias is particularly likely in social situations (due to reactivity), nearly all social psychology experiments use some form of single-blind design.

The behaviours that create subject bias are very understandable: subjects are simply reacting to the situation as they perceive it; when the information available changes, their behaviour changes as well. While such reactions complicate the task of the researcher, they also represent part of the complexity which makes human behaviour fascinating; studying behaviour would certainly be less interesting if people were not so responsive to their environment. Unfortunately, it is harder to find redeeming value in a second form of bias, called **experimenter bias**. The term was coined by a social psychologist named Robert Rosenthal, who was interested in how people's expectations affect their interactions with others.

To understand experimenter bias, we must clarify how it differs from simple perceptual interpretation. As we have already discussed, perception depends in part on our existing schemata – hence, what we perceive is influenced by our expectations. For instance, a **halo effect** occurs when our knowledge of *one* characteristic which is positive or negative about a person leads to similar expectations of *other* characteristics. For example, people are likely to perceive

subject bias in an experiment, systematic error created because the subjects in different groups have different information (for example, knowing whether they are in the control group or experimental group).

single-blind design an experiment set up in such a way that subjects are kept uninformed of any details which might lead to bias.

experimenter bias systematic error created when an experimenter's knowledge and expectations about the experiment influence the behaviour of subjects.

halo effect a form of perceptual bias which occurs when our rating of a person on one characteristic as being positive or negative leads to similar expectations for other characteristics of the individual.

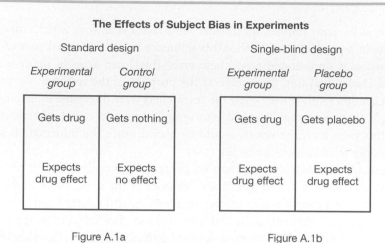

Figure A.1 Subject Bias in Experiments – In doing drug research, experimenters normally use a placebo with the control group, rather than giving nothing, in order to prevent subject bias. As the two figures show, providing a placebo changes the expectations of those in the control group so that they are consistent with the expectations of those in the experimental group.

someone who is intelligent as honest rather than dishonest, sincere rather than insincere, and so on. Note that a halo effect refers only to the perception; it does *not* specify what the person perceived is actually like.

While perceptual effects like the halo effect could pose a threat to scientific objectivity, experimenter bias takes this process one step further. In exploring experimenter bias, Rosenthal was asking if our expectations can alter the way others actually *behave* (as opposed to our *perception* of them). To explore this idea, he did a study with Lenore Jacobson in which they looked at the influence of teachers' expectations on the behaviour of their students (Rosenthal and Jacobson 1968). The teachers were told that certain students had been identified as 'late bloomers', who could be expected to blossom during the school year. Sure enough, those students actually did improve, not only in the eyes of their teacher, but according to independent assessments as well.

self-fulfilling prophecy a phenomenon whereby our expectations about other people lead to acting in ways which elicit the expected response from them; the everyday equivalent to experimenter bias.

What made this surprising was that the only *real* difference between these students and their classmates was the label 'late bloomers', which Rosenthal and Jacobson had applied to randomly chosen students. That is, other than the teachers' expectations, nothing was different about the late bloomers! Rosenthal subsequently called this expectancy effect a **self-fulfilling prophecy**. That is, we tend to produce in others the type of behaviour which our expectations lead us to predict. For example, if I visit a foreign country with the expectation that the people are unfriendly, my own behaviour is likely to lead to experiences which justify my original expectation. While there has been considerable subsequent research on how expectations affect behaviour, it is not clear how significant the phenomenon is in everyday life – in part, because it is so difficult to identify in non-experimental situations.

In experiments, however, such expectancy effects raise a real concern about the objectivity of research. If an experimenter's knowledge and expectations about the experiment could alter the behaviour of subjects, this would be a form of bias (hence the term *experimenter bias*). For

double-blind design a rigorous form of experimental control, whereby both the subject and experimenter are kept uninformed about details of the experiment which could result in bias (both subject bias and experimenter bias).

example, by unconsciously smiling or frowning, the researcher might lead subjects to respond in ways consistent with the experimental hypothesis. (We assume, of course, that there is no conscious intent to bias the results.) Rosenthal went on to do a number of experiments, which suggested that the risks were potentially very significant. How can a researcher cope with this risk? By analogy to subject bias, where one uses a single-blind design, one would seek to keep the experimenter uninformed about the details of the experiment; when both the subject and experimenter are kept uninformed, the experiment is called a **double-blind design**.

Unfortunately, the requirements of a double-blind design can pose considerable difficulties to the execution of the research. In medical experiments, it is possible to use placebos and complex procedures so that neither the person giving nor the person receiving a 'drug' know whether it is a placebo or a real drug – but it requires careful record-keeping to ensure everything proceeds properly. Other situations, particularly those involving social variables, can be even more problematical. For example, in Latané and Darley's field experiment, the independent variables dealt with the number of people present. Since anyone involved, whether the store clerk or an observer recording the results, would be aware of this, there would be no simple way to conduct a double-blind study. Consequently, while Rosenthal would argue that ideally all research should be double-blind, in practice, only the minority of psychology experiments are actually designed in this way. Instead, most researchers would suggest that replication provides a check on possible experimenter bias: if someone does a study which seems inconsistent with previous research, others who disbelieve it are likely to try to repeat the experiment; if the results come out the same, it tends to suggest that the result is genuine, not a product of the original researcher's bias. Still, no one would dispute that use of a double-blind design is desirable when circumstances make it possible.

Try it Yourself

Have you ever created a self-fulfilling prophecy? What was the result? In what ways are self-fulfilling prophecies related to our cognitive schemata?

Going from Observation to Interpretation

Whatever the question and whatever the research design, one ends up with a set of observations – the *data*. (The word *data* sometimes confuses readers, because it is a *plural* noun, borrowed from Latin. One should say, for example, 'The data *are* clear.' The singular, used to refer to a single observation, is *datum*.) One must then look at the results in terms of the original question, to determine if the hypothesis is supported or not. For example, suppose that one wanted to know if there are differences in the attitudes of men and women towards violence in sports. A survey is done, and the results show that 55 per cent of women say there is too much violence, 34 per cent say it is not a problem, and 11 per cent have no opinion. In contrast, 38 per cent of men say there is too much violence, 58 per cent say it is not a problem, and 4 per cent have no opinion. Does this mean that women are more opposed to violence in sports? How can we decide?

This example highlights the problem of how to *interpret* the results of research. The research design is intended to produce observations which are relevant to the original question; once

falsification in research, the process of using observations to prove that a hypothesis is wrong.
confirmation in research, the process of determining that observations are consistent with the hypothesis being true.

we have those observations, however, we must still decide whether they support the hypothesis or not. This is actually not as simple as it seems. At first glance, it may appear that we have two choices: to conclude that the results support the hypothesis, or that they contradict it. It turns out, however, that **falsification** (proving a hypothesis is wrong) is much simpler than **confirmation** (deciding that a hypothesis is true). For example, if I visit a remote tropical island, and the first seagull I encounter is black (instead of the usual white), I may be surprised. If the next several seagulls I see are also black, I may be tempted to propose a hypothesis: on this island, all the seagulls are a mutant form which is black. Now, all it would take to *falsify* this hypothesis would be seeing one white seagull. That is, one clearly contradictory observation is enough to prove it wrong. On the other hand, what would it take to be sure the hypothesis is *true*? It would seem that I would have to observe every seagull on the island (the entire population) in order to be absolutely sure. If I depend on a sample, even a large one, there is still the chance that I will miss one or more white seagulls.

Thus, it turns out that proving a hypothesis is false is a lot simpler than proving it is true. In large part, this is because of the need to depend on samples; if we could observe every relevant case (the entire population), in theory we could prove a hypothesis to be true. In practice, psychologists wish to generalize about such large populations (for instance, all human beings) that observing everyone becomes impossible. As a result, researchers end up framing the original question in terms of a **null hypothesis**, which essentially says the results are random. If one can prove this is *false*, then it implies that there *is* a difference. For example, in the survey mentioned above, the null hypothesis would say, 'There is no difference between the attitudes of men and women towards violence in sports.' If we can show that this statement is *false*, then we can show that there *is* a difference. In order to do that, we use *statistics*.

null hypothesis in research, a hypothesis which asserts that any differences observed between groups are random rather than representing an experimental effect; normally the contrary of the experimental hypothesis, it is used for statistical purposes to evaluate results.

STATISTICS – MAKING SENSE OF THE DATA

The very word 'statistics' seems to strike fear into many students. The reasons for this are varied, but may include a fear of mathematics and an aversion to things which are 'boring'. While it is true that statistics is a form of applied mathematics, it need not be boring. When properly understood, many of the questions it tries to answer are very provocative and challenging. This section will try to show that the fears are largely unjustified, and that the issues are in fact both understandable and interesting.

statistics the branch of mathematics that is concerned with the description and interpretation of sets of scores, such as scientific data.
descriptive statistics the branch of statistics which is concerned with describing and summarizing sets of scores.
inferential statistics the branch of statistics which deals with the interpretation of data, particularly in terms of generalizing from the observed sample to the larger population.

In essence, **statistics** is concerned with the description and interpretation of scientific data. That is, it is used to describe and summarize research results, and to assist in understanding what the results mean. The first function, describing and summarizing results, is referred to as the domain of **descriptive statistics**. The second function, the interpretation of the results, particularly in terms of generalizing from the observed sample to the larger population, is the domain of **inferential statistics**. Since one must know what the results are before one can decide what they mean, we will first consider descriptive statistics.

(a) Test grades

CA	67	AM	64
DB	74	LM	70
FC	58	TM	66
GC	70	BN	63
YC	64	EN	46
ED	78	CO	54
SD	69	LO	73
LE	58	SQ	84
JE	69	FR	81
SF	70	TR	78
PG	63	AS	89
YG	64	KS	55
DH	52	PS	63
RH	52	MT	60
SI	73	RT	77
LJ	84	WT	58
NJ	79	AV	69
FL	68	DY	48
RL	49	Total number of scores	37

(b) Frequency distribution (raw scores)

Score	Frequency	Score	Frequency
46	2	69	3
49	1	70	3
52	2	73	2
54	1	74	1
55	1	77	1
58	3	78	2
60	1	79	1
63	3	81	1
64	3	84	2
66	1	89	1
67	1	Total number of scores	37
68	1		

Note: scores with zero frequency omitted in order to simplify table.

(c) Frequency distribution (using intervals)

Score range	Midpoint	Frequency
40–44	42	0
45–49	47	2
50–54	52	3
55–59	57	4
60–64	62	6
65–69	67	7
70–74	72	5
75–79	77	4
80–84	82	3
85–89	87	1
90–94	92	0
Total number of scores		37

Figure A.2 Analysing the Frequency Distribution for a set of Data – The three tables are as follows: (a) The original scores, expressed in the order they appeared in my grade book; (b) a frequency analysis of the original scores, arranged in order of score value; (c) a frequency analysis based on combining scores into intervals of five.

Descriptive Statistics – Describing the Data

In doing psychological research, one gathers information about behaviour, in the form of observations of one or more variables. These observations then comprise a set of data – typically, numbers of some sort. For example, one could measure students' performance on a test, with performance represented by grades expressed as percentages. In Figure A.2a, the results of an actual test are given. The results are listed in the order in which they appeared in my grade book, though I have substituted letter codes for student names. If you look at them, you will note that there is considerable variation. The question is, what do these grades tell us? As they stand, they present a rather random picture. In order to make sense of them, we need some way to summarize the information.

Frequency Distributions

frequency distribution a statistical analysis of a set of data which tells how frequently each value occurs.

One way to approach the task is to try rearranging the scores in order of size, and then see how many people got each score. If we do this for the numbers in Figure A.2a, we would end up with the result shown in Figure A.2b. This is called a **frequency distribution**, because it tells us how frequently each value occurs. As you can see, a few scores are repeated, but most occur only once. So, it is still somewhat difficult to make much sense out of the data.

If we group the scores into *intervals* (for example, 45–49, 50–54, etc.), then we might simplify the overall frequency distribution (there will be fewer categories), and also perhaps get a clearer picture of where scores are clustered. The result for this is shown in Figure A.2c. Now we get a clearer idea of overall performance – looking at the frequencies, it is evident that more people are near the middle than at either extreme. If we want to visualize this, we can represent it graphically, as in Figure A.3. In making a graph like this, the convention is to put the frequency scale on the vertical axis, and place data points based on using the midpoint of each interval. In effect, the graph assumes all the people in any interval scored at the midpoint. If you look at the original data, you'll see that this is an over-simplification, although not a very extreme one. This points out one of the basic principles of descriptive statistics: *whenever we seek to summarize data, we inevitably lose a little of the information we started with*. Thus, the challenge in descriptive statistics is to not lose anything that seems *essential*. In the example above, it doesn't seem to distort things very much to use the intervals as we have.

Measures of Central Tendency

While a frequency distribution, particularly in graphical form, gives us a general sense of the data, it still is rather limiting. For instance, it suggests that most people scored near the middle,

measure of central tendency a type of descriptive statistic used to determine what is a representative value for a set of scores.

but doesn't tell us how the typical student did. To describe what is typical of a group of scores, we use a type of statistic called a *measure of central tendency*. (A *statistic* is a number which results from some sort of statistical calculation on a set of data, while *statistics* is the name for the discipline.) In everyday terms, a **measure of central tendency** tells us what is an average score. However, the term 'average' is avoided in statistical discussions, because the word can be used to refer to *any* measure of central tendency – and as we shall see, they are not all the same.

mode a statistic measuring central tendency, calculated as the most frequently occurring value (or interval) in a set of scores.

The simplest measure of central tendency (particularly if one already has a frequency distribution) is the **mode**, which is the most frequently occurring score (or interval). Looking at the graph in

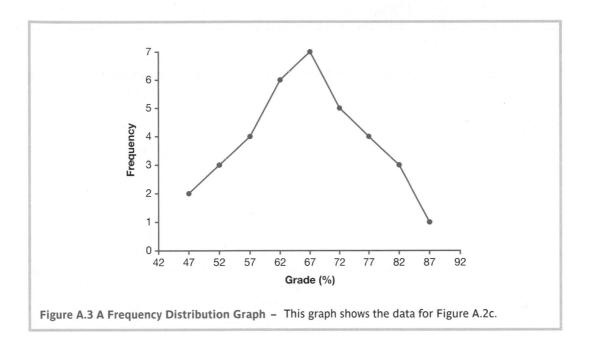

Figure A.3 A Frequency Distribution Graph – This graph shows the data for Figure A.2c.

Figure A.3, it is clear that the peak, representing the most frequent value, occurs in the interval 65–69; using the simplification of the midpoint of the interval, we get a mode of 67 per cent. Note, however, that this does *not* prove that the single score of 67 per cent occurred most often – only that scores were most common in the interval of 65–69 per cent. If we were to determine the mode directly from the original data, we would find that the most frequent single score is actually 64 per cent. While this is close to the value of 67 per cent calculated from the interval data, it also shows how some information gets lost when we summarize. In general, the mode is a measure of popularity – what occurs most frequently defines what is typical.

A second measure of central tendency is the **median** – the score which is in the middle of the frequency distribution. This is actually easier to calculate using the raw frequency data, since we need to find the value which is the midpoint of all the ranked scores. In the current case, the actual value is 67 per cent. (It could also be calculated for interval data, if the original data were not available, but doing so sometimes requires a bit of estimating within the interval. In the present case, it would not be necessary, since the median is the midpoint of the interval.) The median reflects what is typical in the sense of being middle-of-the-road, rather than an extreme. Indeed, one way to remember its meaning is to think of the divider found in the middle of some highways – it is called a median!

edian a statistic measuring central
ndency, calculated as the middle score in
requency distribution.

The most commonly used measure of central tendency is the **mean**, which is sum of all the scores, divided by the number of scores. In our example, the mean is 66.5 per cent. The mean is commonly used because of two characteristics. First, it does not require rearranging the scores in rank order, or creating a frequency distribution, in order to calculate the mean. In many situations, this is a real advantage. Second, unlike either the median or the mode, the mean reflects *all* of the scores – if you change one score, the mean will change, too. By contrast, the mode tells us nothing about any score except itself, while the median tells us only that half the scores are above it, and half below it. In

ean (also called 'arithmetic mean') a static measuring central tendency, calculated
the sum of all the scores, divided by the
mber of scores.

both cases, it would be possible to alter one (or more) scores without altering the value of the central tendency as these measures define it.

If we compare the three values in the current example, they are in reasonably close agreement: using the original scores, the mode is 64 per cent, the median 67 per cent and the mean 66.5 per cent. Since the three measures seem to correspond fairly well, why should we be concerned about differences in how each is derived? The reason is that not all situations are like this example. Consider the data in Figure A.4 and the associated graph (Figure A.5). These data are hypothetical, representing the salaries of employees of a large company (totalling 1000 employees). This lopsided frequency distribution is characteristic of income data, both for companies and nations; in effect, the large majority of individuals have relatively low incomes, while very high incomes are very rare. In analysing the data in this example, we will use the interval data exclusively, because of the large numbers involved (as the number of scores increases, the distortions resulting from simplification typically get smaller, not larger). In this case, both the mode and the median salary are $37,500. The mean, however, is $43,438 – almost $6,000 higher! Now, if one says that the average salary is $43,438 (referring to the mean), this sounds pretty good – until one realizes that at least half the people (those who are at or below the median) earn appreciably *less* than this. Consider further: suppose that the top thirty executives each receive a $25,000 raise. This will raise the average (mean) salary by almost 2 per cent – and yet 97 per cent of employees will have received no increase! Obviously, the word 'average' can be very misleading.

There are two points worth remembering in relation to this example. The first is that one should always be clear on what someone is referring to when they use the term 'average'. The second is that descriptive statistics have limitations, and they are only helpful when used appropriately.

How can one determine when the mean is appropriate or not? Although it is possible to give a technical answer to this, one helpful guide is to look at the shape of the frequency distribution. Very often, the shape is a symmetrical curve that looks something like a bell in profile; this bell-shaped curve is called a **normal distribution** (see Figure A.6). As you can see, the distribution in our example of test grades (Figure A.3) is approximately normal shaped. In a true normal distribution, the highest point occurs at the middle of the distribution – that is, the mode (the highest frequency) is the same as the median (the middle score); in addition, the mean will have the same value. Thus, in a normal distribution, it doesn't matter which measure of central tendency one uses, because they all produce the same result. (Even though our grade example is not perfectly symmetrical, the values come out to be very similar.) By contrast, the frequency distribution in the salary example (Figure A.5) is distinctly lopsided; this is referred to as a **skewed distribution**. Whenever one encounters a very skewed distribution, the mean is unlikely to be representative of the majority of scores. In such circumstances, most researchers prefer to use the median as a way of describing the typical result.

normal distribution a type of frequency distribution which resembles a bell-shaped curve; among its special properties, first identified by Gauss, is that its measures of central tendency are all the same.
skewed distribution an asymmetrical frequency distribution with a single mode; with a skewed distribution the median is usually more representative than the mean as a measure of central tendency.

Measures of Variability

Even when one deals with an approximately normal distribution, as in Figure A.3, measures of central tendency do not give us a full picture of the data. To understand why, let us look at another example. In this case, we will consider two simple distributions of test grades (see Figure A.7a). If

Frequency distribution for salary data

Salary range	Frequency
$0	0
$12,500	250
$37,500	500
$62,500	125
$87,500	60
$112,500	35
$137,500	18
$162,500	6
$187,500	3
$212,500	2
$237,500	1
Total number of employees	1000

Figure A.4 A Frequency Distribution for Salaries in Company 'X' – A hypothetical set of data for salaries.

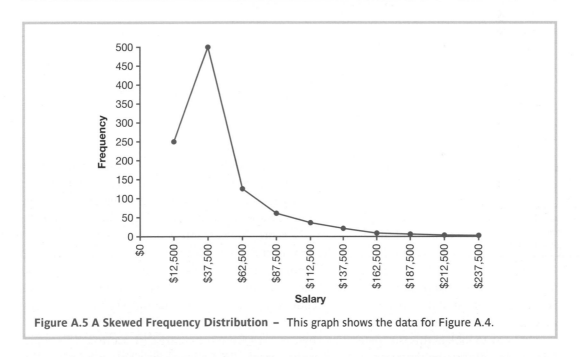

Figure A.5 A Skewed Frequency Distribution – This graph shows the data for Figure A.4.

you look at the two groups, you will note that they have the same mode, the same median and the same mean. Yet, in some sense, they are different. One way to recognize this is by considering the following questions: if you were writing this test, and you were told that you had scored 'below the mean', would you care which group it was? Alternatively, if you were told your performance was 'above the mean', would the group matter? (Look again at the scores.) Most people, asked the first question, would prefer Group 2, because most of the low scores are actually close to the mean. If asked the second question, most people would choose Group 1, because most of the high scores are much higher than the mean. Thus, in a very real sense, these two sets of data are different, even though they have identical measures of central tendency. How is this possible?

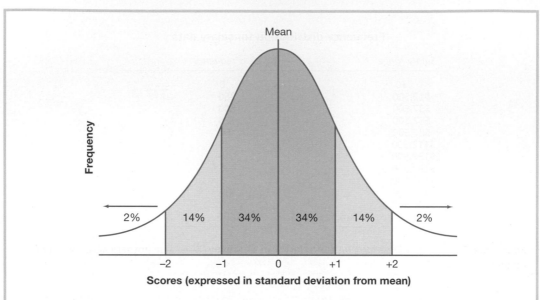

Figure A.6 A Normal Distribution – In a normal distribution, the mean is the same as the median and the mode – hence it also represents the peak of the frequency curve, and the point at which 50 per cent of scores lie on either side. As discussed in the text, in a normal distribution, one can also predict what percentage of people fall into a certain score range by expressing scores in units of the standard deviation. When this is done, the percentages falling within certain regions are as shown in the graph.

variability in statistics, the dispersion of scores within a set of data.
range a statistical measure of variability which is calculated as the difference between the highest score and the lowest score in a frequency distribution.

The answer to this paradox lies in their **variability**, which tells us how the scores are distributed around the centre. One simple indicator of variability is the **range**, which is the difference between the highest score and the lowest score. Interestingly, the range in *both* of these groups is the same – 30 percentage points. Because the range only reflects the two most extreme scores, it is only a crude measure of variability; by ignoring where scores fall *in between* these extremes, it ignores a great deal of information available in the original data. What we would ideally like is a measure of variability that takes into account every score, somewhat the way the mean does as a measure of central tendency.

One way to look at this is to determine *how far away* from the centre each score is. This could be done by subtracting the mean (defined as the centre – in a normal distribution it will be the median as well) from each score. To see how this works, consider Figure A.7b, in which we have calculated the deviations for both groups. You will note that the deviations (ignoring signs) tend to be larger in Group 1 than in Group 2; this tells us that the scores tend to lie further from the mean in this group. Now, if we consider these *deviation scores* as data in themselves, we could ask, 'What is the typical deviation in each group?' If we then proceed to calculate the mean, we will find a strange thing – the mean of these deviation scores is zero in both groups! While this may seem like a strange coincidence, in fact, it is an inevitable result, since it turns out that one can *define* the mean of a distribution as being the number for which the mean of the deviation scores is zero! So, although the deviation scores *do* tell us something about variability, we cannot simply use these scores to measure mean variability.

(a) Data for two sample groups

	Group 1	Group 2
	55	55
	58	64
	60	68
	62	69
	63	69
	70	70
	70	70
	70	70
	77	71
	78	71
	80	72
	82	76
	85	85
Mean	70	70

(b) Data for two sample groups

Group 1	Deviation scores	Group 2	Deviation scores
55	−15	55	−15
58	−12	64	−6
60	−10	68	−2
62	−8	69	−1
63	−7	69	−1
70	0	70	0
70	0	70	0
70	0	70	0
77	7	71	1
78	8	71	1
80	10	72	2
82	12	76	6
85	15	85	15
Mean 70	0	70	0

Figure A.7 Comparing Groups – Table (a) shows the original scores for two groups which have the same central tendency and range; in Table (b), the deviation scores are also calculated (see text for discussion).

If you look closely at the examples, you will see that the difficulty is partly related to the plus and minus signs – if we could focus on just the size of the numbers (what is called the *absolute value*), then we could perhaps get somewhere. Early statisticians recognized this, but found it was cumbersome to extract the signs when doing calculations. However, they also recognized that one could accomplish something similar by *squaring* all the deviation scores, since the squares of both positive *and* negative numbers are positive. The mean of these 'squared deviations' could then be calculated as a measure of variability (which is called the *variance*). While the variance is used in a number of ways by statisticians, in terms of our original question ('How can we describe the typical variability of these groups?'), it gives an inflated number, since it is based on the *squares* of the deviations, *not* the deviations themselves. To circumvent this, one can take the *square root* of the variance, which in one sense scales things back to size. This value is called the **standard deviation**, and

standard deviation a commonly used measure of variability, calculated as the square root of the mean of the squared deviations from the mean of a set of scores.

it provides us with our goal – a measure of variability which reflects the position of every score within the group, expressed in the same units as the original scores. (As we will see below, there are additional reasons why the standard deviation is preferred to the mean deviation.) If we were to define the standard deviation in a single sentence, it would be as 'the square root of the mean of the squared deviations of the scores from the original mean'. Quite a mouthful, to be sure – but if you go back to Figure A.7 and try taking it step by step, it is actually fairly straightforward.

Taken together, the mean and standard deviation tell us a great deal about a set of data. For instance, in the previous example, although the means are identical, the standard deviations are quite different: for Group 1, it is 9.8 per cent, while in Group 2 it is only 6.7 per cent (notice that the standard deviation, like the mean, is expressed in the same units as the original data). This is consistent with our earlier intuition that the scores are more widely scattered in Group 1. In general, the larger the standard deviation, the greater the variability of the scores.

Properties of Normal Distributions

As mentioned earlier, the normal distribution is a symmetrical frequency distribution, with an overall bell-like shape, whose measures of central tendency are all identical. These properties are themselves distinctive, but when combined with the standard deviation, they yield even more surprising results. Because it goes beyond the scope of this overview, we will not try to prove the following points. However, the conclusions have been well established by statisticians.

If you return to the normal distribution in Figure A.6, you will see that the mean has been indicated by a vertical line, which passes through the peak of the curve – hence it is the mode as well. In addition, since this line marks the median, we know that 50 per cent of the scores will lie on either side of this line. Now, if we also mark a line at a distance equal to the standard deviation on either side of the mean, then we break up the 50 per cent into two portions, one of which is larger in area than the other (note it is marked in Figure A.6 as '±1 standard deviation units'). In fact, it turns out that approximately 34 per cent (34.13 per cent if one wishes to be a bit more precise) of the scores lie between the standard deviation and the mean (as noted on the graph). If we continue this process, marking lines at a point equal to twice the standard deviation from the mean, we further sub-divide the remaining area. The larger portion will be about 14 per cent (13.59 per cent), leaving about 2 per cent (2.28 per cent) beyond this point.

At this point, you probably have two questions: how do we know this, and why should we care? The first question is too technical to answer fully here, but is well established, as noted earlier. What we *can* say is that normal distributions are found in many aspects of the real world, and they always have these same characteristics. For example, the height of all the men in the world is a normal distribution, as is the waist size of all women, as is the weight of travellers' suitcases taken on aeroplanes, and many other things. Consequently, knowing something is 'normally distributed' immediately tells us some very specific things, including that most scores are near the mean, and that very few scores (only about 2 per cent) lie more than two standard deviations from the mean.

For example, consider IQ test scores, which have a mean of 100 and a standard deviation of about 15 (depending on the test used). This means that just over two-thirds of all people have IQs between 85 and 115 (these scores represent the dividing lines for ±1 standard deviation). Similarly, it also tells us that only about 2 per cent of all people score higher than 130 on this test. This leads to the answer to the second question ('who cares?'), at least in part: knowing these properties of normal distributions becomes very useful in making predictions about scores, and in our ability to interpret the results of research. For example, airlines depend on statistics about the weight of suitcases in order to plan cargo capacity. Knowing how many people will be on a particular plane, they can also make predictions about the total weight of all luggage. This follows from knowing the mean weight of suitcases, and also the likelihood that unusually heavy ones will occur. To understand how this works, we need to consider how statistics are used in the interpretation of data – that is, *inferential statistics*. However, before doing so, let us take a look at a different type of descriptive statistic, which is used to identify relationships between two sets of observations.

Correlations

As discussed in Chapter 1, there are many situations in which a researcher is unable or disinclined to do an experiment. When using non-experimental research methods such as surveys or naturalistic observation, any relationships perceived between variables are *correlational*, and do not directly identify causal factors. Nonetheless, correlational data can be very useful in identifying patterns or relationships which merit further research.

While Chapter 1 discusses the logic behind the use of correlations, it is worth considering further how statistics are used to describe correlational data. Correlational patterns typically fit one of two types: a positive correlation or a negative correlation. A **positive correlation** occurs when increases in one variable are associated with increases in the other variable. For example, if we were to record the height and weight of a group of people, we would find a positive correlation – generally, taller people also weigh more. A **negative correlation** occurs when increases in one variable occur as the value of the other variable decreases (in mathematics, this is called an inverse relationship). For example, there is a negative correlation between age and fitness – that is, as age increases among adults, fitness level (measured by maximum heart rate) generally declines (see Figure A.8). Typically, correlational patterns are measured using a statistical measure called a *correlation coefficient*. This is a number which varies between 0.0 and +1.0 for positive correlations, and between 0.0 and −1.0 for negative correlations. In both cases, as the value moves from zero towards the maximum, the degree of relationship between the variables becomes stronger. For example, the correlation between height and political success is about +0.20 (tall individuals are slightly more likely to be elected than shorter individuals); by comparison, the correlation between IQ test scores and grade average in high school is about +0.60 (people with above average IQs tend to do well in school). In these examples, there is a stronger relationship between IQ and grades than between height and political success.

positive correlation a relationship observed between two variables in which increases in the value of one variable are associated with increases in the value of the other variable.
negative correlation a relationship observed between two variables in which increases in one variable occur as the value of the other variable decreases.

Technically, the examples in Figure A.8 represent what is called a linear correlation, where the underlying relationship between the two variables is linear (that is, it can be represented as a straight line function). In principle, it is possible for two variables to be related in more complex ways, represented by curvilinear functions (curved lines). For example, the relationship between motivational level and performance is frequently curvilinear, and can be represented by an upside-down U-shape: people tend to perform badly when motivation is very low or very high, and perform best when motivation is moderate. If one were to calculate a linear correlation for the variables of motivation and performance, it would appear to be very low, because a straight line does not accurately represent the relationship between the variables. It is beyond the scope of this Appendix to pursue this issue in detail, but it is worth noting that not all relationships observed in the world are simple straight lines.

Inferential Statistics

As noted, inferential statistics are used for making inferences about the meaning of our observations – that is, they aid us in interpreting a set of data. In essence, this involves making some assumptions, and then seeing what one can conclude, based on those assumptions. In a way, using inferential statistics is like being a detective who tries to interpret a set of clues.

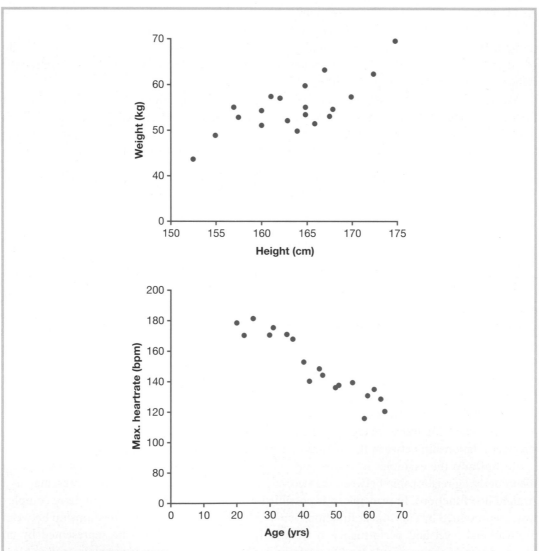

Figure A.8 Correlational Patterns – Correlations are relationships observed between two variables which do not directly tell us about causation. In the top figure, there is a positive correlation between height and weight; in the lower figure, there is a negative correlation between age and fitness, measured by maximum heart rate.

Sampling and Variability

Psychologists almost always depend on observing samples when doing research, even though they want to draw conclusions about a larger population. Ideally, proper sampling procedures will lead to a representative sample. However, even when proper procedures are used, one cannot be absolutely certain that the sample will match the population. To understand why, we must return to the idea of variability. Suppose that the local candy store has a contest: a large barrel is filled with red and yellow jelly beans, and one must guess the ratio of the two in the barrel. As part of the contest, you are allowed to buy a handful, which can then be examined as a way of determining the contents of the barrel. If you examine a handful, and find eight red and five yellow jelly beans, what does this tell us about what is in the barrel? It *might* mean that there are more red ones than yellow ones. But could one get a sample like this if the ratio is actually equal? And what are the chances that a second sample (another handful) will be identical to the first sample?

Intuitively, we recognize that not all samples will be alike, and that any particular sample may differ from the population. Both of these facts are the result of **sampling variability** – the fact that samples randomly drawn from the same population will tend to vary. As a result, using a sample to decide what the population is like can be filled with uncertainty. While this is relatively easy to understand in an example like the jelly-bean contest, the same thing holds true in *any* sampling situation, such as doing research. For example, a cognitive psychologist may test the short-term memory capacity of a group of thirty individuals. The mean capacity is 7.2 chunks of information. Does this mean that people in general would show the same result? Could this be a fluke result, either higher or lower than the proper value in the population? How can one decide? Inferential statistics are concerned with providing guidelines for evaluating situations like this.

sampling variability   variability due to chance variations among samples randomly drawn from the same population.

Drawing Inferences from a Normal Distribution

Perhaps the simplest situation for making inferences involves looking at a single score in relation to a set of data. Suppose that as a teacher, I discover that I have overlooked recording a grade for one particular student on a test. Approaching the student directly, I ask what the grade was, and the student says it was 92 per cent. Now, this strikes me as unlikely, but I am reluctant to accuse the student of lying without reasonable grounds. What can I do? As it happens, I know that the mean for the rest of the class is 66 per cent, with a standard deviation of 7 per cent. Furthermore, I know that the grade distribution is approximately normal. Can this information help me to evaluate the student's claimed grade?

Thanks to what we know about the normal distribution, it is possible to ask about the likelihood of *anyone* receiving a grade of 92 per cent. Knowing the mean and standard deviation,

I can refer back to the normal distribution, and note that only about 2 per cent of all students would receive a grade of even 80 per cent or better; the chances of a grade of 92 per cent are much less. (If our graph in Figure A.6 were more detailed, it would show that the chance of such a grade, given the mean and standard deviation, is less than one in a thousand.) Faced with this information, I conclude that the grade is probably false, and I would insist that the student produce the test as corroboration.

In this situation, I have made an **inference** – a logical conclusion based on what I know (in this case, I have used the observed results to generalize about grades). Note that I can only say the grade is *probably false* – in making inferences, one can never have absolute certainty. In using inferential statistics, we try to generalize from our sample to the population. In doing so, the characteristics of the sample are considered *estimates* of the characteristics of the population. Thus, in the case above, my known values of the mean and standard deviation are based on the sample (that is, the class with one score missing), while the population would be represented by the total class. In effect, by using the estimates, I can ask how likely it would be to find a score like 92 per cent in the total class.

> **inference** the process of drawing a conclusion based on logical analysis of what is already known.

Inferences about the Significance of Results

In similar ways, one can make other kinds of inferences about observational data. For example, a medical researcher does an experiment designed to evaluate a new cold remedy. Sixty people who come to a clinic seeking a cold remedy are randomly assigned to either the experimental group (who receive the new drug) or a control group (who receive a placebo). (We will assume that the experiment is a proper double-blind design, and properly conducted.) All individuals are monitored, and it is found that the mean time to recovery for the experimental group is 4.2 days, and for the control group is 6.4 days; the standard deviation of the combined groups is 1.1 days.

> **t-test** a procedure for determining the significance of observed differences; a common use is to decide whether the difference between the means of two groups is due only to sampling variability.

Does this result represent a real effect of the drug, or is the difference between the groups simply a result of sampling variability, like getting different handfuls of jelly beans? In this situation, the experimenter could use a procedure called Student's **t-test**. (Ferguson (1981) has noted that 'Student' was a pen name for W. S. Gossett, who developed the t-test while working for the Guinness brewery company. Since the problems he dealt with concerned quality control in the brewing process, one might say that we owe current beer quality to statistics!)

> **significance tests** the general name given to inferential statistical procedures which are used to determine whether observed results reflect real differences rather than chance variations.
> **significance level** a statement of the probability that an observed outcome is due only to chance.

In essence, the t-test asks how likely it is to find the observed difference between the means, if only sampling variability is at work; in terms of our example, this would mean that the drug is ineffective. Without going into the technical details, the t-test compares the observed results to a normal distribution of possible sample results. In this case, the probability of finding such a difference purely by chance is less than 3 in a 100, which would normally lead a researcher to conclude that the drug most likely works. Results which are interpreted as based on a real effect (that is, not due to chance) are referred to as 'significant'; the statistical tests for evaluating chance vs. real effects are therefore sometimes called **significance tests**. The conclusion one draws, expressed as the probability that the outcome is due to chance, is called the **significance level** of the results.

Thus, inferential statistics use sample data to try to make inferences about a population which cannot be known directly. In doing so, significance tests evaluate the possibility of obtaining a given result based solely on the chance variations associated with sampling variability. This is reflected in the *null hypothesis*, which always asserts that only chance is at work. If one can *reject* the null hypothesis as being *false*, then this makes the desired hypothesis more likely (but does *not* directly *prove* it to be true, for the reasons mentioned earlier in discussing the logic of research). Although various significance tests exist, they always lead to a probability statement, indicating the likelihood that the observed results would occur if the null hypothesis were true. Thus, statistical inference is always a matter of probabilities, never certainty.

In judging these probabilities, there is no magical cut-off where one can say, 'Now I can be *sure* of my conclusion.' Instead, the commonly accepted standard is that the probability of obtaining the results by chance must be fewer than 5 in 100, although even lower probabilities are more comforting (often, this value will be printed as $p < 0.05$). This means that researchers are actually quite conservative, since fewer than 5 chances of being wrong implies better than 95 chances of being *right* – imagine a gambler who wouldn't bet unless the chances of winning were greater than 95 out of 100!

Decision Errors in Interpreting Data

Despite this conservative attitude, researchers must still face the possibility that sometimes a result *is* due to chance, and that therefore their interpretation of the results is wrong. This leads to the basic problem of all inferential reasoning – trying to make statements based on incomplete knowledge of the world. To return to the drug experiment, the doctors want to determine if the drug works or not; their basis for deciding is their examination of the experimental data. However, as we have discussed, sampling variability implies that if they did the experiment again, the results would be different. So how can they be sure if the drug works or not?

In essence, the situation implies four possibilities, which involve the relationship of the observed results to the underlying reality (see Figure A.9). The results will either suggest that the drug works, or that it doesn't work. Similarly, the underlying reality is either that the drug works, or that it doesn't. This leads to four possible decision outcomes, two of which are correct decisions, and two of which are errors. If the drug actually works, and the statistical analysis says it works, then this is obviously a correct decision. Similarly, if the drug doesn't work, and the analysis does not lead to rejecting the null hypothesis that it doesn't, then this is also a correct decision. The potential problems arise with the other two possible outcomes, which reflect different types of errors. If the drug does not work, but chance factors in the results lead to *concluding* that it does, then rejecting the null hypothesis is really an error. This type of error is variously called a *Type I error*, or a **false positive**. If the drug actually works, but the results are *not* strong enough to conclude that it does, then accepting the null hypothesis is an error. This second form of error, which leads to overlooking genuine effects, is called a *Type II error*, or a **false negative**. In each case, the errors are due to the uncertainty inherent in the process of interpreting results. In a world where sampling variability did not exist, such problems would also be non-existent. But sampling variability is a reality, along with random variations like measurement errors, all of which make it more difficult to get unambiguous results in doing research.

False positive concluding that an observed outcome is significant when in fact it reflects only chance variability; also called a Type I error.

False negative concluding that the observed results are due only to chance variability when in fact a significant effect exists; also called a Type II error.

Decision Table for Evaluating Hypotheses

Reality in population

Decision from sample	Drug works	Drug doesn't work
Reject null hypothesis (conclude drug works)	Correct decision	Type 1 error (false positive)
Accept null hypothesis (conclude drug doesn't work)	Type 2 error (false negative)	Correct decision

Figure A.9 Errors in Evaluating Hypotheses – No statistical procedure can ensure that researchers never make an error in interpreting what the results of a study mean. This chart shows the various ways in which either correct or incorrect decisions can be made. (See text for discussion of the types of errors.)

These effects may seem rather abstract, but in fact, they can be all too real. In the case of drug research, false negatives can lead to abandoning the development of a potentially useful drug, while false positives can lead to wasted effort pursuing an ineffective drug. This type of situation can also arise in situations remote from research – indeed, wherever we must make decisions based on imperfect information.

Increasingly, individuals are faced with making decisions in situations like healthcare. For example, in the past few years, a blood test has been developed for pregnant women, which is designed to detect defects called *neural tube disorders* in the developing embryo. While the test is simple to do, its interpretation is more difficult. Since neural tube disorders are rare, the test results are mostly negative (meaning the embryo is normal). However, of those which are *positive* (suggesting a defect in the embryo), 19 out of 20 are false positives! When a test is positive, the mother must undergo further tests over several weeks. The uncertainty created can cause significant distress, while some of the additional tests (like *amniocentesis*) themselves pose risks. After all this, 95 per cent of those initially told the test is positive will discover that in fact there is nothing wrong with the embryo. In addition, while they occur much less often, the test can also occasionally give false negatives; such a result would lead to the conclusion that the embryo is normal, even when a neural tube disorder exists. Given these realities, many prospective mothers, if informed, might ask whether the test is worth taking.

It should be emphasized that the difficulties described are not unique to the test for neural tube disorders. Similar decision problems arise with other types of medical tests, including mammograms for breast cancer and PSA blood tests for prostate cancer. Similarly, false positives and false negatives can arise in other kinds of situations – for example, if employers concerned about theft ask employees to take a lie detector test (Lykken 1988).

The dilemma which decisions of this nature create cannot be avoided by simple refinements of technology – the limitations are inherent to the process of interpreting the meaning of samples. What one *can* do, if so inclined, is to decide which type of error is more serious, and therefore more important to avoid. Traditionally, the preference in science is to avoid false positives (Type I errors), which would lead to concluding there is support for a theory when in fact it is false. That is why the *minimum* criterion (i.e., *significance level*) for rejecting the null hypothesis is a less than 5 per cent chance that the null hypothesis is correct. In the extreme case, one could avoid *all* false positives by *never* concluding that the results are significant; of course, this would lead to many false negatives, since some data due to real effects would *also* be rejected as inconclusive (similarly, the only way to avoid *all* false negatives is by calling all results significant). Ultimately, uncertainty is an inherent part of the interpretation of data: it is part of the reason that we can never speak of absolute proof in science. To most researchers in psychology, living with such uncertainty is simply part of the larger challenge of understanding behaviour.

Try it Yourself

Suppose that your doctor proposed doing a new test as a means of diagnosing why you don't feel well. What would you want to know about the accuracy and interpretation of the test?

CONCLUSION

Doing research is a complex and challenging process, involving many possible ways that things can go wrong – from the design of the study, to the process of gathering data, to the interpretations that are made once the data have been collected. At the same time, research offers the chance to ask new questions, to be creative in developing a research design, and ultimately, to experience the thrill of discovering something previously unknown. For many people, the rewards far outweigh the risks.

While some individuals reading this book may go on to become professional psychologists, and make discoveries of their own, most readers probably won't. So what value does this material have? In part, this Appendix is intended to appeal to a sense of curiosity, to the desire to understand a bit more about what is actually involved in doing research. Beyond that, it also has a more practical intent: in today's world, we all encounter the results of research, whether in news reports or in our personal lives (as with medical tests). By understanding something about the process which underlies research and statistical analysis, one can be better equipped to evaluate the information we receive. In this sense, the old saying is true: knowledge *is* power. May the knowledge included here add to the power of your understanding as you continue in psychology, and in your life.

CHAPTER SUMMARY

- As a science, psychology makes use of systematic methods for doing research and analysing the resulting data; these topics are referred to as *research methods* and *statistics*.

- In planning research, researchers must consider how observations are made (measurement), what observations to make (*sampling*), and how the hypothesis is to be tested (*research design*).

- In experimental research, the researcher must pay particular attention to the possibility of *error* due to *confounds* or *bias*.

- Statistical analysis involves summarizing the data (*descriptive statistics*) and interpreting the meaning of the results (*inferential statistics*).

- Descriptive statistics include *frequency distributions, measures of central tendency* and *measures of variability*, and *correlations*.

- The most important form of frequency distribution is the *normal distribution*, which is useful both for its particular characteristics and its relevance to many everyday types of data.

- Inferential statistics are necessary in evaluating results because of the occurrence of *variability* when sampling.

- *Significance tests* like the *t-test* are used to estimate the likelihood of obtaining the observed results by chance.

- In using inferential statistics, there is never absolute certainty about one's interpretation; instead, *decision errors* (*false positives and false negatives*) can arise.

- Despite the challenges, research provides opportunities to be creative and to explore the unknown.

🔓 Key terms and concepts

reliability	null hypothesis
validity	descriptive statistics
sample	frequency distribution
population	mode
random sample	median
cross-sectional sample	mean
sampling error	range
internal validity	standard deviation
confound	normal distribution
subject bias	positive correlation
single-blind design	negative correlation
experimenter bias	correlation coefficient
halo effect	sampling variability
self-fulfilling prophecy	significance tests
double-blind design	false positive
falsification	false negative
hypothesis	

When you have read this chapter, log onto the Online Learning Centre website at
www.openup.co.uk/glassman where you will find answers to these Test Yourself questions and
suggested answers to the Try it Yourself activities, plus many more learning resources to help
you study psychology.

Suggestions for Further Reading

- For an entertaining exploration of the ways in which scientific evidence can be misused in everyday life, read **Peter Huber's book,** *Galileo's Revenge: Junk Science in the Courtroom* (1991).
- *Pygmalion in the Classroom*, by **Rosenthal and Jacobson** (1968), provides a vivid and entertaining exploration of how experimenter bias and self-fulfilling prophecies can affect behaviour in the real world.
- If you wish to know more about research design, there are a number of texts available. *Research Methods in Psychology*, by **Hammond** *et al.* (2000), is an established title that provides relatively comprehenisive coverage.
- While statistics is not likely to be considered a topic for light reading, for those who wish to investigate the subject further, **Minium and King's** *Statistical Reasoning in Psychology and Education* (2002) does a better job than most of explaining the logic behind concepts and procedures, and has survived through several editions.

Glossary

abnormal behaviour behaviour which is regarded by society as deviant or maladaptive; according to DSM-IV, an individual must be suffering or show maladaptive functioning in order for behaviour to be described as abnormal.

accessibility in LTM, the principle that remembering and forgetting are dependent on effective retrieval; without the proper cues, information which exists in LTM may not be accessible.

accommodation in Piaget's theory of cognitive development, a process of modifying our cognitive schemata in response to new knowledge or experience.

actualizing tendency in Rogers's theory, an innate drive which reflects the desire to grow, to develop and to enhance one's capacities.

adrenal glands endocrine glands, located just above the kidneys, which play an important role in arousal and stress; the outer layer, the cortex, secretes corticosteroids and the medulla (the inner core) secretes epinephrine (adrenaline) and norepinephrine (noradrenaline).

aetiology the study of the causes of a disease or mental disorder.

aggression behaviour which causes intentional harm to another person.

agoraphobia anxiety disorder in which a person feels anxiety about experiencing panic attacks in public, and therefore avoids public situations.

algorithm a procedure for problem solving which, when used appropriately, always leads to the solution of a particular type of problem.

altered state of consciousness any state of awareness which differs from normal waking awareness; examples could include meditation, sleep, drug states and psychosis.

altruism behaviour intended to help others, independently of any self-interest.

ambiguous figure any stimulus which can be perceived in more than one way.

amphetamine delusional disorder a form of mental disorder resulting from the excessive use of amphetamines; its primary symptom, extreme paranoid delusions, can make it appear symptomatically identical to paranoid schizophrenia.

amygdala an almond-shaped structure in the limbic system which plays a role in basic emotions, and possible memory and stimulus evaluation.

anal stage in Freud's theory of psychosexual development, the second stage (15 months to 3 years); during this stage the focus of drive energy shifts to the lower end of the digestive tract, and the major conflict is toilet training.

androgens hormones whose functions are related to masculine characteristics; the most important is testosterone.

animism Piaget's term for the small child's tendency to ascribe humanlike qualities to inanimate objects.

anti-anxiety drug a drug which functions as a CNS depressant, but whose primary behavioural effect is the reduction of anxiety.

antidepressant a drug which is used to treat clinical depression, primarily by enhancing the activity of the neurotransmitter serotonin.

anti-social personality disorder a behaviour pattern in which an individual shows a history of disregard and violence towards others, unaccompanied by guilt; although these individuals may not report either suffering or unsatisfactory functioning (the generally-accepted standard for abnormality), their behaviour is still deemed abnormal because it violates society's norms in such significant ways.

anxiety a negative emotional state associated with threat to the self; in Freud's theory, it arises when the ego is faced with an influx of stimuli with which it cannot cope, as a result of either external danger or the demands of id or superego.

archetypes in Jung's theory, patterns or frameworks within the collective unconscious which serve to organize our experiences, providing the basis of many fantasies, myths and symbols.

artificial intelligence in computer science, the attempt to build machines which can function intelligently, and the use of such machines to test our understanding of human intelligence.

assimilation in Piaget's theory of cognitive development, a process of integrating new knowledge or experience into our existing cognitive schemata.

association areas areas of the cortex which have no primary function (such as receiving direct sensory data), but rather play a role in integrating activity from other brain areas.

associationism the doctrine, supported by Aristotle, Hume and others, that mental processes, particularly learning, are based on forming connections between ideas and/or events.

attention the process of selectively focusing on particular stimulus elements, typically those deemed most significant.

attitude a personal belief of an evaluative nature, such as good or bad, likeable or not likeable, which influences our reactions towards people or things.

attribution theory a theory dealing with the inferences we make about the causes of our own behaviour, and that of other people; the interpretations made are called attributions.

autonomic conditioning (also called 'learned operant control of autonomic responses') the conditioning of changes in autonomic (involuntary) responses (such as heart rate or blood pressure) by means of operant reinforcement.

availability in memory, the principle that remembering is determined by whether the information exists in LTM or not; forgetting implies that the information is destroyed.

aversive conditioning a form of behaviour modification which is designed to induce an aversive response to stimuli which are associated with existing undesirable behaviours.

axon the relatively elongated portion of a neuron between the cell body and the terminals which provides the signal pathway for a nerve impulse.

basic anxiety in Horney's psychodynamic theory, an intense sense of isolation and helplessness which is the primary source of human motivation.

behaviour modification the application of conditioning techniques to altering human behaviour, particularly those behaviours identified as abnormal.

bias a source of error which results in a systematic distortion of results.

biofeedback a general term for applications of the process of autonomic conditioning; the name refers to the fact that in humans reinforcement is based on providing an individual with information (feedback) about physiological processes (bio) which are normally not observable.

brain the portion of the central nervous system which lies within the skull.

brain stem the region at the top of the spinal cord, composed of three primary structures: the medulla, the pons and the midbrain.

bystander apathy the failure of onlookers to intervene in an emergency; despite the label, the cause is often unrelated to apathy.

bystander intervention the act of assisting strangers in an emergency.

case study a detailed description of a single individual, typically used to provide information on the person's history and to aid in interpreting the person's behaviour.

catharsis the release of drive energy in indirect form, either through the process of recalling emotionally charged experiences or involvement in symbolic activity.

causality the study of how actions or events produce (cause) a particular outcome.

central nervous system (CNS) the brain, together with the nerve pathways of the spinal cord.

cerebellum ('little brain' in Latin) two small hemispheres located beneath the cortical hemispheres, at the back of the head; the cerebellum plays an important role in directing movements and balance.

cerebral dominance the tendency for one hemisphere to be superior for particular functions.

cerebral hemispheres two half spheres, made up of the cortex and underlying structures, which comprise the major portion of the brain.

chaos theory a branch of mathematics dealing with non-linear functions which has been applied to the modelling of situations such as the weather and stock markets; non-linear systems are not predictable, because very small changes in initial conditions can result in radical differences at a later point.

chromosomes thread-like genetic structures composed of double strands of DNA and proteins, containing the genes; in humans, there are 23 pairs of chromosomes.

chunk the basic measure of STM capacity, representing a meaningful unit, such as random letters, numbers or words.

classical conditioning the study of learning which involves reflex responses, in which a neutral stimulus comes to elicit an existing reflex response.

client-centred therapy an approach to therapy developed by Carl Rogers, in which the person seeking treatment (termed a client), not the therapist, is seen as directing the process of therapy; later called person-centred therapy.

closure in perception, the tendency to fill in incomplete patterns to produce a coherent whole.

cognitive appraisal theory a theory of emotion which argues our emotional state is based on our assessment of the situation and its significance to our well-being.

cognitive behaviour modification an extension of behaviour modification which uses cognitive mediation (such as observing a model) in addition to basic conditioning techniques.

cognitive dissonance in Festinger's theory, a state of tension created when there are conflicts between an individual's behaviour and beliefs, or between two beliefs.

cognitive map Tolman's term for the mental representation of learned relationships among stimuli.

cognitive neo-association theory Berkowitz's theory that thoughts, memories and behaviour may be triggered by affective states and/or priming.

cognitive neuroscience a hybrid discipline aimed at identifying the biological bases of cognitive processes by combining techniques for the study of cognitive processes with measures of physiological processes.

cognitive pathology a phenomenon whereby researchers selectively ignore simplifying assumptions and other limitations which are part of the foundations of their theories and methods.

cognitive restructuring in Ellis's rational-emotive therapy, a process for modifying faulty beliefs and the negative emotions they produce, in order to develop realistic beliefs and self-acceptance.

cognitive social learning theory (sometimes simply 'social learning theory') a theory derived from the cognitive approach which asserts that behaviour can be learned from observing other people, and that behaviour is mediated by cognitive schemata.

cognitive therapy a form of therapy which focuses on the role of faulty beliefs and thought patterns in abnormal behaviour; because it also encourages testing beliefs via behavioural strategies, it is sometimes called 'cognitive behavioural therapy'. See also **rational emotive therapy**.

collective unconscious in Jung's theory, a biologically-based portion of the unconscious which reflects universal themes and ideas, not individual experience.

collectivism an orientation which emphasizes a person's connections and obligations to a social group (family, tribe, etc.); when applied to describe a culture, typically contrasted to **individualism**.

compensation in Adler's theory, a process of engaging in activities intended to produce a feeling of superiority over others, in order to overcome feelings of inferiority.

competitive altruism (also called 'costly signalling theory') the concept that individuals will make large public sacrifices if they believe there is a long-term personal benefit.

complementarity a concept developed by physicists to deal with the existence of two models which are both useful, but not directly reconcilable.

complexity a characteristic of systems composed of large numbers of interacting units (such as neurons in the brain), resulting in new patterns or phenomena not found in individual units.

computerized imaging techniques for studying brain function which use computers to convert information into a three-dimensional model of the brain which can be viewed on a television monitor.

concordance a technique for studying inheritance by examining characteristics of individuals whose genetic relationship is known.

conditional positive regard in Rogers's theory, acceptance and caring given to a person only for meeting certain standards of behaviour.

conditioned emotional response an emotional response such as fear which is established through classical conditioning.

conditioned reinforcer in operant conditioning, stimuli which act as reinforcers but are not based on biological survival, such as attention, praise or money.

conditioned response in classical conditioning, a response to a previously neutral stimulus which has become a conditioned stimulus by repeated pairing with an unconditioned stimulus.

conditioned stimulus in classical conditioning a stimulus which by repeated pairings with an unconditioned stimulus comes to elicit a conditioned response.

conditions for growth the conditions under which healthy development of personality occurs; defined by Rogers as unconditional positive regard, openness and empathy.

conditions of worth in Rogers's theory, restrictions imposed on self-expression in order to earn positive regard.

confirmation in research, the process of determining that observations are consistent with the hypothesis being true.

confirmation bias a form of cognitive error based on the tendency to seek out information which supports one's beliefs, and ignore contradictory information.

conformity the tendency to adjust one's opinions and behaviour to comply with group norms in response to explicit or implicit social pressure.

confound in experimental research, a situation where two variables change simultaneously, making it impossible to determine their relative influence.

confounding variable a factor in research which varies jointly with a variable of interest, making it impossible to properly identify the role each variable has in affecting behaviour; typically, a confounding variable represents something which has been overlooked in planning the research, and is only identified after the data have been collected.

congruence in Rogers's theory, a feeling of integration experienced when the self and ideal self match.

conscious in Freud's theory, that aspect of the mind which contains those thoughts and feelings of which we are immediately aware at a given moment.

context-dependent forgetting failure to retrieve information from LTM due to the absence of appropriate contextual cues.

contiguity in behaviourism, the principle that a reinforcer must occur immediately after a response in order for learning to occur.

contingency of reinforcement in operant conditioning, a description of the relationship between a response and a reinforcer.

continuity in developmental theory, the view that changes occur through a continuous gradual process, rather than as a series of discrete stages; continuity is an assertion about the processes that underlie development, as well as the changes observed in behaviour.

continuous reinforcement a reinforcement schedule in which every response is followed by a reinforcer; equivalent to an FR 1 schedule.

convenience sample a quasi-random sampling procedure in which the potential sample pool actually differs from the population – for example, selecting university students instead of people in general; the impact on representativeness (if any) often depends on which behaviour is being studied.

convergent problem a problem which has a single solution, and all elements lead towards that solution; also called closed-end or well-defined problems.

corpus callosum a wide band of nerve fibres which connect the two hemispheres of the brain.

correlation a pattern or relationship observed between two variables.

correlation coefficient a descriptive statistic measuring the degree of relationship between two variables; for positive correlations, it is a number which varies between 0.0 and $+1.0$, and for negative correlations between 0.0 and -1.0; in both cases, the closer the value is to 1, the stronger the relationship between the two variables.

cortex the pink, somewhat wrinkled outer layer of the brain which controls many of our higher functions like speech and perception; from the Greek for 'bark' (as on a tree).

creativity the capacity to produce something which is both unique and useful.

critical period in development, the concept that there are optimal periods for the learning of certain behaviours.

cross-sectional sample a sample which is deliberately selected in such a way that the sample matches the population for particular characteristics, such as age and income.

cross-sectional study a research design based on selecting representative groups who vary on a particular characteristic; when the characteristic is age, this design provides a means of making developmental comparisons.

cue-dependent coding the concept that all information is stored in memory as a set of relationships called the context; remembering is seen as dependent on restoring the cues which formed the original context.

culture a relatively organized set of meanings, shared by members of a group, which affect the way that people, objects and events are interpreted.

debriefing discussing the nature of a research study with participants at its conclusion, in order to explain the true nature and goals of the research and to answer any questions or concerns.

decay in memory, the spontaneous loss of information with the passage of time.

deception in research, the deliberate misinforming of participants concerning the nature of the study and of their role.

deduction the process of drawing specific conclusions from a set of general principles.

defective attention theory a theory which argues that schizophrenia is due to difficulties in selecting and attending to the relevant stimuli in a situation.

defence mechanism in Freud's theory, a technique used by the ego to protect itself from anxiety and the threats which give rise to it; many psychologists use the terms for specific defences as descriptions of behaviour patterns, without endorsing the Freudian interpretation of their origin.

deficiency motives in Maslow's theory, needs whose motivating power is triggered by the absence of the underlying requirements, such as the physiological or esteem needs.

delusions false beliefs which are maintained in the absence of clear evidence to the contrary.

demand characteristics the overt and covert cues present in an experimental situation which can influence how participants behave.

dependent variable in an experiment, the behaviour measured in order to evaluate the effects of the independent variable.

depersonalization a type of dissociative reaction in which the individual psychologically withdraws from a situation, often accompanied by feeling that their body is not real or belongs to someone else.

depressant a drug which reduces CNS activity; in large doses, depressants can cause coma and even death.

depression a mood disorder characterized by sleep disturbances, fatigue and low self-esteem; in major depressive disorder, the symptoms are severe enough to seriously hamper normal functioning, and can be accompanied by thoughts of suicide.

descriptive statistics the branch of statistics which is concerned with describing and summarizing sets of scores.

determinism the assumption that all behaviour has specific causes.

developmental psychology the study of the processes which underlie growth and change in behaviour over time.

diathesis-stress model a theory which views abnormal behaviour as being due to a combination of a physiological predisposition (diathesis) and a stressful environment.

diffusion of responsibility a lessening of an individual's feeling of responsibility in a situation which involves other people.

direct observation any observational technique which depends on direct measurement of behaviour by the researcher, rather than asking an individual to report their behaviour.

discriminative stimulus in operant conditioning, a stimulus which signals the contingency of reinforcement available.

displacement in memory, forgetting (in STM) due to new incoming information pushing out the previous contents; in psychoanalysis, a defence mechanism which involves the redirection of drive energy from one object to a substitute object.

distal cause a factor which has an indirect effect on behaviour, such as previous experiences in similar situations.

divergent problem a problem which does not have a single optimal solution, except according to the criteria one may adopt; rather, the problem tends to lead in several different directions; equivalent to an ill-defined problem.

domain-general model a theory which attempts to account for many aspects of behaviour in terms of a single set of principles.

domain-specific model a theory which focuses on only a single aspect of behaviour in the belief that different aspects of behaviour involve different processes, and therefore require different theoretical explanations.

dopamine hypothesis a theory which argues that schizophrenia is based on overactivity in neural pathways which depend on dopamine as a neurotransmitter.

double-bind hypothesis a theory of schizophrenia developed by anthropologist Gregory Bateson and his colleagues, which argues that faulty communication patterns within the family are the cause of schizophrenia.

double-blind design a rigorous form of experimental control, whereby both the subject and experimenter are kept uninformed about details of the experiment which could result in bias (both subject bias and experimenter bias).

dream censor in Freud's theory, the psychic mechanism whose function is to ensure that sleep is not disturbed by the unconsciously expressed desires that are the basis of dreams; to accomplish this, the dream censor converts the content of the dream into symbolic form (the manifest content).

dualism the view, first attributed to Descartes, that mind and body are distinct; Descartes believed the two could interact via the pineal gland in the brain.

efficacy the measured effectiveness of a treatment technique in medicine or psychotherapy.

ego (Latin for 'I') in psychoanalysis, the element of the psyche which provides the integrating of personality by mediating between the id and the superego, and also mediates the links with the outside world; in Jung's theory, the element of the self which provides the conscious direction of one's life.

egocentrism Piaget's term for the small child's tendency to assume that their perspective of the world is the only one possible.

elaborative rehearsal the active processing of items in STM in order to code the information for LTM; material may be processed in various ways, ranging from an emphasis on sensory characteristics (visual appearance, sound) to a focus on the semantic content (meaning) of information.

electrical stimulation of the brain (ESB) artificial stimulation of neurons by means of a current applied through an implanted electrode.

electroencephalograph (EEG – 'writing the electricity of the brain') a device for recording the electrical activity of the brain.

empathy the ability to understand another person's perceptions and feelings; seen by Rogers as a condition for growth.

empirical based on making observations, as in an empirical theory.

empiricism the philosophical position, first attributed to John Locke, that all knowledge is based on experience; hence, the basis of the view that behaviour is learned.

encoding the processing of stimulus information for retention in memory.

endocrine glands (ductless glands) glands which secrete chemicals called hormones directly into the bloodstream.

endorphin (endogenous – naturally occurring – morphine) a neuropeptide which plays a significant role in pain and mood states.

epigenetic effects in genetics, a term to describe processes whereby stable changes in the expression of genes occur during development; such changes can be transmitted during cell division, but do not involve mutations of DNA itself.

episodic memory the portion of LTM which contains personal experiences, organized according to where and when events happened, such as what happened on your last birthday.

equilibration in Piaget's theory of cognitive development, the process of maintaining balance between our environment and the mental structures which we use to represent that environment.

equipotentiality premise an assumption made by some behaviourists which states that the principles of conditioning should apply equally to all behaviour, in any species.

ethical hedonism the principle that individuals engage in moral behaviour, such as altruism, because it provides some personal benefit.

ethology the study of the behaviour of animals in their natural environments.

evolution a theory to account for the development of species diversity by means of variations which are transmitted to offspring by inheritance; Darwin's theory of natural selection proposed that variations which enhance adaptability, and thereby enhance survival and reproduction rates, are the most likely to be transmitted.

evolutionary psychology the application of evolutionary principles to the understanding of behaviour.

existentialism a twentieth-century philosophical movement concerned with the meaning of individual existence in a universe which lacks objective meaning or purpose.

experiment a research design in which the experimenter uses a controlled situation and manipulates one or more factors (called independent variables) in order to determine their effect on one or more measures of behaviour (called dependent variables).

experimental realism a quality of involvement whereby research participants respond without regard for the laboratory context, as they would in an ordinary situation.

experimenter bias systematic error created when an experimenter's knowledge and expectations about the experiment influence the behaviour of subjects.

expressed emotion a pattern of communication within families which is characterized by high levels of criticism, hostility and emotional intensity.

external validity an assessment of the degree to which one can generalize research results beyond the specific situation studied.

extinction in classical conditioning, the cessation of responding when the CS is presented repeatedly without being paired with the UCS; in operant conditioning, a drop in responding when reinforcement is discontinued.

false negative in inferential statistics, concluding that the observed results are due only to chance variability when in fact a significant effect exists; also called a Type II error.

false positive in inferential statistics, concluding that an observed outcome is significant when in fact it reflects only chance variability; also called a Type I error.

false recognition a form of memory error whereby the presence of familiar cues leads one to believe the stimulus matches a previously experienced stimulus.

falsifiability a criterion for evaluating a theory which states the theory should specify circumstances wherein it could be proven wrong.

falsification in research, the process of using observations to prove that a hypothesis is wrong.

faulty reference an error involving misinterpreting the significance of stimuli and events; while sometimes considered a form of delusion, it can also arise through faulty perceptual processing.

field experiment an experiment done in a natural setting, usually without the explicit awareness of participants; as contrasted to experiments done in a laboratory setting.

fixation in Freud's theory, the incomplete release of drive energy associated with a particular stage of psychosexual development, resulting in a preference for that mode of gratification.

fixed interval schedule in operant conditioning, a reinforcement contingency defined by the amount of time that must pass since the previous reinforcer was given, before a response will receive a reinforcer; thus, FI 5 min. means a fixed interval of five minutes.

fixed ratio schedule in operant conditioning, a reinforcement contingency defined by the number of responses the organism must make in order to get a reinforcer; the ratio is measured as FR x, where x is the required number of responses.

flow Csikszentmihalyi's term for a positive state of subjective experience associated with engaging in tasks which are involving and challenging.

free association a technique originated by Freud for studying the mind, based on asking a person to simply say whatever words floated into their mind, and then looking for patterns.

frequency distribution a statistical analysis of a set of data which tells how frequently each value occurs.

frontal lobe the area of the cortex in front of the central fissure, and above the lateral fissure; it is involved in the interpretation of emotion and experience.

frontal lobotomy an operation, popular in the 1940s and 1950s, which involved sectioning or removing portions of the frontal lobes, in an attempt to treat cases of bipolar mood disorder or chronic pain; later shown to be largely ineffective as a therapeutic procedure.

frontal motor area the area of the frontal lobes just before the central fissure which controls all voluntary movements of the muscles.

frustration–aggression hypothesis a theory of aggression developed by Dollard and Miller which states that frustration (defined as blocking a goal-oriented response) is the sole cause of aggression.

fully functioning person described by Rogers as the ideal of growth, closely related to congruence; healthy growth is characterized by openness, a high degree of spontaneity, compassion and self-direction.

functional fixedness in Gestalt theory, perceiving an object as having only one use.

functionalism an approach to the study of behaviour pioneered by William James, which emphasizes the analysis of the processes by which the mind works (compare **structuralism**).

fundamental attribution error the tendency to underestimate the importance of situational influences, and overestimate the importance of internal factors in interpreting the causes of people's behaviour.

gender identity an individual's belief about whether they are male or female.

gender roles patterns of behaviour which a culture defines as being appropriate for each gender.

gender schema (pl., schemata) a cognitive representation which organizes an individual's knowledge of cultural norms for male or female behaviour.

gene the basic unit of heredity, made up of sequences of 'building blocks' called amino acids; it is estimated that humans possess about 30,000 different genes, each regulating production of various proteins.

general adaptation syndrome a model of stages of stress identified by Hans Selye, ranging from acute stress (alarm) to outward coping (resistance) to finally depletion of bodily resources (exhaustion).

general aggression model (GAM) a theory of aggression developed by Anderson and Bushman which attempts to integrate cognitive social learning theory, cognitive neo-association theory, and biological data on arousal.

generality a criterion for evaluating a theory, which refers to the range of application of a theory; a good theory should apply to a wide range of situations.

genital stage in Freud's theory, the final stage of psychosexual development (from puberty onward), when drive energy is focused on the genitals, with adult expression of sexuality.

genotype the genetic code which an individual carries in the DNA of their cells.

genuine altruism the principle that individuals will assist others without deriving any personal benefit.

Gestalt theory a theory of behaviour pioneered in the early part of the twentieth century by Kohler, Wertheimer and others, which emphasized the active, creative nature of perception and learning (Gestalt is German, and means roughly 'organized whole').

goal state in problem solving, the desired outcome of a problem.

guilt in the recovery movement, a feeling of negative worth in response to behaviour which we recognize as harming others; for Freud, guilt is a form of anxiety associated with behaviours which violate the standards of the superego.

habituation a reduction in neural response due to continual stimulation.

hallucinations false perceptions in the absence of relevant sensory stimuli, such as hearing voices or seeing objects which are not present.

halo effect a form of perceptual bias which occurs when our rating of a person on one characteristic as being positive or negative leads to similar expectations for other characteristics of the individual.

heredity the biological transmission of characteristics from one generation to another.

heuristic a guide to thinking; in problem solving, heuristics provide informal strategies which are usually better than random search, but less effective than algorithms.

hierarchy of fears in systematic desensitization, a list of fear-evoking stimuli, ranging from very mild to very intense, arranged in order of the intensity of fear which they elicit.

hierarchy of needs Maslow's model of basic human needs, which he saw as organized in a hierarchical structure; needs range from physiological (most basic) to self-actualization (top of hierarchy).

higher order conditioning a form of classical conditioning in which a previously-established conditioned stimulus is used as if it were an unconditioned stimulus to create conditioning to a new stimulus.

hippocampus a structure within the limbic system which is important to memory function.

history of reinforcement in operant conditioning, the sum of all prior reinforcement for a particular behaviour; behaviourists assert that the cumulative history of reinforcement is more important than any single reinforcement in determining behaviour.

hormone a chemical secreted by an endocrine gland; hormones are involved in many aspects of metabolism and long-term functioning of the body.

hypothalamus one of the most important elements in the limbic system, the hypothalamus both regulates behaviours associated with hunger, thirst, sex and other basic drives, and also plays a role in regulating hormonal functions.

hypothesis a statement describing a proposed relationship between variables; a specific outcome or prediction derived from a theory which can be evaluated by making further observations.

hysteria a disorder characterized by physical symptoms for which there is no apparent physical cause; the term was used by Freud but actually predates him.

id (Latin for 'it') in Freud's theory, the element of the psyche which is the source of all basic drives.

ideal self in Rogers's theory, a dynamically changing construct which represents an individual's goals and aspirations.

identification in Freud's theory, a defence mechanism which involves incorporating characteristics of a drive object into one's own ego.

illusory correlation a cognitive error in which an individual perceives a relationship between variables where none actually exists.

imitation the learning of behaviour by observing the behaviour of others; sometimes called 'modelling' or 'observational learning'.

implicit personality theories a general cognitive schema about human behaviour, which is used in making interpretations of the behaviour of other people.

incongruence in Rogers's theory, a feeling of conflict or unease experienced when there is a mismatch between the self and ideal self.

incubation in the Gestalt model of problem solving, a process of ceasing to actively work on a problem, in order to modify one's mental set.

independent variable a variable in an experiment which is systematically varied by the researcher, in order to see what effect it has on behaviour.

individualism an orientation which emphasizes personal freedom and independence as important values; when applied to describe a culture, typically contrasted to collectivism.

individuation Jung's conception of the goal of development, which he described as the expansion of conscious awareness by the ego making contact with the unconscious portions of the self.

induction a process of reasoning based on forming general principles from specific observations.

inference the process of drawing a conclusion based on logical analysis of what is already known.

inferential statistics the branch of statistics which deals with the interpretation of data, particularly in terms of generalizing from the observed sample to the larger population.

inferiority for Adler, the notion that all children experience a sense of helplessness because of their size and dependence on others; this feeling can also be intensified by real or imagined physical defects, social rejection and other factors.

inferiority complex in Adler's theory, an intense feeling of insecurity based on failure to resolve the feelings evoked by childhood experiences of helplessness.

information processing a term borrowed from computer science by cognitive psychologists to describe the mental functions which occur between stimulus and response.

initial state in problem solving, the situation at the outset of a problem, including any existing constraints (such as time limits or restrictions on permitted actions).

insight in Gestalt theory, a sudden change in the way one organizes a problem situation, typically characterized by a change in behaviour from random responding to rule-based responding; in psychotherapy, awareness of the underlying conflicts which are regarded as the causes of behaviour.

instrumental aggression aggressive behaviour which is maintained because it is positively reinforced.

interference according to associationism, competition between items which can hamper learning and produce forgetting.

internal validity the assessment of the degree to which the design and execution of an experiment are free from bias, confounds and other sources of error.

interpersonal psychotherapy (IPT) a short-term, focused psychodynamic therapy which emphasizes current interpersonal problems and the development of strategies for dealing with them.

intersubjective verification a process for validating observations based on agreement by two observers; proposed by Rogers as a means of making subjective impressions useful as scientific data.

interview a method of gathering data in which a researcher asks an individual questions; the format may be pre-planned and highly structured, or relatively free-flowing and unstructured.

introjection of values for Rogers, the incorporation of values into the ideal self due to accepting conditions of worth imposed by others; the term was first used by Freud to refer to a defence mechanism.

introspectionism a method of gathering data in which the individual attempts to analyse the content of their conscious mind; associated with the structuralist approach.

kin altruism in evolutionary psychology, the concept that individuals help those who are close relatives, because it fosters the transmission of their genes.

language a system of communication based on symbols or gestures which can vary across individuals and allow for new forms and meanings.

language acquisition device a hypothetical mechanism in the brain that provides an innate understanding of the basic principles of language.

latency stage in Freud's psychosexual developmental theory, the stage which begins at about age 5 and extends until puberty, during which the drives appear to be relatively inactive.

latent content in Freud's theory of dreams, the true meaning of a dream, which is transformed by the dream censor into symbolic form as the manifest content.

latent learning a term used by Tolman to describe situations in which learning is distinct from the performance of a behaviour.

law of effect a principle of learning developed by Edwin Thorndike, stating that any response which leads to a satisfying outcome for the organism is likely to be repeated, and any response which leads to an unpleasant outcome is not likely to be repeated.

learned helplessness a condition found in animals exposed for prolonged periods to unavoidable aversive stimuli, resulting in passive, helpless behaviour.

learning in behaviourism, a change in behaviour which occurs as the result of experience; in cognitive psychology, the process of gathering information and organizing it into mental schemata.

learning set a learned strategy or set which enables the individual to deal efficiently with problems of the same type; similar in meaning to the Gestalt concept of mental set, except that it emphasizes that the set develops as the result of experience.

limbic system a series of subcortical structures which connect the cortex with other parts of the brain and which are important in many basic functions; among the main parts of the limbic system are the thalamus, hypothalamus, amygdala and hippocampus.

localization of function the assumption that specific functions are associated with specific areas of the brain.

logical empiricism in philosophy of science, the assumption that it is possible to compare and evaluate theories in terms of how well they account for the evidence.

logotherapy Viktor Frankl's theory of development and therapy, which is based on the argument that finding a meaning for life is central to individual growth and happiness.

longitudinal study a research design in which a given group of individuals are studied over a period of time.

long-term memory (LTM) the component of memory which is involved with retention over relatively long periods (hours, days, weeks or longer).

maintenance rehearsal the retention of material in STM by means of rote repetition.

manifest content in Freud's theory of dreams, the symbolic form of a dream (disguised by the dream censor) which the conscious mind is aware of, both during sleep and on waking.

materialism the assumption that all behaviour has a physiological basis.

maturation processes in development which seem to be relatively independent of environmental influences, such as depth perception and walking; implied in the term is the assumption that the characteristics are governed by heredity.

mean (also called 'arithmetic mean') a statistic measuring central tendency, calculated as the sum of all the scores, divided by the number of scores.

measure of central tendency a type of descriptive statistic used to determine what is a representative value for a set of scores.

median a statistic measuring central tendency, calculated as the middle score in a frequency distribution.

mediator a process or event within the individual which comes between a stimulus and a response.

medical model a theory of abnormal behaviour which assumes that all such disorders have physiological causes.

meditation a technique or practice that seeks to achieve mental and physical relaxation, a more passive, receptive awareness, and harmony of mind and nature.

medulla a small swelling at the top of the spinal cord composed of the cell bodies of neurons whose axons extend to the heart and other internal organs; its role is to regulate basic bodily processes.

memory the retention and use of prior learning.

mental set in Gestalt theory, the cognitive schema an individual uses to organize their perception of a particular situation, such as a problem.

metaneeds in Maslow's theory, need states which are based on a desire to grow rather than an underlying deficiency; expressed as the need for self-actualization.

mind the inner subjective experience of conscious awareness; the term has no direct reference to physical form.

mnemonics the study and use of techniques for improving memory (from the Greek for 'memory').

mode a statistic measuring central tendency, calculated as the most frequently occurring value (or interval) in a set of scores.

mode of gratification in Freud's theory of development, the way in which the individual satisfies basic drives – for example, in the oral stage, the mouth is the focus for obtaining pleasure (by sucking, eating, biting, etc.).

monism the belief that mind and body are a single entity.

motor nerves those neurons which are responsible for initiating muscle activity.

multiple-personality disorder a severe form of dissociative reaction which can result in several independent personalities being manifested.

mutation a change in the genetic material of a cell; while rare, mutations can result in new characteristics which may be transmitted to descendants of the original cell.

myelin in a neuron, an insulating sheath around the axon, composed of the spirally-wound membrane of Schwann cells, which serves to improve the efficiency of neural conduction.

nativism the philosophical view, held by Plato and others, that knowledge and behaviour are innate in origin.

need for positive regard a need for positive social contacts like love, which Rogers regarded as universal.

negative correlation a relationship observed between two variables in which increases in one variable occur as the value of the other variable decreases.

negative feedback in systems theory, a process within a system which serves to dampen disturbances, promoting stable functioning.

negative reinforcement in operant conditioning, a process for increasing the probability of a response in which a response immediately leads to termination or withholding of an aversive stimulus (negative reinforcer); note that since the response increases in frequency, it is not equivalent to punishment.

negative reinforcer in operant conditioning, an aversive stimulus which, when it follows a response, serves to decrease the probability of the response in the future.

negative symptoms in abnormal psychology, particularly with reference to schizophrenia, the absence of expected behaviours; negative symptoms include bodily immobility, limited speech, flattened affect (absence of emotional expression) and social withdrawal.

nerve impulse the electrical signal generated when a neuron is active, which normally passes from the dendrites, along the axon, to the terminals.

neuron (alt., 'nerve cell') a cell of the nervous system.

neuropeptide a chemical, comprised of a short chain of amino acids, which can function both as a neurotransmitter and as a hormone; also called a neurohormone.

neurosis Freud's term for disorders in which high levels of anxiety are a primary symptom.

neurotransmitter a chemical released by the terminals of a neuron which plays a role in communication between neurons, across the synapse.

neutral stimulus in classical conditioning, a stimulus which initially produces no specific response other than provoking attention; as conditioning proceeds, the neutral stimulus becomes a conditioned stimulus.

non-contingent reinforcement in operant conditioning, a situation where reinforcers sometimes occur independently of any specific response; chance forms of reinforcement.

non-experimental methods research methods which do not involve direct control of any factor, in contrast to experiments; sometimes called descriptive/correlational designs.

noögenic neuroses in Frankl's theory, conflicts within an individual which are based on existential frustrations, rather than the conflicts of id, ego and superego which Freud saw as the source of anxiety.

norm a statistical description of what is typical (e.g., for height); in social psychology, a shared belief about appropriate behaviour.

normal distribution a type of frequency distribution which resembles a bell-shaped curve; among its special properties, first identified by Gauss, is that its measures of central tendency are all the same.

null hypothesis in research, a hypothesis which asserts that any differences observed between groups are random rather than representing an experimental effect; used for statistical purposes to evaluate results.

obedience the study of how people respond to social situations which involve following instructions from an authority figure which may be contrary to individual preference.

occipital lobe the rearmost portion of the cortex, which is devoted solely to vision.

Oedipal conflict in Freud's theory of development, the major conflict associated with the phallic stage which challenges the developing ego; named after the Greek story of Oedipus, who unknowingly killed his father and married his mother.

omission in operant conditioning, a process whereby a response is followed by terminating or withholding a positive reinforcer, which results in a decrease in the probability of the response.

openness behaviour characterized by a person freely expressing their own sense of self, rather than playing a role or hiding behind a façade; seen by Rogers as a condition for growth.

operant conditioning in the behaviourist approach, the form of learning concerned with changes in emitted responses (voluntary behaviour) as a function of their consequences.

operational definition a term whose meaning is defined by the processes or observable events used to measure it.

operator in problem solving, one of the actions permitted in order to solve a problem.

oral stage in Freud's theory of development, the first stage, extending from birth to about 15 months, when the focus of gratification is on the mouth.

organism in Rogers's theory, the biological being which is the source of basic needs (such as food and water), and also the source of a growth motive termed the actualizing tendency.

paradigm in Kuhn's analysis of science, a super-ordinate framework or world view accepted by a group of researchers, which shapes both theories and evidence; since the paradigm influences the observations one makes, no observations can ever be used to evaluate the paradigm.

paraprax (Freudian slip) an error or verbal slip due to an unconscious conflict.

parietal lobe the portion of the cortex just behind the central fissure and above the lateral fissure, whose primary function is the sense of touch.

parsimony in the philosophy of science, the principle that one should always seek the simplest possible explanation for any event.

partial reinforcement in operant conditioning, a contingency of reinforcement in which reinforcement does not follow every response.

participant (alt., 'subject') in research, an individual who is the object of study or participates in an experiment.

participant observation a non-experimental research method in which the researcher becomes part of a group he/she wishes to observe.

peak experience for Maslow, a transient experience of deep intensity which involve enhanced awareness, often accompanied by feelings of being fully alive.

perception the process of selection, organization and interpretation of information about the world conveyed by the senses.

peripheral nervous system (PNS) those nerve pathways which lie outside the central nervous system, involving sensation, motor control and regulation of internal organs.

persistence of set a phenomenon in problem solving, identified by Gestalt psychologists, in which a mental set developed in a previous problem is maintained even though it is no longer appropriate, and tends to interfere with solving a current problem.

persona in Jung's theory, the conscious character or role we assume in presenting ourselves to the world.

personality patterns of behaviour which are characteristic of an individual and which tend to be consistent across situations and over time.

personal unconscious in Jung's theory, that part of the contents of the unconscious which relates to the experiences of the individual.

person-centred therapy (also called 'client-centred therapy') a form of therapy developed by Carl Rogers which emphasizes the responsibility of the individual to determine the direction of change within therapy.

person–situation debate an ongoing issue concerned with the relative importance of personal characteristics vs. situational variables as influences on behaviour.

phallic stage in Freud's theory, the third stage of psychosexual development, extending from about 3 to 5 years of age, during which gratification is focused on the genitals, although not in the form of adult sexuality.

phantom limb a mysterious phenomenon in which individuals who have lost a limb will often continue to experience sensations which seem to come from the missing limb.

phenomenal field for Rogers, an individual's unique perception of the world.

phenomenological pertaining to the way things appear or are experienced; in the humanistic approach, a reference to the emphasis on an individual's perceptions and feelings as defining the meaning of their behaviour.

phenotype the observed characteristics of the individual, based on the combination of genetic expression and environmental influences.

phobia an irrational fear of a specific object or situation which is severe enough to interfere with an individual's functioning in daily life.

phrenology a now-discredited eighteenth-century theory which asserted that one could assess ability by examining the shape of the skull.

pituitary gland a small gland adjacent to the hypothalamus which regulates many endocrine functions, including growth, and also interacts with the nervous system via hypothalamic connections; in stress, it releases a hormone called ACTH which triggers the release of steroids by the cortex of the adrenal glands; sometimes called 'the master gland' because of its many functions.

placebo effect a phenomenon whereby inert substances labelled as drugs (such as a painkiller) produce effects similar to the real drug.

plateau experience for Maslow, an experience which produces an intensified awareness of the world, and a heightened appreciation for life; a more enduring but less intense state of enhanced awareness than a peak experience.

pleasure principle an early description by Freud of the basis of human motivation, which stated that we are driven to maximize pleasure (Lust in German), and to avoid that which is unpleasant (Unlust).

pons (Latin for 'bridge') a region in the brainstem above the medulla which provides connections between the cortex and cerebellum.

population in statistics, the group whose characteristics one wishes to determine, and from which a sample is chosen.

positive correlation a relationship observed between two variables in which increases in the value of one variable are associated with increases in the value of the other variable.

positive feedback in systems theory, a process within a system which reacts to disturbances by amplifying the effects, triggering a major change in functioning.

positive psychology an initiative to combine objective research and subjective experience, with the aim of improving our understanding of how to foster human growth and happiness.

positive reinforcement in operant conditioning, a process of increasing the probability of a response by immediately following the response with a desirable stimulus (a positive reinforcer).

positive reinforcer in operant conditioning, a stimulus which, when it follows a response, serves to increase the probability of the response in the future.

positive symptoms behaviours associated with a mental disorder which would not occur in a healthy person; for example, hallucinations in schizophrenia or sleep disturbances in depression.

post-traumatic stress disorder (PTSD) a chronic stress-like anxiety disorder that can occur as a result of a terrifying experience, such as being in a car accident or being attacked in wartime.

preconscious in Freud's theory, that part of the subconscious mind which can be accessed by deliberate choice.

preparedness a concept developed by Martin Seligman to describe the degree to which physiological structure influences the occurrence of behaviour.

primary process thinking in Freud's theory, a form of thinking characteristic of the id in which no distinction is made between a wish and its fulfilment.

primary reinforcer in operant conditioning, a stimulus whose capacity to act as a reinforcer is based on an innate biological significance, such as food or water.

priming a phenomenon whereby a thought or memory increases the activation of associated thoughts or memories (the term is analogous to 'priming a pump' by using a small quantity of water to enhance the flow of water).

proactive interference in memory, a form of interference in which prior experiences make learning and recall of subsequent experiences more difficult.

problem solving the process of determining appropriate actions in order to overcome obstacles that interfere with reaching a desired goal.

procedural memory that component of LTM which stores 'how-to' information, such as how to play a piano or cook a turkey.

projective test a type of personality test used by psychodynamic theorists in which an individual is asked to interpret an ambiguous stimulus; since the stimulus itself is ambiguous, the assumption is that whatever the person says reveals the workings of their own unconscious mind.

prosocial behaviour socially desirable behaviour that is beneficial to another person, or to society as a whole.

proximal cause a factor which is a direct influence on behaviour, such as one's attitude or an aspect of the immediate situation.

proximity a Gestalt principle of perception which states that elements which are close together tend to be perceived as a group.

psychiatrists medical doctors who specialize in treating mental disorders; by comparison, clinical psychologists typically have a PhD rather than an MD degree.

psychic determinism the assumption made by Freud which states that all behaviour has a cause, and that the cause is to be found in the mind.

psychoactive drug a chemical agent which has a discernible effect on mental state or behaviour.

psychoimmunology the study of mental states and their effect on health, as expressed through the functions of the immune system; sometimes referred to as psychoneuroimmunology.

psychology the scientific study of behaviour and experience.

psychosis a serious mental disorder characterized by severe disturbances of thought and behaviour (as in schizophrenia); according to Freud's theory, psychosis is the result of overuse of defence mechanisms.

psychotherapy any variety of treatment for abnormal behaviour which is primarily verbal in nature, rather than based on the use of drugs.

punding stereotyped, purposeless behaviour that is maintained for long periods of time.

punishment in operant conditioning, a process whereby a response is followed by a negative reinforcer, which results in a decrease in the probability of the response.

quasi-experiment a research design in which participants are assigned to groups based on variables which cannot be manipulated by the researcher (such as age, height, sex).

radical behaviourism a position adopted by Watson and Skinner which argues that mental states are both inaccessible to scientific study and irrelevant to understanding behaviour.

random error non-systematic error produced by the variability in sampling or other natural processes.

random sample a sample obtained through a selection procedure in which everyone in the population has an equal chance of being selected.

range a statistical measure of variability which is calculated as the difference between the highest score and the lowest score in a frequency distribution.

ratio variable a characteristic whose measurements are based on a continuous scale, with an obvious zero point.

rational-emotive therapy a form of therapy developed by Albert Ellis which focuses on the relationship between thoughts and emotions, particularly negative emotions which arise from an individual's faulty interpretations of experiences.

rationalization in Freud's theory, a defence mechanism in which one explains behaviour by offering a reason acceptable to the ego in place of the true reason.

reaction range in genetics, the limits on the variability of a phenotype (observed characteristic) determined by the genotype; in essence, the limits set by the genes on how environmental influences (whether deprivation or enrichment) can affect the trait.

reaction time the time required to make a response to a stimulus, as measured by the interval between the stimulus and the response.

reactivity the tendency for people to alter their behaviour when they are being observed.

reality principle in Freud's theory, the constraints imposed on the ego by the recognition of the demands of the environment.

recall in memory, the active retrieval of information.

recentring in Gestalt theory, developing an alternative mental set for a situation, such as when trying to solve a problem.

reciprocal altruism in evolutionary psychology, the concept that individuals help strangers if the expected benefit of future help from the strangers exceeds the short-term cost of helping.

recognition in memory, the process of identifying presented information as familiar.

reconstruction in memory, the process of remembering by actively creating a whole out of partial information.

reductionism the assumption that phenomena at one level of description can be understood in terms of principles at a more basic level of analysis; for example, that biology is 'reducible' to chemistry.

reflex an unlearned response that can be triggered by specific environmental stimuli, such as a baby's sucking on an object placed in the mouth.

regression in Freud's theory, a defence mechanism in which the individual reverts to behaviours characteristic of an earlier mode of gratification.

reinforcement in operant conditioning, the process by which a reinforcer increases the probability of a response.

reinforcer in operant conditioning, a stimulus which, when it follows a response, alters the probability of the response recurring.

relearning in memory, an improvement in performance which occurs by reviewing, despite the inability to recall or recognize the information.

reliability a criterion for evaluating a measurement process, which assesses the consistency of measurements; often measured by comparing the correlation between repeated observations.

representative sample in statistics, a sample whose composition matches the population from which it is drawn.

repression in Freud's theory, a defence mechanism in which impulses, memories or ideas are actively blocked from the conscious mind.

research method a procedure for examining a problem and gathering observations; in broad terms, research methods are either experimental or non-experimental.

research setting the context in which research is conducted, either a laboratory setting (which involves having participants come to a special location), or a field setting (which requires going to where the people are whom the researcher wishes to study).

resistance in psychoanalysis, the rejection by an individual of the analyst's interpretations of the meaning of behaviour; regarded as a defence mechanism.

response (often abbreviated as R) in general, any reaction to a stimulus, whether overt or mental; for the behaviourists, a measurable change in behaviour.

reticular formation a diffuse network of nerve fibres which runs through the brainstem and limbic system, with connections both up to the cortex and down to the spinal cord; the reticular formation acts as a relay network controlling sensory inputs, and thereby plays a key role in regulating arousal level, alertness and sleep.

retroactive interference in memory, a form of interference in recent experiences that makes it difficult to recall something learned earlier.

sample in statistics, a sub-group drawn from a population; in research, the group which one actually studies.

sampling the process by which one selects observations for research (the sample).

sampling error an error caused by having a non-representative sample, due either to using a biased sampling procedure or the inherent variability associated with the sampling process.

sampling variability variability due to chance variations among samples randomly drawn from the same population.

schedule of reinforcement in operant conditioning, a description of the conditions which determine when a response will be followed by a reinforcer.

schema (pl., 'schemata') a mental framework which organizes knowledge, beliefs and expectations, and is used to guide behaviour.

schizophrenia a severe form of mental disorder in which there can be distortions of perception, thought, language and emotions.

secondary process thinking in Freud's theory, a form of thinking used by the ego to direct the gratification of drives; unlike primary process thinking, secondary process thinking is accessible to conscious awareness, and recognizes constraints imposed by the external world.

selective attention the perceptual process of selectively focusing on particular stimulus elements.

self in Jung's theory, the self comprises the totality of the person, both conscious and unconscious, and is distinct from both the ego and the persona (conscious aspects of personality); for Rogers, the self is a fluid perceptual structure based on our experience of our own being.

self-actualization for Maslow, self-actualization is the most advanced human need, and is based on the desire to grow and use one's capacities to their fullest; as such, it is process-oriented, not based on an underlying deficiency.

self-awareness the capacity for individuals or other living organisms to consciously observe their own behaviour.

self-fulfilling prophecy a phenomenon whereby our expectations about other people lead to acting in ways which elicit the expected response from them; the everyday equivalent to experimenter bias.

self-report a method of gathering data which involves asking an individual to describe their behaviour or mental state in some way, such as an interview, survey or psychological inventory.

self-selected sample a sampling procedure which allows members of the population to decide whether to be included or not, as when a survey has a low rate of response.

self-serving bias the tendency to distort our assessment of our own behaviour, by attributing our successes to personal factors, and our failures to situational factors.

self theory a general term for theories of behaviour which focus on an individual's self-concept and subjective experience of the world.

semantic memory the component of LTM which involves general knowledge of the world.

sensory memory a modality-specific transient form of memory which serves as a buffer between the senses and short-term memory.

sensory nerves neural pathways in the PNS which carry information from the sense receptors to the CNS.

sequential design a research design which combines features of both longitudinal and cross-sectional studies by selecting groups of different ages (like a cross-sectional design), and then following them over a period of time (like a longitudinal study) sufficient to create overlap in the ages represented by different groups.

shame a negative feeling evoked by a perceived loss of self-esteem associated with a particular behaviour.

shaping in operant conditioning, the process of guiding the acquisition of a new response by reinforcing successive approximations to the desired response.

short-term memory (STM) the component of memory which handles retention over relatively brief intervals of up to approximately 15 seconds.

sign stimuli in ethology, environmental cues which regulate the expression of behaviours related to innate drives.

significance level in inferential statistics, a statement of the probability that an observed outcome is due only to chance.

significance tests in statistics, the general name given to inferential statistical procedures which are used to determine whether observed results reflect real differences rather than chance variations.

similarity in the Gestalt theory of perception, a principle of organization based on grouping together similar elements (e.g., based on shape or size).

single-blind design an experiment set up in such a way that subjects are kept uninformed of any details which might lead to bias.

skewed distribution an asymmetrical frequency distribution with a single mode; with a skewed distribution the median is usually more representative than the mean as a measure of central tendency.

social behaviour any behaviour which involves others or is implicitly oriented towards others (for example, both conformity and social expectations that become part of our mental schemata).

social cognition the mental processes involved in the way people perceive and react to social situations.

social constructionism in philosophy of science, the idea that the formation and assessment of theories are primarily influenced by social processes rather than empirical evidence.

social influence a general term for the various ways in which an individual's behaviour is affected by others, such as conformity pressures and group dynamics.

social perception the study of the social aspects of perception – how we see other people, and ourselves in relation to others; part of **social cognition**.

social psychology the study of how interactions with other people affect an individual's thinking and behaviour.

species-specific behaviour behaviours which are characteristic of all members of a particular species. These response patterns (sometimes popularly called 'instincts') apply to behaviours such as mating, finding food, defence and raising offspring.

spontaneous recovery in classical conditioning, the reoccurrence of the CR when the CS is presented after some time has elapsed since extinction training.

spontaneous remission in medicine or therapy, improvement in an individual's condition in the absence of treatment.

stages in developmental theory, the belief that development is based on distinct periods with clear boundaries, with behaviour at each stage governed by different underlying processes; Freud's theory of psychosexual stages is one such theory.

standard deviation a commonly used measure of variability, calculated as the square root of the mean of the squared deviations from the mean of a set of scores.

state-dependent forgetting forgetting related to changes in context associated with internal cues of physical and mental state, as opposed to the context defined by the external environment.

statistics the branch of mathematics that is concerned with the description and interpretation of sets of scores, such as scientific data.

stereotype an oversimplified and often inaccurate perception of an individual based on generalizing from schemata related to the individual's group membership.

steroids hormones produced by the cortex of the adrenal glands which are involved in the regulation of water and sugar metabolism, immune system function and other basic bodily processes; sometimes called 'corticosteroids'.

stigma a mark or label which identifies an individual as deviant, resulting in social rejection.

stimulant a drug which increases activation of the CNS and the autonomic nervous system; these drugs tend to decrease fatigue, increase physical activity and alertness, diminish hunger, and produce a temporary elevation of mood.

stimulus (often abbreviated as S) in general, any event, situation, object or factor that may affect behaviour; for the behaviourists, a stimulus must be a measurable change in the environment.

stimulus discrimination in classical conditioning, selective responding to the CS, but not to stimuli which are similar in some way, as a result of training.

stimulus generalization in classical conditioning, the tendency to produce a CR to both the original CS and to stimuli which are similar to it in some way.

storage the retention of information in memory.

stress a term coined by Hans Selye to describe the non-specific response of the body to any demand on it.

stressor any factor which triggers a stress response in an individual.

structuralism an approach to psychology pioneered by Wundt which attempted to analyse the contents of the mind, using the introspectionist method (compare **functionalism**).

style of life a term used by Adler to describe an individual's unique way of adapting to and interacting with the world, which is an expression of the person's life history and goals.

subconscious in Freud's theory, the portions of the mind which are below the level of conscious awareness.

subject bias in an experiment, systematic error created because the subjects in different groups have different information (for example, knowing whether they are in the control group or experimental group).

sublimation in Freud's theory, a defence mechanism in which drive energy is redirected towards a socially desirable creative activity.

superego in Freud's theory, that portion of the psyche which represents the moral demands of family and society, and is therefore governed by moral constraints.

superiority complex in Adler's theory, a response to feelings of inferiority in which the individual attempts to mask their weakness by adopting an attitude of exaggerated self-importance.

survey a technique for determining attitudes of many individuals by providing a pre-planned series of questions to which individuals respond.

symptom substitution in psychodynamic theory, the assumption that changing overt behaviour without addressing the underlying dynamics will lead to the expression of the problem in a new way.

synapse the junction between two neurons, represented by a small physical gap which is bridged by the flow of neurotransmitter chemicals from the terminals of the 'sending' neuron.

systematic desensitization a technique based on classical conditioning which is designed to treat phobias (unrealistic fears) and related anxiety disorders by gradually diminishing the undesired response.

systems theory a theoretical framework designed for understanding phenomena which involve multiple interrelated elements, where the properties of the whole are different from the properties of the parts; systems are viewed as governed by processes of negative feedback (which promotes stability) and positive feedback (which promotes instability).

temperament behavioural tendencies which are believed to be determined by heredity; examples include emotionality, sociability and fearfulness.

temporal lobe the region of the cortex below the lateral fissure; its primary functions are hearing and memory.

theory a structured set of principles intended to explain a set of phenomena.

think-aloud protocol a transcript of the comments made when an individual is asked to describe their thoughts and behaviour while working on a task such as problem solving.

thought disturbances in abnormal psychology, distortions of thinking processes such as violations of logic, incoherent speech and inappropriate shifts in word usage.

token economy a form of behaviour modification based on operant conditioning; most commonly used in institutional settings, it involves giving conditioned reinforcers (tokens) for doing specific behaviours.

trait a behaviour pattern which occurs consistently across a range of situations; a specific personality characteristic.

transference in psychoanalysis, the displacement of drive energy from past relationships, often between the individual and a parent, to the relationship between the individual and the therapist.

t-test in inferential statistics, a procedure for determining the significance of observed differences; a common use is to decide whether the difference between the means of two groups is due only to sampling variability.

unconditional positive regard in Rogers's theory, acceptance and caring given to a person as a human being, without imposing conditions on how the person behaves.

unconditioned response in classical conditioning, a reflexive response produced by a specific stimulus, such as pupil contraction to bright light.

unconditioned stimulus in classical conditioning, a stimulus which elicits a reflexive (unconditioned) response.

unconscious in Freud's theory, that portion of the subconscious which cannot be directly accessed by the conscious mind; nonetheless, impulses and thoughts from the unconscious can 'leak out' in fragmentary intrusions into conscious awareness, either directly or in symbolic form.

unigenic inheritance genetic transmission which is dependent on the action of a single pair of genes; also called Mendelian inheritance, in recognition of Gregor Mendel's pioneering work.

unlearning an alternative interpretation of the interference theory of memory which holds that the build-up of interference can lead to the breaking of associations, and therefore the destruction of memories.

unobtrusive measure an indirect measure of behaviour intended to avoid the reactivity which can occur with direct observation; such measures typically require making complex assumptions about the relationship of the measure to actual behaviour.

vacuum activities in ethology, behaviours which arise in the absence of appropriate environmental stimuli when drive levels are very high.

validity a criterion for evaluating a measurement process, which assesses whether the variable measures the intended characteristic, as opposed to some other characteristic.

variability in statistics, the dispersion of scores within a set of data.

variable any measured characteristic which shows variation across cases or conditions.

variable interval schedule in operant conditioning, a reinforcement contingency defined by the average time interval which must elapse since the last reinforcer before a response will be reinforced; thus, on a VI 15 sec. schedule, over a long period the average duration would be 15 seconds.

variable ratio schedule in operant conditioning, a reinforcement contingency defined in terms of the average number of responses required to receive a reinforcer; thus, VR 10 means that on average every tenth response is reinforced.

visual agnosia a general term for disorders which result in disruption of visual recognition.

voluntary response a response which is controlled by the individual (i.e., emitted) rather than being triggered (elicited) by specific stimuli the way reflexes are.

wish fulfilment in Freud's theory, the symbolic expression of drives in fantasy form, as in dreams.

would–should dilemma in Rogers's theory, the conflict between one's own needs, expressed through the actualizing tendency, and the demands of others, expressed through the ideal self.

References

Ader, R. (2000) On the development of psychoneuroimmunology, *European Journal of Pharmacology*, 405(1–3), 167–76.

Ader, R. (2003) Conditioned immunomodulation: research needs and directions, *Brain, Behavior and Immunity*, 17 (Suppl. 1), S51–7.

Ader, R. and Cohen, N. (1975) Behaviorally conditioned immunosuppression, *Psychosomatic Medicine*, 37, 333–40.

Ader, R. and Cohen, N. (1985) CNS-immune system interactions: conditioning phenomena, *Behavioral and Brain Sciences*, 8, 379–94.

Aeschleman, S. R., Rosen, C. C. and Williams, M. R. (2003) The effect of non-contingent negative and positive reinforcement operations on the acquisition of superstitious behaviours, *Behavioural Processes*, 61(1–2), 37–45.

Agnew, C. R., Thompson, V. D. and Gaines, S. O., Jr (2000) Incorporating proximal and distal influences on prejudice: testing a general model across outgroups, *Personality & Social Psychology Bulletin*, 26(4), 403–18.

Ahlberg, S. W. and Sharps, M. J. (2002) Bartlett revisited: reconfiguration of long-term memory in young and older adults, *The Journal of Genetic Psychology*, 2002, 163(2), 211–18.

Albee, G. W. (2002) Review of *Mad in America* by Robert Whitaker, *Journal of Community & Applied Social Psychology*, 12(6), 446–9.

Alexander, G. M. and Evardone, M. (2008) Blocks and bodies: sex differences in a novel version of the Mental Rotations Test, *Hormones and Behavior*, 53, 177–84.

Alexander, G. M. and Son, T. (2007) Androgens and eye movements in women and men during a test of mental rotation ability, *Hormones and Behavior*, 52, 197–204.

Allen, B. P. (2005) *Personality Theories: Development, Growth, and Diversity*, 5th edn. New York: Allyn & Bacon.

Allport, G. W. (1937) *Personality: A Psychological Interpretation*. New York: Henry Holt.

Allport, G. W. (1955) *Becoming*. New Haven CT: Yale University Press.

al' Mahdi, M. (2002) *Shaping Excellent Character: A Manual for Parents*. Kuala Lumpur, Malaysia: Women's Club of Universiti Kebangsaan Malaysia.

Alonso, L. and Jeffery, W. D. (1988) Mental illness complicated by the santeria belief in spirit possession, *Hospital and Community Psychiatry*, 39, 1188–91.

Alvarez-Borda, B., Ramirez-Amaya, V., Perez-Montfort, R. and Bermudez-Rattoni, F. (1995) Enhancement of antibody production by a learning paradigm, *Neurobiology of Learning and Memory*, 64, 103–5.

Alvarez-Moya, E. M., Barrantes-Vidal, N., Navarro, J. B. *et al.* (2007) Exophenotypical profile of adolescents with sustained attention deficit: a 10-year follow-up study, *Psychiatry Research*, 153, 119–30.

Amábile-Cuevas, C. F. and Chicuel, M. E. (1993) Horizontal gene transfer, *American Scientist*, 81, 323–41.

American Psychiatric Association (1994) *Diagnostic and Statistical Manual of Mental Disorders*, 4th edn. Washington, DC: American Psychiatric Association.

American Psychological Association (2002a) *Ethical Principles of Psychologists and Code of Conduct*. Washington, DC: American Psychological Association.

American Psychological Association (2002b) *APA Guidelines on Multicultural Education, Training, Research, Practice, and Organizational Change for Psychologists*. Washington, DC: American Psychological Association.

Amsel, E., Langer, R. and Loutzenhiser, L. (1991) Do lawyers reason differently from psychologists? A comparative design for studying expertise, in R. J. Sternberg and P. A. Frensch (eds) *Complex Problem Solving: Principles and Mechanisms*. Hillsdale, NJ: Lawrence Erlbaum Associates, 223–50.

Anderson, C. A., Anderson, K. B. and Deuser, W. E. (1996) Examining an affective aggression framework: weapon and temperature effects on aggressive thoughts, affect, and attitudes, *Personality and Social Psychology Bulletin*, 22, 366–76.

Anderson, C. A. and Bushman, B. J. (1997) External validity of 'trivial' experiments: the case of laboratory aggression, *Review of General Psychology*, 1, 19–41.

Anderson, C. A. and Bushman, B. J. (2002) Human aggression, *Annual Review of Psychology*, 53, 27–51.

Anderson, E. (1994) The code of the streets, *The Atlantic Monthly*, May, 81–94.

Anderson, J. R. (1995) *Learning and Memory: An Integrated Approach*. New York: Wiley.

Anderson, K. B., Anderson, C. A., Dill, K. E. and Deuser, W. E. (1998) The interactive relations between trait hostility, pain, and aggressive thoughts, *Aggressive Behaviour*, 24, 161–71.

Andreasen, N. C. (1999) Understanding the causes of schizophrenia, *New England Journal of Medicine*, 340(8), 645–7.

Angell, M. (1985) Editorial, *New England Journal of Medicine*, June, 6–7.

Angrist, B. J., Rotrosen, J. and Gershon, S. (1980) Positive and negative symptoms in schizophrenia – differential response to amphetamine and neuroleptics, *Psychopharmacology*, 72, 17–19.

Ansbacher, H. L. and Ansbacher, R. (eds) (1956) *The Individual Psychology of Alfred Adler: A Systematic Presentation in Selections from his Writings*. New York: Harper.

Antonuccio, D. O., Danton, W. G., DeNelsky, G. Y. *et al.* (1999) Raising questions about antidepressants, *Psychotherapy & Psychosomatics*, 68(1), 3–14.

Archer, D. and Gartner, R. (1984) *Violence and Crime in Cross-national Perspective*. New Haven, CT: Yale University Press.

Archer, J. and Latham, M. (2004) Variation in beliefs about aggression as a function of relationship to the opponent, *Personality and Individual Differences*, 37, 33–41.

Arieti, S. (1974) An overview of schizophrenia from a predominantly psychological approach. *American Journal of Psychiatry*, 131(3), 241–9.

Aronson, E. (1976) *The Social Animal,* 2nd edn. San Francisco: W. H. Freeman.

Aronson, E. (2000) *Nobody Left to Hate*. San Francisco: W. H. Freeman.

Aronson, E., Wilson, T. D. and Akert, R. (2006) *Social Psychology*, 6th edn. Upper Saddle River, NJ: Prentice-Hall.

Asch, S. (1951) Effects of group pressure upon the modification and distortion of judgements, in H. Guetzkow (ed.) *Groups, Leadership, and Men*. Pittsburgh, PA: Carnegie.

Asch, S. (1955) Opinions and social pressure, *Scientific American*, 193, 31–5.

Atkinson, R. C. and Shiffrin, R. M. (1968) Human memory: a proposed system and its control processes, in K. W. Spence and J. T. Spence (eds) *The Psychology of Learning and Memory*, Vol. 2. New York: Academic Press.

Atthowe, J. and Krasner, L. (1968) Preliminary report on the application of contingent reinforcement procedures (token economy) on a 'chronic' psychiatric ward, *Journal of Abnormal Psychology*, 73(1), 37–43.

Aupée, A. (2007) A detrimental effect of emotion on picture recollection, *Scandinavian Journal of Psychology*, 48, 7–11.

Auster, C. J. and Ohm, S. C. (2000) Masculinity and femininity in contemporary American society: a reevaluation using the Bem Sex-Role Inventory, *Sex Roles*, 43(7–8), 499–528.

Australian Psychological Association (2008) *The Interest Group in Coaching Psychology*, www.groups.psychology.org.au/igcp/.

Ayllon, T. and Azrin, N. H. (1968) *The Token Economy: A Motivational System for Therapy and Rehabilitation*. Englewood Cliffs, NJ: Prentice-Hall.

Azrin, N. H. and Holz, W. C. (1966) Punishment, in N. K. Honig (ed.) *Operant Behavior*. New York: Appleton-Century-Crofts, 380–447.

Baars, B. J. (1986) *The Cognitive Revolution in Psychology*. New York: Guilford Press.

Babits, M. (2001) The Phoenix Juncture: exploring the dimension of hope in psychotherapy, *Clinical Social Work Journal*, 29(4), 341–50.

Bachrach, H. M., Galatzer-Levy, R., Skolnikoff, A. and Waldron, S. (1991) On the efficacy of psychoanalysis, *Journal of the American Psychoanalytic Association*, 39, 871–916.

Baddeley, A. D. (1992) Working memory, *Science*, 255, 556–9.

Baddeley, A. D. (1994) *Your Memory: A User's Guide*. New York: Penguin Books.

Baeaernhielm, S. and Ekblad, S. (2002) Qualitative research, culture and ethics: a case discussion, *Transcultural Psychiatry*, 39(4), 469–83.

Bahrick, H. P. and Hall, L. K. (1991) Lifetime maintenance of high school mathematics content, *Journal of Experimental Psychology: General*, 120, 20–33.

Baillargeon, R. (2002) The acquisition of physical knowledge in infancy: a summary in eight lessons, in U. Goswami (ed.) *Blackwell Handbook of Childhood Cognitive Development*. Malden, MA: Blackwell Publishers.

Baker, B. L. (1969) Symptom treatment and symptom substitution in enuresis, *Journal of Abnormal Psychology*, 74, 42–9.

Baldessarini, R. J. and Tarzi, F. I. (1996) Brain dopamine receptors: a primer on their current status, basic and clinical, *Harvard Review of Psychiatry*, 3, 301–25.

Baldwin, M. (1992) Relational schemas and the processing of social information, *Psychological Bulletin*, 112, 461–84.

Bandura, A. (1970) Modelling therapy, in W. S. Sahakian (ed.) *Psychopathology Today: Experimentation, Theory, and Research*. Itasca, IL: Peacock Press.

Bandura, A. (1973) *Aggression: A Social Learning Analysis*. Englewood Cliffs, NJ: Prentice-Hall.

Bandura, A. (1977) *Social Learning Theory*. Englewood Cliffs, NJ: Prentice-Hall.

Bandura, A. (1986) *Social Foundations of Thought and Action: A Social Cognitive Theory*. Englewood Cliffs, NJ: Prentice-Hall.

Bandura, A. (1991) Social cognitive theory of self-regulation, *Organizational Behavior and Human Decision Processes*, 50, 248–87.

Bandura, A., Ross, D. and Ross, S. A. (1961) Transmission of aggression through imitation of aggressive models, *Journal of Abnormal and Social Psychology*, 63, 575–82.

Barch, D. M. (2003) Cognition in schizophrenia: does working memory work?, *Current Directions in Psychological Science*, 12(4), 146–50.

Barinag, M. (1997) New imaging methods provide a better view into the brain, *Science*, 276, 1974–6.

Barkow, J., Cosmides, L. and Tooby, J. (eds) (1992) *The Adapted Mind: Evolutionary Psychology and the Generation of Culture*. New York: Oxford University Press.

Barnow, S., Lucht, M. and Freyberger, H-J. (2005) Correlates of aggressive and delinquent conduct problems in adolescence, *Aggressive Behavior*, 31, 24–39.

Baron, R. A. (1983) The control of human aggression: an optimistic perspective, *Journal of Social and Clinical Psychology*, 1, 97–119.

Baronides, S. (1993) *Molecules and Mental Illness.* New York: Scientific American Library.

Barry, H., Josephson, L., Lauer, E. and Marshall, C. (1976) Agents and techniques for childtraining: cultural codes, *Ethnology,* 16, 191–230.

Bartholow, B. D., Anderson, C. A., Carnagey, N. L. and Benjamin Jr., A. J. (2005) Interactive effects of life experience and situational cues on aggression: the weapons priming effect in hunters and nonhunters, *Journal of Experimental Social Psychology,* 41(1), 48–60.

Bartlett, F. C. (1932) *Remembering: A Study in Experimental and Social Psychology.* Cambridge: Cambridge University Press.

Bartlett, M. Y. and DeSteno, D. (2006) Gratitude and prosocial behavior: helping when it costs you, *Psychological Science,* 17(4), 319–25.

Bartoshuk, L. (2003) Classical blunders, *APS Observer,* 16(3), 23.

Bassuk, E. L. and Gerson, S. (1978) Deinstitutionalization and mental health services, *Scientific American,* 238, 46–53.

Bateson, G., Jackson, D. D., Haley, J. and Weakland, J. H. (1956) Toward a theory of schizophrenia, *Behavioral Science,* 1, 251–64.

Batson, C. D. (1991) Evidence for altruism: toward a pluralism of prosocial motives, *Psychological Inquiry,* 2, 107–22.

Batson, C. D. (1998) Altruism and prosocial behavior, in D. T. Gilbert, S. T. Fiske and G. Lindzey (eds) *Handbook of Social Psychology,* Vol. 2, 4th edn. Boston, MA: McGraw-Hill.

Batson, C. D., Ahmad, N., Yin, J. *et al.* (1999) Two threats to the common good: self-interested egoism and empathy and empathy-induced altruism, *Personality & Social Psychology Bulletin,* 25(1), 3–16.

Baumeister, R. F. and Leary, M. R. (1995) The need to belong: desire for interpersonal attachments as a fundamental human motivation, *Psychological Bulletin,* 117, 497–529.

Baumrind, D. (1964) Some thoughts on ethics of research: after reading Milgram's 'Behavioral study of obedience', *American Psychologist,* 19, 421–3.

Baumrind, D. (1991) The influence of parenting style on adolescent competence and substance use, *Journal of Early Adolescence,* 11, 56–95.

Beadle, G. and Beadle, M. (1966) *The Language of Life.* New York: Doubleday.

Beaman, A., Barnes, P. J., Klentz, B. and McQuirk, B. (1978) Increasing helping rates through information dissemination: teaching pays, *Personality and Social Psychology Bulletin,* 4, 406–11.

Beauchamp, G. (1987) The human preference for excess salt, *American Scientist,* 75(1), 27–33.

Beauregard, M. and Paquette, V. (2006) Neural correlates of a mystical experience in Carmelite nuns, *Neuroscience Letters,* 405, 186–90.

Beck, A. T. (1993) Cognitive therapy: past, present, and future, *Journal of Consulting and Clinical Psychology,* 61, 194–8.

Beck, A. T., Sokol, L., Clark, D. A. *et al.* (1992) A crossover study of focused cognitive therapy for panic disorder, *American Journal of Psychiatry,* 149, 778–83.

Beck, J. G., Stanley, M. A., Baldwin, L. E. *et al.* (1994) Comparison of cognitive therapy and relaxation training for panic disorder, *Journal of Consulting and Clinical Psychology,* 62, 818–26.

Becker, E. (1973) *The Denial of Death.* New York: Free Press.

Bell, A. P., Weinberg, M. S. and Hammersmith, S. K. (1981) *Sexual Preference: Its Development in Men and Women.* Bloomington, IN: Indiana University Press.

Bellino, S., Zizza, M., Rinaldi, C. and Bogetto, F. (2007) Concomitant borderline personality disorder: comparison of interpersonal and cognitive psychotherapy, *The Canadian Journal of Psychiatry,* 52(11), 718–25.

Belmaker, R. H. and Agam, G. (2008) Major depressive disorder: mechanisms of disease, *New England Journal of Medicine,* 258(1), 55–68.

Belson, W. A. (1978) *Television Violence and the Adolescent Boy*. Hampshire, UK: Saxon House.

Bem, D. J. (1992) On the uncommon wisdom of our lay personality theory, *Psychological Inquiry*, 3(1), 82–5.

Benedetti, F., Maggi, G., Lopiano, L. *et al.* (2003) Open versus hidden medical treatments: the patient's knowledge about a therapy affects the therapy outcome, *Prevention & Treatment*, 6, np.

Benjamin, L. T. and Dixon, D. N. (1996) Dream analysis by mail: an American woman seeks Freud's advice, *American Psychologist*, 51, 461–8.

Benson, H. (1976) *The Relaxation Response*. New York: Morrow.

Berenbaum, S. A. and Hines, M. (1992) Early androgens are related to childhood sex-typed toy preferences, *Psychological Science*, 3, 203–6.

Berg, M. E. and Karlsen, J. T. (2007) Mental models in project management coaching, *Engineering Management Journal*, 19(3), 3–13.

Bergen, D. (2007) *Human Development: Traditional and Contemporary Theories*. Upper Saddle River, NJ: Pearson/Prentice Hall.

Bergin, L. and Walsh, S. (2005) The role of hope in psychotherapy with older adults, *Aging & Mental Health*, 9(1), 7–15.

Berko, J. (1958) The child's learning of English morphology, *World*, 14, 150–7.

Berkowitz, L. (1975) *A Survey of Social Psychology*. Hinsdale, IL: Dryden Press.

Berkowitz, L. (1978) Whatever happened to the frustration-aggression hypothesis?, *American Behavioral Scientist*, 21, 691–708.

Berkowitz, L. (1983) Aversively stimulated aggression, *American Psychologist*, 38, 1135–44.

Berkowitz, L. (1984) Some effects of thoughts on anti- and prosocial influences of media events: a cognitive-neoassociation analysis, *Psychological Bulletin*, 95, 410–27.

Berkowitz, L. (1989) Frustration-aggression hypothesis: examination and reformulation, *Psychological Bulletin*, 106, 59–73.

Berkowitz, L. (1990) On the formation and regulation of anger and aggression: a cognitive-neoassociationistic analysis, *American Psychologist*, 45, 494–503.

Berkowitz, L. (1993a) Pain and aggression: some findings and implications, *Motivation and Emotion*, 17, 277–93.

Berkowitz, L. (1993b) *Aggression: Its Causes, Consequences, and Control*. New York: McGraw-Hill.

Berkowitz, L. (1998) Aggressive personalities, in D. F. Barone, M. Hersen and V.B. Van Hasselt (eds) *Advanced Personality*. New York: Plenum Press.

Berkowitz, L. and Devine, P. G. (1995) Has social psychology always been cognitive? What is 'cognitive' anyhow?, *Personality and Social Psychology Bulletin*, 21, 696–703.

Berlyne, D. E. (1975) Behaviourism? Cognitive theory? Humanistic psychology? – To Hull with them all!, *Canadian Psychological Review*, 16, 69–80.

Berne, E. (1961) *Transactional Analysis in Psychotherapy*. New York: Grove Press.

Berne, E. (1973) *Games People Play*. New York: Grove Press.

Bernstein, I. L. (1991) Aversion conditioning in response to cancer and cancer treatment, *Clinical Psychology Review*, 11, 185–91.

Berry, J. W., Poortinga, Y. H., Segall, M. H. and Dasen, P. R. (2002) *Cross-cultural Psychology: Research and Applications*, 2nd edn. Cambridge: Cambridge University Press.

Berscheid, E. (1988) Some comments on love's anatomy. Or, whatever happened to an old-fashioned lust?, in R. J. Sternberg and M. L. Barnes (eds) *The Psychology of Love*. New Haven, CT: Yale University Press.

Berscheid, E. (2000) Attraction, in A. Kazdin (ed.), *Encyclopedia of Psychology*. New York: Oxford University Press.

Besharat, M. A. (2003) What are the main differences between behavioral and systems therapy with couples? A critical account, *Journal of Contemporary Psychotherapy*, 33(2), 109–27.

Beutler, L. E. (2002) The dodo bird is extinct, *Clinical Psychology: Science and Practice*, 9(1), 30–4.

Beutler, L. E. and Malik, M. L. (eds) (2002) *Rethinking the DSM: A Psychological Perspective*. Washington, DC: The American Psychological Association.

Bhawuk, D. P. S. (2003) Culture's influence on creativity: the case of Indian spirituality, *International Journal of Intercultural Relations*, 27(1), 1–22.

Bhugra, D. and Bhui, K. (2002) Is the Oedipal complex universal? Problems for sexual and relationship psychotherapy across cultures, *Sexual & Relationship Therapy*, 17(1), 69–86.

Bhugra, D., Hilwig, M., Corridon, B. *et al.* (2000) A comparison of symptoms in cases with first onset of schizophrenia across four groups, *European Journal of Psychiatry*, 14(4), 241–9.

Bhui, K., Bhugra, D., Goldberg, D. *et al.* (2001) Cultural influences on the prevalence of common mental disorder, general practitioners' assessments and help-seeking among Punjabi and English people visiting their general practitioner, *Psychological Medicine*, 31(5), 815–25.

Bick, P. A. and Kinsbourne, M. (1987) Auditory hallucinations and subvocal speech in schizophrenic patients, *American Journal of Psychiatry*, 144, 222–5.

Bjorklund, D. F. (1997) The role of immaturity in human development, *Psychological Bulletin*, 122(2), 153–69.

Blackburn, T. (1971) Sensuous-intellectual complementarity in science, *Science*, 172, 1003–7.

Blakemore, C. (1977) *Mechanisms of the Mind*. Cambridge: Cambridge University Press.

Blakemore, J. E. O. (2003) Children's beliefs about violating gender norms: boys shouldn't look like girls, and girls shouldn't act like boys, *Sex Roles*, 48(9/10), 411–19.

Blanchard-Fields, F. (2007) Everyday problem solving and emotion: an adult developmental perspective, *Current Directions in Psychological Science*, 16(1), 26–31.

Blank, H. and Nestler, S. (2007) Cognitive process models of hindsight bias, *Social Cognition*, 25(1), 132–46.

Blanke, O., Ortigue, S., Landis, T. and Seeck, M. (2002) Stimulating illusory own-body perceptions, *Nature*, 419(6904), 269–70.

Blatt, S. J. (1975) The validity of projective techniques and their research and clinical contribution, *Journal of Personality Assessment*, 39, 327–43.

Blazer, D. G., Kessler, R. C., McGonagle, K. A. and Swartz, M. S. (1994) The prevalence and distribution of major depression in a national community sample: the National Comorbidity Survey, *American Journal of Psychiatry*, 151(7), 979–86.

Block, J. (1971) *Lives Through Time*. Berkeley, CA: Bancroft Press.

Bloom, H. E. (1981) *The Linguistic Shaping of Thought: A Study of the Impact of Language on Thinking in China and the West*. Hillsdale, NJ: Lawrence Erlbaum.

Boden, J. M. and Baumeister, R. F. (1997) Repressive coping: distraction using pleasant thoughts and memories, *Journal of Personality and Social Psychology*, 73, 45–62.

Bohart, A. C. (1995) The person-centered psychotherapies, in A. S. Gurman and S. B. Messer (eds) *Essential Psychotherapies: Theory and Practice*. New York: Guilford Press.

Bohart, A. C. and Greening, T. (2001) Humanistic psychology and positive psychology, *American Psychologist*, 56(1), 81–2.

Bolling, M. Y. (2003) Research and representation: a conundrum for behavior analysts, *Behavior and Social Issues*, 12(1), 19–28.

Bond, M. (1991). Chinese values and health: a cultural level examination. *Psychology and Health*, 5, 137–52.

Bond, M. and Smith, P. B. (1996) Culture and conformity: a meta-analysis of studies using Asch's (1952b, 1956) line judgement task, *Psychological Bulletin*, 119(1), 111–37.

Book, H. E. (1998) Guidelines for the practice of brief psychodynamic therapy, in P. Cameron, J. Ennis and J. Deadman (eds) *Standards and Guidelines for the Psychotherapies*. Toronto: University of Toronto Press.

Borkovec, T. D. and Costello, E. (1993) Efficacy of applied relaxation and cognitive-behavioral therapy in the treatment of generalized anxiety disorder, *Journal of Consulting and Clinical Psychology*, 51, 611–19.

Borkovec, T. D. and Mathews, A. M. (1988) Treatment of nonphobic anxiety disorders: a comparison of nondirective, cognitive, and coping desensitization therapy, *Journal of Consulting and Clinical Psychology*, 56, 877–84.

Bornstein, M. H. (1989) Sensitive periods in development: structural characteristics and causal inter-pretations, *Psychological Bulletin*, 105, 179–97.

Borysenko, J. (1990) *Guilt is the Teacher, Love is the Lesson*. New York: Warner.

Bosch, J. A., De Geus, E. J. C., Kelder, A. *et al.* (2001) Differential effects of active versus passive coping on secretory immunity, *Psychophysiology*, 38(5), 836–46.

Bouchard, T. J., Jr, Lykken, D. T., McGue, M., Segal, N. L. and Tellegen, A. (1990) Sources of human psychological differences: the Minnesota study of twins reared apart, *Science*, 250, 223–8.

Bower, G. H. (1981) Mood and memory, *American Psychologist*, 36, 129–48.

Bower, T. G. R. (1979) *Human Development*. San Francisco: W. H. Freeman.

Bowlby, J. (1969) *Attachment and Loss,* Vol. 1: *Attachment*. London: Hogarth Press.

Bowlby, J. (1988) *A Secure Basis: Parent-child Attachment and Healthy Human Development*. New York: Guilford Press.

Braff, D. L. (1993) Information processing and attention dysfunctions in schizophrenia, *Schizophrenia Bulletin*, 19, 233–59.

Brandt, L. W. (1982) *Psychologists Caught: A Psycho-Logic of Psychology*. Toronto: University of Toronto Press.

Braun, A. (1999) 'The new neuropsychology of sleep: Implications for psychoanalysis': Commentary, *Neuro-psychoanalysis*, 1(2), 196–201.

Bregman, E. (1934) An attempt to modify emotional attitude of infants by the conditioned response technique, *Journal of Genetic Psychology*, 45, 169–98.

Brehm, S. S. (2002) *Intimate Relationships*, 3rd edn. New York: McGraw-Hill.

Bremner, J. D. (2003) The effects of stress on brain function, *Psychiatric Times*, 20(7), 18–22.

Brenner, C. (1955) *An Elementary Textbook of Psychoanalysis*. Garden City, New York: Doubleday Anchor.

Brenner, C. (1957) Appendix, in J. Rickman (ed.) *A General Selection from the Works of Sigmund Freud*. Garden City, New York: Doubleday.

Briere, J. and Conte, J. R. (1993) Self-reported amnesia for abuse in adults molested as children, *Journal of Traumatic Stress*, 6, 21–31.

Brislin, R. (2000) *Understanding Culture's Influence on Behavior*, 2nd edn. Pacific Grove, CA: Wadsworth.

British Psychological Society (2006) *Code of Ethics and Conduct*. Leicester: British Psychological Society.

British Psychological Society (2008) *Special Group in Coaching Psychology*, www.bps.org.uk/coachingpsy/.

Bronfenbrenner, U. and Ceci, S. J. (1994) Nature-nurture reconceptualized in developmental perspective: a bioecological model, *Psychological Review*, 101, 568–86.

Brown, G. W. and Harris, T. O. (eds) (1989) *Life Events and Illness*. New York: Guilford Press.

Brown, R. (1972) Schizophrenia, language, and reality. Eastern Psychological Association Presidential Address, Boston.

Brown, R. (1973) Development of the first language in the human species, *American Psychologist*, 28, 97–106.

Brown, R. and Herrnstein, R. J. (1975) *Psychology*. Boston, MA: Little, Brown.

Brown, S. L., Nesse, R. M., Vinokur, A. D. and Smith, D. M. (2003) Providing social support may be more beneficial than receiving it: results from a prospective study of mortality, *Psychological Science*, 14(4), 320–7.

Brown, T. A. and Barlow, D. H. (2001) *Casebook in Abnormal Psychology*, 2nd edn. Pacific Grove, CA: Wadsworth.

Brown, W. A. (2002) Are antidepressants as ineffective as they look?, *Prevention and Treatment*, 5, np. Online at http://journals.apa.org/prevention/volume5/pre0050026c. html.

Bruner, J. S., Goodnow, J. and Austin, G. A. (1956) *A Study of Thinking*. New York: Wiley.

Brzustowicz, L. M., Hodgkinson, K. A., Chow, E. W. C. *et al.* (2000) Location of a major susceptibility locus for familial schizophrenia on chromosome 1q21–q22, *Science*, 208, 678–82.

Buber, M. (1958) *I and Thou*, 2nd edn. New York: Scribner's.

Buckholtz, J.W. and Meyer-Lindenberg, A. (2008) MAOA and the neurogenetic architecture of human aggression, *Trends in Neurosciences*, 31(3), 120–9.

Buford, B. (1991) *Among the Thugs*. London: Mandarin.

Bugental, J. F. T. and Sterling, M. M. (1995) Existential-humanistic therapy: new perspectives, in A. S. Gurman and S. B. Messer (eds) *Essential Psychotherapies: Theory and Practice*. New York: Guilford Press.

Buller, D. J. (2005) Evolutionary psychology: the emperor's new paradigm, *Trends in Cognitive Sciences*, 9(6), 277–83.

Burnstein, E., Crandall, C. and Kitayama, S. (1994) Some neo-Darwinian decision rules for altruism: weighing cues for inclusive fitness as a function of the biological importance of the decision, *Journal of Personality and Social Psychology*, 67, 773–89.

Bushman, B. J., Baumeister, R. F. and Stack, A. D. (1999) Catharsis, aggression, and persuasive influence: self-fulfilling or self-defeating prophecies? *Journal of Personality and Social Psychology*, 76, 367–76.

Bushman, B. J. and Huesmann, L. R. (2001) Effects of televised violence on aggression, in D. Singer and J. Singer (eds) *Handbook of Children and the Media*. Thousand Oaks, CA: Sage.

Buss, A. (1963) Physical aggression in relation to different frustrations, *Journal of Abnormal and Social Psychology*, 67, 1–7.

Buss, D. M. (1995) Evolutionary psychology: a new paradigm for psychological science, *Psychological Inquiry*, 6, 1–30.

Buss, D. M., Shackelford, T. K., Kirkpatrick, L. A. and Larsen, R. J. (2001) A half century of mate preferences: the cultural evolution of values, *Journal of Marriage & the Family*, 63(2), 491–503.

Butt, A., Testylier, G. and Dykes, R. (1997) Acetylcholine release in rat frontal and somatosensory cortex is enhanced during tactile discrimination learning, *Psychobiology*, 25, 18–33.

Butzlaff, R. L. and Hooley, J. M. (1998) Expressed emotion and psychiatric relapse, *Archives of General Psychiatry*, 55, 547–52.

Byne, W. (1994) The biological evidence challenged, *Scientific American*, 270, May, 50–5.

Byrne, M., Esben Agerbo, E., Bennedsen, B., Eaton, W. W. and Mortensen, P. B. (2007) Obstetric conditions and risk of first admission with schizophrenia: a Danish national register based study, *Schizophrenia Research*, 97, 51–9.

Cacioppo, J. T. and Gardner, W. L. (1999) Emotion, *Annual Review of Psychology*, 50, 191–214.

Caetano, S. C., Fonseca, M., Hatch, J. P. *et al.* (2007) Medial temporal lobe abnormalities in pediatric unipolar depression, *Neuroscience Letters*, 427, 142–7.

Caligiuri, M. P., Hellige, J. B., Cherry, B. J. *et al.* (2005) Lateralized cognitive dysfunction and psychotic symptoms in schizophrenia, *Schizophrenia Research*, 80, 151–61.

Campbell, A., Shirley, L. and Caygill, L. (2002) Sex-typed preferences in three domains: do two-year-olds need cognitive variables?, *British Journal of Psychology*, 93(2), 203–17.

Campbell, D. T. and Stanley, J. C. (1966) *Experimental and Quasi-experimental Designs for Research*. Chicago, IL: Rand-McNally.

Campbell, J. (1968) *The Hero with a Thousand Faces*. Princeton, NJ: Princeton/Bollingen Press.

Campbell, J. (1982) *Grammatical Man: Information, Entropy, Language and Life*. New York: Simon & Schuster.

Campbell, J. D., Tesser, A. and Fairey, P. J. (1986) Conformity and attention to the stimulus: some temporal and contextual dynamics, *Journal of Personality and Social Psychology*, 51, 315–24.

Canadian Mental Health Association (2000) Stigma: the dark shadow of oppression (special issue), *Network*, 16(1), 4–15.

Canadian Psychological Association (2000) *Canadian Code of Ethics for Psychologists*, 3rd edn. Ottawa, ON: Canadian Psychological Association.

Cantor-Graae, E. (2007) The contribution of social factors to the development of schizophrenia: a review of recent findings, *Canadian Journal of Psychiatry*, 52, 277–86.

Caporael, L. R. (1976) Ergotism: the Satan loosed in Salem?, *Science*, 192, 21–6.

Caporael, L. R. and Baron, R. M. (1997) Groups as the mind's natural environment, in J. A. Simpson and Douglas T. Kenrick (eds) *Evolutionary Social Psychology*. Mahwah, NJ: Lawrence Erlbaum Associates.

Caprara, G. V., Barbaranelli, C., Pastorelli, C., Bandura, A. and Zimbardo, P. G. (2000) Prosocial foundations of children's academic achievement, *Psychological Science*, 11(4), 302–6.

Caprara, G. V. and Steca, P. (2007) Prosocial agency: the contribution of values and self-efficacy beliefs to prosocial behavior across ages, *Journal of Social and Clinical Psychology*, 26(2), 218–39.

Carlson, M. (2008) I'd rather go along and be considered a man: masculinity and bystander intervention, *The Journal of Men's Studies*, 16(1), 3–17.

Carlson, N. (1990) *Psychology: The Science of Behavior*. Boston: Allyn & Bacon.

Carmichael, L., Hogan, H. P. and Walter, A. A. (1932) An experimental study of the effect of language on the reproduction of visually perceived items, *Journal of Experimental Psychology*, 15, 73–86.

Carter, R. (1998) *Mapping the Mind*. Berkeley, CA: University of California Press.

Carver, P. R., Yunger, J. L. and Perry, D. G. (2003) Gender identity and adjustment in middle childhood, *Sex Roles*, 49(3/4), 95–109.

Cashdan, E. (2003) Hormones and competitive aggression in women, *Aggressive Behavior*, 29(2), 107–15.

Caspi, A., Elder, G. E. and Herbener, E. (1990) Childhood personality and the prediction of life-course patterns, in L. N. Robins and M. Rutter (eds) *Straight and Devious Pathways from Childhood to Adulthood*. New York: Cambridge University Press.

Caspi, A. and Roberts, B. W. (2001) Personality development across the life course: the argument for change and continuity, *Psychological Inquiry*, 12(2), 9–66.

Caspi, A., Roberts, B. W. and Shiner, R. L. (2005) Personality development: stability and change, *Annual Review of Psychology*, 56, 453–84.

Caspi, A., Sugden, K., Moffitt, T. E. *et al.* (2003) Influence of life stress on depression: moderation by a polymorphism in the 5-HTT gene, *Science*, 301, 386–9.

Castonguay, L. G., Goldfried, M. R., Wiser, S. *et al.* (1996) Predicting the effect of cognitive therapy for depression: a study of unique and common factors, *Journal of Consulting and Clinical Psychology*, 64, 497–504.

Chalmers, A. F. (1999) *What is This Thing Called Science?*, 3rd edn. Indianapolis, IN: Hackett Publishing.

Chambers, R. A., Bickel, W. K. and Potenza, M. N. (2007) A scale-free systems theory of motivation and addiction, *Neuroscience & Biobehavioral Reviews*, 31(7), 1017–45.

Chambless, D. L. (2002) Beware the dodo bird: the dangers of overgeneralization, *Clinical Psychology: Science and Practice*, 9(1), 13–16.

Chance, P. (2008) *Learning and Behavior*, 8th edn. Belmont, CA: Wadsworth.

Chapman, J. (1966) The early symptoms of schizophrenia, *British Journal of Psychiatry*, 112, 225–51.

Chen, C., Kasof, J., Himsel, A. J. *et al.* (2002) Creativity in drawings of geometric shapes: a cross-cultural examination with the consensual assessment technique, *Journal of Cross-Cultural Psychology*, 33(2), 171–87.

Chen, C-W. and Ma, H-H. (2007) Effects of treatment on disruptive behaviors: a quantitative synthesis of single-subject researches using the PEM approach, *The Behavior Analyst Today*, 8(4), 380–97.

Cheour, M., Ceponiené, R., Leppänen, P. *et al.* (2002) The auditory sensory memory trace decays rapidly in newborns, *Scandinavian Journal of Psychology*, 43(1), 33-9.

Chess, S. and Thomas, A. (1987) *Origins and Evolution of Behaviour Disorders: From Infancy to Early Adult Life*. Cambridge, MA: Harvard University Press.

Chick, K., Heilman-Houser, R. A. and Hunter, M. W. (2002) The impact of child care on gender role development and gender stereotypes, *Early Childhood Education Journal*, 29(3), 149–54.

Choi, J. and Silverman, I. (2002) The relationship between testosterone and route-learning strategies in humans, *Brain & Cognition*, 50(1), 116–20.

Chomsky, N. (1972) *Language and Mind*. New York: Harcourt Brace Jovanovich.

Chomsky, N. (1988) *Language and Problems of Knowledge*. Cambridge, MA: MIT Press.

Chomsky, N. (2002) *On Nature and Language* (edited by A. Belletti and L. Rizzi). Cambridge: Cambridge University Press.

Chorover, S. L. (1985) Psychology in cultural context: the division of labor and the fragmentation of experience, in S. Koch and D. E. Leary (eds) *A Century of Psychology as Science*. New York: McGraw-Hill, 870–9.

Choy, Y., Fryer, A. J. and Lipsitz, J. D. (2007) Treatment of specific phobia in adults, *Clinical Psychology Review*, 27, 266–86.

Christensen, A. (1988) Deception in psychological research: when is its use justified?, *Personality and Social Psychology Bulletin*, 14, 664–75.

Christy, C. A. and Voigt, H. (1994) Bystander responses to public episodes of child abuse, *Journal of Applied Social Psychology*, 24(9), 824–47.

Chumbley, J. and Griffiths, M. (2006) Affect and the computer game player: gender, personality, and game reinforcement structure on affective responses to computer game-play, *CyberPsychology & Behavior*, 9(3), 308–16.

Chung, M. C., Fulford, K. W. M. and Graham, G. (2007) *Reconceiving Schizophrenia*. New York: Oxford University Press.

Cialdini, Robert B. (1991) Altruism or egoism? That is (still) the question, *Psychological Inquiry*, 2(2), 124–6.

Clancy, S. A., McNally, R. J. and Schachter, D. L. (1999) Effects of guided imagery on memory distortion in women reporting recovered memories of childhood sexual abuse, *Journal of Traumatic Stress*, 12, 559–69.

Clark, W. C. and Clark, S. B. (1980) Pain responses in Nepalese porters, *Science*, 209(4454), 410–11.

Clausen, J. A. (1981) Stigma and mental disorder: phenomena and mental terminology, *Psychiatry*, 44, 287–96.

Cohen, R., Hsueh, Y, Russell, K. M. and Ray, G. E. (2006) Beyond the individual: a consideration of context for the development of aggression, *Aggression and Violent Behavior*, 11, 341–51.

Cohen, S. and Herbert, T. B. (1996) Health psychology: psychological factors and physical disease from the perspective of human psychoneuroimmunology, *Annual Review of Psychology*, 47, 113–42.

Collier, G., Johnson, D. F. and Morgan, C. (1997) Meal patterns of cats encountering variable food procurement cost, *Journal of Experimental Analysis of Behavior*, 67, 303–10.

Collins, F. S., Green, E. D., Guttmacher, A. E. and Guyer, M. S. (2003) A vision for the future of genomics research, *Nature*, 422(6934), 835–47.

Collins, M. A. and Zebrowitz, L. A. (1995) The contributions of appearance to occupational outcomes in civilian and military settings, *Journal of Applied Social Psychology*, 25, 129–63.

Comunian, A. L. and Gielen, U. P. (1995) Moral reasoning and prosocial action in Italian culture, *Journal of Social Psychology*, 135(6), 699–706.

Connolly, J. F. (2000) Applying cognitive research in the twenty-first century: event-related potentials in assessment, *Brain and Cognition*, 42(1), 99–101.

Constantino, M. J., Arnow, B. A., Blasey, C. and Agras, W. S. (2005) The association between patient characteristics and the therapeutic alliance in cognitive-behavioral and interpersonal therapy for bulimia nervosa, *Journal of Consulting and Clinical Psychology*, 73(2), 203–11.

Cooper, J. R., Bloom, F. E. and Roth, R. H. (1991) *The Biochemical Basis of Neuropharmacology*, 6th edn. New York: Oxford University Press.

Corballis, M. C. (1997) The genetics and evolution of handedness, *Psychological Review*, 104, 714–26.

Corballis, M. C. (2004) FOXP2 and the mirror system, *Trends in Cognitive Science*, 8(3), 95–6.

Coren, S. (1995) Family patterns in handedness: evidence for indirect inheritance mediated by birth stress, *Behavor Genetics*, 25(6), 517–24.

Cornblatt, B. A. and Keilp, J. G. (1994) Impaired attention, genetics, and the pathophysiology of schizophrenia, *Schizophrenia Bulletin*, 20, 31–46.

Corrigan, P. W. (2007) How clinical diagnosis might exacerbate the stigma of mental illness, *Social Work*, 52(1), 31–9.

Costello, E. J., Pine, D. S., Hammen, C. *et al.* (2002) Development and natural history of mood disorders, *Biological Psychiatry*, 52(6), 529–42.

Cousins, N. (1989) *Head First: The Biology of Hope*. New York: E. P. Dutton.

Craik, F. I. M. (2002) Levels of processing: past, present … and future?, *Memory*, 10(5), 305–18.

Craik, F. I. M. and Lockhart, R. S. (1972) Levels of processing: a framework for memory research, *Journal of Verbal Learning and Verbal Behavior*, 11, 671–84.

Crandall, J. E. (1984) Social interest as a moderator of life stress, *Journal of Personality and Social Psychology*, 47, 164–74.

Craven, R. (2002) Lateral thinking, *Nature Reviews Neuroscience*, 3, 414.

Creswell, J. D., Welch, W. T., Taylor, S. E. *et al.* (2005) Affirmation of personal values buffers neuroendocrine and psychological stress responses, *Psychological Science*, 16(11), 846–51.

Crews, F. (ed.) (1998) *Unauthorized Freud: Doubters Confront a Legend*. New York: Viking Press.

Crick, F. (1994) *The Astonishing Hypothesis: The Scientific Search for the Soul*. New York: Scribner.

Crick, F. and Koch, C. (1992) The problem of consciousness, *Scientific American*, September, 153–9.

Crowder, R. and Morton, J. (1969) Pre-categorical acoustic storage (PAS), *Perception and Psychophysics*, 8, 815–20.

Csikszentmihalyi, M. (1990) *Flow: The Psychology of Optimal Experience*. New York: HarperCollins.

Csikszentmihalyi, M. (1999) Implications of a systems perspective for the study of creativity, in R. J. Sternberg (ed.) *Handbook of Creativity*. New York: Cambridge University Press.

Cushing, B. S. and Kramer, K. M. (2005) Mechanisms underlying epigenetic effects of early social experience: the role of neuropeptides and steroids, *Neuroscience and Biobehavioral Reviews*, 29, 1089–105.

Cytowic, R. E. (1993) *The Man Who Tasted Shapes*. New York: Tarcher/Putnam.

Dabbs, J. M. and Morris, R. (1990) Testosterone, social class and antisocial behavior in a sample of 4,462 men, *Psychological Science*, 1, 209–11.

Dagg, A. I. (2004) *'Love of Shopping' is Not a Gene: Problems with Darwinian Psychology*. Montreal: Black Rose Books.

Damasio, A. (1999) *The Feeling of What Happens: Body and Emotion in the Making of Consciousness*. New York: Harcourt Brace.

Damasio, A. (2005) *Descartes' Error: Emotion, Reason and the Human Brain*. New York: Penguin.

Darwin, C. (1859) *On the Origin of Species*. New York: Washington Square Press (reprinted 1963).

Darwin, C. (1872) *The Expression of Emotions in Man and Animals*. Chicago, IL: University of Chicago Press (reprinted 1965).

Dasen, P. (1975) Concrete operational development in three cultures, *Journal of Cross-Cultural Psychology*, 6, 156–72.

Davidson, R. J. and Irwin, W. (1999) The functional neuroanatomy of emotion and affective style, *Trends in Cognitive Science*, 3(1), 11–21.

Davidson, R. J., Pizzagalli, D., Nitschke, J. B. and Putnam, K. (2002) Depression: perspectives from affective neuroscience, *Annual Review of Psychology*, 53, 545–74.

Davis, J. (1994) *Mother Tongue: How Humans Create Language*. New York: Birch Lane Press.

Davis, K. L., Charney, D., Coyle, J. T. and Nemeroff, C. (eds) (2002) *Neuropsychopharmacology: The Fifth Generation of Progress*. Baltimore, MD: Lippincott Williams and Wilkins.

Davis, P. J. and Schwartz, G. E. (1987) Repression and the inaccessibility of affective memories, *Journal of Personality and Social Psychology*, 52, 155–62.

Davison, G. C. and Neale, J. M. (1997) *Abnormal Psychology*, 7th edn. New York: John Wiley & Sons.

Davou, B. (2002) Unconscious processes influencing learning, *Psychodynamic Processes*, 8(3), 277–94.

Day, R., Nielsen, J. A., Korten, A. *et al.* (1987) Stressful life events preceding the acute onset of schizophrenia: a cross-national study from the World Health Organization, *Cultural Medicine and Psychiatry*, 11, 123–205.

Deaux, K. (1985) Sex and gender, *Annual Review of Psychology*, 36, 49–81.

deBono, E. (1976) *Practical Thinking*. Harmondsworth: Penguin.

DeCarvalho, J. (1990) A history of the 'Third Force' in psychology, *Journal of Humanistic Psychology*, 30, 22–44.

Deci, E. L. and Ryan, R. M. (2000) The 'what' and 'why' of goal pursuits: human needs and the self-determination of behavior, *Psychological Inquiry*, 11, 227–68.

Delgado, J. M. R. (1969) *Physical Control of the Mind: Toward a Psycho-Civilized Society*. New York: Harper & Row.

Delgado, J. M. R., Roberts, W. W. and Miller, N. E. (1954) Learning motivated by electrical stimulation of the brain, *American Journal of Physiology*, 179, 587–93.

DelMonte, M. M. (2000) Retrieved memories of childhood sexual abuse, *British Journal of Medical Psychology*, 73(1), 1–13.

Denenberg, V. H. (2000) Evolution proposes and ontogeny disposes, *Brain and Language*, 73(2), 274–96.

de Rivera, J. (1989) Comparing experiences across cultures: shame and guilt in America and Japan, *Hiroshima Forum for Psychology*, 14, 13–20.

Derksen, M. (2007) Cultivating human nature, *New Ideas in Psychology*, (25),189–206.

de Waal, F. (1989) *Peacemaking Among Primates*. Cambridge, MA: Harvard University Press.

de Waal, F. B. M. (2002) Evolutionary psychology: the wheat and the chaff, *Current Directions in Psychological Science*, 11(6), 187–91.

de Win, M. M. L., Reneman, L., Reitsma, J. B. *et al.* (2004) Mood disorders and serotonin transporter density in ecstasy users – the influence of long-term abstention, dose, and gender, *Psychopharmacology*, 173(3/4), 376–82.

Dick, D. M. and Rose, R. J. (2002) Behavior genetics: what's new? What's next?, *Current Directions in Psychological Science*, 11(2), 70–4.

Dickerson, F. B., Tenhula, W. N. and Green-Paden, L. D. (2005) The token economy for schizophrenia: review of the literature and recommendations for future research, *Schizophrenia Research*, 75, 405–16.

Diener, E., Oishi, S. and Lucas, R. E. (2003) Personality, culture, and subjective well-being: emotional and cognitive evaluations of life, *Annual Review of Psychology*, 54, 403–25.

Dijksterhuis, A., Bos, M. W., Nordgren, L. F. and van Baaren, R. B. (2006) On making the right choice: the deliberation-without-attention effect, *Science*, 311, 1005–7.

DiLalla, L. F. (2002) Behavior genetics of aggression in children: review and future directions, *Developmental Review*, 22, 593–622.

Dion, K. K. and Dion, K. L. (1993) Individualistic and collectivistic perspectives on gender and the cultural context of love and intimacy, *Journal of Social Issues*, 49(3), 53–69.

Dobson, K. S. (1989) A meta-analysis of the efficacy of cognitive therapy for depression, *Journal of Consulting and Clinical Psychology*, 57, 414–19.

Dollard, J., Doob, L., Miller, N., Mowrer, O. and Sears, R. (1939) *Frustration and Aggression*. New Haven, CT: Yale University Press.

Dollard, J. and Miller, N. E. (1950) *Personality and Psychotherapy*. New York: McGraw-Hill.

Dourley, J. P. (1992) *A Strategy for a Loss of Faith: Jung's Proposal*. Toronto: Inner City Books.

Draguns, J. (2001) Psychopathological and clinical aspects of personal experience: from selves and values to deficits and symptoms, in L. L. Adler and U. P. Gielen (eds) *Crosscultural Topics in Psychology*, 2nd edn. Westport, CT: Praeger.

Drevets, W. C., Bogers, W. and Raichle, M. E. (2002) Functional anatomical correlates of antidepressant drug treatment assessed using PET measures of regional glucose metabolism. *European Neuropsychopharmacology*, 12(6), 527–44.

Dubertret, C., Hanoun, N., Adès, J. *et al.* (2004) Family-based association studies between 5-HT5A receptor gene and schizophrenia, *Journal of Psychiatric Research*, 38, 371–6.

Eagly, A. H. (1995) The science and politics of comparing men and women, *American Psychologist*, 50, 145–58.

Eagly, A. (2001) Social role theory of sex differences and similarities, in J. Worrell (ed.), *Encyclopedia of Women and Gender*. San Diego, CA: Academic Press.

Eagly, A. H. and Diekman, A. B. (2006) Examining gender gaps in sociopolitical attitudes: it's not Mars and Venus, *Feminism & Psychology*, 16(1), 26–34.

Eakin, E. (2000) Bigotry as mental illness or just another norm, *New York Times*, 15 January, p. A21.

Eaton, W. O. and Enns, L. R. (1986) Sex differences in human motor activity, *Psychological Bulletin*, 100, 19–28.

Ebbinghaus, H. (1885; reprinted 1964) *Memory*. New York: Dover.

Eckes, T. and Trautner, H. M. (eds) (2000) *The Developmental Social Psychology of Gender*. Mahwah, NJ: Lawrence Erlbaum Associates.

Edelman, G. M. (1992) *Bright Air, Brilliant Fire*. New York: Basic Books.

Editors (1993) High anxiety, *Consumer Reports*, January, 19–24.

Edwards, V. (2002) *Depression and Bipolar Disorders*. Toronto: Key Porter Books.

Ehrhardt, A. A. (1985) The psychobiology of gender, in A. S. Rossi (ed.) *Gender and the Life Course*. New York: Aldine.

Eisenberg, N. (2005) The development of empathy-related responding, *Nebraska Symposium on Motivation*, 51, 73–117.

Elkin, I., Shea, M. T., Watkins, J. T. *et al.* (1989) National Institutes of Mental Health treatment of depression collaborative research program: general effectiveness of treatments, *Archives of General Psychiatry*, 46, 971–82.

Ellemers, N., Spears, R. and Doosje, B. (2002) Self and social identity, *Annual Review of Psychology*, 53, 161–86.

Elliott, R., Clark, C., Wexler, M. *et al.* (1990) The impact of experiential therapy on depression: initial results, in G. Lietaer, J. Rombauts and R. Van Balen (eds) *Client-centered and Experiential Psychotherapy in the Nineties*. Leuven, Belgium: Leuven University Press.

Ellis, A. (1993) Fundamentals of rational-emotive therapy for the 1990s, in W. Dryden and L. K. Hill (eds) *Innovations in Rational-Emotive Therapy*. Newbury Park, CA: Sage.

Ellis, A. (1994) *Reason and Emotion in Psychotherapy*. Secaucus, NJ: Birch Lane Press.

Ember, C. R. and Ember, M. (1994) War, socialization, and interpersonal violence: a cross-cultural study, *Journal of Conflict Resolution*, 38, 620–46.

Enard, W., Przeworski, M., Fisher, S. E., *et al.* (2002) Molecular evolution of FOXP2, a gene involved in speech and language, *Nature*, 418, 869–72.

Endler, N. S. (1982) *Holiday of Darkness: A Psychologist's Personal Journey out of His Depression*. New York: Wiley.

Endler, N. S. (1997) Stress, anxiety and coping: the multidimensional interaction model, *Canadian Psychology*, 38, 136–53.

Enmarker, I. (2004) The effects of meaningful irrelevant speech and road traffic noise on teachers' attention, episodic and semantic memory, *Scandinavian Journal of Psychology*, 45, 393–405.

Erdfelder, E. and Brandt, M. (2007) Recollection biases in hindsight judgments, *Social Cognition*, 25(1), 114–31.

Ericsson, K. A. and Chase, W. A. (1982) Exceptional memory, *American Scientist*, 70, 607–15.

Erikson, E. H. (1962) *Young Man Luther*. New York: Norton.

Erikson, E. H. (1963) *Childhood and Society*, 2nd edn. New York: Norton.

Erlenmeyer-Kimling, L., Cornblatt, B. A., Rock, D., Roberts, S. *et al.* (1993) The New York High-Risk Project: anhedonia, attentional deviance, and psychopathology, *Schizophrenia Bulletin*, 19, 141–53.

Eron, L. D. (1963) Relationship of TV viewing habits and aggressive behavior in children, *Journal of Abnormal and Social Psychology*, 67, 193–6.

Eron, L. D. (1982) Parent-child interaction, television violence, and aggression of children, *American Psychologist*, 37, 197–211.

Eron, L. D., Walder, L. O. and Lefkowitz, M. M. (1971) *The Learning of Aggression in Children.* Boston, MA: Little, Brown.

Escobar, J. I. and Vega, W. A. (2006) Cultural issues and psychiatric diagnosis: providing a general background for considering substance use diagnoses, *Addiction*, 101(S1), 40–7.

Esterson, A. (2002) The myth of Freud's ostracism by the medical community in 1896–1905: Jeffrey Masson's assault on truth, *History of Psychology*, 5(2), 115–34.

Euler, H. A. and Weitzel, B. (1996) Discriminative grandparental solicitude as reproductive strategy, *Human Nature*, 7, 39–59.

Everly, G. S., Jr and Lating, J. M. (2002) *A Clinical Guide to the Treatment of the Human Stress Response*, 2nd edn. New York: Kluwer Academic/Plenum.

Eynde, P. O. and Turner, J. E. (2006) Focusing on the complexity of emotion issues in academic learning: a dynamical component systems approach, *Educational Psychology Review*, 18, 361–76.

Eysenck, M. W. (1993) *Principles of Cognitive Psychology*. Hillsdale, NJ: Lawrence Erlbaum.

Fabrega, H. (1994) International systems of diagnosis in psychiatry, *Journal of Nervous and Mental Disease*, 182, 256–63.

Fabrega, H. (1995) Cultural challenges to the psychiatric enterprise, *Comprehensive Psychiatry*, 36, 377–83.

Fadiman, J. and Frager, R. (1976) *Personality and Personal Growth*. New York: Harper & Row.

Fagot, B. I. (1985) Changes in thinking about early sex role development, *Developmental Review*, 5, 83–98.

Faller, K. C. (1988) *Child Sexual Abuse: An Interdisciplinary Manual for Diagnosis, Case Management, and Treatment*. New York: Columbia University Press.

Fancher, R. E. (1996) *Pioneers of Psychology*, 3rd edn. New York: W. W. Norton.

Fancher, R. T. (1995) *Cultures of Healing*. New York: W. H. Freeman.

Fein, S. (2001) Beyond the fundamental attribution era?, *Psychological Inquiry*, 12(1), 16–21.

Ferguson, C. J., Rueda, S. M., Cruz, A. M. *et al.* (2008) Violent video games and aggression: causal relationship or byproduct of family violence and intrinsic violence motivation? *Criminal Justice and Behavior*, 35(3), 311–32.

Ferguson, G. A. (1981) *Statistical Analysis in Psychology and Education*, 5th edn. New York: McGraw-Hill.

Ferster, C. B. and Skinner, B. F. (1957) *Schedules of Reinforcement*. New York: Appleton-Century-Crofts.

Feshbach, S. (1955) The drive-reducing function of fantasy behavior, *Journal of Abnormal and Social Psychology*, 50, 3–11.

Festinger, L. (1957) *A Theory of Cognitive Dissonance*. Stanford, CA: Stanford University Press.

Festinger, L. and Carlsmith, J. M. (1959) Cognitive consequences of forced compliance, *Journal of Abnormal and Social Psychology*, 58, 203–10.

Feynman, R. (1988) *What Do You Care What People Think?: Further Adventures of a Curious Character*. New York: Norton.

Filley, C. M., Price, B. H., Nell, V. *et al.* (2001) Toward an understanding of violence: neurobehavioral aspects of unwarranted physical aggression, *Neuropsychiatry*, 14(1), 1–14.

Fischer, P., Greitemeyer, T. and Pollozek, F. (2006) The unresponsive bystander: are bystanders more responsive in dangerous emergencies? *European Journal of Social Psychology*, 36(2), 267–78.

Fisher, J. E., Mohanty, A., Herrington, J. D. *et al.* (2004). Neuropsychological evidence for dimensional schizotypy: implications for creativity and psychopathology, *Journal of Research in Personality*, 38, 24–31.

Fiske, S. T. (2003) Save the hyphens, *APS Observer*, 16(6), 5.

Flavell, J. H. (1992) Cognitive development: past, present, and future, *Developmental Psychology*, 28, 998–1005.

Follette, W. C. and Houts, A. C. (1996) Models of scientific progress and the role of theory in taxonomy development: a case study of the DSM, *Journal of Consulting and Clinical Psychology*, 64, 1120–32.

Fonagy, P., Roth, A. and Higgitt, A. (2005) The outcome of psychodynamic psychotherapy for psychological disorders, *Clinical Neuroscience Research*, 4, 367–77.

Ford, C. S. and Beach. F. A. (1951) *Patterns of Sexual Behavior*. New York: Harper and Row.

Forest, D. V. (1976) Nonsense and sense in schizophrenic language, *Schizophrenia Bulletin*, 2, 286–381.

Forrest, G. G. (1985) Antabuse treatment, in T. E. Bratter and G. G. Forrest (eds), *Alcoholism and Substance Abuse: Strategies for Clinical Intervention*. New York: Free Press.

Fortman, B. de G. (2005) Violence among peoples in the light of human frustration and aggression, *European Journal of Pharmacology*, 526, 2–8.

Fortune, R. F. (1963) *Sorcerers of Dobu*. New York: E. P. Dutton & Co., Inc.

Foucault, M. (1965) *Madness and Civilization: A History of Insanity in the Age of Reason* (English translation). New York: Random House.

Fouts, R. S., Hirsch, A. and Fouts, D. (1983) Cultural transmission of a human language in a chimpanzee mother/infant relationship, in H. E. Fitzgerald, J. A. Mullins and P. Page (eds) *Psychological Perspectives: Child Nurturance Series*, Vol. III. New York: Plenum Press.

Fox, R. M. (1998) A comprehensive treatment program for impatient adolescents, *Behavioral Interventions*, 13, 67–77.

Frager, R. and Fadiman, J. (1998) *Personality and Personal Growth*, 4th edn. New York: Longman.

Frances, A. J. and Egger, H. L. (1999) Whither psychiatric diagnosis, *Australian & New Zealand Journal of Psychiatry*, 33(2), 161–5.

Frank, J. D. (1963) *Persuasion and Healing*. New York: Schocken Books.

Frankl, V. E. (1992) *Man's Search for Meaning*, 4th edn. Boston, MA: Beacon Press.

Fraser, C. (1987) Social psychology, in R. L. Gregory (ed.), *The Oxford Companion to the Mind*. New York: Oxford University Press, 721–3.

Freedman, J. L. (1984) Effect of television violence on aggressiveness, *Psychological Bulletin*, 96, 227–46.

Freedman, J. L. (1986) Television violence and aggression: a rejoinder, *Psychological Bulletin*, 100, 372–8.

Freeman, A. and Reinecke, M. A. (1995) Cognitive therapy, in A. S. Gurman and S. B. Messer (eds) *Essential Psychotherapies: Theory and Practice*. New York: Guilford Press.

Freeman, D. (2007) Suspicious minds: the psychology of persecutory delusions, *Clinical Psychology Review*, 27, 425–57.

Freeman, W. J. (2000) *How the Brain Makes Up Its Mind*. New York: Columbia University Press.

Freidrich-Cofer, L. and Huston, A. C. (1986) Television violence and aggression: the debate continues, *Psychological Bulletin*, 98, 1–20.

Freud, A. (1936) *The Ego and the Mechanisms of Defense* (trans. C. M. Baines). New York: International Universities Press (reprinted 1946).

Freud, A. (1958) Adolescence, *Psychoanalytic Study of the Child*, 15, 255–78.

Freud, S. (1900) *The Interpretation of Dreams*. (Note: where no specific reference is given, this and other references refer to the original German date of publication for volumes later printed in translation as part of J. Strachey (ed.), *The Standard Edition of the Complete Psychological Works of Sigmund Freud*, Vols 1–24. London: Hogarth Press, 1953–66.)

Freud, S. (1904) *Psychopathology in Everyday Life*. Reprinted in Freud, S., *A General Introduction to Psychoanalysis* (trans. J. Riviere). New York: Washington Square Press (reprinted 1952).

Freud, S. (1905) *Three Essays on Sexuality*.

Freud, S. (1913) *Totem and Taboo*.

Freud, S. (1920) *Beyond the Pleasure Principle*.

Freud, S. (1923) *The Ego and the Id*.

Freud, S. (1924) *A General Introduction to Psychoanalysis* (trans. J. Riviere). New York: Washington Square Press (reprinted 1952).

Freud, S. (1926) *The Problem of Anxiety* (trans. H. A. Bunker). New York: W. W. Norton (reprinted 1936).

Freud, S. (1930) *Civilization and its Discontents*.

Frey, D. (1986) Recent research on selective exposure to information, *Advances in Experimental Social Psychology*, 19, 41–80.

Fromkin, V. A. (1973) *Speech Errors as Linguistic Evidence*. The Hague: Mouton.

Funnell, M. G., Colvin, M. K. and Gazzaniga, M. S. (2007) The calculating hemispheres: studies of a split-brain patient, *Neuropsychologia*, 45, 2378–86.

Gabbard, G. O. (2005) Does psychoanalysis have a future? Yes, *Canadian Journal of Psychiatry*, 50(12), 741–2.

Gabrenya, W. K., Wang, Y-E. and Latané, B. (1985) Social loafing on an optimizing task: cross-cultural differences among Chinese and Americans, *Journal of Cross-Cultural Psychology*, 16(2). 223–42.

Gantt, W. H. (1966) Reflexology, schizokinesis, and autokinesis, *Conditioned Reflex*, 1, 57–68.

Gao, J.-H., Parsons, L. M., Bower, J. M., Xiong, J. and Fox, P. (1996) Cerebellum implicated in sensory acquisition and discrimination rather than motor control, *Science*, 272, 545–7.

Garcia, J., Hankins, W. G. and Rusniak, K. (1974) Behavioral regulation of the milieu intern in man and rat, *Science*, 185, 824–31.

Gardiner, H. W. and Kosmitzki, C. (2008) *Lives Across Cultures: Cross-cultural Human Development*, 4th edn. Boston, MA: Pearson.

Gardner, A. and Gardner, B. (1969) Teaching sign language to a chimpanzee, *Science*, 165, 664–77.

Gardner, B. C., Burr, B. K. and Wiedower, S. E. (2006) Reconceptualizing strategic family therapy: insights from a dynamic systems perspective, *Contemporary Family Therapy*, 28, 339–52.

Gardner, H. (1985) *The Mind's New Science: A History of the Cognitive Revolution*. New York: Basic Books.

Garver, D. L. (1997) The etiologic heterogeneity of schizophrenia, *Harvard Review of Psychiatry*, 4, 317–27.

Garver, D. L., Steinberg, J. L., McDermott, B. *et al.* (1997) Etiologic heterogeneity of the psychoses: is there a dopamine psychosis?, *Neuropsychopharmacology*, 16, 191–201.

Gay, P. (1988) *Freud: A Life for Our Time*. New York: W. W. Norton.

Gazzaniga, M. S., Ivry, R. B. and Mangun, G. R. (1998) *Cognitive Neuroscience: The Biology of the Mind*. New York: Norton.

Gedo, J. E. (2002) The enduring scientific contributions of Sigmund Freud, *Perspectives in Biology and Medicine*, 45(2), 200–11.

Geen, R. G., Stonner, D. and Shope, G. I. (1975) The facilitation of aggression by aggression: a study in response inhibition and disinhibition, *Journal of Personality and Social Psychology*, 31, 721–6.

Geeraert, N. and Yzerbyt, V. Y. (2007) Cultural differences in the correction of social inferences: does the dispositional rebound occur in an interdependent culture? *British Journal of Social Psychology*, 46, 423–35.

Geertz, C. (1984) 'From the native's point of view': on the nature of anthropological understanding, in R. A. Shweder and R. A. LeVine (eds), *Culture Theory: Essays on Mind, Self, and Emotion*. Cambridge: Cambridge University Press.

Gemma, S., Vichi, S. and Testai, E. (2007) Metabolic and genetic factors contributing to alcohol induced effects and fetal alcohol syndrome, *Neuroscience & Biobehavioral Reviews*, 31(2), 221–9.

Gerrie, M. P., Belcher, L. E. and Garry, M. (2006) 'Mind the gap': false memories for missing aspects of an event, *Applied Cognitive Psychology*, 20, 689–96.

Gershoff, E. T. (2002) Corporal punishment by parents and associated child behaviors and experiences: a meta-analytic and theoretical review, *Psychological Bulletin*, 128(4), 539–79.

Gershon, E. S. and Rieder, R. O. (1992) Major disorders of mind and brain, *Scientific American*, September, 127–33.

Ghazanfar, A. A. and Logothetis, N. K. (2003) Facial expressions linked to monkey calls, *Nature*, 423, 937–8.

Gibbons, J. L. (2000) Gender development in cross-cultural perspective, in T. Eckes and H. M. Trautner (eds) *The Developmental Social Psychology of Gender*. Mahwah, NJ: Lawrence Erlbaum Associates.

Gil, E. F. and Bob, S. (1999) Culturally competent research: an ethical perspective, *Clinical Psychology Review*, 19(1), 45–55.

Gilbert, D. T., Fiske, S. T. and Lindzey, G. (eds) (1998) *The Handbook of Social Psychology*, 4th edn. New York: McGraw-Hill.

Gillen, K. and Muncer, S. J. (1995) Sex differences in the perceived causal structure of date rape: a preliminary report, *Aggressive Behavior*, 21(2), 101–12.

Giumetti, G. W. and Markey, P. M. (2007) Violent video games and anger as predictors of aggression, *Journal of Research in Personality*, 41(6), 1234–43.

Glass, D. C. and Singer, J. E. (1972) *Urban Stress*. New York: Academic Press.

Glassman, W. E. (1972) Subvocal activity and acoustic confusions in short-term memory, *Journal of Experimental Psychology*, 96, 164–9.

Gleick, J. (1997) *Chaos: Making a New Science*. New York: Penguin.

Godden, D. and Baddeley, A. D. (1975) Context-dependent memory in two natural environments, *British Journal of Psychology*, 66, 325–31.

Goff, D. C. and Coyle, J. T. (2001) The emerging role of glutamate in the pathophysiology and treatment of schizophrenia, *The American Journal of Psychiatry*, 158(9), 1367–77.

Goffman, E. (1963) *Stigma*. Englewood Cliffs, NJ: Prentice-Hall.

Goldberg, E. (2001) *The Executive Brain: Frontal Lobes and the Civilized Mind*. New York: Oxford University Press.

Goldfried, M. R. and Davison, G. C. (1994) *Clinical Behavior Therapy*, 2nd edn. New York: Holt, Rinehart & Winston.

Goldfried, M. R. and Wolfe, B. E. (1998) Toward a more clinically valid approach to therapy research, *Journal of Consulting and Clinical Psychology*, 66, 143–50.

Goldiamond, I. (1973) A diary of self-modification, *Psychology Today*, November, 53–7.

Goldstein, K. (1939) *The Organism*. New York: American Book Co.

Goldstein, K. (1950) Prefrontal lobotomy: analysis and warning, *Scientific American*, February, 36–41.

Goldstein, M. H., King, A. P. and West, M. J. (2003) Social interaction shapes babbling: testing parallels between birdsong and speech, *Proceedings of the National Academy of Science*, 100(13), 8030–5.

Goleman, D. (1993) Studying the pivotal role of bystanders, *The New York Times*, 22 June, C1, C6.

Good, M. I. (1995) Karl Abraham, Sigmund Freud, and the fate of the seduction theory, *Journal of the American Psychoanalytic Association*, 43(4), 1137–67.

Goodall, J. (1990) *Through a Window: My Thirty Years with the Chimpanzees of Gombe.* Boston, MA: Houghton Mifflin.

Gorcynski, R. M., Macrae, S. and Kennedy, M. (1982) Conditioned immune response associated with allogenic skin grafts in mice, *Journal of Immunology*, 29, 704–9.

Gould, S. J. (1981) *The Mismeasure of Man.* New York: Norton.

Gould, S. J. and Vrba, E. (1981) Exaptation: a missing term in the science of form, *Paleobiology*, 8, 4–15.

Graf, P. and Riddle, J. C. (1972) Helping behaviour as a function of interpersonal perception, *Journal of Social Psychology*, 86, 227–31.

Grammar, K. and Thornhill, R. (1994) Human (*Homo Sapiens*) facial attractiveness and sexual selection: the role of symmetry and averageness, *Journal of Comparative Psychology*, 108, 233–42.

Granic, I., Hollenstein, T., Dishion, T. J. and Patterson, G. R. (2003) Longitudinal analysis of flexibility and reorganization in early adolescence: a dynamic systems study of family interactions, *Developmental Psychology*, 39(3), 606–17.

Grant, A. M. (2006) A personal perspective on professional coaching and the development of coaching psychology, *International Coaching Psychology Review*, 1(1), 12–22.

Grant, B. F., Dawson, D. A., Stinson, F. S. *et al.* (2006) Trends in DSM-IV alcohol abuse and dependence: United States, 1991–1992 and 2001–2002, *Alcohol Research & Health*, 29(2), 79–91.

Grazzi, L. (2007) Behavioural treatments: rationale and overview of the most common therapeutic protocols, *Neurological Science*, 28, S67–9.

Green, C. D. (1996) Where did the term 'cognitive' come from anyway?, *Canadian Psychology*, 37, 31–9.

Green, M. E. (1993) Cognitive remediation in schizophrenia: is it time yet?, *American Journal of Psychiatry*, 150, 178–87.

Greenberg, J. (2006) *Comprehensive Stress Management.* New York: McGraw-Hill.

Greene, L. and Burke, J. (2007) Beyond self-actualization, *Journal of Health & Human Services Administration*, 30(2), 116–28.

Greenfield, P. M., Keller, H., Fuligni, A. and Maynard, A. (2003) Cultural pathways through universal development, *Annual Review of Psychology*, 54, 461–90.

Greenwald, A. G. (1992) New look 3: unconscious cognition reclaimed, *American Psychologist*, 47, 766–79.

Grice, G. R. and Hunter, J. J. (1964) Stimulus intensity effects depend on the type of experimental design, *Psychological Review*, 71, 247–56.

Guerin, B. (1992) Social behavior as discriminative stimulus and consequence in social anthropology, *Behavior Analyst*, 15, 31–41.

Guilford, J. P. (1967) *The Nature of Human Intelligence.* New York: McGraw-Hill.

Gurman, A. S. and Messer, S. B. (eds) (1995) *Essential Psychotherapies: Theory and Practice.* New York: Guilford Press.

Haaga, D. and Davison, G. (1993) An appraisal of rational-emotive therapy, *Journal of Consulting and Clinical Psychology*, 61, 215–20.

Hadad, M. and Reed, M. J. (2007) *The Post-secondary Learning Experience.* Toronto: Thomson-Nelson.

Hakuta, K., Bialystok, E. and Wiley, E. (2003) Critical evidence: a test of the critical-period hypothesis for second-language acquisition, *Psychological Science*, 14(1), 31–8.

Hall, C. S. and Nordby, V. J. (1973) *A Primer of Jungian Psychology.* New York: New American Library.

Hall, E. T. (1981) *The Silent Language*. New York: Anchor.

Hall, G. S. (1924) Preface to the American edition, in S. Freud, *A General Introduction to Psychoanalysis* (trans. J. Riviere). New York: Washington Square Press (reprinted 1952).

Hall, M. H. (1968) A conversation with Abraham Maslow, *Psychology Today*, 2(2), 34–7, 54–7.

Halpern, D. (1989) *Thought and Knowledge: An Introduction to Critical Thinking*, 2nd edn. Hillsdale, NJ: Lawrence Erlbaum.

Hamm, J. V. (2000) Do birds of a feather flock together? The variable bases for African American, Asian American, and European American adolescents' selection of similar friends, *Developmental Psychology*, 36(2), 209–19.

Hammond, S. M., Breakwell, G. M. and Fife-Schaw, C. (eds) (2000) *Research Methods in Psychology*, 2nd edn. Thousand Oaks, CA: Sage Publications.

Hardaway, R. A. (1990) Subliminally activated symbiotic fantasies: facts and artifacts, *Psychological Bulletin*, 107, 177–95.

Haridakis, P. M. (2006) Men, women, and televised violence: predicting viewer aggression in male and female television viewers, *Communication Quarterly*, 54(2), 227–55.

Harley, T. R. (1995) *The Psychology of Language: From Data to Theory*. Hove, UK: Psychology Press.

Harlow, H. F. (1949) The formation of learning sets, *Psychological Review*, 56, 51–65.

Harmon-Jones, E. and Mills, J. (eds) (1999) *Cognitive Dissonance*. Washington, DC: American Psychological Association.

Harris, B. (1979) Whatever happened to little Albert?, *American Psychologist*, 34, 151–60.

Harris, J. R. (1995) Where is the child's environment? A group socialization theory of development, *Psychological Review*, 102, 458–89.

Harris, J. R. (1998) *The Nurture Assumption*. New York: Free Press.

Harris, M. (1974) *Cows, Pigs, Wars, and Witches: The Riddle of Culture*. New York: Random House.

Harris, M. B. and Knight-Bohnhoff, K. (1996) Gender and aggression: II. Personal aggressiveness, *Sex Roles*, 35(1–2), 27–42.

Harrison, P. J. and Owen, M. J. (2003) Genes for schizophrenia? Recent findings and their pathophysiological implications, *The Lancet*, 361, 417–19.

Hartup, W. W. and Coates, B. (1967) Imitation of a peer as a function of reinforcement from the peer group and rewardingness of the model, *Child Development*, 38, 1003–16.

Haslam, S. A. and McGarty, C. (2001) A 100 years of certitude? Social psychology, the experimental method and the management of scientific uncertainty, *British Journal of Social Psychology*, 40, 1–21.

Hauser, M. D., Chomsky, N. and Fitch, W. T. (2002) The faculty of language: what it is, who has it, and how did it evolve? *Science*, 298(5598), 1569–79.

Hayes, A. M., Laurenceau, J-P., Feldman, G., Strauss, J. L. and Cardaciotto, L. (2007) Change is not always linear: the study of nonlinear and discontinuous patterns of change in psychotherapy, *Clinical Psychology Review*, 27(6), 715–23.

Hayes, S. C., Follette, W. C. and Follette, V. M. (1995) Behavior therapy, in A. S. Gurman and S. B. Messer (eds) *Essential Psychotherapies: Theory and Practice*. New York: Guilford Press.

Haynes, J.-D. and Rees, G. (2006) Decoding mental states from brain activity in humans, *Nature Reviews: Neuroscience*, 7, 523–34.

Haythornthwaite, J. A., Menefee, L. A., Heinberg, L. J. and Clark, M. R. (1998) Pain coping strategies predict perceived control over pain, *Pain*, 77(1), 33–9.

Heath, R. G. (1972) Pleasure and brain activity in man, *The Journal of Nervous and Mental Disease*, 154, 3–18.

Hebb, D. O. (1953) Heredity and environment in mammalian behaviour, *British Journal of Animal Behaviour*, 1, 43–7.

Heider, F. (1958) *The Psychology of Interpersonal Relations*. New York: Wiley.

Heine, S. J. and Lehman, D. R. (1997) Culture, dissonance, and self-affirmation, *Personality and Social Psychology Bulletin*, 23, 389–400.

Heinrichs, R. W. (1993) Schizophrenia and the brain: conditions for a neuropsychology of madness, *American Psychologist*, 48, 221–33.

Heinrichs, R. W. (2001) *In Search of Madness: Schizophrenia and Neuroscience*. New York: Oxford University Press.

Helzer, J. E. and Canino, G. J. (1992) *Alcoholism in North America, Europe, and Asia*. New York: Oxford University Press.

Heninger, G. R. (1995) Neuroimmunology of stress, in M. J. Friedman, D. S. Charnery and A. Y. Deutch (eds) *Neurobiological and Clinical Consequences of Stress: From Normal Adaptation to PTSD*. Philadephia, PA: Lippincott-Raven.

Herbert, D. M. B. and Burt, J. S. (2004) What do students remember? Episodic memory and the development of schematization, *Applied Cognitive Psychology*, 18, 77–88.

Herdt, G. H. and Davidson, J. (1988) The Sambia 'turnim-man': sociocultural and clinical aspects of gender formation in male pseudohermaphrodites with 5–alpha-reductase deficiency in Papua New Guinea, *Archives of Sexual Behavior*, 17, 33–56.

Herman, J. L. (1992) *Trauma and Recovery: The Aftermath of Violence – From Domestic Violence to Political Terror*. New York: Basic Books.

Hermans, E. J., Ramsey, N. F., and van Honk, J. (2008) Exogenous testosterone enhances responsiveness to social threat in the neural circuitry of social aggression in humans, *Biological Psychiatry*, 63(3), 263–70.

Herwig, U., Abler, B., Walter, H. and Erk, S. (2007) Expecting unpleasant stimuli – an fMRI study, *Psychiatry Research: Neuroimaging*, 154, 1–12.

Hetherington, E. M. and Frankie, G. (1967) Effect of parental dominance, warmth, and conflict on imitation in children, *Journal of Personality and Social Psychology*, 6, 119–25.

Higbee, K. L. (2001) *Your Memory: How It Works and How to Improve It*, 2nd edn. London: Marlowe & Co.

Hilborn, R. C. (1994) *Chaos and Nonlinear Dynamics: An Introduction for Scientists and Engineers*. New York: Oxford University Press.

Hirai, T. (1978) *Zen and the Mind*. Tokyo: Japan Publications.

Hirsch, J. (1963) Behavior genetics and individuality understood, *Science*, 142, 1436–42.

Hirvonen, J., van Erp, T. G. M., Huttunen, J. *et al.* (2005) Increased caudate dopamine D2 receptor availability as a genetic marker for schizophrenia, *Archives of General Psychiatry*, 62, 371–8.

Hite, S. (1987) *The Hite Report: Women and Love: A Cultural Revolution in Progress*. New York: Knopf.

Hoffman, E. (1989) *The Right to Be Human: A Biography of Abraham Maslow*, Wellingborough: Crucible.

Hoffman, P. (1997) The endorphin hypothesis, in W. P. Morgan (ed.) *Physical Activity and Mental Health. Series in Health Psychology and Behavioral Medicine*. Washington: Taylor & Francis.

Hofling, C. K., Brotzman, E., Dalrymple, S., Graves, N. and Pierce, C. M. (1966) An experimental study in nurse-physician relationships, *Journal of Nervous and Mental Disease*, 143, 171–80.

Hofstadter, D. R. (1979) *Gödel, Escher, Bach: An Eternal Golden Braid*. New York: Basic Books.

Hohmann, G. W. (1966) Some effects of spinal cord lesions on experienced emotional feelings, *Psychophysiology*, 3, 143–56.

Holden, C. (2003a) Deconstructing schizophrenia, *Science*, 299, 333–5.

Holden, C. (2003b) Getting the short end of the allele, *Science*, 301, 291–3.

Hollon, S. D., DeRubeis, R. J. and Seligman, M. E. P. (1992) Cognitive therapy and the prevention of depression, *Applied and Preventive Psychology*, 1, 89–95.

Hollon, S. D., Thase, M. E. and Markowitz, J. C. (2002) Treatment and prevention of depression, *Psychological Science in the Public Interest*, 3(2), 39–77.

Hooley, J. M. and Campbell, C. (2002) Control and controllability: beliefs and behaviour in high and low expressed emotion relatives, *Psychological Medicine*, 32(6), 1091–9.

Hooper, J. (1999) A new germ theory, *Atlantic Monthly*, 283(2), 41–53.

Horney, K. (1950) *Neurosis and Human Growth: The Struggle Toward Self-Realization*. New York: Norton.

Horney, K. (1967) *Feminine Psychology*. New York: W. W. Norton.

Hornsey, M. J. and Jetten, J. (2005) Loyalty without conformity: tailoring self-perception as a means of balancing belonging and differentiation, *Self and Identity*, 4, 81–95.

Huber, P. (1991) *Galileo's Revenge: Junk Science in the Courtroom*. New York: Basic Books.

Huber, R. (2007) Memory formation: sleep enough before learning, *Current Biology*, 17(10), R367–8.

Hudson, P. (1996) Using a learning set to increase the test performance of students with learning disabilities in social studies classes, *Learning Disabilities Research and Practice*, 11(2), 78–85.

Huesmann, L. R., Lagerspetz, K. and Eron, L. D. (1984) Intervening variables in the TV violence-aggression relation: evidence from two countries, *Developmental Psychology*, 20, 746–75.

Hunt, E. (1991) Some comments on the study of complexity, in R. J. Sternberg and P. A. Frensch (eds) *Complex Problem Solving: Principles and Mechanisms*. Hillsdale, NJ: Lawrence Erlbaum.

Hunt, M. (1993) *The Story of Psychology*. New York: Doubleday.

Hunter, J. P. and Csikszentmihalyi, M. (2003) The positive psychology of interested adolescents, *Journal of Youth and Adolescence*, 32(1), 27–35.

Huston, A. C., Carpenter, C. J. and Atwater, J. B. (1986) Gender, adult structuring of activities, and social behavior in middle childhood, *Child Development*, 57, 1200–9.

Hutchinson, G. and Haasen, C. (2004) Migration and schizophrenia: the challenges for European psychiatry and implications for the future, *Social Psychiatry & Psychiatric Epidemiology*, 39(5), 350–7.

Ilechukwu, S. T. C. (1999) Oedipal anxiety and culture variations in the incest taboo: a psychotherapy case study in the Nigerian setting, *Transcultural Psychiatry*, 36(2), 211–25.

Imperato-McGinley, J., Peterson, R. E., Gautier, T. and Sturla, E. (1979) Androgyns and the evolution of male gender identity among male pseudohermaphrodites with 5–a-reductase deficiency, *New England Journal of Medicine*, 300, 1233–7.

Inglehart, R. (1990) *Culture Shift in Advanced Industrial Society*. Princeton, NJ: Princeton University Press.

Irwin, M. R. (2008) Human psychoneuroimmunology: 20 years of discovery, *Brain, Behavior, and Immunity*, 22, 129–39.

Isaacs, W., Thomas, J. and Goldiamond, I. (1960) Application of operant conditioning to reinstate verbal behavior in psychotics, *Journal of Speech and Hearing Disorders*, 25, 8–12.

Ito, M., Okazaki, M., Takahashi, S., Muramatsu, R., Kato, M. and Onuma, T. (2007) Subacute postictal aggression in patients with epilepsy, *Epilepsy & Behavior*, 10, 611–14.

Jablensky, A. (2000) Epidemiology of schizophrenia: the global burden of disease and disability, *European Archives of Psychiatry and Clinical Neuroscience*, 250(6), 274–85.

Jablensky, A., Sartorius, N., Ernberg, G. *et al.* (1992) Schizophrenia: manifestations, incidence and course in different cultures. A World Health Organization ten-country study, *Psychological Medicine, Monograph Supplements*, 20 (entire).

James, T. W., Humphrey, G. K., Gati, J. S. *et al.* (2002) Haptic study of three-dimensional objects activates extrastriate visual areas, *Neuropsychologia*, 40(10), 1706–14.

James, W. (1884) Some omissions of introspective psychology, *Mind*, 9 (January), 1–26.

James, W. (1890) *The Principles of Psychology*. New York: Dover (reprinted 1950).

James, W. (1902) *The Varieties of Religious Experience*. New York: Collier (reprinted 1961).

Jamison, K. R. (1995) *An Unquiet Mind*. New York: Alfred A. Knopf.

Jang, K. L., Livesley, W. J., Ando, J. *et al.* (2006) Behavioral genetics of the higher order of the Big Five, *Personality and Individual Differences*, 41, 261–72.

Jenkins, J. G. and Dallenbach, K. M. (1924) Oblivescence during sleep and waking, *American Journal of Psychology*, 35, 605–12.

Jenkins, J. H. and Karno, M. (1992) The meaning of expressed emotion: theoretical issues raised by cross-cultural research, *American Journal of Psychiatry*, 149, 9–21.

Jervis, R. (1998) *System Effects*. Princeton, NJ: Princeton University Press.

Jones, E. E. and Pulos, S. M. (1993) Comparing the process in psychodynamic and cognitive-behavioral therapies, *Journal of Consulting and Clinical Psychology*, 61, 306–16.

Jones, J. L. (1995) *Understanding Psychological Research*. New York: HarperCollins.

Joseph, S. (2005) Person-centred coaching psychology, *The Coaching Psychologist*, 2(2), 3–5.

Joseph, S. (2006) Person-centred coaching psychology: a meta-theoretical perspective, *International Coaching Psychology Review*, 1(1), 47–54.

Joy, L. A., Kimball, M. M., and Zabrack, M. I. (1986) Television and children's aggressive behavior, in T. W. Williams (ed.) *The Impact of Television: A Natural Experiment in Three Communities*. New York: Academic Press, 303–60.

Jung, C. G. (1958) The psychology of the child archetype, in V. S. deLaszlo (ed.) *Psyche and Symbol*. Garden City, NY: Doubleday.

Jung, C. G. (1963) *Memories, Dreams, Reflections*. New York: Pantheon Books.

Jung, C. G. (1967) *Collected Works of C. G. Jung, Volume 9 Part I: The Archetypes and the Collective Unconscious*, H. Read, M. Fordham and G. Adler (eds). Princeton, NJ: Princeton University Press.

Jung, C. G. and von Franz, M.-L. (eds) (1964) *Man and His Symbols*. London: Aldus.

Jusczyk, P. W. (2002) How infants adapt speech-processing capacities to native-language structure, *Current Directions in Psychological Science*, 11(1), 15–18.

Kabat-Zinn, J., Lipworth, L. and Burney, R. (1985) The clinical use of mindfulness meditation for the self-regulation of chronic pain, *Journal of Behavioral Medicine*, 8, 163–90.

Kagan, J. (1989) Temperamental contributions to social behavior, *American Psychologist*, 44, 668–74.

Kagan, J. (1998) *Three Seductive Ideas*. Cambridge, MA: Harvard University Press.

Kahn, R. S., Davidson, M. and Davis, K. L. (1996) Dopamine and schizophrenia revisited, in S. J. Watson *et al.* (eds) *Biology of Schizophrenia and Affective Disease*. Washington, DC: American Psychiatric Press.

Kahneman, D. and Tversky, A. (eds) (2000) *Choices, Values, and Frames*. Cambridge: Cambridge University Press.

Kamin, L. J. (1969) Predictability, surprise, attention, and conditioning, in B. A. Campbell and R. M. Church (eds) *Punishment and Aversive Behavior*. New York: Appleton-Century-Crofts.

Kane, E. W. (2006) 'No way my boys are going to be like that!' Parents' responses to children's gender nonconformity, *Gender & Society*, 20(2), 149–76.

Kantor, J. W., Kohlenberg, R. J. and Loftus, E. F. (2004) Experimental and psychotherapeutic demand characteristics and the cognitive therapy rationale: an analogue study, *Cognitive Therapy and Research*, 28(2), 229–39.

Karen, R. (1992) Shame, *The Atlantic Monthly*, February, 40–70.

Kashima, Y. and Triandis, H. C. (1986) The self-serving bias in attributions as a coping strategy: a cross-cultural study, *Journal of Cross-Cultural Psychology*, 17, 83–97.

Kasper, S., Tauscher, J., Willeit, M. *et al.* (2002) Receptor and transporter imaging studies in schizophrenia, depression, bulimia and Tourette's disorder – implications for psychopharmacology, *World Journal of Biological Psychiatry*, 3(3), 133–46.

Kazdin, A. E. and Wilson, G. T. (1980) *Evaluation of Behavior Therapy: Issues, Evidence, and Research Strategies*. Lincoln, NE: University of Nebraska Press.

Keen, R. (2003) Representation of objects and events: why do infants look so smart and toddlers look so dumb?, *Current Directions in Psychological Science*, 12(3), 79–83.

Kellogg, R. (1967) *The Psychology of Children's Art*. San Diego, CA: CRM.

Kelly, G. A. (1955) *A Theory of Personality: The Psychology of Personal Constructs*. New York: Norton.

Kelly, M. A. R., Cyranowski, J. M. and Frank, E. (2007) Sudden gains in interpersonal psychotherapy for depression, *Behaviour Research and Therapy*, 45, 2563–72.

Kelman, H. C. (1967) Human use of human subjects: the problem of deception in social psychological experiments, *Psychological Bulletin*, 67, 1–11.

Kelsoe, J. R., Ginns, E. I., Egeland, J. A., Gerhard, D. S. *et al.* (1989) Re-evaluation of the linkage relationship between chromosome 11p loci and the gene for bipolar disorder in the Old Order Amish, *Nature*, 342, 238–43.

Keltner, D. and Buswell, B. N. (1996) Evidence for the distinctiveness of embarrassment, shame, and guilt: a study of recalled antecedents and facial expressions of emotion, *Cognition and Emotion*, 10, 155–71.

Kendell, R. E. (1987) Schizophrenia, in R. L Gregory (ed.) *The Oxford Companion to the Mind*. New York: Oxford University Press, pp. 697–9.

Keneally, T. (1982) *Schindler's List*. New York: Simon and Schuster.

Kenrick, D. T. and Luce, C. L. (2000) An evolutionary life-history model of gender differences and similarities, in T. Eckes and H. M. Trautner (eds) *The Developmental Social Psychology of Gender*. Mahwah, NJ: Lawrence Erlbaum Associates.

Kensinger, E. A. and Schacter, D. L. (2007) Remembering the specific visual details of presented objects: neuroimaging evidence for effects of emotion, *Neuropsychologia*, 45, 2951–62.

Kesebir, P. and Diener, E. (2008) In pursuit of happiness: empirical answers to philosophical questions, *Perspectives on Psychological Science*, 3(2), 117–25.

Kety, S., S., Wender, P. H., Jacobsen, B., Ingraham, L. J. *et al.* (1994) Mental illness in the biological and adoptive relatives of schizophrenic adoptees: replication of the Copenhagen study in the rest of Denmark, *Archives of General Psychiatry*, 51, 442–55.

Kevles, B. H. (1996) *Naked to the Bone: Medical Imaging in the Twentieth Century*. Rutgers, NJ: Rutgers University Press.

Kiecolt-Glaser, J. K., Bane, C., Glaser, R. and Malarkey, W. B. (2003) Love, marriage, and divorce: newlyweds' stress hormones foreshadow relationship changes, *Journal of Consulting & Clinical Psychology*, 71(1), 176–88.

Kiecolt-Glaser, J. K., McGuire, L., Robles, T. F. and Glaser, R. (2002) Emotions, morbidity, and mortality: new perspectives from psychoneuroimmunology, *Annual Review of Psychology*, 53(1), 83–107.

Kiecolt-Glaser, J. K. and Newton, T. L. (2001) Marriage and health: his and hers, *Psychological Bulletin*, 127(4), 472–503.

Kihlstrom, J. F. (1994) Commentary: Psychodynamics and social cognition: notes on the fusion of psychoanalysis and psychology, *Journal of Personality*, 62, 681–96.

Kihlstrom, J. F., Barnhardt, T. M. and Tataryn, D. J. (1992) The psychological unconscious: found, lost, reclaimed, *American Psychologist*, 47, 788–91.

Kim, K. H. S., Relkin, N. R., Lee, K.-M. and Hirsch, J. (1997) Distinct cortical areas associated with native and second languages, *Nature*, 388(6638), 171–4.

Kim-Cohen, J., Caspi, A., Taylor, A. *et al.* (2006) MAOA, maltreatment, and gene–environment interaction predicting children's mental health: new evidence and a meta-analysis, *Molecular Psychiatry*, 11, 903–13.

Kim-Prieto, C. and Eid, M. (2004) Norms for experiencing emotion in sub-Saharan Africa, *Journal of Happiness Studies*, 5, 241–68.

Kimura, D. (1999) *Sex and Cognition*. Cambridge, MA: MIT Press.

King, A. (1971) *A Married Couple*. Toronto: NFB Films.

Kirsch, I. (2002) Yes, there is a placebo effect, but is there a powerful antidepressant drug effect? *Prevention and Treatment*, 5, np. Online at http://journals.apa.org/prevention/volume5/pre0050022i.html

Kirsch, I., Moore, T. J., Scoboria, A. and Nicholls, S. S. (2002) The emperor's new drugs: an analysis of antidepressant medication data submitted to the US Food and Drug Administration, *Prevention and Treatment*, 5, np. Online at http://journals.apa.org/prevention/volume5/pre0050023a.html

Kirsh, S. J. (2006) Cartoon violence and aggression in youth, *Aggression and Violent Behavior*, 11, 547–57.

Kirschenbaum, H. and Jourdan, A. (2005) The current status of Carl Rogers and the person-centered approach, *Psychotherapy: Theory/Research/Training*, 42(1), 37–51.

Kitayama, S. (2002) Culture and basic psychological processes – Toward a system view of culture: Comment on D. Oyserman *et al.* (2002) *Psychological Bulletin*, 128(1), 89–96.

Klama, J. (1988) *Aggression: Conflict in Animals and Humans Reconsidered*. London: Longman.

Klar, A. J. (1999) Genetic models for handedness, brain lateralization, schizophrenia, and manic-depression, *Schizophrenia Research*, 39(3), 207–18.

Klar, A. J. S. (2003) Human handedness and scalp hair-whorl direction develop from a common genetic mechanism, *Genetics*, 165(1), 269–76.

Klein, J. (2003) How to build a better democracy, *Time*, 161(20), 16–24.

Klinesmith, J., Kasser, T. and McAndrew, F. T. (2006) Guns, testosterone, and aggression: an experimental test of a mediational hypothesis, *Psychological Science*, 17(7), 568–71.

Kluver, H. (1966) *Mescal and Mechanisms of Hallucinations*. Chicago, IL: University of Chicago Press.

Knauft, B. M. (1987) Reconsidering violence in simple human societies: homicide among the Gebusi of New Guinea, *Current Anthropology*, 28, 457–500.

Knight, G. P., Fabes, R. A. and Higgins, D. A. (1996) Concerns about drawing causal inferences from meta-analyses: an example in the study of gender differences in aggression, *Psychological Bulletin*, 119(3), 410–21.

Knight, Z. G. (2006) Some thoughts on the psychological roots of the behaviour of serial killers as narcissists: an object relations perspective, *Social Behavior and Personality: An International Journal*, 34, 1189–206.

Knight, Z. G. (2007) Sexually motivated serial killers and the psychology of aggression and 'evil' within a contemporary psychoanalytical perspective, *Journal of Sexual Aggression*, 13(1), 21–35.

Knott, V., Cosgrove, M., Villeneuve, C. *et al.* (2008) EEG correlates of imagery-induced cigarette craving in male and female smokers, *Addictive Behaviors*, 33, 616–21.

Knox, J. M. (2001) Memories, fantasies, archetypes: an exploration of some connections between cognitive science and analytical psychology, *Journal of Analytical Psychology*, 46(4), 613–35.

Koch, S. (1985) The nature and limits of psychological knowledge: lessons of a century *qua* 'science', in S. Koch and D. E. Leary (eds) *A Century of Psychology as a Science*. New York: McGraw-Hill, pp. 75–97.

Koch, S. and Leary, D. E. (eds) (1985) *A Century of Psychology as a Science*. New York: McGraw-Hill.

Koepp, M. J., Gunn, R. N., Lawrence, A. D. *et al.* (1998) Evidence for striatal dopamine release during a video game, *Nature*, 393, 266–8.

Kohlberg, L. (1966) A cognitive-developmental analysis of children's sex-role concepts and attitudes, in E. E. Maccoby (ed.) *The Development of Sex Differences*. Stanford, CA: Stanford University Press.

Kohlberg, L. (1969) Stage and sequence: the cognitive-developmental approach to socialization, in D. S. Goslin (ed.) *Handbook of Socialization Theory and Research*. Chicago, IL: Rand McNally.

Kohler, W. (1925) *The Mentality of Apes*. New York: Harcourt, Brace, and World.

Kohut, H. (1977) *The Restoration of the Self*. New York: International Universities Press.

Konjin, E. A., Bijvank, M. N. and Bushman, B. J. (2007) I wish I were a warrior: the role of wishful identification in the effects of violent video games on aggression in adolescent boys, *Developmental Psychology*, 43(4), 1038–44.

Konner, M. (1982) *The Tangled Web: Biological Constraints on the Human Spirit*. New York: Holt, Rinehart & Winston.

Kramer, P. D. (1993) *Listening to Prozac: A Psychiatrist Explores Antidepressant Drugs and the Remaking of the Self*. New York: Viking.

Krampe, H., Stawicki, S., Wagner, T. *et al.* (2006) Follow-up of 180 alcoholic patients for up to 7 years after outpatient treatment: impact of alcohol deterrents on outcome, *Alcoholism: Clinical and Experimental Research*, 30(1), 86–95.

Krantz, D. S., Sheps, D. S., Carney, R. M. and Natelson, B. H. (2000) Effects of mental stress in patients with coronary artery disease: evidence and clinical implications, *Journal of the American Medical Association*, 283(14), 1800–2.

Krasner, L. (1976) On the death of behavior modification: some comments from a mourner, *American Psychologist*, 31, 387–8.

Kraus, S. J. (1995) Attitudes and the prediction of behavior: a meta-analysis of the empirical literature, *Personality and Social Psychology Bulletin*, 21, 58–75.

Krebs, D. L. (1991) Altruism and egoism: a false dichotomy?, *Psychological Inquiry*, 2(2), 137–9.

Kriegman, D. (1990) Compassion and altruism in psychoanalytic theory: an evolutionary analysis of self psychology, *Journal of the American Academy of Psychoanalysis*, 18, 342–67.

Krippner, S. (ed.) (1972) The plateau experience: A. H. Maslow and others, *Journal of Transpersonal Psychology*, 4, 107–20.

Kristin, N., Hunnicutt-Ferguson, K., Reidy, D. E. *et al.* (2007) Relationship of pain tolerance with human aggression, *Psychological Reports*, 101(1), 141–4.

Krøjgaard, P. (2005) Infants' search for hidden persons, *International Journal of Behavioral Development*, 29(1), 70–9.

Kubo, C. and Chida, C. (2006) Psychoneuroimmunology of the mind and body, *International Congress Series*, 1287, 5–11.

Kuhn, T. (1970) *The Structure of Scientific Revolutions*, 2nd edn. London: Cambridge University Press.

Kumar, S. (2005) Punding in Parkinson's disease related to high-dose levodopa therapy, *Neurology India*, 53(3), 362.

Kunkel, J. H. (1996) What have the behaviourists accomplished – and what more can they do?, *Psychological Record*, 46, 21–37.

Kuyken, W., Dalgleish, T. and Holden, E. R. (2007) Advances in cognitive-behavioural therapy for unipolar depression, *The Canadian Journal of Psychiatry*, 52(1), 5–12.

LaBar, K. S. and Cabeza, R. (2006) Cognitive neuroscience of emotional memory, *Nature Reviews: Neuroscience*, 7, 54–64.

Labouvie-Vief, G. (1985) Intelligence and cognition, in J. E. Birren and K. W. Schaie, *Handbook of the Psychology of Aging*, 2nd edn. New York: Van Nostrand.

Lacerda, F., von Hofsten, C. and Heimann, M. (eds) (2001) *Emerging Cognitive Abilities in Early Infancy*. Mahwah, NJ: Lawrence Erlbaum Associates.

LaFond, J. Q. and Durham, M. L. (1992) *Back to the Asylum*. New York: Oxford University Press.

Laing, D. G., Preskott, J., Bell, G.A. *et al.* (1993) A crosscultural study of taste discrimination with Australians and Japanese, *Chemical Senses*, 18(2), 161–8.

Laing, R. D. (1965) *The Divided Self: An Existential Study in Sanity and Madness*. Baltimore, MD: Penguin.

Laing, R. D. (1967) *The Politics of Experience*. New York: Pantheon.

Lamb, C. S., Jackson, L. A., Cassiday, P. B. and Priest, D. J. (1993) Body figure preferences of men and women: a comparison of two generations, *Sex Roles*, 28, 345–58.

Lang, P. J. (1994) The varieties of emotional experience: a meditation on James-Lange theory, *Psychological Review*, 101, 212–21.

Langen, B., Dietze, S. and Fink, H. (2002) Acute effect of ethanol on anxiety and 5–HT in the prefrontal cortex of rats, *Alcohol*, 27(2), 135–41.

Langer, E. J. and Rodin, J. (1976) The effects of choice and enhanced personal responsibility for the aged: a field experiment in an institutional setting, *Journal of Personality and Social Psychology*, 34, 191–8.

Langhoff, C., Baer, T., Zubraegel, D. and Linden, M. (2008) Therapist–patient alliance, patient–therapist alliance, mutual therapeutic alliance, therapist–patient concordance, and outcome of CBT in GAD, *Journal of Cognitive Psychotherapy: An International Quarterly*, 22(1), 68–79.

Langleben, D. D., Loughead, J. W., Bilker, W. B. *et.al.* (2005) Telling truth from lie in individual subjects with fast event-related fMRI, *Human Brain Mapping*, 26, 262–72.

LaPiere, R. T. (1934) Attitudes and actions, *Social Forces*, 13, 230–7.

Latané, B. and Darley, J. (1969) Bystander 'apathy', *American Scientist*, 57, 222–68.

Latané, B. and Nida, S. (1981) Ten years of research on group size and helping, *Psychological Bulletin*, 89(2), 308–24.

Laungani, P. (2001) The influence of culture on stress: India and England, in L. L. Adler and U. P. Gielen (eds), *Crosscultural Topics in Psychology*. Westport, CT: Praeger.

Laungani, P. (2002) Cross-cultural psychology: a handmaiden to mainstream Western psychology, *Counselling Psychology Quarterly*, 15(4), 385–97.

Laungani, P. (2007) *Understanding Cross-cultural Psychology: Eastern and Western Perspectives*. London: Sage.

Lauronen, E., Veijola, J., Isohanni, I. *et al.* (2004) Links between creativity and mental disorder, *Psychiatry*, 67(1), 81–98.

Laursen, B., Coy, K. C. and Collins, W. A. (1998) Reconsidering changes in parent–child conflict across adolescence: a meta-analysis, *Child Development*, 69(3), 817–32.

Lazarus, R. S. (1993) From psychological stress to the emotions: a history of changing outlooks, *Annual Review of Psychology*, 44, 1–21.

Lazarus, R. S. (1995) Vexing research problems inherent in cognitive-mediational theories of emotion – and some solutions, *Psychological Inquiry*, 6(3), 183–96.

Lazarus, R. S. and Folkman, S. (1984) *Stress, Appraisal, & Coping*. New York: Springer.

Lazev, A. B., Herzog, T. A. and Brandon, T. H. (1999) Classical conditioning of environmental cues to cigarette smoking, *Experimental & Clinical Psychopharmacology*, 7(1), 56–63.

Leach, P. (1997) *Your Baby and Child: From Birth to Age Five*, 5th edn. New York: Knopf.

LeDoux, J. E. (1995) Emotion: clues from the brain, *Annual Review of Psychology*, 46, 209–35.

Lee, R. and Ackerman, S. (1980) The sociocultural dynamics of mass hysteria: a case study of social conflict in West Malaysia, *Journal of Cross-Cultural Psychology*, 23, 78–88.

Lee, T. F. (1991) *The Human Genome Project: Cracking the Genetic Code of Life*. New York: Plenum Press.

Lefkowitz, M. M., Huesmann, L. R. and Eron, L. D. (1978) Parental punishment: a longitudinal analysis of effects, *Archives of General Psychiatry*, 35, 186–91.

Le Foll, D., Rascle, O. and Higgins, N. C. (2008) Attributional feedback-induced changes in functional and dysfunctional attributions, expectations of success, hopefulness, and short-term persistence in a novel sport, *Psychology of Sport and Exercise*, 9, 77–101.

Leibman, M. and Salzinger, K. (1998) A theory-based treatment of psychotic symptoms in schizophrenia: treatment successes and obstacles to implementation, *Journal of Genetic Psychology*, 159(4), 404–20.

Lenneberg, E. H. (1967) *Biological Foundations of Language*. New York: Wiley.

Lenzenweger, M. F. and Dworkin, R. H. (eds) (1998) *Origins and Development of Schizophrenia: Advances in Experimental Psychopathology*. Washington, DC: American Psychological Association.

Leo, J. (1985) A therapist in every corner, *Time*, 23 December, 39.

Lerman, D. C. and Vorndran, C. M. (2002) On the status of knowledge for using punishment: implications for treating behavior disorders, *Journal of Applied Behavior Analysis*, 35(4), 431–64.

Lettvin, J. Y., Maturana, H. R., McCulloch, W. S. and Pitts, W. H. (1959) What the frog's eye tells the frog's brain, *Proceedings of the Institute of Radio Engineers*, 47, 1940–51.

Leung, K. and Bond, M. H. (1984) The impact of cultural collectivism on reward allocation, *Journal of Personality and Social Psychology*, 47, 793–804.

Levanthal, H. and Tomarken, A. J. (1986) Emotion: today's problems, *Annual Review of Psychology*, 37, 565–610.

LeVay, S. (1993) *The Sexual Brain*. Cambridge, MA: MIT Press.

LeVay, S. and Hamer, D. H. (1994) Evidence for a biological influence in male homosexuality, *Scientific American*, 270 (May), 44–9.

Levine, E. S. and Padilla, A. M. (1980) *Crossing Cultures in Therapy: Pluralistic Counselling for the Hispanic*. Monterey, CA: Brooks-Cole.

Levine, M. (1976) Hunting for hypotheses, in M. H. Siegel and H. P. Ziegler (eds) *Psychological Research: The Inside Story*. New York: Harper & Row.

Levine, M. (1999) Rethinking bystander nonintervention: social categorization and the evidence of witnesses at the James Bulger murder trial, *Human Relations*, 52(9), 1133–55.

Levine, M. and Thompson, K. (2004) Identity, place, and bystander intervention: social categories and helping after natural disasters, *The Journal of Social Psychology*, 144(3), 229–45.

Levine, R. V. (2003) The kindness of strangers, *American Scientist*, 91(3), 226–33.

Levine, R. V., Martinez, T. S., Brase, G. and Sorenson, K. (1994) Helping in 36 US cities, *Journal of Personality & Social Psychology*, 67(1), 69–82.

Lewin, K. (1948) *Solving Social Conflicts*. New York: Harper.

Lewinsohn, P. M., Zinbarg, R., Seeley, J. R. *et al.* (1997) Lifetime comorbidity among anxiety disorders and between anxiety disorders and other mental disorders in adolescents, *Journal of Anxiety Disorders*, 11(4), 377–94.

Lewis, D. J. (1952) Partial reinforcement in a gambling situation, *Journal of Experimental Psychology*, 43, 447–50.

Lewis, M. (2001) Issues in the study of personality development, *Psychological Inquiry*, 12(2), 67–83.

Li, P. and Gleitman, L. (2002) Turning the tables: language and spatial reasoning, *Cognition*, 83(3), 265–94.

Li, Y. (2007) Recovering from spousal bereavement in later life: does volunteer participation play a role? *The Journals of Gerontology*, 62B(4), S257–66.

Liebert, R. M. and Sprafkin, J. (1988) *The Early Window: Effects of Television on Children and Youth*, 3rd edn. Oxford: Pergamon Press.

Lilienfeld, S. O., Wood, J. M. and Garb, H. N. (2001) What's wrong with this picture? *Scientific American*, 284, May, 80–7.

Lin, K. and Kleinman, A. M. (1988) Psychopathology and clinical course of schizophrenia: a cross-cultural perspective, *Schizophrenia Bulletin*, 14, 555–67.

Linder-Pelz, S. and Hall, L. M. (2007) The theoretical roots of NLP-based coaching, *The Coaching Psychologist*, 3(1), 12–17.

Linley, P. A. (2006) Coaching psychology and positive psychology: points of convergence and new perspectives, Keynote Address, 2006 Special Group in Coaching Psychology 1st International Conference, London.

Little, A. C., Jones, B. C. and Burriss, R. P. (2007) Preferences for masculinity in male bodies change across the menstrual cycle, *Hormones and Behavior*, 51, 633–9.

Locke, J. (1690) *An Essay Concerning Human Understanding*. Oxford: P. H. Nidditch (reprinted 1975).

Loftus, E. (1997) Creating false memories, *Scientific American*, 277, 70–5.

Loftus, E., Garry, M. and Feldman, J. (1994) Forgetting sexual trauma: what does it mean when 38% forget?, *Journal of Consulting and Clinical Psychology*, 62, 1177–81.

Loftus, E. and Hoffman, H. (1989) Misinformation and memory: the creation of new memories, *Journal of Experimental Psychology: General*, 118, 100–4.

Loftus, E. and Ketcham, K. (1991) *Witness for the Defense: The Accused, the Eyewitness, and the Expert Who Puts Memory on Trial*. New York: St Martin's Press.

Loftus, E. and Klinger, M. R. (1992) Is the conscious smart or dumb?, *American Psychologist*, 47, 761–5.

Loftus, E. and Pickerel, J. E. (1995) The formation of false memories, *Psychiatric Annals*, 25, 720–5.

Logie, R. (1996) The seven ages of working memory, in J. T. E. Richardson, R. W. Engle, L. Hasher *et al.* (eds) *Working Memory and Human Cognition*. New York: Oxford University Press.

Logue, A. W. (1988) A comparison of taste aversion learning in humans and other vertebrates: evolutionary pressures in common, in R. C. Bolles and M. D. Beecher (eds) *Evolution and Learning*. Hillsdale, NJ: Lawrence Erlbaum.

London, P. (1974) From the long couch for the sick to the push button for the bored, *Psychology Today*, June, 63–8.

Lore, R. and Schultz, L. A. (1993) Control of human aggression: a comparative perspective, *American Psychologist*, 48, 16–25.

Lorenz, E. N. (1993) *The Essence of Chaos*. Seattle, WA: University of Washington Press.

Lorenz, K. (1967) *On Aggression*. New York: Bantam.

Lorist, M. and Tops, M. (2003) Caffeine, fatigue, and cognition, *Brain and Cognition*, 53, 82–94.

Lu, Z-L., Neuse, J., Madigan, S. and Dosher, B. A. (2005) Fast decay of iconic memory in observers with mild cognitive impairments, *Proceedings of the National Academy of Sciences*, 102(5), 1797–802.

Luborsky, L., Rosenthal, R., Diguer, L. *et al.* (2002) The Dodo bird verdict is alive and well – mostly, *Clinical Psychology: Science and Practice*, 9(1), 2–12.

Luborsky, L. and Spence, D. P. (1978) Quantitative research on psychoanalytic therapy, in A. E. Bergin and S. L. Garfield (eds) *Handbook of Psychotherapy and Behavior Change: An Empirical Analysis*, 2nd edn. New York: John Wiley.

Luchins, A. S. (1942) Mechanization in problem-solving: the effect of *Einstellung*, *Psychological Monographs*, 54, No. 248 (whole).

Luke, K.-K., Liu, H.-L., Wai, Y.-Y., Wan, Y.-L. and Tan, L. H. (2002) Functional anatomy of syntactic and semantic processing in language comprehension, *Human Brain Mapping*, 16(3), 133–45.

Luria, A. R. (1968) *The Mind of a Mnemonist*. New York: Basic Books.

Luyten, P., Blatt, S. J., Van Houdenhove, B. and Corveleyn, J. (2006) Depression research and treatment: are we skating to where the puck is going to be? *Clinical Psychology Review*, 26, 985–99.

Lykken, D. T. (1988) The case against polygraph testing, in A. Gale (ed.) *The Polygraph Test: Lies, Truth, and Science*. London: Sage Publications.

Lykken, D. T., Bouchard, T. J., McGue, M. and Tellegen, A. (1993) Heritability of interests: a twin study, *Journal of Applied Psychology*, 78, 649–61.

Lysaker, P. H., Davis, L. W., Warman, D. M. *et al.* (2007) Stigma, social function and symptoms in schizophrenia and schizoaffective disorder: associations across 6 months, *Psychiatry Research*, 149, 89–95.

Maccoby, E. E. (1992) The role of parents in the socialization of children: an historical overview, *Developmental Psychology*, 28, 1006–17.

Maccoby, E. E. and Jacklin, C. N. (1974) *The Psychology of Sex Differences*. Stanford, CA: Stanford University Press.

Macgregor, S., Visscher, P. M., Knott, S. *et al.* (2002) Is schizophrenia linked to chromosome 1q? *Science*, 298, 2277.

MacKinnon-Lewis, C., Starnes, R., Volling, B. and Johnson, S. (1997) Perceptions of parenting as predictors of boys' sibling and peer relations, *Developmental Psychology*, 33, 1024–31.

MacLean, P. D. (1990) *The Triune Brain in Evolution: Role in Paleocerebral Functions*. New York: Plenum Press.

Macmillan, M. (2001) Limitations to free association and interpretation, *Psychological Inquiry*, 12(3), 113–28.

MacRae, J. R., Scholes, M. T. and Siegel, S. (1987) The contribution of Pavlovian conditioning to drug tolerance and dependence, *British Journal of Addiction*, 82(4), 371–80.

Maddi, S. (1974) Freud's most famous patient: the victimization of Dora, *Psychology Today*, September, 32–5.

Maher, B. (1972) The language of schizophrenia: a review and interpretation, *British Journal of Psychiatry*, 120, 3–17.

Mahler, M. S., Pine, F. and Bergman, A. (1975) *The Psychological Birth of the Human Infant*. New York: Basic Books.

Maier, S. F. and Laudenslager, M. (1985) Stress and health: exploring the links, *Psychology Today*, August, 44–9.

Maier, S. F. and Watkins, L. R. (1998) Stressor controllability, anxiety, and serotonin, *Cognitive Therapy & Research. Special Issue: Cognition and Anxiety*, 22(6), 595–613.

Maikovich, A. K. (2005) A new understanding of terrorism using cognitive dissonance principles, *Journal for the Theory of Social Behaviour*, 35(4), 373–97.

Majid, A., Bowerman, M., Kita, S. *et al.* (2004) Can language restructure cognition? The case for space, *Trends in Cognitive Sciences*, 8(3), 108–14.

Maltby, N., Kirsch, I., Mayers, M. and Allen, G. J. (2002) Virtual reality exposure therapy for the treatment of fear of flying: a controlled investigation, *Journal of Consulting and Clinical Psychology*, 70(5), 1112–18.

Manning, R., Levine, M. and Collins, A. (2007) The Kitty Genovese murder and the social psychology of helping, *American Psychologist*, 62(6), 555–62.

Marcus, D. E. and Overton, W. F. (1978) The development of cognitive gender constancy and sex-role preferences, *Child Development*, 49, 434–44.

Mari, S. and Karayanni, M. (1982) Creativity in Arab culture: two decades of research, *Journal of Creative Behaviour*, 16, 227–38.

Mark, V. H. and Ervin, F. R. (1970) *Violence and the Brain*. New York: Harper & Row.

Markus, H. and Kitayama, S. (1991) Culture and the self: implications for cognition, emotion, and motivation, *Psychological Review*, 98, 224–53.

Marler, P. (1970) A comparative approach to vocal learning: song development in white-crowned sparrows, *Journal of Comparative and Physiological Psychology*, 7, 1–25.

Marsh, A. A. and Ambady, N. (2007) The influence of the fear facial expression on prosocial responding, *Cognition and Emotion*, 21(2), 225–47.

Marsh, E. J. (2007) Retelling is not the same as recalling, *Current Directions in Psychological Science*, 16(1), 16–20.

Marshall, H. (2004) Midlife loss of parents: the transition from adult child to orphan, *Ageing International*, 29(4), 351–67.

Martin, C. L. and Halverson, C. E., Jr (1983) The effects of sex-typing schemas on young children's memory, *Child Development*, 54, 563–74.

Martin, C. L. and Halverson, C. E., Jr (1987) The role of cognition in sex-roles and sex-typing, in D. B. Carter (ed.) *Current Conceptions of Sex Roles and Sex-typing: Theory and Research*. New York: Praeger.

Martin, C. L., Ruble, D. N. and Szkrybalo, J. (2002) Cognitive theories of early gender development, *Psychological Bulletin*, 128(6), 903–33.

Martin, G. L. and Pear, J. (2006) *Behavior Modification: What It Is and How to Do It*, 8th edn. Upper Saddle River, NJ: Prentice-Hall.

Martin, J. and Sugarman, J. (2001) Is the self a kind of understanding?, *Journal for the Theory of Social Behaviour*, 31(1), 103–14.

Martin, R. A. (2002) Is laughter the best medicine? Humor, laughter, and physical health, *Current Directions in Psychological Science*, 11(6), 216–20.

Maryn, Y., De Bodt, M. and Van Cauwenberge, P. (2006) Effects of biofeedback in phonatory disorders and phonatory performance: a systematic literature review, *Applied Psychophysiology and Biofeedback*, 31(1), 65–83.

Maslow, A. (1964) *Religions, Values and Peak Experiences*. Columbus, OH: State University Press.

Maslow, A. (1968) *Toward a Psychology of Being*, 2nd edn. New York: Van Nostrand.

Maslow, A. (1970) *Motivation and Personality*, 2nd edn. New York: Harper & Row.

Maslow, A. H. (1971) *The Farther Reaches of Human Nature*. New York: Viking Press.

Massimini, F. and Delle Fave, A. (2000) Individual development in a bio-cultural perspective. *American Psychologist*, 55(1), 24–33.

Masson, J. (1984) *The Assault on Truth: Freud's Suppression of the Seduction Theory*. New York: Farrar, Strauss & Giroux.

Masters, J. C., Ford, M. E., Arend, R., Grotevant, H. D. and Clark, L. V. (1979) Modeling and labeling as integrated determinants of children's sex-typed imitative behavior, *Child Development*, 50, 364–71.

Matsumoto, D. (1997) *Culture and Modern Life*. Pacific Grove, CA: Brooks/Cole.

Mattern, K. K. and Lindholm, B. W. (1985) Maternal condemnation of TV violence during mother and child viewing, perceptions of violence and aggressive behavior in 61–73 month olds: extension of research by B. F. Fontes, *Journal of Genetic Psychology*, 146, 133–4.

Mauro, R., Sato, K. and Tucker, J. (1992) The role of appraisal in human emotions: a cross-cultural study, *Journal of Personality and Social Psychology*, 62, 301–17.

May, R. (1961) The emergence of existential psychology, in R. May (ed.) *Existential Psychology*. New York: Random House.

May, R. (1972) *Power and Innocence*. New York: W. W. Norton & Co.

Mayer, El. L. (2002) Freud and Jung: the boundaried mind and the radically connected mind, *Journal of Analytical Psychology*, 47(1), 91–9.

McAndrew, F. T. (2002) New evolutionary perspectives on altruism: multilevel-selection and costly-signaling theories, *Current Directions in Psychological Science*, 11(2), 79–82.

McCambridge, J., Mitcheson, L., Winstock, A. and Hunt, N. (2005) Five-year trends in patterns of drug use among people who use stimulants in dance contexts in the United Kingdom, *Addiction*, 100(8), 1140–9.

McCarley, R. W., Salisbury, D. F., Hirayasu, Y. *et al.* (2002) Association between smaller left posterior superior temporal gyrus volume on magnetic resonance imaging and smaller left temporal P300 amplitude in first-episode schizophrenia, *Archives of General Psychiatry*, 59(4), 321–31.

McCarthy, M. (2004) Shopping 'til we drop: can psychology save us from our lust for possessions? *Lancet*, 363, 296–7.

McClelland, D. C., Atkinson, J. W., Clark, R. and Lowell, E. L. (1953) *The Achievement Motive*. New York: Appleton-Century-Crofts.

McCloskey, M. and Zaragoza, M. (1985) Misleading postevent information and memory for events: arguments and evidence against memory impairment hypotheses, *Journal of Experimental Psychology: General*, 114, 1–16.

McClure, S. M., Li, J., Tomlin, D. *et al.* (2004) Neural correlates of behavioral preference for culturally familiar drinks, *Neuron*, 44, 379–87.

McConnell, J. V. (1974) Behavior mod. Letter-to-the-editor, *APA Monitor*, 5(8), 2–3.

McCord, W., McCord, J. and Howard, A. (1961) Familial correlates of aggression in nondelinquent male children, *Journal of Abnormal and Social Psychology*, 62, 79–93.

McDonald, J. L. (1997) Language acquisition: the acquisition of linguistic structure in normal and special populations, *Annual Review of Psychology*, 48, 215–41.

McDonald, R. V. and Siegel, S. (2004) Intra-admininstration association and withdrawal symptoms: morphine-elicited morphine withdrawal, *Experimental and Clinical Psychopharmacology*, 12, 3–11.

McDougall, W. (1908) *An Introduction to Social Psychology*. London: Methuen.

McEwen, B. S. (2002) Sex, stress and the hippocampus: allostasis, allostatic load and the aging process, *Neurobiology of Aging*, 23(5), 921–39.

McEwen, B. S. (2005) Stressed or stressed out: what is the difference? *Journal of Psychiatry and Neuroscience*, 30(5), 315–18.

McEwen, B. S. and Wingfield, J. C. (2003) The concept of allostasis in biology and biomedicine, *Hormones and Behavior*, 43(1), 2–15.

McFarland, C. and Buehler, R. (1997) Negative affective states and the motivated retrieval of positive life events: the role of affect acknowledgment, *Journal of Personality and Social Psychology*, 73, 200–14.

McGinn, L. K. (1997) Interview: Albert Ellis on rational emotive behavior therapy, *American Journal of Psychotherapy*, 51(3), 309–16.

McGrady, A. (1996) Good news – bad press: applied psychophysiology in cardiovascular disorder, *Biofeedback and Self Regulation*, 21, 335–46.

McGuire, W. J. (1973) The yin and yang of progress in social psychology: seven koan, *Journal of Personality & Social Psychology*, 26(3), 446–56.

McGuire, W. J. (1985) Toward social psychology's second century, in S. Koch and D. E. Leary (eds) *A Century of Psychology as a Science*. New York: McGraw-Hill, pp. 558–90.

McHale, S. M., Updegraff, K. A., Helms-Erikson, H. and Crouter, A. C. (2001) Sibling influences on gender development in middle childhood and early adolescence: a longitudinal study, *Developmental Psychology*, 37(1), 115–25.

McKeon, A., Josephs, K. A., Klos, K. J. *et al.* (2007) Unusual compulsive behaviors primarily related to dopamine agonist therapy in Parkinson's disease and multiple system atrophy, *Parkinsonism and Related Disorders*, 13, 516–19.

McLafferty, C. L., Jr and Kirylo, J. D. (2001) Prior positive psychologists proposed personality and spiritual growth, *American Psychologist*, 56(1), 84–5.

McNab, C., Haslam, N. and Burnett, P. (2007) Expressed emotion, attributions, utility beliefs, and distress in parents of young people with first episode psychosis, *Psychiatry Research*, 151, 97–106.

Mead, G. H. (1934) *Mind, Self, and Society*. Chicago: University of Chicago Press.

Mead, M. (1935) *Sex and Temperament in Three Primitive Societies*. New York: William Morrow.

Meador, B. D. and Rogers, C. R. (1979) Person-centered therapy, in R. J. Corsini (ed.) *Current Psychotherapies*, 2nd edn. Itasca, IL: Peacock Press.

Meador-Woodruff, J. H. and Kleinman, J. E. (2002) Neurochemistry of schizophrenia: glutamatergic abnormalities, in K. L. Davis, D. Charney, J. T. Coyle and C. Nemeroff (eds) *Neuropsychopharmacology: The Fifth Generation of Progress*. Baltimore, MD: Lippincott Williams & Wilkins.

Mednick, S. A., Watson, J. B., Huttunen, M. *et al.* (1998) A two-hit working model of the etiology of schizophrenia, in M. F. Lenzenweger and R. H. Dworkin (eds) *Origins and Development of Schizophrenia: Advances in Experimental Psychopathology*. Washington, DC: American Psychological Association.

Meehl, P. (1971) Law and the fireside inductions: some reflections of a clinical psychologist, *Journal of Social Issues*, 27, 65–100.

Meichenbaum, D. (1977) *Cognitive-Behavior Modification: An Integrative Approach*. New York: Plenum.

Meltzer, H. Y. (2002) Mechanism of action of atypical antipsychotic drugs, in K. L. Davis, D. Charney, J. T. Coyle and C. Nemeroff (eds) *Neuropsychopharmacology: The Fifth Generation of Progress*. Baltimore, MD: Lippincott Williams & Wilkins.

Melzack, R. (1973) *The Puzzle of Pain*. New York: Basic Books.

Melzack, R. (1992) Phantom limbs, *Scientific American*, April, 120–6.

Melzack, R. (2005) Evolution of the neuromatrix theory of pain, *Pain Practice*, 5(2), 85–94.

Melzack, R. and Wall, P. D. (1982) *The Challenge of Pain*. New York: Basic Books.

Mennella, J. A. and Beauchamp, G. K. (1997) The ontogeny of human flavor perception, in G. K. Beauchamp and L. Bartoshuk (eds) *Tasting and Smelling: Handbook of Perception and Cognition*, 2nd edn. San Diego, CA: Academic Press.

Mercer, D. (1986) *Biofeedback and Related Therapies in Clinical Practice*, Rockville, MD: Aspen Systems.

Mestel, R. (2003) Rorschach tested, *LA Times*, 19 May, F1, F5.

Michelson, D., Licinio, J. and Gold, P. W. (1995) Mediation of the stress response by the hypothalamic-pituitary-adrenal axis, in M. J. Friedman, D. S. Charnery and A. Y. Deutch (eds) *Neurobiological and Clinical Consequences of Stress: From Normal Adaptation to PTSD*. Philadelphia, PA: Lippincott-Raven.

Michinov, E. and Monteil, J.-M. (2002) The similarity-attraction relationship revisited: divergence between the affective and behavioral facets of attraction, *European Journal of Social Psychology*, 32(4), 485–500.

Milgram, S. (1963) A behavioral study of obedience. *Journal of Abnormal and Social Psychology*, 67, 371–8.

Milgram, S. (1964) Issues in the study of obedience: a reply to Baumrind. *American Psychologist*, 19, 848–52.

Milgram, S. (1970) The experience of living in cities, *Science*, 167, 1461–8.

Milgram, S., Liberty, H. J., Toledo, R. and Wackenhut, J. (1986) Response to intrusion in waiting lines, *Journal of Personality and Social Psychology*, 51, 683–9.

Miller, G. A. (1956) The magical number seven plus or minus two: some limits on our capacity for processing information, *Psychological Review*, 63, 81–97.

Miller, G. A. (1985) The constitutive problem of psychology, in S. Koch and D. E. Leary (eds) *A Century of Psychology as a Science*. New York: McGraw-Hill, pp. 40–5.

Miller, G. F. (2000) *The Mating Mind: How Sexual Choice Shaped the Evolution of Human Nature*. New York: Doubleday.

Miller, J. G. (1984) Culture and the development of everyday social explanation, *Journal of Personality and Social Psychology*, 46, 961–78.

Miller, N. (1941) The frustration-aggression hypothesis, *Psychological Review*, 48, 337–42.

Miller, N. (1969) Learning of visceral and glandular responses, *Science*, 163, 434–45.

Miller, N. (1985) The value of behavioral research on animals, *American Psychologist*, 40, 423–40.

Mills, J., Cooper, D. and Forest, D. (2002) Polarization of interpersonal attraction: the effect of perceived potency, *Basic & Applied Social Psychology*, 24(2), 156–62.

Milner, B. (1965) Memory disturbance after bilateral hippocampal lesions, in P. Milner and S. Glickman (eds), *Cognitive Processes and the Brain*. Princeton, NJ: Van Nostrand.

Minium, E. W. and King, B. M. (2002) *Statistical Reasoning in Psychology and Education*, 4th edn. New York: John Wiley & Sons.

Mischel, W. (1968) *Personality and Assessment*. New York: Wiley.

Mischel, W. (2004) Toward an integrative science of the person, *Annual Review of Psychology*, 55, 1–22.

Mischel, W. and Shoda, Y. (1995) A cognitive-affective system theory of personality: reconceptualizing situations, dispositions, dynamics, and invariance in personality structure, *Psychological Review*, 102, 246–68.

Miwa, H. and Kondo, T. (2005) Increased writing activity in Parkinson's disease: a punding-like behavior? *Parkinsonism and Related Disorders*, 11, 323–5.

Miyamoto, Y. and Kitayama, S. (2002) Cultural variation in correspondence bias: the critical role of attitude diagnosticity of socially constrained behavior, *Journal of Personality & Social Psychology*, 83(5), 1239–48.

Moghaddam, F. M., Taylor, D. M. and Wright, S. C. (1993) *Social Psychology in Cross-Cultural Perspective*. New York: W. H. Freeman.

Momsen, J. (2003) *Gender and Development*, 2nd edn. London: Routledge.

Money, J. and Tucker, P. (1975) *Sexual Signatures: On Being a Man or a Woman*. Boston, MA: Little, Brown.

Moore, D. (2003) *The Dependent Gene: The Fallacy of 'Nature vs. Nurture'*. New York: Henry Holt/ Owl Books.

Morf, M. E. (1994) Sperry's leap, *American Psychologist*, 49, 817–18.

Morgan, G. and Kegl, J. (2006) Nicaraguan sign language and theory of mind: the issue of critical periods and abilities, *Journal of Child Psychology and Psychiatry*, 47(8), 811–19.

Mortenson, P. B., Pederson, C. B., Westergaard, T. *et al.* (1999) Effects of family history and place and season of birth on the risk of schizophrenia, *New England Journal of Medicine*, 340(8), 603–8.

Moskowitz, B. A. (1978) The acquisition of language, *Scientific American*, 239(11), 92–108.

Motley, M. T. (1985) Slips of the tongue, *Scientific American*, September, 116–27.

Mottaghipour, Y., Pourmand, D., Maleki, H. and Davidian, L. (2001) Expressed emotion and the course of schizophrenia in Iran, *Social Psychiatry & Psychiatric Epidemiology*, 36(4), 195–9.

Mowrer, O. H. (1956) Two-factor learning theory reconsidered, with special reference to secondary reinforcement and the concept of habit, *Psychological Review*, 63, 114–28.

Moyer, K. (1976) *The Psychobiology of Aggression*. New York: Harper & Row.

Moyer, K. (1983) Violence, in S. H. Kadish (ed.) *Encyclopedia of Crime and Justice*, Vol. 4. New York: Free Press, pp. 1618–25.

Moyers, B. (1993) *Healing and the Mind*. New York: Doubleday.

Muris, P. (2006) Freud was right ... about the origins of abnormal behavior, *Journal of Child and Family Studies*, 15(1), 1–12.

Murray, B. (2003) A primer on teaching positive psychology, *Monitor on Psychology*, 34(9), 52–3.

Myers, D. G. (2000) The funds, friends, and faith of happy people, *American Psychologist*, 55(1), 56–67.

Nairne, J. S. (2002) Remembering over the short-term: the case against the standard model, *Annual Review of Psychology*, 53(1), 53–81.

Narrow, W. E., Rae, D. S., Robins, L. N. and Regier, D. A. (2002) Revised prevalence estimates of mental disorders in the United States: using a clinical significance criterion to reconcile 2 surveys' estimates, *Archives of General Psychiatry*, 59, 115–23.

Nasar, S. (1998) *A Beautiful Mind*. New York: Simon & Schuster.

National Institute of Mental Health (2002) *Medications*, 4th edn. Bethesda, MD: Department of Health and Human Services.

National Institute of Mental Health (2008) The numbers count: mental disorders in America, www. nimh.nih.gov/health/publications/the-numbers-count-mental-disorders-in-america.shtml.

Neath, I. and Suprenant, A. M. (2003) *Human Memory: An Introduction to Research, Data, and Theory*, 2nd edn. Belmont CA: Thomson-Wadsworth.

Neill, J. (1990) Whatever became of the schizophrenogenic mother?, *American Journal of Psychotherapy*, 44, 499–505.

Neisser, U. and Harsh, N. (1992) Phantom flashbulbs: false recollections of hearing the news about the Challenger, in E. Winograd and U. Neisser (eds) *Affect and Accuracy in Recall: Studies of 'Flashbulb Memory'*. New York: Cambridge University Press.

Nettle, D. (2006) Schizotypy and mental health amongst poets, visual artists, and mathematicians, *Journal of Research in Personality*, 40, 876–90.

Neuhauser, C. (2007) Project manager leadership behaviors and frequency of use by female project managers, *Project Management Journal*, 38(1), 21–31.

Nevis, E. C. (1983) Using an American perspective in understanding another culture: towards a hierarchy of needs for the People's Republic of China, *Journal of Applied Behavioral Science*, 19(3), 249–64.

Newcomer, J. W., Selke, G., Melson, A. K. *et al.* (1999) Decreased memory performance in healthy humans induced by stress-level cortisol treatment, *Archives of General Psychiatry*, 56(6), 527–33.

Newell, A., Shaw, J. C. and Simon, H. A. (1958) Elements of a theory of human problem solving, *Psychological Review*, 65, 151–66.

Newell, A. and Simon, H. A. (1972) *Human Problem Solving.* Englewood Cliffs, NJ: Prentice-Hall.

Newman, J. (1995) Thalamic contributions to attention and consciousness, *Consciousness and Cognition*, 4, 171–93.

Newmann, S. C. and Bland, R. C. (1998) Incidence of mental disorders in Edmonton: estimates of rates and methodological issues, *Journal of Psychiatric Research*, 32(5), 273–82.

Nicol, S. E. and Gottesman, I. I. (1983) Clues to the genetics and neurobiology of schizophrenia, *American Scientist*, 71, 398–404.

Nisbett, R. E. and Ross, L. (1980) *Human Inference: Strategies and Shortcomings of Social Judgement.* Englewood Cliffs, NJ: Prentice-Hall.

Niu, W. and Sternberg, R. J. (2001) Cultural influences on artistic creativity and its evaluation, *International Journal of Psychology*, 36(4), 225–41.

Niu, W. and Sternberg, R. J. (2002) Contemporary studies on the concept of creativity: the East and the West, *Journal of Creative Behavior*, 36(4), 269–88.

Nixon, P. D. and Passingham, R. E. (2001) Predicting sensory events: the role of the cerebellum in motor learning, *Experimental Brain Research*, 138(2), 251–7.

Oakes, W., Chapman, S., Borland, R. *et al.* (2004) 'Bulletproof sceptics in life's jungle': which self-exempting beliefs about smoking most predict lack of progression towards quitting? *Preventive Medicine*, 39, 776–82.

Oatley, K., Keltner, D. and Jenkins, J. M. (2006) *Understanding Emotions.* New York: Wiley-Blackwell.

Ochse, R. and Plug, C. (1986) Cross-cultural investigation of the validity of Erikson's theory of personality development, *Journal of Personality & Society Psychology*, 50(6), 1240–52.

Oh, J. S., Jun, S.-A., Knightly, L. M. and Au, T. K.-F. (2003) Holding on to childhood language memory, *Cognition*, 86(3), B53–B64.

Ohman, A. (1986) Face the beast and fear the face: animal and social fears as prototypes for evolutionary analysis of emotion, *Psychophysiology*, 23, 123–45.

Ohman, A. (2002) Automaticity and the amygdala: non-conscious responses to emotional faces, *Current Directions in Psychological Science*, 11(2), 62–6.

Ohman, A. and Mineka, S. (2003) The malicious serpent: snakes as a prototypical stimulus for an evolved module of fear, *Current Directions in Psychological Science*, 12(1), 5–9.

Ohman, A. and Soares, J. F. (1998) Emotional conditioning to masked stimuli: expectancies for aversive outcomes following non-recognized fear-relevant stimuli, *Journal of Experimental Psychology: General*, 127, 69–82.

Olds, J. and Milner, P. (1954) Positive reinforcement produced by electrical stimulation of septal area and other regions of the rat brain, *Journal of Comparative and Physiological Psychology*, 47, 419–27.

O'Leary, A., Brown, S. and Suarez-Al-Adam, M. (1997) Stress and immune function, in T. W. Miller (ed.) *Clinical Disorders and Stressful Life Events.* Madison, CT: International Universities Press.

Olson, P. O. (2007) The 'war' that may have ended before it begun. The Norwegian coaching standards: a personal perspective from Norway, *The Coaching Psychologist*, 3(1), 38–9.

Ono, Koichi (1987) Superstitious behavior in humans, *Journal of the Experimental Analysis of Behavior*, 47(3), 261–71.

Orgler, H. (1976) Alfred Adler, *International Journal of Social Psychiatry*, 22, 67–8.

Orne, M. T. (1962) On the social psychology of the psychological experiment: with particular reference to demand characteristics and their implications, *American Psychologist*, 17, 776–83.

Ornstein, R. (1972) *The Psychology of Consciousness*. San Francisco, CA: W. H. Freeman.

Osherson, D. N. and Smith, E. S. (eds) (1990) *An Invitation to Cognitive Science* (3 vols). Cambridge, MA: MIT Press.

Ost, J. (2003) Seeking the middle ground in the 'memory wars', *British Journal of Psychology*, 94(1), 125–39.

Ost, J. and Costall, A. (2002) Misremembering Bartlett: a study in serial reproduction, *British Journal of Psychology*, 93(2), 243–55.

Owens, R. E. Jr. (2007) *Language Development: An Introduction*, 7th edn. New York: Allyn & Bacon.

Oxman, T. E., Freeman, D. H. and Manheimer, E. D. (1995) Lack of social participation or religious strength and comfort as risk factors for death after cardiac surgery in the elderly, *Psychosomatic Medicine*, 57(1), 5–13.

Oyserman, D., Coon, H. M. and Kemmelmeier, M. (2002) Rethinking individualism and collectivism: evaluation of theoretical assumptions and meta-analyses, *Psychological Bulletin*, 128(1), 3–72.

Padel, J. H. (1987) Freudianism: later developments, in R. L. Gregory (ed.) *The Oxford Companion to the Mind*. New York: Oxford University Press, pp. 270–4.

Page, R. C. and Berkow, D. N. (1991) Concepts of the self: Western and Eastern perspectives. *Journal of Multicultural Counseling and Development*, 19, 83–93.

Paivio, A. (1971) *Imagery and Verbal Processes*. New York: Holt, Rinehart & Winston.

Pajer, K., Tabbah, R., Gardner, W. *et al*. (2006) Adrenal androgen and gonadal hormone levels in adolescent girls with conduct disorder, *Psychoneuroendocrinology*, 31, 1245–56.

Palumbo, R. and Gillman, I. (1984) Effects of subliminal activation of Oedipal fantasies on competitive performance, *Journal of Nervous and Mental Disease*, 72, 737–41.

Papafragou, A., Massey, C. and Gleitman, L. (2002) Shake, rattle, 'n' roll: the representation of motion in language and cognition, *Cognition*, 84(2), 189–219.

Papalia, D. E., Olds, S. W. and Feldman, R. D. (2007) *Human Development*, 10th edn. New York: McGraw-Hill.

Paris, B. J. (1994) *Karen Horney: A Psychoanalyst's Search for Self-understanding*. New Haven, CT: Yale University Press.

Parrott, A. C. (2001) Human psychopharmacology of Ecstasy (MDMA): a review of 15 years of empirical research, *Human Psychopharmacology: Clinical & Experimental*, 16(8), 557–77.

Parrott, A. C. (2004) Is Ecstasy MDMA? A review of the proportion of Ecstasy tablets containing MDMA, their dosage levels, and the changing perceptions of purity, *Psychopharmacology*, 173(3/4), 234–41.

Patterson, F. G. and Linden, E. (1981) *The Education of Koko*. New York: Holt, Rinehart & Winston.

Pavlov, I. P. (1927) *Conditioned Reflexes* (ed. and trans. by G. V. Anrep). New York: Dover (reprinted 1960).

Payne, B. K. and Corrigan, E. (2007) Emotional constraints on intentional forgetting, *Journal of Experimental Social Psychology*, 43, 780–6.

Penfield, W. (1975) *The Mystery of the Mind*. Princeton, NJ: Princeton University Press.

Penfield, W. and Rasmussen, T. (1957) *The Cerebral Cortex of Man*. New York: Macmillan.

Penke, L., Denisson, J. J. A. and Miller, G. F. (2007) The evolutionary genetics of personality, *European Journal of Personality*, 21, 549–87.

Peretti-Watel, P., Halfen, S. and Grémy, I. (2007) Risk denial about smoking hazards and readiness to quit among French smokers: an exploratory study, *Addictive Behaviors*, 32, 377–83.

Perry, G. D. and Bussey, K. (1979) The social learning of sex differences: imitation is alive and well, *Journal of Personality and Social Psychology*, 37, 1699–712.

Persons, J. (1991) Psychotherapy outcome studies do not accurately represent current models of psychotherapy, *American Psychologist*, 46, 99–106.

Pert, C. B. (1990) The wisdom of the receptors: neuropeptides, the emotions, and body-mind, in R. Ornstein and C. Swencionis (eds) *The Healing Brain: A Scientific Reader*. New York: Guilford Press, pp. 147–58.

Petersen, S. and Rafuls, S. E. (1998) Receiving the scepter: the generational transition and impact of parent death on adults, *Death Studies*, 22, 493–524.

Peterson, C. (2006) *A Primer in Positive Psychology*. New York: Oxford University Press.

Peterson, C., Maier, S. F. and Seligman, M. E. (1993). *Learned Helplessness: A Theory for the Age of Personal Control*. New York: Oxford University Press.

Peterson, C., Ruch, W., Beermann, U., Park, N. and Seligman, M. E. P. (2007) Strengths of character, orientations to happiness, and life satisfaction, *The Journal of Positive Psychology*, 2(3), 149–56.

Peterson, D. (ed.) (1982) *A Mad People's History of Madness*. Pittsburgh, PA: University of Pittsburgh Press.

Peterson, N. (1962) Effect of monochromatic rearing on the control of responding by wavelength, *Science*, 136, 774–5.

Pfungst, O. (1911) *Clever Hans: The Horse of Mr von Osten* (trans. C. L. Rahn) New York: Holt, Rinehart & Winston (reprinted 1965).

Phillips, M. D., Lowe, M. J., Lurito, J. T., Dzemidzic, M. and Mathews, V. P. (2001) Temporal lobe activation demonstrates sex-based differences during passive listening, *Radiology*, 220(1), 202–7.

Piaget, J. (1954) *The Construction of Reality in the Child*. New York: Basic Books.

Pinker, S. (1994) *The Language Instinct*. New York: William Morrow.

Piper, B. J. (2007) A developmental comparison of the neurobehavioral effects of ecstasy (MDMA), *Neurotoxicology and Teratology*, 29, 288–300.

Plomin, R. and Bergemen, C. S. (1991) The nature of nurture: genetic influence on 'environmental' measures, *Behavioural and Brain Sciences*, 14, 373–427.

Plomin, R. and Daniels, D. (1987) Why are children in the same family so different from one another?, *Behavioral and Brain Sciences*, 10, 1–60.

Plomin, R., DeFries, J. C., Craig, I. W. and McGuffin, P. (eds) (2003) *Behavioral Genetics in the Postgenomic Era*. Washington, DC: American Psychological Association.

Plomin, R., DeFries, J. C. and Fulker, D. W. (1988) *Nature and Nurture during Infancy and Early Childhood*. New York: Cambridge University Press.

Plomin, R. and McGuffin, P. (2003) Psychopathology in the postgenomic era, *Annual Review of Psychology*, 54, 205–28.

Polidoro, M. (2007) The magic in the brain: how conjuring works to deceive our minds, in S. Della Salla (ed.) *Tall Tales About the Mind and Brain: Separating Fact from Fiction*. Oxford: Oxford University Press.

Pomerlau, A., Bolduc, D., Malcuit, G. and Cossette, L. (1990) Pink or blue: environmental gender stereotypes in the first two years of life, *Sex Roles*, 22, 359–67.

Poole, D. A., Lindsay, D. S., Memon, A. and Bull, R. (1995) Psychotherapy and the recovered memories of child sexual abuse: U.S. and British therapists' beliefs, practices, and experiences, *Journal of Consulting and Clinical Psychology*, 63, 426–37.

Pope, A. (2005) Personal transformation in midlife orphanhood: an empirical phenomenological study, *Omega*, 51(2), 107–23.

Popovic, M. R., Thrasher, T. A., Adams, M. E. *et al.* (2006) Functional electrical therapy: retraining grasping in spinal cord injury, *Spinal Cord*, 44, 143–51.

Porter, R. (2002) *Madness: A Brief History*. New York: Oxford University Press.

Potter, M. C. (1990) Remembering, in D. N. Osherson and E. S. Smith (eds) *An Invitation to Cognitive Science: Thinking* (Vol. 3). Cambridge, MA: MIT Press.

Potts, G. F., O'Donnell, B. F., Hirayasu, Y. and McCarley, R. W. (2002) Disruption of neural systems of visual attention in schizophrenia, *Archives of General Psychiatry*, 59(5), 418–24.

Pramling, N. (2006) 'The clouds are alive because they fly in the air as if they were birds': a re-analysis of what children say and mean in clinical interviews in the work of Jean Piaget, *European Journal of Psychology of Education*, 21, 453–66.

Prather, E. M., Hedrick, D. L. and Kern, C. A. (1975) Articulation development in children aged two to four years, *Journal of Speech and Hearing Disorders*, 40, 179–91.

Premack, D. (1983) The codes of man and beasts, *Behavioral and Brain Sciences*, 6, 125–67.

Previc, F. H. (1991) A general theory concerning the prenatal origins of cerebral lateralization in humans, *Psychological Review*, 98, 299–334.

Price, W. F. and Crapo, R. H. (2002) *Cross-cultural Perspectives in Introductory Psychology*, 4th edn. Pacific Grove, CA: Wadsworth.

Priel, B. and Besser, A. (2001) Bridging the gap between attachment and object relations theories: a study of the transition to motherhood, *British Journal of Medical Psychology*, 74, 85–100.

Prouty, G. F. (1990) Pre-therapy: a theoretical evolution in the person-centered/experiential psychotherapy of schizophrenia and retardation, in G. Lietaer, J. Rombauts and R. Van Balen (eds) *Client-centered and Experiential Psychotherapy in the Nineties*. Leuven, Belgium: Leuven University Press.

Pruessner, M., Hellhammer, D. H., Pruessner, J. C. and Lupien, S. J. (2003) Self-reported depressive symptoms and stress levels in healthy young men: associations with the cortisol response to awakening, *Psychosomatic Medicine*, 65(1), 92–9.

Pryor, D. B. and Tollerud, T. R. (1999) Applications of Adlerian principles in school settings, *Professional School Counseling*, 2(4), 299–304.

Purnell, B. (2003) To every thing there is a season, *Science*, 301(5631), 325.

Quednow, B. B., Kühn, K-U., Hoppe, C. *et al.* (2007) Elevated impulsivity and impaired decision-making cognition in heavy users of MDMA ('Ecstasy'), *Psychopharmacology*, 189, 517–30.

Rahe, R. H. (1972) Subjects' recent life changes and their near-future illness susceptibility, *Advances in Psychosomatic Medicine*, 8, 2–19.

Raskin, N. J. and Rogers, C. R. (1989) Person-centered therapy, in R. J. Corsini and D. J. Wedding (eds) *Current Psychotherapies*, 4th edn. Itasca, IL: Peacock Press.

Ravnkilde, B., Videbech, P., Rosenberg, R., Gjedde, A. and Gade, A. (2002) Putative tests of frontal lobe function: a PET-study of brain activation during Stroop's test and verbal fluency, *Journal of Clinical & Experimental Neuropsychology*, 24(4), 534–47.

Regier, D. A., Boyd, J. H., Burke, J. D. *et al.* (1988) One-month prevalence of mental disorders in the United States, *Archives of General Psychiatry*, 45, 977–86.

Repovš, G. and Baddeley, A. (2006) The multi-component model of working memory: explorations in experimental cognitive psychology, *Neuroscience*, 139, 5–21.

Rescorla, R. A. (2000) Associative changes with a random CS-US relationship, *Quarterly Journal of Experimental Psychology: Comparative & Physiological Psychology*, 53B(4), 325–40.

Rescorla, R. A. (2001) Retraining of extinguished Pavlovian stimuli, *Journal of Experimental Psychology: Animal Behavior Processes*, 27(2), 115–24.

Rescorla, R. A. and Solomon, R. I. (1967) Two-process learning theory: relationships between Pavlovian conditioning and instrumental learning, *Psychological Review*, 74, 212–21.

Resnick, S. M., Gottesman, I. I. and McGue, M. (1993) Sensation-seeking in opposite-sex twins: an effect of prenatal hormones?, *Behavior Genetics*, 23, 323–9.

Resnick, S., Warmoth, A. and Serlin, I. A. (2001) The humanistic psychology and positive psychology connection: implications for psychotherapy, *Journal of Humanistic Psychology*, 41(1), 73–101.

Ricaurte, G.A., Yuan, J., Hatzidimitriou, G. *et al.* (2002) Severe dopaminergic neurotoxicity in primates after a common recreational dose regimen of MDMA ('Ecstasy'), *Science*, 297(5590), 2260–3.

Ricaurte, G.A., Yuan, J., Hatzidimitriou, G., *et al.* (2003) Retraction of Ricaurte *et al.*, *Science*, 297(5590), 2260–3, 301(5639), 1479.

Rice, N. and O'Donohue, W. (2002) Cultural sensitivity: a critical examination, *New Ideas in Psychology*, 20, 35–48.

Rice, P. L. (1999) *Stress and Health*, 3rd edn. Pacific Grove, CA: Brooks/Cole.

Richards, A. K. (1999) Freud and feminism: a critical appraisal, *Journal of the American Psychoanalytic Association*, 47(4), 1213–37.

Richards, J. E. and Rader, N. (1983) Affective, behavioral, and avoidance responses on the visual cliff: effect of crawling onset age, crawling experience, and testing age, *Psychophysiology*, 20, 633–42.

Richman, A. L., LeVine, R. A., New, R. S. *et al.* (1988) Maternal behavior to infants in five cultures, in R. A. LeVine, P. M. Miller and M. M. West (eds) *Parental Behavior in Diverse Societies: New Directions for Child Development*. San Francisco, CA: Jossey-Bass.

Ridley, M. (2003) *Nature Via Nurture: Genes, Experience, and What Makes Us Human.* New York: HarperCollins.

Rieber, R. W. and Salzinger, K. (eds) (1998) *Psychology: Theoretical-Historical Perspectives*, 2nd edn. Washington, DC: American Psychological Association.

Rime, B. and Giovannini, D. (1986) The physiological patterns of reported emotional states, in K. R. Scherer, H. G. Wallbot and A. B. Summerfield (eds), *Experiencing Emotion: A Crosscultural Study*. Cambridge: Cambridge University Press.

Roazen, P. (1975) *Freud and His Followers.* New York: Knopf.

Roberts, B. W. and Caspi, A. (2001) Authors' response: personality development and the person-situation debate: It's deja vu all over again, *Psychological Inquiry*, 12(2), 104–9.

Roberts, S. and Pashler, H. (2000) How persuasive is a good fit? A comment on theory testing, *Psychological Review*, 107(2), 358–67.

Robins, R. W., Gosling, S. D. and Craik, K. H. (1999) An empirical analysis of trends in psychology, *American Psychologist*, 54(2), 117–28.

Robins, R. W., Trzesniewski, K. H., Tracy, J. L., Gosling, S. D. and Potter, J. (2002) Global self-esteem across the life span, *Psychology & Aging*, 17(3), 423–34.

Robinson, D. N. (1979) *Systems of Modern Psychology.* New York: Columbia University Press.

Robinson, D. N. (1985) Science, psychology, and explanation: synonyms or antonyms?, in S. Koch and D. E. Leary (eds) *A Century of Psychology as a Science*. New York: McGraw-Hill.

Rochester, S. R. (1977) A hard look at studies of language in schizophrenia. Paper presented at Canadian Psychological Association annual meeting, Vancouver, 9 June.

Rodriguez, E., George, N., LaChaux, J.-P. *et al.* (1999) Perception's shadow: long-distance synchronization of human brain activity, *Nature*, 397, 430–3.

Roediger III, H. L., Bergman, E. T. and Meade, M. L. (2000) Repeated reproduction from memory, in Akiko Saito (ed.) *Bartlett, Culture and Cognition*. Philadelphia, PA: Psychology Press.

Rogers, C. R. (1939) *The Clinical Treatment of the Problem Child.* Boston, MA: Houghton-Mifflin.

Rogers, C. R. (1951) *Client-Centered Therapy.* Boston, MA: Houghton-Mifflin.

Rogers, C. R. (1959) A theory of therapy, theory, and interpersonal relationships, as developed in the client-centred framework, in S. Koch (ed.) *Psychology: The Study of a Science*, Vol. 3. New York: McGraw-Hill.

Rogers, C. R. (1964) Towards a science of the person, in T. W. Wann (ed.) *Behaviorism and Phenomenology: Contrasting Bases for Modern Psychology*. Chicago, IL: University of Chicago Press, pp. 109–33.

Rogers, C. R. (1969) *Freedom to Learn*. Columbus, OH: Charles E. Merrill.

Rogers, C. R. (1973) My philosophy of interpersonal relationships and how it grew. *Journal of Humanistic Psychology*, 13, 3–16.

Rogers, C. R. (1985) Toward a more human science of the person, *Journal of Humanistic Psychology*, 25, 7–24.

Rogers, C. R. and Dymond, R. E. (1954) *Psychotherapy and Personality Change*. Chicago: University of Chicago Press.

Rogers, C. R., Gendlin, E. T., Kiesler, D. J. and Truax, C. B. (eds) (1967) *The Therapeutic Relationship and its Impact: A Study of Psychotherapy with Schizophrenics*. Madison, WI: University of Wisconsin Press.

Rogers, C. R. and Skinner, B. F. (1956) Some issues concerning the control of human behavior, *Science*, 124, 1057–66.

Roiser, J.P., Cook, L. J., Cooper, J. D. *et al.* (2005) Association of a functional polymorphism in the serotonin transporter gene with abnormal emotional processing in Ecstasy users, *The American Journal of Psychiatry*, 162(3), 609.

Rokach, A. and Neto, F. (2001) The experience of loneliness in adolescence: a cross-cultural comparison, *International Journal of Adolescence & Youth*, 9(2–3), 159–73.

Rokeach, M. (1981) *The Three Christs of Ypsilanti*. New York: Columbia University Press.

Roper, R. and Shewan, D. (2002) Compliance and eyewitness testimony: do eyewitnesses comply with misleading 'expert pressure' during investigative interviewing?, *Legal and Criminological Psychology*, 7, 155–63.

Rosch, E. (1973) On the internal structures of perceptual and semantic categories, in T. E. Moore (ed.) *Cognitive Development and the Acquisition of Language*. New York: Academic Press.

Roseman, I. J., Antoniou, A. A. and Jose, P. E. (1996) Appraisal determinants of emotions: constructing a more accurate and comprehensive theory, *Cognition and Emotion*, 10, 241–77.

Rosenbaum, R. S., Köhler, S., Schacter, D. L. *et al.* (2005) The case of K. C.: contributions of a memory-impaired person to memory theory, *Neuropsychologia*, 43, 989–1021.

Rosenberg, A. (2008) *The Philosophy of Social Science*. Boulder, CO: Westview Press.

Rosenhan, D. L. (1973) On being sane in insane places, *Science*, 179, 250–8.

Rosenthal, R. (1966) *Experimenter Effects in Behavioral Research*. New York: Appleton-Century-Crofts.

Rosenthal, R. and Jacobson, L. (1968) *Pygmalion in the Classroom*. New York: Holt, Rinehart & Winston.

Rosnow, R. L. (2002) The nature and role of demand characteristics in scientific inquiry, *Prevention & Treatment*, 5, np. Online at http://journals.apa.org/prevention/volume5/pre0050037c.html.

Ross, E. A. (1908) *Society Psychology: An Outline and Source Book*. New York: Macmillan.

Ross, L. (1977) The intuitive psychologist and his shortcomings: distortions in the attribution process, in L. Berkowitz (ed.) *Advances in Experimental Social Psychology*. New York: Academic Press.

Ross, L. (2001) Getting down to fundamentals: lay dispositionism and the attributions of psychologists, *Psychological Inquiry*, 12(1), 37–40.

Ross, L. and Nisbett, R. E. (1991) *The Person and the Situation: Perspectives of Social Psychology*. New York: McGraw-Hill.

Ross, R. (1996). *Returning to the Teachings: Exploring Aboriginal Justice*. Toronto: Penguin Books.

Rosser, R. (1994) *Cognitive Development: Psychological and Biological Perspectives*. Toronto: Allyn & Bacon.

Rostan, S. M., Pariser, D. and Gruber, H. E. (2002) A cross-cultural study of the development of artistic talent, creativity and giftedness, *High Ability Studies*, 13(2), 125–55.

Rotblat, J. (1999) Science and ethical behaviour, address to UNESCO conference, London, 3 June.

Rothbart, M. K. (1981) Measurement of temperament in infancy, *Child Development*, 52, 569–78.

Roughgarden, J. (2005) *Evolution's Rainbow: Diversity, Gender, and Sexuality in Nature and People.* Berkeley, CA: University of California Press.

Royal Society for the Prevention of Accidents (2004) *The Risk of Using a Mobile Phone While Driving.* Birmingham: Royal Society for the Prevention of Accidents.

Rubenstein, E. A., Liebert, R. M., Neale, J. M. and Poulos, R. W. (1974) *Assessing Television's Influence on Children's Prosocial Behavior.* New York: Brookdale International Institute.

Ruble, T. L. (1983) Sexual stereotypes: issues of change in the 70s, *Sex Roles*, 9, 397–402.

Rumbaugh, D. M. (1992) Learning about primates' learning, language, and cognition, in G. G. Brannigan and M. R. Merrens (eds) *The Undaunted Psychologist: Adventures in Research.* New York: McGraw-Hill.

Rumbaugh, D. M. (1997) The psychology of Harry F. Harlow: a bridge from radical to rational behaviorism, *Philosophical Psychology*, 10(2), 197–210.

Rush, A. J. and Ryan, N. D. (2002) Current and emerging therapeutics for depression, in K. L. Davis, D. Charney, J. T. Coyle and C. Nemeroff (eds) *Neuropsychopharmacology: The Fifth Generation of Progress.* Baltimore, MD: Lippincott Williams & Wilkins.

Ruskin, R. and Beiser, M. (1998) Cultural issues in psychotherapy, in P. Cameron, J. Ennis and J. Deadman (eds) *Standards and Guidelines for Psychotherapies.* Toronto: University of Toronto Press.

Rutter, M., Moffitt, T. E. and Caspi, A. (2006) Gene–environment interplay and psychopathology: multiple varieties but real effects, *Journal of Child Psychology and Psychiatry*, 47(3/4), 226–61.

Rutter, V. (2002) Review of: Laumann, Edward O. (ed.), Michael, Robert T., *Sex, Love, and Health in America: Private Choices and Public Policies, Contemporary Sociology*, 31(4), 479–81.

Ruvolo, A. P. and Rotondo, J. L. (1998) Diamonds in the rough: implicit personality theories and views of partner and self, *Personality & Social Psychology Bulletin*, 24(7), 750–8.

Sacks, O. (1985) *The Man Who Mistook His Wife for a Hat.* New York: Summit.

Sagie, A., Elizur, D. and Yamauchi, H. (1996) The structure and strength of achievement motivation: a cross-cultural comparison, *Journal of Organizational Behavior*, 17(5), 431–44.

Salzinger, K. (1995) A behavior-analytic view of anger and aggression, in H. Kassinove (ed.) *Anger Disorders: Definition, Diagnosis, and Treatment.* Philadelphia, PA: Taylor & Francis.

Salzinger, K. (1996) Reinforcement history: a concept underutilized in behavior analysts, *Journal of Behavior Therapy & Experimental Psychiatry*, 27(3), 199–207.

Salzinger, K. (1998) Schizophrenia: from behavior theory to behavior therapy, in J. J. Plaud and G. H. Eifert (eds) *From Behavior Theory to Behavior Therapy.* Needham Heights, MA: Allyn & Bacon.

Sandell, R. (2001) Can psychoanalysis become empirically supported? *International Forum of Psychoanalysis*, 10, 184–90.

Sander, D., Grandjean, D. and Scherer, K. R. (2005) A systems approach to appraisal mechanisms in emotion, *Neural Networks*, 18(4), 317–52.

Sanford, K. (2006) Gendered literary experiences: the effects of expectation and opportunity for boys' and girls' learning, *Journal of Adolescent & Adult Literacy*, 49(4), 302–15.

Sarbin, T. and Mancuso, J. (1980) *Schizophrenia: Medical Diagnosis or Moral Verdict?* Elmsford, NY: Pergamon Press.

Sartre, J. P. (1948) *Existentialism and Humanism* (trans. P. Mariet). London: Methuen.

Savage, C. W. (ed.) (1990) *Scientific Theories*, Vol. 14, in Minnesota Studies in the Philosophy of Science. Minneapolis, MN: University of Minnesota Press.

Savazzi, S., Fabri, M., Rubboli, G. *et al.* (2007) Interhemispheric transfer following callosotomy in humans: role of the superior colliculus, *Neuropsychologia*, 45, 2417–27.

Scarr, S. and McCartney, K. (1983) How people make their own environments: a theory of genotype environment effects, *Child Development*, 54, 424–35.

Schachter, S. and Singer, J. E. (1962) Cognitive, social, and physiological determinants of emotional state, *Psychological Review*, 69, 379–99.

Schacter, D. L. (2001) *The Seven Sins of Memory: How the Mind Forgets and Remembers*. Boston, MA: Houghton Mifflin.

Schaefer, H. H. and Martin, P. L. (1966) Behavioral therapy for 'apathy' of hospitalized schizophrenics, *Psychological Reports*, 19, 1147–58.

Schank, R. C. (1984) *The Cognitive Computer: On Language, Learning, and Artificial Intelligence*. Reading, MA: Addison-Wesley.

Schatzberg, A. F. (2002) Pharmacological principles of antidepressant efficacy, *Human Psychopharmacology: Clinical & Experimental*, 17(Supplement 1), S17–S22.

Schlaug, G., Jaencke, L., Huang, Y. and Steinmetz, H. (1995) In vivo evidence of structural brain asymmetry in musicians, *Science*, 267(5198), 699–701.

Schleicher, D. J. and McConnell, A. R. (2005) The complexity of self-complexity: an associated systems theory approach, *Social Cognition*, 23(5), 387–416.

Schwartz, C. E., Wright, C. I., Shin, L. M., Kagan, J. and Rauch, S. L. (2003) Inhibited and uninhibited infants 'grown up': adult amygdalar response to novelty, *Science*, 300, 1952–3.

Schwartz, M. S. (ed.) (1995) *Biofeedback: A Practitioner's Guide*, 2nd edn. New York: Guilford Press.

Schwartz, M. S. and Andrasik, F. (2005) *Biofeedback: A Practitioner's Guide*, 3rd edn. New York: Guilford Press.

Schwarz, N. and Oyserman, D. (2001) Asking questions about behavior: cognition, communication, and questionnaire construction, *American Journal of Evaluation*, 22(2), 127–60.

Scott, J. (2000) Treatment of chronic depression, *New England Journal of Medicine*, 342(20), 1518–20.

Sears, D. O. (1986) College sophomores in the laboratory: influences of a narrow data base on psychology's view of human nature, *Journal of Personality and Social Psychology*, 51, 515–30.

Segal, L. (2001) Nature's way? Inventing the natural history of rape, *Psychology, Evolution & Gender*, 3(1), 87–93.

Segall, M. H., Dasen, P. R., Berry, J. W. and Poortinga, Y. H. (1999) *Human Behavior in Global Perspective: An Introduction to Cross-Cultural Psychology*, 2nd edn. Boston, MA: Allyn & Bacon.

Seligman, M. E. P. (1970) On the generality of the laws of learning, *Psychological Review*, 77, 406–18.

Seligman, M. E. P. (1975) *Helplessness: On Depression, Development, and Death*. San Francisco, CA: W. H. Freeman.

Seligman, M. E. P. (1995) The effectiveness of psychotherapy: the *Consumer Reports* study, *American Psychologist*, 50, 965–74.

Seligman, M. E. P. (2002) *Authentic Happiness: Using the New Positive Psychology to Realize Your Potential for Lasting Fulfillment*. New York: Free Press/Simon & Schuster.

Seligman, M. E. P. (2007) Coaching and positive psychology, *Australian Psychologist*, 42(4), 266–7.

Seligman, M. E. P. and Csikszentmihalyi, M. (2000) Positive psychology: an introduction. *American Psychologist*, 55(1), 5–14.

Seligman, S. (2005) Dynamic systems theories as a metaframework for psychoanalysis, *Psychoanalytic Dialogues*, 15(2), 285–319.

Selye, H. (1976) *The Stress of Life*. New York: McGraw-Hill.

Selye, H. (1978) They all looked sick to me, *Human Nature*, February, 58–63.

Serbin, L. A., Poulin-Dubois, D. and Eichstedt, J. A. (2002) Infants' response to gender-inconsistent events, *Infancy*, 3(4), 531–42.

Serpell, R. (1993) *The Significance of Schooling: Life Journeys in an African Society*. Cambridge: Cambridge University Press.

Servos, P., Engel, S. A., Gati, J. and Menon, R. (1999) fMRI evidence for an inverted face representation in human somatosensory cortex, *NeuroReport*, 10, 1393–95.

Shah, I. (1981) *A Perfumed Scorpion: The Way to the Way*. San Francisco: Harper & Row.

Shapiro, Y. and Gabbard, G. O. (1994) A reconsideration of altruism from an evolutionary and psychodynamic perspective, *Ethics and Behavior*, 4(1), 23–42.

Sheldon, K. M. and Kasser, T. (2001) Goals, congruence, and positive well-being: new empirical support for humanistic theories, *Journal of Humanistic Psychology*, 41(1), 30–50.

Shepard, R. N. and Metzler, J. (1971) Mental rotation of three-dimensional objects, *Science*, 171, 701–3.

Sherif, M. (1936) *The Psychology of Social Norms*. New York: Harper.

Shettleworth, S. (1972) Constraints on learning, in D. S. Lehrman, R. A. Hinde and H. Shaw (eds) *Advances in the Study of Behavior*, Vol. 4. New York: Academic Press.

Shields, J. (1962) *Monozygotic Twins Brought Up Apart and Brought Up Together*. London: Oxford University Press.

Shiraev, E. and Levy, D. (2001) *Introduction to Cross-Cultural Psychology: Critical Thinking and Contemporary Applications*. Boston, MA: Allyn & Bacon.

Shiu, L. and Chan, T. (2006) Unlearning a stimulus-response association, *Psychological Research*, 70, 193–9.

Shorter, E. (1997) *A History of Psychiatry*. New York: John Wiley & Sons.

Sideridis, G. D. (2006) Coping is not an 'either' 'or': the interaction of coping strategies in regulating affect, arousal and performance, *Stress and Health*, 22, 315–27.

Siegel, D. J. (1999) *The Developing Mind: Toward a Neurobiology of Interpersonal Experience*. New York: Guilford Press.

Siegel, S. (1976) Morphine analgesia tolerance: its situation specificity supports a Pavlovian conditioning model, *Science*, 193, 323–5.

Siegel, S. (2005) Drug tolerance, drug addiction, and drug anticipation, *Current Directions in Psychological Science*, 14(6), 296–300.

Siegel, S. and Ramos, B. M. C. (2002) Applying laboratory research: drug anticipation and the treatment of drug addiction, *Experimental and Clinical Psychopharmacology*, 10(3), 162–83.

Silverman, I. and Phillips, K. (1997) Evolutionary theory and spatial sex differences, in C. Crawford and D. Krebs (eds), *Handbook of Evolutionary Psychology: Ideas, Issues, and Applications*. Hillsdale, NJ: Lawrence Erlbaum.

Simon, H. A. (1990) A mechanism for social selection and successful altruism, *Science*, 250, 1665–8.

Simons, R. C. and Hughes, C. C. (1985) *The Culturebound Syndromes: Folk Illnesses of Psychiatric and Anthropological Interest*. Boston, MA: Reidel.

Singer, D. and Singer, J. (eds) (2001) *Handbook of Children and the Media*. Thousand Oaks, CA: Sage.

Singer, J. (1992) Me, myself, and I: toward the scientific study of personal representations, *Psychological Inquiry*, 3(1), 62–4.

Singer, J. L. and Singer, D. G. (1981) *Television, Imagination, and Aggression: A Study of Preschoolers*. Hillsdale, NJ: Lawrence Erlbaum.

Skinner, B. F. (1948a) Superstition in the pigeon, *Journal of Experimental Psychology*, 38, 168–72.

Skinner, B. F. (1948b) *Walden Two*. New York: Macmillan.

Skinner, B. F. (1950) Are theories of learning necessary?, *Psychological Review*, 57, 193–216.

Skinner, B. F. (1957) *Verbal Behavior*. New York: Appleton-Century-Crofts.

Skinner, B. F. (1967) B. F. Skinner, in E. G. Boring and G. Lindzey (eds) *A History of Psychology in Autobiography*, Vol. 5. New York: Appleton-Century-Crofts.

Skinner, B. F. (1971) *Beyond Freedom and Dignity*. New York: Vintage.

Skinner, B. F. (1974) *About Behaviorism*. New York: Alfred A. Knopf.

Skinner, B. F. (1987) Behaviourism, Skinner on, in R. L. Gregory (ed.) *The Oxford Companion to the Mind*. New York: Oxford University Press, pp. 74–5.

Sloane, R. B., Staples, F. R., Cristo, A. H., Yorkston, N. J. and Whipple, K. (1975) *Psychotherapy Versus Behavior Therapy*. Cambridge, MA: Harvard University Press.

Smith, D. (1982) Trends in counselling and psychotherapy, *American Psychologist*, 37, 802–9.

Smith, D. L. (1992) *Understanding Canadian Prescription Drugs*, revised edn. Toronto: Key Porter Books.

Smith, E. R. and Mackie, D. M. (1995) *Social Psychology*. New York: Worth.

Smith, M. B. (2003) Moral foundations in research with human participants, in Alan E. Kazdin (ed.) *Methodological Issues and Strategies in Clinical Research*, 3rd edn, pp. 771–8. Washington, DC: American Psychological Association.

Smith, M. L., Glass, G. V. and Miller, T. I. (1980) *The Benefits of Psychotherapy*. Baltimore, MD: Johns Hopkins University Press.

Smith, P. B. and Bond, M. H. (1999) *Social Psychology Across Cultures*, 2nd edn. Boston: Allyn & Bacon.

Snyder, C. R. and Lopez, S. J. (eds) (2002) *Handbook of Positive Psychology*. London: Oxford University Press.

Snyder, C. R. and Lopez, S. J. (2006) *Positive Psychology: The Scientific and Practical Explorations of Human Strengths*. Thousand Oaks, CA: Sage.

Snyder, S. (1980) *Biological Aspects of Mental Disorder*. New York: Oxford University Press.

Sober, E. (2002) Kindness and cruelty in evolution, in R. J. Davidson and A. Harrington (eds) *Visions of Compassion: Western Scientists and Tibetan Buddhists Examine Human Nature*. London: Oxford University Press.

Solms, M. (1995) New findings on the neurological organization of dreaming: implications for psychoanalysis, *Psychoanalytic Quarterly*, 64(1), 43–67.

Solomon, G. F. (1990) Emotions, stress, and immunity, in R. Ornstein and C. Swencionis (eds) *The Healing Brain: A Scientific Reader*. New York: Guilford Press.

Spence, D. P. (2001) Filling the gap, *Psychological Inquiry*, 12(3), 148–50.

Sperling, G. (1960) The information available in brief visual presentations, *Psychological Monographs*, 74 (11, Whole No. 498).

Sperry, R. (1968) Hemispheric deconnection and unity in conscious awareness, *American Psychologist*, 23, 723–33.

Sperry, R. (1969) A modified concept of consciousness, *Psychological Review*, 76, 532–6.

Sperry, R. (1993) The impact and promise of the cognitive revolution, *American Psychologist*, 48, 878–85.

Sperry, R. (1995) The riddle of consciousness and the changing scientific worldview, *Journal of Humanistic Psychology*, 35, 7–33.

Spiro, M. E. (1982) *Oedipus in the Trobriands*. Chicago: University of Chicago Press.

Spradlin, J. E. (2002) Punishment: a primary process?, *Journal of Applied Behavior Analysis*, 35(4), 475–7.

Sprafkin, J. N., Liebert, R. M. and Poulos, R. W. (1975) Effects of a prosocial televised example on children's helping, *Journal of Experimental Child Psychology*, 20, 119–26.

Stanley, C. M. and Raskin, J. D. (2002) Abnormality: does it define us or do we define it?, in J. D. Raskin and S. K. Bridges (eds) *Studies in Meaning: Exploring Constructivist Psychology*. New York: Pace University Press.

Staub, E. (2003) *The Psychology of Good and Evil: Why Children, Adults, and Groups Help and Harm Others*. New York: Cambridge University Press.

Steffensen, M. and Calker, L. (1982) Intercultural misunderstandings about health care: recall of descriptions of illness and treatments, *Social Science and Medicine*, 16, 1949–54.

Steiner, C. (1974) *Scripts People Live – Transactional Analysis of Life Scripts*. New York: Grove Press.

Stelter, R. (2007) Coaching: a process of personal and social meaning making, *International Coaching Psychology Review*, 2(2), 191–201.

Stephane, M., Pellizzer, G., Fletcher, C. R. and McClannahan, K. (2006) Empirical evaluation of language disorder in schizophrenia, *Journal of Psychiatry & Neuroscience*, 32(4), 250–8.

Sterman, M. B. (1978) Biofeedback and epilepsy, *Human Nature*, May, 50–7.

Sternberg, E. M. and Gold, P. W. (1997) The mind-body interaction in disease, *Scientific American, Special Issue: The Mind*, 7(1), 8–15.

Sternberg, R. J. and Grigorenko, E. L. (2001) Unified psychology, *American Psychologist*, 56(12), 1069–79.

Sternberg, R. J. and Vroom, V. (2002) The person versus the situation in leadership, *Leadership Quarterly*, 13(3), 301–23.

Stevenson, M. R. and Black, K. N. (1988) Paternal absence and sex-role development: a meta-analysis, *Child Development*, 59, 793–814.

Stiles, W. B., Shapiro, D. A. and Elliott, R. (1986) Are all psychotherapies equivalent?, *American Psychologist*, 41, 165–80.

Stockhorst, U., Mahl, N., Krueger, M. *et al.* (2004) Classical conditioning and conditionability of insulin and glucose effects in healthy humans, *Physiology & Behavior*, 81(3), 375–88.

Stone, J. (1988) Sex and the single gorilla, *Discover*, August, 78, 80.

Stone, M. H. (2002) Individual psychology of depression, in M. A. Reinecke and M. R. Davison (eds) *Comparative Treatments of Depression*. New York: Springer.

Stowell, J. R., Kiecolt-Glaser, J. K. and Glaser, R. (2001) Perceived stress and cellular immunity: when coping counts, *Journal of Behavioral Medicine*, 24(4), 323–39.

Strand, B. Z. (1975) Effects of instructions for category organization on long-term retention, *Journal of Experimental Psychology: Human Learning & Memory* 1(6), 780–6.

Straub, R. E. (1994) Possible vulnerability locus for bipolar affective disorder on chromosome 21q22.3, *Nature Genetics*, 8, 291–4.

Straus, T. (1982) The structure of the self in Northern Cheyenne culture, in B. Lee (ed.) *Psychosocial Theories of the Self*. New York: Plenum Press.

Strayer, D. L. and Drews, F. A. (2007) Cell-phone-induced driver distraction, *Current Directions In Psychological Science*, 16, 128–31.

Strümpfer, D. J. W. (2005) Standing on the shoulders of giants: notes on early positive psychology (psychofortology), *South African Journal of Psychology*, 35(1), 21–45.

Strupp, H. H. (1989) Psychotherapy: can the practitioner learn from the researcher?, *American Psychologist*, 44, 717–24.

Sue, S., Fujino, D. C., Hu, L. *et al.* (1991) Community mental health services for ethnic minority groups: a test of the cultural responsiveness hypothesis, *Journal of Consulting and Clinical Psychology*, 59, 533–40.

Suhail, K. and Cochrane, R. (2002) Effect of culture and environment on the phenomenology of delusions and hallucinations, *International Journal of Social Psychiatry*, 48(2), 126–38.

Sulloway, F. (1979) *Freud: Biologist of the Mind*. New York: Basic Books.

Summers, A. O. (2006) Genetic linkage and horizontal gene transfer: the roots of the antibiotic multi-resistance problem, *Animal Biotechnology*, 17, 125–35.

Swindle, R., Jr, Heller, K., Pescosolido, B. and Kikuzawa, S. (2000) Responses to nervous breakdowns in America over a 40–year period: mental health policy implications, *American Psychologist*, 55(7), 740–9.

Szasz, T. S. (1974) *The Myth of Mental Illness*, revised edn. New York: Harper & Row.

Taeyoung, S., Kraemer, D., Pryor, J. *et al.* (2002) A cat cloned by nuclear transplantation, *Nature*, 415, 859.

Talwar, S. K., Xu, S., Hawley, E. S. *et al.* (2002) Rat navigation guided by remote control, *Nature*, 417(6884), 37–8.

Tandon, R. and Kane, J. M. (1993) Neuropharmacologic basis for clozapine's unique profile, *Archives of General Psychiatry*, 50, 158–9.

Taylor, E. (2001) Positive psychology and humanistic psychology: a reply to Seligman, *Journal of Humanistic Psychology*, 41(1), 13–29.

Taylor, S. E. and Brown, J. D. (1988) Illusion and well-being: a social psychological perspective on mental health, *Psychological Bulletin*, 103, 193–210.

Taylor, S. E., Klein, L. C., Lewis, B. P. *et al.* (2000) Biobehavioral responses to stress in females: tend-and-befriend, not fight-or-flight, *Psychological Review*, 108(3), 411–29.

Tellegen, A., Lykken, D. T., Bouchard, T. J., Wilcox, K. J. and Rich, S. (1988) Personality similarity in twins reared apart and together, *Journal of Personality and Social Psychology*, 54, 1031–9.

Terrace, H. S., Petitto, L. A., Sanders, R. J. and Bever, T. G. (1979) Can an ape create a sentence?, *Science*, 206, 891–902.

Teusch, L. (1990) Positive effects and limitations of client-centered therapy with schizophrenic patients, in G. Lietaer, J. Rombauts and R. Van Balen (eds) *Client-centered and Experiential Psychotherapy in the Nineties*. Leuven, Belgium: Leuven University Press.

Thaler, R. H. and Sunstein, C. R. (2008) *Nudge*. New Haven, CT: Yale University Press.

Thomas, A. and Chess, A. (1977) *Temperament and Development*. New York: Brunner/Mazel.

Thomas, L. (1981) On the need for asylums, *Discover*, December, 68–71.

Thompson, S. K. (1975) Gender labels and early sex-role development, *Child Development*, 46, 339–47.

Thorndike, E. L. (1898) Animal intelligence, *Psychological Review Monograph Supplement*, 2 (4, Whole No. 8).

Thornhill, R. and Palmer, C. T. (2000) *A Natural History of Rape: Biological Bases of Sexual Coercion*. Cambridge, MA: MIT Press.

Till, B. D. and Priluck, R. L. (2000) Stimulus generalization in classical conditioning: an initial investigation and extension, *Psychology & Marketing*, 17(1), 55–72.

Tincoff, R., Hauser, M., Tsao, F. *et al.* (2005) The role of speech rhythm in language discrimination: further tests with a non-human primate, *Developmental Science*, 8(1), 26–35.

Tolman, E. C. (1932) *Purposive Behavior in Animals and Man*. New York: Appleton-Century-Crofts.

Toulin, A. (1993) Liberals head to majority, new poll says, *The Financial Post*, 2 October, 1.

Trevarthen, C. (1987) Split-brain and the mind, in R. L. Gregory (ed.) *The Oxford Companion to the Mind*. New York: Oxford University Press, pp. 740–7.

Triandis, H. C. (1990) Cross-cultural studies of individualism and collectivism, in J. J. Berman (ed.) *Cross-cultural Perspectives: Nebraska Symposium on Motivation, 1989.* Lincoln, NE: University of Nebraska Press.

Trivers, R. L. (1971) The evolution of reciprocal altruism, *Quarterly Review of Biology*, 46, 35–57.

Trope, Y. (2004) Theory in social psychology: seeing the forest and the trees, *Personality and Social Psychology Review*, 8(2), 193–200.

Truax, C. B. (1966) Reinforcement and non-reinforcement in Rogerian psychotherapy, *Journal of Abnormal Psychology*, 71, 1–9.

Tschacher, W. and Kupper, Z. (2007) A dynamics-oriented approach to psychopathology, *Nebraska Symposium on Motivation*, 52, 85–122.

Tucker, Gary J. (1998) Putting DSM-IV in perspective, *American Journal of Psychiatry*, 155(2), 159–61.

Tulving, E. (1974) Recall and recognition of semantically encoded words, *Journal of Experimental Psychology*, 102, 778–87.

Tulving, E. (1985) How many memory systems are there?, *American Psychologist*, 40, 385–98.

Tulving, E. (1986) What kind of hypothesis is the distinction between episodic and semantic memory?, *Journal of Experimental Psychology: Learning, Memory, and Cognition*, 12, 307–11.

Tulving, E. (2002) Episodic memory: from mind to brain, *Annual Review of Psychology*, 53, 1–25.

Tulving, E. and Madigan, S. (1970) Memory and verbal learning, *Annual Review of Psychology*, 21, 457–84.

Tulving, E. and Thompson, D. M. (1971) Retrieval processes in recognition memory, *Journal of Experimental Psychology*, 87, 116–24.

US Department of Health and Human Services (2001) *Mental Health: Culture, Race, and Ethnicity – A Supplement to Mental Health: A Report of the Surgeon General.* Rockville, MD: US Department of Health and Human Services.

US National Institute of Justice (1996) *Convicted by Juries, Exonerated by Science: Case Studies in the Use of DNA Evidence to Establish Innocence After Trial.* Washington, DC: Department of Justice.

Vaillancourt, T., Miller, J. L., Fagbemi, J. *et al.* (2007) Trajectories and predictors of indirect aggression: results from a nationally representative longitudinal study of Canadian children aged 2–10, *Aggressive Behavior*, 33, 314–26.

Vaillant, G. E. (2000) Adaptive mental mechanisms: their role in positive psychology, *American Psychologist*, 55(1), 89–98.

Valins, S. (1966) Cognitive effects of false heart-rate feedback, *Journal of Personality and Social Psychology*, 4, 400–8.

van Bokhoven, I., van Goozen, S. H. M., van Engeland, H. *et al.* (2006) Salivary testosterone and aggression, delinquency, and social dominance in a population-based longitudinal study of adolescent males, *Hormones and Behavior*, 50, 118–25.

Vandenberg, B. (1993) Existentialism and development, *American Psychologist*, 46, 296–7.

Van Den Haak, M. J., De Jong, M. D. T. and Schellens, P. J. (2003) Restrospective vs. concurrent think-aloud protocols: testing the usability of an online library catalogue, *Behaviour & Information Technology*, 22(5), 339–51.

van der Hart, O. and Nijenhuis, E. (2001) Generalized dissociative amnesia: episodic, semantic and procedural memories lost and found, *Australian & New Zealand Journal of Psychiatry*, 35(5), 589–600.

van de Vijver, F. J. R. and Poortinga, Y. H. (2002) On the study of culture in developmental science, *Human Development*, 45(4), 246–56.

V.Bijl, R., de Graaf, R., Ravelli, A. *et al.* (2002) Gender and age-specific first incidence of DSM-III-R psychiatric disorders in the general population: results from the Netherlands Mental Health Survey and Incidence Study (NEMESIS), *Social Psychiatry & Psychiatric Epidemiology*, 37(8), 372–9.

Venables, P. H. (1996) Schizotypy and maternal exposure to influenza and to cold temperature: the Mauritius study, *Journal of Abnormal Psychology*, 105, 53–60.

Vierikko, E., Pulkkinen, L., Kaprio, J. *et al.* (2003) Sex differences in genetic and environmental effects on aggression, *Aggressive Behavior*, 29(2), 55–68.

Viglione, D. J. and Taylor, N. (2003) Empirical support for interrater reliability of Rorschach comprehensive system coding, *Journal of Clinical Psychology*, 59(1), 111–21.

Viinamaeki, H., Koskela, K. and Niskanen, L. (1996) Rapidly declining mental well being during unemployment, *European Journal of Psychiatry*, 10, 215–21.

Villet, B. (1978) Opiates of the mind, *The Atlantic Monthly*, June, 82–9.

Vohs, K. D. and Schooler, J. W. (2008) The value of believing in free will: encouraging a belief in determinism increases cheating, *Psychological Science*, 19(1), 49–54.

Volkow, N. D., Wang, G.-J., Fischman, M. W. *et al.* (1997) Relationship between subjective effects of cocaine and dopamine transporter occupancy, *Nature*, 386(6627), 827–30.

Vollmer, T. R. (2002) Punishment happens: some comments on Lerman and Vorndran's review, *Journal of Applied Behaviour Analysis*, 35(4), 469–73.

Vonnegut, M. (1975) *The Eden Express*. New York: Bantam.

von Wild, K., Rabischong, P., Brunelli, G., Benichou, M. and Krishnan, K. (2002) Computer aided locomotion by implanted electrical stimulation in paraplegic patients, *Acta Neurochirurgica Suppl.*, 79, 99–104.

Wachtel, P. L. (1977) *Psychoanalysis and Behavior Therapy*. New York: Basic Books.

Wachtel, P. L. (1997) *Psychoanalysis, Behavior Therapy, and the Relational World*. Washington, DC: American Psychological Association.

Wade, C. (2006) Some cautions about jumping on the brain-scan bandwagon, *APS Observer*, 19(9), 23–4.

Wadnerkar, M. B., Cowell, P. E. and Whiteside, S. P. (2006) Speech across the menstrual cycle: a replication and extension study, *Neuroscience Letters*, 408, 21–4.

Wager, T. D. (2005) The neural bases of placebo effects in pain, *Current Directions in Psychological Science*, 14(4), 175–9.

Walker, E. F. and Diforio, D. (1997) Schizophrenia: a neural diathesis-stress model, *Psychological Bulletin*, 104, 667–85.

Walker, T. (2008) Could sexual selection have made us psychological altruists?, *Studies in History and Philosophy of Biological and Biomedical Sciences*, 39, 153–62.

Wallace, R. K. and Benson, H. (1972) The physiology of meditation, *Scientific American*, February, 84–90.

Wallerstein, R. S. (1989) The psychotherapy research project of the Meninger Foundation: an overview, *Journal of Consulting and Clinical Psychology*, 57, 195–205.

Wang, Q. (2003) Infantile amnesia reconsidered: a cross-cultural analysis, *Memory*, 11(1), 65–80.

Warner, R. E. (1991) A survey of theoretical orientations of Canadian clinical psychologists, *Canadian Psychology*, 32, 525–8.

Warwick, D. P. (1975) Deceptive research: social scientists ought to stop lying, *Psychology Today*, February, 63–5.

Watanabe, S., Sakamoto, J. and Wakita, M. (1995) Pigeons' discrimination of painting by Monet and Picasso, *Journal of the Experimental Analysis of Behaviour*, 63, 165–74.

Watson, J. B. (1930) *Behaviorism*. New York: W. W. Norton (reprinted 1970).

Watson, J. B. and Rayner, L. (1920) Conditioned emotional reactions, *Journal of Experimental Psychology*, 3, 1–14.

Waugh, N. C. and Norman, D. A. (1965) Primary memory, *Psychological Review*, 72, 89–104.

Webb, E. J., Campbell, D. T., Schwartz, R. D. and Sechrest, L. (1972) *Unobtrusive Measures: Non-reactive Research in the Social Sciences*. Chicago, IL: Rand McNally.

Weimer, W. B. (1973) Psycholinguistics and Plato's paradoxes of the Meno, *American Psychologist*, January, 15–33.

Weinberger, D. A., Schwartz, G. E. and Davidson, R. J. (1979) Low-anxious, high-anxious, and repressive coping styles: psychometric patterns and behavioral and physiological responses to stress, *Journal of Abnormal Psychology*, 88, 369–80.

Weinberger, D. R. (2002) Schizophrenia and related disorders, in K. L. Davis, D. Charney, J. T. Coyle and C. Nemeroff (eds) *Neuropsychopharmacology: The Fifth Generation of Progress*. Baltimore, MD: Lippincott Williams & Wilkins.

Weiner, M. J. (1972) Emotionality and attribution: an instance of the control of the response to private events by external stimuli, *Journal of General Psychology*, 86(2), 207–16.

Weisberg, P. and Waldrop, P. B. (1972) Fixed interval work habits of Congress, *Journal of Applied Behavior Analysis*, 5, 93–7.

Weiss, D. J. and Newport, E. L. (2006) Mechanisms underlying language acquisition: benefits from a comparative approach, *Infancy*, 9(2), 241–57.

Weissman, M. M., Markowitz, J. C. and Klerman, G. L. (2000) *Comprehensive Guide to Interpersonal Psychotherapy*. New York: Basic Books.

Weisz, J. R., Rothbaum, F. M. and Blackburn, T. C. (1984) Standing out and standing in: the psychology of control in America and Japan, *American Psychologist*, 39, 955–69.

Weiten, W. and Lloyd, M. A. (2003) *Psychology Applied to Modern Life: Adjustment in the 21st Century*, 7th edn. Toronto: Wadsworth.

Wells, G. L. and Bradfield, A. L. (1998) 'Good, you identified the suspect': feedback to eyewitnesses distorts their reports of the witnessing experience, *Journal of Applied Psychology*, 83, 360–76.

Wells, G. L., Memon, A. and Penrod, S. D. (2006) Eyewitness evidence: improving its probative value, *Psychological Science in the Public Interest*, 7(2), 45–75.

Wells, G. L. and Olson, E. A. (2003) Eyewitness testimony, *Annual Review of Psychology*, 54, 277–95.

Wender, P. H. and Klein, D. F. (1981) The promise of biological psychiatry, *Psychology Today*, February, 25–41.

Werner, A. and Malterud, K. (2005) 'The pain isn't as disabling as it used to be': how can the patient experience empowerment instead of vulnerability in the consultation? *Scandinavian Journal of Public Health*, 33 (Suppl. 66), 41–6.

Westen, D. (1992) The cognitive self and the psychoanalytic self: can we put our selves together?, *Psychological Inquiry*, 3(1), 1–12.

Westen, D. (1998) The scientific legacy of Sigmund Freud: toward a psychodynamically informed psychological science, *Psychological Bulletin*, 124(3), 333–71.

Westen, D. (1999a) *Psychology: Mind, Brain, & Culture*, 2nd edn. New York: John Wiley & Sons.

Westen, D. (1999b) The scientific status of unconscious processes: is Freud really dead?, *Journal of the American Psychoanalytic Association*, 47(4), 1061–106.

Wheeler, M. A., Stuss, D. T. and Tulving, E. (1997) Toward a theory of episodic memory: the frontal lobes and autonoetic consciousness, *Psychological Bulletin*, 121, 331–54.

Whitaker, R. (2002) *Mad in America: Bad Science, Bad Medicine, and the Enduring Mistreatment of the Mentally Ill*. Cambridge, MA: Perseus Publishing.

White, J. W. (2001) Aggression and gender, in J. Worell (ed.) *Encyclopedia of Gender and Women*. San Diego, CA: Academic Press.

White, R. W. (1975) *Lives in Progress: A Study of the Natural Growth of Personality*, 3rd edn. New York: Holt, Rinehart & Winston.

Whiting, B. B. and Edwards, C. P. (1988) *Children of Different Worlds: The Formation of Social Behavior*. Cambridge, MA: Harvard University Press.

Whittle, P. (1999) Experimental psychology and psychoanalysis: what we can learn from a century of misunderstanding, *Neuro-psychoanalysis*, 1(2), 233–45.

Whorf, B. L. (1956) *Language, Thought, and Reality*. Cambridge, MA: MIT Press.

Whybrow, A. and Palmer, S. (2006) Taking stock: a survey of coaching psychologists' practices and perspectives, *International Coaching Psychology Review*, 1(1), 56–70.

Wicker, A. (1971) Attitudes vs. action: the relationship between verbal and overt behavior responses to attitude objects, *Journal of Social Issues*, 25, 41–78.

Wiederhold, B. K., Gevirtz, R. N. and Spira, J. L. (2001) Virtual reality exposure therapy vs. imagery desensitization therapy in the treatment of flying phobia, in Giuseppe Riva and Carlo Galimberti (eds) *Towards Cyberpsychology: Mind, Cognition and Society in the Internet Age*. Amsterdam, Netherlands: IOS Press.

Wilding, J. and Valentine, E. (1994) Mnemonic wizardry with the telephone directory: but stories are another story, *British Journal of Psychology*, 85(4), 501–9.

Wilkenfeld, A. J., Audu, M. L. and Triolo, R. J. (2006) Feasibility of functional electrical stimulation for control of seated posture after spinal cord injury: a simulation study, *Journal of Rehabilitation Research & Development*, 43(2), 139–52.

Williams, J. E. and Best, D. L. (1982) *Measuring Sex Stereotypes: A Thirty-Nation Study*. Beverly Hills, CA: Sage.

Williams, J. E. and Best, D. L. (1990) *Sex and Psyche: Gender and Self Viewed Cross-culturally*. Newbury Park, CA: Sage.

Williams, L. M. (1994a) Recall of childhood trauma: a prospective study of women's memories of child sexual abuse, *Journal of Consulting and Clinical Psychology*, 62, 1167–76.

Williams, L. M. (1994b) What does it mean to forget child sexual abuse? A reply to Loftus, Garry and Feldman, *Journal of Consulting and Clinical Psychology*, 62, 1182–6.

Williams, L. M. and Banyard, V. L. (eds) (1999) *Trauma and Memory*. Thousand Oaks, CA: Sage.

Wilson, E. O. (1975) *Sociobiology: A New Synthesis*. Cambridge, MA: Harvard University Press.

Wilson, E. O. (1998) *Consilience*. New York: Alfred Knopf.

Winholz, G. (1997) Ivan P. Pavlov: an overview of his life and psychological work, *American Psychologist*, 52, 941–6.

Wirga, M. and De Bernardi, M. (2002) The ABCs of cognition, emotion, and action, *Archives of Psychiatry & Psychotherapy*, 4(1), 5–16.

Wittkower, E. D. and Robertson, B. M. (1979) Sex differences in psychoanalytic treatment, *American Journal of Psychotherapy*, 19, 66–75.

Wolf, O. T., Schommer, N. C., Hellhammer, D. H., McEwen, B. S. and Kirchbaum, C. (2001) The relationship between stress induced cortisol levels and memory differs between men and women, *Psychoneuroendocrinology*, 26(7), 711–20.

Wolpe, J. (1973) *The Practice of Behavior Therapy*, 2nd edn. New York: Pergamon Press.

Wood, R. T. A., Griffiths, M. D., Chappell, D. and Davies, M. N. O. (2004) The structural characteristics of video games: a psycho-structural analysis, *CyberPsychology & Behavior*, 7(1), 1–10.

Wood, W., Wong, F. Y. and Chachere, J. G. (1991) Effects of media violence on viewers' aggression in unconstrained social interaction, *Psychological Bulletin*, 109, 371–83.

Wright, J. C. and Mischel, W. (1987) A conditional approach to dispositional constructs: the local predictability of social behavior, *Journal of Personality & Social Psychology*, 53(6), 1159–77.

Yalom, I. D. (1980) *Existential Psychotherapy*. New York: Basic Books.

Yap, P. (1965) Koro: a culturebound depersonalization syndrome, *British Journal of Psychiatry,* 111, 43–50.

Yates, F. A. (1966) *The Art of Memory.* Chicago, IL: University of Chicago Press.

Yeo, M. (2004) *Harry Potter and the Chamber of Secrets:* feminist interpretations/Jungian dreams, *Simile,* 4(1), n.p.

Zakowski, S. G., Hall, M. H., Klein, L. C. and Baum, A. (2001) Appraised control, coping, and stress in a community sample: a test of the goodness-of-fit hypothesis, *Annals of Behavioral Medicine,* 23(3), 158–65.

Zaner, R. M. (1985) The *logos* of *Psyche*: phenomenological variations on a theme, in S. Koch and D. E. Leary (eds) *A Century of Psychology as a Science.* New York: McGraw-Hill.

Zangwill, O. (1987) Sigmund Freud, in R. L Gregory (ed.) *The Oxford Companion to the Mind.* New York: Oxford University Press.

Zeig, J. (ed.) (1987) *The Evolution of Psychotherapy.* New York: Brunner/Mazell.

Zimbardo, P. G. (1992) *Psychology and Life,* 13th edn. New York: HarperCollins.

Zion-Golumbic, E., Golan, T., Anaki, D. and Bentin, S. (2008) Human face preference in gamma-frequency EEG activity, *Neuroimage,* 39(4), 1980–7.

Zuberbühler, K. (2005) The phylogenetic roots of language, *Current Trends in Psychological Science,* 14(3), 126–30.

Zubin, J. and Spring, B. (1977) Vulnerability – a new view of schizophrenia, *Journal of Abnormal Psychology,* 86, 103–26.

Zuckerman, M. (1991) *Psychobiology of Personality.* Cambridge: Cambridge University Press.

Index

Page numbers in *italics* refer to figures and tables; those in **bold** indicate chapters; *a* and *g* denote appendix and glossary references respectively.